CIVIL PROCEDURE

TWENTY-FIFTH EDITION

STEVEN L. EMANUEL

Founder & Editor-in-Chief, *Emanuel Law Outlines* and
Emanuel Bar Review
Harvard Law School, J.D. 1976
Member, NY, CT, MD and VA bars

The *Emanuel® Law Outlines* Series

Wolters Kluwer
Law & Business

Printed in the United States of America.

1 2 3 4 5 6 7 8 9 0

ISBN 978-1-4548-4088-6

This book is intended as a general review of a legal subject. It is not intended as a source of advice for the solution of legal matters or problems. For advice on legal matters, the reader should consult an attorney.

About Wolters Kluwer Law & Business

Wolters Kluwer Law & Business is a leading global provider of intelligent information and digital solutions for legal and business professionals in key specialty areas, and respected educational resources for professors and law students. Wolters Kluwer Law & Business connects legal and business professionals as well as those in the education market with timely, specialized authoritative content and information-enabled solutions to support success through productivity, accuracy and mobility.

Serving customers worldwide, Wolters Kluwer Law & Business products include those under the Aspen Publishers, CCH, Kluwer Law International, Loislaw, ftwilliam.com and MediRegs family of products.

CCH products have been a trusted resource since 1913, and are highly regarded resources for legal, securities, antitrust and trade regulation, government contracting, banking, pension, payroll, employment and labor, and healthcare reimbursement and compliance professionals.

Aspen Publishers products provide essential information to attorneys, business professionals and law students. Written by preeminent authorities, the product line offers analytical and practical information in a range of specialty practice areas from securities law and intellectual property to mergers and acquisitions and pension/benefits. Aspen's trusted legal education resources provide professors and students with high-quality, up-to-date and effective resources for successful instruction and study in all areas of the law.

Kluwer Law International products provide the global business community with reliable international legal information in English. Legal practitioners, corporate counsel and business executives around the world rely on Kluwer Law journals, looseleafs, books, and electronic products for comprehensive information in many areas of international legal practice.

Loislaw is a comprehensive online legal research product providing legal content to law firm practitioners of various specializations. Loislaw provides attorneys with the ability to quickly and efficiently find the necessary legal information they need, when and where they need it, by facilitating access to primary law as well as state-specific law, records, forms and treatises.

ftwilliam.com offers employee benefits professionals the highest quality plan documents (retirement, welfare and non-qualified) and government forms (5500/PBGC, 1099 and IRS) software at highly competitive prices.

MediRegs products provide integrated health care compliance content and software solutions for professionals in healthcare, higher education and life sciences, including professionals in accounting, law and consulting.

Wolters Kluwer Law & Business, a division of Wolters Kluwer, is headquartered in New York. Wolters Kluwer is a market-leading global information services company focused on professionals.

Dedication

To my beloved wife Marilyn,
mother of my five children

Abbreviations Used in Text

CASEBOOKS

F,K&C — Field, Kaplan and Clermont, *Materials for a Basic Course in Civil Procedure* (7th Ed. 1997)

F,M,S&H — Friedenthal, Miller, Sexton & Hershkoff, *Civil Procedure* (11th Ed. 2013)

G,P&R— Glannon, Perlman and Raven-Hansen, "*Civil Procedure: A Coursebook*" (2d Ed. 2014)

M,RS&P — Marcus, Reddish, Sherman and Pfander, *Civil Procedure: A Modern Approach* (6th Ed. 2013)

Y — Yeazell, *Civil Procedure* (7th Ed. 2008).

Y (8th) — Yeazell, *Civil Procedure* (8th Ed. 2012).

HORNBOOKS & OTHER SECONDARY MATERIALS

F,K&M (4th) — Friedenthal, Kane and Miller, *Civil Procedure* (4th Ed. 2005)

James & Hazard — James, Hazard & Leubsdorf, *Civil Procedure* (4th Ed. 1992)

J & H (3d Ed.) — James and Hazard, *Civil Procedure* (3rd Ed. 1985)

James (1st Ed.) — Fleming James, Jr., *Civil Procedure* (1965)

Jurisdiction Nutshell — Ehrenzweig, Louisell, and Hazard, *Jurisdiction in a Nutshell* (4th Ed. 1980)

Moore's Manual — Moore, Vestal and Kurland, *Moore's Manual —Federal Practice and Procedure* (2 Vols. 1980)

Res Judicata Nutshell — Robert C. Casad, *Res Judicata in a Nutshell* (1976)

Study... — American Law Institute, *Study of the Division of Jurisdiction between State and Federal Courts*

W&K — Wright and Kane, *Law of Federal Courts* (7th Ed. 2011)

W&M — Wright and Miller, *Federal Practice and Procedure* (multi-volume treatise, with annual supplementation)

Wr. — Charles A. Wright, *Law of Federal Courts* (5th Ed. 1994 — this is a prior edition of what is now W&K above)

SUMMARY OF CONTENTS

Table of Contents xi

Preface xxvii

Casebook Correlation Chart xxix

Capsule Summary C-1

1. INTRODUCTION 1

2. JURISDICTION OVER THE PARTIES 7

3. SUBJECT MATTER JURISDICTION 119

4. PLEADING 169

5. DISCOVERY AND PRETRIAL CONFERENCE 203

6. ASCERTAINING APPLICABLE LAW 253

7. TRIAL PROCEDURE 281

8. MULTI-PARTY AND MULTI-CLAIM LITIGATION 335

9. FORMER ADJUDICATION 415

    ESSAY EXAM QUESTIONS AND ANSWERS 455

    TABLE OF CASES 467

    TABLE OF REFERENCES TO THE
    FEDERAL RULES OF CIVIL PROCEDURE 471

    TABLE OF REFERENCES TO TITLE 28,
    UNITED STATES CODE 475

    SUBJECT MATTER INDEX 477

TABLE OF CONTENTS

Preface xxvii

Casebook Correlation Chart xxix

Capsule Summary C-1

Chapter 1

INTRODUCTION

I. CIVIL PROCEDURE GENERALLY 1

   A. "Civil" procedure vs. "criminal" procedure 1

   B. Two court systems 1

   C. Grounds for federal court jurisdiction 3

   D. Both systems studied 3

   E. A road map 3

      1. Personal jurisdiction 3

      2. Venue 3

      3. Subject matter jurisdiction 3

      4. Pleading 4

      5. Discovery 4

      6. Ascertaining applicable law 4

      7. Trial procedure 4

      8. Multi-party and multi-claim litigation 4

      9. Former adjudication 6

Chapter 2

JURISDICTION OVER THE PARTIES

I. GENERAL PRINCIPLES 7

II. JURISDICTION OVER INDIVIDUALS 11

   A. Individual's presence 11

   B. Domicile 13

   C. Residence 14

   D. Consent 15

   E. Non-resident motorist statutes 16

   F. In-state tortious acts 17

   G. Owners of in-state property 18

   H. Conducting business 19

   I. Modern statutory treatment (Illinois) 19

   J. Foreign nationals 20

   K. Statutes going to limits of due process 20

    L. **Limits of "due process" undefined for suits against individuals** 20

III. JURISDICTION OVER CORPORATIONS 21

    A. **Issues covered** 21

    B. **Some general principles** 22

    C. **"Minimum contacts" as basis for jurisdiction (*Int'l Shoe*)** 23

    D. **The meaning of "minimum contacts"** 24

    E. **Suit based on products shipped into the forum state** 28

        1. Suit asserts "specific jurisdiction" 28

        2. Long-arms allow 29

        3. Due process issues 29

        4. Several Supreme Court cases 29

        5. Intentional effort to market in-state (*World-Wide Volkswagen* case) 30

        6. Awareness of sales in foreign state (*Asahi*) 32

        7. Sale by D's distributor into forum state (*McIntyre*) 34

        8. Summary on out-of-state vendors 39

    F. **Establishing "minimum contacts" by use of an Internet Website** 43

    G. **Suits based on contractual relationship** 46

    H. **Class action plaintiffs** 49

    I. **Plaintiff's lack of contacts** 50

IV. "GENERAL" JURISDICTION 51

    A. **Where we are now** 51

    B. **The original "systematic and continuous" test** 51

    C. **The new "at home in the state" requirement** 53

    D. **Meaning of "at home" (*Daimler v. Bauman*)** 56

    E. **Use of agents by out-of-state defendant** 61

        1. Use of corporate subsidiary 61

        2. Two-prong test for attributing subsidiary's contacts to parent 62

        3. General vs. specific jurisdiction 64

Quiz Yourself on
JURISDICTION OVER INDIVIDUALS AND CORPORATIONS;
GENERAL JURISDICTION 65

V. FEDERAL JURISDICTION OVER THE PARTIES 68

    A. **General principles** 68

    B. **Territory for service** 68

        1. Not imposed by Constitution 69

        2. Service out of state 70

        3. 100-mile bulge 70

        4. Foreign defendant not servable in any state 71

        5. Gaps possible 72

    C. **Manner of service** 72

        1. Individual 72

        2. Corporation 72

        3. Waiver of service 73

4. Time for service 74
  D. Amenability to suit 74
    1. Federal question 74
    2. Diversity 75

Quiz Yourself on
FEDERAL JURISDICTION OVER THE PARTIES 75

VI. JURISDICTION OVER THINGS 77
  A. General principles 77
    1. In rem actions 77
    2. Quasi in rem actions 77
    3. Method of attachment 77
  B. In rem jurisdiction 77
  C. Quasi in rem jurisdiction 78
  D. Limited appearances 82
  E. Federal quasi in rem jurisdiction 83

Quiz Yourself on 83
JURISDICTION OVER THINGS 83

VII. NOTICE AND OPPORTUNITY TO BE HEARD 84
  A. General principles 84
  B. Traditional notice requirements 84
  C. Modern notice requirements 85
  D. Statutory provisions vs. actual results 88
  E. Opportunity to be heard 89
  F. Prejudgment remedies, including attachment 89

Quiz Yourself on
NOTICE AND OPPORTUNITY TO BE HEARD 92

VIII. DEFENSES TO CLAIMS OF JURISDICTION 93
  A. General principles 93
  B. Special appearance 93
  C. Enforcement of judgments 94
  D. Collateral attack 95
  E. Defense of fraud or duress 96
  F. Immunity 97
    1. Witnesses 97
    2. Defendants 97
    3. Plaintiffs 98
    4. Federal immunity 98

Quiz Yourself on 98
DEFENSES TO CLAIMS OF JURISDICTION 98

IX. VENUE 99
  A. General principles 99

B. Venue in state actions 100

C. Transitory vs. local actions 100

D. Forum non conveniens 101

E. Venue in federal actions 103

    1. Federal statute 103

    2. "Defendant's residence" venue 105

    3. "Place of events or property" venue 105

    4. The "escape hatch" provision 106

    5. No "plaintiff's residence" venue 107

    6. Corporation 107

    7. Unincorporated associations 108

    8. Waiver of venue claims 108

    9. Venue in federal removal cases 108

    10. Federal forum non conveniens 108

Quiz Yourself on
VENUE 114

Exam Tips on
JURISDICTION OVER THE PARTIES 116

Chapter 3

SUBJECT MATTER JURISDICTION

I. GENERAL PRINCIPLES 119

II. FEDERAL SUBJECT MATTER JURISDICTION GENERALLY 120

III. DIVERSITY JURISDICTION 122

    A. Constitutional provision 122

    B. Complete diversity required 122

    C. Nominal parties ignored 124

    D. Refusal to exercise jurisdiction 124

    E. Date of determination 124

    F. Domicile, not residence, is what counts 125

    G. Citizens of D.C. 125

    H. Jurisdiction involving aliens 125

    I. Diversity involving partnerships and corporations 127

    J. Devices to create or destroy diversity 128

Quiz Yourself on
DIVERSITY JURISDICTION 130

IV. FEDERAL QUESTION JURISDICTION 131

    A. Statutory basis 131

        1. Interpretation constricted 131

2. No adequate definition 131

3. Federal claim 131

4. State-created claim needs interpretation of federal law 132

5. Must be revealed by the complaint 132

6. Claim based on the merits 132

7. Exception for cases raising substantial federal issue 133

Quiz Yourself on
FEDERAL QUESTION JURISDICTION 137

V. AMOUNT IN CONTROVERSY 138

A. General rule 138

B. Proof not required 138

C. Eventual recovery irrelevant 138

D. Whose point of view followed 138

E. Aggregation of claims 139

F. Effect of counterclaim 140

Quiz Yourself on
AMOUNT IN CONTROVERSY 141

VI. SUPPLEMENTAL (FORMERLY "ANCILLARY" AND "PENDENT") JURISDICTION 142

A. Background 142

　1. 1990 amendments 142

B. The traditional "pendent" and "ancillary" ideas 142

　1. Pendent jurisdiction 142

　2. Ancillary jurisdiction 144

C. The present "supplemental" provision 145

　1. Provision generally 145

　2. Federal question cases 146

　3. Diversity exclusions 146

　4. Aggregation to satisfy the amount in controversy (the *Allapattah* case) 150

　5. Discretionary rejection of supplemental jurisdiction 153

　6. No effect on personal jurisdiction 154

　7. Venue not required 154

Quiz Yourself on
SUPPLEMENTAL JURISDICTION 155

VII. REMOVAL OF CASES TO THE FEDERAL COURTS 158

A. General right to remove 158

B. Removal statute 158

C. Diversity and amount rules applicable 159

　1. Anomaly 159

D. Removal not allowed by plaintiff 159

　1. Shamrock case 160

E. Certain kinds of cases not removable 160

F. Original state-court jurisdiction not required 160
G. Pleadings not pierced 160
H. Removal of multiple claims 161
I. Remand 162
J. Waiver 163
K. Mechanics of removal 163

Quiz Yourself on
REMOVAL OF CASES TO THE FEDERAL COURTS 163

Exam Tips on
SUBJECT MATTER JURISDICTION 165

Chapter 4

PLEADING

I.   HISTORY AND GENERAL PRINCIPLES 170

II. MODERN FEDERAL PLEADING GENERALLY 170
A. Purpose 170
B. General principles 171
C. Mechanics of pleadings 171
    1. Kinds of pleadings 171
    2. Verification of pleadings 171
    3. Attorney must not file frivolous pleading (Rule 11) 172
    4. Pleading in the alternative 175

III. THE COMPLAINT 175
A. Definition of complaint 175
B. Elements of complaint 175
C. Jurisdictional allegation 175
D. Degree of specificity required 176
E. Single or separate counts 176
F. Demand for judgment 176
G. Special matters 177

IV. MOTIONS AGAINST THE COMPLAINT 178
A. Motions generally 178
B. 12(b)(6) motion to dismiss for failure to state claim 179
    1. Standard for granting 179
    2. Historical standard for granting 179
    3. Twombly "plausibility" standard 179
    4. "Plausibility" test given extra teeth (*Ashcroft v. Iqbal*) . . . 181
    5. 12(b)(6) dismissal motions after *Twombly* and *Iqbal* . . . 186
    6. Amendment following dismissal 187
C. Motion for judgment on the pleadings 187

D. Motion for more definite statement 187

E. Motion to strike 188

Quiz Yourself on
PLEADING GENERALLY, THE COMPLAINT AND
MOTIONS AGAINST IT 188

V. THE ANSWER 190

A. The answer generally 190

B. Denials 191

C. Signed by defendant's attorney 191

D. Affirmative defenses 192

E. Counterclaims 192

VI. TIME FOR VARIOUS PLEADINGS 193

VII.AMENDMENT OF THE PLEADINGS 193

A. Liberal policy 193

B. Amendment as of right 193

C. Amendment by leave of court 194

D. Relation back 194

   1. Utility 195

   2. When action is deemed "commenced" 195

   3. Easier state "relation back" rule followed 195

   4. What's a single "conduct, transaction, or occurrence" 195

   5. Change of party 196

VIII.VARIANCE OF PROOF FROM PLEADINGS 198

Quiz Yourself on
THE ANSWER, TIMING, AMENDMENTS AND VARIANCE 199

Exam Tips on
PLEADING. 201

Chapter 5

DISCOVERY AND
PRETRIAL CONFERENCE

I. GENERAL PRINCIPLES 204

II. SCOPE OF DISCOVERY 205

A. Scope covered by Rule 26(b) 205

B. General scheme 205

C. Relevance 206

D. Privilege 206

E. Trial preparation immunity 207

1. Conflict 207

2. Distinction 207

3. Absolute or qualified 207

4. *Hickman v. Taylor* 208

5. Rules not adequate 209

6. Revision of Rules 209

7. Qualified immunity 209

8. Absolute immunity 210

9. Statements by witnesses 212

10. Names of witnesses 212

F. Discovery concerning experts 213

   1. Classes of experts 213

   2. Experts to be called at trial 213

   3. Experts retained by counsel, but not to be called at trial 214

   4. Unretained experts not to be called at trial 215

   5. Participant experts 215

G. Impeachment material 215

H. Insurance agreements 216

I. Mandatory disclosure 217

   1. Automatic pre-discovery disclosure 217

   2. Disclosure of expert testimony 219

   3. Trial witnesses and exhibits 219

   4. Exclusion at trial 220

J. Duty to supplement 220

K. Privilege log 220

L. Required meetings 221

Quiz Yourself on
SCOPE OF DISCOVERY 221

III. METHODS OF DISCOVERY 224

A. General characteristics 224

B. Persons affected 225

C. Times usable 225

D. Oral depositions (Rule 30) 226

E. Depositions upon written questions 228

F. Interrogatories to the parties 229

G. Requests for admission (Rule 36) 230

H. Requests to produce documents and to inspect land 231

I. Physical and mental examinations (Rule 35) 234

Quiz Yourself on
METHODS OF DISCOVERY 236

IV. ORDERS AND SANCTIONS 237

A. General availability of sanctions 237

B. Abuse of discovery 237

C. **Compelling discovery** 239

D. **Sanctions** 240

    1. Financial sanctions 240

    2. Other sanctions 241

    3. Wilfulness usually required 242

    4. Which court may issue 242

    5. Physical exam 242

    6. Where allowed 243

    7. Sanctions prior to issuance of order 243

V. USE OF DISCOVERY RESULTS AT TRIAL 243

A. **Use of results generally** 243

B. **Rules on use** 243

C. **Rule 34 requests to produce** 243

D. **Depositions** 244

E. **Interrogatories** 246

F. **Admissions** 246

G. **Physical and mental examinations** 246

H. **Use in subsequent proceedings** 246

Quiz Yourself on
ORDERS AND SANCTIONS; USE OF DISCOVERY
RESULTS AT TRIAL 248

VI. PRETRIAL CONFERENCE 250

Exam Tips on
DISCOVERY AND PRETRIAL CONFERENCE. 250

Chapter 6

ASCERTAINING APPLICABLE LAW

I. NATURE OF PROBLEM 254

II. THE *ERIE* DECISION AND OTHER FUNDAMENTALS 254

A. **Rules of Decision Act** 254

B. **Federal procedural law** 257

III. *ERIE* PROBLEMS 258

A. **Ascertaining state law** 258

B. **Conflict of laws** 259

C. **Burden of proof** 259

D. **Procedure/substance problems** 260

    1. Federal Rules always take precedence 260

    2. Rule's validity under Enabling Act 260

    3. Little protection of state substantive interests 260

4. Reliance on *Erie* to construe Rules 260
5. Outcome-determination and the Federal Rules 261
6. *Byrd v. Blue Ridge* 262
7. *Hanna v. Plumer* 263
8. Conflict must exist 265
9. Conflict between congressional statute and state policy 271

Quiz Yourself on
ERIE PROBLEMS 271

IV. FEDERAL COMMON LAW 274

  A. Federal common law still exists 274

  B. Federal common law in diversity cases 275

  C. Federal common law in state courts 276

Exam Tips on
ASCERTAINING APPLICABLE LAW 278

Chapter 7

TRIAL PROCEDURE

I. BURDEN OF PROOF 282

  A. Two meanings of "burden of proof" 282

  B. Factors in allocation 282

  C. What meets burden 283

II. PRESUMPTIONS 283

  A. Definition 283

  B. Assumptions for discussion 283

    1. Burden of production 283

    2. Burden of persuasion 283

III. PREPONDERANCE OF THE EVIDENCE 284

Quiz Yourself on
BURDEN OF PROOF, PRESUMPTIONS AND
PREPONDERANCE OF EVIDENCE 285

IV. ADJUDICATION WITHOUT TRIAL 286

  A. Trial sometimes unnecessary 286

  B. Voluntary dismissal by plaintiff 287

  C. Involuntary dismissal 287

  D. Summary judgment 288

Quiz Yourself on
ADJUDICATION WITHOUT TRIAL 290

V. TRIALS WITHOUT A JURY 291

A. When tried to court 291

B. Effect 291

C. Evidence rules 291

D. Findings of fact 291

E. Appellate review of factual findings from bench trials 292

Quiz Yourself on
TRIALS WITHOUT A JURY 293

VI. THE JURY 294

A. Seventh Amendment 294

B. Number of jurors 294

C. Unanimity 294

D. Jury selection 294

E. Instructions 295

F. Juror misconduct 296

Quiz Yourself on
THE JURY 297

VII. CHALLENGING THE JUDGE FOR BIAS 298

A. Judicial bias generally 298

B. The federal recusal statute 298

C. Bias great enough to violate due process 299

VIII. DIRECTED VERDICT / JUDGMENT AS A MATTER OF LAW 299

A. Effect 299

B. Standard for granting directed verdict 300

C. *Erie* effect of directed verdict standards 300

D. Use of JNOV 300

Quiz Yourself on
DIRECTED VERDICT; JUDGMENT AS A MATTER OF LAW 301

IX. SPECIAL VERDICT AND INTERROGATORIES 302

X. NEW TRIAL 302

A. Judge's discretion 302

B. Federal new trials 302

C. New trial so judge can correct own error 303

D. New trial for prejudicial conduct by party, witness or counsel 303

E. New trial for jury misconduct 303

F. New trial where verdict against the weight of the evidence 304

G. New trial where verdict is excessive or inadequate 304

H. Remittitur and Additur 305

I. Partial new trial on damages 305

J. New trial for newly discovered evidence 305

    K. Appealability of new trial order 306

Quiz Yourself on
NEW TRIAL 306

**XI. JUDGMENT NOTWITHSTANDING VERDICT (JNOV) /
JUDGMENT AS A MATTER OF LAW (JML)** 306

XII. CONSTITUTIONAL RIGHT TO JURY TRIAL 308

    A. Seventh Amendment 308

    **B. Modern statutes and procedural devices, and their effect on
the jury-trial right** 308

    C. Mixed legal and equitable claims 309

    D. Deciding whether a particular statutory claim is legal or equitable . . . 311

    E. Procedural devices and the expansion of legal claims 313

    F. Limitations on jury trial right 314

Quiz Yourself on
CONSTITUTIONAL RIGHT TO JURY TRIAL 315

XIII. REMEDIES 316

    A. Introduction 316

    B. Damages generally 316

    C. Compensatory damages 316

    D. Punitive damages 317

        1. Due process limits 317

    E. Equitable remedies 318

XIV. APPEALS 319

    A. Appeals generally 319

    B. The scope of appellate review 320

    C. The "final judgment" rule, and exceptions to it 323

        1. The rule in general 323

        2. When is a judgment "final" 325

        3. Multi-claim and multi-party federal litigations (FRCP 54(b)) 326

        4. Certifying the issue 326

        5. The "collateral issue" exception 327

        6. Orders involving the grant or denial of an injunction 329

Quiz Yourself on
APPEALS 330

Exam Tips on
TRIAL PROCEDURE 331

Chapter 8

MULTI-PARTY AND MULTI-CLAIM LITIGATION

I. **BACKGROUND** 336

II. **COUNTERCLAIMS** 337
   A. **Generally** 337
   B. **Federal Rules** 337
      1. Permissive counterclaim 337
      2. Compulsory counterclaim 338
   C. **"Transaction or occurrence"** 339
   D. **Counterclaims by third parties** 339
   E. **Failure to raise a compulsory counterclaim** 340
   F. **Jurisdictional requirements for counterclaims** 340
      1. Supplemental jurisdiction 340
      2. Permissive counterclaims not supplemental 341
   G. **Pleading of counterclaims** 341
   H. **Statutes of limitations for counterclaims** 341

   Quiz Yourself on
   COUNTERCLAIMS. 342

III. **JOINDER OF CLAIMS** 343
   A. **Joinder of claims generally** 343

IV. **JOINDER OF PARTIES** 345
   A. **Reason for joinder** 345
   B. **Permissive joinder** 345
   C. **Use in multi-plaintiff product liability cases** 346
   D. **Jurisdiction in permissive joinder cases** 346
      1. In personam jurisdiction 346
      2. Subject matter jurisdiction 347
      3. Venue 348
   E. **Compulsory joinder (Rule 19)** 348

   Quiz Yourself on
   JOINDER OF CLAIMS AND JOINDER OF PARTIES 351

V. **CLASS ACTIONS** 355
   A. **Background** 355
   B. **Rule 23 generally** 356
   C. **Rule 23(a)'s prerequisites for class actions** 357
   D. **"Common questions of law or fact"** (*Wal-Mart* case) . . . 358
   E. **"Fair and adequate" representation of class** 361
   F. **23(b)(1) actions** 362

G. 23(b)(2) actions 363
H. 23(b)(3) actions 366
I. Requirement of notice 367
J. Binding effect of class action decision 368
K. Subject-matter jurisdiction issues 369
L. Determination that no valid class action exists 371
M. Waiver of the right to bring class action 372
N. Settlements 375
    1. Notice requirement 376
    2. Financial condition 376
    3. Settlement-only class actions 376
O. Attorneys' fees 378
P. Mass tort cases 378

Quiz Yourself on
CLASS ACTIONS 385

VI. INTERVENTION 389
A. Intervention generally 389
B. Intervention as of right 389
C. Permissive intervention 390

Quiz Yourself on
INTERVENTION 391

VII. INTERPLEADER 392
A. Definition 392
B. Need for jurisdiction over both claimants 393
C. Federal statutory interpleader 394
D. Federal Rule interpleader 396

Quiz Yourself on
INTERPLEADER 397

VIII. REAL PARTY IN INTEREST 398
A. Assignment 398
B. Suit in assignee's name 398
C. Representative 399

IX. THIRD-PARTY PRACTICE (IMPLEADER) 399
A. Third-party defendant 399
B. Claim must be derivative 399
C. When leave of court not needed 400
D. Impleader by plaintiff 400
E. Jurisdictional requirements relaxed 400
F. Claims involving third-party defendant 401

Quiz Yourself on
THIRD-PARTY PRACTICE (IMPLEADER) 403

X. CROSS-CLAIMS 406

   A. Definition of cross-claim 406

   B. Requirements 406

   C. Jurisdiction 406

Quiz Yourself on
CROSS-CLAIMS 406

Exam Tips on
MULTI-PARTY AND MULTI-CLAIM LITIGATION 407

Chapter 9

FORMER
ADJUDICATION

I. GENERAL PRINCIPLES 416

II. CLAIM PRECLUSION (MERGER AND BAR) 417

   A. Definition 417

   B. Scope of claim 418

   C. Adjudication on the merits 421

   D. Counterclaims 422

      1. No splitting 422

      2. Collateral estoppel danger 422

      3. Compulsory counterclaims 422

   E. Change of law 422

   F. Persons not party to first action 423

Quiz Yourself on
CLAIM PRECLUSION (MERGER AND BAR) 426

III. COLLATERAL ESTOPPEL 427

   A. Effect 427

   B. Issues to which collateral estoppel applies 428

      1. Same issue 428

      2. Actually litigated and decided 428

      3. Issue essential to verdict 429

      4. Foreseeability of future litigation 429

      5. Courts of limited jurisdiction 430

      6. Differences in burden of proof 431

      7. Settlement 431

      8. Findings of law 431

      9. Where second decision fails to apply estoppel 432

   C. Persons bound by collateral estoppel 433

D. Persons who can benefit from estoppel 433
  1. Mutuality 434
  2. Demise of mutuality 434
  3. Offensive/defensive distinction 434
  4. Offensive estoppel approved by Supreme Court 436
  5. Factors in case-by-case analysis 437
  6. Use of criminal conviction 438

Quiz Yourself on
COLLATERAL ESTOPPEL 439

IV. FULL FAITH AND CREDIT 443
  A. Scope 443
  B. Effect 443
  C. Misinterpretation of another state's law 444
  D. No duty to decisions of other countries 444
  E. Full Faith and Credit to res judicata effect 444
  F. Federal suit follows state suit 444
  G. State suit follows federal suit 446

Quiz Yourself on
FULL FAITH AND CREDIT 449

Exam Tips on
FORMER ADJUDICATION 450

ESSAY EXAM QUESTIONS AND ANSWERS 455

TABLE OF CASES 467

**TABLE OF REFERENCES TO THE
FEDERAL RULES OF CIVIL PROCEDURE** 471

**TABLE OF REFERENCES TO TITLE 28,
UNITED STATES CODE** 475

SUBJECT MATTER INDEX 477

Preface

Thank you for buying this book. It covers all Supreme Court cases decided through March 30, 2014.

We think the special features that are part of this edition will help you a lot. These include:

- **Capsule Summary** — We've boiled the black-letter law of Civil Procedure down to 107 pages. We've designed this Capsule Summary to be read in the last week or so (maybe even the last night) before your exam. If you want to know more about a topic, cross-references in the Capsule point you to the pages in the main text that cover the topic more thoroughly.

- **Casebook Correlation Chart** — This chart shows you, for the leading Civil Procedure casebooks, where in the *Emanuel* any topic from your casebook is covered.

- **Exam Tips** — We've compiled these by reviewing dozens of actual past essay questions, and 100s of multiple-choice questions, asked in past law-school and bar exams. The *Exam Tips* are at the end of each chapter.

- **Quiz Yourself** questions — These short-answer questions will help you test whether you've absorbed the material. You'll find these distributed within each chapter, usually at the end of a roman-numeraled section. Each "pod" of Quiz Yourself questions can easily be located by using the Table of Contents.

I intend for you to use this book both throughout the semester and for exam preparation.

Here are some suggestions about how to use it:[1]

1. During the semester, use the book in preparing each night for the next day's class. To do this, first read your casebook. Then, use the *Casebook Correlation Chart* at the front of the outline to get an idea of what part of the outline to read. Reading the outline will give you a sense of how the particular cases you've just read in your casebook fit into the overall structure of the subject. You may want to use a yellow highlighter to mark key portions of the *Emanuel*.

2. If you make your own outline for the course, use the *Emanuel* to give you a structure, and to supply black letter principles. You may want to rely especially on the *Capsule Summary* for this purpose. You are hereby authorized to copy small portions of the *Emanuel* into your own outline, provided that your outline will be used only by you or your study group, and provided that you are the owner of the *Emanuel*.

3. When you first start studying for exams, read the *Capsule Summary* to get an overview. This will probably take you all or part of two days.

4. Either during exam study or earlier in the semester, do some or all of the *Quiz Yourself* short-answer questions, supplied at the end of most sub-chapters. You can find these quickly by looking for *Quiz Yourself* entries in the Table of Contents. When you do these questions: (1) record your short "answer" on the small blank line provided after the question, but also: (2) try to write out a

---

1. The suggestions below relate only to this book. I don't talk here about taking or reviewing class notes, using hornbooks or other study aids, joining a study group, or anything else. This doesn't mean I don't think these other steps are important — it's just that on this one page I've chosen to focus on how I think you can use this outline.

"mini essay" on a separate piece of paper. Remember that the only way to get good at writing essays is to write essays.

5. A couple of days before the exam, review the *Exam Tips* that appear at the end of each chapter. You may want to combine this step with step (4), so that you use the *Tips* to help you spot the issues in the short-answer questions. You'll also probably want to follow up from many of the *Tips* to the main outline's discussion of the topic; the number references after some of the *Tips* (e.g., "[145]") point you to the main outline's discussion.

6. Some time during the week or so before the exam, do some or all of the full-scale essay exams at the back of the book. Write out a full essay answer under exam-like conditions (e.g., closed-book if your exam will be closed book). If you can, exchange papers with a classmate and critique each other's answer.

7. The night before the exam: (1) do some *Quiz Yourself* questions, just to get your writing juices flowing; and (2) re-read the various *Exam Tips* sections (you should be able to do this in 1-2 hours).

My deepest thanks go to two of my colleages at Wolters Kluwer, Barbara Lasoff and Barbara Roth, who have helped greatly to assure the reliability and readability of this and my other books for many years.

Good luck in your Civil Procedure course. If you'd like any other publication from Aspen, you can find it at your bookstore or at **www.AspenLaw.com**.

If you'd like to contact me, you can email me at **semanuel@westnet.com**.

Steve Emanuel

Larchmont NY

July 2014

CASEBOOK CORRELATION CHART

(**Note:** general sections of the outline are omitted from this chart. **NC** = not directly covered by this casebook.)

Emanuel's Civil Procedure Outline *(by chapter and section heading)*	Friedenthal, Miller, Sexton & Hershkoff **Civil Procedure** (11th Ed. 2013)	Yeazell **Civil Procedure** (8th Ed. 2012)	Marcus, Redish, Sherman & Pfander **Civil Procedure: A Modern Approach** (6th Ed. 2013)	Friedenthal, Miller, Sexton & Hershkoff **Civil Procedure** (Compact 11th Ed. 2013)	Subrin, Minow, Brodin, Main & Lahar **Civil Procedure** (4th Ed. 2012)
CHAPTER 2 **JURISDICTION OVER THE PARTIES**					
II. **Jurisdiction over Individuals**	8, 75-89, 97-103, 180-196	66-76, 148-154, 170-174	744-756, 760-763, 778-781, 874-885	35-48, 56-61, 130-141	208-209, 682-699, 809-825, 837-845
III. **Jurisdiction over Corporations**	89-96, 103-150, 158-165	79-91, 103-131	763-778, 784-857	49-56, 61-104, 112-118	699-711, 714-793
IV. **General Jurisdiction**	150-158	87-88, 132-147	895-905	105-112	825-837
V. **Federal Jurisdiction over the Parties**	196-198, 216-234	12, 164-169	782-784, 908-910	141-142, 158-175	711-713
VI. **Jurisdiction over Things**	165-180	73, 91-103	752-760, 857-873	118-130	793-809
VII. **Notice and Opportunity to be Heard**	9-10, 201-215, 243-258	154-169, 345-363	29-69, 905-910	145-158, 182-191	24-82, 846-855
VIII. **Defenses to Claims of Jurisdiction**	198-200, 234-243	76-78, 203-206	755-756, 898-904	12-16, 142-143, 175-182, 193-196, 243-246	692-693
IX. **Venue**	9, 359-396	174-189	910-930	247-275	855-867
CHAPTER 3 **SUBJECT MATTER JURISDICTION**					
III. **Diversity Jurisdiction**	8, 266-291	6-12, 206-221	932-947	193-211	207-208, 880-890
IV. **Federal Question Jurisdiction**	8, 291-318	195-206	947-974	211-231	207-208, 871-880
V. **Amount in Controversy**	8, 282-289	217-221	942-947	208-209	887-890
VI. **Supplemental (Formerly "Ancillary" and "Pendent") Jurisdiction**	318-345	221-229	974-1000	231-240	890-908
VII. **Removal of Cases to the Federal Courts**	345-352	229-238	1000-1012	240-243	908-913

CASEBOOK CORRELATION CHART (continued)

Emanuel's Civil Procedure Outline *(by chapter and section heading)*	Friedenthal, Miller, Sexton & Hershkoff **Civil Procedure** (11th Ed. 2013)	Yeazell **Civil Procedure** (8th Ed. 2012)	Marcus, Redish, Sherman & Pfander **Civil Procedure: A Modern Approach** (6th Ed. 2013)	Friedenthal, Miller, Sexton & Hershkoff **Civil Procedure** (Compact 11th Ed. 2013)	Subrin, Minow, Brodin, Main & Lahar **Civil Procedure** (4th Ed. 2012)
CHAPTER 4 **PLEADING**					
II. Modern Federal Pleading Generally	550-551, 598, 641-657	12-15, 368, 413-426	136-164	348-351, 390, 403-407	215-219, 325-337
III. The Complaint	10-12, 553-610	370-389, 401-406, 412-413	130-136, 171-218	16-18, 351-354, 381-385	215-251
IV. Motions Against the Complaint	12-13, 23-24, 34-40, 610-618	20-23, 370-383, 390-401, 427-432	139-144, 164-171, 219-220	18, 29-30, 354-381, 386-389	257-261
V. The Answer	618-627	23-25, 432-442	229-242	18-19, 389-391	209, 261-269
VI. Time for Various Pleadings	610	NC	NC	386	NC
VII. Amendment of the Pleadings	627-640	26, 443-456	245-263	391-402	269-294
VIII. Variance of Proof from Pleadings	630-632	26	249	395	270
CHAPTER 5 **DISCOVERY AND PRETRIAL CONFERENCE**					
II. Scope of Discovery	40-44, 831-855, 885-909	29-35, 457-474, 487-503	382-393, 401-402, 409-466	519-533, 553-570	210, 380-420, 430-458
III. Methods of Discovery Oral Depositions	855-859	31, 480-484	396-399	19-20, 534-536	210, 425-427
Written Depositions	13, 859	NC	399	536	NC
Interrogatories to Parties	13, 860-866	30, 478-480	395-396	20, 536-539	427-428
Requests for Admission	14, 878-880	478-480	406	20, 551-553	429
Requests to Produce Documents	14, 866-870	31, 474-477	393-395, 402-405	20, 539-543	428
Physical and Mental Exams	14, 870-877	31, 476, 507-508	399-401	20, 543-551	428-429
IV. Orders and Sanctions	909-916	485-487, 503-507, 508-522	405-409, 466-474	570-572	417, 437-439
V. Use of Discovery Results at Trial	881-885	NC	407	NC	NC
VI. Pretrial Conference	917-931	598-602	20-27, 518-540	573-586	379, 418-420, 436
CHAPTER 6 **ASCERTAINING APPLICABLE LAW**					
II. *Erie* and Other Fundamentals	398-409	239-250	1013-1024	278-287	306-311, 916-927
III. *Erie* Problems	409-478	250-274	1024-1102	287-326	927-984
IV. Federal Common Law	478-496	248-249	1093-1110	326-342	925-926

CASEBOOK CORRELATION CHART (continued)

Emanuel's Civil Procedure Outline *(by chapter and section heading)*	Friedenthal, Miller, Sexton & Hershkoff **Civil Procedure** (11th Ed. 2013)	Yeazell **Civil Procedure** (8th Ed. 2012)	Marcus, Redish, Sherman & Pfander **Civil Procedure: A Modern Approach** (6th Ed. 2013)	Friedenthal, Miller, Sexton & Hershkoff **Civil Procedure** (Compact 11th Ed. 2013)	Subrin, Minow, Brodin, Main & Lahar **Civil Procedure** (4th Ed. 2012)
CHAPTER 7 **TRIAL PROCEDURE**					
I. **Burden of Proof**	1048-1050	41-42, 407-411	NC	650-651	211
II. **Presumptions**	NC	NC	NC	NC	NC
III. **Preponderance of the Evidence**	NC	NC	NC	NC	211
IV. **Adjudication Without Trial**					
Voluntary Dismissal	976-978	41, 529-531, 538	242-245	609-611	564
Involuntary Dismissal	978-980	41, 528-529, 538	NC	611	564-565
Summary Judgment	14-15, 44-47, 947-976	35-41, 581-596	475-516	21-22, 588-609	212, 521-562
V. **Trials Without a Jury**	1048, 1091-1094, 1198-1203	311, 606-607, 703-710	1183-1194	650	NC
VI. **The Jury**	16, 18-19, 47-50, 56-65, 1030-1047, 1072-1083	616-646, 664-671	732-741	22, 24-45, 644-648	509-521, 603-606
VII. **Challenging the Judge for Bias**	NC	625-642	NC	NC	NC
VIII. **Directed Verdict/ Judgment as a Matter of Law**	1061-1070	42-46, 646-656, 662-664	650-666, 679-689	652-655	211, 565-566, 572-597
IX. **Special Verdict and Interrogatories**	18-19, 51-56, 1083-1090	670	721-732	25	598, 1020
X. **New Trial**	19, 1095-1131	656-664	690-721	26, 656-659	568-597, 606-609
XI. **Judgment Notwithstanding the Verdict / Judgment as A Matter of Law**	19, 1070-1072	42-46, 658-662	666-679	652-655	212, 566-567, 572-597
XII. **Constitutional Right to Jury Trial**	987-1028	41, 607-615	583-650	618-644	497-508
XIII. **Remedies**	24-26, 1134-1158	288-315	70-99	30-33	115-149
XIV. **Appeals**	65-70, 1159-1210	52-57, 673-713	1111-1198	661-679	615-619

CASEBOOK CORRELATION CHART (continued)

Emanuel's Civil Procedure Outline *(by chapter and section heading)*	Friedenthal, Miller, Sexton & Hershkoff **Civil Procedure** (11th Ed. 2013)	Yeazell **Civil Procedure** (8th Ed. 2012)	Marcus, Redish, Sherman & Pfander **Civil Procedure: A Modern Approach** (6th Ed. 2013)	Friedenthal, Miller, Sexton & Hershkoff **Civil Procedure** (Compact 11th Ed. 2013)	Subrin, Minow, Brodin, Main & Lahar **Civil Procedure** (4th Ed. 2012)
CHAPTER 8 **MULTI-CLAIM AND MULTI-PARTY LITIGATION**					
II. Counterclaims	663-674	797-806	305-306	411-415	209, 346-349
III. Joinder of Claims	659-663	793-806	272	409-411	209, 337-338
IV. Joinder of Parties	38-40, 683-705	26-29, 806-850	273-298	418-431	209, 337-345, 355-368
V. Class Actions	747-829	859-909	329-379	453-517	210, 1063-1133
VI. Intervention	737-745	839-852	316-329	443-451	210, 369-372
VII. Interpleader	713-736	852-859	306-316	433-443	210, 368-369
VIII. Real Party in Interest	680-683	NC	265-267	416-418	251-257
IX. Third Party Practice (Impleader)	706-13	812-818	298-304	432	210, 350-355
X. Cross-Claims	674-680	819-820	305-306	416	346-349
CHAPTER 9 **FORMER ADJUDICATION**					
II. Claim Preclusion (Merger and Bar)	70-74, 1213-1235	46-52, 716-748, 772-773	1202-1327	682-700	214-215, 988-1016, 1041-1050
III. Collateral Estoppel	70-74, 1235-1309	46-52, 749-772, 773-778	1252-1275	700-737	214-215, 1016-1041
IV. Full Faith and Credit	1309-1325	778-790	NC	738-743	1050-1058

CAPSULE SUMMARY

This Capsule Summary is intended for review at the end of the semester. Reading it is not a substitute for mastering the material in the main outline. Numbers in brackets refer to the pages in the main outline where the topic is discussed.

CHAPTER 1

INTRODUCTION

I. CIVIL PROCEDURE GENERALLY

A. A road map: Here is a *"road map"* for analyzing a Civil Procedure problem:

1. **Personal jurisdiction:** First, make sure that the court has *"personal jurisdiction"* or *"jurisdiction over the parties."* You must check to make sure that: (1) D had *minimum contacts* with the forum state (whether the court is a state or federal court); and (2) D received such *notice and opportunity to be heard* as to satisfy the constitutional requirement of due process. [7-98]

2. **Venue:** Then, check whether *venue* was correct. In federal court suits, the venue requirement describes what judicial *district* the case may be heard in. Essentially, the case must be heard either: (1) in any district where the *defendant resides* (with special rules for multi-defendant cases; or (2) in any district in which a *substantial part of the events* giving rise to the claim occurred. See 28 U.S.C. §1391. [103]

3. **Subject matter jurisdiction:** If the case is a federal case, you must then ask whether the court has *subject matter* jurisdiction. Essentially, this means that one of the following two things must be true: [119-163]

   a. **Diversity:** Either the case is between *citizens of different states* (with "complete diversity" required, so that no plaintiff is a citizen of the same state as any defendant) and at least $75,000 is at stake; or

   b. **Federal question:** The case raises a *"federal question."* Essentially, this means that plaintiff's right to recover stems from the U.S. Constitution, a federal treaty, or an act of Congress. (There is no minimum amount required to be at stake in federal question cases.)

4. **Pleading:** Next, you must examine whether the *pleadings* are proper. [169-201]

5. **Discovery:** Next, you may have a complex of issues relating to pre-trial *discovery*. [203-250]

6. **Ascertaining applicable law:** Now, figure out *what jurisdiction's law* should be used in the case. The most important problem of this type is: In a diversity case, may the federal court apply its own concepts of "federal common law", or must the court apply the law of the state where the federal court sits? If the state has a *substantive law* (whether a statute or a judge-made principle) that is on point, *the federal court sitting in diversity must apply that law*. This is the "rule" of *Erie v. Tompkins*. (*Example:* In a diversity case concerning negligence, the federal court must normally apply the negligence law of the state where the court sits.) [253-278]

7. **Trial procedure:** Next, you may face a series of issues relating to *trial procedure*. [281-331]

8. **Multi-party and multi-claim litigation:** If there is more than one claim in the case, or more than the basic two parties (a single plaintiff and a single defendant), you will face a whole host of issues related to the *multi-party* or *multi-claim* nature of the litigation. You must be prepared to deal with the various methods of bringing multiple parties and multiple claims into a case. In federal courts: [335-407]

   a. **Counterclaim:** D may make a claim against P, by use of the *counterclaim*. See FRCP 13. Check whether the counterclaim is *"permissive"* or *"compulsory."* (Also, remember that third parties, who are neither the original plaintiff nor the original defendant, may make a counterclaim.) [339]

   b. **Joinder of claims:** Once a party has made a claim against some other party, she may then make *any other claim* she wishes against that party. This is *"joinder of claims."* See Rule 18(a). [343]

   c. **Joinder of parties:** Multiple parties may *join* their actions together. Check to see whether either *"permissive* joinder" or *"compulsory* joinder" is applicable. Also, remember that each of these two types of joinder can apply to *either multiple plaintiffs* or *multiple defendants*. See FRCP 19 and 20. [345]

   d. **Class actions:** Check whether a *class action* is available as a device to handle the claims of many similarly-situated plaintiffs, or claims against many similarly-situated defendants. See FRCP 23. Look for the possibility of a class action wherever there are 25 or more similarly-situated plaintiffs or similarly-situated defendants. [355]

   e. **Intervention:** A person who is not initially part of a lawsuit may be able to enter the suit on his own initiative, under the doctrine of *intervention*. See FRCP 24. Check whether the intervention is "of right" or "permissive." [389]

   f. **Interpleader:** Where a party owes something to two or more other persons, but isn't sure which, that party may want to use the device of *interpleader* to prevent being made to pay the same claim twice. After checking whether interpleader might be desirable, decide whether the stakeholder should use *"statutory* interpleader" or "Rule interpleader." See 28 U.S.C. §1335 (statutory interpleader) and FRCP 22 (Rule interpleader). [392]

   g. **Third-party practice (impleader):** Anytime D has a potential claim against some *third person* who is not already in the lawsuit, by which that third person will be liable to D for some or all of P's recovery against D, D should be able to *"implead"* the third person. (*Example:* Employee, while working for Employer, hits Victim with a company car. Victim sues Employer in diversity, under the doctrine of *respondeat superior*. Under traditional concepts of indemnity, Employer will be able to recover from Employee for any amount that Employer is forced to pay Victim. Therefore, Employer should "implead" Employee as a "third party defendant" to the Victim-Employer action.) See FRCP 14(a). Once a third-party defendant is brought into the case, consider what other claims might now be available (e.g., a counterclaim by the third-party defendant against the third-party plaintiff, a cross-claim against some other third-party defendant, a counterclaim against the original plaintiff, etc.). [399]

   h. **Cross-claims:** Check to see whether any party has made, or should make, a claim against a *co-party*. This is a *cross-claim*. See FRCP 13(g). [406]

    i. **Jurisdiction:** For any of these multi-party or multi-claim devices, check to see whether the requirements of *personal jurisdiction* and *subject matter jurisdiction* have been satisfied. To do this, you will need to know whether the doctrine of *"supplemental"* jurisdiction applies to the particular device in question. If it does not, the new claim, or the new party, will typically have to *independently* meet the requirements of federal subject matter jurisdiction. (*Example:* P, from Massachusetts, sues D, from Connecticut, in diversity. X, from Massachusetts, wants to intervene in the case on the side of D. Because supplemental jurisdiction does not apply to intervention, X must independently satisfy the requirement of diversity, which he cannot do because he is a citizen of the same state as P. Therefore, X cannot intervene.)

  9. **Former adjudication:** Lastly, check whether the results in some *prior litigation* are *binding* in the current suit. Distinguish between situations in which the *judgment* in the prior suit is binding on an entire cause of action in the present suit (under the doctrines of *merger* and *bar*), and the situation where a *finding of fact* is binding on the current suit, even though the judgment itself is not binding (the *"collateral estoppel"* situation).

    a. **Non-mutual collateral estoppel:** Where a *"stranger"* to the first action (one not a party to that first action) now seeks to take advantage of a finding of fact in that first suit, consider whether this *"non-mutual"* collateral estoppel should be allowed. [427]

    b. **Full Faith and Credit:** Lastly, if the two suits have taken place in *different jurisdictions*, consider to what extent the principles of *Full Faith and Credit* limit the second court's freedom to ignore what happened in the first suit. [443]

CHAPTER 2

JURISDICTION OVER THE PARTIES

I. GENERAL PRINCIPLES

A. **Two kinds of jurisdiction:** Before a court can decide a case, it must have jurisdiction over the *parties* as well as over the *subject matter*. [7]

  1. **Subject matter jurisdiction:** *Subject matter* jurisdiction refers to the court's power to decide the *kind* of case before it. (*Examples of subject matter jurisdiction issues:* (1) Does the federal court for the District of New Jersey have the power to decide cases in which the two parties are citizens of different states? (2) Does the Binghamton Municipal Court have the power to decide cases involving more than $1,000?)

  2. **Jurisdiction over the parties:** Jurisdiction over the *parties* refers to whether the court has jurisdiction to decide a case *between the particular parties*, or *concerning the property*, before it. (*Examples of issues concerning jurisdiction over the parties:* (1) Does Court X have jurisdiction over D, who is a citizen of State X, but who is temporarily out of the state? (2) Does Court Y have jurisdiction over property in State Y where the action is one by P to register title to the land in his name?)

B. **Jurisdiction over the parties:** There are two distinct requirements which must be met before a court has jurisdiction over the *parties*: [8]

  1. **Substantive due process:** The court must have *power* to act, either upon given property, or on a given person so as to subject her to personal liability. The Constitution's 14th Amendment Due Process Clause imposes this requirement of power to act, as a matter of *"substantive due process."*

2. **Procedural due process:** Also, the court must have given the defendant *adequate notice* of the action against him, and an *opportunity to be heard*. These, taken together, are requirements of *procedural due process*, also imposed by the 14th Amendment's Due Process Clause.

C. **Three kinds of jurisdiction over the parties:** There are *three different kinds* of jurisdiction which a court may exercise over the parties — one of these three *must be present* for the case to go forward. [8]

1. **In personam:** *In personam* jurisdiction, or jurisdiction over the defendant's "person," gives the court power to issue a judgment against her *personally*. Thus *all* of the person's *assets* may be seized to satisfy the judgment, and the judgment can be sued upon in other states as well. [8]

2. **In rem:** *In rem* jurisdiction, or jurisdiction over a *thing*, gives the court power to adjudicate a claim made about a *piece of property* or about a *status*. (*Examples:* An action to quiet title to real estate, or an action to pronounce a marriage dissolved.) [8]

3. **Quasi in rem jurisdiction:** In *quasi in rem* jurisdiction, the action is begun by seizing property owned by (*attachment*), or a debt owed to (*garnishment*) the defendant, within the forum state. The thing seized is a pretext for the court to decide the case without having jurisdiction over the defendant's person. Any judgment affects only the property seized, and the judgment cannot be sued upon in any other court. [8]

4. **"Minimum contacts" requirement:** If jurisdiction in the case is *in personam* or *quasi in rem*, the court may not exercise that jurisdiction unless D has *"minimum contacts"* with the state in which the court sits.

   a. **"Purposefully directed" towards the forum state:** The requirement of minimum contacts usually means that D has to have taken *actions* that were *purposefully directed* towards the forum state.

   Examples of the required action: (1) D sold goods in the state, or (2) D is a corporation that has incorporated in the state, (3) D has visited the state, and been served with process while there, or (4) D has bought property in the state, etc.

   b. **Consequence of lack of contacts:** Without such minimum contacts between D and the forum state, exercise of jurisdiction would violate D's 14th Amendment federal constitutional right to due process. [9] For more about due process, see Par. (D), "Due process," below.

D. **Due process:** The exercise of jurisdiction by a state court must satisfy the defendant's rights under the *due process* clause of the *14th Amendment*. Thus if D is entirely lacking in *connections with the forum state*, it will violate D's 14th Amendment due process rights for a court of the forum state to exercise *in personam* jurisdiction over D. Nearly all of the Supreme Court cases about jurisdiction in Civil Procedure courses concern this due process requirement. [9]

1. **"Specific" versus "general" jurisdiction:** The Supreme Court's cases on the due process aspects of *in personam* jurisdiction make an important distinction between two categories of personal jurisdiction: (1) *"specific"* jurisdiction; and (2) *"general"* jurisdiction.

a. **"Specific" jurisdiction:** *"Specific"* jurisdiction refers to a court's exercise of personal jurisdiction to hear a claim ***related to, and arising out of,*** the defendant's voluntary ***contacts with the forum state.*** [9]

   i. **Lesser contacts required:** In general, a ***smaller degree*** of contact between the defendant and the forum state is required for a state court to exercise specific jurisdiction over the defendant than for it to exercise general jurisdiction. But the defendant will still be required to have some voluntary contacts (also referred to as ***"minimum contacts"***) with the forum state.

   Example: D, an individual, contracts to sell a laptop computer to P, also an individual. D lives in Texas and P resides in Arkansas. D assembles the laptop in Texas and personally delivers it to P's Arkansas home address, where D installs it. D has no business connections with Arkansas other than this one sale and delivery to P. Ten months later, the laptop's batteries malfunction, the laptop catches on fire, and P is burned. P sues D in Arkansas state court for his injuries.

   If the Arkansas state court hears the case and decides whether D should be personally liable for damages, the type of personal jurisdiction that the court will be exercising is *"specific* jurisdiction" — that is, the suit relates to and arises out of D's contacts with the forum state, Arkansas (since the suit relates to a computer as to which D voluntarily traveled to Arkansas to make delivery and installation).

   Because the suit is based on specific jurisdiction, all that's required is that D have "minimum contacts" with Arkansas. And here, even the relatively small degree of voluntary connection between D and Arkansas amounts to "minimum contacts," thereby preventing the Arkansas court's hearing of the case from being a violation of D's 14th Amendment due process rights. [10]

b. **"General" jurisdiction:** By contrast, ***"general"*** jurisdiction refers to a situation in which the state court is exercising *in personam* jurisdiction to hear a claim that ***does not arise out of or relate to the defendant's contacts with the forum state***. [10]

   i. **Extensive contacts required:** The U.S. Supreme Court requires, as a matter of fairness to the defendant, ***much more extensive contacts*** between the defendant and the forum state when the state court is exercising general jurisdiction (as opposed to specific jurisdiction) over that defendant.

   In fact, where the defendant is an ***individual***, in most cases a state court may as a constitutional due process matter exercise general jurisdiction over that defendant ***only*** if the defendant is ***domiciled in***, or else ***personally served with process in***, that state.

   Example: Same basic fact pattern as in the above example. Now, however, some time after D has delivered the computer to P in Arkansas, P drives through Texas on a vacation, and happens to stop off to see D at D's house there. Towards the end of the visit, when P is standing in D's driveway, D accidentally runs him over. P brings a negligence suit against D in Arkansas for P's injuries from the Texas accident.

   This suit, unlike the one in the prior Example, will have to be based on ***"general"*** (not specific) jurisdiction, since P's claim has nothing to do with any voluntary contact between D and Arkansas (the forum state). Since the case has to be based on general jurisdiction over D or not brought at all, D's federal constitutional due process rights probably mean that the Arkansas court will not have personal jurisdiction over D to hear the case, unless either (1) D changes his domicile to Arkansas prior to suit; or (2) D is served by P at a moment when D happens to be temporarily in Arkansas. [10]

    c. **"Specific" form more common:** The substantial majority of state-court litigations that you will encounter in your *Civil Procedure* course — including most of the Supreme Court opinions you'll read — involve specific rather than general jurisdiction. [11]

E. Long-arm statutes: Even where the requirements of due process (minimum contacts between D and the forum state, etc.) are satisfied, the defendant may not be served *outside* of the forum state unless the forum state has enacted a *statute* authorizing out-of-state service under certain circumstances. Such statutes allowing the courts of a state to obtain jurisdiction over persons *not physically present* within the state at the time of the service are called "*long-arm* statutes."

    1. Links to forum state: Long-arm statutes allow jurisdiction on the basis of specified *links between the defendant and the forum state*, such as domicile there, ownership of property in the state, commission of a tortious act inside the state, etc. [11]

    2. Substitute service: Long-arms typically provide for "substitute" means of *service*, since in-state personal service is not possible. (*Example:* A long-arm statute might allow the plaintiff to cause the defendant to be served out of state by registered mail.)

II. JURISDICTION OVER INDIVIDUALS

A. Different categories: In most states, there are a number of different criteria which will enable the court to take personal jurisdiction over an individual. Some of the most common (each of which will be considered in detail below) are: [11]

    1. *Presence* within the forum state;

    2. *Domicile* or *residence* within the forum state;

    3. *Consent* to be sued within the forum state;

    4. *Driving a car* within the forum state;

    5. Committing a *tortious act* within the state (or, perhaps, committing an out-of-state act with in-state tortious consequences);

    6. Ownership of *property* in the forum state;

    7. Conducting *business* in the forum state;

    8. Being *married in*, or living while married in, the forum state.

        Note: Regardless of the criteria used by the state and its long-arm for establishing personal jurisdiction over the individual, due process requires that the individual have *minimum contacts* with the forum state before personal jurisdiction may be exercised over her. The meaning of "minimum contacts" is discussed further below in the treatment of jurisdiction over corporations.

B. Presence: Jurisdiction may be exercised over an individual by virtue of his *presence within the forum state* at the time he is served with process. That is, even if the individual is an out-of-state resident who comes into the forum state only briefly, personal jurisdiction over him may be gotten as long as *service was made* on him while he was in the forum state. [12]

Example: D and his wife, P, separate while residing in New Jersey. P moves to California with their children. D visits California on business, and stops briefly to visit the children. While D is visiting, P serves him with process in a California suit for divorce. D never visits the state again.

Held, California can constitutionally assert personal jurisdiction over D based on his presence in the state at the time of service, even though that presence was brief, and even though D had virtually no other contacts with the state. [*Burnham v. Superior Court*].

C. Domicile: Jurisdiction may be exercised over a person who is **domiciled** within the forum state, even if service takes place outside of the forum state.

   1. Meaning of "domicile": A person is considered to be domiciled in the place where he has his **current dwelling place**, if he also has the **intention to remain** in that place for an **indefinite period**. [13-14]

D. Residence: Some states allow jurisdiction to be exercised on the basis of D's **residence in the forum state**, even though he is absent from the state. A person may have several residences simultaneously. (The Supreme Court has not yet passed on the due process validity of jurisdiction based solely on residence, so this remains presumptively a valid method of gaining jurisdiction.) [14]

E. Consent: Jurisdiction over a party can be exercised by virtue of her **consent**, even if she has no contacts whatsoever with the forum state. [15]

   Example: P, who does not reside in Ohio or have any other contacts with Ohio, brings suit against D in Ohio. By filing the suit in Ohio, P will be deemed to have consented to Ohio's jurisdiction. D may then counterclaim against P. Even if P dismisses his own suit, his consent to the action will be binding, and the Ohio courts will have personal jurisdiction over him on the counterclaim.

F. Non-resident motorist: Most states have statutes allowing the courts to exercise jurisdiction over **non-resident motorists** who have been involved in **accidents in the state**. [16]

   Example: P is a resident of the forum state. D, not a resident of the forum state, is driving his car in the forum state, and has a collision with P's car. Even if D has no other contacts with the state, a non-resident motorist statute will probably be in force in the state, and will probably give the forum state's courts jurisdiction over a tort suit by P against D.

   1. Service on state official: Most of the non-resident motorist statutes provide for in-state service of process on a **designated state official** (e.g., the Director of Motor Vehicles) and for **registered mail service** on the out-of-state defendant himself. [17]

   2. Specific jurisdiction only: Non-resident motorist statutes, when they exist, confer only **specific jurisdiction**. That is, they confer jurisdiction only for a suit involving the in-state auto accident.

G. In-state tortiousness: Many states have statutes allowing their courts jurisdiction over persons committing **tortious acts within the state**. [17]

   Example: D, an out-of-stater, gets into a fight with P at a bar in P's home state. P wants to bring a civil battery claim against D in the state. If, as is likely, the state has a long-arm provision governing tortious acts within the state, P will be able to get personal jurisdiction over D in the battery action.

   1. **Out-of-state acts with in-state consequences:**   Some "in-state tortious acts" long-arm clauses have been interpreted to include acts done *outside the state* which produce *tortious consequences within the state*. In a *products liability* situation, a vendor who sells products that he knows will be used in the state may constitutionally be required to defend in the state, if the product causes injury in the state. [*Gray v. American Radiator Corp.*] [17]

H. Owners of in-state property: Many states exercise jurisdiction over *owners of in-state property* in causes of action arising from that property. [18]

I. Conducting business: States often exercise jurisdiction over non-residents who conduct *businesses* within the state. Since states may regulate an individual's business conduct in the state, they may constitutionally exercise jurisdiction relating to that doing of business. [19]

   1. **Limited to specific jurisdiction:** Again, however, the statement that this type of unincorporated-business long-arm is constitutional assumes that the jurisdiction being exercised under the long-arm is *specific*, rather than general, jurisdiction. In other words, probably the statute can constitutionally apply only to a suit *arising out of the non-resident unincorporated business' in-state business activities*.

J. Limits of "due process" undefined for suits against individuals: The Supreme Court has never squarely articulated a test for determining whether a state's exercise of personal jurisdiction over an out-of-state individual violates that person's right to *constitutional due process.* [20]

   1. **Rules for cases involving corporations:**   But cases involving *corporate* defendants suggest that a defendant who is an individual *cannot constitutionally be subjected to a state's jurisdiction unless either:*

      [1] **General jurisdiction based on domicile:** The defendant is *domiciled in* (or, perhaps, has a residence in) the forum state. And in that case, it's probably constitutional for even *general* jurisdiction to be exercised over her — i.e., even jurisdiction for a suit having nothing to do with the defendant's in-forum-state activities. [20]

   or ...

      [2] **Specific jurisdiction based on minimum contacts:** The suit relates to and arises out of the defendant's *voluntary ties to the forum state* (e.g., conduct that the defendant voluntarily took in the forum state, such as driving a car in the forum state). That is, the situation is one in which the defendant can be said to have *"minimum contacts"* with the forum state. And in this minimum-contacts situation, probably *only specific* jurisdiction — jurisdiction for a claim arising out of the voluntary in-state activities — would satisfy D's right to due process. [21]

III. JURISDICTION OVER CORPORATIONS

A. Domestic corporations: Virtually all of our discussion of jurisdiction over corporations will involve defendants who are *neither* incorporated in, nor have a principal place of business in, the forum state. That's because there are *no personal jurisdiction impediments* to a plaintiff's right to bring a suit in the state against a *"domestic"* corporation, i.e., one that *is* incorporated in the forum state or that has its principal place of business in the forum state. [22]

B. Foreign corporations generally: A state is much more limited in its ability to exercise jurisdiction over a *foreign* corporation (i.e., a corporation not incorporated in the forum state and not headquartered there) than over a domestic corporation. [23-28]

1. **Minimum contacts:** The forum state may exercise personal jurisdiction over the foreign corporation only if the corporation has *"minimum contacts"* with the forum state "such that the maintenance of the suit does not offend 'traditional notions of *fair play* and substantial justice.' " [*International Shoe Co. v. Washington*] [23-24]

2. **Dealings with residents of forum state:** Usually, a corporation will be found to have the requisite "minimum contacts" with the forum state only if the corporation has somehow *voluntarily sought* to *do business* in, or with the residents of, the forum state. [24-28]

    Example 1 (minimum contacts found): D has no activities in Washington except for the activities of its salesmen, who live in the state and work from their homes. All orders are sent by the salesmen to the home office, and approved at the home office. The salesmen earn a total of $31,000 per year in commissions.

    Held, the company has minimum contacts with Washington. [*International Shoe Co.*]

    Example 2 (minimum contacts found): D is a Texas insurance company. It does not solicit business in California. However, it takes over, from a previous insurance company, a policy written on the life of X, a California resident. D sends X a new policy; X sends premiums from his California home to D's out-of-state office. X dies; P (the beneficiary under the policy) is a California resident. P sues D in California for payment under the policy.

    Held, D has minimum contacts with California, and can thus be sued *in personam* there in a suit by P for payment on the policy. [*McGee v. International Life Insur. Co.*]

    Example 3 (minimum contacts not found): D is a Delaware bank, which acts as trustee of a certain trust. S, the settlor of the trust, is a Pennsylvania resident at the time she sets up the trust. Years later, she moves to Florida. Later, her two children, also Florida residents, want to sue D in Florida for a judgment that they are entitled to the remaining trust assets. D has no other contacts with Florida.

    Held, D does not have minimum contacts with Florida, and therefore, cannot be sued *in personam* there. [*Hanson v. Denckla*]

    Note: The key idea is that D will be found to have minimum contacts with the state only if D has *purposely availed* itself of the chance to do business in the forum state. Thus in *McGee* (Example 2 above), the insurance company offered a policy to someone who it knew was a resident of the forum state. In *Hanson* (Example 3 above), by contrast, the trustee never voluntarily initiated business transactions with a resident of the forum state or otherwise voluntarily did business in the state — it was only S's unilateral decision to move to the forum state that established any kind of connection with that state, so minimum contacts did not exist.

C. **Suit based on products shipped into the forum state:** Personal jurisdiction issues are especially important in *products liability* suits in which the plaintiff claims that the out-of-state defendant corporation made or sold — from a location outside the forum state — a product that was later *shipped into the forum state* and caused personal injury to the plaintiff there. Often, these cases are brought in the courts of the *plaintiff's home state*, and the defendant has few or no contacts with that state apart from the fact that the plaintiff's injury occurred there.

1. **Suit asserts "specific jurisdiction":** Throughout the discussion of product-liability cases in this Par. (C), we'll be assuming that the suit by the injured plaintiff asserts *"specific jurisdiction"* over the manufacturer. Remember, "specific" jurisdiction means jurisdiction in a case relating to or arising out of the defendant's *activities in the forum state*.

2. **Summary on out-of-state vendors:** As of this writing (mid-2014), the law is still quite unclear about when an out-of-state or foreign product seller should be required to defend a product liability suit brought in the state where the injury occurred. But here is an attempt to summarize some of the relevant principles.

3. **"Purposeful availment" required:** The mere fact that a product *finds its way* into a state and *causes injury there* is *not enough* to subject the out-of-state manufacturer or vendor to personal jurisdiction there. Instead, the defendant must be shown to have made some conscious *effort to market in the forum state* (a/k/a a *"purposeful availment"* of the privilege of doing business in the forum state).

    Example: The Ps purchase a car in New York while they are New York residents. Some time later, the Ps are driving the car through Oklahoma when an accident occurs. The Ps sue the Ds in Oklahoma for their injuries, alleging that the car was defective. The Ds are the distributor of the car (a non-Oklahoma resident who distributes only in New York, New Jersey and Connecticut) and the dealer (a non-Oklahoma resident whose showroom is in New York). Neither the distributor nor the dealer have ever sold cars in Oklahoma or done any other business there.

    Held, for the Ds — it would be a violation of the Ds' due process rights for the Oklahoma court to exercise personal jurisdiction over them. A "mere *likelihood that a product will find its way* into the forum State" does *not* suffice for jurisdiction over a defendant. The court must find that each D had enough "*conduct* and *connection with the forum state*" to cause him to "*reasonably anticipate being haled into court there.*" If either of the Ds had made *efforts "to serve, directly or indirectly, the market for its products"* in Oklahoma, it would not be unreasonable for the Oklahoma courts to subject that defendant to Oklahoma's jurisdiction. But P has not shown that about either of the Ds. *World-Wide Volkswagen Corp. v. Woodson.* [30]

    a. **Sold via distributor:** However, the "purposeful availment" of the privilege of doing business in the forum state — i.e., "targeting" of the forum state — probably need *not* be done *directly* by the defendant. Instead, if the defendant manufacturer *selects a distributor* — and intends that the distributor will *attempt to make meaningful sales in the forum state* — this act of selection probably suffices to trigger jurisdiction over the manufacturer.

    b. **An "extra" focus on the forum state's market:** Also, once the defendant is shown to have been merely *aware* that one of its products is likely to find its way into a particular state, even a relatively *small degree* of voluntary *"targeting"* by the defendant on that particular state market will probably be *enough* to show that the defendant has crossed the line from mere-awareness into "purposeful availment" of that state's market.

        Example: D is a British-based manufacturer of metal-working machines. D selects Distrib, a Colorado company, as D's exclusive American distributor, with D intending that Distrib will pursue the overall American market. D approves an ad designed by Distrib for marketing D's machines. D knows and intends that Distrib will run this ad in a monthly trade journal directed mainly at scrap-metal processors located in New Jersey, and Distrib runs the ad. Later, a machine made in the U.K. by D is sold by Distrib from its Colorado offices to Recy, a New Jersey-based recycling firm. At Recy's New Jersey premises, the machine slices off two of the fingers of P, who works for Recy. P sues D in New Jersey state court on a product-liability theory. D defends on ground that the court's exercise of jurisdiction over D would violate D's due process rights.

It's likely that D's approval of the New Jersey-focused ad to be run by Distrib, coupled with D's choice of Distrib to make sales across the U.S., would be enough to justify the conclusion that D consciously "targeted" New Jersey. In that event, it would not violate D's due process rights for the New Jersey court to hear the suit. And that's probably true even if the particular machine that injured P was *not* one the sale of which had anything to do with the ad. Cf. *J. McIntyre v. Nicastro* [34] (whose facts have been modified here — including by adding the ad directed at New Jersey customers — in a way that changes the result of the actual case).

    c. **Efforts as to U.S. as a whole:** Where D is a foreign corporation that takes steps to sell lots of units in *America as a whole* — but does *not* take any steps to *single out the forum state as a particular sales target* — the absence of efforts by D to target the forum state will likely be enough to *deprive* the forum state of specific jurisdiction. [Cf. *J. McIntyre.*] [41]

    d. **Shipment of significant quantity of goods into the state:** Where the defendant *knows that a substantial number of items* it manufactures are flowing into the forum state, that known flow will likely *suffice* for specific jurisdiction, even if the defendant has not consciously decided to focus on the particular market represented by that state. [42]

D. **Unfairness despite minimum contacts:** Even if D *has* "minimum contacts" with the forum state, D's connection with the state might be *so minor* that it is *"unreasonable and unfair"* — and thus violative of due process — to allow the state to hear the case. That's especially likely if D is a truly *foreign* (non-U.S.-based) corporation with slender contacts to the forum state.

    Example: P is injured in California when his motorcyle tire's inner tube blows out. P sues X, the maker of the cycle for products liability in California state court. X impleads Y, the non-U.S.-based maker of the tire, asserting that if X has to pay anything to P, Y, as maker of the defective product, has to reimburse X. Y impleads Z, the foreign maker of the tire's inner tube. Neither Y nor Z directly market any products in California or even in the U.S. But both know that their products are part of motorcycles sold by X in California. P and X settle, so that only the impleader claim by Y against Z is left in the case.

    Even if the California court decides that Z had minimum contacts with California, it will violate Z's due process rights to require Z to defend Y's impleader claim in California. That's in part due to the fact that the advantage to Y of being allowed to sue Z in a country in which neither Y nor Z directly does business is so small that allowing the suit would be "unreasonable" and "unfair" to Z. (Cf. *Asahi Metal Industry Co. v. Superior Court*, involving similar but not identical facts.) [34]

E. **Operation of an Internet Website that reaches in-staters:** A hot question today is whether the operation of an *Internet Website* that's hosted outside the forum state, but that's accessed by some in-staters, constitutes minimum contacts with the state. The main issue is, did the Website operator *intended to "target" residents* of the forum state? If yes, there are probably minimum contacts; if no, there probably aren't. [28-45]

1. **Passive site that just posts information:** So if an out-of-state local business just passively *posts info* on the Web, and doesn't especially want to reach in-staters or conduct transactions with them, this probably doesn't amount to minimum contacts, even if some in-staters happen to access the site. [44]

> **Example:** D operates a local jazz cafe in a small town in Kansas. He puts up a Website with a schedule of upcoming events, and uses a trademark belonging to P on the site. P, based in New York, sues D in N.Y. federal court for trademark infringement. Even though a few New Yorkers may have accessed D's site, this won't be enough to constitute minimum contacts with N.Y., because D wasn't trying to attract business from N.Y.

2. **Conducting transactions with in-staters:** But if D runs an *"e-commerce"* site that actively *tries to get in-staters to buy stuff* from the site, and a significant number do, that probably *will* be enough to constitute minimum contacts with the state, at least where the suit *relates to the in-staters' transactions* (i.e., the suit is based on *specific* jurisdiction). [44]

   a. **Rationale:** The court would likely conclude that D, by hosting an out-of-state site that tries to get business from in-state customers, has *purposely availed itself of the opportunity* to do business in the forum state (i.e., has *"targeted"* the forum state for business opportunities).

   b. **General jurisdiction:** But now, let's consider a suit brought against a defendant who uses the Internet to target customers in the forum state, but where the suit *does not arise out of any in-forum-state contacts* between that defendant and the forum state (i.e., the case involves *general* rather than specific jurisdiction). Here, unless the defendant is *incorporated in or headquartered in* the forum state, *no amount* of forum-state-targeted Internet activity (or for that matter in-forum-state sales) will be enough for the state to exercise for jurisdiction over the defendant. [*Daimler AG v. Bauman*] [45]

F. **Suits based on contractual relationship:** The requisite "minimum contacts" are more likely to be found where one party to a *contract* is a resident of the forum state. But the fact that one party to a contract is a resident does not by itself automatically mean that the other party has "minimum contacts" — the existence of a contract is just one factor to look at. [46-49]

1. **Contractual relationship involving the state:** Where the contract itself somehow ties the parties' business activities into the forum state, this will be an important factor tending to show the existence of minimum contacts. For instance, if one party is to make payments to the other, and the latter will be receiving the payments in the forum state, this stream of payments coming into the state is likely to establish minimum contacts and thus to permit suit against the payor.

   > **Example:** D runs a fast food restaurant in Michigan under franchise from P, which has its headquarters in Florida. The contract requires D to make royalty payments to P in Florida.
   >
   > *Held*, P may sue D in Florida. The fact that the payment stream comes into Florida is an important factor, though not by itself dispositive, in the court's conclusion that there were minimum contacts with Florida. [*Burger King Corp. v. Rudzewicz*]

2. **Choice-of-law clause:** Where there is a contract between the parties to the suit, the fact that the contract contains a *choice of law clause* requiring use of the forum state's law will also be a factor (though not a dispositive one) tending towards a finding of minimum contacts. (*Exam-*

ple: On the facts of the above example, the franchise contract stated that Florida law would be used. This was a factor helping lead the court to conclude that D had minimum contacts with Florida.) [48]

3. **"Reasonable anticipation" of defendant:** In suits relating to a contract, as with any other kind of suit, the minimum contacts issue always boils down to this: *Could the defendant have reasonably anticipated being required to litigate in the forum state?* The fact that the other party was a resident of the forum state, the fact that a stream of payments went into the forum state, and the fact that the forum state's law was to be used in the contract, are all non-dispositive, but important, factors tending towards the conclusion that the out-of-stater had minimum contacts with the forum state. [49]

G. **Class action plaintiffs:** An "absent" plaintiff in a class action that takes place in the forum state may be *bound* by the decision in the case, even if that plaintiff did not have minimum contacts with the forum state. [*Phillips Petroleum Co. v. Shutts*] [49-50]

H. **Plaintiff's lack of contacts:** The fact that the *plaintiff has no contacts* with the forum state will *not block* jurisdiction.

> **Example:** P is a New York resident who brings a libel suit against D (a magazine) in New Hampshire. P has chosen New Hampshire only because that is the sole state where the suit would not be been barred by the statute of limitations. Plaintiff has had no contacts with New Hampshire at all, except for the fact that her reputation in that state (as in every other state) has been allegedly libeled. D claims that P's complete lack of connections with New Hampshire blocks the state from exercising jurisdiction over D.
>
> *Held,* for P. "Plaintiff's residence in the forum state is not a separate requirement, and lack of residence will not defeat jurisdiction established on the basis of Defendant's contacts." [*Keeton v. Hustler Magazine*] [50-51]

IV. "GENERAL" JURISDICTION

A. **Where we are now:** So far, most of the cases we've covered involved *"specific* jurisdiction." That is, the claim against the defendant *arose out of the defendant's contacts with the forum state.* But it's now time to take a look at *"general jurisdiction."* That is, we're going to look at the rules governing when personal jurisdiction may be exercised with respect to a claim that does *not* arise out of the defendant's contacts with the forum state.

1. **Individuals:** Where the defendant is an *individual,* general jurisdiction over her will exist if she is *"domiciled"* in the forum state. In fact, it seems probable that for individuals, *nothing less* than domicile in the forum state will suffice for general jurisdiction. [*Goodyear Dunlop Tires Operations, S.A. v. Brown*] [51]

2. **Corporations:** Where the defendant is a *corporation,* the defendant must have such extensive contacts with the forum state that the defendant can be said to be *"essentially at home"* in that state. *Goodyear, supra.* And to be "essentially at home" in the forum state, the corporation must — except in exceptional cases — either:

   [1] be *incorporated* in the forum state, or

   [2] have its *principal place of business* in that state.

Daimler AG v. Bauman. [51]

Example: P, a resident of North Carolina, is riding in a bus in Paris when a tire blowout causes the bus to crash, injuring P. The bus was made by X, a French company. The tire was made by D, a corporation headquartered in Paris, incorporated in France and with all operations in France. About 10% of D's worldwide sales are made to U.S.-based customers (mainly vehicle manufacturers). As D knows, about one-half of 1% of D's annual worldwide sales (worth about $3 million per year) are made by D to North Carolina-based customers. The particular tire that blew out was not one of these — it was sold to by D's sales staff directly to X in France. P sues D in North Carolina state court based on product liability. D asserts that the North Carolina courts cannot constitutionally assert personal jurisdiction over it.

D is correct — it would violate D's federal constitutional rights for the court to exercise general jurisdiction over D. D's knowingly making of $3 million of annual sales into the forum state would probably be enough for *specific* jurisdiction (i.e., jurisdiction in a suit arising out of D's North Carolina-related activities), since all that's required for specific jurisdiction is that D have "targeted" the forum state. But except in exceptional circumstances, a U.S. court may not constitutionally exercise *general* jurisdiction over a corporate defendant unless that corporation is either incorporated in the forum state or has its principal place of business there. And we know that neither of these things is true of D, since both of these elements are located in France. [Cf. *Daimler AG v. Bauman*; *Goodyear Dunlop Tires Operations, S.A. v. Brown.*] (Note that these facts are a modified version of the facts in *Goodyear*.) [53-61]

V. FEDERAL JURISDICTION OVER THE PARTIES

A. General principles: To determine whether a ***federal*** court has personal jurisdiction over the defendant, you must check ***three things***: [68]

1. **Territory for service:** Whether service took place within the appropriate ***territory***;

2. **Manner of service:** Whether the service was carried out in the correct ***manner***; and

3. **Amenability:** Whether the defendant was ***"amenable"*** to the federal suit.

B. Territory for service: Here are the rules about the territory in which service may be made on the defendant in a federal action [68-72]:

1. **General rule:** As a general rule, in both ***diversity*** actions and ***federal question*** cases, ***service of process*** may be made only:

   [1] ***within the territorial limits*** of the ***state in which the District Court sits***; or

   [2] ***anywhere else permitted by the state law*** of the ***state where the District Court sits.***

   FRCP 4(k)(1)(A); 4(k)(2). [68]

   Example (within the territorial limits of state): P sues D in a federal action in the Northern District of Ohio. Whether the suit is based on diversity or federal question, service will be territorially valid if D is served with process anywhere within the state of Ohio, since this is the state where the district court sits. This is true even if service is physically made in the Southern District of Ohio.

   Example (out-of-state service based on state law): Under the New Jersey long-arm statute, if a non-resident is involved in a motor vehicle accident inside New Jersey with a New

Jersey resident, the New Jersey resident may serve the non-resident outside New Jersey, and the New Jersey courts may then exercise personal jurisdiction. P, a New Jersey resident, and D, a California resident, have an accident in New Jersey. P may sue D in diversity in federal District Court for New Jersey; P may serve D with process in California, because the long-arm of the state where the district court sits (New Jersey) would allow such service. FRCP 4(k)(1)(A).

2. **100-mile bulge:** A special *100-mile bulge* provision (FRCP 4(k)(1)(B)) allows for out-of-state service sometimes, even if local law does not permit it. When the provision applies, it allows service anywhere (even across a state boundary) within a 100-mile radius of the federal courthouse where suit is pending. The bulge provision applies only where out-of-staters will be brought in as **additional parties** to an **already pending** action. There are two types of parties against whom it can be used: [70]

   a. **Third-party defendants:** *Third-party defendants* (FRCP 14) may be served within the bulge.

      Example: P sues D in a New Jersey federal district court diversity action. D claims that if D is liable to P, X is liable to D as an indemnitor. The suit is pending in Newark, less than 100 miles from New York City. D may serve X in New York City, even if no New Jersey long-arm statute would allow the suit.

   b. **Indispensable parties:** So-called *"indispensable parties"* — that is, persons who are needed in the action for just adjudication, and whose joinder will not involve subject matter jurisdiction problems — may also be served if they are within the bulge.

      Example: P sues D for copyright infringement in federal district court for the Eastern District of Kentucky, located in Lexington. D files a counterclaim against P. D wants to join X as a co-defendant to this counterclaim, arguing that P and X conspired to violate D's copyrights. X resides in Cincinnati, Ohio, located 78 miles from Lexington. If the court agrees that X is required for just adjudication of D's counterclaim, service on X in Cincinnati is valid, even if the Kentucky long-arm would not allow service there.

3. **Nationwide service of process:** In several kinds of cases, Congress has provided for *nationwide* service of process. Suits against *federal officials and agencies*, and suits based on *statutory interpleader*, are examples of nationwide service. [69]

4. **Foreign defendant not servable in any state:** Rule 4(k)(2)(A) allows a *federal question* suit to be brought against any person or organization who cannot be sued in *any state* court (almost always because they are a *foreigner*).

   Example: D, a French company, without setting foot in the U.S., solicits business by phone and mail from residents of a large number of states. D does not solicit enough from the residents of any one state to satisfy that state's long-arm. Therefore, D could not be sued in any state court for a claim concerning its activities. P, a New York investor, brings a suit based upon the federal securities laws against D in the federal district court for the Southern District of New York.

      Assuming that D can be said to have had minimum contacts with the United States as a whole, the New York federal court will have personal jurisdiction over D for this federal-question claim, because D is not subject to the jurisdiction of the courts of any state. FRCP 4(k)(2)(A).

5. **Gaps possible:** A defendant who is not located in the state where the district court sits may **not** be served if he does not fall within one of the four special cases described above (servable pursuant to state long-arm, 100-mile bulge, nationwide service or foreign defendant not servable in any state), **even if he has the constitutionally-required minimum contacts** with the forum. This is true whether the case is based on diversity or federal question. [72]

> **Example:** P, a Connecticut resident, wants to bring a federal diversity suit in Connecticut against D, a New Yorker. The suit involves an accident that occurred in New York. D owns a second home in Connecticut, as well as lots of other real estate there. Assume that this ownership gives him not only minimum contacts but "systematic and continuous" contacts with Connecticut. However, Connecticut has a very narrow long-arm, which would not allow service on D in New York for a Connecticut state action.
>
> P will not be able to serve D in New York in his federal action, because none of the special cases is satisfied. This is true even though it would not be a violation of due process for either the Connecticut courts or the federal court in Connecticut to exercise personal jurisdiction over D.

C. **Manner of service:** Once you determine that the party to be served lies within the territory described above, you must determine if the service was carried out in the correct **manner**.

1. **Individual:** Service on an **individual** (Rule 4(e)) may be made in any of several ways:

   a. **Personal:** By serving him **personally**;

   b. **Substitute:** By handing the summons and complaint to a person of **"suitable age and discretion"** residing at D's residence;

   c. **Agent:** By serving an **agent** appointed or designated by law to receive process. (*Example:* Many states designate the Director of Motor Vehicles as the agent to receive process in suits involving car accidents);

   d. **Local state law:** By serving D in the manner provided by either: (1) the **law of the state where the district court sits**, if that state has such a provision, or (2) the **law of the state where the person is being served**. (*Example*: P brings an action against D, a resident of California, in New Jersey federal court, and wishes to serve him by certified mail. Service will be possible if **either** the courts of New Jersey **or** California allow certified-mail service.)

2. **Corporation:** Service on a **corporation** may be made by leaving the papers with an **officer**, a managing or general **agent**, or any other agent authorized by appointment or by law to receive process for the corporation. FRCP 4(h)(1).

   a. **Local state law:** As with individuals, service on a corporation may also be made in the manner provided by the local law of (i) the state where the **action is pending** or (ii) the state where the **service is made**. FRCP 4(h)(1)(A).

3. **Waiver of service:** Rule 4(d) allows plaintiff to in effect serve the summons and complaint by **mail**, provided that the **defendant cooperates**. P mails to D a **"request for waiver of service"**; if D agrees, no actual in-person service is needed.

   a. **Incentives:** D is free to refuse to grant the waiver, in which case P must serve the summons by the in-person methods described above. But, if D refuses the waiver, the court will impose the **costs** subsequently incurred by P in effecting service on D unless "good cause" is shown for D's refusal. (FRCP 4(d)(2).)

D. Amenability to suit: If D was served in an appropriate territory, and in an appropriate manner, you still have to determine whether D is closely-enough linked to the state where the federal district court sits to make him *"amenable to suit"* in that court. [74-75]

    1. Federal question: In *federal question* cases, most courts hold that D is amenable to suit in their court if jurisdiction could *constitutionally be exercised* over him in the **state courts** of the state where the federal court is sitting, even if the state court itself would not (because of a limited long-arm) have jurisdiction. [74]

        Example: P sues D for copyright infringement. The suit is brought in the Northern District of Ohio. D's only contact with Ohio is that he sold 100 copies of the allegedly infringing book in Ohio. The state courts of Ohio, although they could constitutionally take personal jurisdiction over D in a similar state-created claim — libel, for instance — would not do so because the Ohio long-arm is very limited and would not cover any action growing out of these facts. However, the federal district court will hear the federal question copyright claim against D, because P has minimum contacts with the state where the federal court sits.

        a. Foreign defendants: In general, if the defendant is a *foreign* corporation or resident, most federal courts will exercise jurisdiction over the defendant only if that defendant has minimum contacts with the state where the federal court sits, not merely minimum contacts with the United States as a whole. (Again, as with an out-of-state but not foreign defendant, the federal court will hear the federal question claim even though the state courts might not exercise jurisdiction over the defendant due to a limited state long-arm.)

            i. Narrow exception: If a foreign defendant could not be sued in *any state*, he may be sued on a federal-question claim in any federal judicial district, assuming that he has minimum contacts with the U.S. as a whole. (FRCP 4(k)(2).) But assuming that the foreign defendant could be sued in at least some state court, the general rule described in the prior paragraph (D must have minimum contacts with the state where the federal court sits, not just with the U.S. as a whole) continues to apply.

    2. Diversity: In *diversity* cases, as a matter of practice the federal courts exercise only the jurisdiction that is allowed *by the statutory law of the state in which they sit*. So if the state statutory law does not go to the limits of due process, the federal court will follow suit. [75]

VI. JURISDICTION OVER THINGS

A. Two types of actions: There are two types of actions that relate primarily to *"things"* rather than to people: (1) *in rem* actions; and (2) *quasi in rem* actions. [77-83]

    1. *In rem* actions: *In rem* actions are ones which do not seek to impose personal liability on anyone, but instead seek to affect the interests of persons in a specific thing (or *res*). (*Examples:* Probate court actions; admiralty actions concerning title to a ship; actions to quiet title to real estate or to foreclose a lien upon it; actions for divorce.)

    2. *Quasi in rem* actions: *Quasi in rem* actions are actions that would have been *in personam* if jurisdiction over D's person had been attainable. Instead, property or intangibles are seized not as the object of the litigation, but merely as a *means of satisfying a possible judgment* against D.

B. *In rem* jurisdiction:

1. **No personal liability:** In *in rem* actions, *no* judgment imposing *personal liability* on anyone results — all that happens is that the *status of a thing* is adjudicated.

   Example: In a quiet title action, a determination is reached that A, rather than B, is the owner of Blackacre. This is an *in rem* action, and does not result in the imposition of personal liability on anyone. [77]

2. **No effect from *Shaffer*:** The landmark case of *Shaffer v. Heitner*, discussed below, has *no effect* on *in rem* suits. *Shaffer* holds that there must be minimum contacts before a *quasi in rem* action may proceed; but no minimum contacts are needed for the court to adjudicate the status of property or some other thing located in the state, even though it affects the rights of an out-of-state defendant. [78]

C. ***Quasi in rem* jurisdiction:** [78-82]

1. **Definition:** As noted, a *quasi in rem* action is one that would have been *in personam* if jurisdiction over D's person had been attainable. Instead, property or intangibles are seized not as the *object* of the litigation, but merely as a means of satisfying a possible judgment against D. D has no liability beyond the value of the property or intangibles seized. [78]

   Example: P wants to sue D on a contract claim in California state court. The contract has no connection with California, nor does D himself have sufficient contacts with California to allow that state to exercise personal jurisdiction over him. D does, however, own a bank account in California. Putting aside constitutional due process problems, P could attach that bank account as a basis of jurisdiction, and bring a *quasi in rem* action on the contract claim. If P wins, he will be able to collect only the value of the bank account, and D will not be personally liable for the remainder if the damages exceed the value of the account.

2. **No *res judicata* value:** *Quasi in rem* judgments have *no res judicata value*. (*Example:* If P wins against D in a *quasi in rem* action in Connecticut, he cannot in a later suit against D in California claim that the matter has been decided for all time. Instead, he must go through another trial on the merits if he wishes to subject D to further liability.) [79]

   a. **Possible exception:** Some courts hold that if D makes a *limited appearance* (an appearance that does not confer personal jurisdiction over him) and fully litigates certain issues, he will not be allowed to re-litigate those issues in a subsequent trial. But other courts hold that even here, the first suit will not prevent D from re-litigating the same issues later on.

3. **Requirement of minimum contacts (*Shaffer*):** *Quasi in rem* jurisdiction over D cannot be exercised unless D had such *"minimum contacts"* with the forum state that *in personam jurisdiction could be exercised over him*. This is the holding of the landmark case of ***Shaffer v. Heitner*.** [79-82]

   Example: P brings a shareholder's derivative suit in Delaware on behalf of XYZ Corp. against 28 of XYZ's non-resident directors and officers. None of the activities complained of took place in Delaware, nor did any D have any other contact with Delaware. P takes advantage of a Delaware statute providing that any stock in a Delaware corporation is deemed to be present in Delaware, allowing that stock to be attached to provide *quasi in rem* jurisdiction against its owner. Thus P is able to tie up each D's XYZ stockholdings even though there is no other connection with Delaware.

   Held, this use of *quasi in rem* jurisdiction violates constitutional due process. No D may be subjected to *quasi in rem* jurisdiction unless he has minimum contacts with the forum state. Here, neither the Ds' actions nor the fact that those actions related to a Delaware corporation were sufficient to create minimum contacts, so the exercise of jurisdiction was improper. [*Shaffer v. Heitner*]

    a. Utility wiped out: Generally speaking, *Shaffer* means that *quasi in rem* jurisdiction has ***very little value today***. Prior to *Shaffer*, *quasi in rem*'s utility came from the fact that where personal jurisdiction was not available, *quasi in rem* provided a "second best" form of jurisdiction, in which the plaintiff could get satisfaction at least to the extent of the in-state property. Once *Shaffer* said that *quasi in rem* jurisdiction could only be exercised where the defendant had minimum contacts with the forum state, *quasi in rem* could rarely do anything that *in personam* jurisdiction couldn't do better. [81]

D. Limited appearance: Some states allow a ***"limited appearance."*** Under a limited appearance, D appears in an *in rem* or *quasi in rem* suit, contests the case on its merits, but is subjected to liability ***only to the extent of the property attached*** by the court. [82]

    1. Distinguished from special appearance: Distinguish limited appearances from *special* appearances — in the latter, a defendant against whom personal jurisdiction is asserted is allowed to argue the invalidity of that jurisdiction without having this argument, or his presence in the court, itself constitute a submission to the court's jurisdiction.

    2. Federal limited appearances: Federal courts usually follow the rule of the ***state in which they are sitting*** in determining whether to allow a limited appearance.

E. Federal *quasi in rem* jurisdiction: *Quasi in rem* jurisdiction is allowed in a ***federal*** court if:

    [1] ***the law of the state in which the federal court sits permits*** such *quasi in rem* jurisdiction, *and*;

    [2] P ***cannot*** obtain ***personal*** jurisdiction over D in the state through reasonable efforts.

Rule 4(n). [83-83]

Examples of conditions satisfying [2]: D is a fugitive, or the local long-arm is too weak to reach D even though he has minimum contacts with the state where the district court sits.

VII. NOTICE AND OPPORTUNITY TO BE HEARD

A. Notice generally: Even if the court has authority to judge the dispute between the parties or over the property before it (covered in the above sections), the court may not proceed unless D received ***adequate notice*** of the case against him. [84-92]

    1. Reasonableness test: In order for D to have received adequate notice, it is not necessary that he ***actually*** have learned of the suit. Rather, the procedures used to alert him must have been ***reasonably likely to inform him***, even if they actually failed to do so. [84]

        Example: P's process server leaves the summons and complaint at D's house, with D's wife. D's wife throws it in the garbage, and D never learns of it. D has received adequate notice, so the court can exercise jurisdiction over him. Conversely, if P's process server had left the papers on the sidewalk outside the house, and D had happened to pick them up, this would ***not*** be adequate notice to D — the procedures used were not reasonably likely to give D notice, and they are not saved by the fact that D in fact learned of the suit.

    2. Substitute service: Personal service — handing the papers to D himself — will always suffice as adequate notice. But all states, and the federal system, also allow ***"substitute service"***

C
A
P
S
U
L
E

S
U
M
M
A
R
Y

in most instances. "Substitute service" means some form of service other than directly handing the papers to the defendant. [85]

    a. Leave at dwelling: The most common substitute service provision allows the process papers to be left at D's **dwelling** within the state, if D is not at home. These provisions usually require the papers to be left with an adult who is reasonably likely to give them to D. (*Example:* FRCP 4(e)(2) allows the papers to be left with a person of "suitable age and discretion who resides there.")

    b. Mail: Some states, and the federal system, allow service to be made by ordinary **first class mail**. However, usually this method is allowable only if D returns an acknowledgement or waiver form to P's lawyer. If D does not return the form, some other method of service must then be used. See FRCP 4(e)(1).

3. Service on out-of-staters: Where D is not present in the forum state, he must somehow be served **out of state**. Remember that in a state court suit, this can only be done if the state has a long-arm statute covering the type of case and defendant in question. Once the long-arm covers the situation, the out-of-state defendant must still be given some sort of notice. [86]

    a. Mail notice: Many states provide for notice by **registered or certified mail** on the out-of-state defendant.

    b. Public official: Sometimes, service may be made by serving a **state official**, plus giving notice by mail to D. (*Example:* Many non-resident motorist statutes allow P to serve the state Director of Motor Vehicles with a matching mailing to the out-of-state defendant.)

    c. Newspaper publication: If D's identity or residence are unknown, some states allow service by **newspaper publication**. But this may only be used where D truly cannot be found by reasonable effort.

4. Corporations: Several means are commonly allowed for giving notice of suit to **corporations**. [86]

    a. Corporate officer: Many states require that a corporation, if it wishes to be incorporated in the state or to do business in the state, must **designate a corporate official** to receive process for suits against the company. Service on this designated official is, of course, deemed to be adequate notice.

    b. Federal Rule: The Federal Rules, and the rules of many states, are more liberal, in that they allow service on any person associated with the corporation who is of sufficiently high placement. Thus FRCP 4(h)(1) provides that service on a corporation may be made by giving the papers to "an officer, a managing or general agent, or any other agent authorized by appointment or by law to receive service of process."

B. Constitutional due process: Just as the Fourteenth Amendment's Due Process Clause prohibits jurisdiction over a defendant who lacks minimum contacts with the forum state (*International Shoe*), so that clause prohibits the exercise of jurisdiction over a defendant who has not been given *"reasonable notice"* of the suit. [*Mullane v. Central Hanover Bank*] [88]

1. Mail notice to all the identifiable parties: For instance, if a party's name and address are "reasonably ascertainable," publication notice will not be sufficient, and instead notice by **mail** (or other means equally likely to ensure actual notice) must be used. [*Mennonite Board of Missions v. Adams*] [88]

2. **Actual receipt doesn't count:** Remember that what matters is the ***appropriateness*** of the notice prescribed by statute and employed, ***not*** whether D actually ***got*** the notice. [88]

C. **Opportunity to be heard:** D must not only be notified of the suit against him, but must also be given an ***opportunity to be heard***. That is, before his property may be taken, he must be given a chance to defend against the claim. This "opportunity to be heard" must be given to D not only when his property will be taken forever, but even before there is any ***significant interference*** with his property rights.

1. **Pre-judgment remedy:** Opportunity-to-be-heard questions arise most frequently in the context of ***pre-judgment remedies***, which protect plaintiff against the defendant's hiding or squandering his assets during litigation. Two common forms of pre-judgment remedies are the ***attachment*** of D's ***bank account*** and the placing of a ***lis pendens*** against her ***real estate***.

2. **Three-part test:** The court will weigh ***three factors*** against each other to determine whether due process was violated when D's property was interfered with through a pre-judgment remedy: [90-92]

   a. First, the degree of ***harm*** to ***D's interest*** from the pre-judgment remedy;

   b. Second, the risk that the deprivation of D's property right will be ***erroneous*** (especially if the state could have used additional procedural safeguards against this but did not); and

   c. Third, the strength of the interest of the party (typically P) ***seeking*** the prejudgment remedy.

   [*Connecticut v. Doehr*] [91]

   Example: A state statute allows P to get a prejudgment attachment of D's real estate without D's having a hearing first, so long as P "verifies by oath" that there is probable cause to sustain his claim. Factor 1 above (the strength of D's interest) works against allowing attachment, since an attachment clouds D's title and affects his credit rating. Factor 2 (risk of erroneous deprivation) also supports not allowing the attachment, since the judge can't accurately determine the likely outcome of the litigation based solely on P's one-sided conclusory statements in the oath. Factor 3 (strength of P's interest) also works against the attachment, since P is not required to show D is dissipating his assets. Consequently, the grant of a prejudgment attachment of D's property violates his due process rights. [*Connecticut v. Doehr*]

VIII. DEFENSES TO CLAIMS OF JURISDICTION

A. **Special appearance:** In a ***"special appearance,"*** D appears in the action with the express purpose of making a jurisdictional objection. By making a special appearance, D has ***not consented*** to the exercise of jurisdiction. [93]

1. **Appeal:** Most courts allow a defendant who has unsuccessfully made a special appearance to then defend on the merits, without losing his right to appeal the jurisdictional issue. [93]

2. **Federal substitute for special appearance:** The federal courts (and the many state courts with rules patterned after the Federal Rules) have ***abolished*** the special appearance. Instead, D makes a ***motion*** to dismiss for lack of jurisdiction over the parties; making this motion does not subject D to the jurisdiction that he is protesting. FRCP 12(b)(2). [94]

a.   **Waiver:** The right to make a motion to dismiss for lack of personal jurisdiction is *waived* in the federal system if: (1) D makes a motion raising any of the defenses listed in Rule 12, and the personal jurisdiction defense is not included; or (2) D neither makes a Rule 12 motion nor raises the defense in his answer.

B. **Collateral attack:** [95]

1. **General enforcement of judgments:** A judgment entered in one jurisdiction may generally be *enforced* in another. That is, if State 1 enters a judgment against D, D's property in State 2 (or wages owed him in State 2) may be seized to satisfy the earlier State 1 judgment. [94]

2. **Collateral attack on default judgment:** If D *defaults* in an action in State 1, she may *collaterally attack* the default judgment when it is sued upon in State 2. Most commonly, D collaterally attacks the earlier judgment on the grounds that State 1 did not have personal jurisdiction over her, or did not have valid subject matter jurisdiction. [95-97]

   Example: D has no contacts with Iowa. P, an Iowa resident, sues D in Iowa court. D never appears in the action, and a default judgment is entered against him for $100,000. P then brings a suit in D's home state of New Jersey to enforce the earlier Iowa judgment. D will be permitted to collaterally attack the Iowa judgment, by arguing that Iowa lacked personal jurisdiction over him. The New Jersey court will undoubtedly agree with D that, because D did not have minimum contacts with Iowa, Iowa could not constitutionally take jurisdiction over him. Therefore, the New Jersey court will decline to enforce the Iowa judgment.

3. **Waiver by D:** A defendant who *appeared in the original action* without objecting to jurisdiction, or one who unsuccessfully litigated the jurisdictional issue in the first action, may *not* collaterally attack the judgment. (Instead, a defendant who unsuccessfully litigates jurisdiction in the first action must appeal to the first state's system, rather than later making a collateral attack.) [96]

C. **Defense of fraud or duress:** A court may constitutionally exercise jurisdiction over a defendant found within the forum state, even if D's presence was the result of *fraud* or *duress* on the part of the plaintiff. But the court may exercise its *discretion* not to exercise jurisdiction. (*Example:* P entices D into the jurisdiction with a false love letter and a false statement that she is leaving the country forever and wants to see D once more. When D arrives at the airport in the forum state, P serves him with papers. *Held*, the forum state will decline to exercise its jurisdiction because of P's fraud. [*Wyman v. Newhouse*]) [96]

D. **Immunity:** Most jurisdictions give to non-residents of the forum state an *immunity* from service of process while they are in state to *attend a trial*. This is true whether the person is a *witness*, a *party*, or an *attorney*. Most states also grant the immunity for related proceedings such as depositions. [97-98]

1. **Federal suits:** Out-of-state parties, witnesses, and attorneys also generally receive immunity from *federal* court suits (whether diversity or federal question). [98]

IX. VENUE

A. **Definition:** *"Venue"* refers to the *place within a sovereign jurisdiction* in which a given action is to be brought. It matters only if jurisdiction over the parties has been established. (*Example:* State X is found to have jurisdiction over the person of B, in a suit against him by A. Venue deter-

C A P S U L E   S U M M A R Y

mines in which *county* or *district* of State X the case should be tried.) [99]

B. State action: In state trials, venue is determined by statute. The states are free to set up virtually any venue rules they wish, without worrying about the federal constitution. [100]

1. **Basis for:** Most commonly, venue is authorized based on the county or city where the *defendant resides*. Many states also allow venue based on where the cause of action arose, where the defendant does business, etc. [100]

2. *Forum non conveniens:* Under the doctrine of *forum non conveniens*, the state may use its discretion not to hear the case in a county where there is statutory venue. Sometimes, this involves shifting the case to a different place within the state. At other times, it involves the state not having the case take place in-state at all. Usually, it is the defendant who moves to have the case dismissed or transferred for *forum non conveniens*. [101-103]

   a. **Factors:** Three factors that state courts often consider in deciding whether to dismiss for *forum non conveniens* are: (1) whether the plaintiff is a state *resident* (if so, he has a stronger claim to be able to have his case heard in his home state); (2) whether the witnesses and sources of proof are more available in a different state or county; and (3) whether the forum's own state laws will govern the action (transfer is more likely if a different state's law controls).

C. Venue in federal actions: In *federal* actions, the venue question is, *"Which federal district court shall try the action?"* Venue is controlled by 28 U.S.C. §1391. [103]

1. **Still need personal jurisdiction:** When you consider a venue problem, remember that venue is *not a substitute* for personal jurisdiction: the fact that venue lies in a particular judicial district does not automatically mean that suit can be brought there. Suit can be brought only in a district that satisfies *both* the venue requirements and the personal jurisdiction requirements as to all defendants. [104]

2. **Three methods:** There are three basic ways by which there might be venue in a particular judicial district:

   [1] if *any* defendant *resides* in that district, and *all defendants reside in the state* containing that district;

   [2] if a "*substantial part of the events*…giving rise to the claim *occurred*, or a substantial part of property that is the subject of the action is situated," in the district; and

   [3] if at *least one defendant* can be subjected to *personal jurisdiction* in the district, and *no other district qualifies* under either of the above two provisions (i.e., the all-defendants-reside and the where-events-occurred provisions).

   We consider each of these separately below, as Paragraphs 3, 4 and 5. [105]

3. **"Defendant's residence" venue:** For both diversity and federal question cases, venue lies in any district where *any defendant resides*, so long as, if there is more than one defendant, *all the defendants* reside in the *state* containing that district. 28 U.S.C. §1391(b)(1). [105]

   Example: P, from Massachusetts, brings a diversity suit against D1, from the Southern District of New York, and D2, from the Eastern District of New York. Venue will lie in either the Southern District of New York or the Eastern District of New York — each of these is home to at least one defendant, and each of these two districts is in a state that is home to all the defendants. But if D2 had been a resident of the District of Connecticut instead of any New York district, there would not be any "defendant's residence" venue anywhere.

4. **"Place of events or property" venue:** For both diversity and federal question cases, venue lies in any district "in which a *substantial part* of the *events* or omissions giving rise to the claim *occurred*, or a substantial part of *property* that is the subject of the action is *situated*...." This is "place of events" venue. 28 U.S.C. §1391(b)(2). [105]

    a. **Multiple districts:** There can be *multiple* districts qualifying for "place of events" venue, as long as each district was the locus for a "substantial part" of the events relating to the claim.

    Example: P, from Massachusetts, sues D, a car dealer from Connecticut. P alleges that D sold P a car in Connecticut, that P drove the car to Massachusetts, and that a defect in the car caused P to be injured in Massachusetts. Probably venue in either the District of Massachusetts or the District of Connecticut would be allowed under the "place of events" provision, since probably both the selling of the defective car and the incurring of the accident were a "substantial part" of the events.

5. **"Escape hatch" provision:** Finally, for both diversity and federal question cases, there is an *"escape hatch,"* by which venue may be founded in a district with which some or all defendants have close ties, if there is *no district in which the action may otherwise be brought*. This escape hatch is used mainly for cases in which nearly all the *events occurred abroad*. § 28 U.S.C. §1391(b)(3). [106-107]

    a. **Federal question cases:** The escape hatch provision gives venue, for both diversity and federal-question suits, in any judicial district as to which *two things* are true:

    [1] there is *no district* in which the action may *otherwise be brought* (i.e., there is no district meeting either the "all defendants reside in the state" or the "substantial part of the events occurred" requirements described above);

    and

    [2] at least one defendant is *"subject to the court's personal jurisdiction"* with respect to the suit.

    28 U.S.C. §1391(b)(3).

    Example: P, from Massachusetts, brings a diversity suit against D1, who resides in the Southern District of New York, and D2, who lives in Mexico. The suit relates solely to matters which occurred in Mexico (a car accident there). P's suit is brought in the Southern District of New York. D1 is served at his residence, and D2 is served when he visits the Southern District of New York.

    The escape hatch applies, to make venue proper in S.D.N.Y. Even though there is no "defendant's residence" venue or "place of events" venue in S.D.N.Y., the escape hatch works as to that district because both requirements of §1391(b)(3) apply. First, there's *no other district* where the suit could have been brought — there's no "defendants' residence" venue since there's no single state in which all defendants reside, and there's no "place of events" venue since everything happened in Mexico. Second, at least one defendant (D1) is subject to personal jurisdiction in S.D.N.Y. by virtue of his residence there (since a federal court follows the jurisdiction rules of the state where the court sits, and the courts of New York could constitutionally exercise jurisdiction over anyone domiciled in the state, as D1 is).

6. **No "plaintiff's residence" venue:** There is *no* venue based on *plaintiff's residence*. [107]

7. **Corporation:** The residence of a *corporation* for venue purposes matters only if the corporation is a defendant.

   a. **Three locations:** In the typical case involving *specific* jurisdiction (i.e., the suit relates to the corporation's in-state activities; see *supra*, p. C-5), a corporation will be deemed to be a resident of at least:

      [1] the district where it has its *principal place of business*;

      [2] any district where it has *substantial operations*; and

      [3] (probably) *any district* in its *state of incorporation.*

   (These categories aren't explicitly stated anywhere in the statute, but can be inferred from 28 U.S.C. §1391(d).)

   On the other hand, it is no longer the case, as it once was, that if a corporation does business anywhere in a state, it is deemed to reside in *all districts* of that state.

   Example: D, a one-store jewelry-retailing corporation, is incorporated in Delaware (which has only one federal judicial district). D's only store is in New York City (in the Southern District of New York), and the corporation makes sales only to people who visit the store. P, a New Jersey resident, buys an expensive diamond ring at D's store, later finds that it's fake, and wants to sue D in diversity for breach of warranty.

   For venue purposes, D is a resident of the District of Delaware and the Southern District of New York. Therefore P may bring suit either in the District of Delaware (based on district-where-all-defendants-reside venue, coupled with an inference based on 28 U.S.C. §1391(d) that a corporation is a resident of any district in its state of incorporation) or the Southern District of New York (based on district-where-all-defendants-reside venue, coupled with an inference from §1391(d) that a corporation is a resident of the district in which the defendant has its principal place of business).

   But P may *not* sue D in, say, the Northern District of New York. The fact that D conducts substantial business operations in one part of New York state (Southern District) does not mean that venue is proper in another part of that state (Northern District).

8. **Removal:** The defendant is sometimes allowed to *remove* a case from state to federal court. (See *infra*, p. C-39.) A case removed from state to federal court passes to "the district court of the U.S. for the district and division embracing the place *where such action is pending*." 28 U.S.C. §1441(a). [108]

9. **Federal *forum non conveniens*:** In the federal system, when a defendant successfully moves for *forum non conveniens*, the original court *transfers* the case to another district, rather than dismissing it. Under 28 U.S.C. §1404(a), "for the *convenience of parties and witnesses* … a district court *may transfer* any civil action to *any other district* or division *where it might have been brought.*" [108-111]

   a. **Defendant's motion:** Usually, it is the defendant who moves for *forum non conveniens*. When this happens, the case may be transferred only to a district where P would have had the right, *independent of the wishes of D*, to bring the action.

Example: Suppose that suit in a particular district would *not* have been possible, as an initial matter, either because one or more of the Ds could not be personally served there, or because venue would not have been proper there. The Ds do not have the right to move to have the case transferred to that not-initially-proper district by saying, in effect, "We consent to this transfer." (*Rationale:* Allowing the Ds to do this would disturb P's right to choose from among the eligible locations for the suit.)

  i. Consent of all parties: But if *all* parties, including P, consented, then the case *could* be transferred even to a district where it could not have originally been brought.

 b. Discretion of judge: The decision whether to transfer the action is left to the *discretion* of the judge where the action is pending, based on the judge's analysis of the convenience of the parties and witnesses.

 c. Transfer where original venue improper: The judge where the action is initially filed may use the federal forum non conveniens provision we've been talking about — §1404(a) — *only* if that original district was a *proper* one. If the case is originally filed in a district in which venue was *not* proper, the judge where the action was (improperly) filed must operate under a *different* statute, 28 U.S.C. §1406. [111]

  i. Judge required to choose: And under §1406, the judge in the place of filing *must* either (a) *dismiss* the suit; or (b) *transfer* the case to a different federal district where it could originally have been brought, if such a transfer is "in the interest of justice."

  ii. Distinction: So if the case was originally filed in a "correct" federal district, the trial judge there considers the forum non conveniens motion under §1404(a), and has discretion to *do nothing* (i.e., to let the case continue in her own court, as originally filed, even if that district might not in fact be the most convenient). *But* if the case was originally filed in a *"wrong"* federal district, then §1406 (not §1404) applies, and the judge does *not* have discretion to let the case remain in her own court. Instead, the judge *must* choose between *dismissing* the case, and *transferring* it to a different federal court where the case *could* properly have been filed. [112]

  iii. Effect of forum-selection clause: Suppose the parties to a contract *designate a particular forum* as the place in which any litigation must occur. The courts will generally *enforce* such a "forum-selection" clause. What happens if the parties agree to such a clause, but one of them later brings suit in a federal court that is proper under the venue statute but that *does not qualify as a permitted forum under the clause?*

   (1) Trial judge must enforce selection clause: When this happens, the relevant provision governing a transfer is §1404(a) (for actions that were brought in a correct district), not §1406 (for actions that were brought in a "wrong" district). But even though a judge hearing a §1404 motion normally has discretion to let the case remain in the judge's own district, if there is a forum selection clause that designates a different federal district court, the judge hearing the §1404 motion (i.e., the judge in the district where the case was filed in disregard of the forum-selection clause) *must enforce the clause*, by transferring the case to the federal court specified by the clause, whether or not this transferee court is more convenient for all the parties. [*Atlantic Marine Constr. Co., Inc. v. United States District Court for the Western District of Texas*] [112]

Example: D is a corporation incorporated in Virginia, with its principal place of business in the Eastern District of Virginia. P is a Texas corporation. They make a contract calling for P to work as a sub-contractor for D on a construction project run by D and located in the Western District of Texas. The contract contains a forum-selection clause drafted by D. The clause says that any suits under the contract must be litigated in federal court for E.D.Va. (not coincidentally, D's home district). P does the work, and isn't paid promptly. P then ignores the clause, and brings a diversity-based collection suit against D in W.D. Texas (P's home district), where venue is valid under the federal venue statute as a place where a substantial part of the underlying events occurred. (1) What provision should D use to try to get the Texas federal judge to dismiss the case or move it to E.D.Va. as required by the forum-selection clause? (2) If D uses the correct provision, what should the Texas court do in response, and on what reasoning?

(1) D should use §140<u>4</u> (to move for discretionary transfer of cases brought in a "correct" district), *not* §140<u>6</u> (to move for mandatory transfer or dismissal of cases brought in a "wrong" district). That's because, when the issue is whether the district in which the suit has been filed is "wrong" (as the term "wrong" is used in §1406), **only** the requirements of the federal **venue** statute are to be considered, not the requirements of any forum-selection clause.

(2) The Texas court should transfer the case to E.D.Va. As the Supreme Court has put it, "[A] forum-selection clause [must] be **given controlling weight** in all but the most exceptional cases." (*Atlantic Marine*, *infra*.) And that's true even though the judge is using §1404, which in theory requires the court to consider the convenience of the parties. Once the parties agree on a forum-selection clause, that fact becomes essentially the **sole issue** to be later considered in deciding whether the case should be transferred under §1404. In other words, the W.D.Tex. judge is *not free* to reason that because of the greater availability of witnesses there than in E.D.Va., the case should stay in W.D.Tex. for the convenience of all participants. Since the forum designated in the clause, E.D.Va., is part of the federal system, the judge *must* transfer the case there. Cf. *Atlantic Marine Constr. Co., Inc. v. United States District Court for the Western District of Texas* (based on facts similar to but not identical to these). [112-114]

Note: Suppose the parties in the above Example had in the forum-selection clause designated a **foreign** court or a **state** court — i.e., a court that **wasn't** part of the federal system. In that event, the W.D.Tex. court would be required to **dismiss** the case. That's because that court wouldn't have power to "transfer" the case to the designated forum (a court may "transfer" a case only to a court that's part of the same judicial system as the transferring court), yet the W.D.Tex. court would be required by the federal policy of enforcing forum-selection clauses to do its best to enforce the clause.

CHAPTER 3

SUBJECT MATTER JURISDICTION

I. GENERAL PRINCIPLES

A. Diversity vs. federal question: In the federal courts, there are two basic kinds of controversies over which the federal judiciary has subject matter jurisdiction: (1) suits between *citizens of different states* (so-called *diversity* jurisdiction); and (2) suits involving a *"federal question."* [119]

   1. Other cases: Certain other kinds of cases specified in the constitution also fall under the federal judicial power. These are cases involving **ambassadors**, cases involving **admiralty**, and cases in which the **United States** is a party. But except in these very unusual cases, when you are considering a case that is brought in the federal courts, you must ask: Does it fall within the diversity jurisdiction or federal question jurisdiction? If it does not fall within either of these, probably it cannot be heard by the federal courts.

B. Amount in controversy: In federal suits based on diversity, an amount in excess of *$75,000* must be in dispute. This is the *"amount in controversy"* requirement. In federal question cases, there is no amount in controversy requirement. [120]

C. Burden: The party seeking to *invoke the jurisdiction* of a federal court must make an *affirmative showing* that the case is within the court's subject matter jurisdiction. (*Example:* If P wants to invoke diversity jurisdiction, in her pleading she must allege the relevant facts about the citizenship of the parties.) [120]

D. Dismissal at any time: *No matter when* a deficiency in the subject matter jurisdiction of a federal court is noticed, the suit must be stopped, and *dismissed* for lack of jurisdiction. See FRCP 12(h)(3), requiring the court to dismiss the action at any time if it appears that the court lacks subject matter jurisdiction. [120-121]

> **Example:** A case brought under federal question jurisdiction goes through trial and through one level of appeals, and is then heard by the Supreme Court. The Supreme Court decides that there was no federal question in the first place. *Held*, the entire case must be dismissed for lack of federal subject matter jurisdiction. [*Louisville & National Railroad v. Mottley*]

II. DIVERSITY JURISDICTION

A. Definition: The Constitution gives the federal courts jurisdiction over *"controversies … between the citizens of different states…."* This is the grant of "diversity jurisdiction." [122-130]

> **Example:** P, a citizen of California, wants to sue D, a citizen of Oregon, for hitting P with D's car. Assuming that P's damages exceed $75,000, P can bring her negligence suit against D in federal court, because it is between citizens of different states.

   1. Date for determining: A party's citizenship for diversity purposes is determined *as of the commencement of the action*.

   a. Later change doesn't defeat diversity: This means that if diversity *existed* between the parties on the filing date, diversity is *not defeated* because one of the parties *later became a citizen of the same state* as his opponent.

    b. **Later change can't create diversity:** Conversely, if parties on opposite sides are citizens of the same state when the action is commenced, there is *no diversity* (and the case must be dismissed), even if by the time of trial the citizenship of one party has changed in such a way that diversity is now present. [124]

  2. **Domicile:** What controls for citizenship is *domicile*, not residence. A person's domicile is where she has her true, fixed and permanent home. (*Example:* P has his main home in New York, but has an expensive second home in Florida. D has her only home in Florida. P can bring a diversity action against D, because P is deemed a citizen only of New York, not Florida, even though P has a "residence" in Florida.) [125]

    a. **Resident alien:** A *resident alien* (an alien who lives in the United States permanently) is deemed a citizen of the state in which he is domiciled.

    b. **Presence of foreigner:** In a suit between citizens of different states, the fact that a *foreign* citizen (or foreign country) is a party does *not destroy* diversity. (Example: P, a citizen of Ohio, sues D1, a citizen of Michigan, and D2, a citizen of Canada. Diversity jurisdiction exists.) (In situations where one side consists *solely* of foreign citizens or foreign countries, "alienage" jurisdiction applies. See below.)

  3. **Complete diversity:** The single most important principle to remember in connection with diversity jurisdiction is that *"complete diversity" is required*. That is, it must be the case that *no plaintiff is a citizen of the same state as any defendant*. [122]

     Example: P, a citizen of New York, brings a suit against D1, a citizen of New York, and D2, a citizen of New Jersey. We ask, "Is there any plaintiff who is a citizen of the same state as any defendant?" Since the answer is "yes," the requirement of complete diversity is not satisfied, and there is no diversity jurisdiction.

  4. **Pleading not dispositive:** In order to determine whether diversity exists, the pleadings do not settle the question of who are adverse parties. Instead, the court looks beyond the pleadings, and arranges the parties according to their real interests in the litigation. [123]

    a. **Nominal parties ignored:** In determining the existence of diversity, *nominal* or purely *formal* parties are ignored. (*Example:* Where a guardian of an infant sues, the guardian is deemed to be a citizen only of the same state as the infant. See 28 U.S.C. §1332(c)(2).) [124]

B. **Alienage jurisdiction:** Related to diversity jurisdiction, but analytically distinct, is *"alienage"* jurisdiction. Alienage jurisdiction exists where there is a suit between citizens of a state, on one side, and foreign states or citizens thereof, on the other.

     Example: P, a citizen of Mexico, sues D, a citizen of Illinois. Even if there is no federal question issue, there will be federal subject matter jurisdiction of the "alienage" variety, assuming that the amount in controversy requirement is satisfied. [125-127]

  1. **Suit solely between or among foreign citizens:** But a suit solely between or among citizens of *foreign countries* does *not* fall within the alienage jurisdiction. [126]

     Example: If P, a citizen of Canada, sues D, a citizen of Mexico, there is no alienage (or other diversity) jurisdiction.

    a. **Resident alien:** A foreigner *living in the U.S.* — i.e., a *resident alien* — is deemed to be a *citizen of the state where she permanently resides*, for diversity purposes. [126]

Example: P, a citizen of Illinois, sues D, a Canadian living permanently in Illinois. D will be deemed to be a citizen of Illinois. Therefore, there's no diversity (of either the regular or alienage variety), so the suit can't go forward without a federal question.

b. Resident alien vs. non-resident alien: Courts are *split* about whether there's diversity in a suit by a *resident alien* against a *non-resident alien* (or against a resident alien who lives in a different state). [126]

Example: P, a Spaniard living in Florida, sues D, a Canadian living in Canada. Courts are split about whether there's diversity. If the same P sued D, a Canadian living permanently in Michigan, courts are similarly split about whether there's diversity.

2. Aliens and U.S. citizens on same side: Jurisdiction is not destroyed by the fact that one or more non-resident foreigners *and* one or more U.S. citizens are *each present* on each side of the litigation. Here, the jurisdiction is deemed to be conventional diversity, rather than alienage jurisdiction. [127]

Example: P1, a citizen of Ohio, and P2, a citizen of Canada (living in Canada), sue D1, a citizen of New Jersey, and D2, a citizen of Canada (living in Canada). The configuration is analyzed as if the foreigners were not present; therefore, the requirements for conventional diversity jurisdiction are satisfied, and the suit may proceed.

C. Diversity involving partnerships and corporations: Often, it will be necessary to determine the citizenship status of non-human entities like *partnerships* and *corporations*. [127]

1. Partnerships: *Partnerships* do *not* have a single state of citizenship. Instead, the citizenship of *each member counts*. [127]

Example: In a diversity suit where one of the parties is a limited partnership, *every member of the partnership* (even the limited partners, who have no say in how the partnership is run) must be diverse with each opposing party.

2. Corporations: A *corporation* is deemed a citizen of both *any state where it is incorporated and* of the state where it has its *"principal place of business."* In other words, for diversity to exist, no adversary of the corporation may be a citizen of *either* the state in which the corporation is incorporated, or of the state in which it has its principal place of business. [127]

Example: XYZ Corp., a corporation which is incorporated in Delaware, has its principal place of business in New York. In order for there to be diversity, no adverse party may be a citizen of *either* Delaware or New York.

a. Principal place of business: What's the test for determining where a corporation's *"principal place of business"* is? The hard case is where the corporation's top managers direct the company from a *headquarters location* that is in *one* state, but where the bulk of the corporation's daily *business activities* take place in a *different* state.

i. "Nerve center" test: In this situation, courts use the *"nerve center"* test, under which the principal place of business will normally be the *headquarters* location. [*Hertz Corp. v. Friend* (2010)] Under the nerve center test, a corporation's principal place of business refers to "the place where the corporation's *high level officers direct, control, and coordinate* the corporation's activities." *Id.* And that place will usually turn out to be the corporate headquarters. [128]

Example: The Ps, California citizens, work for D (a rental-car chain) in California. They sue D in the California state courts on a state-law claim. D, seeking to remove the case to federal district court (see p. C-39), argues that there is diversity because D's "principal place of business" is New Jersey, where D has its corporate headquarters at which its top management works. The Ps retort that D conducts more of its daily business activities in California than in any other single state, so D's principal place of business should be considered to be California.

Held, for D: The phrase "principal place of business" is "the place where the corporation's officers direct, control, and coordinate the corporation's activities." This "nerve center" will normally be the place where the corporation has its *headquarters,* and that's the case here. Therefore, D is a citizen of New Jersey, not California, and there is diversity, so D can remove to federal court. [*Hertz Corp. v. Friend, supra*]

D. **Devices to create or destroy diversity:** The federal courts will not take jurisdiction of a suit in which any party has been *"improperly or collusively joined"* to obtain jurisdiction. 28 U.S.C. §1359. [128-130]

1. **Assignment:** This means that a claimant may *not assign her claim* in order to create diversity. (*Example:* Alex and Dennis are both citizens of Florida. Alex wants to bring a diversity action against Dennis. Alex assigns his claim to Barbara, a Massachusetts citizen, with the understanding that Barbara will remit to Alex 80% of any recovery. The court will not take diversity jurisdiction over the Barbara-vs.-Dennis action, because Barbara's presence in the suit was an improper or collusive joinder. [*Kramer v. Caribbean Mills*]) [128]

2. **Devices to defeat removal:** A plaintiff suing in state court may sometimes seek to defeat her adversary's potential right to *remove to federal court*. There is no federal statute prohibiting "improper or collusive" joinder for the purpose of defeating jurisdiction. However, as a matter of judge-made law, courts will often *disregard* obvious removal-defeating tactics (e.g., joinder of a defendant who has nothing to do with the underlying dispute, but who is a citizen of the same state as a plaintiff.) [129-130]

   a. **Low dollar claim:** But the state-court plaintiff is always free to make a claim for *less than the amount in controversy* ($75,000), in order to defeat removal, even if P has really suffered a loss greater than this amount. (But the less-than-$75,000 amount must be named *before* D removes.)

III. FEDERAL QUESTION JURISDICTION

A. **Generally:** The Constitution gives the federal courts authority to hear *"federal question"* cases. More precisely, under 28 U.S.C. §1331, the federal courts have jurisdiction over "all civil actions *arising under the Constitution, laws, or treaties of the United States*." [131-132]

1. **Federal claim:** There is no precise definition of a case "arising under" the Constitution or laws of the United States. But in the vast majority of cases, the reason there is a federal question is that federal law is the *source of the plaintiff's claim*.

   Examples: A claim of copyright infringement, trademark infringement or patent infringement raises a federal question, because in each of these situations, a federal statute — the federal copyright statute, trademark statute or patent statute — is the source of the right the plaintiff is asserting. [131]

a. **Interpretation of federal law:** It is normally ***not*** enough that P is asserting a ***state-created*** claim which requires ***interpretation*** of federal law. [*Merrell Dow Pharmaceuticals, Inc. v. Thompson*] [132] (But there are exceptions, discussed below.)

b. **Anticipation of defense:** Similarly, the federal question must be ***integral*** to P's cause of action, as revealed by P's complaint. It normally does ***not*** suffice for federal question jurisdiction that P ***anticipates a defense*** based on a federal statute, or even that ***D's answer*** does in fact raise a federal question. Thus the federal question must be part of a "well pleaded complaint." [132]

Example: P claims that D Railroad has breached its agreement to give P free railroad passes. A recently-passed federal statute prohibits the giving of such passes. In P's complaint, he anticipates the railroad's federal statutory defense, claiming that the statute violates the Fifth Amendment.

Held, since P's claim was merely a breach of contract claim, and the federal statute was not essential to that claim, there was no federal question — the fact that federal law was an integral part of D's anticipated defense is irrelevant. [*Louisville & Nashville RR v. Mottley*]

2. **Exception for cases raising substantial federal issue:** Paragraphs 1(a) and 1(b) above, including *Merrell Dow* and *Mottley*, establish a *general* bright-line rule: if the plaintiff's claim is based on state law, then even if an issue of federal law is somehow ***relevant*** in deciding the case (e.g., because federal law gives the defendant a valid defense, or because interpretation of state law requires an understanding of federal law) that's ***not enough*** to make the case a federal-question case. However, there is a narrow (but important) class of ***exceptions*** to this general rule.

   a. **Federal claims — exception for claims arising under state law:** That is, in a ***few*** exceptional instances the Supreme Court has decided that even though the plaintiff's claim ***arises solely under state law***, deciding the validity of the claim would require ***deciding such an important issue of federal law*** that the case should qualify for federal-question jurisdiction.

   b. **"Embedded federal issue":** As a matter of terminology, the federal issue we're examining — the one that is by definition not the source of the plaintiff's cause of action — is called an ***"embedded federal issue."***

   c. **Four requirements for exception:** For the embedded-federal-issue exception to apply (i.e., for a case based on a state-law claim to nonetheless qualify for federal-question jurisdiction), the following ***four requirements*** must all be satisfied:

   [1] the embedded federal issue will be (or has been) ***necessarily raised*** in the federal case;

   [2] the federal issue will be (or has been) ***actually disputed*** during the case;

   [3] the federal issue is a ***"substantial"*** one, whose resolution is ***"importan[t] ... to the federal system as a whole"*** (*Gunn v. Minton, infra*, p. 135); and

   [4] allowing an exception to the general no-jurisdiction rule will ***not "disrupt the federal-state balance"*** of judicial decision-making approved by Congress.

   See generally, *Grable & Sons Metal Products, Inc. v. Darue Engineering & Manufacturing* [134-135] and *Gunn v. Minton* [135]

i. **Two most important factors:** Requirements [1] and [2] above are relatively *easy* to satisfy. So in close cases, the decision on whether the case qualifies for the embedded-federal-issue exception will turn on requirements **[3]** (whether the federal issue is a *substantial one* in terms of its importance to the federal system as a whole) and **[4]** (whether having the federal court hear this and similar cases will disrupt the *congressionally-approved balance* between the federal and state judicial systems).

ii. **Meaning of "substantially important":** As noted, requirement [3] for application of the embedded-federal-issue doctrine is that the federal issue be of *"substantial"* importance. And to meet that requirement, it's *not* enough that the federal issue is merely of substantial importance *to the outcome of the case*, or *to the litigants*; what's required is that resolution of the federal issue be "importan[t] ... to the *federal system as a whole."* *Gunn v. Minton.* [135]

(1) **Federal government's interest:** For instance, if the federal government has a strong interest in having there be a *uniform and well-reasoned resolution* to the embedded federal issue, that interest *will,* typically, satisfy the "substantially important" requirement. And that's especially true where the embedded issue concerns the correctness of the federal government's *own conduct.* [135]

Example: P (Grable) owns real estate in Michigan. The IRS gets a lien on the property on account of P's unpaid federal taxes. The IRS follows certain procedures regarding giving P notice that a tax sale is coming, then sells the property to D (Darue). Five years later, P brings a Michigan state court suit against D to re-establish title in himself (a "quiet title" action). P's claim is that D's record title was invalid because the procedures used by IRS in seizing and selling the property from P violated federal statutes about what notice must be given to the record owner before a seizure-and-sale occurs.

D removes to federal court. He asserts that there is federal-question jurisdiction because, although P's claim is a state-law claim about who holds title to the real estate, correct adjudication of P's claim raises an embedded federal issue (the correct interpretation of the federal statute imposing notice obligations on the IRS). D thus claims that the case involves a federal-question claim by P, giving D the right to remove despite the absence of diversity between P and D.

Held (by the Supreme Court), for D: Because a unit of the federal government (the IRS) has a strong interest in having the federal courts supply a uniform answer to this federal-law question of what notice procedures must be followed, the requirement of a substantially important embedded federal issue is satisfied, creating a federal question even though P's claim is based on state law. Therefore, removal by D was proper. [*Grable & Sons Metal Products, Inc. v. Darue Engineering & Manufacturing*] [135-137]

(2) **Significant only to the litigants:** On the other hand, suppose the resolution of the embedded federal issue is likely to have *no real significance to anyone beyond the parties* to the current litigation. In that case, even if the issue will be completely dispositive of that current suit, the court is very likely to find that the "substantiality requirement" is *not satisfied.* Cf. *Gunn v. Minton* [135].

3. **Claim invalid on the merits:** If P's claim clearly "arises" under federal law, it qualifies for federal question jurisdiction *even if the claim is invalid on the merits*. Here, the federal court

must dismiss for failure to state a claim upon which relief may be granted (FRCP 12(b)(6)), not for lack of subject matter jurisdiction. [137]

IV. AMOUNT IN CONTROVERSY

A. Diversity only: In *diversity* cases, but *not* in federal question cases, plaintiff must satisfy an *"amount in controversy"* requirement. In all diversity cases, the amount in controversy must exceed *$75,000*. [138]

  1. Interest not included: The $75,000 figure does not include interest or court costs.

B. Standard of proof: The party seeking to invoke federal diversity jurisdiction does not have to *prove* that the amount in controversy exceeds $75,000. All she has to show is that there is *some possibility* that that much is in question. [138]

  1. "Legal certainty" test: To put it another way, the claim cannot be dismissed for failing to meet the $75,000 requirement unless it appears to a *legal certainty* that the claim is really for less than the jurisdictional amount. [*St. Paul Mercury Indemnity Co. v. Red Cab*]

  2. Eventual recovery irrelevant: The fact that P *eventually recovers* far *less* than the jurisdictional amount does *not* by itself render the verdict subject to reversal and dismissal on appeal for lack of jurisdiction.

    a. Discretion to deny costs: But the federal court has discretion to *deny costs* to P, and even to impose costs on him, if he recovers less than $75,000. 28 U.S.C. §1332(b).

C. Whose point of view followed: The courts are split as to *which party's* point of view is to be considered in calculating the amount at stake. Most courts hold that the controversy must be worth $75,000 to the *plaintiff* in order to satisfy the jurisdictional amount. [138]

D. Aggregation of claims: In multi-plaintiff or multi-claim litigation, you must understand the rules governing when *aggregation* of claims is permissible for meeting the jurisdictional amount: [139-140]

  1. Aggregation by single plaintiff: If a single plaintiff has a claim in excess of $75,000, he may add to it *any other claim of his against the same defendant*, even though these other claims are for less than the jurisdictional amount. This is done by the doctrine of supplemental jurisdiction. [139]

    a. No claim exceeds $75,000: Even if a plaintiff does *not* have any single claim worth more than $75,000, he may add together all of his claims against a single defendant. So long as these claims against a single defendant *total* more than $75,000, the amount in controversy requirement is satisfied.

    b. Additional defendants: But a plaintiff who has aggregated his claim against a particular defendant, usually may *not* join claims against *other* defendants for less than the jurisdictional amount.

    Example: P has two claims, each for $40,000, against D1. P will be deemed to meet the amount in controversy requirement as to these claims, because they aggregate more than $75,000. But if P tries to bring D2 into the lawsuit, and has a single claim worth $30,000 against D2, most courts will not allow this claim, because P's total claims against D2 do not exceed $75,000, and the doctrine of supplemental jurisdiction does not apply.

2. **Aggregation by multiple plaintiffs:** In suits involving *multiple plaintiffs*, where not all plaintiffs meet the jurisdictional amount, there are two analytically different cases: (1) *at least one* of the plaintiffs meets the amount, but others do not; (2) *none* of the plaintiffs singly meets the amount, but their claims when *aggregated* exceed the amount. [139]

    a. **At least one plaintiff meets amount:** If at least one plaintiff *meets* the amount, other plaintiffs may *join* their related claims against the same defendant. This result is produced by the doctrine of *"supplemental jurisdiction"* (*infra*, p. C-35). [*Exxon Mobil v. Allapattah*]. [139, 150]

    b. **No single claim meets the amount:** If *no single plaintiff* has a claim or claims meeting the jurisdictional amount, aggregation is normally *not allowed*. However, an exception is made where two or more plaintiffs unite to enforce a *single title or right* in which they have a *common and undivided interest.*

    c. **Special rule for class actions:** In diversity-based *class actions*, as long as one named member of the class meets the $75,000 requirement, the others do not have to do so. (They get the benefit of supplemental jurisdiction for amount-in-controversy purposes). See *infra*, p. C-37. [140]

E. **Counterclaims:** [140]

  1. **Suit initially brought in federal court:** If P sues in federal court for less than the jurisdictional amount, and D *counterclaims* for an amount which (either by itself or added to P's claim) exceeds the jurisdictional amount, probably the amount in controversy requirement is *not* met.

  2. **Removal by defendant:** If P originally sues in state court for less than $75,000, and D tries to *remove* to federal court, amount in controversy problems work out as follows:

    a. **Plaintiff removal:** The *plaintiff* may never remove, even if D counterclaims against him for more than $75,000. (The removal statute simply does not apply to plaintiffs, apart from amount-in-controversy problems.)

    b. **Defendant removal:** If the *defendant* counterclaims for more than $75,000, but plaintiff's original claim was for less than $75,000, the result depends on the type of counterclaim. If D's counterclaim was permissive (under state law), all courts agree that D may *not* remove. If D's claim was compulsory under state law, courts are split about whether D may remove.

V. SUPPLEMENTAL JURISDICTION

A. **"Supplemental" jurisdiction:** Suppose new parties or new claims are sought to be added to a basic controversy that by itself satisfies federal subject-matter jurisdictional requirements. Under the doctrine of *"supplemental"* jurisdiction, the new parties and new claims may not have to independently satisfy subject-matter jurisdiction — they can in effect be "tacked on" to the "core" controversy. See 28 U.S.C. §1367. [142-154]

  1. **Pendent and ancillary doctrines replaced:** Supplemental jurisdiction replaces two older judge-made doctrines, "pendent" jurisdiction and "ancillary" jurisdiction.

  2. **Provision generally:** Section 1367(a) says that "in any civil action of which the district courts have original jurisdiction, the district courts *shall have supplemental jurisdiction* over all other claims that are *so related* to claims in the action within such original jurisdiction that

they form part of the **same case or controversy** under Article III of the United States Constitution. Such supplemental jurisdiction shall include claims that involve the joinder or intervention of additional parties." [145]

3. **Federal question cases:** Where the original claim comes within the court's **federal question** jurisdiction, §1367 basically allows the court to hear any **closely related state-law claims**. [146]

   a. **Pendent state claims with no new parties:** Supplemental jurisdiction clearly applies when a related state claim involves the **same parties** as the federal question claim.

      Example: P and D are both citizens of New York. Both sell orange juice nationally. P sues D in federal court for violation of the federal trademark statute, arguing that D's brand name infringes a mark registered to P. P also asserts that D's conduct violates a New York State "unfair competition" statute. There is clearly no independent federal subject matter jurisdiction for P's state law unfair competition claim against D — there is no diversity, and there is no federal question. But by the doctrine of supplemental jurisdiction, since the federal claim satisfies subject-matter jurisdictional requirements, P can add the state law claim that is closely related to it.

   b. **Additional parties to state-law claim:** Section 1367 also allows **additional parties** to the state-law claim to be brought into the case. [146]

      Example: P's husband and children are killed when their small plane hits power lines near an airfield. P sues D1 (the U.S.) in federal court, under the Federal Tort Claims Act, for failing to provide adequate runway lights. Then, P amends her complaint to include state-law tort claims against D2 and D3 (a city and a private company) who maintain the power lines. There is no diversity of citizenship between P and D2 and D3, and no federal-question claim against them. But because P's state-law claim against D2 and D3 arises from the same chain of events as P's federal claim against D1, P may bring D2 and D3 into the suit under the supplemental jurisdiction concept, and the last sentence of §1367(a). [This overrules *Finley v. U.S.*] [146]

4. **Diversity cases:** There is also supplemental jurisdiction in many cases where the "core" claim — the claim as to which there is independent federal subject matter jurisdiction — is based solely on **diversity**. But there are some important **exclusions** to the parties' right to add additional claims and parties to a diversity claim. [146-150]

   a. **Claims covered:** Here are the principal diversity-only situations in which supplemental jurisdiction **applies**: [149-150]

      i. Rule 13(a) **compulsory counterclaims**.

      ii. Rule 13(h) joinder of **additional parties to compulsory counterclaims**.

         Example: P, from New York, brings a diversity suit against D, from New Jersey. The claim is for $60,000. D counterclaims that in the same episode, D was injured not only by P but also by Y; D's injuries total $1,000. Y is from New Jersey. D may bring Y in as a Rule 13(h) additional defendant to D's compulsory counterclaim against P, even though D and Y are both from New Jersey, and even though D's claim does not total $75,000 — supplemental jurisdiction applies, and obviates the need for D-Y diversity or for D to meet the amount in controversy requirement.

      iii. Rule 13(g) **cross-claims**, i.e., claims by one defendant against another.

Example: P, from Ohio, brings a diversity suit against D1 and D2, both from Kentucky. D1 brings a Rule 13(g) cross-claim against D2 — since it is a cross-claim, it necessarily relates to the same subject matter as P's claim. Even though there is no diversity as between D1 and D2, the cross-claim may be heard by the federal court.

iv. Rule 14 *impleader* of third-party defendants, for claims *by and against third-party plaintiffs*, and claims *by third-party defendants*, but *not* claims by the *original plaintiff* against third-party defendants.

Example: P, from California, sues D, a retailer from Arizona, claiming that a product D sold P was defective and injured P. The suit is based solely on diversity. D brings a Rule 14 impleader claim against X, the manufacturer of the item, claiming that if D owes P, X must indemnify D. X is a citizen of Arizona. Because D's suit against X falls within the court's supplemental jurisdiction, the lack of diversity as between D and X makes no difference. Supplemental jurisdiction would also cover any claim by X against P. But any claim by P against X would *not* be within the court's supplemental jurisdiction, so P and X must be diverse and the claim must meet the amount in controversy requirement.

v. *Multiple plaintiffs* who join together under Rule 20's *"permissive joinder"* provision. (More precisely, supplemental jurisdiction applies for amount-in-controversy purposes, but does *not* apply so as to remove the requirement of *complete diversity*.)

Example: P1 and P2, both citizens of New York, bring a diversity-only suit against D, a citizen of New Jersey. P1's claim is worth $100,000, and P2's claim is worth no more than $50,000. The two claims arise out of the same transaction or occurrence. The action may proceed — supplemental jurisdiction allows P2 to ride P1's coattails, for amount-in-controversy purposes. (But supplemental jurisdiction does *not* remove the need for *complete diversity.* So P3, a citizen of New Jersey, would not be permitted to join the action, because she's a citizen of the same state as D.) [*Exxon Mobil Corp. v. Allapattah Services*]. [139, 150]

vi. *Joinder of plaintiffs* for Rule 23 *class actions based on diversity.* (If one or more named plaintiffs meet diversity and amount in controversy requirements, the unnamed plaintiffs *don't* need to meet the amount, because they fall within the court's supplemental jurisdiction.)

Example: In a Rule 23 diversity-only class action, the named plaintiff class members are P1, a citizen of New York with a claim for $100,000 and P2, a citizen of Pennsylvania with a claim for $90,000. The defendants are D1 (a citizen of New Jersey) and D2 (a citizen of California). Because all named plaintiffs (a) meet the amount in controversy requirement and (b) are diverse with all defendants, the class action may go forward even though it includes unnamed class members whose claims are not individually worth in excess of $75,000, and who are citizens of New Jersey and/or California. [*Exxon Mobil Corp. v. Allapattah Services, Inc.*]

b. **Claims not covered:** Where the core claim is based solely on diversity, some important types of claims do *not* get the benefit of supplemental jurisdiction: [147-149]

i. **Claims against third-party defendants:** Claims made by an original plaintiff against a *third-party defendant*, pursuant to Rule 14(a), are *excluded*.

Example: P sues D, and D brings a third-party claim against X, asserting that if D is liable to P, X is liable to D. P and X are citizens of the same state. P does not get supplemental jurisdiction for her claim against X, so the P-vs.-X claim must be dismissed.

ii. **Compulsory joinder:** When a person is joined under Rule 19(a) as a person to be "joined if feasible" (*"compulsory joinder"*), neither a claim *against* such a person, nor a claim *by* that person, comes within the supplemental jurisdiction in a diversity-only case.

iii. **Rule 20 joinder of defendants:** When a plaintiff sues multiple defendants in the same action on common law and facts (Rule 20 *"permissive joinder"* of defendants), supplemental jurisdiction does not apply.

Example: P is hit by D1's car, then negligently ministered to by D2. P is from New York, D1 is from Connecticut, and D2 is from New Jersey. P's claim against D2 is for $20,000. The federal court cannot hear the P-D2 claim, because it does not meet the amount in controversy and does not fall within supplemental jurisdiction.

iv. **Intervention:** Claims by prospective plaintiffs who try to *intervene* under Rule 24 do not get the benefit of supplemental jurisdiction. This is true whether the intervention is permissive or of right.

Example: P1 sues D in diversity. P2, on her own motion, moves for permission to intervene under Rule 24(b), because her claim against D has a question of law or fact in common with P1's claim. P1 is a citizen of Indiana, P2 of Illinois, and D of Illinois. Because there is no supplemental jurisdiction over intervention, the fact that P2 and D are citizens of the same state means that the court may not hear P2's claim. The same result would occur even if P2's claim was so closely related to the main action that P2 would otherwise be entitled to "intervention of right" under Rule 24(a).

c. **Defensive posture required:** If you look at the situations where supplemental jurisdiction is allowed in diversity-only cases, and those where it is not allowed, you will see that basically, additional claims asserted by *defendants* fall within the court's supplemental jurisdiction, but additional claims (or the addition of new parties) by *plaintiffs* are generally not included. So expect supplemental jurisdiction only in cases where the claimant who is trying to benefit from it is in a *"defensive posture."*

5. **Discretion to reject exercise:** Merely because a claim is within the court's supplemental jurisdiction, this does not mean that the court *must* hear that claim. Section 1367(c) gives four reasons for which a court may *decline to exercise* supplemental jurisdiction that exists. Most importantly, the court may abstain if it has already *dismissed all claims* over which it has original jurisdiction. This discretion is especially likely to be used where the case is in its early stages. (*Example:* P sues D1 (the U.S.) under a federal statute, then adds state-law claims against D2 and D3, as to which there is neither diversity nor federal question jurisdiction. Soon after the pleadings are filed, the court dismisses P's claim against D1 under FRCP 12(b)(6). Probably the court will then exercise its discretion to decline to hear the supplemental claims against D2 and D3.) [153]

6. **No effect on personal jurisdiction:** The application of the supplemental jurisdiction doctrine does *not* eliminate the requirement of *jurisdiction over the parties*, nor does it eliminate the requirement of *service of process*. It speaks solely to the question of subject matter jurisdiction. (But often in the supplemental jurisdiction situation, service in the *100-mile bulge*

area will be available.) [154]

    a. Venue: Where supplemental jurisdiction applies, probably *venue* requirements do not have to be satisfied with respect to the new party. But usually, venue will not be a problem anyway in these kinds of situations.

VI. REMOVAL TO THE FEDERAL COURTS

A. Removal generally: Generally, any action brought in *state court* that the plaintiff could have brought in federal court may be *removed* by the defendant to federal district court. [158]

    Example: P, from New Jersey, sues D, from New York, in New Jersey state court. The suit is a garden-variety automobile negligence case. The amount at issue is $100,000. D may remove the case to federal district court for the District of New Jersey.

  1. Diversity limitation: The most important single thing to remember about removal jurisdiction is this: In *diversity* cases, the action may be removed only if *no defendant is a citizen of the state in which the action is pending*.

    Example: P, from New Jersey, brings a negligence action against D, from New York, in the New York state court system. D may not remove the case to federal court for New York, because he is a citizen of the state (New York) in which the action is pending. (But if P's suit was for trademark infringement — a kind of suit that raises a federal question but may be brought in either state or federal court — D would be able to remove, because the "not a citizen of the state where the action is pending" requirement does not apply in suits raising a federal question.)

    a. Exception: There is an exception to this general "no removal allowed if any D is a citizen of the state where the action is pending" rule: most state-court *class actions* can be removed even though one or more defendants are citizens of the forum state. [159]

  2. Where suit goes: When a case is removed, it passes to the federal district court for the district and division embracing the place where the state cause of action is pending. (*Example:* If a suit is brought in the branch of the California state court system located in Sacramento, removal would be to the federal district court in the Eastern District of California encompassing Sacramento.) [158]

B. Diversity and amount in controversy rules applicable: In removal cases, the usual rules governing existence of a federal question or of diversity, and those governing the jurisdictional amount, apply. (*Example:* If there is no federal question, diversity must be "complete.") [159]

C. No plaintiff removal: Only a *defendant* may remove. A plaintiff defending a counterclaim may not remove. (*Example:* P brings a suit for product liability against D. D counterclaims for libel in an amount of $100,000. P is from Ohio; D is from Indiana. The suit is pending in Michigan state court. Even though P is not a resident of the state where the action is pending, P may not remove, because the right of removal is limited to defendants.) [159]

D. Look only at plaintiff's complaint: The right of removal is generally decided from the face of the pleadings. The jurisdictional allegations of plaintiff's complaint control. [160]

    Example: P is badly injured in an automobile accident caused by D's negligence. P's medical bills total $100,000, but P sues only for $60,000, for the express purpose of thwarting D's right to remove. The jurisdictional allegations of P's complaint control, so that D may not remove even though more than $75,000 is "really" at stake.

E. Removal of multiple claims: Where P asserts against D in state court two claims, one of which could be removed if sued upon alone, and the other of which could not, complications arise. [161-162]

  1. Diversity: If the claim for which there is federal jurisdiction is a *diversity* claim, the presence of the second claim (for which there is no original federal jurisdiction) *defeats* the defendant's right of removal entirely — the whole case must stay in state court. [161]

  2. Federal question case: Where the claim for which there is original federal jurisdiction is a *federal question* claim, and there is another, "separate and independent," claim for which there is no original federal jurisdiction, D may remove the whole case. 28 U.S.C. §1441(c). [161]

    Example: P and D1 are both citizens of Kentucky. P brings an action in Kentucky state court alleging federal antitrust violations by D1. P adds to that claim a claim against D1 and D2, also from Kentucky, asserting that the two Ds have violated Kentucky state unfair competition laws. Section 1441(c) will allow D1 and D2 to remove to federal court, if the antitrust claim is "separate and independent" from the state unfair competition claim.

    a. Remand: If §1441(c) applies, and the entire case is removed to federal court, the federal judge need not hear the entire matter. The court may instead remand all matters in which state law predominates.

      i. Remand even the federal claim: In fact, the federal court, after determining that removal is proper, may remand *all claims* — even the properly-removed federal claim — if state law predominates in the whole controversy.

F. Compulsory remand: If the federal judge concludes that the removal did not satisfy the statutory requirements, she *must remand* the case to the state court from which it came. (*Example:* If in a diversity case it turns out that one or more of the Ds was a citizen of the state in which the state suit was commenced, the federal judge must send the case back to the state court where it began.) [162]

G. Mechanics of removal: [163]

  1. Time: D must usually file for removal within *30 days* of the time he receives service of the state-court complaint.

  2. All defendants joined: *All defendants* (except purely nominal ones) must *join* in the notice of removal. (However, if removal occurs under §1441(c)'s "separate and independent federal claim" provision, then only the defendant(s) to the separate and independent federal claim needs to sign the notice of removal.)

CHAPTER 4

PLEADINGS

I.   FEDERAL PLEADING GENERALLY

A. Approach generally: [169-175]

1. **Two types:** In most instances, there are only two types of pleadings in a federal action. These are the **complaint** and the **answer**. The complaint is the document by which the plaintiff begins the case. The answer is the defendant's response to the complaint. [169]

   a. **Reply:** In two circumstances, there will be a third document, called the **reply**. The reply is, in effect, an "answer to the answer." A reply is allowable: (1) if the answer contains a **counterclaim** (in which case a reply is **required**); and (2) at plaintiff's option, if plaintiff obtains a court order allowing the reply.

2. **No verification generally:** Pleadings in a federal action normally need not be **"verified,"** i.e., sworn to by the litigant. However, there are a couple of exceptions, two of which are: (1) the complaint in a stockholders' derivative action (see FRCP 23.1); and (2) when the complaint is seeking a **temporary restraining order** (FRCP 65(b)). [171]

3. **Attorney must sign:** The pleader's **lawyer** must **sign** the pleadings. This is true for both the complaint and the answer. By signing, the lawyer indicates that to the best of her belief, formed after reasonable inquiry, the pleading is not interposed for any **improper purpose** (e.g., harassing or causing unnecessary delays), the claims and defenses are warranted by existing law or a nonfrivolous argument for changing existing law, and (in general) the allegations or denials have evidentiary support. FRCP 11. [172]

   a. **Sanctions:** If Rule 11 is violated (e.g., the complaint, as the lawyer knows, is not well grounded in fact, or supported by any plausible legal argument), the court must impose an **appropriate sanction** on either the signing lawyer, the client, or both. The most common sanction is the award of **attorneys' fees** to the other side.

   b. **Safe harbor:** A party against whom a Rule 11 motion is made has a 21-day **"safe harbor"'** period in which she can withdraw or modify the challenged pleading and thereby avoid any sanction.

4. **Pleading in the alternative:** The pleader, whether plaintiff or defendant, may plead **"in the alternative."** "A party may set forth two or more statements of a claim or defense alternately or hypothetically." FRCP 8(d). (*Example:* In count 1, P claims that work done for D was done under a valid written contract. In count 2, P claims that if the contract was not valid, P rendered value to D and can recover in *quantum meruit* for the value. Such alternative pleading is allowed by Rule 8(d).) [175]

II. THE COMPLAINT

A. **Complaint generally:** The complaint is the initial pleading in a lawsuit, and is filed by the plaintiff. [175]

1. **Commences action:** The filing of the complaint is deemed to "commence" the action. The date of filing of the complaint is what counts for statute of limitation purposes in federal question suits (though in diversity suits, "commencement" for statute-of-limitations purposes depends on how state law defines commencement.)

2. **Elements of complaint:** There are three essential elements that a complaint must have (FRCP 8(a)): [175]

   a. **Jurisdiction:** A short and plain statement of the grounds upon which the court's **jurisdiction** depends;

b. Statement of the claim: A short and plain *statement of the claim* showing that the pleader is entitled to relief; and

c. Relief: A demand for judgment for the *relief* (e.g., money damages, injunction, etc.) which the pleader seeks.

B. Specificity: Plaintiff must make a *"short and plain statement"* of the claim showing that she is entitled to relief. The level of factual detail required is not high — gaps in the facts are usually remedied through discovery.

    1. Dismissal: Even though the level of factual detail required is not high, the complaint may contain such *sparse* factual allegations that the defendant may successfully move to have it dismissed for "failure to state a claim on which relief may be granted" (Rule 12(b)(6)). It's relatively difficult for the defendant to satisfy this standard. But if the court, after assuming that all factual allegations in the complaint are true, cannot *"plausibly infer"* that the defendant is liable, the court will dismiss the complaint for failure to state a claim. See *infra*, p. C-43.

C. Special matters: Certain *"special matters"* must be pleaded with *particularity* if they are to be raised at trial. [177]

    1. Catalog: The special matters (listed in FRCP 9) include: (1) denial of a party's legal *capacity to sue* or be sued; (2) the circumstances giving rise to any allegation of *fraud* or *mistake*; (3) any denial of performance or occurrence of a *condition precedent*; (4) the existence of *judgments* or *official documents* on which the pleader plans to rely; (5) material facts of *time and place*; (6) *special damages*; and (7) certain aspects of admiralty and maritime jurisdiction. [177]

        a. Note: The above matters requiring special pleading apply to the *answer* as well as to the complaint.

    2. Effect of failure to plead: The pleader takes the full risk of failure to plead any special matter.

        Example: P brings a diversity claim for breach of contract against D. P has suffered certain unusual consequential damages, but fails to plead these special damages as required by FRCP 9(g). Even if P proves these items at trial, P may not recover these damages, unless the court agrees to specially permit this "variance" between proof and pleadings. [177]

III. MOTIONS AGAINST THE COMPLAINT

A. Defenses against validity of complaint: Either in the *answer*, or by separate *motion*, defendant may attack the validity of the complaint in a number of respects. Rule 12(b) lists the following such defenses: [178]

    1. Lack of *jurisdiction over the subject matter;*

    2. Lack of *jurisdiction over the person*;

    3. Improper *venue*;

    4. Insufficiency of *process*;

    5. Insufficiency of *service of process*;

6. Failure to *state a claim upon which relief may be granted*; and

7. Failure to *join a necessary party* under Rule 19.

B. 12(b)(6) motion to dismiss for failure to state a claim: Defense (6) above is especially important: if D believes that P's complaint does not state a legally sufficient claim, he can make a Rule 12(b)(6) motion to dismiss for *"failure to state a claim upon which relief can be granted."* The motion asserts that on the facts as pleaded by P, no recovery is possible under *any legal theory*. [179-187]

Example: If P's complaint is barred by the statute of limitations, D should move under 12(b)(6) for failure to state a valid claim. If the court is convinced that under the facts alleged by P, any cause of action would be time-barred, the court will dismiss.

1. "Plausibility" standard: Under recent Supreme Court decisions, the 12(b)(6) motion to dismiss for failure to state a claim can succeed by demonstrating that even if every fact asserted in the complaint is taken as true, no recovery is *"plausible"* under *any legal theory*. This standard is *easier for the defendant to satisfy* than the standard that applied before 2007. [179-187]

    a. Assumption of truth: When the court is deciding whether the complaint should be dismissed for failure to state a claim, all truly *"factual"* allegations in the complaint are to be *assumed to be true*.

    b. Pure legal conclusions: But *pure "legal conclusions" don't qualify* for this assumed-to-be-true treatment. [183]

    Example: P is a Pakistani Muslim who was imprisoned by federal authorities after 9/11. He brings a federal civil-rights action against D1 (the U.S. Attorney General) and D2 (the FBI Director). He alleges that the two Ds knew and approved of their subordinates' plan to imprison P and hundreds of other Muslim men in extra-harsh conditions solely on account of the men's race, religion or national origin, thus violating their constitutional rights. The two Ds move for dismissal under Rule 12(b)(6), alleging that even if the subordinates intentionally violated P's rights, P has not sufficiently alleged facts showing that the two Ds acted with a discriminatory purpose (as is required by the substantive rules for supervisor liability in such cases).

    Held, for the Ds: complaint dismissed. It's true that factual allegations in the complaint must be taken as true. But pure *"legal conclusions" don't qualify* for this "taken as true" treatment. And those allegations that *are* truly factual must *"plausibly suggest"* that P is entitled to relief. In determining whether the complaint meets this "plausible suggestion of entitlement to relief" standard, the trial judge is to draw on his *"judicial experience and common sense."* Here, the complaint does not satisfy the plausibility standard, because even taking P's truly-factual allegations as true, the "more likely explanation" of the Ds' motives is that they were making a *bona fide* pursuit of national security, not acting for forbidden discriminatory purposes. [*Ashcroft v. Iqbal* (2009), a 5-4 vote] [181-185]

    c. Where P lacks personal knowledge: The "plausibility" standard will generally make the most difference where the plaintiff alleges facts as to which he *doesn't have personal knowledge*, and as to which the defendants are in *sole control* of the *relevant records or testimony*. Cases trying to hold *supervisors* liable for violations of *civil rights laws* (as in Iqbal, *supra*) or *employment discrimination laws* are good illustrations. [186]

    d. D is relieved from discovery: When the plausibility requirement makes a difference, the main way it will do so is that D gets ***spared from having to undergo discovery.*** That is, P's case gets dismissed before he gets to examine D's files or take depositions. [186]

C. Amendment: If the complaint is dismissed in response to D's dismissal motion, P will almost always have the opportunity to ***amend*** the complaint. (See *infra,* C-45.)

D. Motion for more definite statement: If the complaint is so "vague or ambiguous that [the defendant] cannot reasonably prepare a response," D may move for a ***more definite statement*** under Rule 12(e). [187]

E. Motion to strike: If P has included "redundant, immaterial, impertinent or scandalous" material in the complaint, D may move to have this material ***stricken*** from the pleading. Rule 12(f). [188]

IV. THE ANSWER

A. The answer generally: The defendant's response to the plaintiff's complaint is called an ***"answer."*** In the answer, D states in short and plain terms his ***defenses*** to each claim asserted, and admits or denies each count of plaintiff's complaint. Rule 8(b). [190]

    1. Alternative pleading: Defenses, like claims, may be pleaded in the ***alternative***. (*Example:* In a breach of contract suit brought by P, D can in count 1 of his answer state that no contract ever existed, and in count 2 state that if such a contract did exist, it was breached by P, not D.)

B. Signed by defendant's attorney: The answer must be ***signed*** by the defendant's lawyer. As with the complaint, the attorney's signature constitutes a certificate that the signer has read the pleading, believes it is well founded, and that it is not interposed for delay. Rule 11. [191]

C. Denials: The defendant may make various kinds of ***denials*** of the truth of plaintiff's allegations. [191]

    1. Where not denied: Averments in a complaint, other than those concerning the amount of damages, are deemed admitted if the allegation is not denied in the answer. Rule 8(b)(6).

    2. Kinds of denials: There are five kinds of denials in federal practice:

        a. General denial: D may make a ***"general"*** denial, by which he denies each and every allegation in P's complaint. (But D must then contest all of P's allegations, or face sanctions.)

        b. Specific denial: D may make a ***"specific"*** denial, which denies all of the allegations of a particular paragraph or count of the complaint.

        c. Qualified denial: D may make a ***"qualified"*** denial, i.e., a denial of a particular ***portion*** of a particular allegation.

        d. Denial of knowledge or information (DKI): D may make a denial of ***knowledge or information*** (DKI), by which he says that he does not have enough knowledge or information sufficient to form a belief as to the truth of P's complaint (but D must do this in good faith).

        e. Denial based on information and belief: D may deny ***"based on information and belief."*** By this, D effectively says, "I don't know for sure, but I reasonably believe that P's allegation is false." This kind of denial is often used by large corporate defendants.

D. Affirmative defenses: There are certain defenses which must be ***explicitly pleaded*** in the answer, if D is to raise them at trial. These are so-called ***"affirmative defenses."*** [192]

1. **Listing:** Rule 8(c) lists 19 specific affirmative defenses, of which the most important are *contributory negligence, fraud, res judicata, statute of limitations,* and *illegality.*

2. **General formulation:** Also, Rule 8(c) contains a more general requirement, by which D must plead affirmatively "any avoidance or affirmative defense." Any defense which relies on facts *particularly within the defendant's knowledge* is likely to be found to be an affirmative defense.

E. **Counterclaim:** In addition to defenses, if D has a claim against P, he may (in all cases) and must (in some cases) plead that claim as a *counterclaim.* If the counterclaim is one which D is *required* to plead, it is called a *compulsory* counterclaim. If it is one which D has the option of pleading or not, it is called a *permissive* counterclaim. A counterclaim is compulsory if it "arises out of the transaction or occurrence that is the subject matter of the [plaintiff's] claim...." Rule 13(a). [192]

V. TIME FOR VARIOUS PLEADINGS

A. **Time table:** Here is the time table for various pleading steps (see Rule 12(a)): [193]

1. **Complaint:** Filing of the complaint usually occurs before it is served. Service must then normally occur within 120 days. Rule 4(m).

2. **Answer:** The *answer* must be served within *21 days* after service of the complaint, except that

   a. **Different state rule:** If P has served D *out of state,* by using the state long-arm (see Rule 4(k)(1)(A)), the time to answer allowed under that state rule (typically longer) controls.

   b. **Rule 12 motion:** If D makes a Rule 12 motion against the complaint and loses, D has 10 days after the court denies the motion to answer.

   c. **Waiver of formal service:** If D *waives* formal service pursuant to Rule 4(d), then he gets *60 days* to answer running from the date the request for waiver was sent by P. Rule 12(a)(1)(A)(ii).

3. **Reply to counterclaim:** If the answer contains a *counterclaim,* P must serve his *reply* within *20 days* after service of the answer.

VI. AMENDMENT OF THE PLEADINGS

A. **Liberal policy:** The Federal Rules are extremely *liberal* in allowing amendment of the pleadings. [193]

B. **Amendment:** Here is a general summary of the rules on when federal pleadings may be amended:

1. **Amendment as of right:** A pleading may be amended once *as a matter of course* (i.e., *without leave* of court) in the following circumstances:

   [1] Amendment of right is *always* allowed if it occurs within *21 days* after the pleader *served the original pleading.* Rule 15(a)(1)(A). [193]

   [2] In those cases in which a *responsive pleading* is required, amendment of right is *also* allowed even if it happens *more* than 21 days after the original pleading was served, as long as the amendment happens within 21 days following the earlier of (a) service of the *responsive pleading* or (b) service of the other side's *motion* under Rule 12(b), (e), or (f).

Rule 15(a)(1)(B). [193]

    a. More time: Point [2] above means that in the case of a ***complaint*** (which requires a "responsive pleading"), the plaintiff can amend of right at any time until 21 days after the defendant has served *either* an ***answer*** or a 12(b), (e) or (f) ***motion***, ***no matter how much time has elapsed*** since the plaintiff served the original complaint. [193]

  2. Amendment by leave of court: If the situation does not fall into one of the above "amendment as of right" categories, then P may amend only by getting ***leave of court*** (i.e., permission). But Rule 15(a)(2) says "the court should *freely* give leave [to amend] when ***justice so requires***." [194]

    a. "Actual prejudice" usually required: Normally, leave to amend should be denied only if it would cause ***actual prejudice*** to the other party.

    b. Amendment after dismissal: And in the case where D has succeeded with a ***motion to dismiss*** the original complaint, the court will almost always give P leave to amend, on the theory that justice so requires.

C. Relation back: When a pleading has been amended, the amendment will ***relate back*** to the date of the original pleading, if the claim or defenses asserted in the amended pleading "arose out of the conduct, transaction or occurrence set out — or attempted to be set out — in the original pleading." Rule 15(c)(1)(B). This "relation back" doctrine is mainly useful in meeting statutes of limitations that have run between filing of the original complaint and the amendment. [194-197]

    Example: On Jan. 1, P files a complaint against D for negligently manufacturing a product that has injured P. The case is brought in diversity in Ohio federal district court. On Feb. 1, the Ohio statute of limitations (which controls in a diversity case) on both negligence and product liability claims arising out of this episode runs. On March 1, P amends to add a count alleging strict products liability. Because the products liability claim arises out of the same conduct or transaction as set forth in the original negligence complaint, the amendment will relate back to Jan. 1, and P will be deemed to have met the statute of limitations for his products liability claim.

  1. A single "conduct, transaction or occurrence": Courts take a fairly *narrow* view of when the amendment and the original pleading involve the same "conduct, transaction or occurrence" (the requirement for relation-back). If what's amended is simply P's ***claim or theory***, the court will typically find that the "same conduct" test *is* satisfied. But where the ***underlying facts*** needed to sustain the new pleading are ***materially different*** from those alleged in the original complaint, the court is likely to find that the "same conduct" standard is ***not*** met. [195]

  2. When action is deemed "commenced": According to Rule 3, an action is deemed "commenced" as of the ***date on which the complaint is filed***. In federal question cases, it is to this date that the amendment relates back. In diversity cases, by contrast, it is the date that state law regards as the date of commencement which controls. [195]

    Example: In a diversity case, assume that state law regards the date on which the complaint is served, not the filing date, as being the commencement. In a diversity action in that state, any relation back will be to the date the complaint was served, not to the filing date.

3. Change of party: Where the amendment to a pleading *changes the party* against whom the claim is asserted, the amendment "relates back" only if, in addition to the "same transaction or occurrence" rule discussed above, it is the case that "within the [120-day] period provided by Rule 4(m) for serving the summons and complaint, the party to be brought in by amendment (i) received such notice of the action that it will *not be prejudiced in defending* on the merits; and (ii) *knew* or *should have known* that the action would have been *brought against it*, but for a *mistake* concerning the *proper party's identity.*" Rule 15(c)(1)(C). [196]

    a. Two scenarios: There are two different scenarios — each involving a mistake by the plaintiff about the identity of the proper party — in which Rule 15(c)(1)(C)'s relation-back doctrine will protect the plaintiff. (We'll refer to the sole defendant against whom P initially and mistakenly files suit as "D1," and to the "correct" defendant whom P serves after the statute of limitations has run as "D2.")

        i. P does not know of D2's existence: The first scenario is where P, at the time the complaint is originally filed, knows *only* of the existence of D1, not D2. Assume that P serves D1 within the limitations period, but by the time P learns that the correct defendant is D2, the limitations period has elapsed. P can bring an amended suit that substitutes D2, as long as two conditions are met:

            [1] before the time for proper service against D2 expired (i.e., before the passage of 120 days following the running of the statute of limitations), D2 *"knew or should have known* that the action *would have been brought* against" D2 had P not made a *"mistake concerning the proper party's identity,"* and

            [2] D2 got sufficient notice that she won't be *prejudiced* in defending the action.

        Example: P's tort complaint names D1 (a corporation), and is filed just prior to the expiration of the statute of limitations. At the time, P has never heard of D2, a corporation owned by the same people as D1; D2 is the real cause of the harm to P. D1's staff immediately forwards the complaint to D2's offices. Ten days after the running of the statute, P is told by D1 that the complaint really should have named D2. P amends the complaint to name D2, and serves D2 60 days after the filing of the original complaint.

        The amendment as to D2 relates back to the original, timely filing, because within 120 days of the original filing, D2 received notice of the action and learned that but for P's mistake about the proper party, the action would have been brought against D2 rather than D1. [196]

        ii. P knows of D2's existence, but thinks D1 is correct party: The second scenario occurs where, at the time the original complaint is filed and served, P *knows of both D1's and D'2s existence,* but (mistakenly) believes that D1 is the proper party, so she brings suit only against D1. Here, too, P *gets the benefit* of the relation-back doctrine as long as D2 learns or should have learned, within the statute-of-limitations-period-plus-120-days, that the suit has been filed and that D2 is the correct party. [*Krupski v. Costa Crociere S.p.A.,* a 2010 Supreme Court decision.] [197-198]

            (1) P's awareness of D2 doesn't hurt P: So it doesn't make any difference that P, at the time she originally filed suit against D1, was aware of D2's existence, as long as P believed that the correct party to sue was D1, not D2.

Example: On Feb. 21, 2007, P trips and falls while on board the cruise ship Costa Magica. Her ticket identifies the carrier as "Costa Crociere," an Italian corporation, but lists "Costa Cruise Lines N.V." as the sales and marketing agent for the cruise and as the "issuer" of the ticket. On Feb. 1, 2008, three weeks before the statute of limitations will run, P brings a diversity action for negligence against only Costa Cruise Lines. During the next several months, Costa Cruise Lines repeatedly tells P's lawyer that the owner/operator of the vessel, and thus the only proper defendant, is Costa Crociere. P eventually files an amended lawsuit against Costa Crociere, and serves Costa Crociere on Aug. 21, 2008 (i.e., more than 120 days after the original statute of limitations would have run). Costa Crociere argues that relation back should not apply because P could see from the face of the ticket that Costa Crociere was the owner of the vessel, and thus the proper party to sue.

Held, for P: relation back applies, preventing P's claim from being time-barred. Rule 15(c)(1)(C)(ii) asks "what the prospective *defendant* knew or should have known ... not what the *plaintiff* knew or should have known at the time of filing her original complaint." Since the complaint made it clear that P meant to sue whichever company owned and operated the ship on which she was injured, Costa Crociere knew or should have known, within the allowable time for service under the statute of limitations, that it, not Costa Cruise Lines, was the party P intended to sue. That's all that matters. (And P's delay in amending once P learned that Crociere was the proper party doesn't matter.) *Krupski v. Costa Crociere S.p.A., supra.* [197-198]

VII. VARIANCE OF PROOF FROM PLEADINGS

A. Federal practice: The Federal Rules allow substantial *deviation* of the proof at trial from the pleadings, so long as the variance does not seriously prejudice the other side. Rule 15(b). Unless omission of the issue from the pleading was intentional, and was designed to lead the objecting party into wasted preparation, the court will almost certainly allow amendment at trial. [198]

Example: P brings a diversity action for breach of contract against D. P's complaint does not allege any special damages. At trial, P shows that P lost considerable business and profits. D objects that special damages were not pleaded. Since D probably cannot show the court that D has wasted preparation, the court will almost certainly allow P to amend his pleadings to allege the special damages. If necessary, the court will give D extra time to develop evidence to rebut P's newly-claimed special damages.

CHAPTER 5

DISCOVERY AND PRETRIAL CONFERENCE

I. GENERAL PRINCIPLES

A. Forms of discovery: Discovery under the Federal Rules includes six main types: [203-204]

1. *Automatic disclosure;*

2. *Depositions*, taken from both written and oral questions;

3. *Interrogatories* addressed to a party;

4. Requests to *inspect documents* or property;

5. Requests for *admission* of facts;

6. Requests for physical or mental *examination*.

II. SCOPE OF DISCOVERY

A. Scope generally: Rule 26(b), which applies to all forms of discovery, provides that the parties "may obtain discovery regarding *any nonprivileged matter that is relevant to any party's claim or defense*[.]" So the two principal requirements for discoverability of material are that it is: (1) *not privileged*; and (2) *relevant* to some claim or defense in the suit. [205-206]

B. Relevant but inadmissible: To be discoverable, it is *not required* that the information necessarily be *admissible*. For example, inadmissible material may be relevant, and thus discoverable, if it: (1) is likely to serve as a *lead* to admissible evidence; or (2) relates to the identity and whereabouts of any *witness* who is thought to have discoverable information. [206]

C. Privilege: Only material which is *not privileged* may be discovered. [206]

    1. Who may assert: Only the *person who could assert the privilege at trial* may resist discovery on the grounds of privilege. (*Example:* P sues D1 and D2 for conversion. At P's deposition of D1, P asks D1 questions relating to the facts. D1 knows the answer and is willing to respond, but D2's lawyer objects on the grounds that the questions may violate D1's privilege against self-incrimination. D2's objection is without substance, because only D1 — the person who could assert the privilege at trial — may assert the privilege during discovery proceedings.)

    2. Determining existence of privilege: Generally, in *diversity cases*, *state law of privilege applies*. See Federal Rule of Evidence 501. (*Example:* P brings a diversity action against D, asserting that D intentionally inflicted emotional distress on him. D seeks to depose P's psychotherapist, to determine the extent of P's anguish. The suit is brought in Ohio Federal District Court. The privilege laws of the state of Ohio, not general federal principles, are looked to to determine whether patient-psychotherapist confidences are privileged.)

D. Trial preparation immunity: Certain immunity from discovery is given to the *materials prepared by counsel for trial purposes*, and to the *opinions of experts* that counsel has consulted in trial preparation. This immunity is often referred to as *"work-product"* immunity. [207-212]

    1. Qualified immunity: *"Qualified"* immunity is given to documents prepared *"in anticipation of litigation"* or for trial, by a party or that party's *representative*. [209-210]

        a. "Representative" defined: A party's "representatives" include his *attorney*, consultant, insurance company, and anybody working for any of these people (e.g., a private investigator hired by the attorney).

        b. Hardship: The privilege is "qualified" rather than "absolute." This means that the other side might be able to get discovery of the materials, but only by showing (i) that it has *"substantial need* for the materials to prepare its case" and (ii) that it "cannot *without undue hardship"* obtain the *"substantial equivalent"* by other means. Rule 26(b)(3)(A)(ii).

Example: A car driven by D runs over P. D's insurance company interviews X, a non-party witness to the accident. The insurer then prepares a transcript of the statement. This transcript was prepared "in anticipation of litigation," so it is protected by the qualified work-product immunity. Therefore, P will be able to obtain discovery of it only if he can show substantial need, and the inability without undue hardship to obtain the substantial equivalent by other means. Since P could conduct his own interview of the witness, the court will probably find that the qualified immunity is not overcome.

2. **Absolute immunity:** In addition to the qualified work-product immunity discussed above, there is also *"absolute"* immunity. Rule 26(b)(3)(B) provides that even where a party has substantial need for materials (in other words, the showing for qualified immunity has been made), the court "must protect against disclosure of the *mental impressions*, *conclusions*, *opinions*, or *legal theories* of a party's attorney or other representative concerning the litigation." [210-212]

> **Example:** Same facts as above example. Now, D's lawyer reads X's statement, and writes a memo to the file stating "X appears to be lying for the following three reasons.…" This lawyer memo, since it reflects the mental impressions and conclusions of an attorney or other representative of a party, will receive absolute immunity, and no showing by P will entitle him to get the memo.

E. **Statements by witnesses:** A person who makes a *statement* to a party or the party's lawyer may obtain a *copy* of that statement without any special showing. Rule 26(b)(3)(C). This is true whether the person making the statement is a party or a non-party. [212]

> **Example:** In an accident suit, D's insurance company takes P's statement about the accident, and transcribes it. D must give P a copy of P's statement, without any special showing of need by P.

F. **Names of witnesses:** The *"identity and location of persons who know of any discoverable matter"* (so-called "occurrence witnesses") are discoverable. Rule 26(b)(1). This means, for instance, that each party must upon request disclose to the other the identity and whereabouts of any *eyewitness* to the events of the lawsuit. (*Example:* In an accident case, D's lawyer and investigator locate all eight people who saw the accident. D must on request furnish this list to P.) [212]

1. **Some disclosure is automatic:** If a person has discoverable information that a party plans to *use in its case,* then that party must *automatically* disclose the person's name and address (even without a specific request from the adversary), early on in the litigation. See Rule 26(a)(1)(A)(i).

G. **Discovery concerning experts:** [213-215]

1. **Experts to be called at trial:** Where one side expects to call an expert *at trial*, the other side gets extensive discovery:

   a. **Identity:** First, a party must automatically (without a request) give the other side a list *identifying* each expert who will be called at trial.

   b. **Report:** Second, the party who intends to call an expert at trial must have the expert prepare and sign a *report* containing, among other things: (i) the expert's *opinions*, and the basis for them; (ii) the *data* considered by the expert; (iii) any *exhibits* to be used by the expert at trial; (iv) the expert's *qualifications*; (v) her *compensation*, and (vi) the names of all *other cases* in which she testified as an expert in the preceding 4 years.

c. **Deposition:** The expert who will be called at trial must also be made available for *deposition* by the other side.

   See Rule 26(a)(2)(A); 26(a)(2)(B); 26(b)(4)(A).

2. **Experts retained by counsel, but not to be called at trial:** Where an expert has been retained by a party, but will *not* be called at trial, discovery concerning that expert (her identity, knowledge and opinions) may be discovered only upon a showing of *exceptional circumstances* making it impractical for the party seeking discovery to obtain the information by other means. Rule 26(b)(4)(B). [214]

3. **Unretained experts not to be called at trial:** Where an expert is *consulted* by a party, but *not retained*, and not to be called at trial, there is virtually no way the other side can discover the identity or opinions of that expert. [215]

4. **Participant experts:** A *participant* expert — one who actually took part in the transactions or occurrences that are part of the subject matter of the lawsuit — is treated like an *ordinary witness*. (*Example:* P's estate sues to compel D, an insurance company, to pay off on a policy covering P's life. D claims that it was a suicide, based on the results of an autopsy conducted by X, a pathologist. P may depose X, even though X is an expert — because X participated in the events, he is treated like an ordinary witness for purposes of discovery.) [215]

   a. **Expert is a party:** Similarly, a *party* who is herself an expert (e.g., a doctor who is a defendant in a malpractice suit) is treated like an ordinary witness for discovery purposes, not like an expert.

H. Insurance: A party may obtain discovery of the existence and contents of any *insurance agreement* under which any insurer will be liable to satisfy any judgment that may result. (*Example:* P brings an automobile negligence suit against D in diversity. P may ask D, in an interrogatory, whether D has insurance, and in what amount by what insurer. P may do this without any special showing of need.) [216]

I. Mandatory disclosure: Certain types of disclosure are *automatic* and *mandatory*. [217-220]

1. **Automatic pre-discovery disclosure:** Under Rule 26(a)(1), a party must, even without a request from the other side, automatically disclose certain things early in the litigation. The most important are:

   a. **All witnesses with discoverable information:** First, each party must disclose the name, address and phone number of *each individual* likely to have *discoverable information* that the party plans to *use in its case.*

      Example: P sues D concerning a car accident in which P and D drove cars that collided. D plans to call W, who saw the accident, as a trial witness. Early in the case, D must automatically disclose W's name and address to P, even without a request from P for this information. (But if D didn't plan to call W, perhaps because W's story favors P, then D would *not* have to disclose W's name unless P specifically asked for this type of information in discovery.)

   b. **Documents:** Second, a party must furnish a *copy*, or else a *description* by category and location, of all *documents* and *tangible* things in that party's possession, that the party plans to *use in its case*.

2. **Other:** Later in the litigation, each party must automatically disclose to the other the details of expert testimony (as discussed above) and witnesses and exhibits to be used at trial.

J. Privilege log: If a party is declining to furnish documents or information because of a claim of *privilege* or *work product* immunity, the party must make the claim *expressly*, and must describe the nature of the documents or communications. (Thus the party can't keep silent about the fact that such a claim is being made or about the nature of the documents/communications as to which it is being made). Rule 26(b)(5). [220]

K. Duty to supplement: A party who makes a disclosure during discovery now normally has a duty to *supplement* that response if the party then learns that the disclosed information is incomplete or incorrect. [220]

   1. How it applies: This "duty to supplement" applies to any *automatic pre-discovery disclosure* (mainly witness names and documents); to any disclosure regarding *experts* to be called at trial; and to any responses to an *interrogatory*, a request for production, or request for admission. Rule 26(e)(1); 26(e)(2).

   > **Example:** P is suing D regarding a car accident in which P was injured. Early in the litigation, P gives D a list of all witnesses to the accident that P knows of, as required by Rule 26(a)(1)(A). If P later learns of another person who saw the accident, P must "supplement" her earlier disclosure by telling D about the new witness.

III. METHODS OF DISCOVERY

A. Characteristics: The various forms of discovery (depositions, interrogatories, requests to produce, requests for admission and requests for examination) have several common characteristics: [224]

   1. Extrajudicial: Each of these methods (except requests for physical examination) operates *without intervention of the court*. Only where one party refuses to comply with the other's discovery request will the court intervene.

   2. Scope: The scope of discovery is the same for all of these forms: the material sought must be relevant to the subject matter for the suit, and unprivileged.

   3. Signature required: Every request for discovery of each of these types, and any response or objection to discovery, must be *signed* by the lawyer preparing it. Rule 26(g).

   4. Only parties: Each of these types — except for depositions — may only be addressed to a *party*. Depositions (whether upon oral or written questions) may be addressed to either a party or to a non-party who possesses relevant information.

B. Oral depositions: After the beginning of an action, any party may take the *oral testimony* of any person thought to have information within the scope of discovery. This is known as an *oral deposition*. Rule 30. [226-228]

   1. Usable against non-party: Not only parties, but any non-party with relevant information, may be deposed.

   2. Subpoena: If a non-party is to be deposed, then the discovering party can only force the deponent to attend by issuing a *subpoena*. This subpoena must require the deposition to be held no more than *100 miles* from the place where the deponent resides, is employed, or regularly transacts business in person. Rule 45(c)(3)(A)(ii).

    a. No subpoena for party: If a *party* is to be deposed, a subpoena is not used. Instead, non-compliance with the notice can be followed up by a motion to compel discovery or to impose sanctions under Rule 37.

    3. Request to produce: The person seeking discovery will often also want documents held by the deponent. If the deponent is a party, the discovering party may attach a Rule 34 *request to produce* to the notice to the party. But if the deponent is a non-party, the discovering party must use a subpoena *duces tecum*. [231]

    4. Limits to ten: Each side is limited to a total of *ten depositions*, unless the adversary agrees to more or the court issues an order allowing more. Rule 30(a)(2)(A)(i).

    5. Method of recording: The party ordering the deposition can arrange to have it recorded by stenography (court reporter), by *audio tape recorder*, or by *video recorder*. Rule 30(b)(3)(A).

C. Depositions upon written questions: Any party may take the oral responses to *written questions*, from *any person* (party or non-party) thought to have discoverable information. Rule 31. This is called a "deposition on written questions." [228]

    1. Distant non-party witnesses: Depositions on written questions are mainly used for deposing *distant non-party witnesses*. Such witnesses cannot be served with interrogatories (since these are limited to parties), and cannot be compelled to travel more than 100 miles from their home or business.

D. Interrogatories to the parties: An *interrogatory* is a set of *written questions* to be *answered in writing* by the person to whom they are addressed. Interrogatories may be addressed *only to a party*. Rule 33(a). [229]

    1. Limit of 25 questions: Each party is limited to *25 interrogatory questions* directed to any other party, unless the parties stipulate otherwise or the court orders otherwise. Rule 33(a).

E. Requests for admission: One party may serve upon another party a written request for the *admission, for the purposes of the pending action only, of the truth of any discoverable matters*. Rule 36. This is a *"request for admission."* [230-231]

    1. Coverage: The statements whose genuineness may be requested include statements or opinions of fact, the application of law to fact, and the genuineness of any documents. (*Example:* P, in a breach of contract action, may request that D admit that the attached document is a contract signed by both P and D.) [230]

    2. Expenses for failure to admit: If a party fails to admit the truth of any matter requested for admission under Rule 36(a), and the party making the request *proves* the truth of the matter at trial, the court may then require the party who refused to admit to pay *reasonable expenses* sustained by the movant in proving the matter. Rule 37(c)(2). (But no expenses may be charged in several situations, including where the party who failed to admit had reasonable grounds to think he might prevail on the issue at trial.) [230]

    3. Effect at trial: If a party makes an admission under Rule 36, the matter is normally *conclusively established at trial*. (However, the court may grant a motion to withdraw or amend the admission, if this would help the action to be presented on its merits, and would not prejudice the other side.) [231]

F. Request to produce documents or to inspect land: A party may require any other party to *produce documents and things*. Rule 34. Thus any papers, photos or objects relevant to the subject matter of the case may be obtained from any other party, but not from a non-party. (*Example:* P sues D1 and D2 for antitrust and price fixing. P believes that the records of both Ds will show that they set prices in concert. P may require D1 and D2 to produce any documents in their control relating to the setting of prices.) [231]

1. **Only to parties:** A request to produce can only be addressed to *parties*. If documents in the possession of a non-party are desired, a subpoena *duces tecum* must be used.

2. **Party's control:** A party may be required to produce only those documents or other objects which are in her *"possession, custody or control."* Rule 34(a). [231]

3. **Land:** Rule 34 also allows a party to demand the right to inspect, photograph and survey any *land* within the control of another party. (*Example:* P sues D, a merchant, for negligence, because P fell on D's slippery floor. P may require D to open the premises so that P may inspect and photograph them.)

G. **Physical and mental examination:** When the mental or physical condition of a *party* is *in controversy*, the court may order the party to submit to a *physical or mental examination* by a suitably licensed or certified examiner. Rule 35. [234-236]

1. **Motion and good cause:** Unlike all other forms of discovery, Rule 35 operates only by *court order*. The discovering party must make a *motion* upon notice to the party to be examined, and must show *good cause* why the examination is needed. [235]

2. **Controversy:** The physical or mental condition of the party must be *in controversy*. In other words, it is not enough (as it is for other forms of discovery) that the condition would be somehow relevant. (*Example:* If P is suing D for medical malpractice arising out of an operation, P's condition would obviously be in controversy, and D would be entitled to have a physician conduct a physical examination of P. But if P were suing D for breach of contract, and D had some suspicion that P was fabricating the whole incident, a mental examination of P to find evidence of delusional behavior would probably not be found to be supported by good cause, so the court order granting the exam would probably not be made.) [235]

3. **Reports from examiner:** The *actual medical report* produced through a Rule 35 examination is discoverable (in contrast to the usual non-discoverability of experts' reports).

   a. **Who may receive:** A *person examined* (typically the opposing party) may request, from the party causing the exam to be made, a copy of the examiner's written report.

   b. **Other examinations:** Once the examined party asks for and receives this report, then the other party is entitled to reports of any *other* examinations made at the request of the examinee for the same condition. (*Example:* P sues D for automobile negligence. D causes P to be examined by a doctor retained by D, to measure the extent of P's injuries. P asks for a copy of the report, and D complies. Now, D is entitled to receive from P copies of any other reports of examinations made of P at P's request. In other words, by asking D for the report, P is deemed to have waived the physician-patient privilege as to exams conducted at P's request.) [235]

IV. ORDERS AND SANCTIONS

A. **Two types:** Discovery normally proceeds without court intervention. But the court where the action is pending may intercede in two main ways, by issuing orders and by awarding sanctions. The court may order abuse of discovery stopped (a protective order) or may order a recalcitrant party to furnish discovery (order compelling discovery). Sanctions can be awarded for failing to handle discovery properly.

B. Abuse of discovery: One party sometimes tries to use discovery to harass her adversary. (*Example:* P requests that D reveal trade secrets, or schedules 10 repetitive depositions of D.) The discoveree may fight back in two ways: (1) by simply *objecting* to a particular request; or (2) by seeking a Rule 26 *protective order*. [237-239]

    1. Objection: A party may *object* to a discovery request the same way a question at trial may be objected to. Typical grounds are that the matter sought is not within the scope of discovery (i.e., not *relevant* to the subject matter) or that it is privileged. [237]

        a. Form of objection: The form depends on the type of discovery. An objection to an *interrogatory* question is written down as part of the set of answers. Similarly, an objection to a request to admit is made in writing. An objection to a *deposition* question, by contrast, is raised as an oral objection by the lawyer representing the deponent or the party opposing the deposition. The deposition then continues, and the objections are later dealt with en masse by the judge.

    2. Protective order: Where more than a few questions are at stake, the party opposing discovery may seek a *"protective order."* Rule 26(c)(1) allows the judge to make "an order to protect a party or person from *annoyance, embarrassment, oppression*, or *undue burden or expense*[.]" [238-239]

        Example 1: In a simple automobile negligence case brought under diversity, D schedules P for ten different depositions, and asks substantially the same questions each time. P may seek a protective order in which the judge orders that no further depositions of P may take place at all. The court will probably grant this request.

        Example 2: P sues D for patent infringement, alleging that D's manufacturing methods violate P's patents. In a deposition of D's vice president, P asks the details of D's secret manufacturing processes. D may seek a protective order preventing P from learning these trade secrets, perhaps on the grounds that P does not need to know these secrets in order to pursue his patent case.

        a. Prohibition of public disclosure: One common type of protective order allows trade secrets or other information to be discovered, but then *bars the public disclosure* of the information by the discovering litigant. (*Example:* On the facts of the above example, the judge might allow P to get discovery of D's trade secrets, but prevent P from disclosing that information to any third party.) [238]

C. Compelling discovery: Conversely, if one party refuses to cooperate in the other's discovery attempts, the aggrieved party may seek an *order compelling discovery* under Rule 37(a). [239-240]

    1. When available: An order to compel discovery may be granted if the discoveree fails to: (1) answer a written or oral deposition question; (2) answer an interrogatory; (3) produce documents, or allow an inspection; (4) designate an officer to answer deposition questions, if the discoveree is a corporation.

D. Sanctions for failing to furnish discovery: The court may order a number of *sanctions* against parties who behave unreasonably during discovery. Principally, these sanctions are used against a party who fails to cooperate in the other party's discovery efforts. [240-243]

C A P S U L E   S U M M A R Y

1. **Financial sanctions:** If a discovering party seeks an order compelling discovery, and the court grants the order, the court may require the discoveree to pay the ***reasonable expenses*** the other party incurred in obtaining the order. These may include attorney's fees for procuring the order. Rule 37(b)(2)(C). [240]

2. **Other sanctions:** Once one party obtains an order compelling the other to submit to discovery, and the latter ***persists in her refusal*** to grant discovery, then the court may (in addition to the financial sanctions mentioned above) impose additional sanctions: [241]

    a. **Facts established:** The court may order that the matters involved in the discovery be taken to be ***established***. (*Example:* In a product liability suit, P wants discovery of D's records, to show that D made the product that injured P. If D refuses to cooperate even after the court issues an order compelling discovery, then the court may treat as established D's having manufactured the item.)

    b. **Claims or defenses barred:** The court may prevent the disobedient party from making certain claims or defenses, or introducing certain matters in evidence.

    c. **Entry of judgment:** The court may also ***dismiss*** the action, or enter a default judgment.

    d. **Contempt:** Finally, the court may hold the disobedient party in ***contempt*** of court.

V. USE OF DISCOVERY RESULTS AT TRIAL

A. Use at same trial: The rules for determining whether the fruits of discovery can be ***introduced at trial*** vary depending on the type of discovery. [243]

B. Request to produce: The admissibility of ***documents*** and ***reports*** that were obtained through a Rule 34 ***request to produce*** is determined ***without regard*** to the fact that these items were obtained through discovery. These documents will thus be admissible unless their contents constitute prejudicial, hearsay, or other inadmissible material. [243]

C. Depositions: The admissibility of ***depositions*** is determined through a two-part test. Both parts must be satisfied: [244-245]

1. **Test 1:** First, determine whether the deposition statement sought to be introduced would be admissible ***if the deponent were giving live testimony***. If not, the statement is automatically inadmissible. (*Example:* Deponent says, "X told me that he committed the murder." If the hearsay rule would prevent deponent from making this statement live at trial, it will also prevent the deposition statement from coming in.)

2. **Test 2:** Second, apply the ***"four categories"*** test. Since the use of a deposition statement rather than live testimony is itself a form of hearsay, the deposition statement must fall within one of the four following categories, which are in effect exceptions to the hearsay rule:

    a. **Adverse party:** The deposition of an ***adverse party***, or of a ***director or officer*** of an adverse ***corporate*** party, may be admitted for ***any purpose at all***. See Rule 32(a)(3). [244]

    b. **Impeachment:** The deposition of any witness, ***party or non-party***, may be used to ***impeach the witness' credibility***. See Rule 32(a)(2).

    c. **Adverse witness' deposition for substantive purposes:** A party may use a deposition of an ***adverse witness*** for ***substantive*** purposes, if it conflicts with that witness' trial testimony. (*Example:* In a suit by P versus D, W, a witness favorable to D and called by D, states at trial, "The light was red when P drove through it." P may introduce W's statement in a deposition, "The light was green when P drove through," not just for impeachment but to prove the substantive fact that the light was green.)

    d. **Other circumstances:** The deposition of any person (party or non-party) can be used for any purpose if one of the following conditions, all relating to the witness' *unavailability*, exists: (1) the deponent is *dead*; (2) the deponent is located *100 or more miles* from the trial; (3) the deponent is *too ill* to testify; (4) the deponent is *not obtainable by subpoena*; or (5) there are *exceptional circumstances* that make it desirable to dispense with the deponent's live testimony. See Rule 32(a)(4).

  3. **Partial offering:** If only *part* of a deposition is offered into evidence by one party, an *adverse* party may introduce *any other parts* of the deposition which in *fairness* ought to be considered with the part introduced. Rule 32(a)(6). (*Example:* If one side reads part of an answer, the other side may almost always read the rest of the answer.)

D. Interrogatories: The *interrogatory answer* of a party can be used by an *adverse party* for *any purpose*. [246]

  1. **Not binding:** Statements made in interrogatories, like statements made in depositions, are *not binding* upon the maker — he may contradict them in court. (Obviously the witness' credibility will suffer, but the witness is not legally bound to the prior statement.)

E. Admissions: *Admissions* obtained under Rule 36 *conclusively establish* the matter admitted. [246]

F. Physical and mental examinations: The results of *physical and mental examinations* made under Rule 35 are almost always *admissible at trial*. (Also, remember that if the examined party requests and obtains a report of the examiner, the examinee is held to waive any privilege associated with the report, such as the doctor/patient privilege.) [246]

> **Note:** All of the above discussion of use at trial assumes that the use takes place during the very proceeding that gave rise to the discovery itself. Where the fruits of discovery in Action 1 are sought to be used in Action 2, different, more complicated, rules apply.

VI. PRETRIAL CONFERENCE

A. Generally: Many states, and the federal system, give the judge the authority to conduct a *pretrial conference*. The judge may use such a conference to simplify or formulate the issues for trial, and to facilitate a settlement. See Rule 16(a) and 16(c). [250-250]

  1. **Scheduling:** The federal judge must issue a *"scheduling order"* within 120 days after filing of the complaint. This order sets a time limit for filing of motions, completion of discovery, etc. Rule 16(b). The trial judge may, but need not, conduct a pretrial conference.

  2. **Pretrial order:** If the judge does hold a pretrial conference, she then must enter a *pretrial order* reciting the actions taken in the conference (e.g., narrowing the issues to be litigated, and summarizing the admissions of fact made by the lawyers).

CHAPTER 6

ASCERTAINING APPLICABLE LAW

I.   NATURE OF PROBLEM

A. Generally: A particular controversy that is litigable in federal court may also, in most situations, be brought in state court. This chapter is about which law — federal law or state law — should be applied in cases brought in federal court. [254]

   1. Forum shopping: A key concept to keep in sight is the federal courts' desire to *discourage "forum shopping."* If a particular case could be brought in either state or federal court, and the state courts would apply rules of law different from those that would be applied by the federal court, the plaintiff (and in situations where removal is possible, the defendant) will have an incentive to *choose the court more favorable to her case*. To prevent forum shopping of this sort, the courts *generally apply state law* in diversity cases. [254]

   2. Rules of Decision Act: The Rules of Decision Act (RDA), 28 U.S.C. §1652, based upon the Supremacy Clause of the Constitution, is the main statute stating when the federal court should apply federal law, and when it should apply state law. [254-257]

   a. Federal law applied: According to the clear language of the RDA, the federal Constitution, treaties, and constitutional *statutes* enacted by Congress, always take precedence, where relevant, over all *state* provisions. (In fact, this rule applies not only to federal proceedings but also to state court proceedings.)

   b. State statutes: The RDA also clearly provides that in the absence of a federal constitutional or statutory provision on point, the federal courts must follow *state constitutions and statutes*. [254]

   c. Dispute about common law: The interesting question, and one on which the RDA is silent, is what the federal court should do where there is *no controlling constitutional or statutory provision*, federal *or* state. In other words, the key question is, what law should the federal court follow where what is at issue is *"common,"* or *judge-made*, law. [254]

   Example: P sues D in a diversity action arising out of an automobile accident that took place in Kansas. The Kansas courts apply common-law contributory negligence. Must the federal judge hearing the case apply Kansas' common-law contributory negligence, or is the court free to make its own determination that comparative negligence is a sounder principle? The answer, as set forth in *Erie v. Tompkins* (discussed below), is that Kansas common law must be followed.

B. *Erie v. Tompkins:* The most important Supreme Court case in all of Civil Procedure is *Erie Railroad v. Tompkins*. That case holds that when the Rules of Decision Act says that the federal courts must apply the "law of the several states, except where the Constitution or … acts of Congress otherwise require…," this language applies to state *common law* as well as state statutory law. The net result is that *in diversity cases, the federal courts must apply state judge-made law on any substantive issue*. [256-257]

   1. Discrimination against citizens: The contrary rule that had been followed before *Erie* — *Swift v. Tyson*'s holding that federal judges could ignore state common law in diversity cases — frequently allowed non-citizens to *discriminate against citizens of the state where the federal court sat*.

Example: P, an Ohio resident, sues D, a Kansas resident, in federal district court for the District of Kansas. Kansas law would be favorable to D. *Swift v. Tyson*, which would allow P to choose federal or state court in Kansas, whichever was more favorable to him, would thus allow P to profit at D's expense. *Erie v. Tompkins*, by forcing the federal court to apply Kansas law, guarantees D, the Kansas citizen, the benefits of his own state's law.

2. **Facts of *Erie*:** The facts of *Erie* remain a good illustration of the case's principle, that state rather than federal common law is to be followed on substantive matters in diversity cases. P, a Pennsylvania citizen, was injured while walking on the right of way maintained by D, a New York railroad. Under Pennsylvania judge-made law, P would probably have lost his negligence suit, because P was a trespasser, to whom D would be liable only for gross, not ordinary, negligence. P instead sued in New York federal district court, expecting the federal court to follow *Swift v. Tyson* and make its own "federal common law" which P hoped would make the railroad liable to him for ordinary negligence.

   a. **Holding:** But the Supreme Court held that the federal court must follow state law on substantive issues, and that "state law" included judge-made (common) law as well as state statutes. So Pennsylvania law on the railroad's duty of care was to be followed (though the Court did not specify why Pennsylvania rather than New York law was what should be followed).

   Note: For an overview of how to analyze an *Erie* problem, see the Flow Chart printed as Figure 6-1 [277].

II. *ERIE* PROBLEMS

A. **Ascertaining state law:** Several problems arise when the federal court tries to determine what *is* the "state law," when there is no state statute on point. Obviously if the highest court of the state where the federal court sits has recently spoken on the issue, the problem is easy. But where this is not the case, life gets trickier. The general principle is that the federal court must try to determine ***how the state's highest court would determine the issue if the case arose before it today***. [258-259]

   1. **Intermediate-court decisions:** If there is no holding by the highest state court, the federal court looking for state law to apply ***considers intermediate-court*** decisions. These intermediate-court decisions will normally be followed, unless there are other reasons to believe that the state's highest court would not follow them. [258]

   2. **Where no state court has spoken:** If no court in the state has ever considered the issue in question, then the court can look to other sources. One important source is decisions in ***prior federal diversity cases*** which have attempted to predict and apply the law of the same state. Similarly, the federal court may look at the practice of other states, other authorities (e.g., Restatements), etc. But the issue is always: What would the highest state court decide today? [258]

   3. **State decision obsolete:** Where there is an ***old*** determination of state law by the highest state court, the federal court hearing the present case is always free to conclude that the state court would decide the issue differently if confronted with the present case. In that situation, the old ruling is not binding. [258]

   4. **Change to conform with new state decision:** The federal court (even an appellate court) must give effect to a ***new*** decision of a state's highest court, even if the state court decision

was handed down *after* the federal district court action was completed. [258]

B. Conflict of laws: The federal court must also apply state law governing *conflict of laws*. In other words, the conflict of laws rules of the state *where the federal court sits* must be followed. [*Klaxon Co. v. Stentor Electric Mfg. Co.*] [259]

> **Example:** The Ps, soldiers, are injured in Cambodia by an explosion of a shell manufactured by D. The Ps sue D in Texas federal court. Texas tort law allows strict liability. The law of Cambodia does not allow strict liability.
>
> *Held*, Texas conflict-of-laws principles must apply. Since the Texas courts would apply the tort law of the place where the accident occurred — Cambodia — so must the federal court. Therefore, strict liability will not be applied, and the Ps lose. [*Day & Zimmermann, Inc. v. Challoner*]

C. Burden of proof: The federal court must also follow the rules governing the *allocation of the burden of proof* in force in the state where the federal court is sitting. [259]

D. Procedure/substance distinction: *Erie v. Tompkins* says that state common law controls in "substantive" matters. But federal rules and policies control on matters that are essentially "procedural." Here are some guidelines for handling the *procedure/substance distinction*: [260-271]

C
A
P
S
U
L
E

S
U
M
M
A
R
Y

1. **Federal Rules take precedence:**   *Erie* is only applicable where there is no controlling federal statute. Since the Federal Rules of Civil Procedure are adopted pursuant to a congressional statute (the Rules Enabling Act), *the FRCP, when applicable, take precedence over state policy*. So if a Federal Rule arguably applies to the situation at hand, ask two questions: (1) Does the Rule in fact apply to the issue at hand? and (2) Is the Rule valid under the Rules Enabling Act? If the answer to both questions is "yes," then the Federal Rule takes precedence. [260]

   a. **Does Rule apply:**   The mere fact that a Federal Rule seems to have something to do with the issue at hand does not mean that the Rule applies — the Rules are *construed narrowly*, to cover just those situations that Congress intended them to cover. [261-262, 265]

   Example: FRCP 3 provides that a civil action "is commenced by filing a complaint with the court." P files a complaint against D with the court on Feb. 1. The statute of limitations on P's right of action expires on Feb. 15. On March 1, P causes D to be served with process. The suit takes place in Kentucky federal district court. Kentucky state law provides that the statute of limitations is satisfied only by service upon the defendant, not by mere filing with the court.

   The federal court for Kentucky must ask, "Does Rule 3 really apply to this situation?" The Supreme Court has held on these facts that Rule 3 does *not* speak to the issue of when a state statute of limitations is tolled, but is merely designed to give a starting point for the measurement of various time periods in the federal suit. Since neither Rule 3 nor any other Federal Rule is on point, state common law — in this case, Kentucky's principle that the date of service is what counts — must be applied in the federal action. [*Ragan v. Merchants Transfer; Walker v. Armco Steel Corp.*]

   b. **Is Rule valid:**   If you conclude that the Rule applies to the issue at hand, the next question is, "Is the Rule valid?" The Rules Enabling Act provides that to be valid, a Rule must not "abridge, enlarge, [or] modify the substantive rights of any litigant." But as long as the Rule is arguably "procedural," it will be found to satisfy this test. *No Federal Rule has*

ever been found to violate the "no abridgement, enlargement or modification of substantive rights" test of the Rules Enabling Act. [260]

c. **Illustrations:**   To see how the two-part test works, consider these two examples, both from important Supreme Court cases. In each case, the Court concluded that (1) the relevant Federal Rule was intended to govern the situation at hand; (2) the Rule was valid under the Enabling Act; and (3) the Rule had to be applied, thereby displacing the relevant state principle, even though this result might be somewhat outcome-determinative. [263-264]

Example 1: P sues D in diversity in Massachusetts federal court. D is the executor of an estate. P causes process to be served on D's wife, by leaving copies of the summons and complaint with her at D's dwelling place. Federal Rule 4(d)(1) (now Rule 4(e)(2)) allows service on a defendant by leaving copies of the summons and complaint at the defendant's dwelling place with a person of suitable age and discretion, a standard met here. But a Massachusetts statute sets special standards for service on an executor of an estate, which were not complied with here.

Held, first, Rule 4(d)(1) is in harmony with the Enabling Act, since it is basically procedural. Second, the Rule clearly applies to the issue here, since it specifies the allowable method of service in a federal action. Therefore, the Rule takes priority over any contrary state policy or statute, even if applying the Rule might help produce a different outcome than had the state rule been applied. [*Hanna v. Plumer*]

Example 2: Shady Grove Orthopedics provides medical care to a patient after she has a car accident. In return, the patient assigns her rights to insurance benefits under a policy she has with D (Allstate). A New York insurance statute requires that insurance companies pay or deny such claims within 30 days, and pay 2%-per-month interest on any claim that is paid late. Shady Grove files a claim, which D pays late and without the statutory interest. Shady Grove then brings a diversity-only class action suit against D in New York federal court, seeking the unpaid interest on behalf of everyone to whom D owes interest under the 2%-per-month New York provision. A different New York statute, §901 of the CPLR (which governs judicial procedure in the New York courts), follows the main principles of FRCP 23 on when class actions may be maintained (see C- 84); but §901 adds an additional requirement, by saying that if a suit is brought "to recover a penalty or a minimum measure of recovery," the suit may not be maintained as a class action. This clause would block a class action n the New York courts for the 2%-per-month interest. D claims that there is no conflict between FRCP 23 and the New York statute, because they are designed to deal with different issues; therefore, D contends, the New York rule barring class actions can and should be applied under *Erie* principles, depriving the federal courts of the right to hear the case as a class action.

Held (by 5-4 on this point), for Shady Grove. There is indeed a conflict between FRCP 23 and the New York statute; Rule 23 lets suits be brought as class actions without regard to whether they are for penalties, and New York would bar such a suit. Since Rule 23 applies to the issue in question and directly conflicts with the state provision, then as long as the Federal Rule does not violate the Enabling Act that Rule will displace state law and will permit the suit to go forward as a diversity class action. And Rule 23 is indeed valid under the Enabling Act (it does not abridge, enlarge or modify any substantive right, since the New York no-class-actions-for-penalties statute is essentially procedural, not substantive). So the suit can proceed as a class action, even though no class action on the same claim could be brought in the New York courts. [*Shady Grove Orthopedic Assoc. v. Allstate Ins. Co.* (2010)]

2. **Case not covered by a Federal Rule:** If the issue at hand is *not* covered by anything in the FRCP, but is nonetheless arguably "procedural," the situation is more complicated: [262-263]

   a. **Rejection of "outcome determination":** At one time, the test was whether the choice between state and federal policy was *"outcome determinative"* — if the choice was at all likely to influence who won the lawsuit, then the litigants' substantive rights would be affected by the choice, and the state policy must be followed. But the Supreme Court has *rejected outcome-determinativeness as the standard*. [*Byrd v. Blue Ridge*] [262]

   b. **Balance state and federal policies:** Today, the federal court *balances* the state and federal policies against each other. *Where the state interest in having its policy followed is fairly weak, and the federal interest strong, the court is likely to hold that the federal procedural policy should be followed*. Here are some illustrations of how this balancing works out: [262-263]

      i. **Judge/Jury allocation:** Where the question is, "Who decides a certain factual issue, judge or jury?" *federal* policies are to be followed. (*Example:* Whether P was an employee rather than an independent contractor is to be determined by following the federal policy of having factual matters determined by a jury, not the state policy of having such an issue decided by the judge, because the federal policy on judge-jury allocation is strong, the state policy is not tightly bound up with the rights of the parties, and the choice is not very outcome determinative. [*Byrd v. Blue Ridge*]) [262]

      ii. **Unanimity for jury trials:** Federal policy requiring a *unanimous jury verdict* will be applied in diversity suits, at the expense of the state policy allowing a verdict based on a less-than-unanimous majority. The state's policy (reducing hung juries) has little weight here, since the case is not taking place in the state system; the federal policy is strong, supported by tradition; the choice is not heavily outcome-determinative.

      iii. **Statute of limitations:** But a state *statute of limitations* must be followed in a diversity case. Here, the state's interest is heavily outcome-determinative, and deeply bound up with the rights of the parties. The federal interest is relatively weak, and there is little to be gained from district-to-district uniformity. [*Guaranty Trust Co. v. York*, an older case that is still valid.] [261]

3. **Federal statute (not Rule) on point:** Where there is a federal procedural *statute* (as distinct from a Federal Rule) that is directly on point, it will control over any state law or policy, even though this may promote forum shopping. [253]

III. FEDERAL COMMON LAW

A. **Federal common law still exists:** Even though *Erie* makes it clear that there is no *general* federal common law, there are still *particular instances* in which federal common law is applied. That is, the federal court is occasionally free to disregard state law in deciding the case. [274]

B. **Federal question cases:** Most importantly, in *federal question* cases, *federal common law, not state common law, usually applies*. (*Example:* P sues D, the United States, in federal district court for the Northern District of Texas. This suit raises a federal question, since it involves the U.S. as a party. Even if there is no federal statute on point, and even if it is clear that under Texas law the

U.S. would not be negligent, the federal court may and should apply general federal common law principles in deciding whether the U.S. was negligent and is thus liable.) [274]

C. Diversity cases: Occasionally, federal common law may even be applied where the basis for federal jurisdiction is diversity. For instance, if P's claim does not raise issues of federal law, but a defense asserted by D does raise federal law, the validity of that defense will be determined under federal common law principles. [275]

D. Federal common law in state courts: Conversely, the *states* are occasionally required to apply *federal* common law. If concurrent jurisdiction (state and federal) exists concerning a particular claim, and the suit is brought in state court, federal common law applies there if it would apply in federal court. [276]

> **Example:** P brings a state-court action against D, a city, under a federal statute giving a cause of action for deprivation of civil rights. State law requires that P give notice to D within 120 days of injury before suing D if D is a city. *Held*, the state court may not impose this state-created procedural rule, since it would abridge federally-granted rights. [*Felder v. Casey*]

CHAPTER 7

TRIAL PROCEDURE

I. BURDEN OF PROOF

A. Two meanings of "burden of proof": There are two kinds of "burden of proof" which a party may have to bear. Assuming that the issue is called *A*: [282]

1. Burden of production: The party bears the "burden of *production*" if the following is true: unless the party produces *some* evidence that *A* exists, the judge must direct the jury to find that *A* does not exist. [282]

2. Burden of persuasion: The party bears the "burden of *persuasion*" if the following is true: at the close of the evidence, if the jury cannot decide whether *A* exists or not, the jury must find that *A* does not exist. [282]

> **Example of two burdens:** P sues D, arguing that D failed to use reasonable care in driving his car, and therefore hit P, a pedestrian. P bears both the burden of production and the burden of persuasion as to D's negligence. To meet the burden of production, P will have to come up with at least some evidence that D was careless; if P does not do so, the judge will not let the jury decide the issue of negligence, and will instead direct the jury to find that there was no negligence. If P comes up with some evidence of negligence, and the case goes to the jury, the fact that P also bears the burden of persuasion means that the judge will tell the jury, "In order to find that D was negligent, you must find it more likely than not that D was negligent. If you find exactly a 50-50 chance that D was negligent, you must find non-negligence."

II. PRESUMPTIONS

A. Definition: A *presumption* is a convention that when a designated *basic fact* exists (call the designated basic fact *B*), another fact, called the *presumed fact* (call it *P*) *must* be taken to exist unless there is rebuttal evidence to show that *P* does not exist. [283]

B. Effect of presumption: The existence of a presumption always has an effect on the burden of production, and sometimes has an effect on the burden of persuasion. (In the following discussion, assume that there is a legal presumption that if *B*, then *P*. Assume also that plaintiff is trying to prove *P*. Also assume that if there were no presumption, plaintiff would bear the burden of persuasion as to *P*.) [283-284]

  1. Effect on burden of production: The party against whom the presumption is directed bears the initial burden of *producing* evidence of non-*P*. If he produces no evidence, he *suffers a directed verdict*. [283]

    Example: A statute establishes a presumption that when a railroad locomotive causes damage, the railroad was negligent. P proves that D's locomotive caused damage to him. Neither party puts on any evidence about D's actual negligence. Assume that if there were no presumption, P would have the burden of production on negligence. By showing damage, P has carried his burden of production; if D does not come up with any rebutting evidence of non-negligence, the judge will direct the jury to find for P on the negligence issue.

  2. Burden of persuasion: If the defendant offers enough evidence of non-*P* that a reasonable jury might find non-*P*, it is clear that defendant has met his production burden, and that the case will go to the jury. But courts are *split* as to who bears the burden of *persuasion*. [283]

    a. Federal Rules of Evidence: Most states, and federal courts in federal-question cases, follow the approach set out in the Federal Rules of Evidence. Under this approach, the presumption has *no* effect on the burden of persuasion, merely on the burden of production. This approach is sometimes called the *"bursting bubble"* approach — *once evidence tending to show the non-existence of the presumed fact is introduced, the presumption bursts like a bubble*. See FRE 301 ("A presumption imposes on the party against whom it is directed the burden of going forward with evidence to rebut or meet the presumption, but does not shift to such party the burden of proof in the sense of the risk of non-persuasion…").

    Example: Same facts as above example. After P shows evidence of damage by the locomotive, D comes forward with evidence that it was not negligent. This is enough to send the case to the jury. Now, under the FRE "bursting bubble" approach, P will still bear the burden of persuasion — unless P convinces the jury that it is more likely than not that D was negligent, D will win on the issue of negligence. This is because the presumption — that where there is locomotive damage, there is railroad negligence — has no effect on the burden of persuasion.

    b. State law in diversity cases: But in *diversity* cases, the federal courts must defer to any contrary state rule concerning the effect of a presumption on the burden of persuasion. See FRE 302. In other words, FRE 301, applying the bursting bubble approach, applies only where a federal claim or defense is at issue, or state law is silent.

III. PREPONDERANCE OF THE EVIDENCE

A. "Preponderance" standard generally: The usual standard of proof in civil actions is the *"preponderance of the evidence"* standard. A proposition is proved by a preponderance of the evidence if the jury is convinced that it is *"more likely than not"* that the proposition is true. [284]

B. Adversary's denials: A party who has the burden of proving a fact by a preponderance of the evidence may ***not rely solely on the jury's disbelief of his adversary's denials of that fact***. [285]

> **Example:** P asserts that D behaved negligently by driving through a red light. P produces no affirmative evidence of this allegation. D takes the stand, and says, "The light was green when I drove through." P does not cross-examine D on this point. There is no other relevant evidence. The court must hold that P could not possibly have satisfied the "preponderance of the evidence" standard as to D's negligence — the fact that the jury might possibly disbelieve D's denials of negligence is not enough, and the court must enter a directed verdict for D on this point.

IV. ADJUDICATION WITHOUT TRIAL

A. Voluntary dismissal by plaintiff: A plaintiff in federal court may ***voluntarily dismiss*** her complaint ***without prejudice*** any time before the defendant serves an answer or moves for summary judgment. The fact that the dismissal is "without prejudice" means that she may ***bring the suit again***. See Rule 41(a)(1). [287]

   1. Only one dismissal: Only the ***first*** dismissal of the claim is without prejudice.

   2. After answer or motion: After D has answered or moved for summary judgment, P may no longer automatically make a voluntary dismissal. Instead, P must get the court's approval. FRCP 41(a)(2).

B. Involuntary dismissal: P's claim may also be ***involuntarily*** dismissed by court order. [287]

   1. Examples: Some of the grounds for which, under FRCP 41(b), the court may grant an involuntary dismissal, are: (1) P's failure to ***prosecute***; (2) P's failure to ***obey court orders***; (3) lack of ***jurisdiction*** or ***venue***; or (4) P's failure to join an ***indispensable party***.

   2. Prejudice: Normally an involuntary dismissal is ***with prejudice***. FRCP 41(b). But some kinds of dismissals are ***not*** with prejudice (and thus the action may be brought anew): (1) dismissal for ***lack of jurisdiction***, of both parties and subject matter, or for insufficient service; (2) improper ***venue***; and (3) failure to ***join*** an indispensable party under Rule 19. *Id.* Also, the court may specify that a dismissal not falling into one of these 3 categories is nonetheless without prejudice. *Id.*

C. Summary judgment: If one party can show that there is ***no "genuine dispute of material fact"*** in the lawsuit, and that she is "entitled to judgment as a matter of law," she can win the case without going to trial. Such a victory without trial is called a ***"summary judgment."*** See FRCP 56. [288-290]

   1. Court goes behind pleadings: The court will go ***"behind the pleadings"*** in deciding a summary judgment motion — even if it appears from the pleadings that the parties are in dispute, the motion may be granted if the movant can show that the disputed factual issues presented by the pleadings are ***illusory***. [288]

   2. How shown: The movant can show the lack of a genuine dispute by a number of means. For example, the movant may produce ***affidavits***, or use the fruits of ***discovery*** (e.g., depositions and interrogatory answers) to show that there is no genuine issue of material fact. [288]

      a. Burden of production: The person moving for summary judgment bears the initial burden of production in the summary judgment motion — that is, the movant must come up with at least some affirmative evidence that there is no genuine issue of material fact.

[288]

3. **Opposition:**   The party *opposing* the summary judgment usually also submits affidavits, depositions and other materials. [289]

    a. **Opponent can't rest on pleadings:**   If the materials from the record submitted by the movant show that there is no genuine material dispute for trial, the party opposing the motion can't avoid summary judgment merely by *repeating his pleadings' denial* of the allegations of the movant's affidavits. Instead, the non-movant who wants to claim that what the movant says is a non-disputed fact really *is* disputed will have to either:

        [1] *point to specific places in the record* (such as depositions, documents, admissions, etc.) showing that the fact in question is disputed, or else

        [2] demonstrate that the movant won't be able to produce *admissible evidence* to establish the fact.

        Rule 56(c)(1)(A) and (B). [289]

        Example: P sues D on a promissory note. P's claim states that the note was validly executed by D. D's answer denies that D signed the note. P moves for a Rule 56 summary judgment, and submits an affidavit by X stating that X saw D sign the note.

        D cannot avoid summary judgment by merely repeating his answer's general denial of the signature. He must do something more. For instance, D can point to something in the record that establishes a genuine dispute about whether he signed (e.g., an affidavit or deposition testimony — even if only his own — asserting that the signature is a forgery, or that it was obtained by duress, etc.). Or, he can show that P won't be able to come up with any admissible evidence at trial that D really signed. But D can't just rest on his pleadings in which he denied signing. Cf. Rule 56(c)(1)(A) and (B).

4. **Partial summary judgment:**   Summary judgment may be granted with respect to *certain claims* in a lawsuit even when it is not granted with respect to all claims. This is called *partial summary judgment*. See Rule 54(b). [290]

    Example: P sues D for breach of contract. The court might grant P partial summary judgment on the issue of liability, on the grounds that there is no genuine dispute about whether a breach occurred. If so, the court would then probably conduct a trial limited to the remaining issue, damages.

V. **TRIALS WITHOUT A JURY**

A. **When tried to court:**   A case will be tried without a jury if *either* of the two following conditions exists: [291]

1. **No right to a jury trial** exists; or

2. **All parties** have **waived** the right to a jury trial.

    a. **When waived:**   A party who wants a jury trial on a particular issue must file a *demand* for jury trial to the other parties within *10 days* after the service of the *last pleading* directed to that issue. FRCP 38(b). Otherwise, the party is deemed to have waived her right to jury trial.

B. Effect: If there is no jury, the trial judge serves as both the ***finder of fact*** and the decider of law. [291]

C. Evidence rules: The rules of evidence followed by the judge (in federal trials, these are the Federal Rules of Evidence) are officially the ***same*** in non-jury trials as in jury trials. However, in practice, judges tend to ***relax the rules*** when there is no jury present. [291]

D. Findings of fact: If an action is tried without a jury, FRCP 52 requires the trial court to "***find the facts*** specially and [to] state its conclusions of law separately[.]" So the trial judge must set forth the facts with ***particularity***, and must in a separate section of her opinion state the law which she believes applies to those facts. [291]

1. Where separate findings required: The federal judge must make separate findings of fact and conclusions of law not only in cases that are fully tried, but also: [291]

    a. Where requests for interlocutory ***injunctions*** are made (whether granted or denied); and

    b. Where ***"judgment on partial findings"*** is given pursuant to Rule 52(c).

2. Separate findings not required: The trial judge is ***not*** obligated to make separate findings of fact and conclusions of law when disposing of a ***motion***, except a Rule 52(c) motion for judgment on partial findings. (*Examples:* If the judge denies a motion for summary judgment, or grants a 12(b)(6) motion to dismiss for failure to state a claim, the judge need not make detailed findings of fact.) [292]

3. Judgment on partial findings: The judge can conduct a ***"mini trial"*** of just one issue, if the judge thinks that this will dispose of the case. If the judge then finds against the party bearing the burden of proof on that issue, the judge issues a "judgment on partial findings." See FRCP 52(c). (*Example:* In an auto accident case, D pleads the three-year statute of limitations. The judge can conduct a mini trial concerning only the date of the accident; if the date is more than three years before P started the action, the judge can issue a judgment in D's favor based on the partial finding that the action is time-barred.) [292]

4. Appellate review of factual findings from bench trials: If the loser of a non-jury trial ***appeals***, the appellate court will be ***reluctant to second-guess*** the trial judge's findings of fact. In the federal system, the trial judge's findings of fact will be set aside only if they are ***"clearly erroneous."*** See FRCP 52(a). Appellate review of findings of fact in bench trials is covered later as part of our general discussion of appeals; see p. C-75 *infra*.

VI. THE JURY

A. Seventh Amendment generally: The Seventh Amendment to the U.S. Constitution says that "in suits at ***common law … the right of trial by jury shall be preserved***.…" This Amendment applies to ***federal trials***, but does ***not*** apply to ***state*** trials. [294]

B. Number of jurors: Traditionally, juries have been composed of 12 members. But this is breaking down today. [294]

1. Federal: Even in federal civil cases, the Seventh Amendment does ***not*** require a 12-member jury. FRCP 48 provides that a jury of at least ***six*** members will be seated.

    a. Too few remaining: Normally the federal court seats more than six jurors, so that if some have to leave the panel, there will be at least six at the time of verdict. If there are fewer than six at the time of verdict, the court must declare a mistrial unless both parties agree to continue.

2. State trials: The number of jurors in *state trials* varies from state to state.

C. Unanimity: [294]

    1. Federal: The verdict of a *federal* civil jury must be *unanimous*, unless the parties stipulate otherwise. FRCP 48.

    2. States: Most states allow a *less-than-unanimous* civil verdict.

D. Jury selection: The process by which the jury is selected is called the *"voir dire."* In most states, the *voir dire* consists of oral questions by both sides' counsel to the prospective jurors. These questions are designed to discover whether a juror would be biased, or has connections with a party or prospective witness. [294]

    1. Dismissal for cause: Any juror who is shown through the *voir dire* to be biased or connected to the case must be dismissed upon motion by a party (dismissal *"for cause"*). There is no limit to the number of for-cause challenges by either party.

    2. Challenges without cause: In addition to the jurors dismissed for cause, each party may dismiss a certain number of other prospective jurors *without showing cause* for their dismissal (*"peremptory challenges"*).

        a. Federal practice: In federal civil trials, each party receives *three* peremptory challenges.

    3. Balanced pool: The Seventh Amendment requires that the jury, and the pool from which it is drawn, be roughly *representative of the overall community*.

    4. Alternates: In most states, the court orders the selection of up to six *alternates* after the "regular" members of the jury have been selected. But under federal practice, alternates are no longer used (FRCP 48).

E. Instructions: The judge must *instruct* the jury as to the *relevant law*. (*Example:* If P sues D for negligence, the judge must instruct the jury about the "reasonable person" standard, and the requirement of proximate cause.) [295]

    1. Objections: A party who wants to raise the inadequacy of the instructions on appeal must *object* to those instructions *before the jury retires*. (Sometimes courts make an exception to this rule for "plain error.")

F. Juror misconduct: A jury verdict may be set aside, and a *new trial* ordered, for certain types of *jury misconduct*. (*Examples:* Talking to a party, receiving a bribe, concealing a bias on voir dire.) [296]

    1. Traditional impeachment rule: The traditional rule, still followed in most states, is that the jury may *not impeach its own verdict*. That is, the verdict will not be set aside because of a juror's testimony of his own or another juror's misconduct — only evidence from a *third party* will suffice. [296]

        a. Federal Rule: But the Federal Rules of Evidence have modified this principle slightly for federal trials. The general "jury can't impeach its own verdict" rule still applies, except that a juror may testify about whether extraneous prejudicial information was improperly brought to the jury's attention, or whether any *outside influence* was improperly brought to bear upon a juror. FRE 606(b). (*Examples:* One juror can testify that another read a newspaper article about the case, or was bribed by one of the parties. But a juror cannot testify that the jury disregarded the judge's instructions.)

CAPSULE SUMMARY

2. **Post-trial discovery of bias:** If, after the trial, it turns out that a juror *failed to disclose* information during voir dire that would have indicated bias, the party may move for a new trial. In federal trials, the movant must show: (1) that the juror failed to answer honestly a material question during the voir dire; and (2) that a correct response would have led to a valid challenge for cause. [*McDonough Power Equipment Inc. v. Greenwood*] (*Example:* A party can get a new trial if he proves that a juror lied about knowing one of the parties, but not if the juror honestly gave a mistaken answer in voir dire because of confusion about the question.) [296]

VII. CHALLENGING THE JUDGE FOR BIAS

A. **Judicial bias generally:** Both federal and state systems try to protect the litigants against *judicial bias*. In general, systems do this by giving a litigant a chance to ask the judge to *"recuse" (i.e., disqualify) herself* from the case where there is a danger of bias. [298-299]

B. **The federal recusal statute:** In federal litigation, a litigant may challenge a judge only for *cause*. That is, unlike some states, the federal system does *not* give litigants any *"peremptory"* challenges analogous to those given as to jurors.

1. **Grounds for recusal:** 28 U.S.C. §455 specifies the circumstances under which there is cause for a judge to recuse herself. Section 455 recognizes *two main categories* in which recusal is required:

   a. **Broad provision:** The first is a *broad*, but *vague*, "appearance-of-bias" category — if the facts are such that it would *look to an observer* as though the judge might well be biased for or against one party, the judge must recuse himself even if he *subjectively* (and reasonably) *believes* that he can in fact be perfectly fair to both sides. 28 U.S.C. §455(a). (But the parties may agree to *waive* any danger of bias under this general provision.) [298]

   b. **Narrow provisions:** Second is a set of narrow, *specific* categories requiring recusal. 28 U.S.C. §455(b). Unlike the above "appearance of bias" category, the parties are *not free to waive* the conflict in a situation covered by §455(b). [298] The specific categories requiring recusal under §455(b) include:

      [1] that the judge has *"personal knowledge* of disputed *evidentiary facts"* that will be involved in the suit;

      [2] that the judge served as a *"lawyer* in the *matter in controversy"* when he was in private practice, or was *associated* with a lawyer who served in that matter while the two practiced law together;

      [3] that when the judge "served in *governmental employment,"* he *"expressed an opinion* concerning the *merits* of the *particular case"*;

      [4] that the judge or a member of his immediate family "has a *financial interest* in the *subject matter* in controversy or in a *party* to the proceeding." (*Example:* If the judge owns even *$1 of stock* in a company that is a party, the judge must recuse himself.)

C. **Bias great enough to violate due process:** In extreme circumstances, a judge's *refusal* to recuse himself for bias, or apparent bias, may constitute a violation of a litigant's *federal constitutional right to due process*.

C
A
P
S
U
L
E

S
U
M
M
A
R
Y

1. **Judicial campaigns:** For instance, recusal may be required where one litigant makes large *campaign expenditures* on behalf of a candidate for a judgeship — the opposing litigant's due process rights may be violated by the judge's post-election refusal to recuse himself from hearing the case. [*Caperton v. A.T. Massey Coal Co., Inc.* (2009)] [299]

> **Example:** The Ps are small mining companies who claim that D, a much larger mining company, has improperly driven them out of business. The Ps obtain a $50 million damage award from a West Virginia jury. D appeals to the West Virginia Supreme Court. While the appeal is pending, the CEO of D spends $3 million in independent campaign expenditures in a successful attempt to have a sitting justice of that court replaced by Brent Benjamin. When the appeal comes before the court, Benjamin refuses to recuse himself; he then votes with a 3-2 majority that throws out the $50 million verdict against D. The Ps now claim that Benjamin's refusal to recuse himself violated their federal constitutional due process rights.
>
> *Held*, by the U.S. Supreme Court on a 5-4 vote, for the Ps. Benjamin's refusal to recuse himself violated the Ps' constitutional due process rights. Due process can be violated not just by proof of "actual bias," but also by a "serious risk of actual bias ... based on objective and reasonable perceptions[.]" That risk of serious bias exists where "a person with a personal stake in a particular case had a significant and disproportionate influence in placing the judge on the case by raising funds or directing the judge's election campaign when the case was pending or imminent." [*Caperton v. A.T. Massey Coal Co., Inc., supra*]

VIII. DIRECTED VERDICT

A. **Defined:** In both state and federal trials, either party may move for a *directed verdict*. Such a verdict *takes the case away from the jury, and determines the outcome as a matter of law*. [299]

1. **Federal trials:** In federal trials, the phrase "directed verdict" is no longer used — instead, a party moves for "judgment as a matter of law."

2. **When made:** Motions for directed verdict or judgment as a matter of law are made when the opposing party has been *fully heard* on the relevant issues. Thus D can move for directed verdict at the close of P's case, and either party may move for directed verdict after both sides have rested.

B. **Standard for granting:** Generally, the court will direct a verdict if the evidence is such that *reasonable people could not differ* as to the result. [300]

1. **Federal standard:** In federal trials, the standard is that the judge may enter judgment as a matter of law "[i]f a party has been fully heard on an issue during a jury trial and the court finds that *a reasonable jury would not have a legally sufficient evidentiary basis to find for the party on that issue*[.]" FRCP 50(a)(1).

IX. SPECIAL VERDICT AND INTERROGATORIES

A. **Special verdict defined:** A "special verdict" is a *specific finding of fact*, as opposed to a general verdict (which merely grants victory to one side or the other). (*Example:* In a contract case, the jury might be asked to render a special verdict as to whether a valid contract existed between the parties.) [302]

B. General verdict with interrogatories: The judge may, instead of requiring a special verdict, require a general verdict, supported by *interrogatories* as to specific findings of fact. See FRCP 49(b). This "general verdict with interrogatories" approach is more common than the specific verdict approach. [302]

X. NEW TRIAL

A. Generally: The trial court, in both state and federal courts, usually has wider discretion to grant a *new trial* motion than to direct a verdict or disregard the jury's verdict (JNOV). The reason is that the grant of a new trial interferes less with the verdict winner's right to jury trial. [302]

B. Federal rules for granting: Here is a summary of the rules on grants of new trials. We concentrate here on federal civil cases, but also sometimes mention state-court rules: [302-303]

1. **Harmless error:** A new trial may not be granted except for errors in the trial which are serious enough that they affect the substantial rights of the parties. FRCP 61. This is the so-called *"harmless error"* doctrine. Basically, unless the trial judge believes that the error *might have made the case come out differently*, she cannot grant a new trial motion. [303]

2. **Evidence error:** One common ground for granting a new trial is that the trial judge *erroneously admitted or excluded evidence*. [302]

3. **Objection:** For most types of error at the trial court level, the party injured by the error must make a *timely objection*, in order to preserve the right to cite that error on appeal as a ground for a new trial. (For more about this, see the discussion of appeals on p. C-75.)

4. **Improper conduct:** A new trial may be granted because of *improper conduct* by a *party*, *witness* or *lawyer*, posing a substantial risk that an unfair verdict will result. Similarly, a new trial may be granted where there is evidence that the *jury* behaved improperly (e.g., a juror was bribed or was contacted by a party). [303]

5. **Verdict against weight of evidence:** The trial judge (or the appeals court) may set aside a verdict as *"against the weight of the evidence."* [304]

   a. **Federal standard:** In federal courts, a verdict must be against the *clear weight* of the evidence, be based upon evidence which is *false*, or result in a miscarriage of justice. It is not enough that there is substantial evidence against the verdict, or that the trial judge disagrees with the verdict and would vote otherwise if he were a juror. (But it is still easier to get a federal judge to grant a new trial as against the weight of the evidence than to get the trial judge to direct judgment as a matter of law.)

6. **Verdict excessive or inadequate:** A new trial may be granted where a verdict is *excessive* or *inadequate*. [304]

   a. *Remittitur* and *additur:* Where the verdict is excessive or inadequate, the judge may grant a *conditional* new trial order — the new trial will occur unless the plaintiff agrees to a reduction of the damages to a specified amount (called *"remittitur"*) or the new trial to occur unless the defendant consents to a *raising* of the damages (called *"additur"*). Most state courts allow both *additur* and *remittitur*. In federal practice, only *remittitur* is allowed. If a party accepts the *remittitur/additur*, he may not thereafter *appeal*.

7. **Partial new trial:** The trial judge may grant a *partial* new trial, i.e., a retrial limited to a particular issue. Most typically, this occurs when the trial judge feels that the jury's conclusion that D is liable is reasonable, but feels that the damages awarded are inadequate or excessive

— the judge can grant a new trial limited to the issue of damages. [305]

8. **Newly-discovered evidence:** The trial judge may grant a new trial because of *newly-discovered evidence*. The person seeking the new trial must show that: (1) the evidence was discovered since the end of the trial; (2) the movant was *"reasonably diligent"* in his search for the evidence before and during the trial, and could not reasonably have found the evidence before the end of the trial; (3) the evidence was *material*, and in fact likely to produce a different result; and (4) injustice would otherwise result. [305]

XI. JUDGMENT NOT WITHSTANDING VERDICT / JUDGMENT AS A MATTER OF LAW

A. Definition: Most states allow the judge to set aside the jury's verdict, and enter judgment for the verdict-loser. This is called a Judgment Notwithstanding Verdict, or *JNOV*. In federal practice, the device is called *"judgment as a matter of law"* (JML). [306-308]

1. **Usefulness:** Judges like the JNOV procedure better than directed verdicts, because it allows the jury to reach a verdict — then, if the judge is reversed on appeal, a new trial is not necessary (as would be the case if the trial judge erroneously directed a verdict).

B. Federal practice: Federal practice for "judgment as a matter of law" is spelled out in FRCP 50: [307]

1. **Motion before jury retires:** The most important thing to remember about JML in federal practice is that the party seeking the JML must make a *motion* for that judgment *before the case is submitted to the jury*. The movant also specifies why (in terms of law and facts) she thinks she is entitled to the JML. The judge reserves decision on the motion, then submits the case to the jury. If the verdict goes against the movant, and the judge agrees that no reasonable jury could have found against the movant, then the judge may effectively overturn the verdict by granting JML. [307]

2. **Appeal:** Appellate courts frequently reverse both grants and denials of JML. Since a JML is granted based on the legal sufficiency of the parties' cases, not a detailed consideration of the evidence, the appellate court is quicker to second-guess the trial judge than in the case of a motion for a new trial. [308-308]

XII. CONSTITUTIONAL RIGHT TO JURY TRIAL

A. Seventh Amendment: The Seventh Amendment provides that "in suits at *common law*…the right of trial by jury shall be preserved…." [308]

1. **No state application:** The Seventh Amendment has never been applicable to *state* trials, only federal ones.

2. **Federal Rule:** The Seventh Amendment does apply to all federal civil jury trials, and is incorporated in Rule 38(a).

   a. **Party must demand:** The right to a jury trial in federal practice is *not* self-executing. A party who wishes a jury trial on a particular issue must file a *demand* for that jury trial to the other parties within *10 days* after the service of the last pleading directed to that issue. (Rule 38(b).)

    b. Equitable claim: There is no jury trial right as to *"equitable"* claims (e.g., a claim for injunction). The distinction between legal and equitable claims is very important, and is discussed further below.

B. Suits with both legal and equitable claims: If a case presents both *legal* and *equitable* claims, and one party wants a jury trial on the legal claims, the court must normally *try the legal claims first.* [*Beacon Theatres v. Westover*] If the court allowed the equitable claims to be tried first, without a jury, this might effectively dispose of some of the legal issues as well, thus thwarting the party's right of jury trial on the legal claims. [309]

> **Example:** P sues D for an injunction against certain contract violations. D counterclaims for damages for breach of contract. D demands a jury trial on its counterclaim. Assuming, as seems likely, the injunction claim is equitable and the damages counterclaim is legal, the judge must try the counterclaim to a jury *before* it conducts a bench trial of the injunction claim, as long as there may be some issues common to both claims.

C. Distinguishing "legal" vs. "equitable" claims: In deciding whether a claim is "legal" rather than "equitable," the issue is whether the claim is a claim "at common law." The main test is whether the claim is one which the courts of law (as opposed to equity) would have recognized prior to the 1791 adoption of the Seventh Amendment. The problem usually arises in the case of a modern statute that has no precise pre-1791 analogue.

    1. Two-part test: The Supreme Court has articulated a *two-part test* for deciding whether a claim based on a modern statute is legal or equitable [311]:

      ❑ First, the court must compare the *statutory action* to the actions available in the courts of England in 1791. If the most similar action available then was legal, that's a factor in favor of the modern action's being considered legal.

      ❑ Second, the court examines the *remedy* sought, and determines whether it would have been considered legal or equitable in nature in 1791.

    [*Tull v. U.S.*] The second of these inquiries — concerning the nature of the *remedy sought* — is the *more important*.

> **Example:** The U.S. government sues D, an alleged polluter, to obtain a civil penalty under the federal Clean Water Act. Under the first part of the test, the court compares this action (which didn't exist in 1791) with actions that did exist then. The most similar is an action to abate a public nuisance, which was equitable; so this factor counts in favor of a finding that the present action is equitable. But under the second part of the test, the court looks at the remedy sought, in this case a civil penalty to punish D. This type of relief would have been legal in 1791. Since the second test is the more important when the two disagree, the claim is legal, and D is entitled to a jury trial on the issue of liability (though not on the issue of damages, since the amount of a civil penalty is not "inherent in ... the system of trial by jury.") [*Tull v. U.S.*] [311]

    2. Examples: Here's how some particular types of claims are treated:

    a. Damages: Claims that basically involve *money damages* are almost always *legal*. (The one exception is a claim for *restitution* of a benefit unfairly kept by D, such as a suit for backpay against an employer — such a claim is equitable, even though it in a sense involves damages.) [311] [*Chauffeurs, Teamsters and Helpers Local 391 v. Terry*]

   b. Injunctions are equitable: An action where the principal relief sought is an *injunction* will almost always be *equitable*.

   c. Declaratory judgment: A *declaratory judgment* suit can be either legal or equitable, depending on the underlying issues in the suit. [314]

XIII. REMEDIES

A. Damages generally: The primary form of judicial relief is *money damages*. We consider here the two major types of damages, compensatory and punitive.

   1. Compensatory damages: The usual form of money damages is *"compensatory"* damages. Compensatory damages attempt to make the plaintiff *"whole"* for the damage she has suffered as the result of the defendant's wrongdoing. For instance, in a contract action, the usual form of damages for breach is a form of compensatory damages called "expectation" damages — the sum of money needed to put the plaintiff in the position she would have been in had the contract been fulfilled.

   2. Punitive damages: A second form of damages is *"punitive"* damages. Punitive damages, as the name implies, are used to *"punish"* the defendant for extreme wrongdoing. Punitive damages are rare in contract suits, but are somewhat common in tort suits, especially those involving serious personal injuries.

      a. Due process limits: The *due process clause* of the 5th and 14th Amendments puts real *limits* on the extent to which federal and state courts can award punitive damages. [317-318]

        i. "Grossly excessive" standard: An award will violate due process if it is *"grossly excessive."* [*BMW of North America v. Gore*]

        ii. Ratio of actual to punitive: One of the most important factors in whether an award of punitive damages is grossly excessive and thus violates due process is the *ratio* of the *punitive damages* to the *actual damages.* As a rule of thumb, the Court will view suspiciously any award that *exceeds* "a *single-digit ratio* between punitive and compensatory damages." [*State Farm Mut. Automobile Insur. Co. v. Campbell*]

        Examples: The Court has struck down awards that were 500 times the amount of compensatory damages [$2 million punitive vs. $4,000 compensatory — *BMW of North America, supra*] and 145 times that amount [$145 million punitive vs. $1 million compensatory —*State Farm v. Campbell, supra*].

        iii. Reprehensibility: The more *reprehensible* D's conduct, the higher the punitive award (and the ratio between the punitive and the compensatory damages) can be without a due process violation. (*Example:* Where D's conduct involves non-disclosure but not trickery or deceit, it's less reprehensible, and a lower amount of punitive damages will nonetheless constitute a violation of due process. [*BMW v. Gore*]

B. Equitable remedies: Money damages are the usual form of relief in civil actions. But occasionally, the appropriate form of relief is *"equitable"* rather than "legal." [318-319]

   1. Two forms of equitable relief: There are two main types of equitable relief: (1) *injunctions*; and (2) *orders of specific performance*.

a. **Injunctions:** An *injunction* is an order of the court *prohibiting* a party from doing something.

> **Example:** P, an author, claims that D, a publisher, is distributing a book that violates P's copyrights. If P can establish that this is true, the court will "enjoin" D from making any further distribution of the book. That is, the court will issue an order telling D not to distribute. If D violates the order, D will be in contempt of court, and can be fined or sent to prison.

b. **Specific performance:** A decree of *specific performance* is a decree ordering a party to *do something* affirmative, typically, to *comply with a contract.*

> **Example:** P and D have a contract under which D is to supply all of P's requirements for uranium to be used in P's nuclear power generation plant for a 10-year period. D violates the contract by refusing to deliver. The court may well issue a decree of specific performance against D, ordering that D comply with the contract by delivering the required amount of uranium (as opposed to just paying damages for uranium not delivered). If D doesn't comply, D will be in contempt of court, and can be fined or (if an individual) sent to jail.

c. **Legal remedy inadequate:** The most important single principle about equitable relief is this: the court may only award equitable relief *if legal relief* (i.e., an award of money damages) is *inadequate in the circumstances*. [319]

> **Example:** Return to the prior example, about uranium supplies. If the court can compute with reasonable precision how much uranium P will need over the remainder of the contract, and what the market price will be over that period, the court can (and will) make P whole by awarding him damages. But if (as is probable) P doesn't know exactly what his requirements for uranium will be (because he doesn't know how much power he'll need to generate), and/or it isn't knowable what the market price of uranium will be during the future course of the contract, then an award of damages *isn't "adequate,"* in which case the court will probably issue a decree of specific performance.

XIV. APPEALS

A. **Appeals generally:** In both federal and state litigation, the party who loses at trial generally has the right to *appeal* the adverse judgment. [319-329]

B. **The scope of appellate review:** Both federal and state systems have various procedural rules that significantly limit *what issues* may be grounds for reversal.

1. **Objection:** Generally, the party who hopes to raise issue X on appeal must promptly make an *"objection"* to the trial court's handling of X, and must state on the record her *grounds* for that objection. [320]

   a. **FRCP 46:** Thus in federal trials, FRCP 46 says that for any ruling or order that's made or denied, the party must "*state* the action that it wants the court to take or *objects* to, along with the *grounds* for the request or objection." If the party doesn't do this, that contention is deemed *waived* on appeal. [320]

   b. **Deference to trial court:** The appellate court will usually make a closer scrutiny of decisions of *law* than of findings of *fact*.

i. Questions of law: If the issue is a *pure question of law*, the appeals court typically decides the issue *from scratch* — it *does not give deference* to the trial court's ruling.

ii. Facts found by judge in bench trial: Appellate courts conduct a somewhat *more probing review* of factfinding by *judges* in *bench* trials, i.e., ones conducted *without a jury,* than of factfinding in *jury trials*. But even in reviewing bench trials, however, appeals courts typically give *significant deference* to the trial court.

(1) FRCP 52(a)(6) for federal practice: FRCP 52(a)(6) expressly *requires* this deference in federal trials. That Rule says that, in appeals from bench trials, "Findings of fact, whether based on *oral or other evidence*, must *not be set aside* unless *clearly erroneous*, and the reviewing court must give *due regard* to the *trial court's opportunity to judge the witnesses' credibility."* [322]

c. "Harmless error" doctrine: All appellate courts apply some version of the *"harmless error"* doctrine. Under this doctrine, the results in the trial court will be reversed only if the appeals court believes that there is a substantial chance that the error *made a difference to the outcome*. [322]

i. Federal standard: In federal cases, the harmless error doctrine is imposed by statute, 28 U.S.C. §2111. That provision says that the appellate court must conduct its review of the record "without regard to errors or defects which *do not affect the substantial rights* of the parties."

Example: P brings a federal diversity action against D for making what P claims was a defective product that injured P. In a jury trial, P puts on no proof that the product was defective. D offers testimony from Expert 1, which is properly admitted, that the product was not defective. D also offers an affidavit to the same effect from Expert 2, which the trial court allows, but which is in fact inadmissible because it is hearsay not within any exception. The jury finds for D. P appeals.

If, as seems likely, the appeals court concludes that even without considering the inadmissible affidavit D has offered so much unrebutted evidence of the product's non-defectiveness that a rational jury could not have found for P, the appeals court will affirm. That is, the appeals court will conclude that the trial judge's error of law in admitting the affidavit was "harmless error," because P was extremely unlikely to win the case even if the affidavit had been excluded. [323]

C. The "final judgment" rule, and exceptions to it: The federal system, and the vast majority of state systems, apply some form of the *final judgment rule.* The basic concept behind the rule is that an appeal is allowed only after *all the issues* involved in the suit have been *finally determined by the trial court.* [323-329]

1. Suit, not just issue, must be finally determined: So even if a particular *issue* in the case has been finally determined, the loser on that issue cannot generally take an immediate appeal. At least in the standard two-party scenario, the final judgment rule means that ordinarily the loser on one or more issues cannot take an appeal until the *entire case has been finished at the trial-court level*, and a judgment in the case has been entered.

a. "Interlocutory" appeals: As a matter of nomenclature, an appeal that is taken when no final judgment has yet been entered is called an *"interlocutory"* appeal.

b. Federal statute: The *federal* court system *applies* the final judgment rule in a fairly rigorous way. 28 U.S.C. §1291 says that except in a few special situations covered by other statutory provisions, the U.S. Courts of Appeal shall only have jurisdiction over *"**final decisions** of the district courts."*

   c. State-court exceptions: The *states* are, whenever they wish, free to decide not to impose the final-judgment rule. A few states in fact allow interlocutory appeals where the federal system would not. Most famously, in *New York*, a very broad range of interlocutory appeals is allowed.

2. Certifying the issue: In the federal courts, one path by which an appeal may be taken before the entire case has been concluded is the *"certification"* method. 28 U.S.C. §1292(b) sometimes allows an interlocutory appeal of an otherwise-unappealable district court order if the judge who rendered the order certifies that order for an immediate appeal. But this certification method requires that *both* the trial court and the court of appeals *approve* the interlocutory appeal. [326]

3. The "collateral issue" exception: The most important exception to the final judgment rule in federal litigation is the so-called *"collateral order"* doctrine. This doctrine holds that even where some part of the case remains unresolved, an order may be immediately appealed from if that order finally determines an important right that is "collateral to" the main issue in the case, and a delay on the appeal would seriously impair the value of that collateral right. [327-329]

   a. Three requirements: The Supreme Court has held that the collateral order doctrine allows for an immediate appeal only if the order satisfies *three requirements*:

     [1] the order must *"conclusively determine* the disputed question";

     [2] the order must "resolve an *important issue completely separate from the merits* of the action"; and

     [3] the order must "be *effectively unreviewable* on appeal from a final judgment."

     [*Lauro Lines s.r.l. v. Chasser*] [327]

   b. "Effectively unreviewable": The third of these requirements — that the order would be *"effectively unreviewable"* if the loser were force to wait until a final overall judgment in the case before appealing — is the requirement that is most often at issue.

     i. Delay damage must be incurable: It's *not enough* that delaying review will *somewhat diminish* the value of the right. Thus if an eventual reversal on appeal would *cure much of the damage* from an incorrect order, the fact that the party who was required to wait has been *somewhat* damaged by the delay won't be enough. [328]

     Example: P, a former employee of D, sues D in federal court for employment discrimination. In discovery, P seeks various documents that D contends are protected by the attorney-client privilege. The trial court rules that D has waived the privilege, and that D must therefore produce the documents. D attempts to take an immediate appeal to the Court of Appeals, on the theory that the trial court's rejection of its claim of privilege is immediately reviewable under the collateral order doctrine. The Court of Appeals rules that the collateral order doctrine does not apply, and D appeals again, to the Supreme Court.

     Held, for P: the collateral order doctrine does not apply to disclosure orders that reject a claim of attorney-client privilege, so the appeal of such an order must wait until after the trial is completed. The collateral order doctrine applies only where the right in question is "effectively unreviewable" during the ultimate appeal from the final judgment in the case. Postjudgment appeals of attorney-client privilege rulings generally protect the privilege adequately, because appellate courts can remedy improper disclosure the same way they handle, say, errors about the admissibility of evidence: by throwing out the final judgment and ordering a new trial. [*Mohawk Industries, Inc. v. Carpenter* (2009)] [328]

    c. **Categories that don't qualify:** Here are some examples of categories where the court has ruled that an interlocutory appeal is *not* permitted:

        [1] Orders *denying or allowing* the *introduction of evidence*.

        [2] Orders compelling *disclosure of materials* that a party claims are *privileged* (as in the attorney-client privilege situation in *Mohawk, supra*).

        [3] Orders denying a party's attempt to have the case *tried somewhere else* on the basis of a *forum-selection clause* in a contract.

        [4] Orders granting or denying a party's attempt to have the other party's *lawyer disqualified on account of a conflict*.

        [5] Orders *denying class action status* (see *infra*, p. C-90).

    d. **Categories that qualify:** There are only a very *small number of categories* that the Supreme Court has found to *qualify* for immediate appeal under the collateral order doctrine. [328-329] Here are the two most important ones:

        [1] Rulings where a *government official* asserts a *qualified or absolute immunity* from suit, and the trial court denies the motion as a *matter of law*. [*Nixon v. Fitzgerald*]

        [2] Rulings where the court *refuses to dismiss* an action against a *governmental entity* which has asserted *Eleventh Amendment immunity* from federal-court suit.

4. **Orders involving the grant or denial of an injunction:** In federal litigation, there is a special provision making it easy to take an interlocutory appeal from a decision granting or denying an *injunction*. 28 U.S.C. §1292(a)(1) allows for an immediate appeal of a federal district court order "*granting*, continuing, *modifying*, *refusing* or dissolving *injunctions*, or *refusing to dissolve or modify* injunctions." [329]

    Example: The Ps claim that D is running an intentionally-segregated school system in violation of the Ps' constitutional rights. The Ps seek both damages and an injunction against continuation of the segregation. If the court *denies* the injunction, the Ps may take an immediate appeal from this denial, even though D's liability, and the Ps' right to damages, have not yet been resolved. Similarly, if the court *grants* the injunction, D may take an immediate appeal (even though here, too, liability and damages have not yet been decided).

CHAPTER 8

MULTI-PARTY AND MULTI-CLAIM LITIGATION

I. COUNTERCLAIMS

A. **Federal Rules generally:** A "counterclaim" is a claim *by a defendant against a plaintiff*. The Federal Rules provide for both *"permissive"* and *"compulsory"* counterclaims. FRCP 13. [337]

1. **Compulsory counterclaim:** If a claim arises "out of the *transaction or occurrence that is the subject matter of the opposing party's claim…*," it is a *"compulsory"* counterclaim. See Rule 13(a). [338]

   a. **Failure to state compulsory counterclaim:** If D does not assert her compulsory counterclaim, she will *lose* that claim in any future litigation. [338]

   Example: Cars driven by P and D collide. P sues D in diversity, alleging personal injury. D makes no counterclaim. Later, D wants to bring either a federal or state suit against P for property damage sustained by D as part of the same car accident. Neither federal nor state courts will permit D to bring this action, because it arises out of the same transaction or occurrence as P's original claim — the car accident — and is thus barred since D did not assert it as a compulsory counterclaim in the initial action.

   i. **Exceptions:** There are a couple of main *exceptions* to the rule that any claim involving the same "transaction or occurrence" as P's claim is compulsory: (1) claims by D which for *"just adjudication"* require the presence of *additional parties* of whom the court *cannot get personal jurisdiction*; and (2) claims by D in which the suit against D is *in rem* or *quasi in rem* (assuming D is not making any other counterclaim in the action). See Rule 13(a), including 13(a)(2).

2. **Permissive counterclaim:** A defendant has *discretion* to assert as a counterclaim "any claim that is *not compulsory.*" This means that *no claim is too far removed from the subject of the plaintiff's claim to be allowed as a counterclaim*. A counterclaim that is not compulsory is known as a *"permissive"* counterclaim. [337]

   Example: P sues D in diversity for a 2007 car accident. D counterclaims for breach of a 2008 contract having nothing to do with the auto accident. D's counterclaim is allowed, and is a "permissive" one because it has nothing to do with the subject matter of P's claim against D.

3. **Default by plaintiff:** If D asserts a counterclaim (whether compulsory or permissive), and P neglects to either serve a reply or make a motion against the counterclaim, a *default judgment* may be entered against P on the counterclaim. Rule 55(a). [338]

B. **Claims by third parties:** A counterclaim may be made by *any party* against *"an opposing party."* Rule 13(a), Rule 13(b). [339]

1. **By third-party defendant:** Thus a *third-party defendant* may counterclaim against either the original defendant, or against the original plaintiff. (In the latter case, a claim by the plaintiff against the third-party defendant must first have been made.) [339]

2. **By plaintiff:** If D has counterclaimed against P, P may then assert a "counterclaim" against D, even though P has already asserted "regular" claims against D. In fact, P's "counter-counterclaim" will be compulsory if it relates to the same subject matter as D's counterclaim. (*Example:* P sues D about a car accident. D sues P for breach of an unrelated contract. Any claims P might have against D relating to that same contract are now compulsory counterclaims.) [339]

3. **New parties:** *New parties* to a counterclaim can be brought into a suit. Rule 13(h). (*Example:* P sues D for an auto accident. D believes that P and X conspired to ruin D's business, in an unrelated action. D may not only counterclaim against P for this conspiracy — a permissive counterclaim — but D may bring in X as a new party to D's counterclaim.) [339]

C. **Subject-matter jurisdiction:** The *subject-matter jurisdiction* treatment of counterclaims depends on whether the counterclaim is compulsory or permissive: [340]

1. **Compulsory counterclaim:** A *compulsory* counterclaim in a federal action is within the federal courts' supplemental jurisdiction. Therefore, it requires *no independent subject-matter jurisdictional grounds*.

> **Example:** A, a New Yorker, sues B, from Massachusetts. The suit relates to an accident involving cars driven by A and B. B, in a counterclaim, asserts that A was at fault, and that the accident caused B $30,000 of damages. A's car was owned by C, a Massachusetts resident not yet in the action whom B would also like to sue. B may bring C in as an additional party to his counterclaim. Because supplemental jurisdiction applies to B's compulsory counterclaim, and even to the entrance of the new party defending that counterclaim, the fact that B and C are not diverse, and the fact that B's counterclaim does not meet the jurisdictional amount, are irrelevant.

2. **Permissive counterclaims:** A *permissive* counterclaim is probably *not* within the court's supplemental jurisdiction, and must therefore independently satisfy the requirements of federal subject matter jurisdiction. (*Example:* Same facts as above example, except that now, B's claim against A and C does not relate to the same transaction as A's claim against B. The absence of diversity as between B and C, and the fact that B's claim does not meet the jurisdictional amount, are both fatal, so B's permissive counterclaim may not go forward against either A or C.)

D. **Statute of limitations for counterclaims:** [341]

1. **Time-barred when P sues:** If D's counterclaim was already *time-barred* at the time P sued, few if any federal courts will allow D to make an affirmative recovery. Some courts will allow the counterclaim to be used as a defense; the court is more likely to do this if the counterclaim is compulsory than if it is permissive.

2. **Time-barred after P sued:** Where the statute of limitations on the counterclaim runs *after* P commenced the suit, but before D asserted his counterclaim, a federal court will probably allow the counterclaim. [*Azada v. Carson*]

II. JOINDER OF CLAIMS

A. **Joinder of claims generally:** *Once a party has made a claim against some other party*, he may then make *any other claim he wishes against that party*. Rule 18(a). (*Example:* P sues D, claiming that D intentionally assaulted and battered him. P may join to this claim a claim that D owes P money on a contract entirely unrelated to the tort.) [343]

1. **Never required:** Joinder of claims is *never required* by Rule 18(a), but is left at the claimant's option. (However, the rules on former adjudication, especially the rule against splitting a cause of action, may cause a claimant to lose the ability to bring the unasserted claim in a later suit.)

2. **Subject-matter jurisdiction not affected:** *Supplemental* jurisdiction probably does *not* apply to a claim joined with another under Rule 18(a). Thus the requirements of subject-matter jurisdiction must be *independently satisfied* by the joined claim. However, usually there will not be a subject-matter jurisdiction problem for joinder of claims (since diversity will not be affected, and since P may add all claims together for purposes of meeting the $75,000 requirement, under the aggregation doctrine).

III. JOINDER OF PARTIES

A. Permissive joinder: Joinder under Rule 20, done at the discretion of the plaintiffs, is called *"permissive"* joinder. ("Compulsory" joinder under Rule 19 is described below.) FRCP 20 allows two types of permissive joinder of parties: (1) the right of *multiple plaintiffs* to join together; and (2) a plaintiff's right to make several parties *co-defendants* to her claim. [345-346]

1. **Joinder of plaintiffs:** Multiple *plaintiffs* may voluntarily join together in an action if they satisfy two tests: [345]

   a. **Single transaction or occurrence:** Their claims for relief must arise from a *single "transaction, occurrence, or series of transactions or occurrences,"* and

   b. **Common questions:** There must be a *question of law or fact common to all plaintiffs* which will arise in the action.

2. **Joinder of defendants:** If one or more plaintiffs have a claim against *multiple defendants*, these defendants may be joined based on the same two tests as plaintiff-joinder. That is, claims against the co-defendants must: (a) arise from a *single "transaction*, occurrence, or series of transactions or occurrences"; and (b) contain a *common question* of law or fact. [346]

   a. **At plaintiff's option:** Joinder of multiple defendants is at the *option of the plaintiff* or plaintiffs.

B. Jurisdiction in permissive joinder cases: [346-348]

1. **Personal jurisdiction:** Where joinder of multiple *defendants* is involved, the requirements of personal jurisdiction must be met with regard to *each defendant individually*. That is: [346]

   a. **Service:** Each D must be *personally served*;

   b. **Contacts:** Each D must individually fall within the *in personam jurisdiction* of the court (by having "minimum contacts"); and

   c. **Long-arm limits:** Each D must be *"amenable"* to suit. Since federal courts in diversity suits follow the long-arm of the state where they sit, if a potential co-defendant cannot be reached by the state long-arm, he cannot be part of the federal diversity action even if he has the requisite minimum contacts. (But in federal question suits, it doesn't matter that the state long-arm can't reach D.)

2. **Subject matter jurisdiction:** All parties (whether plaintiffs or defendants) joined under Rule 20 must meet federal *subject matter jurisdiction* requirements. *Supplemental jurisdic-*

tion generally does not apply to Rule 20 joinder of *multiple defendants*; it only partially applies to Rule 20 joinder of *multiple plaintiffs*. [347-348]

   a. **Complete diversity:**   If the action is brought as a diversity action, the diversity must be *complete*. That is, *no state may be represented on both sides of an action.*

   Example: In an action where no federal question is present, there are 12 plaintiffs, 11 from Connecticut and one from New York, and 12 defendants, 11 from New Jersey and one from New York. On these facts there is no diversity, because complete diversity is required. Thus one of the New Yorkers must be dropped if the action is to proceed in federal court. And supplemental jurisdiction does not apply so as to remove the complete-diversity requirement.

   b. **Aggregation where one P meets the amount:** Multiple plaintiffs are *permitted* to *aggregate* their claims to meet the amount in controversy requirement, *if at least one plaintiff meets the amount. Supplemental jurisdiction applies* to this situation. [*Exxon Mobil Corp. v. Allapattah Services, Inc.*] [347]

   Example: P1 is a nine-year-old girl who has been severely injured when she sliced her finger on a tuna can made by D; her claim is for more than $75,000. P2, P3, etc. are members of P1's immediate family, who have claims for less than $75,000 for items like emotional distress and medical expenses.

      Held, P2, P3, etc., may join with P1 as co-plaintiffs under FRCP 20. As long as one plaintiff meets the jurisdictional amounts, additional co-plaintiffs may join the suit under Rule 20 even though their individual claims don't meet the amount, because supplemental jurisdiction applies. [*Exxon Mobil Corp. v. Allapattah Services, Inc.*]

   Note: But remember that in the Rule 20 scenario, supplemental jurisdiction applies only to the amount in controversy, *not the requirement of complete diversity.* So if, on the facts of the above Example, any one of the Ps was a citizen of the same state as D, the suit could not go forward.

      i. **Each defendant must meet:**   Where the Rule 20 joinder involves *multiple defendants*, supplemental jurisdiction does *not* apply even for amount-in-controversy purposes, so *each defendant* must have claims against him equal to the jurisdictional amount. [348]

      Example: P1 has a diversity claim for $80,000 against D1, and a diversity claim for $15,000 against D2 that is closely related to the claim against D1. Supplemental jurisdiction does not apply. Therefore, P1's claim against D2 must be dropped from the suit, since it does not independently meet the amount-in-controversy requirement.

C. **Compulsory joinder:**   There are certain situations in which additional parties *must* be joined, assuming the requirements of jurisdiction can be met. Such joinder, specified by Rule 19, is called *"compulsory"* joinder. The basic idea is that a party must be joined if it would be uneconomical or unfair to litigate a claim without her. [348-351]

   1. **Two categories:**   There are two categories of parties who must be joined where possible:

      a. **"Necessary" parties:**   The "less vital" group consists of parties: (1) who must be joined if this can be done; but (2) in whose absence because of jurisdictional problems the action

C
A
P
S
U
L
E

S
U
M
M
A
R
Y

will nonetheless be permitted to go forward. These parties are called *"necessary"* parties. See Rule 19(a).

    b. **"Indispensable" parties:** The second, "more vital" group consists of parties who are so vital that if their joinder is impossible for jurisdictional reasons, the whole action must be ***dropped***. They are covered in Rule 19(b). Such vital parties are often called *"indispensable"* parties (though 19(b) doesn't use this term).

2. **"Necessary" defined:** A party is "necessary" — and must be joined if jurisdictionally possible — if the party is not "indispensable" (defined below) ***and either*** of the two following tests is met: [349]

    a. **Incomplete relief:** In the person's absence, ***complete relief*** cannot be accorded among those already parties; or

    b. **Impaired interest:** The absentee has an interest relating to the action, and trying the case without the absentee will either ***impair the absentee's interest*** or leave one of the people already parties subject to ***multiple or inconsistent obligations***.

3. **"Indispensable" defined:** If a party meets the test for "necessary" given in paragraph (2) above, but the party's joinder is ***impossible*** because of jurisdictional problems, the court has to decide whether the party is *"indispensable."* [349]

    a. **Consequence of indispensability:** If the party is "indispensable," then the action must be ***dismissed*** in that party's absence.

    b. **Factors:** When the court decides whether a party is "indispensable," the factors are: (1) the extent of ***prejudice*** to the absentee, or to those already parties; (2) the possibility of framing the judgment so as to ***mitigate*** such prejudice; (3) the ***adequacy*** of a ***remedy*** that can be granted in the party's absence; and (4) whether the plaintiff will have an adequate remedy if the action is dismissed. Rule 19(b).

    Example: P sues D, a bank holding some stock. P alleges that although the stock is registered solely in the name of X, P and X in fact co-own the stock. P and D are citizens of different states, but X is a citizen of the same state as P. X thus cannot be joined as a co-defendant, because his presence would destroy diversity. The issue is whether X is "necessary" or "indispensable."

    Held: (1) X is definitely a person who must be joined if feasible under Rule 19(a), because his absence will expose D to the risk of double obligation — a judgment that P owns the stock will not bind X, who can later sue D for the whole value of the stock; (2) X is in fact "indispensable" — his presence is so important that the suit must be dismissed rather than proceed in X's absence. [*Haas v. Jefferson Bank*] [349]

4. **Jurisdiction:** Where a non-party is one who must be "joined if feasible," the doctrine of ***supplemental jurisdiction*** does ***not*** apply to overcome any jurisdictional problems. So if the person who is sought to be joined as a defendant is not diverse with all plaintiffs, or if the claim against that would-be defendant does not meet the amount-in-controversy requirement in a diversity case, the joinder may not take place. [349]

IV. CLASS ACTIONS

A. **Definition:** The class action is a procedure whereby a single person or small group of co-parties may ***represent*** a larger group, or *"class,"* of persons sharing a ***common interest***. [355]

1. **Jurisdiction:** In the class action, ***only the representatives*** must satisfy the requirements of personal jurisdiction, subject-matter jurisdiction, and venue. (*Example:* P1 and P2 are the named co-plaintiffs who bring a diversity class action against D. There are 2,000 non-named class members. Only P1 and P2 must meet the requirements of diversity vis-a-vis D, so the fact that many non-named plaintiffs are citizens of the same state as D is irrelevant.)

2. **Binding on absentees:** The results of a class action are generally ***binding on the absent members***. Therefore, all kinds of procedural rules (discussed below) exist to make sure that these absentees receive ***due process*** (e.g., they must receive notice of the action, and notice of any proposed settlement).

3. **Defendant class:** In federal practice, as well as in states permitting class actions, the class may be composed ***either*** of plaintiffs or defendants. The vast majority of the time, the class will be composed of plaintiffs. [356]

4. **Certification as class:** At some point before trial, a federal court must ***"certify"*** the action, i.e., affirmatively determine that it meets the requirements of FRCP 23. If the judge rejects certification, the action must proceed as a normal action involving only the named parties, or not proceed at all.

   a. **"Putative" designation:** Until certification has occurred, the action is called a ***"putative"*** class action.

   b. **Usually desired by plaintiffs:** Normally, it is the named ***plaintiffs*** (or at least their lawyer(s)) that wish to proceed as a class action, and the defendant(s) typically oppose class certification. But sometimes the reverse is true — the defendant(s) want to turn one or more individual suits into a class action in which absent plaintiff class members will be bound.

B. **Rule 23 generally:** The federal procedures for ***class actions*** are spelled out in FRCP 23. [356]

   1. **Four prerequisites:** ***Four prerequisites*** (discussed below) must be met before there is any possibility of a class action.

   2. **Three categories:** Once these prerequisites are met, a class action will still not be allowed unless the action fits into one of ***three categories***, represented by Rule 23(b)(1), 23(b)(2), and 23(b)(3). (See Table 8-2, "Class Actions" [357].)

C. **Prerequisites:** Here are the four prerequisites which must be met before any federal class action is allowed: [357]

   1. **Size:** The class must be ***so large*** that joinder of all members is impractical. Nearly all class actions involve a class of at least 25 members, and most involve substantially more (potentially tens of thousands). [357]

   2. **Common questions:** There must be ***"questions of law or fact common to the class."*** [357]

   3. **Typical claims:** The claims or defenses of the representatives must be ***"typical"*** of those of the class. [357]

   4. **Fair representation:** Finally, the representatives must show that they can ***"fairly and adequately protect the interests of the class."*** Thus the representatives must not have any ***conflict of interest*** with the absent class members, and they must furnish ***competent legal counsel*** to fight the suit. [358]

D. Detail on the prerequisites: Here is some further detail on these prerequisites that all federal class actions must satisfy:

1. **Common questions:** Of the four Rule 23 prerequisites, the one that is most likely to be in dispute is 23(a)(2)'s requirement that there be *"questions of law or fact common to the class."* In the 2014 case of *Wal-Mart Stores, Inc. v. Duke*, a majority of the Supreme Court held that the common-questions requirement means that before a federal trial judge may certify a class action, the judge must be satisfied, after *"rigorous analysis,"* that the plaintiffs are prepared to demonstrate affirmatively at trial *all* of the following:

   [1] that there is at least one *"common contention"* of law or fact ...

   [2] whose *"truth or falsity"* will ...

   [3] resolve *"in one stroke"* ...

   [4] an *issue* that is *"central to the validity of each one of the claims."*

   This is a new and *much tougher standard* for commonality than the Court had ever previously applied. [359]

   Example: The named Ps are three female employees of D (the Wal-Mart store chain) who have worked in various local stores owned by D. These named Ps bring a class-action for employment discrimination on behalf of a class of all 1.5 million female employees of 3,500 Wal-Mart stores located in all 50 states. The suit claims that D has given each store manager in the U.S. (nearly all of them male) wide discretion over pay and promotion practices at the manager's local store, and that these individual managers have exercised that discretion in a way that has had a disparate impact on women. The Ps claim that this system of giving discretion to individual store managers itself violates the federal statute barring gender discrimination in employment. D opposes certification on the grounds that there is no common question of law or fact.

   Held, for D. The commonality requirement is *not* satisfied merely by the fact that all of the class members (i.e., all of the 1.5 million female employees) claim to have suffered a *violation of the same law* (the statute barring employment discrimination based on gender). There must be a common contention that is "capable of classwide resolution." And this "capable of classwide resolution" requirement means in turn that the determination of the supposedly-common contention's truth or falsity must *resolve an issue* that is "central to the validity of each one of the claims *in one stroke.*" Here, for each class member, the central issue is "the *reason* for a particular employment decision" (e.g., a particular promotion or firing decision). The 1.5 million class members are thus purporting to sue about "literally millions of employment decisions at once." But there is no single common contention (of either law or fact) whose resolution will resolve all of these claims. Therefore, the case does not meet the commonality prerequisite of Rule 23(a), and cannot proceed as a class action of any sort. [*Wal-Mart Stores, Inc. v. Duke*] [358-360]

2. **"Fair and adequate" representation of class:** Recall that one of the four requirements imposed by Rule 23(a) is *adequacy of representation"* — the court must be satisfied that the representatives "will *fairly and adequately protect the interests* of the class." Rule 23(a)(4).

   a. **Class members versus lawyers for class:** Courts differ as to *which* participants should be most closely scrutinized for adequacy of representation: some look mostly at the adequacy of the *named class members*, and others at the adequacy of the *lawyers* representing the class. [361]

b. Avoidance of conflicts: The main function of the adequacy requirement is to ensure that there are no major *conflicts* between the interests of the representatives and the interests of the unnamed class members.

   i. Reps have separate lawsuits: A key reason why the trial court might find an inadequacy of representation is that some of the named representatives have *separate individual pending or potential lawsuits* against the defendant, and the court believes that the representatives' *real reason* for pursuing the class action is to *gain leverage for their own case.* [361]

c. Separate sub-classes: Adequate-representation problems in which different groups of plaintiffs have different incentives can sometimes be overcome if the suit designates *multiple "sub-classes" of plaintiffs,* and has *separate named representatives and lawyers* for each sub-class. [361]

E. Three categories: As noted, there are three categories of class actions, all of which must meet the four prerequisites listed above. They are covered in Rules 23(b)(1), 23(b)(2) and 23(b)(3). [362-367]

1. 23(b)(1) actions: The first of the three categories, *23(b)(1),* applies to situations similar to the circumstances requiring the *joinder of necessary parties* under Rule 19. [362-363]

a. Test: A class action is allowed under 23(b)(1) if individual actions by or against members of the class would create a *risk* of either: (a) *inconsistent decisions* forcing an opponent of the class to observe *incompatible standards of conduct* (Rule 23(b)(1)(A)); or (b) the *impairment of the interests* of the members of the class who are not actually parties to the individual actions (23(b)(1)(B)).

Example: Taxpayers residing in City XYZ are unhappy with a municipal bond issue by XYZ. Some taxpayers want the issue declared invalid; others want merely to have the terms of the issue changed. If each taxpayer brought his own action, as the result of one suit XYZ might have to refrain from floating the issue altogether, but as the result of the other suit might just be forced to limit the size of the issue. XYZ thus faces a risk of incompatible standards of conduct. Therefore, a Rule 23(b)(1) action would be suitable on these facts.

b. No opting out: Members of the 23(b)(1) class *may not "opt out" of the class*. Any absentee will therefore *necessarily be bound* by the decision in the suit.

c. Mass tort claims: Courts are increasingly allowing use of the 23(b)(1) class action in *mass tort cases*, where there are so many claims that D may be *insolvent* before later claimants can collect. See the further discussion of this topic *infra*, p. C-88.

Example: Tens of thousands of women may have been injured by breast implants manufactured by D. If each brings an individual suit, D's financial resources may be exhausted, leaving nothing for those who bring suit later. A federal court might therefore hold that a 23(b)(1) action is suitable for determining, once and for all, whether D sold a defective device and whether it typically caused a certain type of medical injury. Each P would then have a separate claim on causation and damages only. [363]

2. 23(b)(2) actions: The second category, 23(b)(2), allows use of a class action if "the party opposing the class has acted or refused to act on *grounds that apply generally to the class*, so that final *injunctive relief* or corresponding *declaratory relief* is appropriate respecting the class as a whole." In other words, if the suit is for an *injunction* or declaration that would affect all class members, (b)(2) is probably the right category. [364]

   a. **Civil rights case:** The main use of 23(b)(2) is for *civil rights cases*, where the class says that it has been discriminated against, and seeks an *injunction* prohibiting further discrimination.

   Example: A class action is brought on behalf of all black employees of XYZ Corp., alleging that executives of XYZ have as a matter of company-wide policy paid them less money and given them fewer promotions than white employees. The suit seeks an injunction against further discrimination, as well as money damages. This would likely be an appropriate suit for a 23(b)(2) class action.

3. **Equitable relief:** Notice that 23(b)(2) requires, in essence, that the wrong of which the defendant is accused have been a *class-wide* wrong, and that "final *injunctive* relief or corresponding *declaratory* relief" must be "appropriate respecting the *class as a whole*." So it's clear that a b(2) claim must not only allege a class-wide wrong, but seek a *class-wide equitable remedy* (an injunction and/or declaratory judgment that would run in favor of the entire class).

4. **Seeking of back pay:** Suppose an employment discrimination suit seeks not only an injunction against further discrimination against plaintiff class members, but also an award of *back pay* to restore each class member to the financial position he or she would have been in had there been no discrimination. (Such an award of back pay is authorized by Title VII, the federal anti-employment-discrimination statute.) Notice that since the appropriate amount of back pay depends on when (or even whether) the discriminatory action occurred (longer-ago discrimination requires more back pay to make P whole now), the back-pay aspect will require a *separate, individualized, determination* for each class member. Does this need for individualized back-pay findings automatically make the action *unsuitable* for (b)(2) certification?

   a. *Wal-Mart* **rejects (b)(2) suits for back-pay:** The Supreme Court, in *Wal-Mart Stores, Inc. v. Duke* (see C-85), has answered *"yes."* So if the amount of *back pay* would *vary* from member to member, the mere *request* for it *rules out (b)(2) certification*, even if the back-pay being sought is viewed as *"subordinate"* to the class members' main goal of getting an injunction against further discrimination. [364]

       i. **Future of this type of case:** So *Wal-Mart* probably means that in *mass employment-discrimination cases*, plaintiffs lawyers will have to choose between bringing a (b)(2) action that seeks only injunctive and declaratory relief (in which case any court-awarded *attorneys fees* are likely to be *small*, and the plaintiffs' lawyers' bargaining position in post-certification settlement negotiations likely to be weak), and *not bringing a federal class action at all* (since bringing a (b)(3) action, discussed below, requires that the (b)(3) format be a "superior" method, and in mass-employment-discrimination suits the (b)(3) format will usually *not* be superior).

   b. **No opt-out:** Members of a 23(b)(2) class may not *"opt out"* of the class. See Rule 23(c)(3).

5. **23(b)(3) actions:** The final type of class action is given in Rule *23(b)(3)*. This is the *most common* type of class action. [366-367]

   a. **Two requirements:** The court must make *two findings* for a (b)(3) class action:

      i.   **Common questions:** The court must find that the "questions of law or fact ***common*** to class members ***predominate*** over any questions affecting only individual members…"; and

      ii. **Superior method:** The court must also find that "a class action is ***superior to other available methods***" for deciding the controversy. In deciding "superiority," the court will consider four factors listed in 23(b)(3), including:

         [1] the interest of class members in ***individually controlling*** their separate actions;

         [2] the presence of any suits that have ***already been commenced*** involving class members;

         [3] the desirability of ***concentrating the litigation*** of the claims in a ***particular forum***; and

         [4] any difficulties likely to be encountered in the ***management*** of a class action.

  b. **Securities cases:** (b)(3) class actions are especially common in ***securities fraud*** cases, and in ***antitrust*** cases.

  c. **Mass torts:** (b)(3) actions are sometimes brought in ***mass tort*** cases (e.g., airline crashes) and mass ***product liability*** cases (e.g., mass pharmaceutical cases). But many courts still frown on (b)(3) class action status for such suits, because individual elements typically predominate. See *supra*, C-86.

F. **Requirement of notice:** Absent class members (i.e., those other than the representatives) must almost always be given ***notice*** of the fact that the suit is pending. [367-368]

  1. **When required:** The Federal Rules explicitly require notice only in ***(b)(3)*** actions. But courts have the power to require that notice be given in (b)(1) and (b)(2) actions as well.

    a. **Individual notice:** *Individual* notice, almost always ***by mail***, must be given to all those (b)(3) class members whose names and addresses can be obtained with ***reasonable effort***. This is true even if there are millions of class members, each with only small amounts at stake. FRCP 23(c)(2)(B). [*Eisen v. Carlisle & Jacquelin*] [367]

    b. **Publication notice:** For those class members whose names and addresses cannot be obtained with reasonable effort, ***publication*** notice will usually be sufficient.

  2. **Contents:** The most important things notice does is to tell the claimant that he may ***opt out*** of the class if he wishes (in a (b)(3), but not (b)(1) or (b)(2), action); and that the judgment will affect him, favorably or unfavorably, unless he opts out.

  3. **Cost:** The cost of both ***identifying*** and ***notifying*** each class member must normally be borne by the ***representative plaintiffs***. If the plaintiff side is unwilling to bear this cost, the case must be ***dismissed***. [*Eisen v. Carlisle*; *Oppenheimer Fund v. Sanders*] [368]

G. **Binding effect:** Judgment in a class action is ***binding***, whether it is ***for or against the class***, on all those whom the court finds to be members of the class. [368]

  1. **Exclusion:** In the case of a (b)(3) action, a person may ***opt out***, i.e., exclude himself, from the action, by notifying the court to that effect prior to a date specified in the notice of the action sent to him. A person who opts out of the action will not be bound by an adverse judgment, but conversely may not assert collateral estoppel to take advantage of a judgment favorable to the class. (Absent class members in (b)(1) and (b)(2) actions do ***not*** have the right to opt out and thereafter bring their own suit.)

H. Subject-matter jurisdiction issues: In the federal courts, class actions can occasionally raise questions of *subject matter jurisdiction*. [369-371]

1. **Federal question cases:** Where the plaintiffs' claims are based on a *federal question*, there are no significant subject-matter jurisdiction issues. Diversity of citizenship, of course, does not matter. And there is no amount in controversy requirement. So nationwide class actions based upon federal causes of action are quite easy to bring, even where each claim is for a small amount.

2. **Diversity cases:** On the other hand, a federal class action in which all claims are based *solely on diversity* does face subject-matter jurisdiction problems, principally related to amount in controversy. [369]

   a. **Diversity:** In determining whether the required *"complete diversity"* exists, there will rarely be a problem. That's because of the Supreme Court has long held that *only the citizenship of the class representatives*, not the citizenship of the unnamed class members, counts. So as long as none of the named representatives is a citizen of the same state as any defendant, there is no diversity problem. And, since the lawyer for the plaintiff class gets to decide who the named representatives will be, the lawyer can easily assure that no representative is a citizen of the same state as any defendant.

   b. **Amount in controversy:** By contrast, diversity class actions raise issues regarding the *amount in controversy* requirement. [370]

      i. **At least one named member meets amount:** If *at least one named class member satisfies* the jurisdictional amount, other class members *can* be part of the action even though their claim is for *less than this amount.* This result is due to the doctrine of *"supplemental jurisdiction."* [C-35] [*Exxon Mobil Corp. v. Allapattah Services, Inc.*] [370]

         Example: 10,000 Exxon dealers bring a diversity-only class action against Exxon, claiming that Exxon has overcharged them for fuel. Some named members of the class have a claim for the jurisdictional amount ($75,000), but many other class members' claims are for less than the $75,000 amount. *Held*, the dealers whose claims do not meet this amount may remain part of the class — as long as at least one named class member meets the jurisdictional amount, supplemental jurisdiction applies to the claims of the other class members, no matter how small those claims. [*Exxon Mobil Corp. v. Allapattah Services, Inc.*]

      ii. **Named members can't aggregate:** On the other hand, *at least one named class member must independently meet the jurisdictional amount.* So unless the plaintiff's lawyer can find at least one named claimant with $75,000 at stake, the diversity class action cannot go forward. In other words, several named class members, each having a claim of less than $75,000, *cannot "aggregate" their claims* to get over the $75,000 minimum. (There's an exception if the action involves at least $5 million in total, discussed immediately below.)

      iii. **$5 million at stake:** Under the *Class Action Fairness Act of 2005* ("CAFA"), a class action can go forward if: (a) there is minimal diversity (at least one plaintiff is diverse with at least one defendant); and (b) there is *at least $5 million in controversy in the aggregate,* even if *no class member's claim is for more than $75,000.* [370]

I. Certification and denial of class status: Soon after an action purporting to be a class action is brought, the court must decide whether to *"certify"* the action. By certifying, the court agrees that the class action requirements have been met, and allows the suit to go forward as a class action. If the court refuses to certify the action: [371]

    1. Continued by representative: The suit may still be continued by the "representatives," but with no *res judicata* effect for or against the absent would-be class members. Usually, the representatives will not want to proceed on this non-class action basis. [371]

    2. Sub-class: Alternatively, the suit may be continued by a *sub-class* of the original class. If so, *res judicata* extends to the members of the sub-class, but not to the other members of the original class. [371]

    3. No appeal: The denial of class action status may *not* be immediately appealed, because it is not deemed to be a *"final order."* [371]

J. Waiver of the right to bring class action: An increasingly important issue is whether a party to a contract may agree in advance to *waive* her right to bring a class action if litigation should ensue. The issue typically arises where the contract contains a boilerplate clause stating that all disputes will be subject to one-plaintiff-at-a-time *arbitration*.

    1. Waivers are valid: The general principle is that such waivers are *valid*, and will be *enforced*. In fact, a federal statute — the *Federal Arbitration Act (FAA)* —essentially *compels* both state and federal courts to *enforce as drafted any arbitration* clause. [373]

        a. Unconscionability doesn't avoid the waiver: The FAA will usually require judicial enforcement of an agreement to arbitrate even if the court believes that the contract's arbitration clause would be otherwise be *unenforceable* due to the state-law doctrine of *unconscionability*. *AT&T Mobility LLC v. Concepcion*. [374]

K. Settlements: Any proposed *settlement* of the class action must be *approved by the court*. FRCP 23(e). The court will approve the settlement only if it is convinced that the interests of the absent class members have been adequately protected (e.g., that settlement is not being urged by greedy contingent-fee lawyers who will pocket most of the settlement money). [375]

    1. Notice requirement: If the class has already been certified, *notice* of any proposed settlement must be given to *each class member*.

L. Attorneys' fees: The court may award *reasonable attorneys fees* to the lawyers for the class. These fees are generally in rough proportion to the size of the recovery on behalf of the class. [378]

    1. Federal statute requires: In the usual case of a class action brought under a *federal statute*, attorneys fees may be awarded *only if a federal statute so provides*. [*Alyeska Pipeline Service Co. v. Wilderness Society*.] Congress has authorized attorneys fees for many important federal statutes that are frequently the subject of class action suits (e.g., civil rights and securities law).

M. Mass tort cases: Class actions have begun to be used increasingly in *"mass tort"* cases. [378-385]

    1. Definition of "mass tort": Mass torts fall into two categories. In a *"mass accident,"* a large number of persons are injured as a result of a single accident. (*Examples:* an airplane crash, the collapse of a building, or the explosion of a factory accompanied by the release of toxic substances.) In a *"mass product liability"* case, a *defective product* is sold to thousands of buyers, who are thereby injured. [378]

2. **Single-accident cases:** In mass-tort cases involving a *single "mass accident,"* or a single "course of conduct" by one defendant, many courts allow class certification. Cases involving a single explosion, or a single toxic dumping by one defendant on one occasion, are examples. [380]

3. **Product liability cases:** In mass-tort cases involving *product liability*, by contrast, most federal courts have held that the federal class action is *not suitable*. Usually courts don't allow it to be used even for the limited purpose of deciding core "all or nothing" issues like D's negligence, or the product's defectiveness. [380]

4. **Factors for mass-tort cases:** Here are some of the factors that courts consider in deciding whether to allow certification in a mass accident or mass product liability case: [381]

   a. **State-by-state law variations:** If the suit is based on diversity (as it usually will be in a product liability case), and involves plaintiffs from many states, and if the federal court would therefore somehow have to apply the *differing laws of many states* (because of *Erie*), the court is *less likely* to grant class status.

   b. **Centrality of single issue:** Where one issue is truly *"central"* to the case, the court is *most likely* to certify the class.

   c. **Size of typical claim:** The *larger each individual claim*, the *less likely* the court is to allow class status (because each claimant could sue on his own).

   d. **Novelty of claim:** Where the plaintiffs' claim is *"novel,"* i.e., untested (e.g., that cigarette companies have fraudulently entrapped young people into addiction to nicotine), certification is *unlikely*, because the court won't want to let the future of a whole industry turn on whether one jury likes the claim.

   e. **Limited funds:** Where there are so many thousands of claimants that there's reason to believe that the defendant(s) will be *insolvent* before the last claimant has recovered, certification is *more likely*.

V. INTERVENTION

A. **Intervention generally:** By the doctrine of *"intervention,"* certain persons who are not initially part of a lawsuit may enter the suit *on their own initiative*. The person who intervenes is called an "intervenor." [389]

   1. **Two forms:** In federal suits, FRCP 24 creates two forms of intervention:

      a. *"Intervention of right"* (Rule 24(a)); and

      b. *"Permissive intervention"* (Rule 24(b)).

   2. **Distinction:** Where the intervention is "of right," *no leave of court* is required for the party's entry into the case. Where the facts are such that only "permissive" intervention is possible, it is up to the court's *discretion* whether to allow intervention.

B. **Intervention of right:** [389-390]

   1. **Three tests:** A stranger to an existing action may intervene *"of right,"* under Rule 24(a), if she meets *all* of the three following criteria: [389]

a. **Interest in subject-matter:** She must "claim[] an interest relating to the ***property or transaction*** that is the ***subject*** of the action";

b. **Impaired interest:** She must be "so situated that disposing of the action may as a ***practical matter impair or impede [her] ability to protect [that] interest***"; and

c. **Inadequate representation:** She must show that this interest is ***not "adequately represented" by existing parties***.

> **Note:** Even if the outsider cannot meet one or more of these criteria, she may nonetheless automatically intervene under Rule 24(a) if a federal ***statute*** gives her such a right. (*Example:* The U.S. may intervene in any action involving the constitutionality of an act of Congress.) [389]

> **Example:** P (the U.S. government) sues D, a local Board of Education, charging that D has drawn school boundaries on racially-discriminatory lines. X, the parent of a black public school student attending D's schools, wants to intervene. Probably X's intervention will be of right, since X has an interest in the subject-matter, and his ability to bring his own action in the future will be compromised if the U.S. loses the case. X will have to show that the U.S. may not adequately represent X's interest, which he can do by showing that the U.S. may be pursuing other objectives, such as settling a lot of suits quickly.

2. **Jurisdiction:** ***Independent subject-matter*** jurisdictional grounds are ***required*** for intervention of right in a diversity case. In other words, such intervention does not fall within the court's ***supplemental*** jurisdiction. [390]

> **Example:** P, from California, sues D, from New York, in a diversity suit. X, from New York, would like to intervene. Even if the court concludes that the requirements of intervention of right are met by X, X cannot intervene because there is no supplemental jurisdiction for intervention of right; after X's intervention there would have to be complete diversity, and this would not be the case since X and D are both citizens of New York.

C. **Permissive intervention:** For a person to seek ***"permissive intervention,"*** she merely has to have a "claim or defense" that involves a ***"common question of law or fact" with the pending action***. [390]

1. **Discretion:** Where the outsider seeks permissive intervention, it is up to the trial court's ***discretion*** whether to allow the intervention. The trial court's decision — whichever way it goes — is rarely reversed on appeal.

2. **Jurisdiction:** Like any intervenor of right, a permissive intervenor in a diversity case must independently meet federal subject-matter jurisdictional requirements. (*Example:* There must be diversity between the intervenor and all defendants.) [390]

VI. INTERPLEADER

A. **Definition:** Interpleader allows a party who owes something to one of two or more other persons, but is not sure whom, to force the other parties to argue out their claims among themselves. The technique is designed to allow the "stakeholder" to avoid being made to pay the same claim twice. [392]

> **Example:** X and Y both claim a bank account at Bank. Y demands the money from Bank. If Bank had to litigate against Y, and then possibly defend a second suit brought by X,

C
A
P
S
U
L
E

S
U
M
M
A
R
Y

Bank might have to pay the amount of the account twice. By using the interpleader doctrine, Bank can force X and Y to litigate between themselves as to the ownership of the account, with Bank paying only the winner.

1. **Federal practice:** In federal practice, *two* kinds of interpleader are allowed:

    a. *"Statutory interpleader"* under 28 U.S.C. §1335; and

    b. *"Rule interpleader"* under FRCP 22.

    Note: See Table 8-3, "Comparison: Statutory and Rule Interpleader" [397].

B. **Federal statutory interpleader:** 28 U.S.C. §1335 allows a person holding property which *is* or *may be* claimed by two or more "adverse claimants" to interplead those claimants. [394-396]

1. **Jurisdictional benefits:** The main benefits to the stakeholder from using statutory interpleader instead of Rule interpleader relate to *jurisdiction* and *service*: [394]

    a. **Nationwide service:** *Nationwide service of process* is allowed in statutory interpleader actions. See 28 U.S.C. §2361. Thus the court where the stakeholder files a statutory interpleader suit may serve its process on any claimant, *no matter where in the U.S. that claimant resides or is found*.

    b. **Diversity:** Diversity is satisfied as long as *some two claimants are citizens of different states*. (*Example:* Two New York residents and a Californian all claim the proceeds of a particular insurance policy. Since either New Yorker and the Californian form a diverse pair, the diversity requirement for statutory interpleader is satisfied. The citizenship of the insurance company is irrelevant.)

    c. **Amount in controversy:** The property which is the subject of the suit must merely exceed *$500* in value, in contrast to the usual $75,000.

2. **How commenced:** A statutory interpleader suit is commenced by the *stakeholder*. The stakeholder must, to begin the suit, *deposit into court* the amount of the property in question, or post a *bond* for that amount. [395]

    a. **Right to deny debt:** Even though the stakeholder must deposit the amount of the property with the court, he is not estopped from claiming at trial that he does *not owe the money to any claimant at all*. [395]

3. **Restraint on other suits:** Once the statutory interpleader suit is begun, the court may *restrain all claimants* from starting or continuing any other action, in any state or federal suit, which would affect the property. (*Example:* On the facts of the above example, the court could prevent the two New Yorkers and the Californian from starting any state action to collect on the policy.) [395-396]

C. **Rule interpleader:** FRCP 22 provides an interpleader remedy for any person who is or may be exposed to "double or multiple liability." This is so-called *"Rule interpleader."* The stakeholder may invoke interpleader by coming into court on his own initiative (i.e., as plaintiff), or by counterclaiming or cross-claiming as *defendant* in an action already commenced against him by one claimant. [396]

1. **Jurisdiction:** The main difference between statutory interpleader and Rule interpleader is that *Rule 22 interpleader has no effect on ordinary jurisdictional and venue requirements*.

    a. **Complete diversity:** Thus *diversity* must be *complete* between the stakeholder on one hand and all claimants on the other (assuming there is no federal question). (*Example:*

Two New Yorkers and a Californian all claim a particular insurance policy, which is issued by a California-based insurer. Rule 22 interpleader cannot be used, because it is not the case that all claimants are of different citizenship than the insurer.)

　　　b.　Service: Service of process must be carried out as in any other diversity action — that is, within the state where the district court sits, or pursuant to the long-arm of the state. There is *no "nationwide service of process"* as in statutory interpleader.

　　　c.　Amount in controversy: The *$75,000* amount in controversy requirement must be met.

2.　No deposit: The stakeholder is *not required* to *deposit* the property or money into the court (as she is in statutory interpleader).

3.　Denial of liability: The stakeholder may "aver that the plaintiff is not liable in whole or in part to any or all of the claimants." FRCP 22(1). In other words, the stakeholder may *deny liability*.

VII.　REAL PARTY IN INTEREST

A.　Generally: FRCP 17, and most states, require that a complaint be in the name of the *"real party in interest."* This means, for instance, that an *assignee* — a person to whom the original holder of a claim assigned that claim — must sue in the assignee's own name. [398]

1.　Subrogation: This "real party in interest" rule covers *subrogation*. An insurer who has compensated its policy holder may sue the tortfeasor in lieu of suit by the policy holder — but the insurance company must sue in its own name, not in the name of the policy holder.

2.　Representatives: Executors, administrators, bailees and other *representatives* are considered to be themselves "real parties in interest." Therefore, they may bring suit in their own names, not in the names of persons they represent (e.g., the estate). But the *citizenship* of the *represented party* (e.g., the estate) generally controls for diversity purposes.

VIII.　THIRD-PARTY PRACTICE (IMPLEADER)

A.　Impleader right generally: A defendant who believes that a third person is *liable to him* "for all or part of the claim against [the defendant]" may *implead* such a person as a *"third party defendant."* FRCP 14(a). [399]

> **Example:** Victim is injured when a van driven by Employee and owned by Employer runs her over. Victim brings a diversity action against Employer, on a *respondeat superior* theory. Employer believes that if Employer is required to pay a judgment to Victim, Employee, under common law indemnity rules, will be required to reimburse Employer. Instead of waiting until the end of the Victim-Employer suit, Employer may instead "implead" Employee. That is, Employer (the third-party plaintiff or TPP) brings Employee into the action as a "third party defendant" (TPD), so that in a single action, the court may conclude that Employer owes Victim, and that Employee owes indemnity to Employer.

B.　Claim must be derivative: For a third-party claim to be valid, the TPP may not claim that the TPD is the *only* one liable to the plaintiff, and that he himself is not liable at all. (*Examples:* Impleader works for claims for *indemnity*, *subrogation*, *contribution* and *breach of warranty*, since as to each of these, the TPD is liable only if the TPP is liable.) [399]

1. **Alternative pleading:** However, the TPP is not precluded from claiming in an *alternative* pleading that neither she nor the TPD is liable.

2. **Partial claim:** Also, the TPP may allege that only a *portion* of the recovery is due from the TPD. (*Example:* If TPP claims that TPD is liable for "contribution" rather than "indemnity," TPP will recover from TPD at most only part of any judgment that TPP owes to P.)

C. **Leave of court:** Leave of court is *not* necessary for impleader, as long as the TPP serves a summons and complaint on a TPD within *10 days* after the time the TPP served his answer to P's claim. FRCP 14(a)(1). After this 10-day period, however, the court's permission to implead is necessary. [400]

D. **Impleader by plaintiff:** Just as the defendant may implead a TPD, so a *plaintiff* against whom a *counterclaim* is filed may implead a third person who is liable to him for any judgment on the counterclaim. FRCP 14(b). [400]

E. **Jurisdictional requirements relaxed:** Both personal and subject-matter *jurisdictional* requirements are *relaxed* with respect to the third-party claim: [400]

1. **100-mile bulge:** Service of the third-party complaint may be made anywhere within the *100-mile bulge* surrounding the courthouse, even if the place of service is outside the state and is beyond the scope of the local long-arm. FRCP 4(k)(1)(B). [401]

   Example: In the above Victim/Employer/Employee example, if the suit is pending in the Southern District of New York (Manhattan), Employee could be served in Newark, New Jersey, even if the New York State long-arm would not reach him.

2. **Supplemental jurisdiction:** A third-party claim generally falls within the court's *supplemental jurisdiction*. Thus the TPD's citizenship is unimportant, and no amount-in-controversy requirement must be satisfied. [401]

3. **Venue:** Similarly, if *venue* is proper between the original parties, it remains valid regardless of the residence of the TPD. [401]

F. **Additional claims involving the TPD:** [401-403]

1. **Claim by TPD:** Once a TPD has been impleaded, she may make *claims of her own*, including: (1) counterclaims against the TPP (either permissive or compulsory); (2) cross-claims against any other TPDs; (3) any claim against the original plaintiff, but only if it arises out of the same transaction or occurrence that is the subject of the plaintiff's claim against the TPP; (4) any counterclaim against the original plaintiff, if the original plaintiff has made a claim against the TPD; and (5) impleader claims against persons not previously part of the suit, if these persons may be liable to the TPD for all or part of the TPP's claim against the TPD. [401]

   a. **Supplemental jurisdiction:** All of the above kinds of claims, except permissive counterclaims, fall within the court's *supplemental jurisdiction*, and thus need no independent federal subject-matter jurisdictional grounds.

   b. **Defenses:** A TPD may also raise against the original plaintiff the same *defenses* that the original defendant could have raised.

2. **Claims by original plaintiff:** The original plaintiff may assert any claims against the TPD arising out of the transaction or occurrence that is the subject-matter of that plaintiff's claim against the TPP. [402]

    a. Jurisdiction: A claim by a plaintiff against the TPD must ***independently satisfy jurisdictional requirements*** — supplemental jurisdiction does not apply in this situation. (*Example:* In a diversity case, the original plaintiff's claim against the TPD must be supported by diversity between the plaintiff and the TPD, and that claim must satisfy the $75,000 amount in controversy.)

G. Dismissal of main claim: If the main claim is ***dismissed*** before or during trial, the court has ***discretion*** whether to hear the third-party claims relating to it (assuming that these are within the court's supplemental jurisdiction, as they will be in the case of an ordinary impleader claim). [403]

IX. CROSS-CLAIMS

A. Definition: A claim by a party against a ***co-party*** is called a ***"cross-claim."*** A cross-claim is made only against a party who is on the ***same side*** of an already-existing claim (e.g., a claim by one co-defendant against another, or by one co-plaintiff against another). [406]

B. Requirements: A cross-claim must meet two main requirements: [406]

    1. Transaction requirements: It must have arisen out of the ***"transaction or occurrence"*** that is the subject of the original action or the subject of a counterclaim. FRCP 13(g). (A cross-claim is thus comparable to a compulsory counterclaim, in terms of how closely related it must be to the original claim.)

    2. Actual relief: The cross-claim must ask for ***actual relief*** from the co-party against whom it is directed. (*Example:* D1 claims that he is blameless, and that D2 is the one who should be liable for all of P's claims. This is not a cross-claim, since D1 is not asking for actual relief from D2 — instead, D1 is merely asserting a defense.)

C. Not compulsory: A cross-claim, no matter how closely related it is to the subject of the existing action, is ***never compulsory***. [406]

D. Jurisdiction: Cross-claims are within the ***supplemental jurisdiction*** of the court, and thus need no independent jurisdictional grounds. [406]

CHAPTER 9

FORMER ADJUDICATION

I. GENERAL PRINCIPLES

A. Former adjudication generally: There is a set of rules that prevents re-litigation of claims and issues; the set is sometimes collectively called the doctrine of ***"res judicata"*** (Latin for "things which have been decided"). [416]

    1. Two categories: There are two main categories of rules governing re-litigation:

        a. Merger and bar: One set of rules prevents a ***claim*** (or "cause of action") from being re-litigated. These rules are collectively called the rules of ***claim preclusion***. They break down into two sub-rules:

            i. Merger: Under the rule of ***"merger,"*** if P ***wins*** the first action, his claim is "merged" into his judgment. He cannot later sue the same D on the same cause of action for higher damages.

    ii. Bar: Under the doctrine of ***"bar,"*** if P *loses* his first action, his claim is extinguished, and he is barred from suing again on that cause of action.

  b. Collateral estoppel: The second main set of rules prevents re-litigation of a particular *issue of fact or law.* When a particular issue of fact or law has been determined in one proceeding, then in a subsequent proceeding between the same parties, ***even on a different cause of action***, each party is ***"collaterally estopped"*** from claiming that that issue should have been decided differently than it was in the first action. This is known as the doctrine of "collateral estoppel" or ***"issue preclusion."***

    i. Use by stranger: Today, even one who is not a party to the first action (a "*stranger* to the first action") may in some circumstances assert in the second suit that her adversary, who was a party to the first action, is collaterally estopped from re-litigating an issue of fact or law decided in that first action.

B. Applicable only to new actions: The rules discussed in this "Former Adjudication" chapter apply only to ***new actions*** subsequent to the action in which the original judgment was rendered — they do not apply to ***further proceedings*** in the same action in which the original judgment was rendered. (*Examples:* These rules do not apply to a party seeking a ***new trial***, or to one seeking to have a judgment reversed on ***appeal***.) [417]

C. Only parties bound: The rules of claim preclusion and collateral estoppel generally apply only to the ***parties*** to the first action, ***not to "strangers"*** to that action.

  1. Exceptions: But there are a few situations in which someone who was not a party to the first action is ***so closely linked*** to someone who was, that the stranger ***will be bound*** by the first result, for claim preclusion and collateral estoppel purposes, as if she had been a party. For instance, a ***successor in interest*** to property (e.g., the purchaser of real estate which has been the subject of an earlier quiet-title action), would be bound by the result in the earlier action. For more about these exceptions see C-97 (claim preclusion) and C-100 (collateral estoppel).

II. CLAIM PRECLUSION (MERGER AND BAR)

A. Definition: If a judgment is rendered for the plaintiff, his claim is "merged" into the judgment — the claim is extinguished and a new claim to enforce the judgment is created. If a judgment is for the defendant on the merits, the claim is extinguished and nothing new is created; plaintiff is "barred" from raising the claim again. [417-418]

    Example 1: P sues D for $1,000 damages resulting from an automobile accident. The verdict and judgment grant P only $500. His claim, or cause of action, is "merged," meaning that P cannot start a new suit for the other $500.

    Example 2: Same as Example 1, but D is found not to be liable at all. P is now "barred" from making the same claim in a second suit against D.

B. No claim-splitting: The basic concept of claim preclusion is that a judgment is conclusive with respect to the ***entire "claim"*** which it adjudicates. Consequently, P ***may not split her claim*** — if she sues upon ***any portion*** of the claim, the other aspects of that claim are merged in her judgment if she wins, and barred if she loses. [418-419]

    Example: P believes that D has breached a contract with him, and that P has lost $100,000 as a result. If P sues for $25,000 and loses, P may not bring a second suit for the other $75,000. The same is true if P wins the $25,000 — the rule is "one suit per claim."

C
A
P
S
U
L
E

S
U
M
M
A
R
Y

1. **Installment contracts:** Where the claim relates to payments due under a *lease* or *installment contract*, generally P must sue at the same time for *all payments* due at the time the suit is filed. (*Example:* If Tenant is six months behind in the rent at the time Landlord brings suit, Landlord must sue for the entire six months at once — any months missed that are not sued for when the suit is brought are waived.) [418-419]

2. **Personal and property damage from accident:** Today, most states hold that claims for *personal injuries* arising from an auto accident are part of the *same cause of action* as a claim for *property damage* sustained in the same accident. Thus generally, P must bring a single suit for property damage and personal injuries from a given accident. [420]

3. **Multi-theory actions:** The rule against splitting a claim also applies where P has several claims, all arising from the same set of facts, but involving *different theories* or remedies. The modern rule is that there will be merger or bar of all of P's rights against D with respect to all or any part of the *transaction*, or series of connected transactions, out of which the action arose. [419-420]

   Example: P works for D, and is then fired. P sues D for breach of an alleged oral contract promising two years of employment. P loses. P then sues D, alleging the same facts, and asserting the right to recover in *quantum meruit* for the reasonable value of services he performed for D. A modern court would probably hold that the two suits related to a single transaction or series of transactions, and that the first judgment against P therefore barred him from bringing the second suit.

   a. **Equitable/legal distinction:** A demand for *legal* relief (generally, money damages) and a demand for *equitable* relief (e.g., an injunction) will both be deemed to be part of the same claim if they relate to the same facts — therefore, demands for both types of relief will have to be made in the same action. (*Example:* If P believes that D is violating P's copyrights, P cannot bring a suit for an injunction, followed by a separate suit for money damages.) [420]

4. **Exceptions based on jurisdictional requirements:** There is one important *exception* to the rule against splitting a cause of action — if the court trying the first action would not have had *subject matter jurisdiction* for a claim now asserted in the second action, there will be no bar or merger. (*Example:* P sues D in state court under state antitrust law, and loses on the merits. P then sues D in federal court alleging the same facts, and charging a violation of federal antitrust laws. Because the federal courts have exclusive jurisdiction of antitrust claims, the state court could not have heard the federal claim. Therefore, the second — federal court — action will not be barred.) [420]

5. **State law followed in diversity cases:** In diversity cases, the federal courts follow *state law* with respect to the application of the rules of claim preclusion (as well as collateral estoppel). In other words, if (and only if) the law of the state where the district court sits would have granted claim preclusion or collateral estoppel effect to an earlier state court judgment, the federal court will do the same. [421]

C. **Adjudication on merits:** Not every loss by the plaintiff in the first action will act as a "bar" to subsequent suits on the same claim. Plaintiff will be barred only if the original adjudication in favor of the defendant was *"on the merits."* [421-422]

1. **Non-prejudicial grounds:** In other words, some of the ways that a plaintiff may "lose" the first suit are deemed to be "without prejudice" to future suits. For instance, if the first suit is

brought in federal court, plaintiff will **not** be barred from bringing a new action if the first action is dismissed because of: (1) lack of jurisdiction; (2) improper venue; or (3) failure to join an indispensable party. See FRCP 41(b). Any other type of dismissal (e.g., dismissal for failure to state a claim under 12(b)(6)) **does** bar a future claim by P, unless the court granting the dismissal specifies otherwise in its order. FRCP 41(b), last sentence. [421]

D. Counterclaims: A defendant who pleads a **counterclaim** is, in effect, a plaintiff with respect to that claim. He is bound by the outcome, just as a plaintiff is bound by the outcome of his original claim. [422-422]

    1. No splitting: Thus D may not split his counterclaim into two parts. (*Example:* P sues D for damages from an auto accident. D counterclaims for his property damage from that same accident, but not for personal injuries. Whether D wins or loses with the counterclaim, he may not bring a second suit against P for personal injury arising from that same accident.) [422]

    2. Compulsory counterclaim: Observe that state and federal rules making certain counterclaims "compulsory" serve a similar function to the merger or bar doctrine. (*Example:* P sues D for damages arising out of an auto accident. The rules of merger and bar do not by themselves force D to assert either his claim for property damage, or for personal injury, arising out of that same accident. But in the federal court and in most state courts, any counterclaim by D for either of these things would be "compulsory," so that D would not be able to use that claim in a subsequent suit against P.) [422]

E. Change of law: Once a final judgment has been rendered (and any appeals resolved), **not even a change in the applicable law** will prevent claim preclusion from operating. The fact that the losing party would, because of such an overruling of legal precedent, win the lawsuit if she were allowed to start it again, is irrelevant. [422]

F. Persons not party to first action: Normally, **only parties** to the initial judgment will be subject to merger or bar. [423-426]

    1. Exceptions: But there are six fairly narrow well-established **exceptions** to the general rule of no-non-party-preclusion, situations in which a non-party may be **so closely tied** to a party to the first judgment that he will be both burdened and benefited by that judgment as if he had been a party to it. (We'll refer to the party to the first suit as "P1" and to the non-party who is suing now, and who is proposed to be bound by that judgment, as "P2," even though the party may have been a defendant in the first suit rather than a plaintiff.) [424]

        [1] P2 **agrees to be bound** by the results in the first action;

        [2] P1 and P2 have any of several pre-existing **"substantive legal relationships"** with each other (e.g., **successive owners** of the same property, or **indemnitor-and-indemnitee**). These relationships establish what is often called **"privity."**

        [3] P2 is deemed to have been **adequately represented** by P1 in the first suit, such as in a properly conducted **class action**, or in a suit in which the beneficiary of a **trust** is represented by the trustee.

        [4] P2 **assumed control** of the first litigation, even though P1 was the named party.

        [5] P1 was the real party in the first suit, and has now **designated P2 as her representative** in the present suit, making P2 P1's **"proxy."** So if P2 is now suing as an **agent** on behalf of P1, the suit will not be permitted to go forward because P1, the real party in interest, has already had her day in court.

[6] Under some special *statutory* scheme (e.g., *bankruptcy* or *probate* proceedings), P2 is expressly precluded from relitigating the claim or issue in question, even though P2 was not a party to that first suit.

[*Taylor v. Sturgell* (2008)]

2. **"Virtual representation" doctrine rejected:** If the situation does not fall into one of the above six exceptions, then (at least in federal practice), a stranger to the first action cannot be subjected to claim preclusion no matter how close his relationship is to a party to that action. The Supreme Court has rejected the so-called *"virtual representation"* doctrine, under which some lower federal courts had previously found that the *practical links* between the stranger and a party to the first suit — such as links of *friendship* or a *shared lawyer* — were so tight that it was fair to bind the stranger based on the outcome of the first suit. [*Taylor v. Sturgell, supra*] [423-426]

> **Example:** P1 and Ps are friends and fellow antique-aircraft enthusiasts. P1 wants to restore a vintage F-45 airplane he owns, which was made 70 years earlier. He therefore files a Freedom of Information Act (FOIA) request with the FAA for any technical information in the agency's files about the F-45 model. The FAA turns down the request on the grounds that a statutory exception to FOIA applies; P1 then sues the FAA in federal court and loses. A month later, P2 brings his own federal FOIA suit against the FAA for the same documents. P1 and P2 turn out to have numerous links (e.g., both are members of the Antique Aircraft Association; P1 asked P2 to help restore P1's plane; P2 is represented in his suit by the same lawyer who represented P1 in the first suit; and P1 gave P2 documents that P1 had previously gotten from the FAA in discovery during P1's suit). The FAA claims that these links are so extensive that P2 should be found to have been "virtually represented" by P1 during the first suit, and therefore barred by P1's loss in that suit.

> *Held* (by the Supreme Court): for P2. The "virtual representation" doctrine is hereby rejected for federal courts, because it goes against the fundamental rule that "a litigant is *not bound by a judgment to which she was not a party."* Unless the situation is found on remand to fall within one of the six traditional narrow exceptions to the no-strangers-are bound rule (listed above), P2 can't be bound. [*Taylor v. Sturgell, supra*]

III. COLLATERAL ESTOPPEL

A. **Definition:** Regardless of which of the parties to an action wins, the judgment decides for all time any ==*issue actually litigated*== in the suit. A party who seeks to re-litigate one of the issues disposed of in the first trial is said to be ==*"collaterally estopped"*== from doing so. [427]

> **Example:** Cars driven by A and B collide. A sues B for property damage. Assume that the jurisdiction has no rules making any counterclaim a compulsory counterclaim. B declines to assert any counterclaim in the suit brought by A. A recovers $1,000 of damages. The jurisdiction follows common-law contributory negligence, by which even a small amount of contributory negligence by A would have barred him from recovery. In a subsequent suit, B sues A for personal injuries arising out of the same accident.

> The court will hold that B is "collaterally estopped" from re-litigating the issue of whether A was negligent — the first judgment in A's favor amounted to a specific finding that A was not negligent, because contributory negligence would have barred recovery if

he had been. Therefore, B cannot recover from A on a negligence theory. [*Little v. Blue Goose*]

1. **Distinguished from merger and bar:** There are two major differences between collateral estoppel and claim preclusion (merger and bar): [428]

   a. **Issue vs. claim:** Whereas claim preclusion applies only where the "cause of action" or "claim" in the second action is the *same* as the one in the first action, collateral estoppel applies as long as any *issue* is the same, even though the causes of action are different.

   b. **Suit not prevented:** Whereas claim preclusion prevents the second suit altogether, collateral estoppel does not prevent suit, but merely compels the court to make the *same finding of fact* that the first court made on the identical issue.

2. **To whom applied:** Collateral estoppel always applies where *both* the parties in the second action were present in the first action. Collateral estoppel sometimes, but not always, applies where only the person against whom estoppel is sought to be used was present in the first action. [433-433]

B. **Issues covered:** For an issue to be subject to collateral estoppel, three requirements concerning that issue must be satisfied: (1) the issue must be the *same* as one that was *fully and fairly litigated* in the first action; (2) it must have been actually *decided* by the first court; and (3) the first court's decision on this issue must have been *necessary* to the outcome in the first suit. [428-432]

1. **Same issue:** For the re-litigation of an issue to be collaterally estopped, that issue must be *identical* to an issue litigated in the earlier trial. [428]

2. **Actually litigated and decided:** The issue must have been actually *litigated* and *decided* at the first trial. [428]

   a. **Need not raise all defenses:** This means that D in the first trial is *not obligated to raise all of his defenses*. D does not forfeit these defenses by not raising them as he would forfeit a compulsory counterclaim. (*Example:* P sues D for an installment of rent under a lease, and wins. In a later suit for subsequent installments due on the same lease, D will not be collaterally estopped from denying that the lease was ever executed — since the issue of execution was not actually litigated and decided in the first action, collateral estoppel does not apply even though D *could* have raised this as a defense the first time. [*Jacobson v. Miller*])

   b. **"Full and fair" litigation:** Also, the party against whom collateral estoppel is sought to be used must have had a *"full and fair opportunity"* to litigate the claim. (*Example:* In a negligence case by P against D, D asserts his own due care, but the trial court unjustly excludes relevant evidence tending to prove that D was careful. In a subsequent suit by D against P for his own injuries, D will not be estopped from contending that he behaved with due care, since he lacked a full and fair opportunity to litigate the due care issue in the first suit.)

3. **Issue essential to verdict:** Not only must the issue have been litigated and decided in the first action, but the finding on that issue must have been *necessary to the judgment*. [429]

   Example: A sues B for common-law negligence, and loses. The court's findings state that both parties were negligent, and recovery is denied on the grounds that A was contributorily negligent. B then sues A. A claims that the earlier finding of B's negligence, together with the doctrine of contributory negligence, mean that B cannot now recover as plaintiff.

Held, collateral estoppel should not be applied against B. The first case's finding that B was negligent was not necessary to the first verdict, since A's contributory negligence would have been enough to dispose of the case. Collateral estoppel applies only to issues whose adjudication was necessary to the verdict in the first action. [*Cambria v. Jeffery*]

a. **Alternate findings:** Where a judgment rests upon *alternate* findings, either of which would be sufficient to sustain it, courts are split about whether either finding should be given collateral estoppel effect. The modern (and Restatement) view is that *neither* should be given collateral estoppel effect, since the case could have turned out the same way without that finding. [429]

4. **Reasonably foreseeable future litigation:** Many courts today apply collateral estoppel in a subsequent action only where that action was *reasonably foreseeable* at the time of the initial suit. Otherwise, "defeat in one suit might entail results beyond all calculation…; a trivial controversy might bring utter disaster in its train." [*The Evergreens v. Nunan*] [429]

5. **Court of limited jurisdiction:** A finding made by a court of *limited jurisdiction* may be denied collateral estoppel effect in a subsequent suit that would have been beyond the first court's jurisdiction. This is especially true where the first court has jurisdiction limited to a dollar amount, and also has *informal procedures*. (*Example:* If the first suit is in a small claims court, most of which have no pleadings, no rules of evidence, and usually no lawyers, a finding will generally not be held to have collateral estoppel effect in a later suit that could not have been brought in the small claims court.) [430-431]

6. **Differences in burden of proof:** If in the first action the allocation of the *burden of proof* was more favorable to the party now seeking to apply collateral estoppel than it was in the second action, collateral estoppel will not be allowed. [431]

7. **Settlement:** In most jurisdictions, the *settlement* of an action by consent of the parties has *no* collateral estoppel effect. (The settlement document may, of course, provide otherwise.) [431]

8. **Findings of law:** A court's conclusion of *law*, like a conclusion of fact, is generally given collateral estoppel effect. [431-432]

a. **Exceptions:** But there are two situations in which a conclusion of law generally will *not* be given collateral estoppel effect: (1) where the two actions involve claims that are *substantially unrelated* to each other; and (2) where there has been a significant *change in legal principles* between the two suits, especially where use of collateral estoppel would impose on one of the parties a significant disadvantage, or confer on him a significant benefit, with respect to his *competitors*.

Example: D is a liquor wholesaler. P, a state liquor licensing agency, sues to have D's license revoked on the grounds that D is really functioning as a retailer. The trial court finds in D's favor. P then sues X, whose conduct is the same as D's; a higher court finds in favor of P, and orders X's license revoked. Now, P brings a second suit against D for revocation.

Collateral estoppel effect will probably not be given to the first P-D suit, since there has been an intervening change in legal principles, and since use of collateral estoppel would give D a perpetual, and unfair, advantage over X and other similar competitors.

C. **Persons who can be estopped:** Generally, only the *actual parties* to the first action can be *bound* by the finding on an issue, i.e., by collateral estoppel. [433]

1. **Exceptions:** There are a few narrowly-defined *exceptions* to the general rule that a person who was not a party to the first action cannot be collateral estopped as to facts found in that action. These are special situations in which the present litigant is so closely related to the previous litigant that it's fair to bind the former to the factual findings made in the first suit. For instance, if the litigant in the second suit (call him P2) is now acting as an *agent* of a party to the first suit (call her P1), P2 will be collaterally estopped.

   a. **Where to find the list:** See *supra*, p. C- 103, in the discussion of claim preclusion, for a list of the six situations in which a non-party to the first action can be bound. (The six situations apply the same way to issue preclusion as to claim preclusion.) Keep in mind that these six exceptions apply in federal litigation; the states are free to set up additional exceptions, as long as they don't violate the non-party's due process rights.

2. **Strangers to first action:** The most important thing to remember is that a true *stranger* to the first action (i.e., one not falling within the six exceptions mentioned above) *cannot be collaterally estopped* by the former judgment. [433]

   Example: A bus owned by Bus Co. collides with a car driven by Driver. In a suit between these two, Bus Co. is held to have full responsibility. Passenger, who was riding in Driver's car, now sues Driver. Even though the court in the first action decided that Driver was not at all at fault, Passenger is not bound by this finding. This is because Passenger was a complete stranger to the first action, and none of the six exceptions to the "no binding of strangers" rule applies to the ordinary passenger-driver situation. Therefore, the usual rule applies that a stranger cannot be bound by any finding of fact in the first action.

D. **Persons who can benefit from estoppel:** [433-438]

1. **Mutuality:** Originally, it was held that a party *not bound* by an earlier judgment (because not a party to it) could not use that judgment to bind his adversary who *was* a party to the first action. This rule prohibiting a stranger's use of collateral estoppel was known as the doctrine of *"mutuality."* [434]

   a. **Abandoned:** Nearly all courts have *abandoned* the general principle of mutuality. While many courts refuse in *particular circumstances* to allow the use of estoppel by one not a party to the first action, it is no longer a general rule that a stranger to the first action cannot benefit from findings of fact made against her adversary.

   Example: A bus owned by Bus Co. and a car driven by Driver collide. Also involved in the collision is Pedestrian, who is badly injured. Bus Co. sues Driver for negligence, and the court decides that Driver was totally at fault. In a separate suit, Pedestrian now sues Driver. Application of the doctrine of mutuality would prevent Pedestrian from collaterally estopping Driver on the issue of negligence. But most courts today would give Pedestrian the benefit of collateral estoppel in this situation, even though Pedestrian was a stranger to the first action.

2. **Offensive/defensive distinction:** Courts are *more willing* to allow the *"defensive"* use of collateral estoppel by a stranger than they are to allow the *"offensive"* use. "Offensive" use refers to use by a stranger to the first action who is a *plaintiff* in the second action; "defensive" use refers to use by a stranger who is a *defendant* in the second action. [434]

   a. **Offensive use sometimes OK:** But even offensive use is sometimes approved by the courts, just not as often as defensive use. (The above example is an illustration of offensive use that would probably be accepted by a court.) [436-437]

Example: The SEC sues D, a corporation, based on a false proxy statement D has issued. The trial court decides in the SEC's favor, concluding that the proxy statement contained certain falsehoods. P then brings a stockholder's derivative action against D, based on the same proxy statement. P wants to collaterally estop D from relitigating the falsity of the proxy statement.

Held, P may use collateral estoppel. This is true even though P was a stranger to the first action, and even though P's use is offensive, in the sense that the person seeking collateral estoppel is the plaintiff in the second action. [*Park Lane Hosiery Co. v. Shore*]

b. **Factors:** Here are some of the factors courts consider in deciding whether to allow offensive non-mutual estoppel in a particular case: [437-438]

   i. **Alignment:** Whether the party sought to be bound (the defendant in the second suit) was a *plaintiff* or *defendant* in the *first* suit. (If she was a defendant, this will militate against use of estoppel.)

   ii. **Incentive to litigate:** Whether the person to be estopped had a reasonable *incentive* to litigate the issue fully in the first suit, which will depend in part on whether the second suit was *foreseeable* at the time of the first suit. (The more incentive the party had to litigate the first time, the fairer it is to bind him now.)

   iii. **Discouraging break-away suits:** Whether the plaintiff in the second action *could have joined* in the first action, but instead sat out that first action in order to derive a tactical advantage.

   iv. **Multiple plaintiff anomaly:** Whether permitting offensive estoppel would present a danger of the *"multiple plaintiff anomaly."* (*Example:* All 200 passengers are killed when a plane owned by D crashes. If each P sues *seriatim*, and offensive estoppel is allowed, D might win the first 20 suits, lose the 21st, and then be estopped from denying liability in the next 179. This would be unfair to D.)

   v. **Procedural opportunities:** Whether there are *procedural opportunities* not available to the party in the first action but available now in the second action — if there are, allowing offensive estoppel is less likely. (*Examples:* There was less extensive discovery available in the first action, or no jury trial right.)

   vi. **Issue of law:** Whether the issue is one of *law* or merely of "fact." (Where the issue is one of law, the court is likely to use the more flexible doctrine of *stare decisis*, rather than collateral estoppel.)

   vii. **Government as party:** Whether the defendant in the second action is the *government* — non-mutual offensive use of collateral estoppel will virtually *never* be allowed against the government. [*U.S. v. Mendoza*]

3. **Criminal conviction:** Courts are split as to whether a party's previous *criminal conviction* may serve to collaterally estop him in the subsequent civil action. (*Example:* D is convicted of drunk driving after getting into an accident in which V is injured. In a subsequent civil suit by V, some but not all courts will allow V to collaterally estop D from denying that he was drunk.) [438]

   a. **Guilty plea:** Courts are also split about whether offensive collateral estoppel effect should be given to a *guilty plea* in the first proceeding.

b. Acquittal: *Acquittal* in a criminal case is ***never binding*** in a subsequent civil action. The main reason is that to grant estoppel effect to an acquittal would be to allow the criminal defendant to bind a non-party. (*Example:* D is prosecuted by the state for drunk driving in an accident in which V was injured. D is acquitted. V now brings a civil action for negligence against D, and seeks to show that D was drunk. V will not be collaterally estopped by the acquittal, because V was not a party to the earlier action. A second reason for rejecting estoppel is that the "beyond a reasonable doubt" standard of proof necessary in a criminal case was tougher for the prosecution to meet than the "preponderance of the evidence" standard used in the later civil suit, so estopping V would be extra unfair to him.) [439]

IV. FULL FAITH AND CREDIT

A. Full Faith and Credit generally: Special problems arise when two related suits occur in ***different jurisdictions***. There may be two different states involved, or a state court and a federal court. In either situation, the second court's handling of the first court's judgment is governed by a general principle called "full faith and credit." [443]

1. Two states: When the courts of ***two different states*** are involved, the result is dictated by the ***Full Faith and Credit*** Clause of the U.S. Constitution (Article IV, Section 1). This clause requires each state to give to the judgment of any other state ***the same effect that that judgment would have in the state which rendered it***. [443]

> **Example:** P wins a judgment against D in Connecticut, but cannot find any property in Connecticut on which to levy. P then locates property held by D in Illinois. P may collect in Illinois by bringing a suit based on the Connecticut judgment. Because of the Full Faith and Credit Clause, the courts of Illinois must accept this judgment at face value, and may not reconsider any issues which it concluded. The Illinois courts must therefore give P all the rights that a judgment creditor would have if he got an Illinois judgment, including the right to have the sheriff sell D's Illinois assets.

a. Misinterpretation: The rule of full faith and credit applies even where the second court is convinced that the first court made a ***mistake*** on law or facts. Indeed, State A must give full faith and credit to an adjudication of State B even if that judgment was based on a ***misinterpretation of the laws of State A***. [*Fauntleroy v. Lum*] [444]

b. Collateral attack on jurisdiction: There is ***one exception*** to the rule that the second court may not reconsider any aspect of the original judgment: the second court may reconsider whether the first court had ***jurisdiction*** (either personal or subject-matter), provided that the jurisdictional question was ***not litigated or waived*** in the first action. This is the doctrine of ***"collateral attack."***

> **Example:** P sues D in Connecticut. D defaults, by never appearing in the suit at all. The Connecticut court enters a judgment in favor of P. P then sues in Illinois, having found property of D there. At D's request, the Illinois court may consider whether the Connecticut court ever had valid personal jurisdiction over D. If it concludes that Connecticut did not, the Illinois court need not enforce the judgment. (But if D had litigated the jurisdictional issue in Connecticut, Illinois could not reconsider the jurisdiction question, even if it was convinced that Connecticut wrongly determined that it had jurisdiction.)

2. State followed by federal court: If the first court is a state court, and the second court is a *federal* court, a similar full faith and credit principle applies, but this is not dictated by the Constitution. Instead a federal statute, 28 U.S.C. §1738, requires every federal court to give to the judgment of any state court the same effect that that judgment would have in the courts of the state which rendered it. [444]

3. Federal followed by state court: Conversely, if the first judgment is in a federal court and the second suit is in a state court, full faith and credit again applies, though the mechanism by which this happens is not so clear. (Probably the Constitution's Supremacy Clause dictates that the state court honor a federal court judgment). [449]

B. Duty to follow the *res judicata* effect of first judgment: The full faith and credit principle — that one jurisdiction's courts must honor the judgments of another jurisdiction — applies not only generally, but specifically to the issue of *res judicata effect*. In other words, the earlier judgment must be given *exactly the same effect*, in terms of claim preclusion and collateral estoppel, as the judgment would have in the court that rendered it. [445]

1. Two states: Thus a state must give to the judgment of any other state at least the *res judicata* effect that that judgment would have in the state of its rendition. (*Example:* P litigates an issue with D in State 1. The issue is decided in favor of P. X now sues D in State 2 in a suit raising the same issue. The State 2 court determines that the courts of State 1 would allow X to use offensive collateral estoppel in this situation. The courts of State 2 must follow suit, even if the State 2 courts do not themselves generally allow offensive collateral estoppel in this situation.) [444]

a. Greater effect: Courts are split about whether they may or should give *greater effect* to another state's judgment than it would have in that other state. Probably no constitutional principle prevents the second state from giving greater effect to the first state's judgment, so it is within the second court's discretion whether to do so. (*Example:* On the facts of the above example, assume that State 2 would allow offensive collateral estoppel, but State 1 would not. Probably State 2 is free to give the State 1 judgment collateral estoppel effect, but State 2 might choose not to do so.)

2. State followed by federal: Similarly, if the *first* judgment is in a *state* court and the *second* suit is in a *federal* court, the federal court must grant the state court judgment the same *res judicata* effect that it would have in that state. [444-446]

a. Right of Congress to specify otherwise: There is an exception to this rule: Congress is always free to provide *otherwise*, in a specific context. If Congress does provide otherwise, then the federal court may be free to deny the earlier state court judgment the *res judicata* effect it would have in the rendering state.

Example: 42 U.S.C. §1983 gives a person the right to bring a federal suit against anyone who violates his constitutional rights "under color of" state law. Suppose Congress added a clause to §1983 saying that any state court criminal proceeding absolving an official of unconstitutional conduct should be ignored by the federal court hearing the §1983 action. If Congress did this, a federal court hearing a §1983 suit would be free to deny any state judgment the collateral estoppel effect it would have in the courts of the state that rendered it. But Congress has not in fact done this in §1983, so the federal courts must honor the collateral estoppel effect of state court judgments in §1983 suits.

   b. Can't give greater effect: The federal court may ***not*** give ***greater*** preclusive effect to the prior state court judgment than that state would give it. [*Migra v. Warren City Board of Ed.*] (*Example:* If the initial state judgment comes from a state that does not allow non-mutual offensive use of collateral estoppel, the federal court hearing the second suit may not apply such collateral estoppel, even if the situation is one in which the Supreme Court allows the use of collateral estoppel.) [446]

C. State suit follows federal suit: Suppose now that the *federal* suit comes *first*, and the *state* suit *second*. [446-449]

   1. First case is a diversity action: First, let's assume that Suit 1 is a *diversity* action. Here, the rule is that the state court in Suit 2 must give to the earlier federal judgment ***the same preclusive effect as such a judgment would have been given by the courts of the state where the first (federal) court sat.*** [*Semtek Int'l Inc. v. Lockheed Martin Corp.*] [446]

   Example: In Suit 1, P sues on a state-law claim, in California federal court sitting in diversity. The court concludes that the claim is barred by California's statute of limitations, and therefore dismisses it. (A federal court sitting in diversity must follow the statute-of-limitations law of the state where the federal court sits, under *Erie*.) Assume that the California courts would not regard a dismissal for failure to meet the statute of limitations a dismissal "on the merits" (i.e., they would not expect that if P re-filed in some state with an unexpired statute, the case would be barred on account of the California dismissal.) Now, in Suit 2, P makes the same claims in Maryland state court.

   The Maryland court must give to the prior federal dismissal the same preclusive effect that California (the state where the federal diversity court sat) would expect a dismissal by it on statute-of-limitations grounds to have in another court. Since California wouldn't expect the Maryland courts to bar the action, Maryland must allow the action. [*Semtek*] [446-448]

   2. First case is a federal-question case: Now, assume that Suit 1 is based on a *federal question*. Here, the federal courts will develop their own case-by-case policies about when their judgment should have preclusive effects. Then, a state court hearing Suit 2 will be required to give the same preclusive effect (whatever that is) when a claim that was decided in Suit 1 is brought in the state court. [449]

CHAPTER 1

INTRODUCTION

I. CIVIL PROCEDURE GENERALLY

A. "Civil" procedure vs. "criminal" procedure: "Civil" procedure refers to the rules of litigation for **"civil" actions**. Civil actions are best defined by contrasting them to "criminal" proceedings. In a criminal proceeding, the state is a party, and is asserting that an individual has committed a crime requiring punishment. In a civil action, by contrast, there is no assertion that the defendant has committed a crime. Instead, one private party (the plaintiff) has brought the suit, and is asserting that the other private party (the defendant) has wronged the plaintiff. Typically, the plaintiff in a private civil action is seeking money damages; however, the plaintiff may also be seeking "equitable" relief, such as an injunction to prevent the defendant from doing something.

> **Example 1 (money damages):** P and D are in an automobile accident. P sues D for $30,000 for personal injury. This is a civil action of the "money damages" type. If P wins, he will get a judgment from the court. This judgment will entitle P to collect (assuming the judgment is for the full amount sought) $30,000 from D. If D does not pay promptly, P will be able to use the state's judgment-collection mechanisms, such as a sheriff's auction, to forcibly collect the money from D.

> **Example 2 (equitable relief):** As part of P's purchase of D's business, D agrees not to start up a competing business within a five-mile radius for five years. D violates the agreement, and opens up a competing business. P sues D to enforce the non-compete. Here, P's action is an "equitable" action, for an injunction. That is, P is not asking principally for money damages (though he may ask for these as well). Instead, he is asking the court to order D not to do something, namely, carry on the new, competing, business. An action for an injunction is known as an **"equitable"** rather than **"legal"** action, because, historically, injunctions were the sort of relief granted by courts of "equity" as opposed to courts of "law."

B. Two court systems: There are **two entirely distinct court systems** in the U.S.

1. State courts: First is the system of **state courts**. Each state has its own system of courts. In a typical state, courts which can entertain civil proceedings are likely to include: (1) **small claims** courts, which are typically limited to suits seeking no more than a certain dollar amount, say $5,000; (2) courts of **general jurisdiction**, in which civil trials are held without any limit on the amount being sought; (3) an **intermediate appeals** court, to which anyone who loses a verdict in the general trial court has a right of appeal; and (4) a highest state court (typically called a "Supreme" court, but bearing a different name in certain states, such as the "Court of Appeals" in New York). In many states, there is no automatic right of appeal to the highest state court, since the litigant has already had an appeal "of right" to the intermediate appeals court; instead, it is up to the state's highest court to decide which requests for appeal it will accept.

a. Appeal to U.S. Supreme Court: The losing litigant in a state court proceeding does *not* have an automatic right to appeal to the *U.S. Supreme Court*. In brief, the Supreme Court may only hear appeals from state court judgments where the state court has decided a *federal question*. For more about this, see *infra*, p. 320.

    i. "Independent and necessary" ground: In fact, the Supreme Court may only hear those state cases in which the federal-question decision was *necessary* to the outcome. As the idea is usually put, the Supreme Court will not hear cases whose outcome rests on an *"independent and adequate state ground."* For a more full discussion of when the Supreme Court can hear an appeal from a state court proceeding, see Emanuel on *Constitutional Law*.

2. The federal courts: There is a second, entirely distinct, set of courts in the U.S.: the *federal* judicial system. This set of courts has three levels: (1) district courts; (2) circuit courts of appeal; and (3) the U.S. Supreme Court.

    a. District courts: Each state is divided into one or more "federal judicial *districts*." Each district has at least one *federal district court*, and some states have multiple courts. (For example, New York has four judicial districts, some of which have district courts in multiple places, each representing a "division" of a district.) The federal district courts are the *trial* courts of the federal system.

    b. Circuit courts of appeal: The federal judicial districts described in the prior paragraph are grouped into 13 *"judicial circuits."* In each of these circuits, there is a *"Court of Appeals."* The circuits are numbered First through Eleventh, plus the District of Columbia Circuit and the Federal Circuit. The First through Eleventh each cover the district courts in three or more states. (For example, the Ninth Circuit covers all districts located in Alaska, Arizona, California, Idaho, Montana, Nevada, Oregon, Washington, Guam and Hawaii, and thus hears all appeals from federal district courts in any of these states.)

        i. Appeal: Any litigant who loses in federal district court has a right to appeal to the Court of Appeals. Typically, an appeal is heard not by the entire Court of Appeals (which contains from 4-23 judges, depending on the circuit), but rather by a 3-judge *panel* of that circuit. (Occasionally, the entire set of judges in the circuit will re-consider a decision by a panel; in that case, the resulting decision is said to be "en banc.")

    c. Supreme Court: When a federal civil litigant loses in the Court of Appeals, she may petition the Supreme Court to hear the case. It is up to the Supreme Court to decide whether to "grant certiorari," i.e., to hear the appeal. The Supreme Court is never *required* to hear an appeal; the Court exercises its discretion to hear the case only if four Justices vote to grant certiorari.

    d. Federal Rules of Civil Procedure: Procedure in the federal courts is mainly governed by the *Federal Rules of Civil Procedure*. Changes in these Rules are proposed from time to time by the U.S. Supreme Court, and go into effect unless Congress specifically objects (which it rarely does).

C. Grounds for federal court jurisdiction: The *jurisdiction* of the federal court system is *limited* by the U.S. Constitution. In other words, it is not the case that the federal courts can hear any controversy they wish to hear. It is not even the case that Congress could, by passing a broad jurisdictional statute, empower the federal courts to hear any case they wish. Instead, the Constitution lists certain types of cases as to which the federal judicial power is deemed to exist, and only cases falling within that power may be heard by the federal system. (Furthermore, Congress can, and frequently has, cut back the federal judicial power to exclude cases that would be within the Constitution's grant.) At present, there are two main kinds of civil cases that the federal district courts may hear:

1. Diversity cases: First, the federal district courts may hear cases arising between *"citizens of different states,"* in which more than $75,000 is involved. See 28 U.S.C. §1332. (Also, the courts may hear a case between a citizen of an American state and any foreign subject.) The right to hear cases between citizens of different states is known as the grant of *"diversity"* jurisdiction, and the cases are called "diversity cases."

2. Federal question cases: Second, the federal district courts may hear any civil action "arising under the Constitution, laws, or treaties of the United States." 28 U.S.C. §1331. Cases falling under this provision are typically called *"federal question"* cases.

D. Both systems studied: In a typical first-year Civil Procedure course, both judicial systems are studied. However, certain "chapters" of the course typically focus on just state-court concerns or just federal concerns. Other chapters relate heavily to both systems. Thus "jurisdiction over the parties" relates to both federal and state systems; "subject matter jurisdiction," on the other hand, is limited to the federal-court context.

E. A road map: Here is a sort of *"road map"* for analyzing a Civil Procedure problem. If you are currently at the beginning of your Civil Procedure course, just look at this road map quickly, to get some sense of the lay of the land. If you are towards the end, and studying for exams, try to memorize this map so that you can use it as a checklist for spotting issues:

1. Personal jurisdiction: First, make sure that the court has *"personal jurisdiction"* or *"jurisdiction over the parties."* In brief, this means that you must check to make sure that the court can hear the case against the particular defendant. You must check to make sure that: (1) D had *minimum contacts* with the forum state (whether the court is a state or federal court); and (2) D received such *notice and opportunity to be heard* as to satisfy the constitutional requirement of due process.

2. Venue: Then, check whether *venue* was correct. In federal court suits (which are the only types of suits as to which venue problems are usually covered in a Civil Procedure course), the venue requirement describes what judicial *district* the case may be heard in. Essentially, the case must be heard either: (1) in any district where the *defendant resides* (with special rules for multi-defendant cases); or (2) in any district in which a *substantial part of the events* giving rise to the claim occurred. See 28 U.S.C. §1391. (There are special provisions giving venue for other districts in special cases, but most of the time you should be concerned with just "defendant's residence" or "place of events" venue.)

3. Subject matter jurisdiction: If the case is a federal case, you must then ask whether the court has *subject matter* jurisdiction. Essentially, this means that one of the following two things must be the case:

a. **Diversity:** Either the case is between *citizens of different states* (with "complete diversity" required, so that no plaintiff is a citizen of the same state as any defendant) and more than $75,000 is at stake; or

b. **Federal question:** The case raises a *"federal question."* Essentially, this means that plaintiff's right to recover stems from the U.S. Constitution, a federal treaty, or an act of Congress. (There is no minimum amount required to be at stake in federal question cases.)

4. **Pleading:** Next, you must examine whether the *pleadings* are proper. This can involve a whole range of questions, most of which will be fairly easy to spot. Typical questions might include: Did D answer in time? Can D make a motion to get the complaint dismissed for failure to state a claim? May P now amend her pleadings?

5. **Discovery:** Next, you may have a complex of issues relating to pretrial *discovery*, the process by which each side finds out details about the other side's case. Again, you should be able to spot discovery questions fairly readily from the fact pattern. Typical issues might include: May P take the oral deposition of W, an expert witness whom D is planning to call at trial? May D obtain court-ordered sanctions against P for failing to cooperate with discovery? May P use at trial the results of a deposition taken of W in a different case?

6. **Ascertaining applicable law:** Now, figure out *what jurisdiction's law* should be used in the case. The most important problem of this type is: In a diversity case, may the federal court apply its own concepts of "federal common law" (i.e., federal judge-made law), or must the court apply the law of the state where the federal court sits? In brief, the answer is that if the state has a *substantive law* (whether a statute or a judge-made principle) that is on point, *the federal court sitting in diversity must apply that law.* (*Example:* In a diversity case concerning negligence, the federal court must normally apply the negligence law of the state where the court sits.) This whole set of problems relating to ascertaining applicable law is commonly referred to as *"Erie"* problems, after *Erie v. Tompkins*, probably the most important case in federal Civil Procedure.

7. **Trial procedure:** Next, you may face a series of issues relating to *trial procedure*. Typical questions here are: What burden of proof does P bear, both to avoid having the case dismissed before it is fully tried, and to prevail in front of the judge or jury? May the case be dismissed before trial pursuant to the doctrine of summary judgment? Is there a right to jury trial here? May the judge order a directed verdict, effectively taking the case away from the jury? Should the judge grant a new trial or a judgment notwithstanding the verdict?

8. **Multi-party and multi-claim litigation:** If there is more than one claim in the case, or more than the basic two parties (a single plaintiff and a single defendant), you will face a whole host of issues related to the *multi-party* or *multi-claim* nature of the litigation. You must be prepared to deal with the various methods of bringing multiple parties and multiple claims into a case.

a. **Various devices:** Following is a brief checklist of devices by which multiple parties, or multiple claims, may be brought into the case. (In most Civil Procedure courses, and for our discussion here, the multi-claim and multi-party discussion focuses on the Federal Rules of Civil Procedure. Most states have roughly similar rules.)

b. **Counterclaim:** D may make a claim against P, by use of the ***counterclaim***. See FRCP 13. Check whether the counterclaim is ***"permissive"*** or ***"compulsory."*** (Also, remember that third parties, who are neither the original plaintiff nor the original defendant, may make a counterclaim.)

c. **Joinder of claims:** Once a party has made a claim against some other party, she may then make ***any other claim*** she wishes against that party. This is ***"joinder of claims."*** See Rule 18(a).

d. **Joinder of parties:** Multiple parties may ***join*** their actions together. Check to see whether either ***"permissive* joinder"** or ***"compulsory* joinder"** is applicable. Also, remember that each of these two types of joinder can apply to ***either multiple plaintiffs*** or ***multiple defendants***. See FRCP 19 and 20.

e. **Class actions:** Check whether a ***class action*** is available as a device to handle the claims of many similarly-situated plaintiffs, or claims against many similarly-situated defendants. See FRCP 23. Look for the possibility of a class action wherever there are 25 or more similarly-situated plaintiffs or similarly-situated defendants.

f. **Intervention:** A person who is not initially part of a lawsuit may be able to enter the suit on his own initiative, under the doctrine of ***intervention***. See FRCP 24. Check whether the intervention is "of right" or "permissive."

g. **Interpleader:** Where a party owes something to two or more other persons, but isn't sure which, that party may want to use the device of ***interpleader*** to prevent being made to pay the same claim twice. After checking whether interpleader might be desirable, decide whether the stakeholder should use "***statutory* interpleader**" or "Rule interpleader." See 28 U.S.C. §1335 (statutory interpleader) and FRCP 22 (Rule interpleader).

h. **Third-party practice (impleader):** Anytime D has a potential claim against some ***third person*** who is not already in the lawsuit, by which that third person will be liable to D for some or all of P's recovery against D, D should be able to ***"implead"*** the third person. (*Example:* Employee, while working for Employer, hits Victim with a company car. Victim sues Employer in diversity, under the doctrine of *respondeat superior*. Under traditional concepts of indemnity, Employer will be able to recover from Employee for any amount that Employer is forced to pay Victim. Therefore, Employer should "implead" Employee as a "third-party defendant" to the Victim-Employer action.) See FRCP 14(a). Once a third-party defendant is brought into the case, consider what other claims might now be available (e.g., a counterclaim by the third-party defendant against the third-party plaintiff, a cross-claim against some other third-party defendant, a counterclaim against the original plaintiff, etc.).

i. **Cross-claims:** Check to see whether any party has made, or should make, a claim against a ***co-party***. This is a ***cross-claim***. See FRCP 13(g).

j. **Jurisdiction:** For any of these multi-party or multi-claim devices, check to see whether the requirements of ***personal jurisdiction*** and ***subject matter jurisdiction*** have been satisfied. To do this, you will need to know whether the doctrine of *"supplemental"* jurisdiction applies to the particular device in question. If it does not, the new claim, or the new party, will typically have to *independently* meet the requirements of federal subject matter jurisdiction. (*Example:* P, from Massachusetts, sues D, from Connecticut, in diversity. X, from Massachusetts, wants to intervene in the case on the side of D. Because supplemental jurisdiction does not apply to intervention, X must independently satisfy the requirement of diversity, which he cannot do because he is a citizen of the same state as P. Therefore, X cannot intervene.)

9. **Former adjudication:** Lastly, check whether the results in some *prior litigation* are *binding* in the current suit. Distinguish between situations in which the *judgment* in the prior suit is binding on an entire cause of action in the present suit (under the doctrines of *merger* and *bar*), and the situation where a *finding of fact* is binding on the current suit, even though the judgment itself is not binding (the *"collateral estoppel"* situation).

   a. **Non-mutual collateral estoppel:** Where a *"stranger"* to the first action (one not a party to that first action) now seeks to take advantage of a finding of fact in that first suit, consider whether this *"non-mutual"* collateral estoppel should be allowed.

   b. **Full Faith and Credit:** Lastly, if the two suits have taken place in *different jurisdictions*, consider to what extent the principles of *Full Faith and Credit* limit the second court's freedom to ignore what happened in the first suit.

CHAPTER 2

JURISDICTION OVER THE PARTIES

ChapterScope

This Chapter examines "jurisdiction over the parties," that is, a court's power to decide a case between the *particular parties* before it. The most important concepts in this Chapter are:

- **Minimum contacts:** Whether the defendant is an individual or a corporation, the court may proceed only if D has *"minimum contacts"* with the state in which the court sits. This is true for all state-court actions and most federal-court actions.

- **Voluntariness:** Usually a corporation will be found to have the requisite minimum contacts with the forum state only if the corporation has somehow *voluntarily sought to do business in*, or *with the residents of*, the forum state.

  ❑ **"At home" requirement for general jurisdiction:** If the plaintiff's claim against a corporate defendant does *not* involve that corporation's *activities inside the forum state* (i.e., the suit is said to be based on *"general"* rather than "specific" jurisdiction), the corporation can't be required to defend unless the corporation is *"at home"* in the forum state, meaning it's either incorporated there or has its principal place of business there.

- **Limits on service of process:** As a general rule, in federal cases (both diversity actions and federal question cases), *service of process* may be made only: (1) *within the territorial limits of the state in which the District Court sits*; or (2) anywhere else permitted by the state law of the state where the District Court sits.

- **Notice:** Even if the court has authority to judge the dispute between the parties or over the property before it, the court may not proceed unless D received *adequate notice* of the case against him.

  ❑ **Reasonableness test:** In order for D to have received adequate notice, it is not necessary that he *actually* have learned of the suit. Rather, the procedures used to alert him must have been *reasonably likely to inform him*, even if they actually failed to do so.

- **Venue:** In addition to requirements of jurisdiction, requirements of *venue* must also be satisfied. Venue refers to the place within a jurisdiction in which a particular action may be brought. In a state-court action, venue determines in what county or district of the state the action may be brought. In federal actions, venue determines which federal district court may try the action.

I. GENERAL PRINCIPLES

A. Two kinds of jurisdiction: Before a court can decide a case, it must have jurisdiction over the *parties* as well as over the *subject matter*. That is, it must have jurisdiction not only to decide the *kind* of case before it (subject matter jurisdiction) but also to decide a case *between the particular parties*, or *concerning the property*, before it.

1. Examples of *subject matter* jurisdictional problems:

    a. *Does Court X have the power to decide cases in which the two parties are citizens of different states?* (The answer would be "yes" if Court X were a federal court; the subject matter jurisdiction would be "diversity jurisdiction." Of course, the amount in controversy requirement, *infra*, p. 138, would also have to be met.)

    b. *Does Court X have the power to decide cases involving more than $1,000?* (The answer might be "no" if Court X were a municipal court.)

    Note: Questions of subject matter jurisdiction are discussed in the chapter on Subject Matter Jurisdiction, *infra*, p. 119.

2. Examples of problems of jurisdiction *over the parties:*

    a. *Does Court X have jurisdiction over a defendant who is a citizen of State X, but who is temporarily out of the state?* (The answer would be "yes" in almost every state, as long as the defendant were given reasonable notice that the Court in X was going to exercise its jurisdiction over him.)

    b. *Does Court Y have jurisdiction over property in State Y where the action is one by the plaintiff to register title to the land in his name?* (The answer is "yes," even though no defendant is personally known to the plaintiff or to the court. Even though the jurisdiction here is over land rather than people, it is still referred to as a kind of jurisdiction *over the parties* as distinguished from *subject matter* jurisdiction.)

B. **Requirements for jurisdiction over the parties:**   There are two distinct requirements which must be met before a court can be said to have jurisdiction over the parties:

1. The court must have *power* to act, either upon given property, or on a given person so as to subject him to personal liability. This is a requirement of *substantive due process.*

2. The court must have given the defendant *adequate notice* of the action against him, and an *opportunity to be heard*. This is a requirement of *procedural due process.*

C. **Three kinds of jurisdiction over the parties:**   There are three kinds of jurisdiction which a court may exercise over the parties. These will be distinguished more fully in the treatment of *in rem* and *quasi in rem* jurisdiction, *infra*, p. 77.

1. *In personam:* *In personam* jurisdiction, or jurisdiction over the defendant's person, gives the court power to issue a judgment against him personally. This judgment can then be sued upon in other states, and *all of his assets* may be seized to satisfy the judgment.

2. *In rem:* *In rem* jurisdiction, or jurisdiction over a *thing*, gives the court power to adjudicate a claim made about a *piece of property* or about a *status*. An action to quiet title to real estate, and an action to pronounce a marriage dissolved, are examples.

3. *Quasi in rem jurisdiction:*   In *quasi in rem* jurisdiction, the action is begun by seizing property owned by (*attachment*), or a debt owed to (*garnishment*) the defendant, within the forum state. This is different from *in rem* jurisdiction because here the action is not really *about* the "thing" seized; instead the thing seized is a pretext for the court to decide

the case without having jurisdiction over the defendant's person. Any judgment affects only the property seized, and the judgment cannot be sued upon in any other court.

D. Minimum contacts requirement: Regardless of which type of jurisdiction over the parties is involved, a court may not exercise it unless the defendant has *"minimum contacts"* with the state in which the court sits. What constitutes "minimum contacts" is a complex issue that is discussed extensively beginning *infra*, p. 23. In brief, the notion is that the defendant must have taken *actions* that were *purposefully directed* toward the forum state. (These might include selling goods in the state, incorporating in the state, visiting the state, etc.) Without such minimum contacts, exercise of jurisdiction would violate the defendant's *federal constitutional right to due process.* In the usual case of a *state* court that is exercising jurisdiction, the relevant clause is the *14th Amendment's* guarantee of due process.

1. **Balancing test:** Furthermore, even if the defendant has the requisite "minimum contacts" with the forum state, the court may not exercise jurisdiction if considerations of *"fair play* and *substantial justice"* would make requiring the defendant to defend the action in the forum state so *unreasonable* as to constitute a due process violation. This might be the case, for instance, if the burden to the defendant of defending in the forum state was unusually great, and the interests of the plaintiff in having the controversy heard in the forum state were very slight. See, e.g., *Asahi Metal Industry Co. v. Superior Court, infra,* p. 32 (*held*, where the only parties remaining in this California suit are foreign corporations that never did business in the U.S., it's unfair to require D to litigate in California).

   a. **Not usually unreasonable:** *Generally*, however, if D has the requisite minimum contacts with the forum state, it will *not be unreasonable* for the case to be tried there, and there will thus be constitutionally-exercisable jurisdiction over D. (So the result in *Asahi, supra* — where the Court found that even though foreign-based D probably had minimum contacts with California, making it defend in California would be so unfair as to violate D's due process rights — will be unusual.)

E. Due process: The exercise of jurisdiction by a state court must meet the requirements of the *due process* clause of the *14th Amendment*, as that clause is interpreted by the U.S. Supreme Court. Thus if D is entirely lacking in *connections with the forum state*, it will violate D's 14th Amendment due process rights for a court of the forum state to exercise *in personam* jurisdiction over D. Nearly all of the Supreme Court cases discussed in this chapter concern this due process requirement.

1. **"Specific" versus "general" jurisdiction:** The Supreme Court's cases on the due process aspects of *in personam* jurisdiction make an important distinction between two categories of personal jurisdiction: (1) *"specific"* jurisdiction; and (2) *"general"* jurisdiction.

   The two terms distinguish between two situations: (a) that in which a state court is hearing a claim arising out of the defendant's voluntary contacts with the "forum state" (the state where the court sits), and (b) that in which the court is instead hearing a claim that does *not* arise out of any voluntary contacts between the defendant and the forum state.

   [1] **"Specific" jurisdiction:** *"Specific"* jurisdiction refers to a court's exercise of personal jurisdiction to hear a claim *related to, and arising out of,* the defendant's voluntary *contacts with the forum state.* In general, a *smaller degree* of contact between

the defendant and the forum state is required for a state court to exercise specific jurisdiction over the defendant than for it to exercise general jurisdiction.[1]

Example: D is a sole proprietor of a one-person computer-assembly business. D lives in Texas and conducts all of his regular business activities there, rarely venturing out of state in connection with the business. In response to a referral from a friend, D gets an order for a single laptop from P, who resides in Arkansas. D assembles a custom laptop in Texas and personally delivers it to P's Arkansas home address, and installs it there. D has no business connections with Arkansas other than this one sale-and-delivery to P. Ten months later, the laptop's batteries malfunction, the laptop catches on fire, and P is burned. P sues D in Arkansas state court for his injuries.

If the Arkansas state court hears the case and decides whether D should be liable for damages, the type of personal jurisdiction that the court will be exercising is *"specific* jurisdiction" — that is, the suit relates to and arises out of D's voluntary contacts with the forum state, Arkansas (since the suit relates to a computer that D voluntarily traveled to Arkansas to deliver and install). Because the suit is based on specific jurisdiction, even the relatively small degree of voluntary connection between D and Arkansas that exists is enough to prevent the Arkansas court's hearing of the case (and its rendition of a personal judgment against D) from being a violation of D's federal constitutional due process rights.

[2] **"General" jurisdiction:** By contrast, *"general"* jurisdiction refers to a situation in which the state court is exercising *in personam* jurisdiction to hear a claim that ***does not arise out of or relate to the defendant's contacts with the forum state***. The U.S. Supreme Court requires, as a matter of fairness to the defendant, ***much more extensive contacts*** between the defendant and the forum state when the state court is exercising general jurisdiction over that defendant. In fact, where the defendant is an individual, in most cases a state court may as a constitutional due process matter exercise general jurisdiction over that defendant only if the defendant is ***domiciled in***, or else ***personally served with process in***, that state. (For more about the requirements of general jurisdiction, see Section IV beginning on p. 51 *infra*.)

Example: Same basic fact pattern as in the above example. Now, however, some time after D has delivered the computer to P in Arkansas, P drives through Texas on a vacation, and happens to stop off to see D at D's house there. Towards the end of the visit, when P is standing in D's driveway, D accidentally runs him over. In part because P knows a lawyer based in P's home state of Arkansas but no lawyers based in Texas, P chooses to bring a negligence suit against D in Arkansas for P's injuries from the Texas accident.

This suit, unlike the one in the prior Example, will have to be based on *"general"* (not specific) jurisdiction, since P's claim has nothing to do with any voluntary contact between D and Arkansas (the forum state). Since the case has to be based on general jurisdiction over D or not brought at all, D's federal constitutional due process

---

1. For more about the minimum contacts between the defendant and the forum state required for specific jurisdiction in the core situation of an out-of-state corporation whose products cause in-state harm, see *infra*, p. 40.

rights probably mean that the Arkansas court will not have personal jurisdiction over D to hear the case, unless either (1) D changes his domicile to Arkansas prior to suit; or (2) D is served by P at a moment when D happens to be temporarily in Arkansas.

    a. **"Specific" form more common:** The substantial majority of state-court litigations that you will encounter in your *Civil Procedure* course — including most of the Supreme Court opinions you'll read — involve specific rather than general jurisdiction.

F. Long-arm statutes: Even where the requirements of due process (minimum contacts between D and the forum state, etc.) are satisfied, the defendant may not be served *outside* of the forum state unless the forum state has enacted a *statute* authorizing out-of-state service under certain circumstances. Such statutes allowing the courts of a state to obtain jurisdiction over persons *not physically present* within the state at the time of the service are called "*long-arm* statutes."

    1. **Links to forum state:** Long-arm statutes allow jurisdiction on the basis of specified *links between the defendant and the forum state*, such as domicile there, ownership of property in the state, commission of a tortious act inside the state, etc.

G. State and federal: Most of the material which follows relates to the exercise of jurisdiction by *state* courts. Federal jurisdiction follows roughly similar principles, and will be outlined in detail in the section on Federal Jurisdiction over the Parties, *infra*, p. 68.

II. JURISDICTION OVER INDIVIDUALS

Note: This section will consider various bases which have been employed for the exercise of jurisdiction over natural persons. These bases include *presence within the forum state, domicile within the state, consent to being sued within the state, tortious acts committed within the state, business done within the state*, etc. *Jurisdiction over corporations* will be considered separately in the section following the present one.

A. Individual's presence: Jurisdiction may be exercised over an individual by virtue of her *presence within the forum state* at the time she is served with process.

    1. **Originally chief basis:** *Originally, presence within the state was the chief, if not sole, basis for personal jurisdiction.* This principle is illustrated by the leading case of *Pennoyer v. Neff*, 95 U.S. 714 (1877). In *Pennoyer* the Supreme Court said that "the authority of every tribunal is necessarily *restricted by the territorial limits of the State in which it is established.*"

        a. **No out-of-state service:** Since the state's *power* only extends to the *edge of its borders*, the Court said in *Pennoyer*, "*Process* from the tribunals of one State cannot *run into another State*, and summon parties there domiciled to leave its territory and respond to proceedings against them."

        b. **In-state presence at time of service suffices:** The actual *holding* of *Pennoyer* is that a nonresident defendant *cannot* be subjected to the personal jurisdiction of the forum state if the defendant is ***not served*** within the state — that's the meaning of the above-quoted statement that a state's process cannot "run into another state." But *Pennoyer* is also significant for the ***converse*** proposition— if a nonresident defendant ***does*** venture into the forum state, and is ***served with process there***, that in-state service ***does*** suffice to allow the forum state to exercise personal jurisdiction over the defendant. As one commentator has summarized this aspect of the decision, "A state court could enter a binding personal judgment against an unwilling nonresident defendant if, and only if, he was ***personally served with process within the state*** or voluntarily appeared before the court." F,K&M (4th), §3.3.

2. **Presence still enough:**   Today, presence within the forum state at the time of service is only one of numerous ways to get jurisdiction over a person. But it continues to be a ***constitutionally valid method*** of getting jurisdiction, even where the individual is an ***out-of-state resident*** who comes into the forum state only briefly. In other words, so long as ***service is made*** on the person while he is in the forum state, the entire case may be tried in the forum state, even though the defendant then leaves the forum state and has no other contacts with it. This is the result of an important Supreme Court decision, ***Burnham v. Superior Court***, 495 U.S. 604 (1990).

   a. **Facts:**   In *Burnham*, Dennis and Francie Burnham, a married couple with children, separated. Mrs. Burnham and the children moved to California, and Mr. Burnham remained in New Jersey. The next year, Mr. Burnham visited California on business. That same trip, he went to visit his children, and was served with process in a California suit by Mrs. Burnham for divorce. Mr. Burnham then returned to New Jersey. Mr. Burnham argued that California could not constitutionally exercise personal jurisdiction over him, because his only contacts with the state were a few short visits there for business, and a few visits with his children.

   b. **Court upholds jurisdiction:**   But the Supreme Court held that on these facts, California ***could*** constitutionally assert jurisdiction. There was no majority opinion. But all members of the court agreed that on these facts, personal jurisdiction was not a violation of Mr. Burnham's due process rights.

      i. **Plurality:**   Four justices seemed to feel that as long as the defendant was personally served while present in the forum state, no matter how briefly, this would always suffice for personal jurisdiction. The plurality reasoned that all American jurisdictions apparently continue to allow in-state service as a basis for jurisdiction, so that this means of jurisdiction cannot be said to violate "traditional notions of fairness," the standard for determining whether a practice violates due process.

      ii. **Other justices:**   The other justices in *Burnham* believed that presence would almost always suffice, but appeared to think that there might be occasional instances where this would lead to great unfairness and might thus be unconstitutional.

   c. **Summary:**   So as the result of *Burnham*, so long as the defendant voluntarily travels to the forum state, and is ***served while present there***, that state will have personal jurisdiction over him in virtually all instances, even though the defendant may have no other contacts with the state at all apart from the visit on which he was served. (If the defendant was *involuntarily* in the forum state at the time of service, e.g., because he was forcibly abducted and brought there, this rationale would presumably not apply, so jurisdiction would probably be a violation of due process. But this rarely happens.)

B. **Domicile:** Jurisdiction may constitutionally be exercised over an individual who is *domiciled* within the forum state, even if service takes place outside of the forum state.

1. *Milliken:* The leading case allowing jurisdiction based on domicile is *Milliken v. Meyer*, 311 U.S. 457 (1940). Meyer was domiciled in Wyoming, and was served in Colorado, pursuant to a Wyoming statute allowing out-of-state service on a resident defendant who has attempted either to escape his creditors or to avoid being served with process. The U.S. Supreme Court held that such service was valid: "Domicile in the state is alone sufficient to bring an absent defendant within the reach of the state's jurisdiction for purposes of a personal judgment. ..." The Court noted that the defendant still had to be served out of state in a way "reasonably calculated to give him actual notice of the proceedings and an opportunity to be heard." (See the section on Notice and Opportunity to be Heard, *infra*, p. 84.)

2. **Rationale for jurisdiction based on domicile:** The rationale for allowing jurisdiction based on domicile was explained in *Milliken* as follows: *"A state which accords privileges and affords protection to [a person] and his property by virtue of his domicile may also exact reciprocal duties."*

3. **Necessity for statutory authorization:** Most courts have held that they have jurisdiction based on domicile only if they have been explicitly given this authorization by statute. (F,K&C, p. 952.)

4. **Domicile and citizenship:** Domicile is usually held to be synonymous with citizenship for personal jurisdiction purposes. A person can have only one domicile at a time for this purpose.

5. **Domicile and residence:** Domicile is more limited than residence, since people can have several residences at one time.

6. **Formula for domicile:** A person is considered to be domiciled in the place where he has his *current dwelling-place*, if he also has an *intention to remain* in that place for an *indefinite period*. The formula is sometimes expressed:

   domicile = current dwelling place + intent to remain indefinitely

   a. **Indefinite plan to return:** A person's general desire to return to a previous domicile at some *indefinite point* in the future does *not* prevent her *present* residence from being her domicile.

   b. **Restatement test:** The 2nd Restatement of Conflicts (§18) says, "To acquire a domicile of choice in a place, a person must intend to make that place his home *for the time at least."*

   Example: A moves to state B to be near his mother, who has cancer, and who will probably die within the next year. A rents an apartment, and plans to stay in State B until his mother dies, at which time he plans to return to his old state of residence. A court would probably hold that he was domiciled in State B, since the date of his mother's death is not known with certainty, and his intention to stay in the state is therefore indefinite.

c. Criteria for determining intention: In determining a person's intention to remain indefinitely or permanently, the court will look at whether he has **registered to vote**, whether he has **left property behind** in his former state of residence, **where he works**, whether his **family has moved** with him, etc.

d. Prior residence as domicile: Observe that the equation given above means that a person is domiciled in the place where he has his current dwelling-place only if he has the intention to remain there indefinitely. What happens if a person has a residence in a particular state, but does *not* intend to remain there indefinitely? Generally, his **prior** residence will be looked at; if there was a time when he intended to remain in that prior state indefinitely (so that it became his domicile), the court will treat it as **continuing** to be his domicile until he both resides in, and intends to remain indefinitely in, some new place. This can produce the anomaly that a person is treated as a domiciliary of a place that he no longer resides in and intends never to return to.

Example: P1 and P2, a husband and wife, sue D in federal court under diversity of citizenship. (See *infra*, p. 122.) It becomes relevant to determine the domicile of P1, the wife. P1 formerly lived in Mississippi. She then moved to Louisiana to attend graduate school; subsequently, she moved to Illinois, where she lives at the time the trial begins. She intends to move back to Louisiana so her husband can complete his schooling there, and does not know where she will reside thereafter.

Held, P1 is domiciled in Mississippi. Her move to Louisiana did not change her domicile since she never intended to remain there indefinitely. Nor did her temporary move to Illinois change her domicile. Therefore, her domicile remains Mississippi, and this will continue to be the case until she moves to a place in which she intends to reside indefinitely. This is true even though she has *no* intent ever to return to Mississippi to live. *Mas v. Perry*, 489 F.2d 1396 (5th Cir. 1974).

e. Avoidance of jurisdiction: As long as the intention to remain indefinitely in the new domicile exists, it is **irrelevant** that a defendant has **moved in order to avoid the jurisdiction** of his former state. (But he must make the move **before** the action against him is begun.)

f. Diversity of citizenship: The same definition of "domicile" described above is used to determine whether diversity of citizenship exists in federal cases. (The *Mas* case, *supra*, illustrates this.) See the discussion of diversity in the Subject Matter Jurisdiction chapter, *infra*, p. 119. See also Wr., pp. 161-63.

g. Service on absent domiciliaries: If the requirements for jurisdiction on the basis of domicile are met, service may be made on the absent defendant by personal service, or by any other method that is reasonably calculated to give him actual notice. (See Section on Notice and Opportunity to be Heard, *infra*, p. 84.)

C. Residence: Some states allow jurisdiction to be exercised on the basis of defendant's **residence in the forum state**, even though he is absent from the state. Since a person may have several residences, but only one domicile, this is a looser ground for jurisdiction than domicile.

1. **Rationale:** The argument that the forum state grants certain privileges and protection to the property owner (police, fire, streets, etc.) and is thus entitled to exert jurisdiction in return, would apply almost as strongly to the resident as to the domiciliary.

2. **No Supreme Court decision:** The U.S. Supreme Court has not yet passed on the due process validity of jurisdiction based solely on residence.

D. Consent: Jurisdiction over a party can be exercised by virtue of his *consent*, even if he has no contacts whatsoever with the forum state. So if the person takes an action that's considered to be a *voluntary submission to the forum state's jurisdiction*, that submission can be the basis for jurisdiction even though the party has no other forum-state contacts.

1. **Consent by filing action:** For instance, if a person *files an action* as plaintiff in the forum state, the person is considered to have submitted to that court's jurisdiction. A counterclaim may therefore be filed against the plaintiff, by service on his attorney. And the plaintiff then cannot escape jurisdiction by dismissing her original action, or by failing to prosecute it. *Adam v. Saenger*, 303 U.S. 59 (1938).

2. **Consent before claim arises:** A party may agree to submit to the jurisdiction of a certain court even before any cause of action has arisen. This is often done as part of a commercial *contract* between the parties.

    Example: Defendants are Michigan farmers who sign a rental equipment leasing contract with a farm equipment company. The contract states that the defendants agree to designate a third person to receive process for them for a suit in New York, should one arise. *Held*, the defendants have consented to the jurisdiction of the New York federal district court. *National Equipment Rental v. Szukhent*, 375 U.S. 311 (1964).

    a. **"Forum selection" clauses:** Some contracts go further than just an agreement to submit to the jurisdiction of a particular court — they obligate each party to *litigate in one particular court*. Such *"forum selection"* clauses will be *enforced*, provided that they are *"fundamentally fair."*

    Example: The Ps take a cruise on the D cruise line. Before the cruise starts, the Ps receive tickets issued by D; each ticket states that any dispute in connection with the trip "shall be litigated, if at all, in and before a Court located in the State of Florida." The cruise originates in Los Angeles. One of the Ps is injured by a fall that occurs while the ship is in international waters off the coast of Mexico. The Ps sue in federal court for the Western District of Washington. D asks that the suit be dismissed, on the grounds that any suit arising out of the cruise must occur in a federal (or state) court located in Florida, not Washington.

    Held (by the U.S. Supreme Court), for D. Forum-selection clauses will be upheld, subject to judicial scrutiny for "fundamental fairness." Here, the clause was not unfair, for several reasons. First, a cruise ship typically carries passengers from many locales, so the ship's owners have a strong interest in not being subject to litigation in multiple fora. Additionally, a cruise line that can centralize its litigation may well be able to offer lower prices to the public. Also, D is based in Florida, and many of its cruises depart from there, so there's no indication that D chose Florida for the forum clause merely to make litigation inconvenient for plaintiffs. *Carnival Cruise Lines, Inc. v. Shute*, 499 U.S. 585 (1991).

3. **Cognovit:** A party may not only agree to submit to the jurisdiction of a certain court in advance of a cause of action, he may even agree to **waive his right of notice and appearance**, and to allow a judgment to be entered against him by consent. The instrument indicating such consent is known as a **cognovit** note. Cognovits are generally enforced, at least where the party signing the note is shown to have read and understood it, and to have received something in exchange for signing.

4. **Implied consent:** Certain state statutes recognize the doctrine of **implied consent**, by which a defendant is said to have impliedly consented to the jurisdiction of a state over him by virtue of acts which he had committed within the state. This doctrine will be discussed more fully in the sections on Non-resident Motorist Statutes, *infra*, and Jurisdiction over Corporations, *infra*, p. 21.

5. **General appearance:** If a suit is brought seeking personal liability over a defendant, his appearance in the court to contest the case **on the merits** constitutes consent to the court's jurisdiction, even if jurisdiction would not otherwise have been valid. Such an appearance on the merits is called a **general appearance**. If defendant first makes an objection to lack of jurisdiction, and then contests the case on the merits, the matter is more complicated — see the Section on Special Appearances, *infra*, p. 93.

E. **Non-resident motorist statutes:** Many states have statutes allowing their courts to exercise jurisdiction over **non-resident motorists** who have been involved in **accidents in the state.**

1. **Implied consent:** Formerly this jurisdiction over non-resident motorists was based on the fiction of **implied consent.**

> **Example:** A Massachusetts statute held that Massachusetts had jurisdiction over anyone who operated a motor vehicle within the state, on the grounds that such a person could be said to have **impliedly consented** to jurisdiction by the act of operating the vehicle. *Hess v. Pawloski*, 274 U.S. 352 (1927).

2. **Rejection of "implied consent" theory:** But the modern trend in non-resident motorist statutes is to **reject the theory of implied consent**, in favor of a theory that the states have the right to use their **police power** and their court system to protect their own citizens who are injured by the automobile, a dangerous object.

3. **Specific jurisdiction only:** Non-resident motorist statutes, when they exist, confer only **specific jurisdiction.** That is, they confer jurisdiction only for a suit involving the in-state auto accident.

4. **Cases where non-resident statutes used:** Here are some of the situations in which non-resident motorist statutes have been applied:

   a. P is a resident of the forum state, and D was driving the car in the forum state, when the accident injuring P occurred. This is the most common situation in which non-resident motorist statutes are applied.

b. Neither P nor D is a resident of the forum state, but the accident occurred there. W&M, v. 4, p. 242.

c. D was never in the state at all, but merely lent his car to a friend, who had the accident in the state. *Id.*

d. D is the representative of the dead motorist. *Id.*

5. Service on state official: Most of the non-resident motorist statutes provide for in-state service of process on a ***designated state official***, such as the Director of Motor Vehicles, and for ***registered mail service*** on the defendant himself.

F. In-state tortious acts: Many states have statutes allowing their courts jurisdiction over persons committing ***tortious acts within the state***.

> **Example:** The Illinois long-arm statute permits Illinois courts to exercise jurisdiction over any person in a cause of action arising from "the commission of a tortious act within this state" by that person or his agent.

1. Measure of proof for jurisdiction: Long-arm statutes based on in-state tortious acts allow jurisdiction if the plaintiff shows at the outset merely that it is ***reasonably likely*** that the defendant has committed a tortious act within the state. Proof of the kind that would suffice at trial is not required.

2. Out-of-state acts with in-state consequences: Do long-arms typically confer jurisdiction for acts by the defendant that are ***done outside the forum state***, but that ***cause injuries inside*** the state? The issue arises most often in ***product-liability*** cases, where the product is made outside the forum state, and ends up causing a personal injury in the forum state. The answer is often ***"yes."***

a. Specifically covered: Many modern long-arms ***explicitly cover*** acts done outside the forum state with in-state consequences, at least where the actor ***regularly does business*** in the forum state.

b. Not specifically covered: Furthermore, even in states where the long-arm ***doesn't*** explicitly cover out-of-state acts with in-state tortious consequences, the long-arm is sometimes ***interpreted*** to reach such out-of-state actors. Thus clauses in long-arm statutes referring to "a tortious act within the state" or "tortious conduct within the state" have sometimes been interpreted to reach out-of-state acts that lead to tortious consequences within the state.

> **Example:** Titan (an Ohio company) makes valves which it sells to another company, which incorporates them into a boiler which it sells to P. The boiler explodes in Illinois, injuring P, who sues Titan in Illinois. The Illinois long-arm allows suit in Illinois based upon a "tortious act within the state." The issue is whether, as P contends, the long-arm gives the Illinois court jurisdiction over Titan.
>
> *Held*, for P. A tortious act is deemed to be committed ***where the resultant damage occurs***. Therefore, the Illinois courts have jurisdiction in the present case. "In law the place of the wrong is where the last event takes place which is necessary to render the actor liable." *Gray v. American Radiator Corp.*, 176 N.E.2d 761 (Ill. 1961)

i.   Limits on *Gray* rationale: But *Gray* deals only with the proper interpretation of the Illinois *long-arm*, not with whether Illinois' exercise of jurisdiction over Titan was consistent with Titan's *constitutional right to due process*. Post-*Gray* decisions by the U.S. Supreme Court have established some tough rules about whether it's constitutional for a state court to exercise jurisdiction in a product-liability suit for injuries caused in that state by products made by out-of-state companies that don't regularly and intentionally sell their products into the forum state. These are discussed in detail *infra*, starting in Par. E on p. 28.

(1)   Mere use in forum state not sufficient: For instance, the Supreme Court has held the mere fact that a product made out of state has *found its way into the forum state, and has caused injury there*, is *not* constitutionally sufficient for the assertion of jurisdiction. See *World-Wide Volkswagen Corp. v. Woodson*, discussed *infra*, pp. 30-31.

(2)   Expectation of use in forum state: On the other hand, the Supreme Court has held that jurisdiction *is* permissible over a corporation that "delivers its products into the [interstate] stream of commerce with the *expectation that they will be purchased by consumers in the forum State.*" *World-Wide Volkswagen.*

Example: Suppose that D, the valve-making defendant in *Gray,* had taken out national ads in trade journals for boilermakers, without D's making any attempt to sell to Illinois-based boilermakers. (In fact, assume that there *are* no Illinois-based boilermakers.) Suppose also that D takes out these national ads with the hope and expectation that some non-Illinois boilermakers will incorporate D's valves into boilers, some of which boilers will then (D hopes and expects) be regularly sold by D's boilermaker customers to Illinois end-users.

Even such a minor and indirect "targeting" by D of the Illinois end-user market likely *would* suffice, constitutionally, for Illinois jurisdiction over D as to P's suit for a boiler explosion in Illinois. And that would be true even if D sold the particular valve that injured P to a *non-Illinois-based* boiler-maker, who without D's direct knowledge or approval sold the resulting boiler to an Illinois resident. Thus the specific result in *Gray* — that D, the non-Illinois maker of the valves, can be sued by someone injured in Illinois even though D didn't directly do business in Illinois — probably survives under modern due process cases like *World-Wide Volkswagen*.

G. Owners of in-state property: Some long-arm statutes allow states to exercise jurisdiction over *owners of in-state property* in causes of action arising from that property.

1.   Constitutional: These statutes are probably constitutional, since a person who chooses to own property in a state may reasonably anticipate that he will be required to defend a lawsuit in the state, at least where the suit relates to the property (i.e., what's being asserted is specific rather than general jurisdiction).

Example: D lives in New York, but owns a vacation home in Florida. P, a Florida resident, slips on the sidewalk in front of D's Florida property, and sues D in Florida for negligently maintaining the sidewalk. Even if D has no other contacts with the state of

Florida, it is almost certainly not a violation of due process for Florida to exercise jurisdiction over this case, since D voluntarily chose to own property in Florida, and should reasonably have anticipated that Florida might require him to defend lawsuits there that related to the property.

H. Conducting business: Some states have statutes allowing jurisdiction over non-residents who conduct *unincorporated businesses* within the state.

1. Constitutionality: It seems clear that such statutes are *constitutional*, i.e., that a state does not violate due process when it exercises jurisdiction over out-of-state individuals who do business within the state.

a. Limited to specific jurisdiction: Again, however, our statement that this type of unincorporated-business long-arm is constitutional assumes that the jurisdiction being exercised under the long-arm is *specific*, rather than general, jurisdiction. In other words, we're saying that the statute can constitutionally apply only to a suit *arising out of the non-resident unincorporated business' in-state business activities*.[2]

Example: D, an individual, resides in Kansas City, Kansas. D operates an unincorporated home-renovation business from an office in that city. He contracts to do a renovation project at the home of P, a resident of Kansas City, Missouri, just over the state line. P pays D an advance of $10,000 for work to be done under the contract. P then sues D in Missouri state court, alleging that D has violated the contract by keeping the deposit and not doing the work. Assume that a Missouri statute allows jurisdiction over an out-of-state unincorporated business.

This statute can be constitutionally applied to P's suit against D. But that's true *only* because the suit here is premised on specific jurisdiction, i.e., P's claim arises from D's voluntary business activities *in Missouri*. If the suit was about, say, D's negligent driving of a car in an accident occurring in Kansas having nothing to do with the P-D home-improvement contract, the fact that D also conducted unincorporated-business activities in Kansas would *not* suffice, constitutionally, for jurisdiction over D. (That's because *general* jurisdiction over a business exists only when the defendant is "at home" in the forum state — see footnote 2 above, and the discussion of the "at home" rule *infra*, p. 53.)

I. Modern statutory treatment (Illinois): For a good illustration of the types of activities that states typically try to reach with their long-arms, let's consider the *Illinois* long-arm statute.

1. Illinois long-arm: Under the Illinois long-arm, any person, whether a resident or not, submits himself to the jurisdiction of the Illinois courts for *any cause of action arising from any of the following acts*, among others:

[1] "The *transaction of any business* within this State."

[2] "The *commission of a tortious act* within this State."

---

2. For *general* jurisdiction to be constitutionally exercised under the long arm, the unincorporated business would have to be "at home" in the state, which would probably mean that all or nearly-all of its operations would need to occur in the forum state. See *infra*, p. 53, describing the "at home" requirement for general jurisdiction over a corporate defendant. The same requirement of being "at home" would presumably apply to a defendant that is an unincorporated business.

[3]   "The ***ownership, use, or possession*** of any real estate situated in this State."

[4]   "The ***making or performance of any contract or promise*** substantially connected with this State."

   a.   Means of service under Illinois statute: When jurisdiction is valid according to the Illinois long-arm, service may be made outside the state in person, and has the same effect as if it had been personally made within the state. Only ***personal*** (this presumably excludes mail) service seems to be contemplated by the statute.

   b.   Out-of-state torts with in-state consequences: the Illinois long-arm does not on its face seem to allow jurisdiction for ***out-of-state*** torts having ***in-state consequences.*** But the statute has been interpreted to reach these kinds of torts. Thus in *Gray v. American Radiator*, *supra*, p.17, where the court was interpreting the Illinois long-arm, the tortious act was held to have taken place ***where the injury occurred***, even though all physical motions by the defendant took place out of state.

J.   Foreign nationals: Some long-arm statutes exercise jurisdiction over non-resident individuals located in ***foreign countries***.

K.   Statutes going to limits of due process: Some states have enacted long-arm statutes that purport to extend jurisdiction ***as far as the due process clause*** of the 14th Amendment will allow.

> **Example:** The California long-arm provides that "A court of this state may exercise jurisdiction ***on any basis not inconsistent with the Constitution of this state or of the United States.***"

L.   Limits of "due process" undefined for suits against individuals: The Supreme Court has never squarely articulated a test for determining whether a state's exercise of personal jurisdiction over an out-of-state individual violates that person's right to ***constitutional due process.***

   1.   Rules for cases involving corporations: That's because all of the Supreme Court's modern-era jurisdiction cases evaluating defendants' right to due process have involved *corporations*, rather than individuals.[3] But these cases involving corporate defendants suggest that an individual defendant ***cannot constitutionally be subjected to a state's jurisdiction unless either:***

   [1]   General jurisdiction based on domicile: The defendant is ***domiciled in*** (or, perhaps, has a residence in) the forum state. And in that case, it's probably constitutional for even *general* jurisdiction to be exercised over her — i.e., even jurisdiction for a suit having nothing to do with the defendant's in-forum-state activities.

   or ...

   [2]   Specific jurisdiction based on minimum contacts: The suit relates to and arises out of the defendant's ***voluntary ties to the forum state*** (e.g., conduct that the defendant voluntarily took in the forum state, such as driving a car in the forum state). That is, the situation is one in which the defendant can be said to have ***"minimum contacts"***

---

3. See, e.g., the line of cases involving jurisdiction over out-of-state corporations who make or sell products that produce in-forum-state harm, *infra*, p. 28.

with the forum state.[4] And in this minimum-contacts situation, probably *only specific jurisdiction* — jurisdiction for a claim arising out of the voluntary in-state activities — would satisfy D's right to due process. [5]

III. JURISDICTION OVER CORPORATIONS

A. Issues covered: We turn now from considering personal jurisdiction over individuals to the topic of personal jurisdiction over *corporations*.

1. **Federal due process issue:** Our discussion of jurisdiction over corporations will consist mainly of one central constitutional issue: when does a state's exercise of personal jurisdiction over an out-of-state corporation *violate the corporation's due process rights*? Since the Supreme Court's 1945 decision in *International Shoe v. Washington* (discussed *infra*, p. 23), nearly all of the Supreme Court's significant opinions about personal jurisdiction have involved some aspect of this due process issue.

2. **U.S.-based versus foreign-based defendant:** As we consider a state's right to hear a suit brought against an out-of-state corporation, we'll be considering the rights of two different types of defendant corporations:

   [1] *"American"* corporations, i.e., corporations incorporated in, and headquartered in, some U.S. state other than the forum state; and

   [2] *"Foreign"* corporations, i.e., corporations incorporated in a foreign country.

   As we'll see, essentially the *same* principles of "fairness" are involved in the two situations — when is it fair, and thus consistent with due process, for the courts of a state to hear a suit against a corporation that is headquartered in, and organized under the law of, someplace other than the forum state? The factors that the Supreme Court considers *do not vary very much* depending on whether the out-of-state defendant corporation is headquartered in the U.S. or abroad.

3. **Specific versus general jurisdiction:** We'll also see that the distinction between *specific jurisdiction* and *general jurisdiction applies* to suits against corporations as it does in the context of suits against individuals. That is, it's much easier for a state to avoid a due process violation when hearing a suit against an out-of-state corporation if the suit arises out of the corporation's voluntary contacts with the forum state (*specific* jurisdiction) than if the suit has nothing to do with any voluntary ties the corporation may have with the forum state (*general* jurisdiction). (For a review of the distinction, see *supra*, p. 9.)

4. **State versus federal court:** Finally, in our discussion of suits against corporations, keep in mind the distinction between a suit brought in a *state* court, and one brought in *federal*

---

4. For the significance of a corporate defendant's "minimum contacts" with the forum state, see *International Shoe* and cases derived from it, discussed beginning *infra*, p. 23.

5. For an illustration of how a forum state probably cannot exercise general jurisdiction over an individual who is a non-forum-state-domiciliary, see the Example on p. 10 *supra*, involving an Arkansas court's lack of general jurisdiction in a suit brought by an Arkansas resident in Arkansas against a Texas resident for damages from a Texas car accident.

court. The majority of the cases we'll be looking at involve the right of a ***state*** judicial system to exercise jurisdiction against an out-of-state corporation. But occasionally, we'll encounter the issue of whether a ***federal*** court — especially one hearing a claim based on state law[6] — is permitted to hear the case even though the corporation is not incorporated in or headquartered in the state where the federal court sits.

   a. Limits on federal court's power to hear the case: Generally, as a matter of ***policy*** and federal ***statutory*** law — *not* constitutional due process — a federal court will only hear a suit against a corporation not based in the state where the federal court sits if the state courts of the state where the federal court suits would be not be violating the defendant corporation's due process rights by hearing the suit. (See *infra*, p. 68, for our treatment of the personal jurisdiction rules that apply to federal suits.)

B. Some general principles: Here are a few general principles about personal jurisdiction over corporate defendants:

1. Domestic corporations: Virtually all of our discussion of jurisdiction over corporations will involve defendants who are neither incorporated in, nor have a principal place of business in, the forum state. The reason for this concentration of discussion is that analysis of personal jurisdiction over ***"in-state"*** corporations is very ***simple***: there are ***no personal jurisdiction impediments*** to a plaintiff's right to bring a suit in the state against a ***"domestic"*** corporation, i.e. one that is incorporated in the forum state or that has its principal place of business in the forum state.

   Example: D Corp. is a service company that's incorporated in Delaware, and that has its principal place of business (i.e., its sole office) in Michigan. D's only customer is P, a wealthy individual living in Louisiana. All services performed by D are performed by D's sole employee, Prez, during trips to P's Louisiana home. P sues D in Delaware for tortious conduct that P says Prez committed in Louisiana while on the job for D.

   Since D chose to incorporate in Delaware, D's constitutional due process rights will not be violated by the Delaware court's hearing of the case (or by that court's rendition of a judgment against all of D's assets). That is, there's no due-process significance to the fact that: (1) P ***has no connection with the forum state*** (Delaware); (2) the claim arose entirely from ***events outside of the forum state***; and (3) D never conducted ***any voluntary activities*** (even ones unconnected to P's claim) having anything to do with the forum state, beyond choosing that state as D's state of incorporation. The same conclusion — jurisdiction over D is valid, with no due process problems — would be true if P sued D in *Michigan* (D's state of principal place of business) for the same Louisiana-based conduct by Prez.

2. Presence of corporate agent: Whereas an individual can be "tagged" by being served with process in a state where his presence is transient, the same ***cannot be done*** with a corporation whose presence is occasional and casual. Thus a corporate agent or employee who comes into the state only occasionally to conduct a small piece of business does not

___
6. As we'll learn, federal courts may generally hear even suits where the plaintiff's claim is based on state rather than federal law, at least where the suit is between citizens of different states (so-called diversity jurisdiction). See *infra*, p. 122.

thereby automatically render the corporation liable to service through him. The corporation must meet minimum standards of contact with a state beyond mere presence by an agent, before that state may exercise jurisdiction over it. These minimum contacts are described below.

> **Example:** Same facts as above example. Now, assume that Prez stops in Dallas Fort Worth Airport on his way to Louisiana to work on a job for P. P sues D by serving Prez at the airport, in a suit against D in the Texas state courts. Assume that D has had no other contacts with Texas. The fact that D's "agent" (and employee), Prez, was present in Texas at the moment of service will *not* suffice to give Texas jurisdiction over D in this suit — as a matter of D's federal constitutional due process rights, only "minimum contacts" by D with Texas (i.e., significant voluntary acts by D *"targeting"* the Texas market in some way) will suffice to give Texas jurisdiction over D. (By contrast, as we saw in *Burnham v. Superior Court, supra,* p. 12, if the suit were against Prez as an individual, Prez' *mere presence* in Texas at the moment of service *would* suffice to give Texas personal jurisdiction over him.)

3. **Cessation of in-state contacts:** Once an act or the systematic doing of in-state business has rendered a corporation subject to the state's jurisdiction — under the principles discussed below — the fact that the corporation has later *ceased to do business* within the state will not undo this "amenability to process." W&M, Vol. 4, p. 262.

C. **"Minimum contacts" as basis for jurisdiction (*Int'l Shoe*):** The case in which the Supreme Court first articulated its modern view of jurisdiction over foreign corporations was *International Shoe Co. v. Washington*, 326 U.S. 310 (1945). That's the case in which the Court first articulated its rule that for a state to exercise personal jurisdiction over a corporate defendant not based in the state, the defendant must be shown to have *"minimum contacts"* with the forum state.

1. **Facts of *International Shoe*:** In *International Shoe,* the state of Washington sought to collect unemployment taxes based on commissions paid by the International Shoe Company to the firm's Washington-based salesmen. The company's status with respect to Washington was as follows:

   a. **Incorporation:** The company was incorporated in Delaware, and its principal place of business was in Missouri.

   b. **Washington activities:** The firm conducted no business in Washington except for the activities of its Washington-based salesmen, who solicited orders for the firm.

   c. **Office:** The firm had no Washington office, but the salesmen sometimes rented display rooms in the state.

   d. **Salesmen's authority:** The salesmen had no authority to enter into contracts; all orders had to be approved by the home office.

   e. **Shipping:** All orders were shipped to Washington from the home office in Missouri.

   f. **Commissions:** Total commissions paid annually to the Washington salesmen were about $31,000.

2. **Holding:** On the basis of the above facts, the Supreme Court concluded that the state of Washington *could constitutionally exercise jurisdiction* over the Shoe Company.

   a. **Test:** The Court established a new test based on *minimum contacts* with the forum state: "Due process requires only that in order to subject a defendant to a judgment *in personam*, if he be not *present within the territory* of the forum, he have *certain minimum contacts with it* such that the maintenance of the suit *does not offend 'traditional notions of fair play and substantial justice'*."

   b. **Applicability to individuals:** *International Shoe* involved a *corporate defendant*, but the language used above, with its implicit rejection of the requirement that jurisdiction be limited by territoriality (the theory of *Pennoyer*) has always been assumed to be applicable to *individuals* as well.

   c. **Inconvenience:** The test of "fair play" may include "an *'estimate of the inconveniences'* which would result to the corporation from a trial away from its 'home' or principal place of business."

   d. **Claims not arising from in-state contacts:** While *Shoe* involved a cause of action arising from activities within the state of Washington (the unemployment taxes sought were based on the payments of commissions by the firm to its salesmen for work done in Washington) the Court left open the possibility that a firm might have sufficient contacts with the forum state to subject it to jurisdiction even on a cause of action *independent* of any in-state activities. (But later cases have established that a corporation may be subjected to suits not tied to its in-state activities *only* if the corporation is *"at home in"* the state, i.e., incorporated there or with its principal place of business there. See *Daimler AG v. Bauman, infra*, p. 56.)

3. **Black's concurrence:** A concurrence in *International Shoe* by Justice Black argued that a state has an *absolute Constitutional right to protect its own citizens* by allowing them to sue a corporation on *any claim arising from their in-state dealings with the firm*.

   a. **"Inconvenience" criterion rejected:** The concurrence strongly rejected the idea that the "inconvenience" to the corporation of being forced to defend away from home should be considered.

   b. **Black's rejection of "fair play" idea:** The concurrence also rejected the majority's decision to based its jurisdictional test on notions of "fair play" and "substantial justice"; "For application of this natural law concept … makes judges the supreme arbiters of the country's laws and practices … and means that tomorrow's judgment may strike down a State or Federal enactment on the ground that it does not conform to this Court's idea of natural justice."

4. **Still good law:** *International Shoe* is *still good law*. That is, its fundamental holding — that a state's federal constitutional authority to exercise *in personam* over an out-of-state corporation depends on the existence of "minimum contacts" between the corporation and the forum state — remains the law.

D. **The meaning of "minimum contacts":** A number of post-*International Shoe* decisions by the U.S. Supreme Court have helped define the types of contacts between the defendant and the forum state that will or won't suffice to constitute the *"minimum contacts"* required for a state to exercise personal jurisdiction over the defendant.

1. ***McGee:*** One of the earliest of these cases was ***McGee v. International Life Insurance Co.***, 335 U.S. 220 (1957). *McGee* was a California case involving an insurance policy written by a Texas-based insurance company on a California resident. The issue was whether the defendant, the Texas insurer, could be subjected to a suit brought in California to collect the policy proceeds.

   a. **Contacts with forum state:** The *contacts* between D (the insurance company) and the forum state (California) were as follows:

      i. **Assumption of obligation:** D assumed the insurance obligations of the deceased's previous insurer, and sent the deceased a reinsurance offer which he accepted.

      ii. **Mailing of premiums:** The deceased *mailed all premiums* to D *from California* until his death.

      iii. **California residents:** Both the deceased and the plaintiff (the beneficiary under the policy) were *California residents*.

      iv. **Witnesses:** D refused to pay the policy benefits, claiming that the deceased's death was a suicide; the *witnesses* to this death were all *residents of California.*

      v. **Offices and solicitation:** D had no offices in California, and had apparently never *solicited or done any business in the state*, apart from the policy in this case.

   b. **Holding:** Even though D's connections with California were slim, the U.S. Supreme Court held that these contacts were *sufficient* to allow jurisdiction there for P's suit.

      i. **State's right to protect its citizens:** The key point in *McGee* was that the Court found that California had a *strong interest* in *protecting its citizens*, by giving them a *local forum* to sue the out-of-state company with which they had dealings. As Justice Black wrote, "It is sufficient for purposes of due process that the suit was based on a *contract* which had *substantial connection* with [the forum state]. … It cannot be denied that California has a manifest interest in *providing effective means of redress for its citizens* when their insurers refuse to pay claims. These *residents would be at a severe disadvantage if they were forced to follow the insurance company to a distant state* in order to hold it legally accountable."

      ii. **Importance of** *McGee:* *McGee* probably represents the *least contact with the forum state* that has been approved by the Supreme Court as the basis for personal jurisdiction.

      iii. **Specific jurisdiction:** Note that the jurisdiction upheld in *McGee* was what we would today call *"specific"* jurisdiction — that is, the cause of action arose out of the defendant's *in-state* activities. In cases where the claim does *not* arise out of the defendant's in-forum-state activities (i.e., cases of *"general"* jurisdiction), *much closer ties* between the defendant and the forum state are required — only if the defendant is *"at home"* in the forum state (i.e., in the case of a corporation, incorporated or headquartered in the forum state) will general jurisdiction be allowed. See *Daimler v. Bauman, infra*, p. 56.

Example: Suppose that in *McGee*, the deceased and the beneficiary had been California residents at the time the deceased died, but that they had both been residents of Texas at all times before that (and that the policy being sued on had never had any connection with California).

In this scenario, the suit against D would have to be based on "general" (not "specific") jurisdiction, i.e., jurisdiction not arising out of the defendant's forum-state contacts. And since D was neither incorporated in or headquartered in California, *no matter how much business D had done in California* (i.e., no matter how great D's "contacts" with California were), California would be violating D's due process rights if the state were to force D to defend the action there.

2. ***Hanson v. Denckla:*** A case decided soon after *McGee* went the other way, finding that the defendant corporation's contacts with the forum state did not suffice for jurisdiction over the defendant. That case, ***Hanson v. Denckla***, 357 U.S. 235 (1958), involved the decisions of two states about the disposition of *funds from a trust.*

   a. **Ongoing significance:** The case remains an important one, because it stands for the still-valid proposition that only the defendant's *voluntary* contacts with the forum state — not forum-state contacts thrust on the defendant by other people's actions — will count in the minimum-contacts analyis.

   b. **Facts:** The general (and unfortunately complicated) facts of *Hanson* are as follows:

      i. A Mrs. Donner, while she was domiciled in Pennsylvania, created a trust, the trustee of which was a Delaware bank. The terms of the trust gave her a life estate in the trust, and gave her the power to dispose of the remainder of the trust either by will or by an instrument taking effect during her lifetime.

      ii. Ten years after making the trust, Mrs. Donner moved to Florida, and several years after that, assigned the remainder of the trust to her grandchildren in trust.

      iii. In her will, the remaining assets of the trust (assuming that her assignment of the trust assets to her grandchildren was invalid) passed to her two daughters, residents of Florida.

      iv. The daughters, claiming that the appointment of the remainder of the trust to the grandchildren was invalid, argued that the trust funds should pass to them through the will. They sued in Florida for a declaratory judgment to that effect; the Delaware trustee was notified by mail and in-state publication, as provided by Florida law.

      v. The Florida court, in a trial at which the Delaware trustee did not appear, found that the funds passed through the will to the daughters.

      vi. Meanwhile, the Delaware trust beneficiaries (the grandchildren) sued in Delaware for a declaratory judgment that the funds passed to them through the assignment Mrs. Donner had made, and not through the will. The daughters, although notified by mail, did not appear. The Delaware court found that the property passed to the grandchildren.

    vii. The two decisions, inconsistent with each other, were appealed to the Supreme Court. The two issues decided by the Court were: (1) Did Florida have jurisdiction over the Delaware trustee? and (2) If so, did Delaware err in refusing to give the Florida judgment full faith and credit?

c. Holding: The Supreme Court in *Hanson* found that the Florida court could ***not*** constitutionally exercise jurisdiction over the Delaware trustee, since the trustee's contacts with Florida were insufficient. The Court emphasized the following:

    i. The trustee bank had never done any other business in Florida.

    ii. The cause of action sued on could not be said to have arisen out of business done in Florida, since the trustee's obligation was created in Pennsylvania, and merely continued when the settlor of the trust, Mrs. Donner, moved to Florida.

d. Importance of *Hanson*: *Hanson* was the first major post-*International Shoe* case in which the Supreme Court ***invalidated*** asserted jurisdiction over a foreign corporation.

    i. Limits on state court personal jurisdiction: The Court noted that it would be a mistake to assume that the liberalized jurisdiction requirements of *International Shoe* heralded the demise of all restraints on the personal jurisdiction of state courts.

    ii. Nature of restraints on jurisdiction: Restrictions on jurisdiction "are more than a guaranty of immunity from inconvenient or distant litigation. They are a consequence of ***territorial limitations on the power of the respective states***. However minimal the burden of defending in a foreign tribunal, a defendant may not be called upon to do so unless he had had the 'minimum contacts' with that state that are a prerequisite to its exercise of power over him."

e. *Hanson* distinguished from *McGee*: The Court distinguished *Hanson* from *McGee* partly on the grounds that in *Hanson*, the contacts with the forum state were initiated by the settlor, not the defendant. "The ***unilateral activities*** of those who claim some relationship with a non-resident defendant cannot satisfy requirements of contact with the forum state. … It is essential that in each case there be ***some act by which the defendant purposely avails itself of the privilege of conducting activities within the forum State***, thus involving the benefit and protections of its laws."

    i. "Center of gravity" ignored: The Court noted that a state court "does ***not*** acquire … jurisdiction by being ***'the center of gravity'*** of the controversy, or the ***most convenient location*** for litigation." 357 U.S. at 254.

f. Full Faith and Credit issue: Since the Florida judgment was void for want of jurisdiction, the Delaware court was not bound to give it full faith and credit.

g. Black's dissent in *Hanson*: A dissent in *Hanson*, by Justice Black, stressed that Florida:

    i. was the home of all the principal contenders for the money;

  ii. was a reasonably convenient forum for all litigants; even the Delaware trustee had maintained correspondence voluntarily with Mrs. Donner for eight years after her move to Florida, and could therefore be subjected to suit there without fundamental unfairness;

  iii. had an interest in the trust funds, since Mrs. Donner's will was probated in that state.

 h. **Minimum contacts still required:** "The principal significance of *Hanson* is that the Court still insists on minimum ***voluntary*** contacts ***between the state and the non-resident defendant.*** It is not enough that the ***subject matter*** of the action has ample connection with the forum state; nor that the ***balance of convenience*** favors allowing the suit to proceed. James (1st Ed.), 643.

3. **Minimum contacts in domestic relations cases:** The minimum contacts rule has been applied in the ***domestic relations*** context. In ***Kulko v. Superior Court***, 436 U.S. 84 (1978), the Supreme Court held that a father residing in New York does not acquire "minimum contacts" with California merely by permitting his minor daughter to go there to live with her mother. The Court therefore refused to allow the mother to bring an *in personam* suit in California against the father for increased child support.

 a. **State interest:** The Court conceded that California had a strong interest in assuring the financial support of children residing in it. But this interest was adequately protected by the Uniform Reciprocal Enforcement of Support Act, in force in both California and New York, which would have allowed the wife to obtain a New York adjudication on the support issue, without requiring her to leave California.

  i. **Distinguished from *McGee*:** The Court therefore distinguished this case from *McGee*, *supra*, p. 25, where citizens of the forum state would have been severely disadvantaged by an inability to bring suit there against out-of-state insurers who refused to pay claims.

 b. **Divorce allowed:** But California's right to grant effect to a Haitian divorce was not questioned — this was adjudication of a status, which is considered to be *in rem* (*infra*, p. 77), and permissible where either spouse is domiciled.

E. **Suit based on products shipped into the forum state:** A lot of issues of personal jurisdiction have arisen in ***products liability*** suits in which the plaintiff claims that the out-of-state defendant corporation made or sold — from a location outside the forum state — a product that was later ***shipped into the forum state*** and caused personal injury to the plaintiff there. Often, these cases are brought in the courts of the plaintiff's home state, and the defendant has few or no contacts with that state apart from the fact that the plaintiff's injury occurred there.

1. **Suit asserts "specific jurisdiction":** Throughout the discussion of product-liability cases in Par. (E), we'll be assuming that the suit by the injured plaintiff asserts ***"specific jurisdiction"*** over the manufacturer. Remember (see *supra*, p. 9), "specific" jurisdiction means jurisdiction in a case relating to or arising out of the defendant's ***activities in the forum state.*** (The opposite of specific jurisdiction is "general" jurisdiction, i.e., jurisdiction in a case *not* relating to the defendant's in-state activities, a topic discussed *infra*, p. 51.) So for purposes of this discussion of products manufactured elsewhere that cause injuries inside the forum state, unless otherwise stated we'll be talking only about claims that the product in question *caused injury to the plaintiff in the forum state.*

2. **Long-arms allow:** An injured plaintiff's attempt to sue in his own home state based on specific jurisdiction is usually supported by the language of that state's *long-arm statute.* For instance, most long-arm statutes allow specific jurisdiction over an out-of-state corporation that *commits a tort within the forum state*, as long as the suit relates to the in-state tort. (See, e.g., the Illinois long-arm, discussed *supra*, p. 19.)

   a. **Out-of-state tort with in-state consequences:** In fact, long-arm provisions asserting jurisdiction over "in-state torts" are often drafted or interpreted to cover tortious conduct that occurs outside the state, but that produces *in-state injury.* (See, e.g., *Gray, supra*, p. 17.)

3. **Due process issues:** However, remember that no matter what circumstances the forum-state's long arm purports to cover, a state court may not constitutionally exercise personal jurisdiction over an out-of-state defendant unless doing so *would be consistent with the defendant's rights under the federal 14th Amendment due process clause.* (See *supra*, p. 9.) And where an out-of-state corporation makes or sells a product that eventually *finds its way* into the forum state and causes injury there, those facts alone will *not necessarily establish* enough contacts between the defendant and the forum state to make it consonant with due process for the defendant to be required to defend in the forum state.

4. **Several Supreme Court cases:** The Supreme Court's rules for determining the constitutionality a state's exercise of specific personal jurisdiction over an out-of-state defendant whose product has caused in-state tort injury continue to evolve, and form an important subject that we cover in this Par. (E).

   a. **Ambiguous results:** As we'll see, the case law on analyzing jurisdiction over product-liability suits for in-state injuries against out-of-state defendants is remarkably *ambiguous.* On some major points, the Court has unfortunately been hopelessly fragmented, so that there has been *no majority* agreeing to any useful rule.

      i. **Three cases:** There are three main modern-era Supreme Court cases — dating from 1980 (*Worldwide Volkswagen*, Par. 4, p. 30), 1987 (*Asahi Metal Industry*, Par. 5, p. 32) and 2011 (*J. McIntyre*, Par. 6, p. 34) — each of which we'll be exploring. Together, the three have left the rules on jurisdiction over out-of-state product manufacturers in a confused state.

   b. **Brief summary:** Here are a few things these three cases *do* allow us to say about when a state has personal jurisdiction over the out-of-state supplier on a claim that the supplier's product has caused an in-state injury to the plaintiff:

      [1] **"Targeting" of state required:** The mere fact that a product *finds its way into a state* and *causes injury there* is *not enough* to subject the out-of-state manufacturer or vendor to personal jurisdiction there. Instead, some conscious *effort by the defendant to market in the forum state* (i.e., to *"target"* that state), either directly or indirectly, is required. [*World-Wide Volkswagen, infra*, p. 30.]

      [2] **"Reasonableness" considered:** In at least some instances, even if D has "minimum contacts" with the forum state, D's connections with the state and with the

underlying controversy might be so *minor* that it is *"unreasonable and unfair"* — and thus violative of due process — to allow the state to hear the case. [*Asahi*, *infra*, p. 32]

[3] **Sales to U.S. as a whole:** Where D is a non-U.S.-baed corporation that takes steps to sell significant quantities of its products to *America as a whole* — but does not take any steps to *single out the forum state as a particular sales target* — the absence of efforts by D to target the forum state will likely be enough to *deprive* the forum state of specific jurisdiction, even though some sales volume occurs in the forum state. (This is the practical result of *J. McIntyre*, *infra*, p. 34, even though there was no majority opinion in that case.)

[4] **Use of distributor who "targets" the forum state:** Where an out-of-forum-state defendant manufacturer relies on a *distributor* to make any in-forum-state sales, it's not enough for jurisdiction over the manufacturer that the *distributor* decided to "target" the forum state. That is, the application of principle [3] above means that unless the *defendant manufacturer itself* takes intentional steps (or directs or encourages the distributor to take steps) targeted to the forum state, the distributor's *own* conscious efforts to serve the forum state — including the distributor's sale of the injury-producing product into the forum state — *won't suffice* for forum-state jurisdiction over the manufacturer. (Again, this result seems to follow from *J. McIntyre*, *infra*, p. 34.)

5. **Intentional effort to market in-state** *(World-Wide Volkswagen* case): The first of our three Supreme Court product-liability cases, ***World-Wide Volkswagen Corp. v. Woodson***, 444 U.S. 286 (1980), demonstrates that the mere fact that a product *finds its way into a state* and *causes injury there* is *not enough* to subject the out-of-state manufacturer or vendor to specific jurisdiction there. Instead, *World-Wide Volkswagen* holds, the defendant must have made some intentional *effort to market in the forum state*, either directly or indirectly, in order for personal jurisdiction over the defendant to meet the requirements of due process.

   a. **Facts of *Volkswagen:*** In *World-Wide Volkswagen*, the Ps sued in Oklahoma for injuries suffered there in an accident involving an allegedly-defective car they were driving. The Ps purchased the car *in New York* while they were New York residents. Some time later, the Ps were driving the car through Oklahoma when the accident occurred. The Ds were, *inter alia*, the distributor of the car (a non-Oklahoma resident who distributed only in New York, New Jersey and Connecticut) and the dealer (a non-Oklahoma resident whose showroom was in New York). Neither the distributor nor the dealer sold cars in Oklahoma or did any other business there.

   b. **Holding:** The Supreme Court held, by a 6-3 vote, that as a matter of due process, even though it may have been *foreseeable* to the distributor and dealer defendants that they would or might derive revenue from a car ultimately used in Oklahoma, this type of foreseeability was *not sufficient to confer jurisdiction* on the Oklahoma courts. The majority opinion by Justice White said that "the foreseeability that is critical to due process analysis is *not* the *mere likelihood that a product will find its way* into the forum State."

i. **"Anticipate being haled into court":** Rather, White said, the foreseeability that counted was this: were the defendant's "*conduct* and *connection with the forum state*" sufficient that he "should *reasonably anticipate being haled into court there.*"

ii. **Application of test:** Thus, White wrote, if either of the defendants had made *efforts "to serve directly or indirectly, the market for its products"* in Oklahoma, it would not be unreasonable for the Oklahoma courts to subject that defendant to Oklahoma's jurisdiction. But here, the use of the defendants' products in Oklahoma was merely an *"isolated occurrence,"* and was completely due to the *unilateral activity of the Ps.*

iii. **Ordered from forum state:** Under White's reasoning in *World-Wide*, one critical fact seems to have been that the Ps bought the car *in New York*, and were *New York residents* at the time they did so. If instead the Ps had *placed the order from Oklahoma*, and had asked the dealer to ship the car directly to them there, they would have had a better chance of subjecting at least the dealer to Oklahoma's jurisdiction, even if that were the only car the dealer shipped directly to the state.

   (1) **Other in-state acts:** Alternatively, if the Ds had *advertised* in Oklahoma, or had *shipped a significant number of cars* into the state, these forum-state-focused acts, too, would probably have been sufficient to confer jurisdiction in Oklahoma even for a suit involving a car delivered by the Ds in New York, at least as to an accident that took place in Oklahoma.[7]

c. **Dissent:** Three Justices dissented in *World-Wide Volkswagen*. One of them, Justice Brennan, noted that the car accident occurred in Oklahoma, the Ps were hospitalized there when they brought the suit, and essential witnesses and evidence were there. Also, he argued, Oklahoma had a legitimate interest in enforcing its laws designed to keep its highway system safe. Together, he said, these facts should have been enough to entitle the Oklahoma courts to assert specific jurisdiction over the defendants for Ps suit.

d. **Remains good law:** The main reasoning of *World-Wide Volkswagen* **remains good law** as of this writing (mid-2014). That is, the mere fact that it's *foreseeable* to the out-of-state defendant — or even *likely* — that one of the defendant's products will or may eventually find its way into the forum state and cause harm in that state is *not enough* to confer jurisdiction on the forum state for a suit involving the in-state harm. The defendant must instead have had sufficient *voluntary connections* with the forum state — most commonly, an intent to *"serve"* or *"target"* the in-forum-state market for that type of product — that the defendant "should reasonably *anticipate being haled into court*" in the forum state. So it's pretty clear that the result in *Volkswagen* — a finding of no jurisdiction over either defendant — would be the same today.

---

7. See the discussion of the implications of *J. McIntyre, infra,* p. 34, a more recent case that raises similar issues of a product sold by an out-of-state manufacturer who took no forum-state-focused acts, but whose product eventually caused in-forum-state injuries.

6. **Awareness of sales in foreign state (*Asahi*):** The second case in our Supreme Court product-liability trilogy of suits again involved, as *World-Wide Volkswagen* had, the issue of what type of contacts between a non-U.S.-based product manufacturer and the forum state would suffice for the state where the injury occurred to exercise specific jurisdiction over the manufacture. That case was ***Asahi Metal Industry Co. v. Superior Court***, 480 U.S. 102 (1987)

a. **"Stream of commerce" issue:** *Asahi* also posed an important additional issue, the effect of an ***intermediate seller*** — if the manufacturer sells to a ***wholesaler*** or ***components-assembler*** who then resells directly into the forum state, does the fact that the manufacturer released its products into the ***"stream of commerce"*** while knowing that some of the released products might be re-sold into the forum state suffice for specific jurisdiction over the manufacturer? As we'll see, the Supreme Court ***split 4-4 on this point***, but was unanimous in holding that the particular procedural facts of the case made jurisdiction over the defendant a violation of due process.

b. **Facts of *Asahi*:** In *Asahi*, Zurcher (the original plaintiff in the case) lost control of his motorcycle while riding in California, and was seriously injured. He brought a products liability suit in California state court against various parties connected with the cyle's distribution chain, claiming that the cycle's rear tire and and the tire's inner tube were defective. One of the co-defendants was Cheng Shin, the Taiwanese manufacturer of the tube. Cheng Shin in turn impleaded (see p. 399, *infra*) Asahi, the Japanese manufacturer of the tube's valve assembly. In the impleader suit, Chen Shin sought indemnity from Asahi for the full amount of any payment Chen Shin eventually made to Zurcher. Zurcher eventually settled all of his claims against the various defendants. By the time the case got to the Supreme Court, the only portion left was Cheng Shin's impleader suit against Asahi to be reimbursed for payments it had made to Zurcher.

c. **Contacts:** Asahi was purely a components seller, and never made any direct sales in California. Asahi had no offices or agents in California, and did not control the system of distribution that carried its products into the state. But Asahi apparently ***knew,*** prior to the accident, that Cheng Shin had been selling a lot of tubes in California that contained valves made by Asahi.

d. **Split decision:** All nine members of the Court concluded that California could not, consonant with due process, ***adjudicate*** Cheng Shin's indemnity claim against Asahi. But the Court was badly split as to the reason.

e. **Split on how to judge "minimum contacts":** *Asahi* is most important today for the way in which the Justices ***split 4-4*** on the proper ***test*** for determining whether an out-of-state manufacturer whose product causes an in-forum-state injury ***has minimum contacts*** with the forum state. The two contrasting views articulated in the case — one by O'Connor and the other by Brennan — remain highly relevant today, so it's worth taking a brief look at each view.

i. **O'Connor's "purposefully directed" view:** O'Connor believed that minimum contacts could only come about "by an action of the defendant ***purposefully directed toward the forum State***." And, she said, "[t]he placement of a product ***into the stream of commerce, without more,*** is ***not an act of the defendant pur-***

posefully directed toward the forum State." So O'Connor advocated a relatively-tough-to-satisfy *"purposefully directed"* standard.

(1) Application: Under O'Connor's "purposefully directed" standard, Asahi *did not have minimum contacts* with California. But, she said, Asahi *would* likely have satisfied the purposefully-directed standard had it been shown to have taken *any* of the following additional steps:

[1] It *designed* the valves with the *needs of the California market* in mind; *or*

[2] It *advertised* or *"solicited business"* in that state, *or*

[3] It established "channels for providing *regular advice to customers"* in the state, *or*

[4] It *controlled the distribution system* by which the company's valves found their way to California.

(2) Only 4 votes: Justice O'Connor's purposefully-directed test for the existence of minimum contacts (like her conclusion that Asahi didn't satisfy the test), was joined *only* by Rehnquist, Powell, and Scalia. So the test got only four votes, and thus never represented a view accepted "by the Supreme Court."

ii. **Brennan's "stream of commerce" test:** A different four Justices in *Asahi* (Brennan, joined by White, Marshall, and Blackmun), disagreed with O'Connor's minimum-contacts analysis.[8] Brennan *endorsed* the *"stream of commerce"* test that O'Connor had rejected.

(1) "Regular and anticipated flow" But Brennan defined "stream of commerce" somewhat differently than O'Connor did. The phrase "stream of commerce" should mean "the *regular and anticipated flow* of products from manufacture to distribution to retail sale." If the defendant was *aware* that its product was entering the so-defined stream of commerce into the forum state (i.e., that D knew there was a "regular and anticipated flow" of D's product into the forum state), then that awareness *was* enough to establish minimum contacts — and no "additional conduct" by the defendant needed to be shown.

(2) No surprise to D: Brennan based his view on the idea that the out-of-state defendant in this situation would *not be unfairly surprised* by having to defend in the state. "[A]s long as a participant in [the manufacturing-to-distribution-to-retail-sale] process is *aware* that the *final product is being marketed in the forum State*, the possibility of a lawsuit there *cannot come as a surprise*."

(3) Test satisfied: By Brennan's stream of commerce test, Asahi *had* minimum contacts with California, merely by virtue of Asahi's knowledge that tires incorporating Asahi's valves were regularly marketed in California.

---

8. The ninth Justice in *Asahi*, Stevens, did not take either side on this minimum-contacts issue; since all justices agreed that it would be unreasonable to make Asahi defend in California, Stevens thought it was unnecessary to decide whether Asahi had minimum contacts there.

    iii. Unfair to make Asahi defend: But Brennan — and indeed *every* member of the Court except Scalia — agreed that whether or not Asahi had "minimum contacts" with California, it would be ***"unreasonable and unfair,"*** and thus a violation of Asahi's due process rights, for California to *hear* the case against Asahi. These eight Justices believed that the unfairness stemmed from several factors:

        [1] the relatively ***large burden*** to Asahi of defending in a ***foreign legal system***;

        [2] the ***slenderness*** of California's and Cheng Shin's ***interests*** in having the indemnity claim heard ***in California*** (as opposed to somewhere more closely connected to the remaining parties); and

        [3] the strong federal and state interest in ***not creating foreign relations problems*** by deciding an indemnity claim between ***two foreign defendants***.

7. Sale by D's distributor into forum state (*McIntyre*): As we've just seen, *Asahi* resulted in a 4-4 split, and thus no majority opinion, on the key issue of what the out-of-state manufacturer had to ***know or intend*** in order to later be subjected to a suit for injuries incurred in-state from the product. As it has turned out,[9] the only post-*Asahi* case in which the Court has faced this issue ***again failed to produce a majority opinion*** about when specific jurisdiction over the out-of-state manufacturer will exist. That disappointing case is ***J. McIntyre Machinery, Ltd. v. Nicastro***, 131 S.Ct. 2780 (2011), which I'll refer to as *McIntyre*. Like *Asahi*, *McIntyre* resulted in a completely split Court — though with an unusual 4-2-3 alignment rather than the 4-4 alignment in *Asahi*.

    a. Facts of *McIntyre*: P (Nicastro) was using a metal-shearing machine manufactured by D ("J. McIntyre Machinery, Ltd."), at P's workplace in New Jersey, a scrap recycling company, when the machine accidentally severed four fingers of P's hand. P sued D in a product liability action in N.J. state court. The machine had been made by D in England, the country in which D was incorporated and had its only place of business. All sales by D into the U.S. market were made by a company that was based in Ohio (which we'll call "Distributor"), and that was owned and operated independently of D.

        i. Connections with U.S.: The two main Supreme Court opinions in *McIntyre* each emphasized a different set of facts about D's contacts with New Jersey and the U.S. For now, here's a summary of just those facts cited by Justice Kennedy's plurality opinion in deciding that New Jersey should not be deemed to have jurisdiction over D:[10]

            [1] Distributor was ***not under D's control***.

            [2] D's ***officials attended annual conventions for the scrap recycling industry***. At these conventions, D's officials appeared alongside Distributor's employees. The conventions occurred in various states, but ***never New Jersey***.

            [3] ***No more than four machines*** made by D ever ended up in New Jersey, and

---

9. As of this writing (mid-2014).

10. This set of four contacts are the sole facts on which the New Jersey Supreme Court had earlier relied in finding that it *had* jurisdiction over D.

it's possible that the machine that injured P was the *only* one that ended up there.

[4] When it was feasible to do so, Distributor *followed D's guidance* about how to *structure* Distributor's *U.S. advertising and sales efforts.*

b. **New Jersey exercises jurisdiction:** The New Jersey Supreme Court held that the New Jersey trial courts *had jurisdiction* over P's claim against D. The court relied essentially on Justice Brennan's "stream of commerce" theory from *Asahi* (*supra*, p. 33): since D knew or should have known that its products were being sold through a nationwide distribution system that might lead to product sales in any of the 50 states, it would not violate D's due process rights for it to be sued in New Jersey for injuries occurring there.

c. **Supreme Court rejects jurisdiction:** But six members of the U.S. Supreme Court concluded that, on the record presented, the New Jersey courts *could not constitutionally exercise jurisdiction over P's suit.* However, only a four-Justice *plurality* agreed on any one rationale; two other justices concurred just in the result, and three others dissented from both the result and the plurality's rationale.

d. **Plurality opinion rejects "stream of commerce" theory:** The plurality opinion was by Justice Kennedy, who was joined by Chief Justice Roberts and Justices Scalia and Thomas. Kennedy said that the New Jersey Court had been *wrong to rely on the "stream of commerce" rationale.* As a general rule, he said, "the exercise of judicial power is *not lawful* unless the defendant '*purposefully avails itself* of the privilege of conducting activities within the forum State' " (quoting *Hanson v. Denckla*, *supra*, p. 27). And "the so-called 'stream-of-commerce' doctrine *cannot displace*" this requirement of purposeful availment, Kennedy said.

   i. **"Seeking to serve" the state's market enough:** It's true, Kennedy said, that a defendant can be found to have purposely availed itself of the privilege of conducting business in the state even if the defendant *never entered the state*. Thus purposeful availment can occur "where manufacturers or distributors '*seek to serve' a given State's market.*" But a *desire to serve* the particular forum state's market — *not* the mere *foreseeability* that one's products will end up in the forum state — is *required for purposeful availment.*

   ii. **Intent to submit to sovereign's power:** Kennedy's analysis then relied on a concept — *"sovereignty"* — that had seldom been mentioned in the Court's previous jurisdiction cases. A forum's exercise of personal jurisdiction over an out-of-state defendant, he said, is an exercise of the forum's sovereignty. And when that exercise of jurisdiction is based on the defendant's products' entry into the state, the issue of whether the defendant "seeks to serve" the state means asking "whether the defendant's activities *manifest an intention to submit to the power of a sovereign.*"

   iii. **Test based on "targeting the forum":** But by what test should a court *determine* whether the defendant manifested the requisite intent to submit to the forum state's sovereign authority? Kennedy answered that a defendant submits to the forum state's sovereignty by transmitting goods into the state "only where the defendant can be said to have **targeted the forum**; as a general rule, it is **not** enough that the defendant might have **predicted** that its goods will reach the forum State."

Note: Kennedy's test based on whether the defendant "*targeted* the forum" sounds virtually indistinguishable from the "purposefully directed" test advocated by Justice O'Connor in her plurality opinion in *Asahi* (see *supra*, p. 32).

iv. **D did not target New Jersey:** Kennedy then concluded that P had **not carried his burden of proving** that D (the British company) had "targeted" New Jersey. That is, D had not established that D "**engaged in conduct purposefully directed at New Jersey.**" In Kennedy's view of the facts (a view limited to those factors relied on by the New Jersey Supreme Court in approving jurisdiction), D's *only* relevant contacts consisted of D's:

[1] engaging a U.S. distributor to sell D's machines throughout the United States;

[2] causing D's officials to attend nationally-oriented trade shows in several states but not New Jersey; and

[3] making sales through the distributor so that between one and four machines ended up in New Jersey.

These three facts might well reveal an intent by D to target the "*U.S.* market" as a whole. But they were not enough to show that D had targeted (i.e., "purposefully availed itself of") the *New Jersey* market in particular.

v. **Small domestic producers:** *McIntyre* involved a **foreign** manufacturer, who Kennedy asserted could not constitutionally be sued in a U.S. state that the company had not targeted. But Kennedy also argued that **small U.S.-based** manufacturers should receive similar constitutional protection from having to defend in a state they had not targeted.

(1) **Stream-of-commerce test criticized:** In fact, Kennedy's fear of the impact on small domestic manufacturers was a major part of the reason he rejected the stream-of-commerce test. Under that test (as advocated by Brennan in *Asahi, supra,* p. 33)*,* as long as a vendor could reasonably **foresee** that a significant number of its products would eventually be used in the forum state, the vendor would automatically be subject to jurisdiction there. But this test would, Kennedy said, produce **"undesirable consequences"** for small or locally-focused domestic producers.

Example: Kennedy gave this example of undesirable consequences: "the owner of a **small Florida farm** might **sell crops to a large nearby distributor.**" Under the foreseeability/stream-of-commerce test, the distributor's unilateral marketing choices could produce the **unfair result** that "the farmer could be **sued in Alaska** or any number of other States' courts **without ever leaving town.**"

e. **Concurrence:** Justice Breyer (joined by Alito), **concurred in the result only**, thus supplying the fifth and sixth votes to hold that New Jersey could not exercise jurisdiction over D. But Breyer **did not agree** with the plurality's **reasoning**, and joined the plurality's result only because he thought that the ***particular facts*** that the New Jersey court had relied on — which were the only ones he was willing to consider — were not enough to confer jurisdiction.

Note: Because Breyer disagreed with the reasoning of both the plurality and the dissent of Justice Ginsburg (discussed below), the Court was left ***without a majority supporting any single rationale*** that would apply beyond the narrow facts of *McIntyre* itself.

i. **Rejects plurality view:** Breyer declined to apply what he called the plurality's new "strict no-jurisdiction rule," a rule that would reject jurisdiction wherever the defendant did not "intend to submit to the power of [the] sovereign" and "cannot be said to have targeted the forum."

ii. **"Single isolated sale" plus "awareness" not enough:** Breyer thought that the case could and should be decided (against P) ***without making new law***. He said that the Court's prior opinions, taken together, had "strongly suggested that a ***single sale*** of a product in a State ***does not constitute an adequate basis*** for asserting jurisdiction over an out-of-state defendant, ***even if that defendant places his goods in the stream of commerce, fully aware (and hoping) that such a sale will take place***." ***"Something more"*** by the defendant is required for jurisdiction, he said, beyond the defendant's simply having placed its product into the nationwide stream of commerce with the awareness that the product might end up in the forum state.

   (1) **No "something more" proven by P:** And under the New Jersey's court's analysis of the facts, Breyer said, P had not proven any such "something more" — P had not for instance shown either that there was a ***"regular course"*** of sales in New Jersey, or that D had ***made any special New Jersey-related efforts*** (e.g., advertising or marketing related to the state). Therefore, the case could be decided against P without any need to make "broad pronouncements that refashion basic jurisdictional rules" (which he claimed the plurality was doing).

iii. **New Jersey's broad approach rejected:** But Breyer *also* indicated potential disagreement with what he called the ***"absolute approach"*** employed by the New Jersey Court. That court had held that a defendant producer can be made subject to jurisdiction for a product-liability action so long as the defendant ***"knows or reasonably should know*** that its products are ***distributed through a nationwide distribution system*** that *might* lead to those products being sold ***in any of the fifty states***."

   (1) **Broad approach rejected:** But Breyer was unhappy with this broad New Jersey approach, too, for several reasons. Most important, he worried that the approach would "***permit every State to assert jurisdiction*** in a products-liability suit against ***any domestic manufacturer who sells its products*** (made anywhere in the United States) ***to a national distributor***, no matter how large or ***small*** the manufacturer, no matter how ***distant*** the forum, and no matter how ***few the number of items*** that end up in the particular forum at issue."

(2) Illustration: Breyer gave an example of how the New Jersey stream-of-commerce approach might be *unfair to smaller and more-locally-focused producers*: "What might appear fair in the case of a *large manufacturer* which specifically seeks, or expects, an equal-sized distributor to sell its product in a distant State might seem *unfair* in the case of a *small manufacturer (say, an Appalachian potter)* who sells his product (cups and saucers) *exclusively to a large distributor,* who *resells a single item (a coffee mug)* to a buyer from a *distant State (Hawaii)."*

(3) Foreign manufacturers: Breyer was also worried about the impact that a New Jersey-type approach might have on smaller *foreign* manufacturers, who he said would be required to understand and evaluate a wide range of *state-specific tort-law risks:* such an approach "would require *every product manufacturer, large or small, selling to American distributors* to understand not only the *tort law of every State*, but also the wide variance in the *way courts within different States apply* that law."

iv. **Not ripe for decision:** Breyer made it clear that he was *not* saying that he would necessarily reject the New Jersey-style stream-of-commerce approach in a *suitable case* that involved *modern* international commercial practices. But the fact pattern in *McIntyre* itself did not *"implicate modern concerns."* And, he said, he didn't want to adopt the stream-of-commerce or any other new rule "without a better understanding of the *relevant contemporary commercial circumstances."*[11] Furthermore, he noted, the record relied on by the New Jersey court had left open many factual questions. Therefore, Breyer said, he was voting to "adhere strictly to our precedents and the *limited facts* found by the New Jersey Supreme Court." And those facts were not enough to establish New Jersey's right to exercise jurisdiction over D.

f. **Dissent:** Justice Ginsburg (joined by Sotomayor and Kagan) dissented in *McIntyre*. Ginsburg phrased the issue as whether it was "fair and reasonable" to "require [an] *international seller to defend at the place its products cause injury."* Her answer was an emphatic *"yes."*

i. **U.S. as "single market":** In contrast to the plurality, Ginsburg believed that a state's right to exercise specific jurisdiction over a foreign seller should be judged by reference to the seller's voluntary *contacts with the entire U.S.,* not just its contacts with the particular state where the seller's products caused injury. D (which Ginsburg referred to as "McIntyre UK") had *"dealt with the United States as a single market."* In doing so, D, like most foreign manufacturers, had been concerned "not with the prospect of suit in State X as opposed to State Y, but rather with its subjection to suit *anywhere in the United States*."

(1) Choice of distributor: Ginsburg then briefly discussed the significance of D's choice to do business in the United States through a *distributor* rather than

---

11. As I suggest below (p. 41, n. 13), perhaps Breyer was signaling that he wanted the Court to refrain from making changes to the law until a case presented itself involving modern techniques such as the *use of the Internet* in marketing or sales.

directly. This choice to use an intermediary *made no difference* to her analysis — when D chose "McIntyre America" as D's exclusive agent for promoting and selling D's machines in the U.S., D thereby " 'purposely availed itself' of the *United States market nationwide*, not a market in a single State or a discrete collection of States." Consequently, D should be deemed to have availed itself of the market of *each state in which the distributor sold any of D's products.*

(2) New Jersey as target market: Furthermore, Ginsburg noted, among the various U.S. states New Jersey was an *especially large potential market* for D's metal-shearing machines. She asked rhetorically, "How could McIntyre UK *not* have intended, by its actions targeting a national market, to sell products in the *fourth largest destination for imports among all States of the United States* and the *largest scrap metal market?*" So even if McIntyre UK might not properly be deemed to have targeted *every* U.S. state when it caused its distributor to market products nationally, McIntyre UK surely intended to address ("target") the large New Jersey market in particular.

ii. Summary: Ginsburg said she would apply the following rule: in cases involving "a local plaintiff injured by the activity of a manufacturer seeking to *exploit a multistate or global market*," jurisdiction is "appropriately exercised by courts of *the place where the product was sold and caused injury.*"

(1) Distinction based on D's focus: In answer to Justice Breyer's concern about the possible unfairness of forcing a *small locally-oriented U.S. manufacturer* to defend in a distant state based solely on the marketing decisions made by a distributor (see *supra*, p. 37), Ginsburg said that this issue could be addressed by assigning weight to the *size of the "stage on which the parties operate."* Ginsburg seemed to be saying that a given set of forum-state activities might simultaneously be sufficient to trigger jurisdiction when taken by a huge multinational serving a world-wide market, but not sufficient when taken by a small U.S.-based manufacturer serving mainly a local market.

8. Summary on out-of-state vendors: Following *Worldwide Volkswagen, Asahi* and *McIntyre,* the law is very unclear about when an out-of-state or foreign product seller should be required to defend a product liability suit brought in the state where the injury occurred. But here is an attempt to summarize some of the relevant principles:

a. "Purposeful availment" required: The mere fact that a product *finds its way* into a state and *causes injury there* is *not enough* to subject the out-of-state manufacturer or vendor to personal jurisdiction there. Instead, some conscious *effort to market in the forum state* (a/k/a a *"purposeful availment"* of the privilege of doing business in the forum state) is required.

i. Sold via distributor: However, the "purposeful availment" of the privilege of doing business in the forum state — i.e., "targeting" of the forum state — probably need *not* be done *directly* by the defendant. Instead, if the defendant *selects a distributor* — and intends that the distributor will *attempt to make meaningful sales in the forum state* — this probably suffices to trigger jurisdiction over the manufacturer. (At least the three dissenters in *McIntyre*, plus the two justices who concurred in the result there, seemed to agree with this analysis.)

ii. **An "extra" focus on the forum state's market:** Also, once the defendant is shown to have been merely **aware** that one of its products is likely to find its way into a particular state, even a relatively **small degree** of voluntary **"targeting"** by the defendant on that particular state market will probably be **enough** to show that the defendant has crossed the line from mere-awareness into "purposeful availment" of that state's market. Thus it likely won't take much more state-specific targeting than P proved in *McIntyre* to induce a majority of the present Court to agree that the state can exercise specific jurisdiction.

(1) **Breyer concurrence's "something more":**   Thus Justice Breyer's concurrence in *McIntyre* indicated that P had not fallen very short of showing enough targeting by D of the New Jersey market to convince Breyer (and presumably Alito, who signed the concurrence) that the New Jersey courts could exercise specific jurisdiction over the case. For instance, Breyer indicated, had P proved **"something more"** connecting D to New Jersey — such as "special **state-related design, advertising, advice** [or] **marketing**" by D — that "something more" would likely have been enough. So if P had merely "introduced [a] list of **potential New Jersey customers** who might, for example, have **regularly attended trade shows**," Breyer suggested, this might well have made a difference. Or, had P introduced evidence about the **large "size and scope of New Jersey's scrap-metal business,"** that, too, might have been enough "extra."

So five members of the *McIntyre* Court (the three dissenters plus Breyer and Alito concurring in result) would apparently have found that evidence illustrating even a **slight focus** by D on the New Jersey market in particular (as opposed to just a focus on the U.S. national market) would have been enough to change the outcome and entitle New Jersey to exercise jurisdiction.

Example: Suppose that in *McIntyre*, P (Nicastro) had shown not only the three facts cited by the New Jersey court (that U.K.-based D selected an exclusive American distributor — call it "Distrib" — with intent that Distrib pursue the overall American market; that the machine that injured P was sold by Distrib to a New Jersey-based customer; and that D's officials attended nationally-oriented trade shows located in states other than New Jersey), but also that D had approved and paid for design of an ad proposed by Distrib for marketing D's machines. Assume also that D knew and intended that Distrib would run this ad in *Garden State Recycling*, a monthly trade journal directed mainly at scrap-metal processors located in New Jersey.

It's likely that D's approval of this New Jersey-focused ad to be run by Distrib **would constitute enough "extra" focus by D** on the particular New Jersey market to justify the conclusion that D had consciously **"targeted"** New Jersey. If such a targeting was found, there would not have been any violation of due process for D to be sued by P in New Jersey for injuries caused to him in-state by D's machine. And that would likely be so even if the particular machine that injured P was *not* one the sale of which had anything to do with the ad.[12]

iii. **Internet advertising directed at in-state customers:** None of our trio of cases, culminating in *McIntyre*, seem to have involved any attempt by the out-of-state manufacturer/defendant to use the ***Internet*** to try to reach customers in the forum state. Where a manufacturer or other out-of-state seller ***maintains a website*** that the seller expects or hopes will be ***accessed by potential customers*** in the forum state, the maintenance of this website may by itself be the "something more" (beyond mere awareness of a few in-state sales) that would cause a majority of the Court to find jurisdiction.[13]

Example: Suppose that on top of all the other facts in *McIntyre*, D knew that its U.S. distributor ***maintained an Internet website*** that was being accessed with some frequency by potential New-Jersey-based customers for D's machines. Suppose further that, as D knew and approved, the distributor's website had a form to solicit the prospective customer's contact information, and that a drop-down box included "New Jersey" as one of the state choices for U.S.-based prospects.

In this scenario, there's a good chance that five members of the Court that decided *McIntyre* would say that the maintenance of this website, when coupled with the fact that a machine made by D and shipped by the distributor into New Jersey caused P's accident, sufficed to give New Jersey specific jurisdiction over P's suit.

Note: For more about the significance of the defendant's use of the Internet to reach forum-state customers, see *infra*, p. 43.

b. **Efforts as to U.S. as a whole:** Where D is a foreign corporation that takes steps to sell lots of units in ***America as a whole*** — but does ***not*** take any steps to ***single out the forum state as a particular sales target*** — the absence of efforts by D to target the forum state will likely be enough to ***deprive*** the forum state of specific jurisdiction, even though a meaningful sales volume occurs in the forum state.

Example: Recall that in *McIntyre*, D (the British company J. McIntyre) had made the decision to target the *entire U.S. market* — it did so by appointing an independent U.S.-based distributor, whom it encouraged to sell as many of D's machines as it could throughout the U.S. But P wasn't able to prove that D had ever "targeted" New Jersey, in the sense of taking any action directed at customers in the state. For a majority of the Court (the 4-justice plurality plus Breyer and Alito in concurrence), the fact that D

---

12. In other words, once a defendant makes a decision to "target" the forum state, in seems likely that the defendant can apparently be made to defend *any* suit arising out of an injury caused in-state by the defendant's defective product, whether or not the defendant had advance notice that the *particular item in question* would likely find its way into the state.

13. Recall (*supra*, p. 38) that Breyer, speaking for himself and Alito, said that before he would announce new rules, he would wait for a case that "implicate[s] modern concerns," so that the Court would be sure that it was considering "the relevant contemporary commercial circumstances." It seems likely that Breyer, writing in 2011, had in mind the desirability of waiting for a future case that would involve the defendant's use — or at least the defendant's *distributor's* use — of the Internet to market to potential customers in the forum state.

targeted the "entire U.S. market" *wasn't enough* to allow an *individual state* into which the distributor sold the injury-causing machine (New Jersey) to assert jurisdiction over D for a suit about that injury.

    i.   Suit in federal court: But if D targets the entire U.S. market (as in the prior example), a *different* majority of the *McIntyre* Court apparently believed that this fact *is* enough to allow a *federal* court located in a state where D's product causes injury to exercise jurisdiction without violating D's due process rights.[14] However, Congress would have to pass a statute (one that doesn't now exist) allowing such jurisdiction.

        Example: On the basic fact-pattern of *McIntyre*, assume that Congress has passed a statute purporting to give, to any federal district court located in any state where a foreign manufacturer sells a product that causes in-state injury, specific jurisdiction to hear a claim relating to that injury. Assume that D (still the British company J. McIntyre) decides to "target" the entire U.S. as a market (as the real D did), but does not target any particular state. D sells one machine to its U.S. distributor Distrib, who sells it to a New Jersey business customer, at whose workplace P is injured by the machine.

        The *federal district court* for New Jersey will constitutionally be able to exercise diversity jurisdiction (see *infra*, p. 122) over P's claim against D based on New Jersey substantive product-liability law. That's because a seven-member majority of the present Supreme Court (the *McIntyre* plurality plus the dissenters) would agree that D, by deciding to market actively in the "U.S.," a ***distinct sovereign power***, had voluntarily submitted to the jurisdiction of the U.S. federal courts for claims arising out of those U.S.-focused marketing activities. This would presumably be so even if D didn't know or authorize the particular sale by Distrib into New Jersey that gave rise to the suit.

   c.   Shipment of significant quantity of goods into the state: In the trio of *Worldwide Volkswagen, Asahi* and *McIntyre,* none involved a defendant who knowingly sent more than one or a very small number of items into the forum state. But where the defendant ***knows that a substantial number of items*** it manufactures are flowing into the forum state, that known flow will likely ***suffice*** for specific jurisdiction, even if the defendant has not consciously decided to focus on the particular market represented by that state.

---

14. In *McIntyre*, Kennedy's plurality opinion noted that under our federal system, the United States is a "distinct sovereign" apart from each of the states. Therefore, Kennedy said, in a given situation a defendant might be "***subject to the jurisdiction of the courts of the United States*** [i.e., federal courts] ***but not of any particular State.***" The three *McIntyre* dissenters would presumably join the four members of the plurality in agreement on this point. So if a foreign manufacturer ("D") decided to target the entire U.S. market, there would be a seven-vote majority agreeing that D had voluntarily submitted itself to the federal government's "sovereign" judicial authority for any claim arising out of a product sold by D anywhere in the U.S. In that event, a federal district court for State X could exercise specific jurisdiction over a federal-law or diversity claim based on injuries from a single product sold in State X (assuming that Congress passed a statute allowing such personal jurisdiction). The example following this footnote is an illustration of this point.

Example: Again, consider the scrap-metal-shearing machines in *McIntyre* manufactured by D (the British-based "J. McIntyre" corporation). The finding of no state jurisdiction by a majority of the Supreme Court was premised on the lack of evidence that any more than four of D's machines — and perhaps *only* the machine that injured P — ever found their way into the state. But suppose instead that P had been able to prove that every year D's distributor shipped a **constant, though small, flow** of D's products sold by D's distributor to New Jersey customers.

In that event, there would likely have been five votes on the Supreme Court in support of a holding that New Jersey *could* exercise jurisdiction. First, there would be the three dissenters, who believed that D's mere targeting of the entire U.S. national market, when coupled with the distributor's shipment into New Jersey of the machine that actually caused the accident, sufficed even without any additional New Jersey sales. These three would presumably have then been joined by Breyer (plus Alito, who joined Breyer's concurrence in result) — Breyer said that had P proved a *"regular flow"* or *"regular course"* of sales in New Jersey, this would have been enough to allow jurisdiction in New Jersey. And Breyer seemed to say that this result would follow even if D had never intentionally "targeted" the New Jersey market — mere **awareness** of a "regular flow" would apparently have been enough for him.

d. **"Unreasonable and unfair" to exercise jurisdiction:** Even if D *has* "minimum contacts" with the forum state, D's connection with the state might be *so minor* that it is *"unreasonable and unfair"* — and thus violative of due process — to allow the state to hear the case. That's especially likely if D is a truly *foreign* (non-U.S.-based) corporation with slender contacts to the forum state. [*Asahi, supra*, p. 34]

Example: Recall that in *Asahi*, the original injured plaintiff, as well as the maker of the allegedly-defective tire (the original defendant), had been dropped from the case, so that by the time the Supreme Court heard the case, only D and another component-maker, neither of whom had sold directly into the U.S., were left as parties battling each other over an indemnity claim.

It's clear that today's Supreme Court would reach the same conclusion as the Court reached in *Asahi* in 1987: even if the remaining third-party-defendant component maker *had* minimum contacts with the state, it would be unreasonable, and thus violative of due process, to require that defendant to defend the claim in the state.

F. **Establishing "minimum contacts" by use of an Internet Website:** Anyone with a computer and a little know-how can establish an *Internet Website* that people in any state across the country (and in fact anywhere around the world) can view. Does having a Website automatically qualify as a sufficient "minimum contact" with any state in which a user views the site? The short answer is, "no."

But a number of recent cases have grappled with just how **much** of a **connection** between the Website and the forum state (beyond the site's mere visibility from the forum state) should be required before minimum contacts are found to exist. In general, courts seem to be adopting a *"sliding scale"* approach — the more extensive the **interaction** between D's Website and persons located in the forum state, the more likely it is that D's Web-related activities will be found to constitute minimum contacts with the forum state.

1. **"Posting" cases:** On one end of the scale are Websites that are relatively *"passive."* These are sites that are used to merely *post information*, and not to conduct business transactions. By merely making information available to people in other states, the operator of a passive Website is *unlikely* to be found to have subjected himself to personal jurisdiction in every state where the site can be viewed.

   Example: Suppose D operates a local jazz cafe in a small town in Kansas. He puts up a Website with a schedule of upcoming events, and uses a trademark belonging to P on the site. P, based in New York, sues D in N.Y. federal court for trademark infringement. Even though a few New Yorkers may have accessed D's site, this won't be enough to constitute minimum contacts with N.Y., because D wasn't trying to attract business from N.Y. (i.e., wasn't "targeting" N.Y. customers).

2. **Conducting transactions over the Internet:** On the other end of the scale are Websites that have been established for the *primary reason of conducting business transactions with residents of other jurisdictions,* including residents of the forum state. Examples of these sites include traditional national "e-commerce" sites such as those of Amazon.com and ebay.com, where forum-state residents are encouraged to consummate commercial transactions on the company's Website.

   a. **Ongoing communications:** Even sites that *don't* encourage or allow the consummation of paid transactions over the site may fall within this "conducting business" category, if they allow forum-state residents to sign up to receive *repeated, ongoing communications* from the host company, and significant numbers of forum-staters do so.

   b. **Jurisdiction available:** In *either* of these scenarios — significant numbers of *paid transactions* by forum-state residents, or *ongoing communications* with significant numbers of forum-state residents — the court will almost certainly find that the host company *can* constitutionally be sued in the forum state in a special-jurisdiction case, on the theory that the host has *purposely availed itself of the opportunity* to do business in the forum state (i.e., has "targeted" the forum state for business opportunities).

3. **Cases in the middle, especially "interactive" sites:** The tough cases are the ones in the *"middle"* of the spectrum, those where there is some real *interaction* between forum-state users and the defendant via the Website, but no significant volume of commercial transactions, or ongoing communications, involving forum-state-based customers. For instance, perhaps the defendant has posted an 800 number on the site, and allows goods or services to be purchased over the site, but has sold just a few items to persons in the forum state. There is no easy way to predict how a case falling in this middle ground will be resolved.

   a. **Targeting:** An important issue is whether D has *"targeted"* residents of the forum state, i.e., *consciously attempted* to *promote a business relationship* with forum-state residents. If there was *no* targeting, the fact that D may have made a few isolated Web-based transactions with forum-staters who happened upon the site typically *won't* suffice.

4. **"Specific" vs "general" jurisdiction and the Internet:** The *only* situation in which the defendant's attempt to develop an Internet presence in the forum state can possibly matter is where the suit is based on *specific* rather than general jurisdiction.

   a. **Claim relates to D's in-state Internet activities (specific jurisdiction):** First, let's consider the *specific*-jurisdiction situation, i.e., the situation in which the plaintiff's claim *arises out of an in-forum-state transaction* that was facilitated by the defendant's intentional use of the Internet to reach in-forum-state plaintiffs.

      Example: Assume D operates a company (and Website) called "Comp-u-Save," which sells inexpensive software packages exclusively through the Internet. The company and its Web server are physically located in Virginia. D's website says, "Orders from all 50 states are welcomed." Fewer than three of D's customers in any year are located in California, and California customers represent only 2% of D's sales volume. One of those three California customers is P1, a California consumer who uses D's website to buy and pay for a license to a software package for $500, and who tells D via the website to ship the product to him at a California address P1 supplies. One month later, P1 sues D in an action in California state court, claiming that D has breached the implied warranty of merchantability because the software does not perform as a reasonable customer would expect it to. D claims that the California court cannot exercise personal jurisdiction over it because D lacks minimum contacts with the state, in view of its failure to target the California market.

      D will almost certainly *lose* with this jurisdiction defense — P1's claim will almost certainly be found to be within the California court's jurisdiction. That's because not only did D have purposeful contacts with the forum state (national ads that mentioned the products' availability in all states, plus D's knowing sale of an item to a California purchaser, P1), but also because the claim *arises out of D's in-state contacts* (the item knowingly shipped by D directly to a California resident). In other words, P1's suit asks California to exercise specific jurisdiction. And even under jurisdiction-restrictive cases like *World-Wide Volkswagen* (*supra*, p. 30) and *J. McIntyre v. Nicastro* (*supra*, p. 34), it's clear that a majority of the Supreme Court believes that the mere fact that D has "targeted" (even in a minor way) California customers will be enough for the state to take jurisdiction over a claim arising out of one of D's contacts with the state.[15]

   b. **General jurisdiction:** But now let's consider a suit brought against a defendant who uses the Internet to target customers in the forum state, but where the suit *does not arise out of any in-forum-state contacts* between that defendant and the forum state.

---

15. Recall that Justice Breyer, one of the two swing votes in *McIntyre*, showed a willingness in a proper case to impose specific jurisdiction over an out-of-state defendant who targets some customers in the forum state — according to Breyer, the problem for the plaintiff in *McIntyre* was that he didn't *show* any such targeting of the forum state by the defendant from use of the Internet or any other method (coupled with the fact that the sale of the machine in question into the forum state was made not by the foreign-based defendant manufacturer, but by an independent distributor). Thus Breyer indicated that a different result — i.e., a finding that specific jurisdiction *could* be exercised in the forum state — might well occur had the case involved "contemporary commercial circumstances," circumstances that would presumably include the defendant's use of the Internet to reach potential forum-state customers. See *supra*, p. 38.

That is, we're now considering the significance of the defendant's Internet use in a case involving ***general*** rather than specific jurisdiction. Here, unless the defendant is ***incorporated in or headquartered in*** the forum state, ***no amount*** of forum-state-targeted Internet activity (or for that matter in-forum-state sales) will be enough for the state to exercise for jurisdiction over the defendant.

Example: Same defendant, D, as in the prior example. That is, D again uses the name "Comp-u-Save," is located in Virginia, and sells and ships software packages from Virginia through the Internet to customers located throughout all states. In this example, too, assume that D's website says, "Orders from all 50 states are welcomed." Let's further assume that 35% of D's sales go directly to California customers, more than go to any other state. On the other hand, let's now assume that the relevant suit is brought against D by P2, a California company that owns the federal trademark for "Comp-u-Save" and that operates a business by that name from California. P2's suit, brought against D in California state court for violation of the federal trademark-protection statute,[16] claims that D's sales to *Virginia* customers (and only those Virginia sales) have interfered with P's ability to effectively use P's trademark in Virginia. D objects to the California court's exercise of jurisdiction over it, on grounds that such jurisdiction will violate D's due process rights.

Unlike the result in the prior example, this time *D will prevail* on the jurisdiction issue. That is, P2's suit here *won't* be found within the court's *in personam* jurisdiction. That's because the essence of P2's trademark claim ***does not relate to anything that occurred in California.*** Thus P2's suit has to fall within the California court's ***"general"*** jurisdiction, or can't be brought at all. And as we'll soon see, under the 2014 case of *Daimler AG v. Bauman*, 134 S.Ct. 746 (2014) (discussed *infra*, p. 56), general jurisdiction against a corporation may almost never be asserted in a state where the corporation is ***not "at home"*** (and a corporation is deemed "at home" only in the state where it is incorporated or has its principal place of business). Therefore, even though D does more business in California (and intentionally so) than ***in any other state***, P2 can't sue D there on P's non-forum-related claim, since D is neither incorporated in nor headquartered in the state.

G. Suits based on contractual relationship: What effect on jurisdictional analysis should result from the fact that the in-state plaintiff and the out-of-state defendant have a ***contractual*** relationship?

The fact that one party to a contract is a forum-state resident ***won't by itself be enough*** to confer specific jurisdiction over the other party in a dispute about the contract. But the fact that one party to the contract resides in the forum state, if ***coupled with*** contractual dealings that have some connection to the forum state (e.g., contract negotiations that take place there), *may* be enough in a particular situation to tip the balance in favor of letting the forum state have jurisdiction over the contractual dispute.

1. ***Burger King* case:** The principal Supreme Court case involving the significance of a contract's connections with the forum state is ***Burger King Corp. v. Rudzewicz***, 471 U.S. 462

---

16. For some types of suits alleging infringement of the federal trademark laws, the plaintiff has a choice between suing in federal or state court.

(1985). There, the Supreme Court held that the courts of Florida (and therefore, a federal district court sitting in Florida — see *infra*, p. 74) *could* constitutionally exercise jurisdiction over a Michigan-resident defendant who had signed a franchise contract with a Florida franchiser, even though the defendant operated the franchise in Michigan.

a. Facts: The contract allowed D, an individual residing in Michigan, to run a fast-food restaurant in Michigan under a franchise from P (Burger King Corp.), which had its headquarters in Florida. The lawsuit was brought by Burger King in order to terminate the franchise agreement and to collect payments alleged to be due under it. The franchise agreement provided that ***Florida law*** would control, but expressly stated that this choice of Florida law "does not require that all suits concerning this Agreement be filed in Florida."

   i. Contacts with state: D never traveled to Florida in connection with the contract or the restaurant (though his partner in the franchise went there once for a training session). D's face-to-face meetings with Burger King officials all involved people from the local Michigan office of Burger King, not from its Florida headquarters. However, there were some phone and mail negotiations between D and the Florida headquarters. Also, the contract required that all payments and notices be sent by D to the Florida office.

   ii. Long-arm: Service was made under a provision of the Florida long-arm statute allowing jurisdiction over one who "[b]reach[es] a contract in this state by failing to perform acts required by the contract to be performed in this state," so long as the cause of action arose from the alleged breach of contract.

b. D found subject to jurisdiction: The Supreme Court concluded that Florida *could* constitutionally entertain personal jurisdiction over D, at least as to a suit arising out of the contract.

   i. Designation of law: In upholding jurisdiction over D, the Court attached special importance to the contract's ***designation of Florida law*** as the controlling substantive law. The Court conceded that under *Hanson v. Denckla* (*supra*, p. 26), the state that is the "center of gravity" of the controversy (i.e., the state whose law will normally control for conflict of laws purposes) is ***not automatically*** entitled to jurisdiction. But, the *Burger King* Court said, the rule is somewhat different where the out-of-stater has ***signed a contract expressly designating the forum state's law as the controlling law.***

   (1) "Purposeful availment" standard: By signing a contract with such a provision, the out-of-stater has ***"purposely availed himself of the benefits*** and protections of [the forum state's] laws." The Court observed that this choice-of-law provision *by itself* would not be sufficient to confer jurisdiction. However, the provision was clearly a major factor in the Court's analysis.

   ii. Other factors: In addition to the mere existence of the contract, the Court said, other significant factors were "prior negotiations and contemplated future consequences, along with the terms of the contract and the parties' actual course of dealing" — all of these must be evaluated to determine "whether the defendant purposefully established minimum contacts within the forum."

iii. **No surprise:** The Court also asserted that D was *not unfairly surprised* by being required to defend in Florida against a suit having to do with the franchise relationship. Both the contractual provisions and the course of dealing should have *put D on notice* that the franchise relationship would be *supervised from Florida*, not from the local Michigan office — the Court implied that P's suit was merely an aspect of its supervision of the franchise relationship.

iv. **Fraud or bargaining advantage:** The Court took pains to point out that had D been able to show that the contract or particular terms in it were obtained through *"fraud, undue influence*, or *overweening bargaining power*," the contractual provisions would *not* have supplied the basis for jurisdiction. Here, however, D was an experienced accountant who spent five months negotiating the contract, and who was represented by counsel. Although Burger King may have had a bargaining advantage, its advantage was not so great as to constitute fraud or economic duress.

v. **Inconvenience:** The Court rejected D's plea that it would be materially *inconvenient* for him to have to defend the suit in Florida (e.g., that he would not be able to obtain witnesses as easily). D did not demonstrate which witnesses he was forced to do without, and in any event any inconvenience could have been relieved by a *change of venue* (see *infra*, p. 108.) Nor was it relevant that Burger King, with its great wealth and national operations, would have found it easier to litigate in Michigan than D found it to litigate in Florida — "absent compelling considerations … a defendant who has purposefully derived commercial benefit from his affiliations in a forum may not defeat jurisdiction simply because of his adversary's greater net wealth."

c. **Dissent:** Justice Stevens (joined by Justice White) dissented. Stevens stressed these points: (1) D's entire conduct of the business took place in Michigan, not Florida; (2) D's face-to-face dealings with Burger King's representatives, and even all or most of his telephone contacts with them, were with people who worked in D's Michigan, not Florida, office; (3) D had reason to believe that since the Michigan office was the office that negotiated and supervised the contract, any suit would be brought in Michigan, not Florida; and (4) there was a substantial inequality in bargaining power, which deprived D of the practical ability to get concessions in return for bearing the risk of having to defend a possible suit in Florida. All in all, the contract and the negotiations leading to it "left [D] bereft of reasonable notice and financially unprepared for the prospect of franchise litigation in Florida."

2. **Significance of case:** *Burger King* establishes several principles:

a. **Significance of contract:** The existence of a *contractual relationship*, one party to which *resides or has its headquarters in the forum state*, will go a significant distance towards establishing the out-of-state party's minimum contacts with the forum state (even though the existence of the contract will not be *dispositive* on the jurisdiction issue);

b. **Choice of law:** The presence in a contract of a *"choice of law"* provision making the forum state's law the law to be used in any lawsuit will carry *significant weight* in the analysis, since such a provision indicates that the out-of-stater has chosen to receive the benefits of the forum state's legal system;

c. **Payment stream:** The fact that the out-of-stater is required by contract to **send payments and reports into the forum state** will also be a significant factor.

d. **Limitations:** However, *Burger King* does **not** mean that just *any* franchiser will be able to sue its franchisee in the franchiser's home state. If the size of the contract claim is small (in contrast to the $228,000 judgment in *Burger King,* a relatively large number of 1987 dollars), if the contract terms are obtained through "fraud, undue influence, or overweening bargaining power," if the franchise is "primarily intrastate in character" or if the franchiser's decision-making structures are different (e.g., more authority is vested in the local office and less in the forum-state-based home office), there may not be jurisdiction. The underlying question is whether the franchisee should **"reasonably anticipate out-of-state litigation."**

H. **Class action plaintiffs:** The vast majority of the time, personal jurisdiction challenges involve *defendants*. There is, however, at least one context in which the issue of the jurisdiction over a **plaintiff** can arise: the **"class action."** The class action (discussed extensively beginning *infra*, p. 355) is a device by which the claims of many similarly-situated parties (usually plaintiffs) can be adjudicated in one proceeding. Not all of these plaintiffs will participate actively in the lawsuit: indeed, some will not even know that it is going on. Yet under federal class action rules, as well as the rules of most states, such an "absent" plaintiff may nonetheless be **bound** by the decision in the case — if the class loses the case, he loses his claim, and if the class wins, the case will determine the size of his award. What contacts, if any, must the "absent plaintiff" have with the state hearing the class action suit in order for the result to be binding upon him? In brief, the Supreme Court has decided that "minimum contacts" of the sort needed for personal jurisdiction over a defendant **need not exist** between the absent plaintiff and the forum state.

1. **Setting of the case:** The case raising this issue was **Phillips Petroleum Co. v. Shutts**, 472 U.S. 797 (1985). The plaintiff class was composed of all persons owning a royalty interest in certain oil and gas leases being exploited by the defendant, Phillips Petroleum. The claim was for interest alleged to be owed by Phillips to the class members on account of late royalty payments. Of the 28,000 members of the class, fewer than 1,000 lived in Kansas, in whose state courts the suit was brought. Only about 1/4 of 1% of the oil and gas leases involved in the suit were on Kansas land.

a. **Defense contention:** The defendant asserted that those members of the class who did not live in Kansas were not properly class members, since they did not have "minimum contacts" with Kansas, and thus could not constitutionally be bound by the decision. Phillips claimed to be worried that if it won, the absent plaintiffs would subsequently make an objection to jurisdiction and would end up not being bound by the result, whereas if Phillips lost, it would be bound, a "heads you win, tails I lose" result.

b. **Opt-out provision:** The Kansas class action rules, like those of most states and the federal system, required that all prospective members of the class be **notified** of the suit, and that they be given the opportunity to **"opt out"** of the class. Those who took advantage of this "opt-out" provision (over 10% of the potential members of the plaintiff class) were not bound by the results in the case, but could not take advantage of the favorable result either. Those to whom notice of the suit could not be delivered were also excluded from the class. But those who received notice and who **remained silent** were made members of the class. It was as to these silent, absent plaintiffs (or at least those who were not Kansas residents and who did not have minimum contacts of the sort that would be sufficient to make them defendants) that Phillips made its jurisdictional challenge.

2. **Result:** The Supreme Court **rejected** Phillips' jurisdictional argument. The Court conceded that these absent class members might, as a result of the suit, lose a constitutionally protected property interest (namely, their claim, or "chose in action"). But this **limited loss** was **far smaller** than the damage that virtually any defendant can suffer as a result of a judgment against him — there could be no monetary recovery against the absent class members, nor were such absent members required to do anything (in contrast to a defendant, who must ordinarily retain counsel and appear). Furthermore, the "opt-out" procedure gave each absentee the ability to escape even this limited impact.

3. **Standard:** However, the Court held in *Phillips*, there are some **safeguards** that must be **observed before absent members who remain silent can be deemed part of the class and thus bound**: the forum state must provide **"minimal procedural due process protection."** The protection must consist of the following elements:

   a. **Notice and opportunity to be heard:** The plaintiff must receive **notice** plus have an opportunity to be heard and participate in the litigation.

      i. **Type of notice:** The notice must be "the best practicable, 'reasonably calculated, under all the circumstances, to apprise interested parties of the pendency of the action …' " (quoting *Mullane v. Central Hanover Bank & Trust, infra*, p. 87).

   b. **Opt-out provision:** The absent plaintiff must be given the opportunity to **"opt out"** of the class by returning a form to the court.

      i. **No "opt-in" requirement:** It is **not** required that the class members affirmatively **"opt in."** Such a requirement would "probably impede the prosecution of those class actions involving an aggregation of small individual claims, where a large number of claims are required to make it economical to bring suit."

   c. **Adequate representation:** The named plaintiff(s) must **adequately represent** the interests of the absent class members.

I. **Plaintiff's lack of contacts:** The fact that the **plaintiff has no contacts** with the forum state will **not block** jurisdiction.

Example: P is a New York resident who has sued D (*Hustler* magazine) in New Hampshire only because that is the sole state where the suit would not be been barred by the statute of limitations. Plaintiff has had no contacts with New Hampshire at all, except for the fact that her reputation in that state (as in every other state) has been allegedly libeled. D claims that P's complete lack of connections with New Hampshire blocks the state from exercising jurisdiction over D.

Held, for P. "Plaintiff's residence in the forum state is not a separate requirement, and lack of residence will not defeat jurisdiction established on the basis of Defendant's contacts." *Keeton v. Hustler Magazine*, 465 U.S. 770 (1984).

IV. "GENERAL" JURISDICTION

A. Where we are now: So far, the vast majority of the cases we've covered involved "*specific* jurisdiction." That is, the claim against the defendant *arose out of the defendant's contacts with the forum state*.[17] But it's now time to take a look at *"general jurisdiction."* That is, we're going to look at the rules governing when personal jurisdiction may be exercised with respect to a claim that does *not* arise out of the defendant's contacts with the forum state.

1. **Tougher rules:** As you might expect, the Supreme Court has required *greater connections* between the defendant and the forum state when the claim does not have anything to do with the defendant's in-state contacts than where the claim arises out of the defendant's in-state contacts. In other words, the Court requires *much more extensive voluntary defendant-to-forum-state contacts* for *general jurisdiction* to exist than for specific jurisdiction.

   a. **Modern trend:** In fact, as the result of a pair of cases decided in 2011 and 2014, the Court has made the requirements for the exercise of general jurisdiction dramatically *tougher* than they had previously seemed to be:

      i. **Individuals:** Where the defendant is an *individual* (rather than an entity such as a corporation), general jurisdiction over her will exist if she is *"domiciled"* in the forum state. See *Goodyear Dunlop Tires Operations, S.A. v. Brown,* 131 S. Ct. 2846 (2011), discussed *infra,* p. 53 ("For an individual, the paradigm forum for the exercise of general jurisdiction is the individual's domicile"). In fact, it seems probable that for individuals, *nothing less* than domicile in the forum state will suffice for general jurisdiction over a person not served in within the state.

      ii. **Corporations:** Where the defendant is a *corporation*, the defendant must have such extensive contacts with the forum state that the defendant can be said to be *"essentially at home"* in that state. *Goodyear, supra.* And to be "essentially at home" in the forum state, the corporation must — except in exceptional cases — either:

         [1] be *incorporated* in the forum state, or

         [2] have its *principal place of business* in that state.

         Daimler AG v. Bauman, 134 S.Ct. 746 (2014), *infra*, p. 56.

B. The original "systematic and continuous" test: Prior to 2011, most lower courts believed that the *only* constitutional requirement for exercising general jurisdiction over an out-of-state corporation (i.e., a corporation not incorporated or headquartered in the forum state) was that the corporation's contacts with the forum state be *"continuous and systematic."*

---

17. *Pennoyer v. Neff, supra*, p. 11, and *Burnham v. Superior Court, supra*, p. 12, both allowing jurisdiction over the defendant on the basis of his *presence in the jurisdiction at the time of service*, are exceptions to my statement that we've concentrated on cases involving specific jurisdiction.

1. ***Perkins v. Benguet*:** This view that "continuous and systematic" contacts between the corporation and the forum state would suffice for general jurisdiction derived mainly from an older Supreme Court case, ***Perkins v. Benguet Consolidated Mining Co.***, 342 U.S. 437 (1952).

   a. **Facts:** In *Perkins*, D (the Benguet mining corporation) was officially based in the Philippines, where it operated gold and silver mines. But during the relevant time — World War II — the company suspended its Philippine operations because of the Japanese occupation, and the company president moved to Ohio. From Ohio, the president kept an office, maintained the company's files, and oversaw the company's activities. P, an Ohio resident, sued D in Ohio on a claim that neither arose in Ohio nor had anything to do with the company's in-Ohio activities.

   b. **Holding:** The Supreme Court held that the Ohio courts ***could constitutionally exercise general jurisdiction*** over D. The Court reasoned that even though D was not incorporated in Ohio, the president had been "carr[ying] on in Ohio a ***continuous and systematic supervision***" of the company's wartime activities. Therefore, the Court said, it did not violate D's constitutional due process rights for Ohio to exercise general jurisdiction over D (i.e., jurisdiction in a case not arising out of D's in-Ohio activities).

2. **Interpretation:** *Perkins* was widely ***interpreted*** by lower courts and commentators to mean that it was sufficient for general jurisdiction that the defendant corporation had ***"continuous and systematic" contacts*** with the forum state. But in the 60 years following *Perkins*, the Supreme Court never squarely said whether this was true. And during that period, no case occurred in which the Court actually found general jurisdiction to exist over a corporation not incorporated in or headquartered in the forum state — so the proposition that an out-of-state corporation's "continuous and systematic" forum-state contacts sufficed for general jurisdiction was never tested, even though widely believed.

   a. **Jurisdiction not found (*Helicopteros*):** In fact, in the only Supreme Court case decided during the 60 post-*Perkins* years that turned on whether the forum state had general jurisdiction, the Court found that there was no such jurisdiction. That case was ***Helicopteros Nacionales de Colombia, S.A. v. Hall***, 466 U.S. 408 (1984), a case in which the defendant corporation's forum-state contacts were found ***not*** to rise to the level of "continuous and systematic," a level the Court seemed to assume was the threshold for general jurisdiction.

      i. **Facts:** *Helicopteros* was a wrongful death action brought in Texas state court by the Ps, who were the estates of four U.S. citizens who died in a helicopter crash in Peru. D was a Colombian corporation that owned and operated the helicopter. D's contacts with Texas were, in the Supreme Court's words, limited to "sending its chief executive officer to Houston for a contract-negotiation session; accepting into its New York bank account checks drawn on a Houston bank; purchasing helicopters, equipment, and training services from [a Texas-based helicopter company] for substantial sums; and sending personnel to [Texas] for training."

         (1) **Contacts unrelated to the claim:** None of these contacts between D and Texas had anything to do with the accident in Peru that gave rise to the Ps'

claims — so if the Texas courts were to have jurisdiction over D, the jurisdiction would have to be "general," not "specific."

ii. No jurisdiction found: The Supreme Court found that D's connections with Texas were ***not sufficient*** to allow Texas to constitutionally exercise general jurisdiction over the corporation. The Court concluded that D's connections with Texas, even when aggregated, were ***not "the kind of continuous and systematic general business contacts the Court found to exist in Perkins."***

iii. Limited reach of *Helicopteros* decision: The particular defendants in *Helicopteros* were found to be beyond the court's general jurisdiction. But *Helicopteros* said nothing to reject *Perkins'* apparent conclusion that even a corporation that was neither incorporated in nor headquartered in the forum state might nonetheless have such extensive contacts with the state — such "systematic and continuous" contacts — that these contacts might suffice for general jurisdiction.

C. The new "at home in the state" requirement: But in a 2011 case, the Court announced a new rule that surprised most observers: unless the defendant corporation could fairly be said to be ***"at home in" the forum state***, the corporation ***cannot constitutionally be subjected to general jurisdiction*** in that state. The case was ***Goodyear Dunlop Tires Operations, S.A. v. Brown***, 131 S.Ct. 2846 (2011).

1. In-state "contacts" not enough: The *Goodyear* Court claimed that its "at home" rule was merely a ***"clarification"*** of what *Perkins* had meant by "continuous and systematic" ties with the forum state. But *Goodyear* made it clear that even ***extensive and voluntary contacts*** by the corporation with the forum state ***won't be enough*** for general jurisdiction if the corporation cannot be said to be "at home" in the state. (And as we'll see shortly below, a post-*Goodyear* case holds that the standard for whether a corporation is "at home" in a given state is ***very demanding***.)

2. Context: *Goodyear* — like *Helicopteros* before it — involved efforts by the families of U.S. citizens killed in a ***foreign accident*** to recover in tort in the ***victims' home state*** against a ***foreign corporation*** whose only ties with the forum state were unrelated to the accident.

3. Facts: The Ps in *Goodyear* were the parents of two young soccer player from North Carolina who were killed outside Paris when the bus carrying them overturned. The parents claimed that the accident was caused by tires defectively designed and manufactured by certain non-U.S. subsidiaries of Goodyear Tire (an Ohio corporation). The parents brought a wrongful death action not only against Goodyear Tire (i.e., the American-based "parent" corporation of these foreign subsidiaries)[18] but also against three of Goodyear Tire's foreign subsidiaries, ones based in and incorporated in Turkey, France and Luxembourg respectively.[19]

a. Subsidiaries' operations: The foreign subsidiaries manufactured tires for sale in Europe and Asia. The particular model of tire that blew out was manufactured by the Turkish subsidiary, and sold by it to customers in Europe.

i. No direct connection with the state: None of the three foreign Goodyear subsidiaries had any direct connection with North Carolina. They were not registered to do business in North Carolina, and didn't have any "place of business" in the state. Nor did they have any in-state employees or bank accounts, advertise their products in the state, or sell or ship tires to North Carolina customers.

    ii.   **Indirect sales:** However, a small percentage of all tires manufactured by the foreign subsidiaries (tens of *thousands* out of tens of *millions* manufactured between 2004 and 2007) were *distributed* within North Carolina by other Goodyear U.S.-based subsidiaries. But the type of tire involved in the accident (made, as noted, by Goodyear Turkey) was never distributed in North Carolina.

4. **"Stream of commerce" theory by lower court:** The North Carolina courts found that North Carolina *could* exercise general jurisdiction over the foreign subsidiaries. The highest North Carolina court to review the case on the merits — the North Carolina Court of Appeals — reasoned that these subsidiaries had intentionally *placed tires into "the stream of commerce"* while *knowing* that some of the tires might end up in North Carolina. Such a placement was enough, the North Carolina court held, to entitle North Carolina to exercise general jurisdiction over the foreign subsidiaries (i.e., jurisdiction even for a suit about an alleged defect and accident that had no connection to North Carolina).

5. **Supreme Court rejects general jurisdiction:** But the U.S. Supreme Court *unanimously rejected* the North Carolina court's stream-of-commerce rationale, and its holding that North Carolina could properly exercise general jurisdiction over Goodyear Tire and its foreign subsidiaries. Justice Ginsburg's opinion for the Court said that the North Carolina court's stream-of-commerce analysis had incorrectly *ignored* "the *essential difference* between *case-specific* and *all-purpose (general)* jurisdiction."

    a. **Prior cases involving in-forum-state sales:** Ginsburg agreed with the plaintiffs that, as the Supreme Court had held, "[f]low of a manufacturer's products into the forum ... may *bolster an affiliation germane to specific jurisdiction*." Thus she quoted *World-Wide Volkswagen* (*supra*, p. 30), for the proposition that when an in-forum-state sale "is not simply an isolated occurrence, but arises from the *efforts of the manufacturer or distributor* to *serve . . . the market for its product in [several] States*, it is *not*

---

18. The *parent* corporation, Ohio-based Goodyear Tire, did *not* contest North Carolina's general jurisdiction over itself, and it's not clear why. The parent may have believed either that (a) even if the parent was subjected to jurisdiction in North Carolina, it wouldn't be held liable for the conduct of a foreign subsidiary (i.e., confident that the "corporate veil" wouldn't be "pierced," so that liability would be limited to the assets of the foreign subsidiaries that had arguably committed the tort out of which the claim arose), or (b) there was no way it, the parent, could win on a claim that North Carolina couldn't exercise general jurisdiction over the parent. But if (b) is the correct explanation, post-*Goodyear* developments show that the decision-makers for the parent made a legal assessment now known to be incorrect: since the parent was neither incorporated in North Carolina nor had its principal place of business there, under the later case of *Daimler* the parent wasn't "at home" in North Carolina, and therefore *couldn't* have been subjected to general jurisdiction there. See *infra*, p. 56. In other words, Goodyear Tire (the parent) *needlessly conceded* that it could be subjected to general jurisdiction in North Carolina.

19. It's not clear why the Ps fought so hard to establish personal jurisdiction over these foreign subsidiaries. One possibility is that the Ps thought that if they could get a judgment in North Carolina against the foreign subsidiaries, they could sue for *enforcement* of the judgment in the foreign subsidiaries' home countries, or in any country where those subsidiaries had assets. (Many foreign countries allow a creditor holding a U.S. judgment against a company doing business in the U.S. to sue to enforce that judgment in the foreign country.)

unreasonable to subject it to suit in one of those States if its allegedly defective merchandise has *there* been the *source of injury* to its owner or to others[.]"

b. **Specific and general jurisdiction distinguished:** But, Ginsburg pointed out, *World-Wide Volkswagen*, and most other prior modern-era Supreme Court cases analyzing whether in-forum-state sales were enough to confer jurisdiction (e.g., *Helicopteros*, *supra*) had involved *specific* jurisdiction, i.e., jurisdiction over cases in which the cause of action arose from ties between the defendant and the forum state. The present case involved whether the forum state could exercise *general* jurisdiction. And, she said, the mere existence of voluntary contacts between the defendant and the forum state was *not* sufficient to establish *that* form of jurisdiction: "[T]ies [between the defendant and the forum state] serving to bolster the exercise of specific jurisdiction *do not warrant* a determination that, based on those ties, the forum has *general* jurisdiction over a defendant."

   i. ***Perkins* as classic case of general jurisdiction:** Ginsburg noted that *Perkins v. Benguet* (*supra*, p. 52) was "[t]he textbook case of general jurisdiction *appropriately exercised* over a foreign corporation that has not consented to suit in the forum." And she agreed that the Supreme Court had been correct to allow general jurisdiction over the corporate defendant on the particular facts of *Perkins*.

   ii. **"Continuous and systematic contacts" not enough:** But Ginsburg implicitly *rejected* the common interpretation of *Perkins* as having held that *"continuous and systematic"* contacts with the forum state sufficed for general jurisdiction. When she summarized the facts of *Perkins*, she portrayed Benguet Mining (the corporate defendant there) as having conducted virtually *all of its world-wide activities in the forum state*, Ohio: "To the extent that the [Benguet] company was conducting *any* business during and immediately after the Japanese occupation of the Philippines, it was doing so in Ohio: the corporation's president maintained his office there, kept the company files in that office, and supervised from the Ohio office 'the necessarily limited wartime activities of the company.' " So for Ginsburg, the availability of general jurisdiction in *Perkins* had turned *not* on the mere fact that the foreign corporation had conducted "continuous and systematic" activities in the forum state, but rather on the fact that virtually *everything* the corporation had voluntarily done *anywhere* during the relevant years (the World War II years) had been done in the forum state.

c. **The "at home" rule:** This analysis led to Ginsburg's formulation of the new, and surprisingly tight, requirement for the forum state's exercise of general jurisdiction: the *"at home"* rule. As she put it, "A court may assert general jurisdiction over foreign (*sister-state* or *foreign-country*) corporations to hear any and all claims against them when their affiliations with the State are *so 'continuous and systematic'* as to *render them essentially at home in the forum State*[.]"

   i. **Compared to individuals:** This "at home" rule, Ginsburg said, was the equivalent of the rule governing general jurisdiction over *individuals*: "For an individual, the *paradigm forum* for the exercise of general jurisdiction is the individual's *domicile*; for a corporation, it is *an equivalent place*, one in which the corporation is *fairly regarded as at home.*"

ii. **Goodyear's contacts not enough:** Ginsburg did not specify, in *Goodyear*, the precise test to be used for determining whether a corporation was "at home" in a particular state.[20] Instead, she simply concluded that Goodyear's non-U.S.-based subsidiaries at issue *"are in no sense at home* in North Carolina." She contrasted their "attenuated connections" to North Carolina[21] with the situation in *Perkins* (*supra*, p. 52), where the defendant corporation's "sole wartime business activity was conducted in [the forum state]." These attenuated connections, she said, "fall far *short* of *'the continuous and systematic general business contacts' "* necessary to empower North Carolina to entertain suit against the subsidiaries on claims unrelated to anything that connected them to that state.

D. **Meaning of "at home" (*Daimler v. Bauman*):** *Goodyear* shows that a corporation may be subjected to general jurisdiction by a state only if the corporation is "at home" in that state. So, what does it *mean* for a corporation to be "at home" in a particular state? A 2014 Supreme Court gives a surprisingly *restrictive* answer: except in an "exceptional case," the corporation *may not* be subjected to general jurisdiction in a state (the forum state) *unless the corporation either:*

[1] is *incorporated* in the forum state or;

[2] has its *principal place of business* in that state.

The case so holding is ***Daimler AG v. Bauman***, 134 S.Ct. 746 (2014).

1. **In-state contacts cannot suffice:** In other words, *Daimler* seems to mean that *no matter how much business* the defendant corporation *voluntarily does in a state*, that state *may not constitutionally hear* a case against the corporation arising out of a claim *unconnected* with those in-state activities, if the corporation is not incorporated in the forum state and doesn't have its principal place of business there.

2. **No American nexus for suit:** The facts cited by the plaintiffs in *Daimler* in support of their claim that a California federal court should have general jurisdiction over the multinational defendant were exceptionally *weak* for their position: not only did the plaintiffs' claim not even arguably relate to anyone's activities connected with *California*, the claim had nothing to do with any actions taken by the defendant or anyone else *anywhere in the United States* — the case alleged solely that a *foreign* (Argentinian) subsidiary of a huge foreign-based multinational (DaimlerChrysler of Germany) had long ago engaged in human-rights abuses in a foreign country (Argentina).

a. **The decision's surprisingly broad scope:** So the *result* in *Daimler,* that a California federal court did not have general jurisdiction over Daimler's non-California (but American) subsidiary, was not too surprising. But the Court's far-reaching *rationale* for that result *was* surprising.

---

20. As we'll see, soon after *Goodyear* the Court articulated such a test in *Daimler*, *infra*, p. 56.

21. Remember, all these subsidiaries did was to manufacture tires abroad, a very small percentage of which (*not* including the tire that caused the accident) indirectly reached the North Carolina market through the work of other Goodyear U.S. affiliates; see *supra*, p. 53.

3. **Facts:** To understand the Court's ruling and analysis in *Daimler*, you have to understand some details of the Daimler company's multinational corporate structure.

    a. **Daimler Corp.:** Daimler Corporation (which we'll call "Daimler" here, and which was the ***only named defendant*** in the case) is a large multinational company headquartered in Germany that makes and sells Mercedes Benz and Chrysler vehicles throughout the world. Daimler's American activities were and are carried out by "MBUSA," a separate wholly-owned American subsidiary of Daimler.

    b. **The plaintiffs and their claim:** The Ps were all ***Argentinian citizens*** (and residents) who sued Daimler in California federal district court. The Ps alleged that employees of Daimler's ***Argentinian*** subsidiary, MB Argentina, had collaborated with Argentina's military dictatorship to kidnap and torture the Ps and/or their relatives in Argentina during Argentina's "Dirty War" of the 1970s and 1980s. The Ps did not name MB Argentina as a defendant, probably because that corporation had no American contacts or assets — the only named defendant was Daimler, the German-based parent corporation.

    c. **No in-state contacts relating to claim:** The essence of Ps' claims was that when employees of MB Argentina collaborated with the Argentinian government, that collaboration violated various federal and California statutes and common-law tort principles, such as the federal Torture Victim Protection Act and California's tort rules against intentional infliction of emotional distress. But the only actions by any Daimler-related party that the complaint cited were ones that employees of MB Argentina allegedly took *in Argentina*. Since the Ps' claims didn't arise out of (or even relate to) any activities in California, the Ps had to rely on general jurisdiction, rather than specific jurisdiction.[22]

        i. **MBUSA's contacts:** Plus, the Ps had another problem: the only contacts that any part of the Daimler world-wide organization had with California were contacts between the Daimler-owned *MBUSA* (which was ***not named*** as a defendant) and California. And MBUSA was neither incorporated in California (but rather, in Delaware), nor had its principal place of business there (that was in New Jersey).

        (1) **MBUSA's California contacts:** But MBUSA *did* have fairly extensive ***contacts*** with California. MBUSA was by contractual agreement Daimler's ***exclusive U.S. importer and distributor*** of Mercedes-Benz cars. MBUSA bought the German-manufactured cars from Daimler, imported them into the U.S., and distributed them to various independent dealerships including quite a number of California ones. MBUSA was the largest supplier of luxury cars to the California market, and the state accounted for over 10% of all MBUSA's new-car sales (as well as 2.4% of Daimler's *worldwide* sales). Plus, MBUSA had several places of business in California (e.g., a regional sales office).

---

22. As we discuss more below, p. 75, in a federal-court action, the *state in which the federal court* sits must normally have and be willing to exercise personal jurisdiction over the defendant — it's not enough that *some* state in the U.S. could constitutionally exercise jurisdiction over the defendant. So the California federal district court would have personal jurisdiction over German-based Daimler (D) only if the state courts of California would also have jurisdiction over D.

(2) Significance: So it's clear that California had enough contacts with MBUSA that had the suit arisen out of *California-related events* (e.g., an accident occurring in California caused by a defect in a car sold by MBUSA to a California-based dealer), the California state courts — and thus by extension a California federal district court — would have had *specific* jurisdiction over the claim. The problem for the Ps, of course, was that the suit had nothing to do with any California activities by MBUSA or Daimler — so unless the case could be premised on *general* jurisdiction, it couldn't be brought in any California-based state or federal court at all.

ii. **Lower court finds D vicariously liable for MBUSA as agent:** A three-judge panel of the Ninth Circuit *agreed with the Ps' contention* that the California courts (state or federal) *could* constitutionally exercise general jurisdiction over Daimler, based on MBUSA's connections with California. In a split 2-1 decision, the Ninth Circuit relied on mainly on an *"agency"* theory in order to ascribe MBUSA's California connections to that company's parent, Daimler.

(1) **Agency theory:** MBUSA served as Daimler's agent in California for the performance of important services, such as all sales and marketing to in-state customers. Therefore, the Ninth Circuit reasoned, MBUSA's contacts with California should be *imputed* to Daimler. Since (the Ninth Circuit found), MBUSA had *"continuous and systematic"* contacts with California, and since such contacts had sufficed for general jurisdiction under cases like *Perkins*, Daimler, too, should be treated as having the continuous and systematic forum-state contacts sufficient for general jurisdiction.

4. **General jurisdiction rejected by the Supreme Court:** The Supreme Court unanimously *reversed* the Ninth Circuit's conclusion that the California courts could exercise general jurisdiction over Daimler. Most importantly, eight of the nine justices agreed that a corporation will ordinarily be deemed to be *"at home in"* — and thus amenable to general jurisdiction in — *only* a state that serves as the corporation's *"formal place of incorporation* or [its] *principal place of business*[.]" Justice Ginsburg wrote the Court's opinion, as she had done in *Goodyear*.

a. **Federal courts follow state law:** Ginsburg began by discussing what principles of personal jurisdiction the federal courts must follow. As Ginsburg noted, under the FRCP and long-standing federal practice, federal courts do not normally exercise personal jurisdiction beyond the personal-jurisdiction limits of the law of the *state where the court sits*.[23] So the first question for Ginsburg was, would the California *state* courts exercise personal jurisdiction over Daimler for the sorts of claims being raised here by the Ps?

i. **California goes to limits of due process:** As Ginsburg pointed out, California is among those states whose long-arm statute is expressly drafted to go to the *limits* of federal constitutional due process. (See Calif. Civ. Proc. Code §410.10.) There-

---

23. Thus FRCP 4(k)(1)(A) says that service of process establishes personal jurisdiction of a defendant "who is subject to the jurisdiction of a court of general jurisdiction in the state where the District Court is located." For more about federal-court rules on personal jurisdiction, see *infra*, p. 68.

fore, as long as the California courts' exercise of personal jurisdiction over Daimler would not violate federal constitutional due process, the California courts (and thus the federal district court) were empowered to exercise jurisdiction. In other words, the question of whether California's exercise of personal jurisdiction would or would not violate the U.S. Constitution's Due Process clause was the *only* issue effectively before the Supreme Court.

b. **General vs specific jurisdiction:** Ginsburg then gave a recap of her analysis from *Goodyear* on the distinction between specific and general jurisdiction. Most of the Court's modern personal-jurisdiction opinions, she said, had dealt with specific jurisdiction. For the rare cases involving general jurisdiction (like this one and *Goodyear*), *Goodyear* held that that form of jurisdiction requires forum-state affiliations ***"so 'continuous and systematic'*** as to render [the foreign corporation] ***essentially at home in the forum State."***

c. **"Agency" rule irrelevant:** This brought Ginsburg to the issue of what the effect should be of the fact that the non-U.S.-based Daimler had a ***subsidiary or other agent*** with extensive forum-state contacts. She noted that the Ninth Circuit had relied on an "***agency*** theory" to find that MBUSA's contacts with California should be attributed to Daimler, MBUSA's parent. But Ginsburg found it ***unnecessary*** for the Supreme Court to decide whether the Ninth Circuit's agency theory was proper, since not even MBUSA could be said to be "at home" in California.[24]

d. **Application of "at home" test:** Ginsburg then came to the core of her *Daimler* ruling, her new test for ***when a corporation should be deemed to be "at home" in a state.*** Only a ***"limited set of affiliations*** with a forum" will make a corporation "at home," she said. And the "paradigm bases" for being at home are the corporation's ***"place of incorporation*** and [its] ***principal place of business."*** She did not cite any previous cases for this proposition, only a 1988 law review article.

    i. **At least one guaranteed forum:** Ginsburg pointed out that as long as a corporation is deemed to be at home in its place-of-incorporation and its principal-place-of-business, this fact ***guarantees*** any plaintiff who wants to sue any corporation "recourse to ***at least one clear and certain forum*** in which [the] corporate defendant may be sued on ***any and all claims***."[25]

    ii. **Broader standard rejected as "grasping":** Ginsburg noted that *Goodyear* had not held that place-of-incorporation and principal-place-of-business are the *only* places that should be available for general jurisdiction. And the Ps in *Daimler* argued that general jurisdiction should be available in *any* state in which a corporation "engages in a substantial, continuous, and systematic course of business."

---

24. For more about how a company's use of an "agent" for in-forum-state tasks affects whether the forum state has jurisdiction over the principal, see *infra*, p. 61.

25. Although Ginsburg did not say so, her "recourse to at least one clear and certain forum" formulation is only true for a corporation that is either incorporated in, or has its principal place of business in, *some American state*. Where a corporate defendant is based ***abroad***, then if one ignores the issue of subsidiaries, there will probably be *no state* that meets either of these tests, even if the corporation voluntarily does a substantial amount of business in a particular American state.

But Ginsburg *disagreed*, saying that this formulation was *"unacceptably grasping."*

iii. **Possible "exceptional cases":** Ginsburg went on to say, in a footnote, that the court was *not "foreclos[ing] the possibility* that in an *exceptional case*, ... a corporation's operations in a forum other than its formal place of incorporation or principal place of business may be *so substantial and of such a nature as to render the corporation at home* in that State." And she cited *Perkins* (*supra*, p. 52) as an example (in fact, the *only* example she mentioned) of a case that would likely qualify as "exceptional," so that general jurisdiction could be exercised.

   (1) **Present case not "exceptional":**   But, she said, the Court did not even have to "explore" the issue of whether the present case involved one of these exceptional situations, because the facts did not even *"approach that level."* That was so because here, not even Daimler's American subsidiary (MBUSA) was incorporated in California or had its principal place of business there.

iv. **Slippery slope:** Ginsburg then made a "slippery slope" type of argument, of the form, "If we recognize general jurisdiction *here*, we'll have to allow it *everywhere*." She said that "[i]f Daimler's California activities sufficed to allow adjudication of this Argentina-rooted case in California ... the same global reach would presumably be available in *every other State in which MBUSA's sales are sizable."* Such an exercise of general jurisdiction would, she said, be *"exorbitant."*

   (1) **D's right to structure primary conduct:** Also, Ginsburg said, a rule allowing general jurisdiction wherever a corporate defendant had sizable sales would deprive such defendants of their due process right *"to structure their primary conduct with some minimum assurance* as to *where that conduct will and will not render them liable to suit"* (a right that the Court had recognized in *Burger King*, *supra*, p. 46).

v. **"Nationwide and worldwide" contacts considered:** Ginsburg conceded, in another footnote, that the Court's "at home" requirement for general jurisdiction would now require trial courts to consider an *additional aspect* of a defendant's activities. Now, in cases raising the issue of general jurisdiction over a large company, the trial court would have to take into account not only the magnitude of the defendant's *in-state contacts*, but also "[the] corporation's activities in *their entirety, nationwide and worldwide."* This is so, she said, because "[a] corporation that *operates in many places can scarcely be deemed at home in all of them.* Otherwise, 'at home' would be synonymous with *'doing business' tests* framed before specific jurisdiction evolved in the United States."

vi. **"International comity" aspect:** Finally, Ginsburg wrote, allowing a state to exercise jurisdiction over claims having nothing to do with the U.S. — like the claims here — *might damage America's relationships with other countries.*

   (1) **Other countries:** She noted that some other nations — all members of the European Union, for example — allow suit against a corporation to be brought *only* where the corporation is "domiciled" (essentially the same place-of-

incorporation-or-principal-place-of-business rule that was being adopted in *Daimler*).

> **(2) Reciprocity in danger:** Therefore, she said, if the U.S. allowed non-U.S. corporations to be sued in all states where the corporation did a sizeable amount of business, other countries might not be willing to sign agreements with the U.S. (and desired by the U.S.) providing for ***reciprocal enforcement of judgments.*** Furthermore, foreign companies' willingness to ***open and invest in U.S.-based subsidiaries*** might be ***impaired***, if doing so would expose the foreign parent to suit in any American state where the subsidiary were to do business.

5. **Sotomayor's concurrence:** The only justice who did not join Ginsburg's opinion was Sotomayor, who concurred in the result but not the rationale. Sotomayor agreed that on the particular facts here, Daimler's due process rights would be violated if the company were subjected to general jurisdiction in California.

   a. **Would keep "continuous and systematic contacts" test:** But Sotomayor rejected the majority's core ruling that an out-of-state corporation — one neither incorporated in nor with its principal place of business in the forum state — cannot be subjected to general jurisdiction no matter how extensive the corporation's forum-state contacts. Sotomayor would have ***maintained*** the standard that pre-*Goodyear* and pre-*Daimler* cases seemed to use: that general jurisdiction is allowable wherever the defendant has such ***continuous and substantial contacts*** with the forum state that it would not be unfair to require the defendant to answer suits there, even suits having nothing to do with the in-state contacts.

   b. **Look only at D's in-state contacts:** Sotomayor argued that pre-*Goodyear* cases had allowed general jurisdiction based on the strength of the defendant's "continuous and systematic general business contacts" with the forum state (quoting *Helicopteros, supra*, p. 52). And when the Court had applied this test, she said, it had "focused solely on the ***magnitude of the defendant's in-state contacts***, not the ***relative magnitude*** of those contacts in ***comparison to the defendant's contacts with other States.***" This "continuous and systematic contacts" test had been "taught to generations of first-year law students," and, Sotomayor said, the majority was wrong to reject it for being (in the majority's terms) "unacceptably grasping[.]"

E. **Use of agents by out-of-state defendant:** Sometimes an out-of-state company does not directly conduct activities within the forum state, but instead uses another company as its ***agent*** to pursue business relating to that state. When that happens, the issue becomes: can the ***agent's contacts*** with the forum state be ***treated as if they were the contacts of the "principal,"*** for purposes of deciding whether the forum state can exercise jurisdiction over the principal? The Supreme Court has never squarely addressed this question.

1. **Use of corporate subsidiary:** The way the agency issue arises most often is where a ***"parent"*** corporation does not itself conduct business activities directed at the forum state, but the parent's wholly- or partly-owned ***subsidiary*** does do business in (or targeted at) the forum state. So the question becomes, ***can the subsidiary's forum-state contacts be ascribed to the parent?*** Again, the Supreme Court has never given a direct answer.

2. **Two-prong test for attributing subsidiary's contacts to parent:**   A number of *lower* courts have applied a ***two-pronged test*** to deal with this parent-subsidiary[26] issue. Under this two-pronged approach, the subsidiary's forum-state contacts ***can be attributed to the parent*** if *either* of two prongs is satisfied: (1) the *"alter ego"* prong; and (2) the *"agency"* prong.

    [1] **"Alter ego" prong:** The first prong, typically the less-often satisfied one, is the *"alter ego"* test: if the parent has ***such complete control*** of the subsidiary that the subsidiary is properly viewed as the *"mere instrumentality"* of the parent, the subsidiary's forum-state contacts will be attributed to the parent.

    [2] **"Agency" prong:** The second prong — typically a somewhat easier test for the plaintiff seeking jurisdiction over the defendant parent to satisfy — is the *"agency"* prong. As one court has put it, the agency prong is satisfied where "the subsidiary ***functions as the parent corporation's representative*** in that it ***performs services that are sufficiently important*** to the foreign corporation that ***if it did not have a representative to perform them***, the corporation's ***own officials*** would ***undertake to perform substantially similar services.***" *Bauman v. DaimlerChrysler Corp.*, 644 F.3d 909 (9th Cir. 2010) (rev'd on other grounds in *Daimler AG v. Bauman*, at 134 S.Ct. 746).

    a. **Supreme Court view unknown:** The U.S. Supreme Court has never decided whether either or both of these prongs should be enough for a conclusion that the subsidiary's forum-state contacts should be attributable to the parent. But we can make some guesses based on things the Court has said.

        i.   **Alter ego test:** As to the *"alter ego"* prong: it seems *likely* that the Supreme Court will ultimately *agree* that this prong is an *appropriate* standard for attributing the subsidiary's contacts to the parent. If the parent really ***controls all actions of the subsidiary*** (as the alter ego test requires), there doesn't seem to be much unfairness in requiring the parent to defend an action in a state where the subsidiary has minimum contacts.[27]

        ii. **Agency test:** As to the *"agency"* prong, the ultimate validity of this prong — at least as articulated in the Ninth Circuit *Bauman* decision quoted above — is *less likely.* In the Supreme Court's opinion in *Daimler AG v. Bauman* (*supra*, p. 56) reversing the Ninth Circuit's *Bauman* decision on other grounds, Justice Ginsburg *disapproved* of the Ninth Circuit's view on agency.

            (1) **Ginsburg's criticism of agency test:** Ginsburg noted that the Ninth Circuit in *Bauman* had found general jurisdiction over the parent (Daimler) based "primarily on its observation that [subsidiary] MBUSA's services were '*import-*

---

26. In the discussion that follows, I refer to the "parent-subsidiary" issue. But by this phrase, I also mean to incorporate other types of agency relationships, such as that between a manufacturer and an independently-owned ***distributor*** that is acting on the manufacturer's behalf. It seems likely that whatever rule for attributing a subsidiary's action to the parent is eventually adopted by the Supreme Court, a similar rule will apply in non-subsidiary agency situations.

27. This statement assumes that the suit is based on *specific* jurisdiction, i.e., on a claim that arises out of the subsidiary's forum-state-related activities. For more about possible differences in analyzing the agency issue as between cases of specific jurisdiction and general jurisdiction, see *infra*, p. 64.

ant' to Daimler, as gauged by Daimler's hypothetical *readiness to perform those services itself* if MBUSA did not exist." But, Ginsburg said, "[f]ormulated this way, the inquiry into importance *stacks the deck*, for it will *always* yield a *pro-jurisdiction* answer." She continued, "[t]he Ninth Circuit's agency theory thus appears to *subject foreign corporations to general jurisdiction whenever they have an in-state subsidiary or affiliate*, an outcome that would *sweep beyond* even the 'sprawling view of general jurisdiction' we [previously] rejected in *Goodyear*."

Although Ginsburg's remark is dictum — not required to reach the outcome — it's quite clear that she herself would *not* regard satisfaction of the Ninth Circuit's "agency" standard as sufficient for jurisdiction, at least in cases involving general jurisdiction (which was the type of case at issue in *Daimler*). (For more about the general/specific distinction, see the discussion that follows shortly below, p. 64.)

(2) Consequence: Seven of the eight other members of the Court *joined* Justice Ginsburg's opinion in *Daimler*. So presumably eight members of the *Daimler* Court would agree that the "agency" test, as articulated by the Ninth Circuit in *Bauman*, is an *inappropriately-easy standard* for deciding that a subsidiary's contacts with the state should be attributed to the parent, at least in cases involving general jurisdiction.

Example: Consider the following version (customized for our present analysis) of the facts of *Daimler v. Bauman, supra*, p. 56: Daimler is a corporation incorporated in, and headquartered in, Germany. All cars made by Daimler are made in Germany. By long-standing contract, all U.S. sales and marketing of any cars made by Daimler is carried out by a corporation called MBUSA, incorporated in Delaware and with a principal place of business (i.e., headquarters) in New Jersey. Assume for this example (contrary to fact) that MBUSA is owned by a private investor who has no direct connection with Daimler. Daimler lets MBUSA make all decisions about whether (and how) to market Daimler's cars throughout the U.S. P, a California resident, is injured in California while riding as a passenger in a German-made Daimler car, sold by MBUSA to a California dealer, who then re-sold the car to the California consumer who was driving it at the time of P's accident. P believes that the accident resulted from a defect in the car's design. P, reasoning that MBUSA has few assets, sues only Daimler in New Jersey state court, asserting that New Jersey may exercise general jurisdiction. To support this argument, P contends that since MBUSA performs major functions for Daimler that Daimler would otherwise have to perform itself (i.e., all U.S.-based sales and marketing of Daimler's products), all of MBUSA's ties to New Jersey (including MBUSA's choice of New Jersey as its headquarters state) should be imputed to Daimler, thereby justifying New Jersey's exercise of general jurisdiction over Daimler.

There's a good chance that the Supreme Court would *refuse* to use the Ninth Circuit agency test to impute MBUSA's New Jersey ties to Daimler — and in the event of such a refusal, P would *not* be able to proceed with suit against Daimler there. Under the Ninth Circuit's version of the agency test, the fact that MBUSA performed for Daimler tasks (all U.S. sales and marketing) "so important" to Daimler that if MBUSA didn't exist, Daimler would perform those tasks itself, would be enough to make MBUSA's New Jersey contacts attributable to Daimler. But most of the Supreme Court would probably agree with Justice Ginsburg's dictum in *Daimler* that at least in general-jurisdiction cases, the agency test is much too pro-jurisdiction; in that event, the Court would refuse to use the test to impute MBUSA's New Jersey connections to Daimler.

If the Supreme Court refused to apply the agency test, the Court would then conclude that the fact that *MBUSA* is "at home" in New Jersey (i.e., has its principal place of business there) is **irrelevant** to whether *Daimler* is "at home" in New Jersey. Then, since Daimler would itself be neither incorporated in, nor with a principal place of business in, New Jersey, New Jersey wouldn't have general jurisdiction over Daimler.[28] (As to a suit based on specific jurisdiction on these facts, see the Example shortly below.)

3. **General vs. specific jurisdiction:** Notice that our present discussion of whether the subsidiary's forum-state connections should be attributed to the parent is part of our discussion of *general* jurisdiction. And, indeed, this subsidiary/parent issue often arises in general-jurisdiction cases. But the problem can also arise where what's involved is **specific** jurisdiction.

   a. **Maybe a difference:** The Supreme Court has not explicitly decided whether the same rule about imputing a subsidiary's acts to a parent (whatever the rule is) should apply in general-jurisdiction cases as in specific-jurisdictional ones. But the majority opinion in *Daimler AG v. Bauman*, *supra*, p. 56, suggests that the subsidiary's or agent's acts should **more readily be attributed** to the parent when the case involves **specific** jurisdiction than where it involves **general** jurisdiction. In *Daimler*, Justice Ginsburg's opinion for the Court said that "[a]gency relationships ... may be relevant to the existence of **specific** jurisdiction. ... [A] corporation can purposefully avail itself of a forum by **directing its agents** or distributors to **take action there**. ... It does **not inevitably follow**, however, that similar reasoning applies to **general** jurisdiction."

   This last-quoted sentence certainly sounds as though Ginsburg believes that courts should be less quick to attribute an agent's forum-state contacts to the principal where the case involves general jurisdiction than where it's based on specific jurisdiction.

   Example: Assume the same basic facts as in the above Example (which featured a modified version of the facts in *Daimler*). But now, assume that MBUSA is a *wholly-owned subsidiary* of Daimler Corp, and Daimler's executives largely dictate how MBUSA is to carry out the sales and marketing of Daimler cars in the U.S. As in the prior Example, the question is whether the New Jersey courts can hear a suit brought against Daimler, if the only contacts that exist are ones between MBUSA and New

---

28. Recall that this rule that general jurisdiction over a corporation normally can occur only in a state that is the corporation's state of incorporation or state of principal place of business is the holding of the actual Supreme Court *Daimler* decision, discussed *supra*, p. 56.

Jersey (i.e., none exist between *Daimler* and New Jersey). If suit concerns, say, an *accident in New Jersey* involving a Daimler-made car — a case of *specific* jurisdiction — the Supreme Court might well be willing to impute MBUSA's New Jersey contacts (e.g., its making of a significant volume of sales in New Jersey) to Daimler, on the theory that MBUSA acted as Daimler's agent in pursuing New Jersey-targeted sales, and Daimler knowingly accepted the benefits of those New Jersey-linked efforts.

By contrast, if the suit involved a *California* accident (so that the suit in New Jersey was based on *general* jurisdiction), the Supreme Court would likely be much **less willing** to hold that whatever relevant ties MBUSA had with New Jersey (e.g., incorporation in the state, or a principal place of business there) should be imputed to Daimler.

Quiz Yourself on

JURISDICTION OVER INDIVIDUALS AND CORPORATIONS; GENERAL JURISDICTION

1. D lived in Connecticut until five years ago. His company then transferred him to California to take over a troubled operation. Even though D expected to return to Connecticut eventually, he sold his Connecticut house, figuring that when he returned there he would buy a different house. D did not know for sure how long he would be residing in California, but he did not expect to remain there for more than two or three years. After D took up residence in California, he was sued in the Connecticut state courts concerning a transaction which he had carried out in New York some years before. Can the Connecticut state courts constitutionally take jurisdiction over this suit? _____

2. D owns and runs a small bakery in Portland, Maine. P is a truck driver who lives in South Carolina. One day, P visited D's bakery just before embarking on the long truck ride from Maine to South Carolina. He bought a dozen cream-filled doughnuts from D, and remarked, "I'm going to eat one of these every two hours, so I'll still have a couple left by the time I get home to South Carolina." P followed this plan, and ate the last two doughnuts while inside the South Carolina state limits. P then fell violently ill of food poisoning, causing him to lose control of his truck, so that it went off the road and flipped over, seriously injuring P. Later, medical evidence showed that it was one of the last two doughnuts, eaten in South Carolina, that caused the food poisoning. P sued D in the South Carolina courts. Not only was P a resident of South Carolina, but at the time of the suit he was hospitalized there, and all witnesses to the accident, as well as all witnesses to the medical findings concerning the food poisoning, resided in South Carolina. Assuming that the South Carolina long-arm statute can fairly be interpreted to give jurisdiction over D on these facts, may the courts of South Carolina constitutionally hear the suit? _____

3. Corporation is a manufacturer of ladies' dresses. In the state of Arkansas, Corporation does not maintain any official office. Corporation conducts no advertising directed at Arkansas residents, and derives only a small portion of its total revenues from that state. Corporation's sole activities in the state consist of the activities of Jones, a commission salesman for Corporation, who works out of his house soliciting orders from Arkansas-based department stores. When an Arkansas department store places an order, the order is not accepted by Jones, but is instead sent to the home office in New York for approval. All orders are shipped from New York directly to the department store which placed the order. P, an Arkansas department store that placed one order with Corporation via Jones, received what it believed to be defective merchandise, and sued Corporation in the Arkansas courts. May the Arkansas courts constitutionally take jurisdiction over Corporation? _____

[handwritten margin note: McIntyre]

4. D is a corporation based in Italy, with no American subsidiaries, that manufactures drill presses in Italy and exports them throughout the world. D appoints Distrib, a corporation, to be the exclusive distributor of D's products in North America. Distrib is owned by persons who have no ownership interest in D. Distrib is incorporated in North Carolina, and has its principal place of business in South Carolina. The distributorship agreement between D and Distrib provides that Distrib "shall use its best efforts to sell as many machines made by D in the United States and Canada as is reasonably practicable." Distrib then asks D to approve (as the distribution agreement requires) Distrib's plan to open, at Distrib's expense, a sales office in New Jersey. Distrib points out to D that New Jersey has many potential customers for the type of drill presses made by D, and that these customers will be more likely to buy if Distrib has a local office. D agrees, and Distrib opens the office. From that N.J. office, Distrib sells a drill press made by D to Cust, a machine shop located in New Jersey. P, an employee of Cust, is injured when the drill press pierces the palm of P's hand. P sues D in tort in New Jersey state court, alleging that the absence of a guard on the press made the product dangerously defective. The New Jersey long-arm allows service on "any defendant, wherever based, who makes a product that causes physical injury within this state." P makes service on D as authorized by the statute. D moves for dismissal, asserting that the New Jersey courts cannot constitutionally exercise personal jurisdiction over D in this case. Should the court grant D's motion? _____

[handwritten margin note (diagram): D-Sub; D-GE · Del.; · VA → Boiler (SP) → Holland → Texas (P) < 1%]

5. D is a corporation that manufactures valves to be used in various heating devices. D is incorporated in Germany, and has its only offices there. D sells many valves to Boiler Co., a Spanish manufacturer of boilers. A boiler made by Boiler Co. and with a valve made by D is installed in a hotel in Amsterdam, Holland. While P, a Texas resident, is visiting that hotel, the boiler explodes, causing P to be burned in the ensuing fire. D has a wholly-owned U.S. subsidiary, D-Sub, that is incorporated in Delaware, and that has its principal place of business in Virginia. From the Virginia office, D-Sub makes sales of D's products throughout the U.S.; these sales collectively represent 12% of D's worldwide sales. About 8% of D-Sub's sales (and thus less than 1% of D's worldwide sales) are made to customers located in Texas. In reliance on D-Sub's sales in Texas, P brings a product liability suit against D and D-Sub in Texas state court, claiming that a defect in the valve that was sold by D to Boiler Co. and incorporated by the latter into the boiler installed in Amsterdam was the cause of P's injuries. D and D-Sub both move to dismiss the suit on grounds that personal jurisdiction may not constitutionally be exercised against either by the Texas court. How should the Texas court rule on the motions? (Answer separately with respect to D and D-Sub.) _____

Answers

1. Yes. It is quite clear that a court may constitutionally exercise both general and specific jurisdiction over anyone who is *domiciled* in that state. Even though D has temporarily changed his residence to California, his domicile remains Connecticut. This is because one's domicile is the last place of which it was true both that one resided there and that one had the indefinite intent to remain there. Since D does not intend to remain in California, California cannot be his domicile, so we look at the next prior place he resided, Connecticut. (In fact, Connecticut would still be D's domicile even if he intended to move to New York after he finished his California job.)

2. No, probably. According to *Worldwide Volkswagen v. Woodson*, 444 U.S. 286 (1980), the mere fact that a product finds its way into a state and causes injury there is not enough to subject the out-of-state manufacturer or vendor to personal jurisdiction there. Instead, the defendant must have made some effort to *market* in the forum state. Here, D was not attempting to market in South Carolina, even though he knew that the doughnuts in question would find their way to South Carolina. Therefore, even though P resides in and is presently located in South Carolina, and all the witnesses are there, it would probably be a violation of due process for the South Carolina courts to subject D to personal jurisdiction there.

3. **Yes.** These facts are quite similar to those of *International Shoe v. Washington*, 326 U.S. 310 (1945), in which the Supreme Court held that the out-of-state company had the requisite *"minimum contacts"* with the forum state, so that it did not violate the company's due process rights for the forum state to exercise jurisdiction over the company (at least assuming that the suit related to the company's in-state activities, as was the case in Int'l Shoe itself, and as is the case here). Since Corporation sought business from within Arkansas, and had a salesman based there, the fact that it had no office, conducted no advertising directed at the state, and derived only a small portion of its total revenues from the state, are all irrelevant. The basic idea is that Corporation purposefully availed itself of the opportunity to sell goods within Arkansas, so it is therefore not unfair for Corporation to be required to defend suits there relating to those sales. Notice that it's key that this suit involves *"specific"* jurisdiction (i.e., the suit involves the defendant's *forum-state-related* activities); the fact that Corporation had minimum contacts would *not* be sufficient to support *"general"* jurisdiction by Arkansas over Corporation (i.e., jurisdiction in a suit *not* involving Corporation's Arkansas-related activities) — only the fact that Corporation was incorporated in, or had its principal place of business in, Arkansas would suffice for general jurisdiction.

4. **No.** First, notice that P's suit requires only *specific* jurisdiction, not *general* jurisdiction, over D. That is, P's claim arises out of the contacts between D and the forum state (the sale, through D's authorized distributor, of a machine made by D to a New Jersey-based customer, and the consequent in-state injury to P caused by that machine). Next, we need to know what kinds of connections between an out-of-state or foreign manufacturer and the forum state will suffice for specific jurisdiction. The Supreme Court has held that for a state to constitutionally exercise specific jurisdiction over an out-of-state or foreign manufacturer of an item that causes in-state injuries, it is *not* enough that it was merely *foreseeable* to the manufacturer that the item would find its way into the forum state and cause injury there (*World-Wide Volkswagen*). Instead, something more of a connection between the manufacturer and the forum state is required. But a majority of the Supreme Court agrees that specific jurisdiction *can* be constitutionally exercised if the defendant manufacturer *"purposefully availed itself"* of the opportunity to serve the forum state's market. (*J. McIntyre v. Nicastro*.) Here, this "purposeful availment" (or "targeting") test is satisfied, because D not only urged Distrib to make as many American sales as possible, but approved Distrib's plan to open a New Jersey office from which, as D knew, Distrib intended to serve the lucrative New Jersey market. That's enough to constitute a targeting by D of the New Jersey market, making this fact pattern different from the one in *McIntyre* itself (where specific jurisdiction was found lacking, on the ground that neither the foreign manufacturer nor the American distributor there had targeted the forum state).

5. **The court should grant both motions.** First, notice that P's suit requires *general* (not specific) jurisdiction over both D and D-Sub in order to proceed. That's because the suit arises out of a valve made and installed abroad, so that the suit does not arise out of whatever contacts D and/or D-Sub might have with the forum state. (Remember that when the plaintiff's claim does not arise out of any connection between the defendant and the forum state, the resulting exercise of jurisdiction is "general" rather than "specific.") For a court to exercise general jurisdiction, the due process clause of the U.S. Constitution's 14th Amendment requires much greater voluntary connections between the defendant and the forum state than

where "specific" jurisdiction is involved. In fact, where the defendant is a corporation, the forum state may normally exercise general jurisdiction over it only if the corporation is *"at home"* in the forum state. And a corporation is deemed to be "at home" in a state only if the corporation is either **incorporated in** that state or has its **principal place of business there**. *Daimler AG v. Bauman.*

Since neither D nor D-Sub is either incorporated in Texas or has a principal place of business in Texas, neither defendant is "at home" in Texas. Therefore, Texas cannot exercise general jurisdiction against either defendant. So although P would be able to sue both D and D-Sub for an accident occurring *in Texas* arising out of a defective valve sold by D-Sub to a *Texas-based* boiler customer (that would be an exercise of *specific* jurisdiction, making the defendant's purposeful availment of the Texas market sufficient for jurisdiction), P may not sue either D or D-Sub for this *non-Texas-based* accident. And notice that this result does not depend solely on the fact that the accident occurred outside the U.S. — the same result (no general jurisdiction by Texas) would occur if the accident had occurred somewhere in the U.S. but outside of Texas.

V.   FEDERAL JURISDICTION OVER THE PARTIES

A. General principles: To determine whether a *federal* court has personal jurisdiction over the defendant, you must check *three things*:

1. **Territory for service:**   Whether service took place within the appropriate *territory*;

2. **Manner of service:**   Whether the service was carried out in the correct *manner*; and

3. **Amenability:**   Whether the defendant is *"amenable"* to the federal suit.

   > **Note:** *All three* of these requirements must be satisfied, in order for there to be federal-court personal jurisdiction over the defendant. You should check these things in the order listed above — that way, if service didn't take place within the appropriate territory (which must usually happen by using the long-arm statute of the state where the district court sits), you don't have to go further.

B. Territory for service: As a general rule, in **both diversity actions and federal question cases**, **service of process** may be made **only**:

   [1]   **within the territorial limits** of the **state in which the District Court sits**; or

   [2]   **anywhere else that the long-arm of the state where the District Court sits permits**.

FRCP 4(k)(1)(A); 4(k)(2).[29] There are some additional possibilities for special situations, such as the "100-mile bulge" provision discussed *infra*, p. 70, and the "foreign defendant not servable in any state" provision discussed *infra*, p. 71. But for most cases, if the local state long-arm couldn't or wouldn't allow service on an out-of-state defendant, the federal court won't do so either.

---

29. 4(k)(1)(A) deals with service in diversity cases; 4(k)(2) deals with service in federal-question cases.

Example 1 (service within the territorial limits of state): P sues D in a federal action in the Northern District of Ohio. Whether the suit is based on diversity or federal question, service will be territorially valid if D is served with process anywhere within the state of Ohio, since this is the state where the district court sits. This is true even if service is physically made in the Southern District of Ohio.

Example 2 (out-of-state service based on state law): Assume that under the Montana long-arm statute, if a non-resident is involved in a motor vehicle accident inside Montana with a Montana resident, the Montana resident may serve the non-resident outside Montana, and the Montana courts may then exercise personal jurisdiction. P, a Montana resident, and D, a Texas resident, have an accident in Montana. P may sue D in diversity in federal District Court for Montana; P may serve D with process in Texas, because the long-arm of the state where the district court sits (Montana) would allow such service. FRCP 4(k)(1)(A).

Example 3 (no territory available for service): P and D are involved in an auto accident in Nevada. P is a Nevada resident. D is a Vermont resident. Because P is an invalid, he cannot leave Nevada to litigate. Assume that the Nevada long-arm statute is extremely limited, and would not allow service to be made on D anywhere outside of Nevada for the Nevada negligence action. Assume further that D has never set foot in Nevada again after the accident, and is unlikely to do so in the future. There is no way that P can bring a federal court *diversity* action in Nevada against D. He cannot serve D within Nevada, because D will not be physically there to receive service. He cannot serve D in Vermont (or anywhere else), because the Nevada long-arm would not allow out-of-state service on these facts. Therefore, even though there is diversity of citizenship between P and D, there is no way for P to make service for his Nevada federal court action, and he is stuck.

The same result would follow if P's suit against D was based on a ***federal question*** (say a violation of the federal securities laws) rather than on diversity — since P cannot make service on D within Nevada, and the local long-arm does not allow out-of-state service, P cannot bring his federal suit in Nevada. FRCP 4(k)(2) (see *infra*, p. 71) looks as though it might help P, but it doesn't — the section only applies to allow jurisdiction over a defendant for a federal-question claim where the defendant "is not subject to jurisdiction in ***any state's*** courts of general jurisdiction." Since D is subject to jurisdiction in the courts of his home state, Vermont (any resident of a state can always be sued in that state), Rule 4(k)(2) does not apply.

1. **Not imposed by Constitution:** These limits — requiring service to be made either within the state where the District Court sits or where permitted by the local law of that state — are ***not*** imposed by the U.S. ***Constitution***. "The sovereignty of the U.S. is, of course, nationwide and Congress could constitutionally provide for the service of process, issuing out of any federal court, throughout the length and breadth of the land, just as New York may provide that process of a state court in Manhattan may be served in Buffalo." James (1st Ed.), 616. Rather, these limits come principally from the Federal Rules of Civil Procedure and the way the federal courts have interpreted those Rules.

   a. **Nationwide service of process:** In fact, in several kinds of cases, Congress has provided for ***nationwide service of process***. An example of such a statute is 28 U.S.C.

§1391(e), permitting service by registered mail anywhere in the country in a suit against *federal officials and agencies*. See also the Federal Interpleader Act, 28 U.S.C. §2361, discussed *infra*, p. 394. See FRCP 4(k)(1)(C), referring to federal statutes (including interpleader) allowing for nationwide service.

2. **Service out of state:** As noted, service outside the state where the District Court sits may be made *if the law of that state so permits*. Federal Rule 4(k)(1)(A).

> **Example:** New Jersey enacts a long-arm statute which provides that if a non-resident is involved in a motor vehicle accident inside New Jersey with a New Jersey resident, the New Jersey resident may serve the non-resident outside New Jersey, and the New Jersey courts may then exercise personal jurisdiction over the non-resident in a suit relating to the accident. P, a New Jersey resident, and D, a California resident, are involved in an automobile accident in New Jersey.
>
> P may bring a diversity suit against D in federal district court for New Jersey. Since the New Jersey long-arm would allow service to be made on D (in California) if P sued on the accident in the New Jersey courts, Federal Rule 4(k)(1)(A) allows service in the federal action to be made on D in California under similar circumstances. (The "manner" of service — for instance, service by certified mail, or service by a process server licensed to make service in California — may be made either as expressly permitted in the federal rules, as provided in the New Jersey long-arm, or as allowed under the law of the state where service is made (California). See *infra*, pp. 72-74.)

3. **100-mile bulge:** A special *100-mile bulge* provision (FRCP 4(k)(1)(B)) allows for out-of-state service sometimes, even if local law does not permit it. When the provision applies, it allows service anywhere (even across a state boundary) within a *100-mile radius of the federal courthouse where suit is pending*. The bulge provision applies only where out-of-staters will be brought in as *additional parties* to an *already pending* action.

    a. **Two types of parties:** There are two types of parties against whom the 100-mile bulge can be used:

        i. **Third-party defendants:** First, *third-party defendants* (FRCP 14) may be served within the bulge.

            > **Example:** P sues D in a New Jersey federal district court diversity action. D claims that if D is liable to P, X is liable to D as an indemnitor. The suit is pending in Newark, less than 100 miles from New York City. D may serve X in New York City, even if no New Jersey long-arm statute would allow the suit.

        ii. **Necessary parties:** Second, so-called *"necessary parties"* (FRCP 19(a)) — that is, persons who are needed in the action for just adjudication, and whose joinder will not involve subject matter jurisdictional problems — may also be served if they are within the bulge.

            > **Example:** P sues D for copyright infringement in federal district court for the Eastern District of Kentucky, located in Lexington. D files a counterclaim against P. D wants to join X as a co-defendant to this counterclaim, arguing that P and X conspired to violate D's copyrights. X resides in Cincinnati, Ohio, located 78 miles from Lexington. If the court agrees that X is required for just adjudication of

D's counterclaim, service on X in Cincinnati is valid, even if the Kentucky long-arm would not allow service there.

b. Minimum contacts with the bulge: As noted above, an out-of-state defendant in a diversity suit may only be required to defend if she would be reachable by the long-arm of the state where the District Court sits for purposes of a state suit. Does this limitation apply to out-of-state defendants served in the "bulge"? The case law on this question is quite confused; most federal courts seem to hold that the defendant may be required to defend so long as he is reachable by the long-arm of the state *where service is made* (i.e., the "bulge state"), even if he could not be reached according to the law of the state where the federal suit is pending.

4. Foreign defendant not servable in any state: Another special provision in Rule 4 allows a *federal-question* suit to be brought against a person or organization who cannot be sued in *any state* court (almost always because they are a *foreigner*). FRCP 4(k)(2) provides that "For a claim that arises under federal law, serving a summons ... establishes personal jurisdiction over a defendant if: (A) the defendant is *not subject to jurisdiction in any state's courts* of general jurisdiction, and (b) exercising jurisdiction is consistent with the United States constitution and laws."

> **Example:** P, a citizen of New York, sues D, a corporation domiciled in France, for securities fraud (a federal-law cause of action). The suit is brought in the Southern District of New York. D's only activities that relate to the U.S. are to take out advertisements in the *International Herald Tribune* (published in Paris, but read by some U.S. subscribers) offering investments. P was one of the investors recruited in this manner. Assume that because D's contacts with New York state were so minimal, the New York long-arm wouldn't allow D to be sued in a New York state-court suit. Assume further that *no state* has a long-arm that would allow service on D, because D's contacts with the U.S. are so limited, and so spread out. Finally, assume that D has enough contacts with the U.S. that it would not be a violation of federal due process to make D defend P's suit in the S.D.N.Y. Under these facts, P's service on D would be allowable, because: (1) the suit is based on a federal-question; (2) D is not subject to "jurisdiction in any state's courts of general jurisdiction"; and (3) D has enough contacts with the U.S. that it's not a violation of D's due process rights to have to defend in the S.D.N.Y.

> **Note:** But observe how limited 4(k)(2) really is — if there were a *single state* anywhere in the U.S. that would permit P to sue D, then P can't use 4(k)(2). So if D had enough contacts with, say, California (and California had a generous enough long-arm) that P could bring a California state action against D, then P wouldn't be able to use 4(k)(2) for his S.D.N.Y. action. Yet the availability of a California action would probably be cold comfort indeed to a New York plaintiff in P's position.

a. Not applicable to diversity claim standing alone: Also, observe that 4(k)(2) applies only to a *federal question* claim. If the only claim against D is based on diversity, then even though D has minimum contacts with the United States as a whole, and does not have minimum contacts with any particular state, P is out of luck. (But if P does have a federal claim against D, then a related diversity claim could be added to the suit, under the doctrine of "supplemental jurisdiction," discussed *infra*, p. 142.)

5. **Gaps possible:** Even with 4(k)(2), there can be *"gaps of service,"* whereby a person will not be servable in a federal action even though the person has minimum contacts with the state where the federal court sits. A defendant who is not located in the state where the District Court sits may *not* be served if she does not fall within one of the four special cases described above (servable pursuant to state long-arm, 100-mile bulge, special nationwide-service provision, or 4(k)(2)'s "foreign defendant not servable in any state" provision), *even if she has the constitutionally-required minimum contacts* with the forum. Example 3, *supra*, p. 69, shows how this can be true, both as to a case based on diversity and one based on federal question.

C. **Manner of service:** Once you determine that the party to be served lies within the territory described above, you must determine whether the service was carried out in the correct *manner*. The allowable manner of service is somewhat different, depending on whether the defendant is an individual or a corporation.

1. **Individual:** The manner for serving an *individual* is set out in 4(e). Service on the individual may be made in any of several ways:

   a. **Personal:** By serving him *personally* (4(e)(2)(A));

   b. **Substitute:** By leaving the summons and complaint at D's *residence* with a person of *"suitable age and discretion"* residing there (4(e)(2)(B));

   c. **Agent:** By serving an *agent* appointed or designated by law to receive process. (4(e)(2)(C)). (For instance, many states designate the Director of Motor Vehicles as the agent to receive process in suits involving car accidents);

   d. **Local state law:** By serving D in the manner provided by either: (1) the *law of the state where the District Court sits*, if that state has such a provision; or (2) in the manner provided by the *law of the state where the person is being served*. (4(e)(1).)

      Example: P sues D in an action brought in federal court for the District of New Jersey. D resides in California. P wishes to serve D by certified mail. If *either* the New Jersey courts or the California courts allow service by certified mail, P may use this method for serving D. (Prior to the 1993 amendments to Rule 4, only the law of the state where the action was pending, not the state where the service was to be effected, could be relied on by the plaintiff.)

   e. **Foreign defendants:** A special rule governs service *outside the United States* on an individual. Essentially, any method allowed by a particular international treaty (the Hague Convention) or any method allowed by the country where service occurs, can be used. See FRCP 4(f).

2. **Corporation:** Service on a *corporation* may be made by leaving the papers with an *officer*, a managing or general *agent*, or any other agent authorized by appointment or by law to receive process for the corporation. FRCP 4(h)(1)(B).

   a. **Test for suitability:** Whether a given corporate employee is an "officer or managing or general agent" and is thus qualified to receive process is established by examining her position within the corporation; if that position makes her likely to pass the papers on to the lawyers or directors who would be expected to prepare the defense, she is qualified. Wr., 446.

b. **Local state law:** As with individuals, service on a corporation may also be made in the manner provided by the law of the *state* where the action is *pending* or the law of the *state* where the *service is made*. FRCP 4(h)(1)(A).

c. **Foreign defendants:** As with individuals, special rules for serving corporations that are *not present in the U.S.* are provided, in Rule 4(h)(2). These rules are essentially the same as for individuals.

3. **Waiver of service:** Nearly all the methods of service discussed above require a person acting as the plaintiff's agent to personally deliver the summons and complaint to the defendant or to someone acting on behalf of the defendant. But Rule 4(d) (added in 1993) allows the plaintiff to in effect serve the summons and complaint by *mail*, provided that the *defendant cooperates*. Actually, what the plaintiff does is to mail to the defendant a *"request for waiver of service;"* if the defendant agrees, no actual in-person service is needed. The rule gives the defendant financial and other incentives to grant the waiver request.

a. **Procedure:** The plaintiff begins the waiver-of-service procedure by sending the defendant a notice that the action is being commenced, two copies of a waiver-of-service form, a copy of the complaint, and a prepaid return envelope. The documents may be sent "by *first-class mail* or *other reliable means*" (4(d)(1)(G)).

b. **Time to respond:** The defendant has 30 days to respond to the request for waiver (60 days for a foreign defendant).

c. **Incentives:** The defendant is free to refuse to grant the waiver, in which case the plaintiff must serve the summons by the in-person methods described above (personal service, substitute service, service on agent, or service pursuant to local state law; see *supra*, p. 72). But Rule 4(d) gives the defendant two significant incentives, one a "carrot" and the other a "stick," to grant the waiver:

   i. **Additional time to answer:** The "carrot" is that if the defendant grants the waiver, she gets *60 days* following the date on which the request for waiver was sent, in which to *answer* the complaint (compared with 21 days from service of process, provided by Rule 12(a)). (Foreign defendants get 90 days.)

   ii. **D must pay costs of service:** Probably more significantly, the "stick" is that if the defendant refuses the waiver without good cause, and requires plaintiff to bear the expense of serving the summons, the court *"must impose"* on the defendant the *expenses later incurred in making service*, and the costs of any *motion* to collect those service expenses. (4(d)(2).) So the costs of hiring a process server (even the attorneys fees involved in moving to collect the cost of the process server) will normally be assessed against the defendant. (But these rules only apply to a defendant "located within the United States"; foreign defendants suffer no monetary sanction if they refuse to grant the waiver.)

d.   No waiver of personal jurisdiction or venue: A defendant who grants the waiver of personal service will **not** be deemed to have **waived** any objection to venue or personal jurisdiction over him. Rule 4(d)(5). So D can still make a motion for dismissal on either of these counts, under FRCP 12(b)(2) and (3). See *infra*, p. 94.

4.   Time for service: Service on the defendant must be made **within 120 days** after the filing of the complaint. Rule 4(m). If the plaintiff fails to serve the defendant within this time, the court can dismiss the action without prejudice (i.e., plaintiff gets to start a new action). *Id.* But if the statute of limitations has run in the interim, dismissal will mean that the plaintiff is out of luck. (Alternatively, the court can give additional time, instead of dismissing; this will save the plaintiff from statute of limitations problems. *Id.*)

D. Amenability to suit: Even if D was served in an appropriate territory[30] and in an appropriate manner, you still have to determine whether D is **closely-enough linked** to the state where the federal district court sits to make him **"amenable to suit"** in that court. That is, there's a separate test for whether D's **contacts** with the forum state are sufficiently great to justify requiring D to defend there. The standard for measuring "amenability" varies depending on whether the suit is brought based on existence of a federal question or on diversity.

1.   Federal question: In federal question cases, amenability to suit depends solely on **federal law** and federal concepts of due process. Wr. 448-51.

a.   Same as state court limits: Most federal courts in federal question cases have held a defendant to be amenable to suit in their court if jurisdiction **could constitutionally be exercised** over him in the **state courts** of the state where the federal court is sitting. The result of this rule is that it will be possible to bring a federal question suit against the defendant in federal court even if the courts of the state where the federal court sits would conclude that the defendant's contacts with the state were too attenuated to make it wise for the state to exercise jurisdiction over him. In other words, the federal courts will allow suit whenever the state court **could** constitutionally hear the suit (assuming that the state long-arm would allow service of process over the defendant), not merely in those cases where the state courts **will** hear the suit.

Example: P sues D for copyright infringement. The suit is brought in the Northern District of Ohio. P is an Ohio resident. D is a corporation located in, and organized under the law of, California. D's only contact with Ohio is that he sold 100 copies of the allegedly infringing book in Ohio. Assume that the state courts of Ohio, although they could constitutionally take personal jurisdiction over D in a similar state-created claim — libel, for instance — would not do so because they would conclude that D's contacts with Ohio are simply too sparse to make it "fair" for him to have to defend there. (But also assume that the Ohio long-arm would allow D to be served by mail anywhere in the U.S. if the suit related to, say, "a tort committed against an Ohio resident.")

---

30. Remember, in most cases "appropriate territory" will be determined by **the forum state's long-arm:** if the long-arm of the state where the federal court sits wouldn't reach the defendant, the federal court won't hear the suit, whether the suit is in diversity or based on a federal question. See *supra*, p. 68.

Even though the Ohio state courts wouldn't hear the suit, the federal district court will nonetheless hear the federal question copyright claim against D, because P has minimum contacts with the state where the federal court sits. (But if the Ohio long-arm wouldn't even allow service on D on these facts, then this would block the federal suit in Ohio — it's only where the local long-arm allows service on the defendant that the federal court can even reach the further question of whether the defendant's ties to the forum state are broad enough to satisfy general federal principles of due process.

2. **Diversity:** In *diversity* cases, by contrast, the federal courts exercise *only* the jurisdiction that is allowed *by the law of the state in which they sit*, even if this state law does not go to the limits of what the state could do commensurate with due process.

   a. **Supreme Court silent:** The Supreme Court has never said whether this restraint is constitutionally required (which it probably is not) or even desirable as a matter of policy. But it's clear that at least as a matter of *practice*, the federal court won't hear the diversity case if the courts of the state where the federal court sits wouldn't hear it because they would conclude that the defendant's contacts with the forum state weren't extensive enough.

   Example: P sues D for breach of contract, in a diversity action in Ohio. D is an Oklahoma corporation, which has never done business in Ohio (except that it made the contract in question with P while P was an Ohio resident). Assume that the Ohio long-arm allows service to be made by mail in "any contract action brought by an Ohio resident." Assume further that as a matter of policy, the Ohio courts would not hear P's suit, because they would conclude that D's contacts with Ohio are so limited that it would be unfair to make D defend in Ohio.

   Under these facts, as a matter of federal judicial policy the federal court in Ohio won't hear the diversity suit — it will honor the "amenability to suit" rules of the state in which it sits.

Quiz Yourself on
FEDERAL JURISDICTION OVER THE PARTIES

6. D is a toy manufacturer whose sole office is located in New York. P is a young Florida citizen who claims to have been seriously injured in Florida by a toy made by D in New York and shipped to a store in Florida, from which P's mother bought it. P has brought a diversity action against D, based on strict product liability, in the U.S. District Court, Southern District of Florida. Assume that if the action had been brought in the Florida state courts, no Florida statute would have permitted P to serve process on D outside the boundaries of Florida. In the federal action, P caused a licensed process server to travel to New York, where the process server visited D's headquarters, and personally handed the summons and complaint to D's president. Does the federal court for the Southern District of Florida now have personal jurisdiction over D? _____

7. Same facts as prior question. Now, however, assume that Florida has a long-arm statute that provides that service may be made on a corporation located outside of the state, by first-class mail sent to any officer of that corporation, in any suit in which the claim arises out of a tort allegedly committed by the defendant outside of the state but causing injury in the state. P caused a summons in his Florida federal court action to be sent by first-class mail to the president of D in New York. May the U.S. District Court for the South-

ern District of Florida take jurisdiction over D? _____

8. Software Co. is a Washington-based publisher of computer software, particularly a program called "3-2-1." Clone Co., which is also a software publisher, has come out with a competing program called "4-3-2." Clone Co. has sold over 1,000 copies of 4-3-2 in the state of Washington. Software Co. has sued Clone Co. for federal copyright infringement in U.S. District Court for the Western District of Washington. The complaint alleges that 4-3-2 is so similar to 3-2-1 that it has the same "look and feel," and is therefore a violation of Software Co.'s copyrights. Assume that Clone Co., by selling over 1,000 copies in Washington, has the constitutionally-required minimum contacts with Washington to make it not violative of due process for Clone Co. to have to defend a suit there. Assume further, however, that due to the Washington courts' desire to cut down on the "litigation explosion," those courts would not exercise jurisdiction over any suit against a company which, like Clone Co., has no contacts with the state except for selling 1,000 copies of a product in the state. May the federal court for the Western District of Washington take personal jurisdiction over Clone Co. for purposes of the Software Co. copyright suit? (Assume that the method by which service is made on Clone Co. is satisfactory.) _____

9. Driver borrowed a car owned by Owner (a New Mexico resident), with Owner's permission. While Driver was driving the car in Arizona, he hit and injured Pedestrian, an Arizona resident. Pedestrian, realizing that Driver is so poor as to be judgment-proof, has brought a diversity action against Owner in Arizona Federal District Court. Applicable Supreme Court decisions indicate that Owner, by permitting his car to be driven into Arizona, has such minimum contacts with Arizona that it is not a violation of due process for him to be required to defend a suit brought in the Arizona state courts arising out of the accident. However, Arizona's non-resident motorist statute is relatively restrictive; it allows suit against one who is the driver in an Arizona-based accident, but not against one who owns a car (which he is not driving) that is involved in an Arizona accident. Therefore, Pedestrian would not have been permitted to sue Owner in the Arizona courts unless Owner was served while in Arizona. Pedestrian instituted his federal court suit by making personal service on Owner in New Mexico. May the Arizona district court hear the suit against Owner? _____

———————

Answers

6. **No.** Normally, service in a federal court action (whether based on diversity or federal question) must either take place within the confines of the state where the federal court sits, or must be made out of state in a way that is expressly permitted by that state's own long-arm statute. (There is an exception for situations where Congress has allowed for nationwide service of process, and for the 100-mile bulge provision of Federal Rule 4(f), neither of which is applicable here.) Since the facts tell us that Florida would not allow service on the New York corporation to be made in New York on these facts, and since D is not found within Florida (as it would be if, say, it had its principal place of business there), the federal court may not take jurisdiction either.

7. **Yes.** According to Federal Rule 4(e), if the long-arm statute of the state in which the District Court is located would permit a particular type of out-of-state service on a particular defendant, that same form of out-of-state service will suffice to confer jurisdiction on the federal district court (whether the case is based on diversity or federal question).

8. **Yes.** Software Co.'s suit is a "federal question" suit. That is, Software Co.'s claim "arises under the constitution, laws, or treaties of the United States," since the source of the claim is the federal copyright statute. In federal question suits, the federal court will hear the case if the defendant has minimum contacts with the forum state, even though the courts of the state might not (for reasons of fairness or judicial economy)

have heard a suit against that defendant. So the fact that the Washington courts would not hear any suit against Clone Co. is irrelevant — since Clone Co. has the constitutionally-required minimum contacts with Washington, the federal court will hear the suit. (But this is not the rule for suits based on diversity.)

9. No. In diversity cases, the federal courts only exercise the personal jurisdiction that is allowed by the law of the state in which they sit, even if the state law does not go to the limits of what the state could do commensurate with due process. So the rule for diversity actions is quite different from that for federal question actions — this fact pattern is virtually identical to the fact pattern of the prior question, except for the fact that we are dealing with diversity rather than federal question, yet the result is that here there is no federal-court jurisdiction and in the prior question there is.

VI. JURISDICTION OVER THINGS

A. General principles:

1. *In rem* actions: *In rem* actions are ones which do not seek to impose personal liability on anyone, but seek rather to affect the interests of persons in a specific thing (or *res*).

   a. Illustrations: Typical examples are actions to **quiet title** to, or to **foreclose a lien** on, real estate.

   b. Status as *res*: The concept of *in rem* has been extended to cover actions which seek to affect **status**, for instance, **divorce** actions. In such an action, the marital status is considered to be the "thing" on which jurisdiction is exercised; it is often considered to be located wherever one of the two spouses is domiciled.

2. *Quasi in rem* actions: *Quasi in rem* actions are those which would have been *in personam* if jurisdiction over the defendant's person had been attainable. Instead, property or intangibles are seized not as the **object** of the litigation, but merely as a **means of satisfying a possible judgment** against the defendant.

3. Method of attachment: In an *in rem* action, a **description** of the property in the papers filed with the court is sufficient to bring the property within the control of the court for the purposes of the suit. But in a *quasi in rem* action, the property must be actually **attached**, or seized (generally by having the sheriff post official notice on the land). This is the actual holding of *Pennoyer*. (The statements about the lack of personal jurisdiction in that case are essentially dicta.)

B. *In rem* jurisdiction

1. Constitutionality of *in rem* judgments: The constitutionality of *in rem* judgments has never been seriously in question.

> **Example:** Virtually all jurisdictions allow "quiet title" actions, by which a person claiming sole ownership of a piece of real estate can eliminate any other claims. Quiet title statutes typically call for mail notice to anyone known to claim an interest in the property, and newspaper publication about the suit in an attempt to reach unknown claimants. It's clear that such quiet title actions do not violate the due process rights of unknown claimants, since otherwise it would not be possible to clear title as against

the world. Cf. *Tyler v. Judges of the Court of Registration*, 55 N.E. 812 (Mass. 1900) (Holmes, J.).

2. **Effect of *Shaffer*:** *Shaffer v. Heitner*, discussed *infra*, p. 79, which largely wipes out the use of *quasi in rem* jurisdiction, has little effect on *in rem* jurisdiction.

> **Example:** *Shaffer* doesn't prevent a court from ordering **specific performance** of a **contract to convey land located within the state's borders**, even if the defendant resides out-of-state. By owning in-state real estate, the defendant has evidenced his expectation of receiving the benefit of the state's laws, and it's reasonable to require him to litigate claims regarding that land in-state. This is different from the usual *quasi in rem* case, where the property has nothing to do with the litigation.

3. **Federal *in rem* jurisdiction:** If federal subject matter jurisdiction exists (either diversity or federal question), a ***federal in rem*** case may be brought concerning land (e.g., to clear title, or to foreclose a lien).

   a. **Nationwide service:** 28 U.S.C. §1655 allows **nationwide service** on defendants in District Court actions "to enforce any lien upon or claim to, or to remove any incumbrance or lien or cloud upon the title to, real or personal property within the district. …"

   b. **Only lien property affected by default:** If the defendant in a §1655 suit defaults, the judgment affects **only the property involved in the lien**, and not the defendant's other assets.

C. ***Quasi in rem* jurisdiction**

1. **Nature of *quasi in rem*:** A *quasi in rem* action is one which would have been *in personam* if jurisdiction over the defendant's person had been attainable. Instead property or intangibles are seized not as the **object** of the litigation, but merely as a **means of satisfying a possible judgment** against the defendant.

   > **Example:** P wishes to sue D on a contract claim in California state court. The contract has no connection with California, nor does D himself have sufficient contacts with California to allow it to exercise *in personam* jurisdiction over him. D does, however, own some property in California. Putting aside constitutional due process problems, P could attach that property as a basis of jurisdiction, and bring a *quasi in rem* action on the contract claim. If P wins, he will be able to collect only the value of the attached property, and D will not be personally liable for the remainder if the damages exceed the value of the property.

2. **"Half-way house":** *Quasi in rem* jurisdiction has been referred to as a ***"half-way house"*** between *in rem* and *in personam* jurisdiction; it is *in rem* in the sense that the court is able to adjudicate the case only because the defendant has property within the state that has been attached by the court; it is *in personam* in the sense that the subject matter of the suit is unrelated to the property seized.

3. **Means of satisfying judgment:** *Quasi in rem* actions are generally for money damages, which are awarded by **selling the property**, or **garnishing the debt**, owned by or owed to the defendant within the forum state.

a. **Limited to attached property:** A *quasi in rem* judgment may be satisfied ***only out of the attached property***. Even if there is other property belonging to the defendant within the forum state, unless this property has been attached prior to the suit, it may not be seized and sold to satisfy the judgment subsequently. A new action must be brought, and litigated on the merits, in order to reach this new property.

b. **No *res judicata*:** *Quasi in rem* judgments have **no *res judicata* value;** if P wins against D in a *quasi in rem* action in State X, he cannot in a later suit against D in State Y claim that the matter has been decided for all time. Instead, he must go through another trial on the merits if he wishes to subject D to further liability.

    i. **Exception:** Some courts recognize one exception to the general rule that *quasi in rem* judgments to do not have res judicata value. These courts hold that if the defendant makes a ***limited appearance*** (*infra*, p. 82) and fully litigates certain issues, he will not be allowed to re-litigate those issues in a subsequent trial. Nor will the plaintiff be allowed to re-litigate those issues. The Restatement, Second, Judgments §75(c), takes this view.

    ii. **Contrary view:** Other courts, however, hold that even if the defendant makes a limited appearance and litigates all the issues, the judgment has no *res judicata* effect. These courts point out that to allow res judicata in this situation would destroy the utility of the limited appearance (a device which allows the defendant to contest on the merits without subjecting himself to personal liability) since the defendant will be bound as to all his other property by the results of the first *quasi in rem* suit. See Res Judicata in a Nutshell, p. 236.

4. ***Shaffer v. Heitner:*** The utility of *quasi in rem* jurisdiction was radically curtailed in the landmark Supreme Court case, ***Shaffer v. Heitner***, 433 U.S. 186 (1977). That case held that *quasi in rem* jurisdiction over a defendant could not be exercised unless the defendant had such ***"minimum contacts"*** with the forum state that ***in personam jurisdiction could be exercised over him*** under *International Shoe*.

a. **Facts of *Shaffer*:** Plaintiff Heitner brought a shareholder's derivative suit in Delaware on behalf of Greyhound Corporation against 28 of the corporation's non-resident directors and officers. The suit alleged that wrongdoing by the defendants had caused the corporation to be liable for large antitrust damages and fines.

    i. **Place of activities complained of:** None of the activities complained of took place in Delaware, nor had any of the defendants had any other contacts with Delaware. The corporation's business activities were conducted mostly at its home headquarters in Phoenix, Arizona.

    ii. **Sequestration of stock:** In order to gain jurisdiction, the plaintiff took advantage of a Delaware statute providing that any stock in a Delaware corporation could be ***"sequestered,"*** i.e. attached, to provide *quasi in rem* jurisdiction against its owner. The shares themselves were not physically present in Delaware, but the statute provided that the situs of stock in a Delaware corporation should be "deemed" to be Delaware, regardless of its actual physical location. 21 of the 28 defendants owned Greyhound stock, so jurisdiction was obtained only as to their property.

iii. Consequence: The consequence of all this was that the plaintiff was able to attach over $1 million worth of stock as a basis for *quasi in rem* jurisdiction against most of the defendants. Furthermore, since Delaware ***does not allow a limited appearance***, these defendants had to choose between not defending the action, and forfeiting the $1 million in stock, or defending it, and subjecting themselves to possibly unlimited personal liability. Instead, they maintained that *quasi in rem* jurisdiction violated their due process rights, because of their lack of contacts with Delaware.

b. Holding: The Court, in an opinion by Justice Marshall, agreed that Delaware's statute ***violated the defendants' due process rights.*** The Court noted that all actions, even true *in rem* ones, adjudicate the interests of ***people*** in things, and are therefore really "against" people. Where, as here, the suit is not even "about" the in-state property, and the property is merely a means of giving the court jurisdiction, the suit is even more clearly against the owner than in the true *in rem* case. And this is still more obviously the case insofar as Delaware allows no limited appearance, and the express purpose of its sequestration statute is to force the defendant to enter a general appearance.

c. Conclusion: Therefore, the Court concluded, "If a direct assertion of personal jurisdiction over the defendant would violate the Constitution, it would seem that an indirect assertion of that jurisdiction should be equally impermissible." ***The same test, the "minimum contacts" test of International Shoe, should therefore apply to determine whether the exercise of quasi in rem in a particular case is constitutional.***

i. Arguments for *quasi in rem* rejected: The Court rejected several traditional arguments in favor of *quasi in rem*. The most important of these was the argument that a defendant "should not be able to avoid payment of his obligations by the expedient of removing his assets to a place where he is not subject to an *in personam* suit." Even if the defendant attempts to do this, the Court said, the plaintiff is always free to bring an *in personam* suit where the defendant resides, regardless of the presence of assets, and then after recovering a judgment, sue to enforce that judgment in the state where the assets are. He has a right to bring the second suit under the Full Faith and Credit Clause (see *infra*, p. 95).

d. Lack of minimum contacts: The Court also found that Delaware did not have an interest in adjudicating the controversy sufficient to make such an adjudication fair to the defendant.

i. Lack of connection between state and cause of action: First, no acts alleged in the complaint had any contact with Delaware.

ii. Regulatory interest: Secondly, Delaware's interest in "supervising the management of a Delaware corporation" was insufficient. This interest couldn't really be that strong, the Court said, or the sequestration statute wouldn't have been designed as it was. That statute would not allow the court to exercise *quasi in rem* jurisdiction over a director or officer who owned no stock in the Delaware corporation, or other Delaware property (as was indeed the case with 7 of the 28 defendants). Furthermore, the statute was overinclusive, since it would grant jurisdiction over any stockholder of a Delaware corporation, even on a claim having nothing to do with the corporation, or Delaware, at all (e.g., a claim for a personal breach of contract occurring in California).

iii. **Delaware law applies:** Delaware's interest in supervising corporations was given adequate protection, the Court said, by the fact that Delaware *law* would apply to this suit no matter where it was brought, because of conflict of laws principles. But, the Court stated, the fact that a state's laws apply does not mean that that state has the right to adjudicate the controversy; the Court quoted *Hanson v. Denckla*: "[The State] does not acquire … jurisdiction by being the 'center of gravity' of the controversy, or the most convenient location for the litigation. The issue is personal jurisdiction, not choice of law."

iv. **Implied consent:** The Court also rejected the plaintiff's *"implied consent"* argument, i.e., that by accepting positions as officers or directors of a Delaware corporation, the defendants had impliedly consented to be subject to Delaware law. Again, the Court stated, the fact that they may have consented to be bound by Delaware law did not mean that they had agreed to be sued in Delaware courts. Furthermore, "It strains reason … to suggest that anyone buying securities in a corporation formed in Delaware 'impliedly consents' to subject himself to Delaware's … jurisdiction on any cause of action."

e. **Concurrences:** Justice Powell concurred, but indicated that there might be some kinds of property "whose situs is indisputably and permanently located within a State" and which might therefore, and without anything else, provide the necessary contacts to make *quasi in rem* jurisdiction constitutional. He thought that this was particularly likely to be true of real estate, and that such jurisdiction "would avoid the uncertainty of the general *International Shoe* standard. …" Justice Stevens concurred in the result only, stating that the test should be whether the defendant had a *"fair warning"* of the chance of litigation within a particular forum; one who owns real estate or keeps a bank account within the state probably has received such warning, he indicated, but someone who buys a share of stock in a Delaware corporation on a national stock exchange certainly has not.

i. **Brennan's concurrence and dissent:** Justice Brennan concurred in part and dissented in part. He agreed that "minimum contacts" should be required to sustain *quasi in rem* jurisdiction. However, he felt that such contacts should be found to exist whenever a shareholders' derivative suit is brought in the state where the corporation is chartered, in view of the chartering state's "unusually powerful interest in insuring the availability of a convenient forum for litigating claims involving a possible multiplicity of defendant fiduciaries and for vindicating the State's substantive policies regarding the management of its domestic corporations." He argued that the defendants, by associating themselves with a Delaware corporation, had invoked the "benefits and protections" of Delaware law, and should have been apprised that "the State may seek to offer a convenient forum for redressing claims of fiduciary breach of trust."

5. **Significance of *Shaffer*:** Generally speaking, *Shaffer ended the utility of quasi in rem jurisdiction.* Prior to *Shaffer*, *quasi in rem*'s utility lay precisely in the fact that where personal jurisdiction was not available, *quasi in rem* provided a "second best" form of juris-

diction, in which the plaintiff could get satisfaction at least to the extent of the in-state property (and perhaps induce the defendant into a general appearance). Once *Shaffer* said that *quasi in rem* jurisdiction could only be exercised where the *International Shoe* minimum contacts test is satisfied, *quasi in rem* could virtually never do anything that *in personam* jurisdiction couldn't do better.

6. **Scope of *Shaffer*:**   Here are some questions that *Shaffer* raised but didn't answer:

   a. **Transient presence:** Is mere ***presence in the forum state*** at the time of service enough for *in personam* jurisdiction, if the defendant has no other contacts? The answer to this turned out to be ***"yes"*** — the Supreme Court held in 1990 that because virtually all states continue to allow presence in the forum state at the time of service as a basis for jurisdiction, use of presence does not violate "traditional notions of fairness," and thus does not violate due process. See *Burnham v. Superior Court, supra,* p. 12.

   b. ***In rem* jurisdiction:** What becomes of the familiar kinds of ***in rem*** jurisdiction, such as mortgage foreclosures, specific performance actions involving land sale contracts, etc.? Since these actions are "about" the property in the state, they are not affected by *Shaffer*.

   c. **Suit to enforce judgments:** If the plaintiff obtains a personal judgment against the defendant in one state, may he sue to ***enforce it*** against the defendant's assets in another state with which the defendant does not have minimum contacts? The answer is "yes," judgments may be sued on for enforcement under the Full Faith and Credit Clause, just as pre-*Shaffer*.

D. **Limited appearances:** Some states allow what is called a ***limited appearance***. In a limited appearance, the defendant appears in an *in rem* or *quasi in rem* suit, contests the case on its merits, but is subjected to liability ***only to the extent of the property or debt attached or garnished by the court.***

   > **Example:** In order to sue D in State X (where personal jurisdiction over D cannot be obtained), P has the court garnish wages owed to D by T, a State X corporation. P claims $10,000 damages for the wrong done by D, but the garnished wages only amount to $2,000. If D is allowed to make a limited appearance, he may contest the case on the merits (that is, argue that he does not in fact owe P the money) without subjecting himself to unlimited personal liability. If he loses, he loses only the $2,000 in wages. If P sues him again in another state where jurisdiction is obtained, P must retry the case on the merits — there is no *res judicata* effect of the judgment, even though D contested on the merits in the original action.

1. **Distinguished from special appearance:** The doctrine of ***limited appearance*** should be distinguished from that of ***special appearance***. The former allows the defendant to contest on the merits while limiting his liability to the property previously attached or garnished by the court. The latter allows a defendant against whom personal jurisdiction is asserted to argue the invalidity of that jurisdiction, without having his argument, or presence in the court, itself constitute a submission to the court's jurisdiction. See the discussion of special appearances, *infra,* p. 93.

2. **Federal limited appearances:** A limited appearance is sometimes allowed in *federal* actions. See *infra*, p. 83.

E. **Federal *quasi in rem* jurisdiction:** In *federal* suits, *quasi in rem* jurisdiction will sometimes be available. In brief, a plaintiff can use *quasi in rem* jurisdiction in a federal suit only if (and in the manner that) the **state where the court sits** would allow such jurisdiction, and not always even then.

1. **FRCP 4(n):** FRCP 4(n) allows a court to exercise *quasi in rem* jurisdiction over a person by seizure of his assets within the jurisdiction, "under the circumstances and in the manner provided by state law" of the district in which the federal court is located. 4(n)(2). Thus *quasi in rem* may be used only **if the law of the state in which the federal court sits permits** such *quasi in rem* jurisdiction.

   a. **Can't get personal jurisdiction:** Furthermore, *quasi in rem* jurisdiction may be used only "on a showing that **personal** jurisdiction over a defendant **cannot be obtained in the district where the action is brought by reasonable efforts** to serve a summons under this rule. …" Rule 4(n). So no matter what state law says, federal *quasi in rem* jurisdiction is available **only if personal jurisdiction** for an action in that federal district **cannot** be obtained. Thus in a diversity case, if the **forum state's long-arm** could reach D, and she has **minimum contacts** with the state (giving the federal court potential personal jurisdiction over D), federal *quasi in rem* **can't be used** even if state law would allow it under comparable circumstances.

   b. **Limited circumstances:** This means that even assuming that the state where the district court sits allows *quasi in rem* jurisdiction, the plaintiff will likely get some benefit from federal *quasi in rem* jurisdiction only if one of these circumstances occurs: (1) D is a **fugitive** who cannot be located (though he has minimum contacts with the state where the District Court sits); (2) the **assets** themselves are in imminent danger of **disappearing**, or (3) the local state **long-arm** is **too narrow** to reach D even though he has minimum contacts with the forum state. See Advisory Committee Notes to Rule 4(n).

2. **Limited appearance:** The federal courts are split on whether a **limited appearance** may be made, i.e., whether the defendant may defend on the merits in a federal *quasi in rem* suit without thereby subjecting himself to unlimited personal liability.

   a. **Federal Rules silent:** The Federal Rules of Civil Procedure neither allow nor prohibit limited appearances — these are simply not mentioned at all.

   b. **Follow state law:** Most federal courts that have considered the issue have followed the rule of the **state in which they are sitting** in determining whether to allow a limited appearance. That is, if the state would allow a limited appearance in a state-court *quasi in rem* suit, the federal court similarly allows it; if not, not.

Quiz Yourself on

JURISDICTION OVER THINGS

10. D is a resident of Pennsylvania. While driving one day in Pennsylvania, D collided with P, a pedestrian, who is an Ohio resident who happened to be visiting his sister in Pennsylvania. D has no contacts with Ohio except for the fact that D works in Pennsylvania for a corporation whose state of incorporation and

principal place of business are Ohio. P commenced an action for negligence against D in the Ohio state courts. P obtained from the Ohio state courts an order of pre-judgment garnishment (authorized by Ohio statutes) whereby D's employer was required to deposit with the court each week 20% of D's take-home pay until the action is resolved. Under the terms of the garnishment order, if P prevails, P will be given the garnished amount (up to the amount of his judgment), but D will have no other liability, assuming that he does not make a general appearance. May the Ohio courts constitutionally proceed with P's action on this basis? _____

———————————————   ·

Answer

10. **No.** The landmark case of *Shaffer v. Heitner* states that *quasi in rem* jurisdiction over a defendant may not be exercised unless the defendant has such minimum contacts with the forum state that *in personam* jurisdiction could be exercised over him. Since D has no contacts at all with Ohio (except for the very fortuitous fact that D's Pennsylvania-based job is with an Ohio-headquartered company), the Ohio courts could not exercise personal jurisdiction over D. Consequently, under *Shaffer v. Heitner*, Ohio may not achieve the same result by seizing part of D's wages to serve as the means for satisfying a possible judgment. The fact that P happens to be an Ohio resident is irrelevant — what counts is D's contacts with the forum state.

VII. NOTICE AND OPPORTUNITY TO BE HEARD

A. **General principles:** Here are some general principles governing a defendant's right to notice of the action, and her right to have an opportunity to be heard, i.e., her right to defend:

1. **Notice:** Once it has been established that the court has the ***authority*** to adjudicate a dispute between the parties or over the property before it, it must still be established that the defendant received ***adequate notice*** of the case against him.

   a. **Reasonableness test:** In order for the defendant to have received adequate notice, it is not necessary that he ***actually*** have learned of the suit. Rather, the procedures used to alert him must have been ***reasonably likely to inform him***, even if they actually failed to do so.

   b. ***In rem and quasi in rem:*** Less strict notice requirements are generally applied in *in rem* and *quasi in rem* cases than in *in personam* cases.

   c. **Mail notice:** Many statutes today allow service by registered mail or certified mail, in addition to the traditional personal "in-hand" service required in the 19th century (as in *Pennoyer*). The applicability of these "constructive" service statutes will be considered more fully below.

2. **Opportunity to defend:** The defendant must be given ***adequate time*** to prepare a defense, and an ***opportunity*** to present that defense. This requirement is in addition to the requirement that he be given reasonable notice of the case against him.

3. **Constitutional standard:** The adequacy of notice and hearing are measured by a Constitutional due process standard.

B. **Traditional notice requirements:**

1. **In-hand service:** In *in personam* cases, until the 20th century, ***personal*** "in-hand" service within the forum state was generally required. Personal service is still the best and surest means of satisfying the notice requirement.

2. **Attachment:** In *in rem* and *quasi in rem* cases, if the suit is begun by the attachment of ***tangible property***, the traditional view has been that this attachment suffices to give the defendant property owner notice.

   a. **Rationale:** This rule was based on the idea that the act of attaching tangible property (by sending the sheriff to post notices on the land) would be almost certain to effectively inform the absent owner of the land of the suit against him.

   b. **Modern requirement:** Since, however, the owner of the land was usually an out-of-state resident (hence an *in rem* or *quasi in rem* suit, rather than one *in personam*) attachment might well not give him actual notice. Most modern statutes therefore require some ***additional*** means of informing the defendant, such as publication of the fact of the impending suit, or mailing of notice to the defendant.

C. Modern notice requirements:

1. **"Substitute" service:** When personal "in-hand" service was required, an unscrupulous defendant could thwart a plaintiff either by staying out of the forum state (since only in-state personal service was allowed) or by remaining ***hidden within the state***. To deal with such evasion of process-servers, the concept of ***"substitute service"*** was established.

   a. **Papers left at dwelling:** The most common substitute service provision allows the process papers to be left at the defendant's dwelling house or usual place of abode within the state.

   b. **Court order:** Some statutes make substitute service available only after a court order is obtained showing personal service was unsuccessfully attempted.

   c. **"Suitable age and discretion" standard:** Some statutes require that the papers be left "at the individual's dwelling … with someone of suitable age and discretion who resides there" (as the formula is phrased in Federal Rule 4(e)(2)(B)) or some similar formula.

   d. **Left at unattended dwelling:** Some states permit papers in certain types of actions to be left even at an ***unattended dwelling***; usually such statutes require that the papers be ***affixed to the door***. However, in some fact situations, use of provisions like these may violate the constitutional due process right to adequate notice.

      i. *Greene* **case:** For instance, in *Greene v. Lindsey*, 456 U.S. 444 (1982), notice of eviction proceedings was given by posting copies of summonses on the door of several tenants' apartments. The tenants claimed that they never saw the posted summonses, and that they did not learn of the eviction proceedings until default judgments had been taken. The Court held that, at least on these facts, service had ***not*** met the requirements of due process — there was substantial risk that the summonses would be torn down by children in the building (a factor which presumably would not be present if the defendant lived in a house). Even more importantly, ***use of the mails*** was a better way to ensure that the tenants actually received service; this more effective means should have been used.

e. Service by mail: Some states (e.g., California) and the federal court system allow service to be made by ordinary *first-class mail*, if the defendant returns an acknowledgment or waiver form to the plaintiff's lawyer. For a more complete description of the federal mail service provision, see *supra*, p. 73.

f. Domicile requirement: Some states have statutes requiring that the defendant must have his *domicile* in the forum state in order for substitute service to be performed. Other statutes, however, have been construed to allow substitute service on the *temporary residence* of a transient, such as a hotel room, as long as the service is made during the period when the dwelling is still the defendant's local residence.

2. **"Constructive" notice to out-of-staters:** The notion of *"constructive service"* was developed to notify defendants who could not be located within the state. (The growth of long-arm statutes has made the need for a means of notifying out-of-state defendants increasingly pressing.)

a. Mail notice: These statutes generally provide for notice by *registered or certified mail*, or sometimes by publication, upon defendants over whom jurisdiction has been asserted. Such defendants include in-state domiciliaries or residents who are temporarily absent, non-resident tortfeasors, etc., as described in the discussion of Jurisdiction over Individuals, *supra*, pp. 11-21.

b. Reasonableness test: The standard that has generally been used for determining whether such constructive service is constitutionally adequate has been whether the procedure used was *reasonably likely* to give the defendant actual notice.

c. Service on state official: Many of the non-resident motorist statutes described *supra*, p. 16, provide for constructive service on a *state official* (e.g., the State Director of Motor Vehicles) plus notice by mail to the defendant. *Hess v. Pawloski*, 274 U.S. 352 (1927).

d. Estoppel of defendant: A manner of notice otherwise insufficient may be sufficient by virtue of the fact that it is the *defendant's own acts* which make traditional service impossible. F,K&C, pp. 1091-92.

Example: An automobile owner who has moved from the address at which his car is registered without informing any authority of his move might be constructively served by service on his insurance company, if the insurer's identity is known.

e. Publication: Service by *newspaper publication* announcing the suit has been upheld in certain cases, e.g., where the defendant's identity is unknown. (This is discussed more fully in the analysis of *Mullane v. Central Hanover Bank, infra*.)

  i. Service on domiciliary in hiding: Service by publication has been upheld against a domiciliary of the forum state who *hides himself* within the state.

  ii. Publication insufficient: But service by publication will virtually never be constitutionally sufficient if the defendant's *name and address* are *known*. See, e.g., *Walker v. City of Hutchinson*, 352 U.S. 112 (1956).

3. **Service on corporations:** There are several means which are commonly allowed for giving notice of suit to *corporations.*

a. Official to receive process: The licensing procedures of many states require that a corporation, if it wishes to do business within the state, must **designate a corporate official** to receive process for suits against the company.

b. Notice to official: Many other statutes merely provide for notice to be given to any corporation official or manager.

   i. Constitutional test: Under such general statutes, the constitutional test seems to be whether the official occupies a position within the firm such that it is likely that he will pass on the process papers to the corporate lawyers or directors who will prepare the defense. Wr., 445-46.

c. Federal Rule: Federal Rule 4(h)(1)(B) states that service on a corporation may be made by giving the papers to "an officer, a managing or general agent, or any other agent authorized by appointment or by law to receive service of process." (See *supra*, p. 72.)

4. The *Mullane* balancing test: A **balancing test** is used to determine whether the particular form of notice meets the requirements of due process. The Supreme Court set forth this balancing test in ***Mullane v. Central Hanover Bank,*** 339 U.S. 306 (1950), a case posing the issue of whether notice by **publication** could suffice in cases involving relatively small sums.

a. Facts: The facts of *Mullane* were as follows:

   i. The Hanover Bank administered numerous **small trust funds**. The bank wished to settle the year's accounts for the funds, which it had pooled together for investment purposes.

   ii. The Bank brought proceedings to certify the settlement of the accounts, pursuant to state law. The court appointed Mullane to represent all those who had an interest in the trust funds.

   iii. The only notice given to the beneficiaries of the trust funds was through a newspaper announcement. The Bank had available to it the names and addresses of the beneficiaries, but claimed that it would be too costly for it to notify them all of the proceedings to settle the accounts, in view of the small sums involved in most of the accounts.

   iv. Mullane, the court-appointed beneficiaries' representative, objected to the court's jurisdiction, claiming that the requirement of reasonable notice to the beneficiaries was not met, and that therefore the court's certification of the accounts could not be binding.

b. Holding: The Court held that the **expense** of notification by mail, and the **availability of names and addresses** of beneficiaries, were factors that could be taken into account in determining whether publication was sufficient notice.

   i. Reasonableness standard: "The means [of notice] employed must be such as one desirous of actually informing the absentee might reasonably adopt to accomplish it." But this could be **limited by reasonable considerations of economy.**

      ii. **Names and addresses known:** Publication was ***insufficient*** notice to those beneficiaries whose names and addresses were ***known*** to the Bank.

      iii. **Names and addresses unknown:** But for those beneficiaries who were unknown or unlocatable, ***publication was a reasonable method of notice***.

5. ***Mullane* reasonableness test curtailed:** But the *Mullane* test of "reasonableness in view of all the circumstances" has been ***undercut*** by later cases.

    a. **Class actions:** For instance, the Court has held post-*Mullane* that the plaintiff in a ***federal class action*** must pay the costs of notifying by mail ***all*** members of the class whose names and addresses can be ascertained by "reasonable effort." *Eisen v. Carlisle & Jacquelin*, 417 U.S. 156 (1974). Since the class in *Eisen* numbered 2,250,000, and the individual plaintiff's stake in the litigation was only $70, the reasonableness test of *Mullane* does not seem to have been followed.

    b. **Mail notice to all "reasonable ascertainable" parties:** More generally, the Court seems not to apply the *Mullane* "reasonableness in view of all the circumstances" test as to ***any party*** who has any liberty or property interest in the controversy, if the party's name and address are ***"reasonably ascertainable."*** *Mennonite Board of Missions v. Adams*, 462 U.S. 791 (1983). Instead, notice by ***mail,*** or other means equally likely to insure actual notice, must be used.

    c. **Summary:** So the *Mullane* "reasonableness" test probably survives today, but only as a very general principle. That general principle is ***overridden*** by the more specific rule that ***publication*** notice will ***not*** be enough as to any party with an interest in the controversy whose name and address are ***reasonably ascertainable***. In the "reasonably ascertainable" situation, notice by mail or other personalized means must be used, even if its cost is very high relative to the interest at stake.

D. **Statutory provisions vs. actual results:** Generally what matters is the ***appropriateness*** of the notice prescribed by statute and employed, ***not*** whether the defendant actually ***got*** the notice.

1. **Actual notice not required:** Thus if a reasonable means of notification is prescribed by statute, and followed in the individual case, it does not matter that the defendant did not ***in fact*** receive notice. F,K&C, p. 1091. (Most states allow a statutory period after the entry of default judgments for defendants to claim their failure to receive actual notice, and to prepare a defense on the merits.)

2. **Actual notice not sufficient:** Conversely, if the prescribed statutory method is either insufficient, or is not followed, the fact that the individual defendant actually received notice does ***not*** make the service valid.

      Example: In *Wuchter v. Pizzutti*, 276 U.S. 13 (1928), the state notice statute (of the non-resident motorist variety) did not provide for actual mail notice on the defendant, but merely for constructive service on a state official. The Supreme Court held that the statute's notice provisions were invalid, even though in this case the state official mailed a copy of the summons to the defendant on his own initiative. ***Notice in the actual case did not resuscitate a formally invalid statute***, and service under the statute was held invalid.

E. Opportunity to be heard: The defendant must not only be notified of the suit against him, but must also be given an ***opportunity to be heard***. That is, in order for the state to "take" defendant's property from him (even if the taking is only temporary), the defendant must be given a chance to appear in court to tell his side of the story. This hearing requirement is imposed by the Due Process Clause of the 14th Amendment.

    1. Notice alone not enough: For instance, suppose that a state were to provide that P can serve D with a summons and complaint alleging that D is liable to P for money damages, and that without any further fact-finding by the state, D must pay the amount demanded to P. (Obviously, no rational state would enact such a statute.) Clearly, it would be a violation of due process for the state to give plaintiffs this kind of power over defendants — it is not enough that the defendant be given notice that the state (acting on behalf of the plaintiff) will be taking the defendant's property; the defendant must be given a chance to show a neutral state fact-finder (e.g., a judge) that on the merits, P's claim is wrong.

F. Prejudgment remedies, including attachment: Actually, it has always been pretty clear that states must give the defendant notice and an opportunity to be heard before the state renders a *final* decision on the defendant's civil liability. What is not so clear is the procedures that must be observed before states give plaintiffs ***temporary prejudgment relief***. Litigation can take a long time, and a plaintiff may reasonably fear that during the course of litigation, a defendant may hide his assets, fraudulently dispose of them, move from the jurisdiction, or otherwise act in such a way that the plaintiff will end up with a judgment but also an assetless defendant. Therefore, all states give plaintiffs various ways to try to prevent this kind of during-the-litigation dissipation of assets. Most commonly, states let the plaintiff under certain circumstances ***"attach"*** (i.e., tie up) the defendant's property after the litigation begins. Once the litigation is finished, if plaintiff wins, the attached assets can be used to satisfy the judgment; if defendant wins, the attachment is released.

    1. Illustrative techniques: Thus, states typically allow a plaintiff who meets certain requirements to (1) attach the defendant's real property by placing a "lis pendens" on it, which has the effect of preventing defendant from selling the property to anyone else; and (2) attach the defendant's bank accounts, by informing the bank that the account proceeds are to be frozen and not released to the defendant. Other devices help a plaintiff gain possession of property which, the plaintiff alleges, the plaintiff owns or has rights to even though the property is still in the defendant's possession. An example of this kind of procedural help is a statute allowing a creditor to ***repossess*** goods which the creditor claims to have sold to the defendant under agreements giving the creditor the right to repossess if the defendant does not pay. However, since federal and state laws limit the garnishment rights even of a creditor who has obtained a final judgment against a defendant, in all of these situations, the question becomes: ***What procedures must be followed before the state*** (acting on behalf of the creditor) ***impairs the defendant's interest in the property in question?***

    2. Significant property interest: Before we look at the detailed procedures that are required, we must first understand the circumstances under which the defendant has some right to procedural due process. Essentially, the rule is that the defendant has the right to notice and a hearing before there is a state-sponsored deprivation of ***any significant property interest*** on the part of the defendant. In other words, it is not just a final taking of the defendant's property that triggers due process, but even a *temporary* and *less-than-total* taking. For instance, if the state lets the plaintiff block the defendant from selling the defendant's real estate for even a few days, this is still a sufficiently significant property deprivation that due process must be obeyed.

a. **Significance of prior hearing:** Furthermore, the mere fact that the state gives some sort of a *hearing* before the deprivation is not enough to automatically establish that due process has been respected. Most battles over pre-judgment attachment techniques have focused on techniques that do not give the defendant a hearing until after the deprivation has already begun. (The recent leading case of *Connecticut v. Doehr*, discussed extensively below, is one illustration of this.) But even if the state gives the defendant notice and some sort of hearing before the deprivation occurs, the deprivation may violate due process if the hearing itself is conducted in such a way that it is too easy for the plaintiff, and too hard for the defendant, to win. For instance, if a state statute required a hearing before defendant's bank account could be attached, but provided that the attachment should be granted if, as a result of the hearing, "the court finds that there is *some possibility* that the plaintiff will prevail at trial and that the defendant will not have sufficient assets to satisfy a judgment," the Supreme Court would almost certainly hold that the rules of the game had been so rigged in favor of the plaintiff that due process was not followed.

3. **Test for due process:** Here, then, are the rules for determining when a state-sponsored deprivation of any significant property interest on the part of the defendant, made before a full trial on the merits, violates the defendant's due process rights:

a. **Three-part test:** A *three-part test* is to be used, the Supreme Court held in *Connecticut v. Doehr*, 501 U.S. 1 (1991). In judging the validity of a state statute that enables an individual to enlist the aid of the state to deprive another person of his property by means of a prejudgment attachment or similar procedure, the following three factors must be *balanced* against one another:

i. **Strength of D's private interest:** First, the interest of the private party who is being *harmed* by the prejudgment attachment or other procedure. The more important the defendant's property right (or the greater the interference with that property right), the harder it is for due process to be satisfied.

ii. **Risk of erroneous deprivation:** Second, the risk of an *erroneous determination*. The greater the risk that the particular *procedures* being used will result in an erroneous interference with defendant's property rights, the harder it is for the procedure to pass due process scrutiny. For instance, a procedure that makes it probable that the attachment will be granted even in circumstances where the defendant would eventually prevail on the merits is less likely to satisfy due process than a procedure that grants the prejudgment relief only to a plaintiff who shows that she is very likely to prevail ultimately on the merits. (The availability of *alternative procedural safeguards* is part of this examination of the risk of an erroneous deprivation.)

iii. **Interest of the party seeking the remedy:** Finally, on the other side of the scale, the strength of the interest of the party *seeking the prejudgment remedy*. For instance, where plaintiff has a large sum at stake and will probably prevail at trial, and it is also likely that the defendant will dissipate or conceal his assets if the pre-judgment remedy is not granted, this "plaintiff's interest" factor weighs more strongly in favor of a finding that due process has been observed than where, say, a large percentage of the defendant's property is being tied up to protect a small or weak claim on the part of the plaintiff which the defendant will probably be able to satisfy anyway even without prejudgment relief.

Example applying the three-part test: The facts of *Connecticut v. Doehr* show how the three-part test will be applied in practice (and, in fact, represent the only Supreme Court case so far applying this test, which originated in *Doehr.*) A Connecticut statute allows prejudgment attachment of D's real estate without giving D opportunity for a prior hearing, if P "verifies by oath" that there is probable cause to sustain the validity of his claim.

As to the first factor — the strength of the private interest (D's) that will be hurt by the prejudgment measure — here, the impact on D is significant; the attachment clouds title to the property, prevents D from selling it, affects his credit rating, and prevents him from getting a home equity loan or new mortgage. As to the second factor — the risk of erroneous deprivation — this, too, is substantial here. Even if the statute is read to mean that a judge must independently find that P will probably prevail (as opposed to determining merely that plaintiff honestly believes that he will prevail), "the judge could make no realistic assessment concerning the likelihood of an action's success based upon these one-sided, self-serving, and conclusory submissions." This factor also weighs against the validity of the procedure because the state fails to use other protections that it might have used, such as requiring the plaintiff to post a bond. (The fact that the property owner can get a reasonably prompt *post-attachment* hearing helps somewhat, but even a temporary interference with one's property rights is significant.) Finally, the last factor — the strength of the interest in favor of the attachment — works against a finding of validity; for instance, P was not required to show that D was about transfer or encumber his real estate or do anything else that would impair P's ability to collect a judgment if he should obtain one.

In summary, these three factors all mean that the Connecticut practice of allowing a pre-judgment attachment of real estate without a prior hearing, without a bond and without a showing of exigent circumstances, violates the property owner's 14th Amendment due process rights. *Connecticut v. Doehr, supra.*

4. **Some other examples of bad statutes:** Here are some other examples of statutes which have been found to be violations of a property owner's due process rights (these are all pre-*Doehr* decisions, but they probably remain valid).

a. **Wage garnishment:** A defendant's *wages* may not be *garnished* unless she has first been given a chance to show that the garnishor has no right to garnish. See *Sniadach v. Family Finance Corp.*, 395 U.S. 337 (1969).

b. **Bank account attachment:** A defendant's *bank account* may not be attached unless he is given the right to argue against the attachment either before it occurs or immediately thereafter. See *North Georgia Finishing, Inc. v. Di-Chem*, 419 U.S. 601 (1975).

   c. **Repossession of goods:**   A statute allowing a creditor to obtain ***repossession of goods*** before a hearing violates due process where it (1) allows repossession merely on the creditor's conclusory statement that he owns the property; (2) provides for a writ of possession issued by a clerk rather than a judge; and (3) does not provide for an immediate post-repossession hearing. See *Fuentes v. Shevin*, 407 U.S. 67 (1972). (But a statute allowing repossession by a creditor will be valid if it requires presentation of specific facts about the claim, requires that the facts be presented to a judge rather than to a clerk, and provides for an immediate post-repossession hearing at which the defendant can present his case. See *Mitchell v. W.T. Grant Co.*, 416 U.S. 600 (1974).)

  5. **Clues to a bad statute:**   Here are some statutory provisions that make it more likely that a due process violation will be found:

   a. **No bond by P:**   Due process is likely to be violated if the provision for pre-judgment attachment does ***not*** require the plaintiff to ***post a bond***, from which damages to the defendant can be paid if the attachment turns out to have been wrongful. See *Connecticut v. Doehr, supra* (four Justices conclude that due process virtually always requires the plaintiff to post a bond or other security even if a hearing and some showing of exigency are also required).

   b. **Deprivation before hearing:**   If the defendant does not get notice or opportunity for a hearing until sometime ***after*** the attachment, a due process violation is much more likely to be found than where the notice and hearing come before the deprivation. (But even a pre-attachment hearing does not insulate the procedure from due process attack, if the risk of an erroneous deprivation is too high or the plaintiff's interest in having the attachment is too weak.)

   c. **Clerk rather than judge:**   If the decision whether to allow the attachment is made by a ***clerk*** rather than by a judge, a due process violation is more likely to be found.

   d. **Conclusory statements:**   If the plaintiff is able to obtain the attachment by making ***conclusory statements*** rather than by making detailed disclosure of the underlying facts of the dispute, due process is more likely to be found to be violated.

  6. **State action:**   A due process violation can occur only where the state ***actively participates*** in the interference with the defendant's property rights. Usually, some action by a state official in connection with the particular case is necessary before state action will be found. For instance, the procedure under U.C.C. Article 9, whereby a creditor holding a security interest can repossess property that has not been paid for, does not involve state action and does not, therefore, need to meet due process requirements.

Quiz Yourself on
NOTICE AND OPPORTUNITY TO BE HEARD

  11. A statute of the state of Ames provides that in any action for personal injuries arising out of an automobile accident, the plaintiff may obtain a pre-judgment attachment of the defendant's bank account simultaneously with the filing of the plaintiff's suit. However, the plaintiff may obtain the attachment only by filing an affidavit stating that, to the best of P's knowledge, D was involved in, and was the cause of, the accident; the judge must then find that P appears to be acting in good faith. The statute also provides that the court must grant D a hearing, within one month after issuance of the attachment, at which D may show that he will probably not be found liable in the suit; if D makes such a showing, the attachment must be rescinded. D now attacks the statute as a violation of his right to due process. Should D prevail? _____

Answer

11. Yes. Under *Connecticut v. Doehr*, 501 U.S. 1 (1991), the court is to apply a three-part balancing test in determining whether a statute allowing for prejudgment attachment satisfies the due process rights of the person whose property is being attached (here, D): the court weighs the harm to D's property right, the risk of an erroneous deprivation, and the strength of the other party's (here, P) interest in obtaining the prejudgment attachment. Here, the impact on D is significant, since D can't spend the money in the account (and even a temporary, up-to-one-month deprivation would probably be found to be material). The risk of erroneous deprivation is substantial, because P's one-sided conclusory allegations (with no rebuttal by D or opportunity to cross-examine P or to present witnesses) leave the judge no real ability to assess the likelihood that P will prevail on the merits. The strength of P's interest in the attachment is weak, because the statute does not require P to show that D is about to transfer funds or do anything else that would make it hard for P to collect any judgment he might obtain. All in all, the statute here is marginally better than the one struck down in Doehr, but similar enough to it that it, too, would almost certainly be found to violate due process.

VIII. DEFENSES TO CLAIMS OF JURISDICTION

A. General principles: We examine in this section several defenses to claims of jurisdiction, including (1) the *special appearance* (by which the defendant may litigate the jurisdiction issue without automatically subjecting himself to personal jurisdiction by his mere appearance); (2) the *collateral attack* on another court's default judgment (and the companion issue of enforcement of sister state judgments); (3) the defense that jurisdiction was obtained by *fraud or duress*; and (4) the defense that the defendant is *immune* from service of the process of the court where the suit is in progress.

B. Special appearance: A *special appearance* is distinguished from a *general appearance*; in the latter, the defendant appears before the court to defend *on the merits*, and is thereby concluded to have *consented* or submitted to the court's personal jurisdiction over him. In the special appearance, the defendant appears with the *express purpose of making a jurisdictional objection*; his doing so is *not a consent* to the exercise of jurisdiction.

   1. Appeal: Most courts allow a defendant who has unsuccessfully made a special appearance to then defend on the merits, *without losing his right to appeal* the jurisdictional issue.

   a. Minority rule: Some courts do not follow this majority rule, and thereby force a defendant to make the following unpleasant choice:

   i. Appeal: He can stick to his unsuccessful jurisdictional objection, refuse to defend on the merits, allow a default judgment to be entered against him, and then appeal.

He thereby puts all his hopes on winning the jurisdictional question on appeal; he has lost his right to defend on the merits.

    ii. Defend: Alternatively, he can forget his unsuccessful jurisdictional objection, and defend on the merits. But by so doing, he loses the right to appeal the jurisdictional question.

    iii. Interlocutory appeal: Some of the majority-rule jurisdictions have alleviated the above dilemma by allowing an *interlocutory* appeal when a jurisdictional objection is made unsuccessfully. This lets the defendant make the appeal as soon as the trial court rules against him on jurisdiction — if he wins on appeal, the suit is dismissed; if he loses, he can then defend on the merits.

2. Federal and state substitutes for special appearance: The federal courts, and many state courts whose rules are patterned after the Federal Rules, have *abolished the special appearance*. Instead, a *motion* to dismiss for lack of jurisdiction over the parties may be made, without subjecting the movant to the jurisdiction he is protesting. Fed. Rule 12(b)(2).

    a. Waiver: The right to make a motion to dismiss for lack of jurisdiction of the parties is *waived* in the federal system if:

        i. Omitted from 12(b) motion: a motion is made raising any of the defenses listed in Rule 12 (e.g., failure to state a claim on which relief may be granted — Rule 12(b)(6)), and the personal jurisdiction defense is not included; or

        ii. Not made by motion or answer: the personal jurisdiction defense is not made either by a Rule 12 motion or in the answer. See Rule 12(h)(1).

    b. Distinguished from lack of subject matter jurisdiction: For waiver purposes, an objection to lack of jurisdiction over the *person* must be distinguished from one to lack of *subject matter* jurisdiction. The latter (e.g., "lack of diversity"; "jurisdictional amount not satisfied") may be made *at any time*, even after trial, and even at the court's own initiative. Rule 12(h)(3).

3. Special appearance in *quasi in rem* and *in rem* actions: In state courts, when suit is begun by attachment or garnishment (i.e., the plaintiff proceeds on the basis of asserted *quasi in rem* or *in rem* jurisdiction), the general rule is that D may appear specially to contest the validity of the attachment, without giving the court jurisdiction over his person. But not all courts allow this.

    a. Federal practice: In the *federal courts, both quasi in rem* (Rule 4(n)) and *in rem* (28 U.S.C. §1655) jurisdiction may be protested through a Rule 12(b) jurisdictional objection, just as for lack of *in personam* jurisdiction. This objection, by motion or answer, has the effect of a special appearance.

C. Enforcement of judgments: A judgment entered in one jurisdiction may be *enforced* in another. That is, the defendant's property in one state, or wages owed him in that state, may be seized to satisfy the judgment entered in another state.

1. Procedure: In order to sue on a foreign judgment, the victorious plaintiff must institute a new suit in the second state, and then prove that he has received the original judgment.

The second court must then enter an identical judgment, which serves as the basis for levy and/or garnishment in the second state.

    a. Merits not reviewable: The second court may not reconsider the merits of the original controversy, even if the first court's conclusion was patently incorrect. The only exception to this rule is if the first court is shown to have lacked personal or subject matter jurisdiction, and the jurisdictional issue was *not* litigated in that first court, i.e., a "collateral attack," discussed *infra*, p. 95.

  2. Rules: The following rules govern the effect given to one jurisdiction's judgment in another jurisdiction:

    a. Two state courts (Full Faith and Credit): If both judgments are in *state* courts, the second court is compelled to give the first judgment the same effect it would have had in the first state. This is required by the Full Faith and Credit Clause of the Constitution (Art. IV, § 1).

    b. State judgment followed by federal suit: If the first judgment is in state court, then a federal court is obligated to give the first judgment full faith and credit by a statutory provision, 28 U.S.C. §1738.

    c. Federal judgment followed by state suit: If the first judgment is in federal court, the *Supremacy Clause* of the U.S. Constitution (Art. 6) requires a subsequent state court to give the federal judgment the same effect it would have if sued on in federal court.

    d. Both courts federal: If both judgments are in federal courts, the second court respects the first because they are both arms of the same sovereignty, just as two trial courts in the same state respect each other's judgments.

      i. Registration of judgments: A judgment entered in any federal court may be *registered* in any other federal court, thus abolishing the need for a separate suit for enforcement. 28 U.S.C. §1963.

      ii. State registration: A similar registration procedure has been proposed for the states, and a number of states have adopted it. F,K&C, p. 949.

D. Collateral attack: A defendant who *defaults* in an action in one jurisdiction may *collaterally attack* the default judgment when it is sued upon in a second jurisdiction.

  1. Basis of attack: The defendant may make such a collateral attack either upon the first court's jurisdiction over the parties, or upon its subject matter jurisdiction.

    a. Personal jurisdiction: The defendant may argue that the first court lacked *in personam* jurisdiction over him.

    b. *In rem:* He may argue that the *quasi in rem* or *in rem* jurisdiction purportedly exercised over his property by the first court was invalid.

    c. Extrinsic fraud: He may argue that his failure to appear in the first action was the result of *fraud* by the plaintiff. Fraud inducing a party not to appear is often classified as "extrinsic fraud" (as distinguished from "intrinsic fraud," which relates to the litigation itself, and which is not grounds for collateral attack).

Example: P sues D in Penn. As D is about to move to dismiss, P induces D not to defend the first action because, P says (falsely), the suit will be discontinued. Unbeknownst to D, P goes ahead and gets a default judgment. If P then sues in California to enforce the default judgment, D will probably be able to collaterally attack that judgment on grounds of extrinsic fraud.

    d. Subject matter jurisdiction: The defendant may also argue that the first court had no statutory authority to try the kind of case or grant the kind of relief in question (i.e., that it lacks subject matter jurisdiction). For instance, if the first court, a municipal court not empowered to try matrimonial actions, had granted a divorce, the defendant could attack this.

2. Waiver: A defendant who *appeared in the original action* without objecting to jurisdiction, or one who *unsuccessfully litigated the jurisdictional issue* in the first action, may *not* collaterally attack the judgment. The unsuccessful objection to jurisdiction may, of course, be repeated on appeal to a court superior to the first trial court; but this is a *direct*, rather than *collateral*, attack.

    Example: Defendant makes a special appearance in a Missouri District Court, loses on his jurisdictional objection, then declines to answer. A default judgment is entered against him. Plaintiff then sues in Iowa District Court to enforce the judgment. Defendant raises the jurisdictional objection again. *Held* (by the U.S. Supreme Court), Defendant had no right to raise the jurisdictional objection a second time. *Baldwin v. Iowa State Traveling Men's Ass'n.*, 283 U.S. 522 (1931).

E. Defense of fraud or duress: Presence, however transient, can be a basis for personal jurisdiction. But if this presence is the result of *fraud* or *duress* on the part of the plaintiff, the court may decide not to exercise jurisdiction.

1. Discretionary: If the defendant has been *induced into the jurisdiction* by fraud or duress, it is probably not a violation of Constitutional due process for the court to exercise jurisdiction over him, but most courts will, as a matter of *discretion, refuse to exercise* this jurisdiction. Rest. Conflicts 2nd, §82.

    a. No collateral attack: If the court does decide to exercise jurisdiction where fraud or duress was involved, this jurisdiction may not be collaterally attacked, if this issue or any other was litigated in the first court. (This is by the general principle of Full Faith and Credit — *even if the first court's exercise of jurisdiction was clearly unconstitutional*, the second state court must respect it, if the defendant appeared in the first court. Only the U.S. Supreme Court can overrule a final, non-default, state court judgment.)

    b. Where first court's judgment is by default: But if the first court enters a *default judgment*, the defendant may raise the fraud or duress defense as part of a collateral attack when enforcement is sought in a second state. Cf. *Wyman v. Newhouse*, 93 F.2d 313 (2d Cir. 1937).

2. Person already in state: Where a potential defendant is *already within the forum state*, most jurisdictions hold that he may be served by *resort to subterfuge*. At first glance, it might seem inconsistent to allow subterfuge in this situation, but not to allow it when it is used to induce the defendant into the forum state. The two situations can be distinguished, however: Trickery used to serve a person *already in the jurisdiction voluntarily* does not confer a right which the court would not otherwise have had (since the court has the *power* to exercise jurisdiction over a person just by virtue of that person's presence in the state). When deception is used to *induce a person into the jurisdiction*, by contrast, the trickery puts a person into the court's power who would not otherwise be within that power.

    a. Substitute service: The issue does not arise too often today, since many states have statutes providing for substitute service (e.g., at the last known dwelling place) for one who is known to be within the state but who is in hiding.

  3. Federal practice: The federal courts follow their own, rather than state, principles with respect to fraud or duress. In general, service on a party induced into the jurisdiction by fraud or deceit is *invalid.* Wr., 444-45.

F. Immunity: Most jurisdictions give to nonresidents of the forum state an immunity from service of process while they are in the state to *attend a trial* either as witnesses, parties, or attorneys. James & Hazard, p. 79. Immunity is also granted for a reasonable time period before and after trial, for the journey into and out of the state. Most states also grant the immunity for related proceedings such as *depositions*.

  1. Witnesses: Of the persons listed in the preceding paragraph, the case for immunity is strongest for *witnesses. Id.*

    a. Rationale: Witnesses cannot be forced to testify in a state of which they are not residents. Therefore, the forum state has an interest in having them come in voluntarily, and to the extent to which immunity from service induces them to do so, it is justifiable.

  2. Defendants: Immunity for *defendants* is also probably a good idea on balance. If immunity is not granted, some defendants will not attend trial, resulting in a default judgment being entered against them. Since such a judgment can be collaterally attacked when it is sued on for enforcement in another jurisdiction, plaintiff is forced not only to sue a second time, but also to run the risk that the second court will find that the first lacked jurisdiction.

    a. Actions concerning related facts: The case for defendant immunity is especially strong where the two suits involve *related facts*, and the defendant is making a special or limited appearance in the first suit. If the plaintiff in the case for which a special or limited appearance was being made by the defendant were allowed to serve him on a cause of action closely related to the original cause of action, the doctrines of special and limited appearance would be vitiated; defendants would always be afraid of being subjected to personal jurisdiction if they set foot in the forum state at all.

    b. Immunity for criminal defendants: The courts are split on whether to grant immunity from civil suit to defendants in *criminal actions*. If the defendant comes in voluntarily, there is good reason to grant him this immunity, and thus spare the expense and bother of extradition proceedings. But if the defendant is in the forum state only because extradition proceedings have brought him there, the weight of authority denies him immunity from process, since his presence in the state would not have been facilitated by immunity. James & Hazard, 643-44.

3. **Plaintiffs:** Immunity for ***non-resident plaintiffs*** is harder to justify than for witnesses and defendants, since the plaintiff is pursuing his own self-interest in the forum state. But there is nonetheless good reason for a state to encourage in-state suits against at least those of its citizens who could be reached by the long-arms of other states, since it is more convenient for those citizens to be sued at home than elsewhere.

4. **Federal immunity:** In *federal* suits, both diversity and federal question, the fact that a person would be immune from service in the courts of the state where the federal court sits is irrelevant; the federal courts treat immunity as a matter of *federal*, not state, law. Wr., 445.

    a. **Federal rule:** In general, the federal courts grant immunity from a federal suit to ***parties***, ***witnesses*** and ***attorneys*** coming into the state in connection with a different (state or federal) suit. Wr., p. 445.

Quiz Yourself on
DEFENSES TO CLAIMS OF JURISDICTION

12. P is a resident of New Mexico. D is a resident of Arizona. P sued D in diversity in federal court for New Mexico, and made service on D in Arizona in a manner that he believed to be authorized by the New Mexico long-arm statute. D filed a motion under Federal Rule 12(b)(6) for failure to state a claim upon which relief can be granted; this motion asserted that P's claim was barred by the applicable statute of limitations. The court considered and rejected D's motion. D then made a motion pursuant to Rule 12(b)(2), claiming that the federal court lacked personal jurisdiction over D. D does not in fact have minimum contacts with New Mexico. Should the court grant D's second motion? _____

13. Same facts as prior question. Now, however, assume that D has not made a 12(b)(6) motion or a motion to dismiss for lack of jurisdiction. This is because he has placed his lawyer on a tight budget, and has told her not to make any motions at all. What should D's lawyer do to assert D's claim of lack of personal jurisdiction, without subjecting D to the court's general jurisdiction by the very act of raising the lack-of-jurisdiction objection? _____

14. P is a resident of New York. D is a resident of New Jersey. While P was driving through New Jersey, D (who operates a fast food restaurant) served P a hamburger. P ate the hamburger in New Jersey, but became violently ill upon his return to New York. P sued D in New York state court for negligence and product liability. Service on D was carried out by means authorized by the New York long-arm statute. D never appeared in the New York courts in any way, and thus did not contest New York's jurisdiction over him. The New York court issued a default judgment against him.

Since all of D's assets were in New Jersey, P brought a suit in New Jersey to enforce the New York judgment. In the New Jersey suit on the judgment, D convinced the New Jersey court that under applicable U.S. Supreme Court decisions, the New York court had erred in deciding that it could constitutionally exercise personal jurisdiction over D, because D did not knowingly and voluntarily take action that would bring his products into New York. Must the New Jersey court enforce the New York judgment against D, thus allowing P to seize D's property to satisfy that judgment? _____

Answers

12. **No.** D has *waived* his meritorious claim of lack of personal jurisdiction by failing to make it as part of the initial motion under Rule 12(b) that he made. Under Rule 12(h)(1), a defense of lack of jurisdiction over the person is waived if it is "omitted from a motion in the circumstances described in subdivision (g) …," which is a sub-section that allows a party only one 12(b) motion per case. (If D had not made his 12(b)(6) motion, he could have asserted his claim of lack of personal jurisdiction as part of his answer.)

13. **Assert the defense as part of D's answer.** Any defense, including the defense of lack of jurisdiction, may in the federal system be asserted as part of the defendant's answer. The defendant's right to do this is implied by Federal Rule 12(b) and 12(h)(1)(B).

14. **No.** The Full Faith and Credit Clause of the Constitution (Article IV, Section 1) provides that where a judgment from State 1 is sued upon in State 2, the courts of State 2 must give that judgment the same effect as it would have in State 1. Thus normally, a defendant may not "collaterally attack" the first court's jurisdiction when the judgment is sued upon in the second court. However, there is one exception to this general rule: the defendant *will* be permitted in the State 2 proceedings to collaterally attack the judgment issued against him in State 1 if: State 1 issued a *default judgment* against the defendant, *and* the defendant *did not appear* for *any reason* in the State 1 proceeding (even to unsuccessfully contest jurisdiction there). Observe, however, that D took a big chance by letting a default judgment be issued against him in the New York proceedings: if the New Jersey court had disagreed with D's jurisdictional argument, D would have lost his right to defend on the merits in the New Jersey courts, since under the Full Faith and Credit Clause the New Jersey courts would have had no choice but to enforce New York's judgment against D once the court concluded that the New York court had personal jurisdiction over D.

IX. VENUE

A. **General principles:**

1. **Definition of venue:** Venue refers to the *place within a sovereign jurisdiction* in which a given action is to be brought. It becomes a consideration only when jurisdiction over the parties has been established.

   Example: State X is found to have jurisdiction over the person of B, in a suit against him by A. Venue determines in which *county* or *district* of State X the case shall be tried.

2. **Venue in state courts statutory:** Venue in state trials is almost exclusively determined by statute, and has few if any Constitutional implications.

3. **Land:** Courts frequently refuse to try cases involving certain transactions relating to *land* lying in another jurisdiction. Sometimes the court bases this refusal on *venue* principles, sometimes on *subject matter jurisdictional* ones.

4. *Forum non conveniens:* Courts will sometimes refuse to exercise their jurisdiction over the parties, on the grounds that it would be more convenient to try the case elsewhere,

either in a court of their own jurisdiction, or in one of another jurisdiction. This refusal, based on principles of venue, is known as the doctrine of *forum non conveniens.*

5. **Venue in federal cases:** Venue in federal cases is controlled by 28 U.S.C. §1391, the general federal venue statute. It provides mainly for venue based on the *defendant's residence*, the place where a substantial part of the relevant *events occurred*, or the place where defendant can be made *subject to personal jurisdiction.* See *infra*, p. 103.

B. **Venue in state actions:** Venue in state actions is determined by many different tests. Generally, plaintiff has a choice of several different criteria in determining where he may bring his action.

1. **Places for state court venue:** Among the places (usually a county or judicial district of the state) where venue is sometimes determined to lie are the following: (F,K&C, p. 1053.)

   a. where the *cause of action arose;*

   b. where the *defendant resides;*

   c. where the *defendant has a place of business*, or agent;

   d. where the *plaintiff does business;*

   e. where the *seat of government is located; or*

   f. in the county *designated in plaintiff's complaint.*

2. **Most common test:** "The most common provision today, and the basic one, appears to be venue based upon the *residence of the defendant."* J & H (3d ed.), 607.

3. **Waiver:** Objections to venue are *waived* unless they are seasonably made, generally speaking. The time for making an objection to improper venue is often at an early stage in the proceedings.

4. **Effect of improper venue:** If jurisdiction is good, but venue improper, a judgment is good against a defendant who defaults, and may *not be collaterally attacked* when sued upon for enforcement in another jurisdiction. F,K&C, p. 1053.

   a. **Rationale:** The courts' refusal to allow collateral attacks on venue may be justified as follows: since the venue privilege is purely a matter of convenience for the defendant, and involves no element of the forum state's *power* to adjudicate the case before it, its absence is in a sense less severe than the absence of personal jurisdiction. Thus where a default judgment is open to collateral attack in the state where it is sought to be enforced, on the grounds that personal jurisdiction was lacking, the sovereignty of the original forum is brought into question. But an objection to originally improper venue would involve only the discretionary decision of the original forum state to use the power of adjudication which it had; the objection is thus less serious, since the venue privilege is not mandated by any constitutional principles. (Presumably a state could, once it had jurisdiction over the parties, try an action in any county it wished.)

C. **Transitory vs. local actions:** State courts will sometimes refuse to try actions involving *land* located in other jurisdictions. These actions intimately involving land are often called *local* actions (as distinguished from *transitory* actions).

Example: A sues B for trespass to land lying in State X. State Y may decline to try the suit, even though it may have personal jurisdiction over B. See *Livingston v. Jefferson*, 15 Fed.Cas. 660, No. 8,411 (C.C.D.Va. 1811).

1. **Basis for court's refusal:** It is often unclear whether this refusal to try such a land-related case is based on lack of ***in rem*** jurisdiction (under the theory that the *res* of the suit is land, which is not within the state's boundaries, and thus not within the control of its courts) or on a lack of venue.

   a. **Discretionary:** Probably the refusal to exercise jurisdiction is a discretionary one, mandated not by any constitutional principles, but by considerations of comity and convenience. James & Hazard, 49.

2. **No test:** No clear rule exists for distinguishing ***local*** actions (trial of which a court is likely to decline because the land lies elsewhere) from ***transitory*** ones (which the court will try even though the suit relates in some way to out-of-state land).

   Example: When a plaintiff seeks specific performance of a contract to sell land, it is generally held that any court which has jurisdiction over the defendant's person has jurisdiction to enter a judgment commanding specific performance, although such an action concerns land intimately.

   a. **Trespass:** Almost all states hold that ***trespass*** actions are local (as did the court in *Livingston v. Jefferson*, *supra*, p. 101). Therefore, states generally refuse to try suits for damages from trespass to land lying in other states.

   b. **Conversion; specific performance:** Actions for ***conversion***, and actions for ***specific performance*** of land-sale contracts, are generally ***not considered local*** for venue purposes, and may thus be brought wherever personal jurisdiction may be had. Similarly, where the action affecting land in State X took place in State Y, most courts will allow suit in either place.

D. ***Forum non conveniens:*** Under the doctrine of ***"forum non conveniens,"*** a court having jurisdiction over a particular case may use its ***discretion*** to ***decline to exercise*** that jurisdiction, if the court concludes that the action could be more appropriately tried in ***some other jurisdiction***.

   Example: Suppose that P1, P2 and W, all New York residents, are travelling in a car that crashes while passing through Oklahoma. P1 and P2 are injured. The Ps bring suit in Oklahoma state court against D1 and D2, the retailer and manufacturer of the car, respectively, on a products liability theory. D1 and D2 have their principal place of business in New York, and are incorporated there. Assume that these two defendants have just enough contacts with Oklahoma for it to be constitutional for the Oklahoma courts to hear suits against them. The only witness to the accident is W, who has no other connection with Oklahoma.

   The Oklahoma court clearly has constitutionally-sufficient jurisdiction to hear the suit. But the Oklahoma court might invoke the doctrine of *forum non conveniens* to decline to hear the suit, on the grounds that the parties' and witness' links to New York are far stronger than those to Oklahoma, and that the suit is therefore better heard in New York. (Probably the dismissal on grounds of *forum non conveniens* would come in response to a motion by the defendants, but the Oklahoma court might decide on its own to dismiss.)

1. **Rationale:** Two independent policy considerations seem to be involved in a court's decision to invoke the doctrine of *forum non conveniens* (James & Hazard, p. 87):

    a. **Parties' convenience:** The **parties** have an interest in having the litigation conducted in the **most convenient locale**. (When the doctrine is invoked, it is generally the **defendant** whose convenience is being respected, since the plaintiff has usually indicated his own convenience in his original choice of forum.)

    b. **State's interest:** The state has an interest in **not burdening its courts** with litigation not connected with the state. (This only becomes a consideration when the more convenient forum lies outside the original forum state; a court's decision to transfer the case to another court within the same jurisdiction is also sometimes referred to as invoking the *forum non conveniens* doctrine, but does not reflect the state's interest in being free of litigation unrelated to the state.)

2. **Factors in decision:** Among the factors which have been considered by courts in determining whether to invoke the doctrine are the following (James & Hazard, p. 87):

    a. Is the plaintiff a state **resident** and taxpayer? (If so, he should have a right to the judicial machinery of his state.)

    b. In which forum are the **witnesses** and sources of proof most available?

    c. Which forum will be **familiar with** the state law that must govern the case? Conflict-of-laws principles may require a court to apply the law of a different state; it is generally undesirable to have "a court in some other forum untangle problems in conflict of laws, and in law foreign to itself." *Gulf Oil v. Gilbert*, 330 U.S. 501 (1947).

3. **Unfavorable change in law insufficient:** The mere fact that the law of the alternative forum is **less favorable to the plaintiff** is **not** by itself grounds for denying the defendant's *forum non conveniens* motion. This is illustrated by a Supreme Court case, *Piper Aircraft Co. v. Reyno*, 454 U.S. 235 (1981).

    a. **Facts:** In *Piper*, a plane built by an American manufacturer crashed in Scotland, killing all aboard. Plaintiff, the decedents' representative, brought a wrongful death action in Pennsylvania Federal District Court. (The American manufacturer of the plane's propellers, as well as the plane's manufacturer, were joined as defendants.) The defendants, in moving for a dismissal based on *forum non conveniens*, argued that Scotland was a more appropriate forum: the decedents and their heirs were all Scottish citizens, and the necessary witnesses to the crash and to the prior maintenance of the airplane were located in Scotland and Great Britain. (Also, because of choice-of-law principles, Scottish law would have had to be applied to one, but not the other, defendant.) However, the plaintiff opposed the *non conveniens* motion because Scottish law was much less favorable to her. For instance, it did not recognize strict tort liability, and also limited the items of damages.

    b. **Grant of motion upheld:** The Supreme Court rejected plaintiff's assertion that a *forum non conveniens* motion should be denied wherever it would result in application of law less favorable to the plaintiff than the law applying in the plaintiff's originally-chosen forum. In fact, the Court stated that the likelihood of an unfavorable change in law should not even be given "substantial," let alone "conclusive," weight in the *forum non conveniens* decision.

i. **Rationale:** The Court stressed that the essential purpose of the *forum non conveniens* doctrine is to assure that the litigation takes place in the most **convenient** forum. Since most litigation could take place (at least from the standpoint of jurisdiction) in two or more forums, a rule that *forum non conveniens* will not be applied where the law would be less favorable to the plaintiff would strip *forum non conveniens* of most of its utility, and would lead to trials in "plainly inconvenient" forums.

ii. **Foreign plaintiff:** Where the plaintiff (or, as here, the real party in interest) is a *foreigner*, the considerations against stripping the plaintiff of an American forum are even weaker, the Court noted. The usual presumption that the plaintiff has chosen a convenient forum is not applicable where a foreign plaintiff has selected a United States forum.

iii. **No real remedy available:** But the Court indicated that if the remedy provided by the alternative forum was "so clearly inadequate or unsatisfactory that it is no remedy at all," the unfavorable change in law could be given substantial weight in the *forum non conveniens* decision. For instance, if the alternative forum did not allow litigation of the very **subject matter** of the dispute, this might be a reason for denying the *forum non conveniens* motion. But here, all that would be lost to plaintiff was a more favorable rule on liability and a somewhat broader gamut of damages, not all possibility of a reasonably adequate remedy.

E. **Venue in federal actions:** In *federal* actions, the venue question is: "*Which federal district court* shall try the action?"

1. **Federal statute:** The general federal venue statute is 28 U.S.C. §1391. The main provisions of §1391 are as follows:

   "(b) **Venue in General.** A civil action may be brought in—

   (1) a judicial district in which **any defendant resides**, if **all defendants are residents of the State** in which the district is located;

   (2) a judicial district in which **a substantial part of the events or omissions giving rise to the claim occurred**, or a substantial part of property that is the subject of the action is situated; or

   (3) **if there is no district in which an action may otherwise be brought** as provided in this section, **any judicial district in which any defendant is subject to the court's personal jurisdiction** with respect to such action.

   (c) **Residency.** For all venue purposes—

   (1) a **natural person**, including an alien lawfully admitted for permanent residence in the United States, shall be deemed to reside in **the judicial district in which that person is domiciled;**

   (2) an **entity** with the capacity to sue and be sued in its common name under applica-

ble law, whether or not *incorporated*, shall be deemed to reside, if a *defendant*, in *any judicial district* in which such defendant is *subject to the court's personal jurisdiction* with respect to the civil action in question and, if a *plaintiff*, only in the judicial *district* in which it *maintains its principal place of business*; and

(3) a defendant *not resident in the United States* may be sued in *any judicial district*, and the joinder of such a defendant shall be *disregarded* in determining where the action may be brought with respect to *other* defendants.

(d) Residency of Corporations in States With Multiple Districts. For purposes of venue under this chapter, in a State which has *more than one judicial district* and in which a defendant that is a *corporation* is subject to personal jurisdiction at the time an action is commenced, such corporation shall be deemed to reside *in any district in that State within which its contacts would be sufficient to subject it to personal jurisdiction if that district were a separate State*, and, if there is *no such district*, the corporation shall be deemed to reside in the *district within which it has the most significant contacts*."

a. **Definition of "judicial district":**   The venue statute, as you can see, uses the term *"judicial district."* A federal judicial district can consist either of a whole state, or a portion of a state. Generally, the more populous a state, the more federal judicial districts it is likely to contain. Thus in Rhode Island, there is only one district, and one district court, the Rhode Island federal district court. In New York, on the other hand, there are four districts, the Southern (which includes Manhattan), Eastern, Northern and Western Districts.

b. **Still need personal jurisdiction:**   When you consider a venue problem, remember that venue is *not a substitute* for *personal jurisdiction*: the fact that venue lies in a particular judicial district does not automatically mean that suit can be brought there. Suit can be brought only in a district that satisfies *both* the venue requirements and the personal jurisdiction requirements as to all defendants. (Remember that in federal question cases, the defendant is generally held to be subject to personal jurisdiction as long as jurisdiction could constitutionally be exercised over him in the state courts of the state where the federal court is sitting, and service is validly made. In diversity cases, there is personal jurisdiction only if this would not only be constitutional but also would be allowed by the long-arm of the state in which the federal court sits. See *supra*, p. 73.)

Example: P is a citizen of Massachusetts. D, a car dealer, is a citizen of Connecticut. D sold a Buick to P in Connecticut. P then drove the car to Massachusetts, where he was involved in an accident. P brings suit in Massachusetts federal district court against D, in diversity, alleging that D is liable for P's injuries based on a strict product liability theory. Assume that Massachusetts has a very limited long-arm statute, which covers tortious actions occurring in Massachusetts, but which does not cover the sale of a defective product outside Massachusetts which later causes injury in Massachusetts.

The federal venue statute, 28 U.S.C. §1391, gives P venue in Massachusetts: §1391(b)(2) puts venue in a judicial district "in which a substantial part of the events or omissions giving rise to the claim occurred …," a test which is satisfied here. But the federal district court of Massachusetts will *not* exercise jurisdiction over D. Why?

Because in diversity cases a federal court will exercise only that personal jurisdiction which would be exercised by the state in which the federal court sits, and here, by hypothesis, Massachusetts would not exercise personal jurisdiction over D because of the limited Massachusetts long-arm. Consequently, the fact that there is *venue* in Massachusetts is irrelevant — the case cannot be heard there because of lack of personal jurisdiction over D.

c. **Three methods:**   Section 1391(b) gives *three basic methods* for determining whether there is venue in a particular judicial district. There is venue in a district if *any* of these three things is true:

[1] *any* defendant *resides* in that district, and *all defendants reside in the state* containing that district (a test applicable in *both diversity and federal question* cases);

[2] "a *substantial part* of the *events* or omissions giving rise to the claim *occurred*, or a substantial part of *property* that is the subject of the action is *situated* …" in the district (again, a test that is applicable whether the case is based on diversity or federal question); or

[3] two things are true: (a) there is *no district* in which the action may otherwise be brought (i.e., no district meeting either of the above two requirements); and (b) at least one defendant is *"subject to the court's personal jurisdiction"* with respect to the suit.

We consider each of these three main bases for venue separately below.

2. **"Defendant's residence" venue:**   For both diversity and federal question cases, venue lies in any district where *any defendant resides*, so long as, if there is more than one defendant, *all* the defendants reside in the *state* containing that district.

Example 1: P, a citizen of Massachusetts, brings a diversity suit against D1, a resident of the Southern District of New York, and D2, a resident of the Eastern District of New York. Based on §1391(b)(1), venue will lie in either the Southern District of New York or the Eastern District of New York — each of these is home to at least one defendant, and each is in a state that is home to all defendants.

Example 2: P, a citizen of Massachusetts, brings a diversity suit (or, for that matter, a federal question suit) against D1, a resident of the Southern District of New York, and D2, a resident of the District of Connecticut. Now, §1391(b)(1) does *not* furnish any "defendant's residence" venue anywhere. This is because there is no state in which all defendants reside. P will have to rely either on "place of events" venue, or on the "escape hatch" of §1391(b)(3)).

3. **"Place of events or property" venue:**   For both diversity and federal question cases, venue will lie in any judicial district "in which a *substantial part* of the *events* or omissions giving rise to the claim occurred, or a substantial part of *property* that is the subject of the action is situated. …" §1391(b)(2).

a. **Multiple districts possible:**   Notice that there does not have to be a *single* district where "the claim arose." Instead, there can be *multiple* districts qualifying for "place of events" venue, as long as a ***"substantial part"*** of the events relating to the claim occurred in each of those districts.

Example: P, a citizen of Massachusetts, sues D, a car dealer who is a citizen of Connecticut. The claim alleges that D sold P a car in Connecticut, that P drove the car to Massachusetts, and that a defect in the car caused P to be injured in Massachusetts. Probably venue in ***either*** the District of Massachusetts or the District of Connecticut would be allowed under the "place of events" provision (§1391(b)(2)), since probably both the selling of a defective car, and the incurring of an accident, are a "substantial part" of the events giving rise to P's product liability claim.

4. **The "escape hatch" provision:**   Finally, for both diversity and federal question cases, there is a kind of ***"escape hatch,"*** by which venue may be founded in a district in which at least one defendant is ***subject to the federal court's jurisdiction*** for the claim in question, ***"if there is no district in which an action may otherwise be brought."*** §1391(b)(3).

   a. **Foreign events:** As we describe further below, this escape hatch is mainly used for cases in which ***nearly all of the events occurred abroad.***

   b. **Examples of how the escape hatch works:** Let's look at an examples of how the escape hatch can work:

   Example: P, a resident of Massachusetts, brings a diversity action against D1, a resident of the Southern District of New York, and D2, a resident of Connecticut. P's suit is brought in the Southern District of New York. The suit relates solely to matters which occurred in Mexico. "Defendant's residence" venue, based on §1391(b)(1), does not exist, because it is not the case that *all* the defendants reside in New York state. Similarly, "place of events" venue does not lie in the Southern District, because it is not the case that a "substantial part" of the relevant events occurred in that district. But §1391(b)(3) saves the day — D1 is obviously "subject to personal jurisdiction" in the district in which he resides (and only one defendant has to have that connection with the district).[31]

   Before concluding that §1391(b)(3)'s escape hatch applies, remember that it applies *only* if "there is *no other district* in which the action may otherwise be brought." This requirement is satisfied here: There's no "defendants' residence" venue since there's no single state in which all defendants reside, and there's no "place of events or property" venue since everything happened in Mexico.

   c. **Foreign events:**   Always remember that escape hatch (§1391(b)(3)) applies ***only*** "if there is ***no district in which the action may otherwise be brought.***" Therefore, you must analyze, especially, the places where the ***events occurred*** to make sure that there is no "place of events" venue in a district from which personal jurisdiction over all defendants could be gotten. The main utility of the escape hatch is for cases where

---

31. All defendants will have to be subject to service under the long-arm of the *state* where the district court sits — and have minimum contacts with that state — because of the rules on personal jurisdiction and service in diversity cases; see *supra*, p. 74. But as a matter of venue, only one defendant needs to have this connection with the actual *district*, under §1391(b)(3).

nearly all of the events occurred *abroad* (since this would knock out "place of events" venue anywhere in the U.S.).

    i.   **Other applications:** The escape hatches might also help in the rare situation in which events are *so spread out* that no district accounts for a "substantial part" of the events.

5. **No "plaintiff's residence" venue:** Notice that there is *no* venue based on the *plaintiff's residence*.

6. **Corporation:** The residence of a *corporation* for venue purposes matters only if the corporation is a defendant. A special section, §1391(d), deals with the residence of corporate defendants in multi-district states. That section says, in part:

> [I]n a State which has *more than one judicial district* and in which a defendant that is a *corporation* is subject to personal jurisdiction at the time an action is commenced, such corporation shall be deemed to reside *in any district in that State within which its contacts would be sufficient to subject it to personal jurisdiction if that district were a separate State*, and, if there is no such district, the corporation shall be deemed to reside in the *district within which it has the most significant contacts*.

So in the typical case involving *specific* jurisdiction (i.e., the suit relates to the corporation's in-state activities; see *supra*, p. 9), a corporation will be deemed to be a resident of at least:

    [1] the district where it has its *principal place of business*;

    [2] any district where it has *substantial operations*;

    [3] (probably) *any district* in its *state of incorporation.*

But it is no longer the case, as it once was, that if a corporation does business anywhere in a state, it is automatically deemed to reside in *all districts* of that state.

> **Example:** D, a one-store jewelry-retailing corporation, is incorporated in Delaware (which has only one federal judicial district). D's only store is in New York City (in the Southern District of New York), and the corporation makes sales only to people who visit the store. P, a New Jersey resident, buys an expensive diamond ring at D's store, later finds that it's fake, and wants to sue D in diversity for breach of warranty.
>
> For venue purposes, D is a resident of the District of Delaware and the Southern District of New York. Therefore P may bring suit either in the District of Delaware (based on district-where-all-defendants-reside venue, coupled with the any-district-in-the-state-where-corporate-defendant-is-incorporated provision of §1391(d)) or the Southern District of New York (based on district-where-all-defendants-reside venue, coupled with the any-district-where-corporate-defendant-has-its-principal-place-of-business provision of §1391(d)). But P may *not* sue D in, say, the Northern District of New York. That is, the fact that D conducts substantial business operations in one part of New York state (Southern District) does not mean that venue in another part of that state (Northern District) is proper. Furthermore, we know that D conducts no business operations in N.D.N.Y. Therefore, we know that N.D.N.Y. itself does not satisfy any of the three corporate-venue provisions of §1391(d) (district of principal place of busi-

ness, district where substantial operations occur, and all districts of state of incorporation). Therefore, venue can't be in N.D.N.Y.

7. **Unincorporated associations:** Unincorporated associations (e.g., partnerships, labor unions, etc.) are treated like corporations for venue purposes. Wr., 266.

    a. **Distinction:** Such associations are not treated like corporations for *citizenship* purposes, however. Thus, a union with members in every state is never able to take advantage of diversity jurisdiction, despite proper venue. Since it is a citizen of all states of which its members are citizens, there could never be complete diversity between it and an adversary (except a foreign one).

8. **Waiver of venue claims:** The Federal Rules provide that an objection to improper venue *must be raised at the same time as one to lack of personal jurisdiction*, i.e. either in the answer to the complaint or in the pre-answer motions. Rule 12(h)(1). If not, it is *waived*.

9. **Venue in federal removal cases:** A case *removed* from state to federal court passes to "the district court of the U.S. for the district and division embracing the place *where such action is pending.*" 28 U.S.C. §1441(a). (Some districts are subdivided into divisions.)

    a. **Unusual result:** Observe that there may be situations where a case properly removed from state court to federal district court may *not* end up in a federal district court in which it could have been brought as an original federal action.

        Example: A federal question suit is brought in Massachusetts state court by a Massachusetts resident against a New Jersey defendant, on a cause of action arising in New Jersey. In an original action, venue could lie only in New Jersey, since that is where "defendant's residence" venue would lie, as well as where "place of events" venue would lie; the escape hatch of §1391(b)(3) would not give venue in Massachusetts because there is a district (New Jersey) where the action might "otherwise be brought."

        Notwithstanding the unavailability of original venue in Massachusetts, the case would nonetheless be removed to Massachusetts district court — "the district court of the U.S. for the district and division embracing the place *where such action is pending*" — in accordance with §1441(a).

10. **Federal *forum non conveniens:***

    a. **Transfers for convenience in federal courts:** In a state court, application of the *forum non conveniens* doctrine typically means that the state court *dismisses* the law suit, and the plaintiff must start a new law suit from scratch in a more appropriate state. But in *federal* courts, the court generally does *not* dismiss the original suit on grounds of *forum non conveniens*; instead, generally it *transfers* the action to *another district*. That way, the plaintiff does not have to re-file the suit.

    b. **Statutory standard:** The federal statute authorizing such court-to-court transfers is 28 U.S.C. *§1404(a).* That section says that *"for the convenience of parties and witnesses, … a district court may transfer any civil action to any other district or division where it might have been brought* or to any district or division to which *all parties have consented."*

i.   **Defendant's motion:**   A motion to invoke §1404(a) may be *made by either party.* But most §1404(a) motions for transfer are made *by defendants*.

ii. **Burden on defendant:**   The *burden* is on the party seeking a transfer to make a convincing showing that the overall convenience of the parties will be better served if the action is transferred to a different district. In the usual case where the movant is the defendant, this burden is not an easy one to carry, because granting a transfer to a defendant would disturb the plaintiff's customary right to choose, within limits, where her action should be brought. Thus the Supreme Court has said, "Unless the balance [of convenience] is *strongly in favor of the defendant*, the *plaintiff's choice of forum should rarely be disturbed.*" *Gulf Oil v. Gilbert*, 330 U.S. 501 (1947).

iii. **Initial venue must be proper:**   The §1404(a) transfer-for-convenience provision applies — by judicial interpretation — only if the court where the action is now pending is a district in which the venue is *proper* (even if not the most convenient). Therefore, if the action is filed by the plaintiff in (or removed by the defendant to) a district that is *not in fact a district in which venue is proper,* that district judge *may not use* §1404(a) as authority for transferring to a district where venue is correct. Instead, the judge must proceed under a different statutory provision, 28 U.S.C. *§1406*, designed for correcting errors of venue; we consider §1406 below, p. 111.

c. **Interpretation:** The statutory phrase *"where it might have been brought"* has been interpreted so as to sharply *limit* the choice of districts to which the original judge may transfer the suit:

i.   **Defendant's motion:**   In the usual scenario where it's the defendant who is making the motion, the phrase "where it might have been brought" means that the transfer may be made only to a district where the *plaintiff would have had the right, independent of the wishes of the defendant*, to bring the action. That, in turn, means that the transfer may be made only to a district that *meets two requirements:*

   ❏ the transferee district is in a *state* in which or from which the defendant could *initially have been served* with process (as authorized by the *long-arm of that state,* and under the personal-jurisdiction rules of that state); *and*

   ❏ the transferee district is one in which *venue* would originally *have been proper* (as specified by 28 U.S.C. §1391).

   (1) **D's consent not enough:**   If the proposed transferee district does not satisfy those two requirement, then *"consent"* by the defendant *won't cure* the problem, even though the defendant would like it to. *Hoffman v. Blaski*, 363 U.S. 335 (1960). In other words, the defendant can't move to have the action transfered to the District for State X if, say, venue would not be proper in that district — and the defendant can't make this problem go away by saying *"I waive*

any objection I might have to venue in the District of State X" (assuming that the plaintiff doesn't also agree to waive any objection[32]).

The following Example on transfer of venue, though it's long, is worth reading closely, because it will help you (1) review how the federal venue statute works in general; and (2) understand the implications of the above rule that §1404(a) transfers may be made only to a district where the plaintiff **could have originally brought** the suit.

Example: P is injured in an accident while a passenger on a bus owned by D1 (a corporation) and driven by D2. The accident occurs in Miami, which is in the Southern District of Florida. P lives in the Northern District of Alabama. D1 is headquartered in the Middle District of Florida. D2 lives in the Northern District of Mississippi. P brings a diversity suit against D1 and D2, which he files in the Southern District of Florida (i.e., in the district where the accident occurred). D1 moves the Florida Southern District court to transfer the case to D1's home district, the Middle District of Florida. D2 consents to this transfer (in part because D2's legal bills are being paid by D1, his employer), but P opposes it. D1 argues that the place where the action is pending, the Southern District of Florida, is less convenient for D1, is no more convenient for D2, and is no more convenient for P, than the Middle District of Florida. Assume that the judge hearing the motion agrees, factually, with D1's argument about overall convenience. May that judge transfer the case under §1404(a) to the Middle District of Florida as D1 urges?

No, because the case could not *originally* have been filed by P in the district to which D1 is now seeking to have it transferred (Middle District of Florida). We can see this by verifying that none of the subsections of 28 U.S.C. §1391 would have allowed venue in that Middle District:

(1) Section 1391(b)(1) wouldn't have allowed a Middle District of Florida filing, because although that section allows venue in a district "in which any defendant resides," the section applies only if "*all defendants* are residents of the *state* in which the district is located," and here, D2 resides in Mississippi, not Florida.

(2) Section 1391(b)(2) wouldn't have allowed a Middle District of Florida finally either, because that section applies only in a district where a "substantial **part of the events** or omissions giving rise to the claim occurred" or "a substantial part of property that is the subject of the action is situated," and the only district that qualifies under this provision is the Southern District (not the Middle District) of Florida, since all of the events giving rise to the claim (i.e., the accident) occurred in that Southern District.

(3) Lastly, §1391(b)(3) wouldn't have allowed a Middle District of Florida filing either. That's the "escape hatch" section (*supra*, p. 106), which allows for venue in any district in which "any defendant is subject to the court's personal jurisdiction with respect to [the] action." If the just-quoted language were the *sole* relevant language, the Middle District of Florida *would* qualify, since D1's corpo-

---

32. But if the *plaintiff consents* to the defendant's motion to transfer to a particular federal district or division, this *will* overcome the fact that the action couldn't originally have been brought in that district.

rate headquarter is there, and §1391(d) deems a corporation to reside in any district where the corporation has enough contacts that the district could exercise personal jurisdiction over the corporation if the district were a state, a formulation that makes a corporation always reside at least in the district containing the corporation's place of principal place of business. But (b)(3) applies *only* "if there is *no district* in which an action may *otherwise be brought* as provided in this section[.]" (That's why it's colloquially called the "escape hatch" provision.) And there *is* such a district, namely the place where the action is now pending, the Southern District of Florida — as we saw in the prior paragraph, a district qualifies if it's the district in which "a substantial part of the events or omissions giving rise to the claim occurred," and the place where a motor vehicle accident occurred obviously qualifies under this definition as long as the suit is based on the accident.

Thus the Middle District of Florida is *not* a district in which P *could originally have brought the suit* even if he had wanted to do so. Therefore, §1404(a), as interpreted by the Supreme Court in *Hoffman v. Blaski, supra,* deprives the Southern District of Florida judge of the authority to transfer the case to the Middle District without P's consent. And that's true even if the judge is convinced that the overall convenience of the parties would be better served by such a transfer. In other words, P as a plaintiff has the right to a significant degree of **autonomy** in the selection of a forum, and that autonomy includes the right to insist that the action not be transferred to a different federal district (even one that would be more convenient for all parties), unless that proposed transferee district is one where P could have originally brought the action.

d. **Transfer where original venue improper:** As noted (*supra*, p. 109), the federal judge where the action is initially filed may use §1404(a) as authority to make a transfer for convenience *only* if that original district was a proper one (even if not the most convenient one). What happens if the case is originally filed in a district in which venue was *not* proper? In that scenario, the judge must proceed under a different provision, 28 U.S.C. §1406(a), which says that:

> "The district court of a district in which is filed a case laying venue in the **wrong division or district** shall **dismiss**, or *if it be in the interest of justice, transfer* such case to **any district or division in which it could have been brought.**"

Example: P, a pedestrian, is injured in Colorado, his state of residence, when he is struck by a car driven by D. D is a resident of Kansas. P brings a diversity action, alleging D's negligence, against D in federal court for the District of Wyoming, where P's lawyer happens to reside. D correctly notices that venue in the District of Wyoming is not proper, because that district is not the district of residence of all defendants (i.e., D doesn't live there), is not the district where a substantial part of the events giving rise to the claim arose (since the only such district is Colorado), and does not qualify under the "there is no other district" provision (since venue is as noted proper in the District of Colorado). Assume that D would rather have the action proceed in Colorado, as opposed to Wyoming, federal court. (1) What should D do? and (2) How should the court respond when D does what you recommend?

(1) D should move in the Wyoming federal court for a transfer to Colorado under 28 U.S.C. §1406(a). The District of Wyoming is "the wrong division or district" (the language used by §1406(a)). Therefore, under §1406(a) D is entitled to in effect require the judge to choose between dismissing the case and transferring it to some "district or division in which it could have been brought." The logical choice for D to request as transferee district is the District of Colorado (where the case could have been brought, since the accident occurred there). In support of the request, D should point out that not only is Colorado the place where the events in question arose, but it's also P's home state, thus probably making venue in Colorado something that's "in the interest of justice."

(2) The judge should probably **grant** D's motion, since it's hard to see what would make a transfer to P's home state against the interest of justice. If the court disagrees with transfer to Colorado, and finds no other district that both qualifies for venue and meets the requirements of justice, the court **must dismiss** the action. In other words, under §1406(a), the court is not permitted to allow the action to continue in Wyoming federal court (a "wrong" district), unless D changes his mind and consents to having the action remain there.

i.   **Effect of forum-selection clause:**   Recall that the parties to a contract are free to **designate the forum** in which any litigation must occur, and that the courts will generally enforce such a clause. (See *supra*, p. 15.) When the parties have included such a **"forum-selection" clause** in their contract, what happens if one of them later brings suit in a federal court that is proper under the venue statute, but that does **not qualify as a permitted forum under the clause?** Does the clause transform the plaintiff's choice of location into a "wrong" forum that triggers the defendant's right to use §1406(a) to demand to be given either a dismissal or a transfer-for-convenience? The Supreme Court answered **"no"** to this question: §1406 applies *only* to violations of the federal venue statute, **not to violations of the parties' forum-selection clause.** The case so holding is **Atlantic Marine Constr. Co., Inc. v. United States District Court for the Western District of Texas**, 134 S.Ct. 568 (2013).

   (1) **Not much difference.**   *Atlantic Marine* doesn't actually change prior law very much. It's true that under the case, a defendant who realizes that the plaintiff has violated the forum-selection clause won't be able to use §1406's "wrong district" provision to demand that the federal judge choose between a transfer and a dismissal, and will instead have to use §1404, which seems to give the trial judge discretion about whether to make a transfer for convenience. But the judge hearing the §1404 motion will nonetheless have to **try to enforce** the forum-selection clause, either by transferring the case to a federal court that satisfies the clause, or else dismissing the case.

   (2) **The contract in *Atlantic Marine*:**   Here's what happened in *Atlantic Marine*: D (Atlantic Marine) was a corporation residing solely in Virginia. P (J-Crew) was a corporation residing solely in Texas. They made a contract calling for P to work as a sub-contractor for D on a construction project run by D and located in the Western District of Texas. The contract contained a forum-selec-

tion clause, which said that any suits under the contract would be litigated either in a particular Virginia state court or in federal court for the Eastern District of Virginia.

(3) The suit: P eventually decided to sue D for non-payment. P brought suit in the Western District of Texas (where, under 28 U.S.C. §1391(b)(2), venue was valid as a place where a substantial part of the underlying events occurred). D responded by moving under §1406(a) for either a transfer or a dismissal. D argued that the Western District of Texas was a "wrong" district (since it was not permitted by the forum-selection clause). Therefore, D said, the Texas federal judge was required by §1406 to either dismiss the suit or transfer it to a district that complied with the forum-selection clause (e.g., the federal district court for E.D.Va.).

(4) Lower courts: The lower federal courts sided with P; they held that §1406 wasn't the right provision, and that D had to make its motion for transfer under §140<u>4</u> instead. They also held that in deciding whether a motion for transfer under §1404 should be granted, the trial court should not give sole weight to enforcing the forum-selection clause, but should also balance the various competing interests of the parties about where the suit should be litigated. In this case, since P might have problems requiring witnesses to travel to Virginia to testify (and in any event would have to pay the travel expenses of such witnesses), D had not established that a transfer to Virginia would better serve the convenience of the parties overall. The effect of the lower courts' denial of transfer was that D *lost the benefit of the forum-selection clause* that it had negotiated.

(5) Right to enforcement of selection clause: When the case got to the Supreme Court, the Court found that D was *entitled to the benefit of its forum selection clause* (i.e., to have the case transfered to Virginia or else dismissed) unless there should on remand turn out to be some extraordinary factor in the case that hadn't yet surfaced, and that did not involve the convenience of the parties.

(6) §§ 1404 vs. 1406: On the narrow point in the case, the issue of *which* federal transfer provision should apply, D lost. When a federal district court is deciding whether the district in which the suit has been filed is "wrong" as that term is used in §1406, *only* the requirements of the federal *venue* statute (28 U.S.C. §1391) are to be considered, the Supreme Court said. So here, since the Western District of Texas was a proper place according to the venue statute, that district was not a "wrong" district, meaning that §1406 was not the right provision to use in deciding whether the case should be transferred (or dismissed). Instead, the relevant provision is the basic §1404, which allows a transfer for convenience when the case has been filed in a proper (according to the venue statute) location.

(7) Application to facts: How, then, should the trial court have *applied* §1404 to these facts? The Supreme Court's answer was that "a forum-selection clause [must] be *'given controlling weight* in all but the most exceptional cases.'"

(And there did not seem to be any such extraordinary factors here.) So the Texas court should not even have *considered* convenience issues like the availability of witnesses — once the parties had agreed on a forum-selection clause, that fact became essentially the **sole issue** to be considered in deciding whether the case should be transferred under §1404.

(8) D gets benefit of forum clause: Thus although D in *Atlantic Marine* had to take the case all the way to the U.S. Supreme Court, D ended up with the benefit of its forum-selection bargain — on remand, the Texas federal judge will almost certainly ensure that the case ends up being litigated in Virginia federal or state court.[33] And in all probability, the Texas federal judge will end up using §1404 to transfer the case to the federal court for E.D.Va.

Quiz Yourself on
VENUE

15. P, a resident of Las Vegas (in the District of Nevada) wishes to bring a federal-court suit against D1, a resident of Los Angeles (in the Central District of California) and D2 a resident of San Francisco (in the Northern District of California). The suit would be based on diversity, and concerns an auto accident which occurred in San Diego (in the Southern District of California). In which federal judicial district(s) may the suit be brought? _____

16. Same facts as above question. Now, however, assume that D2 is a resident of Albuquerque, in the District of New Mexico. What district(s) have venue? _____

17. D, a large multinational corporation located in Cleveland, in the Northern District of Ohio, is in the business of drilling for oil. D owns and operates an oil rig located in Omaha, Nebraska. (Nebraska has only one judicial district). When the rig breaks down, D contracts to have the rig repaired at a cost of $200,000 by P, a rig-servicing corporation located in Omaha. The contract (a form contract used by D for repairs on all of its American-based oil rigs) specifies that any litigation in connection with the contract shall occur only in either the Ohio state courts or the federal courts for the Northern District of Ohio. (D wants all litigation to occurs in D's "home district," for D's convenience.) P does the work, but D does not pay. P brings a diversity action against D in federal court for the District of Nebraska. You represent D. Your client would like you to try to have the case moved to the N.D. Ohio federal court, as provided in the contract.

(a) What court should you approach for relief, and what statutory authority should you cite as authority for that relief? _____

(b) What factors should the court consider in deciding whether to give you the relief you asked for in (a)?
_____

---

33. As the Supreme Court noted, a federal judge using §1404 only has the power to transfer the case to another *federal* court, not to a *state* (or *foreign*) court. So where a forum-selection clause specifies that only a state court (or foreign court) will hear any litigation, the federal court hearing a §1404 motion will have to *dismiss* the case rather than transferring it. (In *Atlantic Marine* itself, the forum clause allowed both federal and state courts to hear the case so long as the court was in Virginia, so the Texas judge would have the power to transfer the case to the federal court for the Eastern District of Virginia.)

(c) What decision will the court likely make on your motion? _____

Answers

15. **Central, Northern and Southern Districts of California.** In both diversity and federal question cases, venue lies in any district where any defendant resides, so long as, if there is more than one defendant, all the defendants reside in the state containing that district. 28 U.S.C. §1391(a)(1). This yields the Central and Northern Districts of California. Additionally, for both diversity and federal question cases, venue lies in any judicial district "in which a substantial part of the events or omissions giving rise to the claim occurred, or a substantial part of property that is the subject of the action is situated. …" 28 U.S.C. §1391(a)(2). This yields the Southern District of California, where the accident took place. There is no provision allowing venue based on the residence of the plaintiff.

16. **Southern District of California.** As noted in the prior answer, venue based on defendants' residence exists only if all defendants are at least residents of the same state. Since this is not true here, the fact that the Central District of California and the District of New Mexico are each home to one defendant is irrelevant. Only the "place of events" section, §1391(a)(2), gives venue, which as in the prior question is the Southern District of California.

17. **(a) You should make a motion to the District of Nebraska** federal court, i.e., the court where the action is pending; the motion should cite **28 U.S.C. §1404(a).** §1404(a) says that "for the convenience of parties and witnesses, … a district court may *transfer* any civil action to any other district or division *where it might have been brought*[,]" What's interesting is that your motion may *not* be based on 28 U.S.C. §1406, which requires a federal court in which a case has been filed that "lay[s] venue in the *wrong … district*" to "*dismiss* [it], or if it be in the interest of justice, *transfer* [it]" to a district in which it could have been brought. The Supreme Court has held that where a case is filed in a district that is a correct one under the venue statute, the fact that the district is not proper under a contractual forum-selection clause does *not* make the district a "wrong" one so as to justify the use of §1406 (and instead requires the movant to use §1404). *Atlantic Marine Constr. Co., Inc. v. United States District Court for the Western District of Texas.* So here, even though the District of Nebraska is the "wrong district" in terms of the forum-selection clause, it is a *correct* district in terms of the venue statute (since the District of Nebraska, where the contract work was done, is a district in which "a substantial part of the events ... giving rise to the claim occurred," making venue there correct under 28 U.S.C. §1391(b)(2)). That means that you have to make your motion on behalf of D under §1404 (theoretically a mechanism that leaves the transfer decision to the judge) rather than under §1406 (a mechanism that *requires* the court in the district where the case is presently pending to either dismiss the case or transfer it, if the present district is a "wrong" one in terms of venue).

    (b) The court will only consider what the forum-selection clause says, not the convenience of the parties. §1404(a) *says* that the district of Nebraska federal judge should consider the "convenience of parties and witnesses." But in this special case where the parties have agreed to a forum-selection clause, the Supreme Court has held that the court hearing the §1404 transfer motion may not consider the overall convenience of the parties and/or the witnesses. Instead, the court must attempt to enforce the forum-selection clause as written, whether or not that conforms to the convenience of the parties. *Atlantic Marine, supra.*

    (c) Transfer to N.D. Ohio. Since there exists at least one district (N.D. Ohio) that qualifies both under the forum-selection clause and as a district "where [the action] might have been brought" in terms of the venue statute, the Nebraska judge *must* transfer the case to that district. And that's true even if the

Nebraska judge believes that a transfer to N.D. Ohio would be inconvenient for P, not all that convenient for D, and inconvenient for any witnesses. This result follows directly from *Atlantic Marine, supra.*

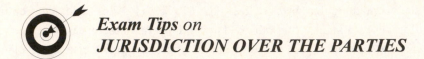

Exam Tips *on*
JURISDICTION OVER THE PARTIES

In any fact pattern involving the starting of a lawsuit or the service of process, you must of course be alert to issues of jurisdiction over the parties. Here are some particular things to check for:

☛ In a state-court suit, if D is served *outside* the forum state, check whether the applicable *long-arm* statute was complied with. (If not, service is invalid even if there are minimum contacts.) [9, 17-21]

   ☞ If D was served *inside* the forum state (even during a brief visit), the long-arm is irrelevant, and service is valid. (You don't even have to check for minimum contacts, since presence at the time of service is treated as the equivalent of minimum contacts).

☛ Always check whether *P's claim derives* from D's *in-state* activities.

   ☞ If it *does*, then the forum state court needs to have only "*specific* jurisdiction" over D, and it's enough for this that D has *minimum contacts* with the forum state.

   ☞ But if P's claim does *not* derive from D's in-state activities, the case requires "*general*" jurisdiction. And it's much tougher for the court to have general jurisdiction than specific jurisdiction:

      ☞ If D is an *individual*, for the court to assert general jurisdiction over D, D probably has to satisfy one of the following: be *domiciled* in the forum state, be *served while physically present* in the forum state, or have *consented* to service.

      ☞ If D is a *corporation*, for the court to assert general jurisdiction over D, D has to be "*at home*" in the forum state. This means that D must either be *incorporated* in the forum state or have its *principal place of business* there. [53]

☛ If the case involves *specific jurisdiction* (P's claim arises from D's in-state contacts), make sure each D has *minimum contacts* with the forum state. [9, 23-49]

   ☞ See whether D *voluntarily did business in*, or with residents of, the forum state. If so, minimum contacts probably exists. If not, D probably doesn't have minimum contacts.

   ☞ If D *made a product outside the state* that *caused in-state injuries*, the jurisdiction issue can go either way depending on D's actions relating to the state:

      ☞ If D *didn't "target"* the forum state for sales, and the injury-causing product just *found its way into the state*, that's *not* enough for minimum contacts, even if it was "*foreseeable*" to D that some products might end up in the forum state and cause injury there. [30]

☞ But if D *did "target"* the forum state for sales (e.g., took out *ads* specifically directed at in-state customers, or *regularly shipped goods* into the state, or *opened an office* in-state), then that targeting *does* constitute minimum contacts with the state (so the court can exercise specific jurisdiction). [40]

☞ If all D did in connection with the forum state was to *operate an out-of-state Internet website* that some in-staters accessed (and there's no evidence that D wanted to *"target"* in-staters as customers), this probably *won't* constitute minimum contacts with the forum state, so an in-stater won't be able to have her home-state court hear a suit against D arising out of that in-state use of the website. [28]

☛ For *federal* suits:

☞ Check that service took place in the correct *place.* This is either: (1) within the *territorial limits* of the state where the District Court sits; or (2) somewhere else *permitted by the state law* (i.e., the long-arm) of the state where the District Court sits. [68-72]

☞ But if D is a *third-party defendant* or *indispensable party,* think *"100-mile bulge."* Rule 4(k)(1)(B) allows service within a 100-mile bulge around the federal courthouse. [70]

☞ Check that service took place in the correct *manner.* This is either a method specified in the Federal Rules (e.g., delivery of summons and complaint to a person of "suitable age and discretion" at D's residence), or else a method allowed by the local law of the state where service is made or where the District Court sits. [72-74]

☞ Check that D is *"amenable"* to service. This means that:

☞ if the case involves a *federal question*, it's enough that D has minimum contacts with the forum state (even if the long-arm of the state where the federal court sits wouldn't allow the state courts to exercise jurisdiction);

☞ if the case is a *diversity* case, the long-arm of the *state* where the federal court sits *must* allow jurisdiction, or the federal court can't exercise jurisdiction. [74-75]

☛ If P is trying to get jurisdiction based on D's *assets* in the forum state (*quasi in rem* jurisdiction), remember that P can't go forward unless D has *minimum contacts* with the forum state, just as if this were an *in personam* suit. [78-82]

☛ Check that D was given *notice*, and a reasonable opportunity to be *heard.* [84-92] (Remember that it doesn't matter whether D got actual notice, merely that the procedures used were ones reasonably calculated to give D notice.)

☛ In federal suits, check for *venue*. [101-114] Venue will usually lie only:

☞ in any district where any defendant resides, if all defendants reside in the *state* containing that district; or

☞ in any district where a "substantial part of the events" giving rise to the claim occurred.

☞ A corporation "resides" (for venue purposes) in the district where it has its principal place of business, and also in any district where it has substantial operations.

CHAPTER 3

SUBJECT MATTER JURISDICTION

ChapterScope

This Chapter examines "subject matter jurisdiction," that is, the court's power to adjudicate the kind of controversy before it. The most important concepts in this Chapter are:

■ **Two basic types:** In the federal courts, there are two basic kinds of controversies over which the federal judiciary has subject matter jurisdiction: (1) suits between *citizens of different states* (so-called *diversity* jurisdiction); and (2) suits involving a *"federal question."*

■ **Diversity suits:** In *diversity* suits:

❑ An amount in excess of *$75,000* must be in dispute. This is the *"amount in controversy"* requirement. (In federal question cases, there is no amount in controversy requirement.)

❑ *"Complete diversity" is required*. That is, it must be the case that *no plaintiff is a citizen of the same state as any defendant*.

❑ A *corporation* is deemed a citizen of *any state where it is incorporated* and of the state where it has its *principal place of business*. In other words, for diversity to exist, no adversary of the corporation may be a citizen of the state in which the corporation is incorporated, or of the state in which it has its principal place of business.

■ **Federal question suits:** A *"federal question"* suit is one "*arising under the Constitution, laws, or treaties of the United States.*" Usually, the reason there is a federal question is that federal law is the *source of the plaintiff's claim*.

■ **Supplemental jurisdiction:** Under the doctrine of *"supplemental"* jurisdiction, if a basic controversy satisfies federal subject matter jurisdictional requirements, *additional claims* and *additional parties* may be brought into the litigation. This is true whether the basic claim is based on federal-question or (with important limits) diversity.

■ **Removal:** Under the doctrine of *"removal"*, any action brought in state court which the plaintiff could have brought in federal court may be transferred ("removed") by the defendant to federal district court. (But in diversity cases, the action may be removed only if no defendant is a citizen of the state in which the action is pending.)

I. GENERAL PRINCIPLES

A. **Definition of subject matter jurisdiction:** Even though a state or federal court has jurisdiction over the *parties* in an action, it cannot try the case unless it has the power to adjudicate that *kind* of controversy. The power to adjudicate a certain kind of controversy is known as *subject matter jurisdiction* or *competency over the litigation.*

Example: A state court has personal jurisdiction over both parties in a divorce action. But unless the court has been granted (usually by the legislature) the power to decide divorce cases, any divorce decree granted by the court is void for lack of subject matter jurisdiction or competency. Restatement of Judgments, §7, comment 6.

B. Consent insufficient: Most courts hold that subject matter jurisdiction, unlike jurisdiction over the parties, may *not* be conferred by consent of the litigants.

C. Kinds of federal subject matter jurisdiction: In the federal courts, there are two basic kinds of controversies over which the federal judiciary has subject matter jurisdiction:

1. Suits between *citizens of different states* (so-called *diversity jurisdiction*);

2. Suits involving a *"federal question"* — this will be defined more fully in the discussion of Federal Question Jurisdiction, *infra*, p. 131.

3. **Other cases:** Certain other kinds of cases specified in the Constitution, Art. III, §2, also fall under the federal judicial power. These are:

   a. Cases involving *ambassadors*, other public ministers and consuls;

   b. Cases of *admiralty* and maritime jurisdiction;

   c. Cases in which the *United States is a party.*

D. Amount in controversy: In a federal suit based on diversity (category 1 above), an amount in excess of $75,000 must be in dispute in the suit. This requirement is known as the *jurisdictional amount* or the *amount in controversy.*

> **Note:** This chapter will be concerned with the subject matter jurisdiction of the *federal courts*. The subject matter jurisdiction of the state courts is generally controlled by state statute; each state is free to allocate the judicial power reserved to it by the 10th Amendment as it wishes among its own state courts. Most states have two or three different kinds of trial courts: a small claims or justice of the peace court, a court of general jurisdiction, a probate court, etc. Often, minimum and maximum limits are placed on the amounts in controversy in these courts. A state's court of general jurisdiction may even hear claims based on *federal* law, unless Congress has specified otherwise as to a particular type of claim. The statutes of the particular state must be consulted to determine the allocation of subject matter among its courts; this allocation will not be discussed further here.

II. FEDERAL SUBJECT MATTER JURISDICTION GENERALLY

A. Burden: The party seeking to invoke the jurisdiction of a federal court must affirmatively show that the case is within the competency of the court. Wr., 27.

> **Example:** A plaintiff seeking to invoke diversity jurisdiction (i.e. jurisdiction based on the fact that the parties are citizens of different states) must in the pleading allege the relevant facts about the citizenship of the parties.

B. Dismissal: *No matter when* a deficiency in the subject matter jurisdiction of a federal court is noticed, the suit must be stopped, and dismissed for lack of jurisdiction.

1. **Objection:** Rule 12(h)(3) of the Federal Rules provides that the parties or the court on its own initiative can ***always*** object to the court's lack of subject matter jurisdiction: "If the court determines at any time that it lacks subject-matter jurisdiction, the court must dismiss the action."

2. **Appeals:** Even at the appellate level, the suit already tried may be dismissed for lack of subject matter jurisdiction. Cf. *American Fire & Casualty Co. v. Finn,* 341 U.S. 6 (1951).

   Example: In *Louisville & Nashville Railroad v. Mottley*, 211 U.S. 149 (1908), the controversy reached the Supreme Court before it was dismissed for lack of subject matter jurisdiction. Neither party had raised the jurisdictional issue, but the Court found that the federal question jurisdiction alleged by the plaintiff did not exist.

   a. **Relief from judgment:** Similarly, after a judgment has been entered and any appellate proceedings concluded, a party may be entitled to have the judgment ***voided*** on the grounds that it was issued in a proceeding as to which the court had no subject matter jurisdiction. FRCP 60(b) allows a court to grant relief from a final judgment for a variety of reasons. Among these are that the judgment is "void" (60(b)(4)) or for "any other reason that justifies relief." (60(b)(6)).

3. **Distinction:** Federal subject matter jurisdiction must be distinguished from jurisdiction over the parties; the latter is a ***waivable*** defect, which must be asserted by the party who would take advantage of it. (See Rule 12(h)(1)). Subject matter jurisdiction, on the other hand, is never waived, and may be made by the court on its own motion, as in *Louisville & Nashville, supra.*

4. **Collateral attack on subject matter jurisdiction:** The rules allowing collateral attack on the decision of the court of another jurisdiction are generally the same for both subject matter and personal jurisdiction. That is, it is only where a party to the first action had a ***default judgment*** entered against him that he may claim, when he is sued on the judgment in a second court, that the first court lacked subject matter jurisdiction. See *Chicot County Drainage District v. Baxter State Bank*, 308 U.S. 371 (1940), discussed *infra*, p. 444.

   Example: A party who appeared in a state action against him, and who did not raise any objection to lack of subject matter jurisdiction, may not generally collaterally attack the state court's judgment when it is sued upon for enforcement in federal court. Nor would he be able usually to collaterally attack if he had made the jurisdictional objection in the state court, and lost.

   a. **Exception:** This policy limiting collateral attack is not followed when there are very strong policy considerations weighing in the opposite direction.

   Example: When a federal statute has given exclusive jurisdiction over a particular type of action to the federal courts, for instance bankruptcy, patent, and copyright actions, the finding by a state court, even in a non-default situation, that it has jurisdiction over such a case will not bar collateral attack on the state court's judgment, when it is sued on for enforcement in either a federal or state court. Wr., 95.

III. DIVERSITY JURISDICTION

A. **Constitutional provision:** The constitutional grant of jurisdiction based on diversity of citizenship extends to "Controversies ... between *Citizens of different states* ... and between a State, or the Citizens thereof, and foreign States, Citizens or Subjects." (Art. III, §2.) This grant is repeated in a statute, 28 U.S.C. §1332.

> **Example:** P, a citizen of New York, sues D, a citizen of California, in a cause of action arising out of an automobile accident. P claims damages of $100,000. Even though this suit does not involve any federal question, and P's right to recover will be determined exclusively by reference to state law, the case may be heard in federal court. This is because P and D are citizens of different states.

1. **Rationale for diversity:** The rationale for the existence of diversity jurisdiction has traditionally been that it offers a federal forum for an out-of-state litigant who would be exposed to *local prejudice* if suit was held in state court.

   a. **Criticism:** But if local prejudice is really the reason for the existence of diversity jurisdiction, it is hard to see why a *plaintiff* who is a citizen of the forum state is able to choose to sue in federal court, even if the out-of-state defendant does not wish a federal forum.

2. **Possible abolition of diversity:** The constitutional grant of diversity jurisdiction is permissive, rather than mandatory, in nature. Therefore, Congress is free to redraft the federal jurisdiction statutes to *curtail or abolish diversity.* Several recent sessions of Congress have seen attempts to do this. There appears to be substantial Congressional support for either a complete abolition of diversity jurisdiction or a substantial curtailment of it (e.g., a limitation to *cases where the plaintiff is a non-resident* of the state where the district court sits).

3. **Amount in controversy:** In all cases in which diversity is the sole basis for jurisdiction, the amount in controversy must exceed $75,000. See the section on Jurisdictional Amount, *infra*, p. 138.

B. **Complete diversity required:** In order to invoke diversity, it must be the case that *no plaintiff is a citizen of the same state as any defendant.* (This does not prevent a pair of plaintiffs, or a pair of defendants, from being co-citizens.) This is the rule of *"complete diversity,"* and is probably the single most important thing to remember about diversity jurisdiction.

> **Example:** P1, P2 and P3 are all citizens of Michigan. P4 is a citizen of Ohio. D1, D2 and D3 are all citizens of California. D4 is a citizen of Ohio. These plaintiffs cannot bring a joint diversity suit against these defendants, because P4 and D4 are citizens of the same state. Because it is not the case that no plaintiff is a citizen of the same state as any defendant, the required "complete diversity" is absent.

1. **Basis:** The requirement of complete diversity is *not* a Constitutional requirement. It is instead merely a *judge-made* interpretation of 28 U.S.C. §1332, first set forth by Justice Marshall in *Strawbridge v. Curtiss*, 3 Cranch 267 (1806). Thus Congress is free at any time to specify that "partial" diversity (e.g., one plaintiff is from a different state than some one defendant) will suffice.

2. **Congressional modification:** In fact, Congress has ***removed*** the requirement of complete diversity in certain types of cases.

    a. **Interpleader:** One common example in which complete diversity is not required is cases filed under the federal ***interpleader*** statute. In such cases, diversity is deemed to exist as long as there are "two or more adverse claimants, of diverse citizenship." 28 U.S.C. §1335(a)(1).

        Example: Three competing beneficiaries, two from N.Y. and one from N.J., claim money owed to them under an insurance policy. The insurance company, by invoking the federal interpleader statute, effectively tells them, "fight it out in court and we'll pay the winner." Since there are two adverse parties from different states, the fact that there are also two adverse parties from the same state does not destroy diversity, as it would in a non-interpleader action.

        Note: Of course, diversity is only a requirement when there is no other basis for federal jurisdiction, such as the existence of a federal question, or the presence of the U.S. as a party, etc.

    b. **High-stakes class actions:** Another situation in which Congress has removed the requirement of complete diversity is for certain high-stakes ***class actions.*** Under the Class Action Fairness Act of 2005 ("CAFA"), in most diversity-based suits where ***more than $5 million is at stake in total***, the diversity requirement is satisfied so long as any member of the plaintiff class is diverse with any defendant. See 28 U.S.C. § 1332(d)(2)(A).

3. **Presence of foreigner:** In a suit between citizens of different states, the fact that a ***foreign*** citizen (or foreign country) is a party does ***not destroy*** diversity. 28 U.S.C. §1332(a)(3).

    Example: P, a citizen of Ohio, sues D1, a citizen of Michigan, and D2, a citizen of Canada. Diversity jurisdiction exists. (In situations where one side consists ***solely*** of foreign citizens or foreign countries, "alienage" jurisdiction applies. See *infra*, p. 125.)

4. **Pleadings not dispositive:** In order to determine whether complete diversity exists, the pleadings do not settle the question of who should be considered adverse parties. Instead, the court will ***look beyond the pleadings***, and arrange the parties according to their ***substantive sides in the dispute.***

    Example: An insured tortfeasor, A, brings an action against Insurer, his liability insurer, for a declaratory judgment holding Insurer liable for certain coverage under the policy. A names B, the person suing him in tort, as a defendant along with Insurer. For the purposes of determining whether complete diversity exists, the court will probably classify B as a plaintiff, since he and A have an identical interest in having it held that the insurance covers the accident in question. Thus, as long as neither A nor B is a citizen of the same state as Insurer (for the citizenship of a corporation, see *infra*, p. 127), diversity will not be destroyed by the fact that A and B are citizens of the same state.

C. Nominal parties ignored: In determining the existence of diversity, *nominal* or *purely formal* parties may be *ignored*.

   1. Citizenship of trust: A *trustee's* citizenship may or may not count for diversity purposes. If the trustee has real powers, her citizenship will count. But if the trustee is just a formal holder of title (e.g., a "straw man" in a real estate transaction), with no real decision-making authority, the trustee's citizenship will be ignored and the beneficiaries' citizenship used instead.

   2. Representatives and administrators: *Representatives* and *administrators* will generally be treated as having the citizenship of the *party they represent*. Thus according to §1332(c)(2), "The legal representative of the *estate* of a decedent shall be deemed to be a citizen only of the same State as the decedent, and the legal representative of an *infant* or incompetent shall be deemed to be a citizen only of the same State as the infant or incompetent."

   a. Can't be used to affect diversity: So a representative can't be selected based on his own citizenship, for the purpose of creating (or defeating, in the case of removal) diversity jurisdiction.

   Note: Apart from the rule, just discussed, that nominal or purely formal parties may be ignored, there is a separate doctrine that parties who are "improperly or collusively joined" shall be ignored, for citizenship purposes. See the discussion of this rule *infra*, p. 128.

D. Refusal to exercise jurisdiction: Even where diversity jurisdiction as spelled out in 28 U.S.C. §1332 exists, the federal courts may still *decline to exercise* jurisdiction under certain circumstances. Among such circumstances preventing the exercise of federal jurisdiction are:

   1. where diversity is the result of *improper or collusive joinder* of parties, (*infra*, p. 128);

   2. where *domestic relations* (i.e., *divorce* and *child custody*) constitute the main subject matter of the suit (but civil child abuse actions don't fall within this exception, and can be heard in diversity; see *Ankenbrandt v. Richards*, 504 U.S. 689 (1992);

   3. where *probate* matters are the essence of the suit;

   4. where the *"abstention doctrine"* is invoked. This doctrine permits a federal court to decline jurisdiction where congestion of the federal court's docket, the difficulty of the questions of state law presented by the case, the existence of related litigation in state court, etc., make it wiser to defer to a state court. Wr., 323.

E. Date of determination: A party's citizenship for diversity purposes is determined *as of the commencement of the action*. If diversity existed between the parties at that date, it is *not defeated* because one of the parties *later became a citizen of the same state* as his opponent. Conversely, if parties on opposite sides are citizens of the same state when the action is commenced, there is *no diversity* (and the case must be dismissed), even if by the time of trial the citizenship of one party has changed in such a way that diversity is now present.

   Example: Atlas, a partnership, sues Dataflux, a Mexican corporation, in November 1997, on a diversity-only claim. The complaint asserts that Atlas is a citizen of Texas. Unbeknownst to Dataflux, at the time of suit Atlas has two Mexican partners, making it a citizen of Mexico at that time.[1] Since the case consists solely of foreigners on each side, the required complete diversity (in this case diversity of the "alienage" variety) is lacking at that moment.[2] Three years later, just before the case is tried to a jury, the Mexican partners in Atlas leave the partnership, making Atlas no longer a citizen of Mexico and thus now completely diverse with Dataflux. Atlas wins at trial, and Dataflux now argues on appeal that the case should be dismissed because the required diversity did not exist at the moment the suit was filed.

Held, for Dataflux. Under the traditional "time of filing" rule, "all challenges to subject-matter jurisdiction premised upon diversity of citizenship [must be measured] against the state of facts that existed at the time of filing — whether the challenge be brought shortly after filing, after the trial, or even for the first time on appeal." The time-of-filing rule is used "precisely because the facts determining jurisdiction are subject to change, and because constant litigation in response to that change would be wasteful[.]" *Grupo Dataflux v. Atlas Global Group, L.P.*, 541 U.S. 567 (2004).

1. **Motive for moving irrelevant:** A person's ***motive for changing her state of citizenship*** is ***irrelevant***. So if a person, by moving, meets the test of domicile in his new state of residence, it is immaterial for diversity purposes that he moved in order to create or destroy diversity. But of course, as *Grupo Dataflux, supra*, illustrates, the move must be made *before* the commencement of the action. Cf. Wr., 162-63.

F. **Domicile, not residence, is what counts:** Residence, by itself, is not enough to make a person a citizen of a state in the sense in which the term is used in Art. III, §2 of the Constitution. Instead, ***domicile*** is controlling. Wr., 161. For an extended discussion of what constitutes domicile, see *supra*, p. 13.

   1. **General principle:** "A person's domicile is that place where he has his ***true, fixed, and permanent home*** and principal establishment, and to which he has the intention of returning whenever he is absent therefrom." Wr., 161.

   2. **Motive for moving irrelevant:** If a person, by moving, meets the test of domicile in his new state of residence, it is immaterial for diversity purposes that he moved in order to create or destroy diversity. (But of course, as noted in (E) above, the move must be made before the commencement of the action.)

G. **Citizens of D.C.:** Citizens of the ***District of Columbia*** are regarded as citizens of a state, for purposes of diversity. 28 U.S.C. §1332(e). Wr., 155-56.

   Example: P, a citizen of D.C., may bring a diversity suit against D, a citizen of any one of the 50 states.

H. **Jurisdiction involving aliens:** Federal jurisdiction exists where there is a suit between a citizen of a state, on one side, and foreign countries, or citizens or subjects thereof, on the other.

---

1. As we'll see below, p. 127, a partnership is deemed a citizen of every state and every country of which any partner is a citizen.

2. See "Suit solely between or among foreign citizens," *infra*, p. 126, for the proposition that diversity of the alienage variety does not exist where the only parties are foreign citizens.

Wr. 154; U.S. Const. Art. III, §2. This is sometimes referred to as ***alienage jurisdiction***. See 28 U.S.C. §1332(a)(2).

> **Example:** P, a citizen of Mexico, sues D, a citizen of Illinois. Even if there is no federal question at issue, there will be federal subject matter jurisdiction (assuming the amount in controversy requirement is satisfied). This is because the case falls under the alienage jurisdiction, since it is between a citizen of a foreign state and a citizen of an American state.

1. **Suit solely between or among foreign citizens:** But a suit solely between or among citizens of ***foreign countries*** does ***not*** fall within the alienage jurisdiction. Thus if P, a citizen of Canada, sues D, a citizen of Mexico, there is no alienage jurisdiction; there must be a citizen of an American state on one side of the controversy.

2. **Resident alien:** A foreigner living in the U.S. (i.e., a ***resident alien***) is deemed to be a citizen of whatever state in which the alien is domiciled. 28 U.S.C. §1332(a), last sentence.[3] So a resident alien is not really treated like a foreigner at all, for diversity purposes.

> **Example:** Suppose that P, a citizen of Illinois, sues D, a Canadian citizen who now has permanent resident status in the U.S. and who lives in Illinois. Because D will be treated as a citizen of the state in which he is now domiciled, there is no diversity, and the suit cannot proceed.

   a. **Resident alien vs. non-resident alien:** Suppose that the case consists solely of a ***resident alien*** on one side, and a ***non-resident alien*** on the other. Let's assume, for instance, that P is a Spaniard living in Florida, and D is a Canadian living in Canada. Is there diversity? Courts are ***split*** on the answer, and the Supreme Court has never decided it.[4]

       i. **Literal reading says "yes":** A ***literal reading*** of the last sentence of § 1332(a) suggests that the answer is ***"yes,"*** there is diversity, because P is deemed to be a citizen of Florida, and a suit between a U.S. citizens and a foreigner falls within the alienage jurisdiction given by § 1332(a)(2) (see the Mexican vs. Illinois citizen example on p. 126 above). A few courts have indeed applied this literal approach. See, e.g., *Singh v. Daimler-Benz*, 9 F.3d 303 (3d Cir. 1993).

       ii. **Most courts say "no":** But most courts that have considered the issue have rejected the literal reading, and have ***declined*** to find a diversity in this resident-vs.-non-resident-alien situation. These courts have reasoned that when Congress amended § 1332(a) to make resident aliens citizens of the states where they reside, Congress did ***not intend*** to grant diversity jurisdiction for suits in which ***all parties are aliens***. See, e.g., *Saadeh v. Farouki*, 107 F.3d 52 (D.C. Cir. 1997), holding that the literal reading would probably be ***unconstitutional***: "[The literal

---

3. This provision was added by Congress in 1988, in order to eliminate diversity in cases between a U.S. citizen and an alien permanently residing in the same state.

4. Essentially the same question is posed by a suit between a ***resident alien*** and ***another resident alien*** residing in a different state (e.g., a Canadian permanently residing in Florida vs. a Spaniard permanently residing in Texas). Probably the answer (whatever it is) would be the same here as in the resident-alien-vs.-non-resident-alien scenario discussed in the main text.

reading] would ... create federal diversity jurisdiction over a lawsuit brought by one alien against another alien, without a citizen of a state on either side of the litigation. The *judicial power* of the United States does *not extend* to such an action under the diversity clause of Article III." In any event, the *Saadeh* court reasoned, when Congress amended § 1332(a) to treat resident aliens as citizens of the state where they reside, Congress was trying to "*eliminate* diversity jurisdiction in cases between a citizen and an alien permanently residing in the same state," and it would be illogical to assume that Congress intended at the same time to *expand* diversity to cover the alien-vs.-alien scenario.

3. **Aliens and U.S. citizens on same side:** Jurisdiction is not destroyed by the fact that one or more non-resident foreigners and one or more U.S. citizens are each present on each side of the litigation. Here, the jurisdiction is deemed to be conventional diversity, rather than alienage jurisdiction.

> **Example:** P1, a citizen of Ohio, and P2, a citizen of Canada (living in Canada), sue D1, a citizen of New Jersey, and D2, a citizen of Canada (living in Canada). The configuration is analyzed as if the foreigners were not present; therefore, the requirements for conventional diversity jurisdiction are satisfied, and the suit may proceed. See 28 U.S.C. §1332(a)(3), which specifies that in a suit between citizens of different states, the fact that "foreign states or citizens or subjects thereof are additional parties" does not destroy diversity.

I. **Diversity involving partnerships and corporations:** Often, it will be necessary to determine the citizenship status of non-human entities like *partnerships* and *corporations*.

1. **Partnerships and other unincorporated associations:** *Unincorporated associations*, such as *partnerships* and *labor unions*, do *not* have a single state of citizenship. Instead, the citizenship of *each member counts*. For instance, in a diversity suit where one of the parties is a limited partnership, every member of the partnership (even the limited partners, who have no say in how the partnership is run) must be diverse with the opposing party; see *Carden v. Arkoma Associates*, 494 U.S. 185 (1990), so holding.

2. **Corporations:** The citizenship of *corporations*, on the other hand, is determined by a special statutory provision. 28 U.S.C. § 1332(c) says that "a corporation shall be deemed to be a citizen of any State by which it has been *incorporated* and of the State where it has its *principal place of business.*" This means that for diversity to exist, *no adversary of the corporation may be a citizen of the state in which the corporation is incorporated, or of the state in which it has its principal place of business*.

> **Example:** Suppose a corporation is incorporated in Delaware, and has its principal place of business in New York. In order for there to be diversity, no adverse party may be a citizen of *either* Delaware or New York.

a. **Meaning of "principal place of business":** What *test* do we use to determine the state in which the corporation's *"principal place of business"* is located? The question is most interesting where the corporation's top managers direct the company from a *headquarters location* that is in *one* state, but where the bulk of the corporation's daily *business activities* take place in a *different* state.

   i.   **"Nerve center" test:** The Supreme Court answered this question in a 2010 case, by adopting the ***"nerve center"*** test, under which the principal place of business will normally be the ***headquarters*** location. ***Hertz Corp. v. Friend***, 130 S.Ct. 1181 (2010). Under this test, a corporation's principal place of business refers to "the place where the corporation's ***high level officers direct, control, and coordinate*** the corporation's activities." *Id*. And that place will usually turn out to be the corporate headquarters.

     Example: The Ps, California citizens, work for D (the Hertz rental-car chain) in California. They sue D in the California state courts, alleging violations of California's wage and hour laws. D, seeking to remove the case to federal district court, argues that there is diversity because D's "principal place of business" is New Jersey, not California. D shows that its corporate headquarters is in New Jersey, and that its top management works out of that headquarters. The Ps retort that D conducts more of its daily business activities in California than in any other single state, so that D's principal place of business should be considered California. If the Ps are right, this would make the Ps and D both citizens of California, thus destroying diversity (and D's right to remove).

     Held, for D: The phrase "principal place of business" is best interpreted as referring to "the place where the corporation's officers direct, control, and coordinate the corporation's activities." This "nerve center" will normally be the place where the corporation has its ***headquarters***. The test urged by the Ps — based on the state in which the corporation conducts the ***largest percentage*** of its general business ***activities*** — "invites greater litigation" because that test is more complex to apply. Furthermore, using the business-activities test would mean that, because California's population is significantly bigger than that of any other state, virtually every national retailer would automatically be deemed to be a citizen of California, not a sensible result. *Hertz Corp. v. Friend, supra*.

J. **Devices to create or destroy diversity:** Suppose a court believes that a party has used procedural tricks — such as assignment of claims, failure to join parties who have a real interest in the litigation, etc. — in order to produce diversity jurisdiction that would otherwise not exist. Congress has passed a statute to prevent such tactics. 28 U.S.C. §1359 provides that "A district court shall not have jurisdiction of a civil action in which any party, by assignment or otherwise, has been ***improperly or collusively … joined*** to invoke the jurisdiction of such court."

  1. **Assignment of claims:** §1359 has been applied with particular strictness to the ***assignment of claims*** for the purpose of creating diversity.

    a. ***Kramer* case:** For instance, in *Kramer v. Caribbean Mills*, 394 U.S. 823 (1969), the defendant Caribbean Mills, a Haitian corporation, bought shares of the stock of the Panama Finance Co., a Panamanian Corp. The shares were bought under an installment contract, the payments for which were never made by Caribbean. Panama couldn't sue in diversity or alienage, so it assigned its contract interest to a Texas lawyer, Kramer, for $1. (Kramer, by personally suing Caribbean, invoked the alienage jurisdiction). By separate agreement, Kramer promised to return to Panama 95% of any recovery "solely as a bonus."

b. Assignment held invalid: The Supreme Court in *Kramer* found that the assignment of the claim to Kramer had been made solely for the purpose of creating jurisdiction, and that the assignment was thus improper and collusive under §1359. Therefore, the court held that jurisdiction was *void*.

2. **Failure to name indispensable parties:** Plaintiff may not create diversity by failing to name, either as defendants or plaintiffs, **"*indispensable parties.*"** That is, where the presence of a person who has not been made a party to the action is vital to the fair carrying out of the litigation, the court may classify the missing person as an "indispensable" party in whose absence the suit may not proceed. The standards for doing this are spelled out in FRCP 19(b). See the discussion of indispensable parties (and of "necessary" parties, a related category) *infra*, p. 349.

3. **Devices to defeat removal:** A plaintiff suing in state court may sometimes seek to defeat his adversary's potential right to *remove* to federal court (*infra*, p. 158). There is *no* federal statute prohibiting "improper or collusive" joinder to *defeat* jurisdiction, and the courts have given plaintiffs fairly free rein in their attempts to block removal.

a. **Assignment of part of claim:** Some courts have even held that a plaintiff bringing a state court action may *assign* a portion of his claim in order to defeat an undesired removal by the defendant. But the modern trend seems to be to hold that such a removal-defeating assignment *fails*. Wr., p. 187.

Example: P, a Vermont resident, sues D, a California resident, in Vermont state court. Before the action is commenced, P assigns (for a nominal consideration) 1/50th of his claim to X, a friend of his who is a California resident. X joins as co-plaintiff. By doing this, the required complete diversity for a federal action is destroyed, in an attempt to block D from removing to federal court.

Courts are split on whether this ploy should succeed. The traditional view has been that the ploy does succeed, since there is no federal statute which exists to prevent improper and collusive joinder to *defeat* (rather than create) jurisdiction. However, most recent decisions have gone the other way, especially where the portion of the claim assigned was small, and the original owner of the claim remained as a party to benefit from local state court prejudice against the out-of-state defendant.

b. **Joinder of non-diverse defendant:** Removal may *not* be defeated by the plaintiff's *joinder as defendant* of a party against whom *no bona fide claim exists*.

Example: P (baseball great Pete Rose) brings a state-court action in Ohio against three Ds (the Commissioner of Baseball, "Major League Baseball," and the Cincinnati Reds) to prevent the Commissioner from conducting a hearing into charges that Rose gambled on baseball. The Ds remove to federal court. P claims that removal is improper, on the grounds that Major League Baseball and the Reds are citizens of Ohio, as is Rose, so that there is not complete diversity.

Held, for the Ds. Removal is proper because neither "Major League Baseball" nor the Reds are important to the case — they are both "formal or nominal" parties, with no "actual interest or control over the subject matter of the litigation." Major League

Baseball and the Reds are thus, in the formal sense, "fraudulently joined," and their joinder will not prevent removal. *Rose v. Giamatti*, 721 F.Supp. 906 (S.D. Ohio 1989).

> **i.   Valid claim but no assets:**   But if there is a valid claim against the defendant whose presence destroys diversity, the fact that he has **no assets** out of which a judgment could be satisfied does not prevent diversity from being destroyed. Wr., 188.

> **c.   Low dollar claim to defeat removal:**   A claim for *less than the jurisdictional amount* will destroy removal jurisdiction, but this low amount must be named *before* the defendant removes. Wr., 189.

Quiz Yourself on
DIVERSITY JURISDICTION

18. D's sole residence is in Connecticut. Under a contract with P, D performed some construction work on P's weekend home in Connecticut. P also has a principal residence, located in New York (where P resides during the week). When D failed to do the work in the contracted-for manner, P sued D in federal court for the District of Connecticut for $100,000 (a reasonable assessment of the damages suffered by P). No federal questions are presented by P's suit. May the federal court for Connecticut hear the case?

_____

19. P1 is a citizen of New York. P2 is a citizen of New Jersey. D1 is a citizen of California. D2 is a citizen of New Jersey. P1 and P2 have brought a federal court action in the Southern District of New York against D1 and D2, alleging that D1 and D2 have breached a contract. No federal question is present. The Southern District of New York is the district where the claim arose. The amount at stake is $100,000. May the Southern District of New York hear the case?

_____

20. P1 is a citizen of Delaware; P2 is a citizen of New Jersey. They have brought a federal court action against D, a corporation with its principal place of business in New York and incorporated in Delaware. No federal question is present. $80,000 is at stake. Putting aside questions of venue, does the federal court have subject matter jurisdiction over the dispute? _____

21. Peter is a citizen of South Carolina. A car he was driving was involved in an accident with a car driven by Dennis, also a citizen of South Carolina. Peter wished to sue Dennis for negligence. He was aware that procedural rules would be more favorable for him in the federal court for South Carolina than in the South Carolina state courts. However, he realized that he would not be able to obtain diversity of citizenship in an action against Dennis. Therefore, he assigned his claim to his sister Paula, a citizen of North Carolina, for $1. Such an assignment is fully enforceable under the laws of both South Carolina and North Carolina. Peter and Paula had an implicit understanding that if Paula recovered, she would return the vast bulk of the award to Peter. Paula then sued Dennis on the claim in South Carolina federal court. The amount in controversy requirement is satisfied. Does the South Carolina federal district court have subject matter jurisdiction over the case? _____

Answers

18. Yes. For there to be subject matter jurisdiction, there must of course be diversity of citizenship. That is, P and D must be "citizens" of different states. "Citizenship" for this purpose is not synonymous with "residence." Instead, a person is a "citizen" only of the state where he is *domiciled*, i.e., has his principal residence. On these facts, P's principal residence is clearly New York, and Connecticut is merely his secondary residence. Therefore, P is a "citizen" of New York, and he has diversity of citizenship with D. Consequently, the court may hear the case.

19. **No.** Since there is no federal question present, the federal subject matter jurisdiction must be supplied by diversity if at all. But by a judge-made construction of the federal diversity statute, there must be *"complete"* diversity. That is, it must be the case that no plaintiff is a citizen of the same state as any defendant. Since P2 and D2 are both citizens of New Jersey, diversity is deemed not to exist even though there is also a pair of opponents (P1 and D1) who are citizens of different states from each other. See *Strawbridge v. Curtiss*, 3 Cranch 267 (1806).

20. **No.** A corporation (whether plaintiff or defendant) is deemed to be a citizen *both* of the state where it has its principal place of business *and* the state where it is incorporated. 28 U.S.C. §1332(c)(1). Putting this rule together with the rule requiring complete diversity, it becomes the case that D can be sued only if none of the Ps is a citizen of *either* Delaware or New York. Since P1 is a citizen of Delaware, complete diversity is lacking and there is no diversity jurisdiction.

21. **No.** 28 U.S.C. §1359 provides that "a district court shall not have jurisdiction of a civil action in which any party, by assignment or otherwise, has been improperly or collusively … joined to invoke the jurisdiction of such court." Since the sole reason for which Peter made the assignment to Paula was to create diversity, and since this assignment was collusive in the sense that it was not the product of an arm's-length economic bargain between Peter and Paula, the court will invoke §1359 and refuse to take jurisdiction. The fact that the assignment may have been valid and enforceable under South Carolina law is irrelevant for purposes of §1359.

IV. FEDERAL QUESTION JURISDICTION

A. **Statutory basis:** The grant of original jurisdiction over federal question cases is given in 28 U.S.C. §1331: "[Jurisdiction extends to] all civil actions *arising under the Constitution, laws, or treaties of the United States.*" This language is similar to that used by Art. III, §2 of the Constitution, which gives the federal courts authority to hear federal question cases.

1. **Interpretation constricted:** The interpretation given to the statute has been narrower than that given to the Constitutional language (which applies not only to *original*, but also to *appellate*, jurisdiction).

2. **No adequate definition:** No really satisfactory definition of a case "arising under" the Constitution, etc., exists. The one that is most generally accepted is that the suit must be on *"a substantial claim founded 'directly' upon federal law."* The Supreme Court has formulated a somewhat more specific test: In order for a federal question to exist, it must be the case "either that federal law *creates the cause of action* or that the plaintiff's right to relief necessarily *depends on resolution of a substantial question* of federal law." See *Franchise Tax Bd. v. Construction Laborers Vacation Trust*, 463 U.S. 1 (1983).

3. **Federal claim:** In the vast majority of federal-question cases, federal law will be the *source of the cause of action*. For instance, a claim for copyright or trademark violation

clearly presents a federal question, because a federal statute (the federal copyright statute or trademark statute) is the source of the right the plaintiff is asserting. Conversely, if the plaintiff's cause of action derives from federal law, the case necessarily is one falling within the federal-question jurisdiction.

4. **State-created claim needs interpretation of federal law:**   Suppose, however, that the claim being asserted is one *created by state law*, but adjudication of that claim requires *interpretation* of a federal law. The Supreme Court has held that this is normally *not* sufficient to bring the case within the federal-question jurisdiction. See, e.g., *Merrell Dow Pharmaceuticals, Inc. v. Thompson*, 478 U.S. 804 (1986). (But there's an important exception, which we discuss starting on p. 133.)

5. **Must be revealed by the complaint:**   What does it mean to say that the source of the cause of action must normally be federal law? It means that the federal question must be *integral* to plaintiff's cause of action, as revealed by *plaintiff's complaint*. As the idea is often put, the federal question must be *part of a "well pleaded complaint."* F,K&M, 20-23.

   a. **Anticipation of federal defense not sufficient:** Therefore, it does *not* suffice for federal question jurisdiction that the plaintiff *anticipates a defense* based on a federal statute, or even that *defendant's answer does in fact raise a federal question*. This principle is illustrated by the classic Supreme Court case set forth in the following example.

      Example: The Ps claim in a federal suit that D, a railroad, has breached its agreement to give the Ps free passes in return for their release of tort claims against it. A federal statute has recently been passed which prohibits the giving of such passes. The Ps, anticipating that D will raise the federal statute as a defense, assert in their complaint that the statute does not apply to their case or, alternatively, that if it applies it would violate their Fifth Amendment right not to be deprived of property without due process. The matter goes to trial, where D does in fact claim the federal statute as a defense.

      Held (by the U.S. Supreme Court on appeal), no federal question jurisdiction existed, because the federal statute was *not essential to the plaintiffs' cause of action.* It is not sufficient that the complaint mentions some anticipated defense and asserts that the validity of the defense is governed by federal law. *Louisville & Nashville R.R. v. Mottley*, 211 U.S. 149 (1908).

6. **Claim based on the merits**:   If the plaintiff's claim is clearly based upon federal law, it qualifies for federal-question jurisdiction *even if it is invalid on the merits*. In this situation, the federal court will dismiss for *failure to state a claim on which relief may be granted* (see Rule 12(b)(6)), not for lack of subject matter jurisdiction.

   a. **Insubstantial claim:**   However, if the "federal claim" is clearly made *solely for the purpose of obtaining jurisdiction*, or is "wholly insubstantial and frivolous," the court will dismiss for lack of federal-question jurisdiction. *Id.*

   b. **Supplemental claims:**   It might not be obvious why there would be any practical difference between a dismissal for failure to state a claim on which relief may be granted and a dismissal for lack of subject matter jurisdiction. However, the plaintiff may be asserting *multiple claims*, one of which is a federal-question claim and the other of which is a state-law claim that falls within the federal court's "*supplemental*" jurisdiction. (See *infra*, p. 142 for a discussion of supplemental jurisdiction.) As a matter of subject matter jurisdiction, the federal court can (though need not) hear the state-created supplemental claim even if it dismisses the federal-law claim for failure under Rule 12(b)(6); but it can't hear the supplemental claim if it has no subject matter jurisdiction over what is *falsely alleged* to be the federal-question claim.

7. **Exception for cases raising substantial federal issue:** As we've just seen, the *general* rule is that if the plaintiff's claim is based on state law, the fact that an issue of federal law might be somehow *relevant* in deciding the case (e.g., because federal law gives the defendant a valid *defense*, or because interpretation of state law requires an *understanding* of federal law) is *not enough* to make the case a federal-question case. However, there is a narrow (but important) class of *exceptions* to this general rule.

   a. **Exception:** That is, in a *few* exceptional instances the Supreme Court has decided that even though the plaintiff's claim *arises solely under state law*, deciding the validity of the claim would require *deciding such an important issue of federal law* that the case should qualify for federal-question jurisdiction.

   b. **"Embedded federal issue":** As a matter of terminology, the federal issue we're examining — the one that is by definition not the source of the plaintiff's cause of action — is called an *"embedded federal issue."* Most of the time, the embedded federal issue will be either:

      (1) a federal-law issue that will be central to determining whether a *defense* asserted or expected to be asserted by the defendant is valid; or

      (2) a federal-law issue whose resolution will help *determine the validity of the plaintiff's state-law claim*, even though the direct source of plaintiff's claim is state rather than federal law. An example is where the plaintiff asserts a state-law *legal-malpractice claim,* and the core issue of whether D committed legal malpractice will depend on some aspect of federal law that was relevant in the underlying case that gave rise to the malpractice claim. See *Gunn v. Minton, infra*, p. 137, for an illustration.

   c. **Four requirements for exception:** For the embedded-federal-issue exception to apply (i.e., for a case based on a state-law claim to nonetheless qualify for federal-question jurisdiction), the following *four requirements* must all be satisfied:

      [1] the embedded federal issue will be (or has been) *necessarily raised* in the federal case;

      [2] the federal issue will be (or has been) *actually disputed* during the case;

      [3] the federal issue is a *"substantial"* one, whose resolution is *"importan[t] ... to the federal system as a whole"* (*Gunn v. Minton, infra*, p. 137); and

      [4] allowing an exception to the general no-jurisdiction rule will *not "disrupt the federal-state balance"* of judicial decision-making approved by Congress.

See generally, *Grable & Sons Metal Products, Inc. v. Darue Engineering & Manufacturing, infra,* p. 135, and *Gunn v. Minton, infra,* p. 137.

i.   Two most important factors: Requirements [1] and [2] above are relatively *easy* to satisfy. So in close cases, the decision on whether the case qualifies for the embedded-federal-issue exception will turn on requirements **[3]** (whether the federal issue is a *substantial one* in terms of its importance to the federal system as a whole) and **[4]** (whether having the federal court hear this and similar cases will disrupt the *congressionally-approved balance* between the federal and state judicial systems).

d.   Illustration of qualifying federal issue: The case in the following example is the most prominent modern case applying the embedded-federal-issue exception, i.e., finding that there was federal-question jurisdiction even though the federal issue did not appear in the plaintiff's complaint.

Example: P (Grable) owns real estate in Michigan. The IRS gets a lien on the property on account of P's unpaid federal taxes. The IRS gives P actual certified-mail notice that it will soon seize the property and sell it. The IRS then seizes the property, sells it to D (Darue), and gives P notice of the sale. Federal tax law gives P a 180-day post-sale period in which to redeem the property, but P doesn't exercise that right. Five years later, P brings a Michigan state court suit against D to re-establish title in himself (a "quiet title" action). P's claim is that D's record title was invalid because when the IRS gave P the initial notice of the upcoming seizure, the federal tax statute required (P asserts) personal service, not mere certified-mail service. D removes to federal court; he asserts that there is federal-question jurisdiction because, although P's claim is a state-law claim about who holds title to the real estate, correct adjudication of P's claim requires an interpretation of a federal statute (the notice provision in the federal tax law). P opposes removal, arguing that his claim does *not* present a federal question, so that he could not have brought it as a federal-question case in federal court in the first instance (the test for whether the defendant may remove where there is no diversity).

Held, for D: P's claim "arises under" federal law, so there is federal-question jurisdiction over it, and D is entitled to remove. It's true that *generally*, a plaintiff's claim will be found to "arise under" federal law only if the cause of action was created by federal law. But there is a long-standing, though rarely-applied, second variety of "arising under" jurisdiction, covering "state-law claims that *implicate significant federal issues.*" This exception applies where, even though the claim is created under state law, the claim *"turns on substantial questions of federal law"* in such a way that federal courts' experience, and the need for *nationwide uniformity*, justify having the case heard in federal court. But this exception applies only where having the federal court decide the state-law claim will not "*disturb* any *congressionally approved balance* of federal and state judicial responsibilities."

This narrow exception should *apply* here. The only contested legal or factual issue in the case is an important issue of federal law: whether the federal tax statute requires personal (as opposed to certified-mail) service before a federal tax seizure. The federal government has a strong interest in having a *federal forum* in which to uphold the government's ***chosen method*** of administering federal tax laws. And applying the exception here will have only a "***microscopic effect*** on the federal-state ***division of [judicial] labor***" — it will not "materially affect, or threaten to affect, the ***normal currents of litigation***." *Grable & Sons Metal Products, Inc. v. Darue Engineering & Manufacturing*, 545 U.S. 308 (2005).

i. **Meaning of "substantially important":** One of the two most significant requirements for the embedded-federal-issue doctrine to apply is that the federal issue must be of ***"substantial"*** importance. And to meet that requirement, it's ***not*** enough that the federal issue is merely of substantial importance ***to the outcome of the case***, or ***to the litigants***; what's required is that resolution of the federal issue be "importan[t] ... to the ***federal system as a whole." Gunn v. Minton***, 133 S.Ct. 1059 (2013).

    (1) **Federal government's interest:** For instance, if the federal government has a strong interest in having there be a ***uniform and well-reasoned resolution*** to the embedded federal issue, that interest ***will***, typically, satisfy the "substantially important" requirement. And that's especially true where the embedded issue concerns the correctness of the federal government's ***own conduct.***

        Example: Recall the facts of *Grable*, *supra*. There, the embedded factual issue was the correctness of the IRS' own procedures for seizing property (i.e., whether the IRS was required to give personal service before seizing the taxpayer's property for non-payment of taxes). The Supreme Court concluded that because the federal government (the IRS) had a strong interest in having the courts supply a uniform answer to this federal-law question of what notice procedures must be followed, the requirement of a substantially important issue was satisfied. That in turn meant that the embedded federal issue gave rise to federal-question jurisdiction, even though the suit was between two private parties, and the plaintiff's claim ("I still own the property") was not based on federal law.

    (2) **Significant only to the litigants:** On the other hand, suppose the resolution of the embedded federal issue is likely to have ***no real significance to anyone beyond the parties*** to the current litigation. In that case, even if the issue will be completely dispositive of that current suit, the court is very likely to find that the "substantiality requirement" is ***not satisfied.***

        A good example of "no substantiality" arises in cases of ***legal malpractice.*** Suppose P claims that her lawyer, D, committed malpractice in a prior matter, and the validity of P's claim depends on some issue of federal law that arose in the prior matter. In this scenario, it's very unlikely that this previously-arising federal-law issue will meet the "substantially important" requirement so as to confer federal-question jurisdiction on the malpractice action.

        Example: In what we'll call "Suit 1," Minton brings a federal suit against NASDAQ for infringing a patent that Minton has been awarded by the U.S. Patent and Trademark Office. Gunn, a lawyer, represents Minton in this suit. Minton loses the suit at the summary judgment stage — the federal judge decides that the patent had been improperly awarded to Minton in the first place, because he hadn't filed for the patent within one year after he put the invention on sale to one Stark. In the summary judgment proceeding, Gunn fails to timely make a theoretically-available argument about why the one-year time limit shouldn't apply (that the "sale" to Stark fell within an "experimental use" exception).

Now, in Suit 2, Minton sues Gunn in Texas state court for legal malpractice — he claims that it was malpractice for Gunn not to have timely raised the experimental-use exception in Suit 1, and that if Gunn had raised it, the result in Suit 1 would likely have been different. D defends Suit 2 on the grounds that the sale to Stark never in fact qualified for the experimental-use exception, so that even had Gunn timely asserted that exception, the federal court would have rejected the defense and P would still have lost Suit 1. The state judge in Suit 2 agrees with D's defense, and awards summary judgment to D. On appeal to the state appellate system in Suit 2, Minton makes a new chain of arguments: (1) that the federal courts have exclusive jurisdiction over patent-infringement claims (which is true); (2) that Minton's legal malpractice claim in Suit 2 contains a "substantial" embedded federal-patent-law issue of whether the experimental-use argument would likely have succeeded in Suit 1 had it been timely asserted there; (3) that therefore, not only do the federal courts have federal-question jurisdiction over Suit 2, but that jurisdiction is *"exclusive"* (because the case "involves" a patent issue even though Minton's claim isn't directly based on federal law); and (4) consequently, the Texas appellate courts must dismiss the entire Texas-based Suit 2, leaving Minton free to commence a *new* "Suit 2" for legal malpractice in federal district court, based on federal-question jurisdiction. The Texas Supreme Court agrees with Minton's chain of argument; the court thus dismisses Suit 2 and leaves Minton free to refile his malpractice claim in federal court, as a case falling within the exclusive jurisdiction of the federal courts for patent-law cases. Gunn then appeals to the U.S. Supreme Court.

Held (by the U.S. Supreme Court), for Gunn — the federal issue here does not meet the requirement of being "substantially important," so that this issue *does not qualify* for the embedded-federal-issue exception to the general rule that federal-question jurisdiction exists only if the plaintiff's claim arises from federal law. "[It] is not enough [for 'substantiality'] that the federal issue be significant *to the particular parties in the immediate suit*; that will *always* be true when the state claim 'necessarily raise[s]' a disputed federal issue, as *Grable* (*supra*) separately requires. The substantiality inquiry under *Grable* looks instead to *the importance of the issue to the federal system as a whole.*"

Here (as in any other legal malpractice case), the claim is "backward-looking" and "hypothetical": "*If* Minton's lawyers had raised a timely experimental-use argument, would the result in the patent infringement proceeding have been different?" And no matter how the state courts resolve that hypothetical "case within a case" in Suit 2, Minton's patent will *remain invalid* because of the actual result of the (federal court) Suit 1 proceeding. So no matter what the result in Suit 2 turns out to be, that result *won't affect anyone except for the immediate parties to Suit 2.* This reality alone prevents the federal-law issue from being "substantial." Furthermore, allowing malpractice cases to proceed in state court, even where the case involves an issue of federal patent law, *will not "undermine the development of a uniform body of [patent] law"* — that's so because anything the state courts decide while hearing such malpractice suits will not stand as a precedent binding federal courts in later patent-infringement cases.

Therefore, there is no serious interest on the part of the federal government in having Suit 2 proceed as a federal-question case in federal courts. That fact prevents the federal courts from having exclusive jurisdiction over Minton's Suit 2 malpractice claim. Consequently, the Texas Supreme Court was incorrect in concluding that the Texas courts never had subject-matter jurisdiction over Suit 2. *Gunn v. Minton*, 133 S.Ct. 1059 (2013) (also discussed *supra*, p. 135).

Quiz Yourself on
FEDERAL QUESTION JURISDICTION

22. P is a franchiser of fast food restaurants. D holds a franchise issued by P for a particular restaurant location. P is incorporated in Delaware, and has its principal place of business in New York. D is incorporated in Delaware, and has its principal place of business in Florida. P wishes to terminate D's franchise. Therefore, P has brought an action in Florida federal district court for a declaratory judgment that by the terms of the franchise contract, P is entitled to terminate D's franchise. P's complaint raises no substantive issues other than issues of state contract law. D has submitted an answer asserting that P wishes to terminate D's franchise so that P can operate D's store itself; D asserts that this cancellation would be a violation of federal antitrust laws. Both P and D wish the action to proceed in federal court, to avoid the congestion of the Florida state courts. The federal judge is convinced that D's antitrust defense is not frivolous. Any applicable amount in controversy requirement is satisfied. Does the federal court for Florida have subject matter jurisdiction over the case? _____

Answer

22. **No.** Clearly there is no diversity of citizenship (since both parties are incorporated in Delaware, and are thus deemed to be citizens of Delaware as well as of the state where they have their principal place of business). Therefore, the subject matter jurisdiction must be of the federal question sort. But it is well established that the federal question must be part of a "well-pleaded complaint." In other words, the federal question must be an integral part of the plaintiff's cause of action (as revealed by the plaintiff's complaint); it is not enough that the plaintiff anticipates a defense based on federal law, or even that the defendant's answer explicitly states a federal defense. Since P's claim is founded solely upon state law (contract law), it is irrelevant that D has asserted a defense that derives entirely from a federal statute. See *Louisville & Nashville R.R. v. Mottley.*

V.   AMOUNT IN CONTROVERSY

A. General rule: In *all diversity cases*, the amount in controversy must exceed *$75,000*. 28 U.S.C. §1332(a).

   1. Interest not included: The $75,000 figure does not include interest or court costs.

   2. Federal question cases: In all *federal question* cases, there is *no* amount in controversy requirement, as the result of a 1980 amendment to 28 U.S.C. §1331.

B. Proof not required: The party seeking to invoke federal diversity jurisdiction does not have to *prove* that the amount in controversy exceeds $75,000. All he has to show is that there is *some possibility* that that much is in question.

   1. Standard of proof: The usual standard of proof is that "it must appear to a *legal certainty* that the claim is really for less than the jurisdictional amount to justify dismissal." *St. Paul Mercury Indemnity Co. v. Red Cab*, 303 U.S. 283 (1938).

      a. State law followed: State law is consulted in determining whether it is a "legal certainty" that plaintiff cannot recover more than $75,000.

      Example: P claims $50,000 actual damages in a negligence action, and $50,000 punitive damages. If state law does not allow punitive damages for negligence, the jurisdictional amount is not satisfied in a diversity case.

   2. Good faith: "The sum claimed by the plaintiff controls if the claim is apparently made in *good faith*." *St. Paul Mercury, supra*.

C. Eventual recovery irrelevant: The fact that plaintiff *eventually recovers far less* than the jurisdictional amount does *not* by itself render the verdict subject to reversal and dismissal on appeal for lack of jurisdiction. "The inability of the plaintiff to recover an amount adequate to give the court jurisdiction does not show his bad faith or oust the jurisdiction. … [But] if, from the proofs, the court is satisfied to a legal certainty that the plaintiff never was entitled to recover that amount, and that his claim was therefore colorable for the purpose of conferring jurisdiction, the suit will be dismissed." *St. Paul Mercury, supra*.

   1. Discretion to deny costs: Congress has given the federal courts the discretionary power to deny costs to plaintiff, and even to impose costs on him, if he recovers less than $75,000. 28 U.S.C. §1332(b). But this power has rarely been used by the courts. F,K&C, p. 896.

D. Whose point of view followed: The courts are divided on the question of which party's point of view is to be considered in calculating the amount at stake.

   1. "Plaintiff" test: Most courts have held that the controversy must be *worth more than $75,000 to the plaintiff* in order to satisfy the jurisdictional amount. F,K&M, p. 46.

   2. "Either party" test: Other courts, however, have rejected this "plaintiff viewpoint" approach, and have held that as long as the possible benefit or cost to *one of the two parties* is greater than the jurisdictional amount, the requirement is satisfied. This would seem to serve the Congressional policy of keeping petty cases out of the courts, since any controversy which is worth more than $75,000 to *someone* is not petty. Wr., 206-07.

3. **Removal cases:** In cases which have been ***removed*** to federal court, the court is likely to be much less suspicious about whether plaintiff's claim meets the jurisdictional amount, if the plaintiff has stated it as being for a sum in excess of $75,000. This is because if the action meets the criteria for removal, it could have almost always been brought as an original action in the district to which it is removed. Therefore, since the plaintiff, by bringing the suit in state court, has indicated his lack of interest in having the suit tried in federal court, the amount of his claim can usually be automatically considered to have been made in good faith, if it exceeds $75,000.

   a. **Plaintiff may defeat removal:** But the ***plaintiff is master of his complaint***, in removal cases as in other ones — if a plaintiff wishes to defeat removal, he may claim ***less than what his cause of action is really worth***. See *supra*, p. 129.

E. **Aggregation of claims:** In multi-plaintiff and/or multi-claim litigation, it will often be the case that not all claims of all individual plaintiffs meet the jurisdictional amount. It then becomes important to determine whether some or all claims may be ***added together*** (***"aggregated"***) in order to satisfy the jurisdictional amount.

   1. **Aggregation by single plaintiff:** If a plaintiff has a claim in excess of $75,000, he may add to it ***any other claim of his against the same defendant***, even though these other claims are for less than the jurisdictional amount. These lesser claims may be "tacked on" to the big claim under the doctrine of ***"supplemental jurisdiction,"*** discussed *infra*, p. 142.

   a. **No claim exceeds $75,000:** Even if a plaintiff does ***not*** have any single claim worth more than $75,000, he may add together ***all of his claims against a single defendant.*** If these claims against a single defendant total more than $75,000, the amount in controversy requirement is satisfied. The plaintiff is thus permitted to ***aggregate*** his claims against a particular defendant.

   2. **Aggregation by multiple plaintiffs:** In suits involving ***multiple plaintiffs***, where not all plaintiffs meet the jurisdictional amount, there are two analytically different cases: (1) ***at least one*** of the plaintiffs meets the amount, but others do not; (2) ***none*** of the plaintiffs singly meets the amount, but their claims when ***aggregated*** exceed the amount. Let's consider these two cases separately:

   a. **At least one plaintiff meets amount:** If at least one plaintiff ***meets*** the amount, other plaintiffs may join their related claims against the same defendant. The doctrine of ***"supplemental jurisdiction"*** (*infra*, p. 142) enables the low-amount plaintiffs to join their claims together with the plaintiff who independently satisfies the jurisdictional amount. The Supreme Court so held in *Exxon Mobil Corp. v. Allapattah Services, Inc.*, 125 S.Ct. 2611 (2005), discussed further *infra*, p. 150.

   b. **No single claim meets the amount:** If ***no single plaintiff*** has a claim or claims meeting the jurisdictional amount, aggregation is normally ***not allowed***. However, an exception is made where two or more plaintiffs unite to enforce a ***single title or right*** in which they have a ***common and undivided interest.***

   c. **Special restrictions for class actions:** In ***class actions***, here are the rules on aggregation:

i. **No plaintiff meets amount:** It's pretty clear that if no single plaintiff has a claim that by itself meets the jurisdictional amount, the amount requirement is not met. *Snyder v. Harris*, 394 U.S. 332 (1969). (But see (iii) below for the special case of a class action with $5 million or more at stake in total.)

ii. **At least one plaintiff meets amount:** Where *at least one* plaintiff class member meets the amount but others don't, the doctrine of **supplemental jurisdiction** (*infra*, p. 142) now allows aggregation. Thus if one class member has a valid diversity claim for more than $75,000 against a defendant, other plaintiffs may be made part of the class even if they don't separately satisfy the jurisdictional amount. The Supreme Court so held in *Exxon Mobil Corp. v. Allapattah Services, Inc.*, 125 S.Ct. 2611 (2005), discussed further *infra*, p. 150.

iii. **Class actions with $5 million or more at stake:** Also, if the class action involves *$5 million or more in total,* the action can often go forward even though no individual claimant meets the jurisdictional amount, as the result of the Class Action Fairness Act of 2005. See 28 U.S.C. § 1332(d)(2), discussed further *infra*, p. 370.

iv. **Federal question in class actions:** Finally, class actions are available without regard to jurisdictional amount in *federal question* cases, since there is no amount in controversy requirement in such cases.

F. **Effect of counterclaim:** The presence of *counterclaims* by the defendant against the plaintiff can raise questions as to jurisdictional amount.

1. **Suit brought in federal court:** If the plaintiff sues in federal court for less than the jurisdictional amount, and the defendant counterclaims for an amount which, either by itself or added to the plaintiff's claim, exceeds the jurisdictional amount, it is not clear whether "aggregation" occurs, or whether the court must instead dismiss. Wright suggests (pp. 202-03) that the amount in controversy requirement is not met, by reference to the rule that the existence of federal subject jurisdiction must appear from the *plaintiff's claim*, without reference to that of the defendant.

2. **Removal where counterclaim present:** If the plaintiff originally sued in state court, and the defendant *removed* to federal court, amount in controversy questions also arise if a counterclaim is present. The following general rules seem to be applied:

    a. **Plaintiff removal:** A *plaintiff may never remove*, even if the defendant counterclaims against him for more than $75,000. The removal statute, 28 U.S.C. §1441, has been held not to apply to plaintiffs, even those who are really defendants against counterclaims. Wr., 217. See *Shamrock Oil v. Sheets*, *infra*, p. 160.

    b. **Defendant removal:** If *defendant* makes a *permissive* (by state law) counterclaim for more than $75,000, but plaintiff's original claim is for less than $75,000, defendant may *not* remove. Wr., 217.

    c. **Compulsory counterclaim:** Under the same facts as (b.), but where the counterclaim is *compulsory* under the state law, some courts allow defendant to remove, and some do not. Wr., 217.

Quiz Yourself on

AMOUNT IN CONTROVERSY

23. P is an individual who is a citizen of Missouri. D, also an individual, is a citizen of Indiana. P asserts that he sold goods to D under a contract whereby D was to pay him $65,000, and that D has not paid for the goods. If suit is brought in federal court for the Southern District of Indiana (the district in which D resides), may that court hear the suit? _____

24. P, an individual, is a citizen of Vermont. D, a corporation, is incorporated in and has its principal place of business in Washington. In 1988, P signed a contract with D giving D marketing rights to a software program developed by P, 4-3-2. In 1989, D issued a press release (unrelated to the P-D contract), stating that P "is a good programmer, but he's not a very good or honest guy, as evidenced by his 1986 conviction for armed robbery." P has brought suit against D in federal district court for Vermont alleging: (1) in count 1, breach of the contractual royalty provisions, for which P claims damages of $55,000; and (2) in count 2, libel, for which P claims damages of $70,000. Assume the court has personal jurisdiction over D. May the court hear the case? _____

25. P1 and P2 are individuals who are citizens of Kentucky. D is a corporation that is a citizen of North Carolina. The Ps both signed identically worded contracts with D, whereby the Ps were each to raise broiler chickens, which they would sell to D for a stated price per pound. D unilaterally cancelled both contracts at the same time. The Ps wish to sue jointly in North Carolina federal court for breach of contract, and plan to join together as plaintiffs against D under Federal Rule 20. (Assume that the claims are properly joinable under Rule 20(a) in that they arise out of the same "series of transactions" and involve at least one "question of law or fact [in] common.") The damages asserted by P1 are $80,000, and the damages asserted by P2 equal $40,000. May the claims by P1 and P2 be heard together in a single federal action? _____

26. Same facts as prior question. Now, however, assume that P1 and P2 each have a claim for $45,000. May they join their claims against D together pursuant to Rule 20, so that they can be adjudicated in a single federal court suit? _____

Answers

23. **No.** For diversity actions, the **amount in controversy** must exceed $75,000. See 28 U.S.C. §1332(a). Since P is claiming only the amount of money due under the contract, and that amount comes to less than $75,000, this requirement is not satisfied. (Nor can costs, interest or attorney's fees generally be included to meet the amount.)

24. **Yes.** A plaintiff may **"aggregate,"** i.e., add together, all of his claims against a single defendant, for purposes of meeting the $75,000 diversity amount in controversy requirement. This is true even if no single claim meets the jurisdictional amount by itself.

25. **Yes.** In *Exxon Mobil Corp. v. Allapattah Services, Inc.*, 125 S.Ct. 2611 (2005), the Supreme Court held that when multiple plaintiffs join under Rule 20, as long as one satisfies the amount in controversy requirement, the doctrine of supplemental jurisdiction permits the other(s) to join in with claims that don't meet the requirement. So here, because P1's claim is for more than $75,000, P2 can join the action under Rule 20(b) even though P2's claim is for less than $75,000.

26. **No.** Unlike the fact pattern in which one claimant does meet the jurisdictional amount and others do not

(dealt with in the prior question), here *neither* plaintiff independently satisfies the amount in controversy requirement. Therefore, in this situation supplemental jurisdiction does not apply — supplemental jurisdiction can't be triggered unless at least one plaintiff independently satisfies all subject-matter-jurisdictional requirements.

Given that supplemental jurisdiction does not apply, the question is whether aggregation among multiple plaintiffs is permitted. The answer is that aggregation is *not* permitted so long as the claims are "separate and distinct." See *Snyder v. Harris*, 394 U.S. 332 (1969). Here, even though the Ps both signed similarly-worded contracts, and even though the alleged breach was carried out by D in a similar manner and at a similar time towards both Ps, a court would almost certainly regard the claims as "separate and distinct." Consequently, aggregation will not be allowed, and the case cannot go forward.

VI. SUPPLEMENTAL (FORMERLY "ANCILLARY" AND "PENDENT") JURISDICTION

A. **Background:** Modern federal litigation typically involves more than just the basic two parties, and more than one claim. These additional claims and parties frequently present subject matter jurisdictional problems. For instance, if P brings a diversity suit against D, and D wants to "implead" X (i.e., D wants to hold X liable for any damages that D may have to pay to P; see *infra*, p. 399), what happens if D and X are citizens of the same state — is diversity ruined? Or, suppose that P sues D on an antitrust theory (clearly a federal question claim), and wants to add to the case a claim founded solely on state law (e.g., a claim for unfair competition) — may this state claim be added on to the federal case, even though there would be no federal subject matter jurisdiction if P brought just the state-law claim against D? We examine now the doctrine called *"supplemental jurisdiction,"* by which *additional claims and parties* may be brought into a federal case without independently satisfying subject matter jurisdictional requirements, once there is a basic controversy as to which there *is* subject matter jurisdiction.

　　1. **1990 amendments:** Congress completely codified this area of jurisdiction in 1990, as part of the Judicial Improvements Act of 1990. That Act added 28 U.S.C. §1367. Basically, §1367 establishes the doctrine of "supplemental jurisdiction," which is a reworking and combination of two older judge-made doctrines, "ancillary" jurisdiction and "pendent" jurisdiction.

B. **The traditional "pendent" and "ancillary" ideas:** Before we can understand the 1990 statute creating supplemental jurisdiction, we first need some sense of how courts before 1990 handled subject matter jurisdiction where new parties or new claims were sought to be added to a basic controversy that by itself satisfied federal subject matter jurisdictional requirements.

　　1. **Pendent jurisdiction:** By the doctrine of *"pendent"* jurisdiction, if a federal court had jurisdiction over a *federal question claim* between two parties, it could sometimes adjudicate a *state-created claim* between those same parties, even though it would not have jurisdiction if the claim were brought separately.

a. **Utility:**   The pendent doctrine was useful in those situations where the parties were citizens of the same state, so that diversity did not exist. In such a situation, the plaintiff could gain a federal forum for her state-created claim by linking it to a federal question claim, provided that the two claims were sufficiently closely related to justify use of the pendent doctrine.

Example: P and D are both citizens of New York. Both sell orange juice nationally. P sues D in federal court for violation of the federal trademark infringement statute, arguing that D's brand name infringes a trademark registered to P. P also believes that D's conduct violates a New York state "unfair competition" statute, in that the name of D's brand unfairly confuses New York consumers by making them think that it is P's product they are buying. There is clearly no independent federal subject matter jurisdiction for P's state-law unfair competition claim against D — there is no diversity, and there is no federal question. But by the doctrine of pendent jurisdiction, P can add the state-law claim to the federal claim, since both are closely related and stem from a "common nucleus of operative fact."

b. **Must be similar:**   For the pendent doctrine to be applied, the Supreme Court has required fairly close *similarity* between the facts underlying the federal claim and those underlying the state-law claim. As the test was articulated in the leading case on the subject, the state and federal claims must ***"derive from a common nucleus of operative fact,"*** and must be so closely related that usually a plaintiff "would be expected to try them all in one judicial proceeding." *United Mine Workers v. Gibbs*, 383 U.S. 715 (1966). Initially, this meant that both must arise out of the *same event* or *transaction*. Thus in the above example, the reason pendent jurisdiction could be used is that a single act or series of acts by D — selling orange juice bearing a certain name and label — formed the basis for both the state-law claim and the federal-law one.

c. **"Pendent party" jurisdiction:**   Suppose there was an ***additional party*** against whom the state-law claim was brought, but who was not a defendant to the federal-law claim. Under the doctrine of ***"pendent party"*** jurisdiction, this third party could be made to defend the state-law claim in federal court, even though she was not a defendant to any federal-law claim, and thus was not a defendant to any claim for which there was independent federal subject matter jurisdiction.

Example: Suppose that on the facts of the above example, P claimed that X, a retailer, orally told customers that the product that was in fact made by D was really made by P (a more prestigious and better-known producer). X is a New York citizen. P would like to be able to join X as a co-defendant to P's state-law unfair competition claim. But P has no federal trademark law claim against X. If the "pendent party" doctrine were applied, P could add X as a co-defendant to the state-law claim — X would be a "pendent party."

i. **Restricted by case law:**   But the Supreme Court, in a series of decisions ending in 1989, made it very tough to use the pendent party doctrine. The Court held that only where Congress had ***affirmatively*** indicated that it wanted to allow new parties to be brought in on pendent state claims may such additional parties be added without separate jurisdictional grounds. Even if the federal claim was of a type that could *only* be brought in federal court, this fact would not itself be enough to allow pendent parties to be brought in, with the result that two separate actions might be required. See *Finley v. U.S.*, 490 U.S. 545 (1989).

    ii. Reversed by statute: One of the most important results of the "supplemental jurisdiction" statute added in 1990 is that the result and logic of *Finley, supra,* were *reversed* — new parties may be brought in to defend against the state-law claims even though they don't independently satisfy federal subject-matter jurisdiction requirements. See *infra*, p. 146.

2. Ancillary jurisdiction: The second judge-made jurisdictional doctrine was *"ancillary"* jurisdiction. The line between "pendent" and "ancillary" jurisdictions was always somewhat blurry. But the basic use of ancillary jurisdiction was in cases where there was *diversity jurisdiction* for at least one claim between one plaintiff and one defendant, and *additional parties*, or additional *claims*, were sought to be joined to that "core" claim. Mostly, ancillary jurisdiction was used to give the federal courts jurisdiction over certain types of claims made by *parties other than the plaintiff*, claims as to which there would not be independent federal subject matter jurisdiction because of either lack of diversity or failure to meet the amount in controversy.

    Example: P, a citizen of Connecticut, brings suit against D1 and D2, both citizens of New York. The suit is based solely on diversity, and alleges that D1 and D2 simultaneously hit P, a pedestrian, while driving their cars. Since D1 sustained injuries of her own in the suit, D1 would like to make a claim against D2 as part of the basic federal court action brought by P. Federal Rule 13(g) allows one defendant to make a *"cross-claim"* against another defendant, if that cross-claim arises out of the "transaction or occurrence that is the subject matter … of the original action. …" So 13(g) authorizes D1's proposed claim against D2. But there is no diversity as between D1 and D2, so there would not be independent federal subject matter jurisdiction of D1's claim against D2. However, by the ancillary jurisdiction doctrine, D1's cross-claim against D2 was allowed to be added to the action already commenced by P, and the lack of diversity was disregarded. (The 1990 supplemental jurisdiction statute in force today, 28 U.S.C. §1367, *preserves* this result — D1 can bring the claim against D2 despite the lack of diversity.)

    Note: Ancillary jurisdiction also eliminated the need to satisfy the *amount in controversy* requirement. For instance, suppose that on the facts of the above example, D1's injuries amounted to only $12,000. D1 would not be able to sue D2 in a stand-alone federal action (even putting aside the lack-of-diversity problem), because D1's claim is for less than $75,000. But since ancillary jurisdiction applied to D1's cross claim against D2, her claim need did not need to meet the amount in controversy requirement.

    a. Generally not allowed for plaintiffs: The Supreme Court generally restricted the ancillary doctrine to claims asserted by litigants in a *defensive posture*, who would otherwise either lose forever their right to assert the claim (as in the case of a compulsory counterclaim) or be burdened by being required to start a whole new state court proceeding to litigate the right. Thus in the above example, it's not coincidence that it was a defendant who got the benefit of ancillary jurisdiction. Conversely, the original plaintiff's right to use ancillary jurisdiction was **cut back** to almost nothing by the Supreme Court. For instance, a plaintiff was not allowed to use ancillary jurisdiction to assert a claim against the **third-party defendant**, even if that third-party defendant had already been brought into the action by the ancillary doctrine. **Owen Equipment & Erection Co. v. Kroger**, 437 U.S. 365 (1978).

Example: P brings a wrongful death diversity action against D, a utility, for negligently maintaining a power line that electrocutes P's husband. P is a resident of Iowa, and D is a Nebraska corporation. D then makes a third-party claim against X, a contractor, alleging that X caused the accident by its negligence in operating a crane, and that X must therefore indemnify D against any judgment that P may obtain against D. X is an Iowa corporation. P now tries to make a claim against X, arguing that X is liable directly to P for X's negligence. Since P and X are citizens of the same state, P's claim may be heard by the court only if ancillary jurisdiction recognizes it.

Held (by the Supreme Court), ancillary jurisdiction may *not* be used to cover P's claim against X. If the ancillary jurisdiction doctrine were allowed in cases of a plaintiff's claim against a third-party defendant, "a plaintiff could defeat the statutory requirement of complete diversity by the simple expedient of suing only those defendants who were of diverse citizenship and waiting for them to implead non-diverse defendants." This is quite different from the situation where "a defending party [is] haled into court against his will," the kind of situation where the ancillary doctrine is allowed. *Owen Equipment & Erection Co. v. Kroger, supra.*

   i. **Distinction maintained:** The 1990 codification of the pendent and ancillary doctrines **maintains** the plaintiff/defendant distinction drawn by *Owen Equipment*. It remains the case, for instance, that a diversity plaintiff may not use the ancillary doctrine against a third-party defendant, so that the result in *Owen* would be the same under the new statute. See *infra*, p. 146.

C. The present "supplemental" provision: 28 U.S.C. §1367, added in 1990, codifies the "ancillary" and "pendent" concepts, and combines them into a single notion of *"supplemental"* jurisdiction.

   1. **Provision generally:** The core of §1367 comes in subsection (a), which says generally that "in any civil action of which the district courts have original jurisdiction, the district courts **shall have supplemental jurisdiction** over all other claims that are *so related* to claims in the action within such original jurisdiction that they form part of the same *case or controversy* under Article III of the United States Constitution. Such supplemental jurisdiction shall include claims that involve the joinder or intervention of additional parties."

      a. **Exceptions:** This broad grant of jurisdiction is made subject to certain specific exceptions given in subsection (b) (which apply where the original action is based solely on diversity) and subject to the trial court's right, given in subsection (c), to decline to *exercise* the supplemental jurisdiction. But with these two exceptions, the grant of supplemental jurisdiction is a broad one — the federal district courts are given jurisdiction to add any claim (and any party to an additional claim) as long as that claim is so close to the original one as to be part of the same "case or controversy" as that term is used in Article III of the Constitution. The legislative history indicates that Congress was trying to codify the concept of *U.M.W. v. Gibbs, supra,* p. 143, whereby the two claims would be part of the same case or controversy if they "derive from a common nucleus of operative fact," i.e., derive from the same *transaction* or *occurrence*.

2. **Federal question cases:** Where the original claim comes within the court's *federal question* jurisdiction, §1367 basically codifies the prior judge-made *"pendent"* jurisdiction concept. Assuming that the state-law claim involves only the same parties as the federal-law claim, §1367 should produce exactly the same result as the pre-1990 pendent jurisdiction doctrine would have produced.

> **Example:** Suppose P brings a federal-law trademark infringement claim against D, and seeks to add to its suit a state-law unfair competition claim against D. Since the state-law claim is closely related to the federal-law claim, the state-law claim would fall within the supplemental jurisdiction given by 28 U.S.C. §1367(a). Therefore, the fact that there would not be federal subject matter jurisdiction if P's only claim against D was the state-law claim becomes irrelevant.

a. **"Pendent party" jurisdiction:** In one very important respect, the jurisdiction given by §1367 is much *broader* than that developed by case law prior to §1367's enactment. Remember that in the *Finley* case, *supra,* p. 143, the Supreme Court held that the *"pendent party"* doctrine would be severely restricted — additional parties to the state-law claim could only be brought in if Congress affirmatively indicated that it wanted those parties brought in. But §1367 contains no such limit — the last sentence of §1367(a) states that "such supplemental jurisdiction shall include claims that involve the *joinder* or intervention of *additional parties*." The legislative history indicates that this sentence was expressly designed to overturn the result of *Finley*.

> **Example:** P's husband and children are killed when their small plane hits power lines while approaching the San Diego airfield. P sues D1 (the U.S.) in federal court, under the Federal Tort Claims Act, for failing to provide adequate runway lights. (Claims against the U.S. under the FTCA can *only* be brought in federal court.) Then, P adds a state-law claim against D2 and D3 (a city and a private company) arising out of the same transaction, claiming that they, too, inadequately maintained the runway lights. There is no federal claim against D2 and D3, and there is no diversity of citizenship between P and D2/D3. But because P's state-law claim against D2 and D3 arises from the same chain of events as P's federal claim against D1 — all relate to the plane crash and the reasons for it — P is now permitted to bring in D2 and D3 under the supplemental jurisdiction concept and the last sentence of §1367(a).
>
> Under the old *Finley* decision, by contrast (on which these facts are based), D2 and D3, as "pendent parties," were not permitted to be brought in, because Congress, in enacting the FTCA, had not expressly provided that additional parties could be brought in on related state-law claims.

3. **Diversity exclusions:** Where the "core" claim — the claim as to which there is independent federal subject matter jurisdiction — is based solely on *diversity*, §1367's grant of

supplemental jurisdiction is a bit less generous. This situation corresponds to the pre-§1367 concept of "ancillary" jurisdiction. §1367 generally allows claims that would have been ancillary to fall within the Court's supplemental jurisdiction in diversity-only cases, and thus eliminates the requirement of diversity and amount-in-controversy as to the supplemental claim. But §1367(b) sets forth some explicit and important *limits* on supplemental jurisdiction:

> (b) in any civil action of which the district courts have original jurisdiction founded solely on section 1332 of this Title [the diversity grant], the district courts shall *not* have supplemental jurisdiction … over claims *by plaintiffs* against persons made parties under Rule 14, 19, 20, or 24 of the Federal Rules of Civil Procedure, or over claims by persons *proposed to be joined as plaintiffs* under Rule 19 of such Rules or seeking to *intervene* as plaintiffs under Rule 24 of such Rules, when exercising supplemental jurisdiction over such claims would be inconsistent with the jurisdictional requirements of section 1332.

a. **Theory of exclusions:** This section basically applies the same limits as pre-§1367 Supreme Court cases did, especially *Owen Equipment v. Kroger, supra*, p. 145. That is, where the core claim is founded solely on diversity, additional claims asserted by *defendants* are within the Court's supplemental jurisdiction, but additional claims (or the addition of new parties) by *plaintiffs* are severely *restricted*.

   i. **Rationale:** The legislative history explains the reason for this limit as follows: "In diversity-only actions the district courts may not hear plaintiffs' supplemental claims when exercising supplemental jurisdiction would *encourage plaintiffs to evade* the jurisdictional requirement of 28 U.S.C. §1332 by the simple expedient of *naming initially* only those defendants whose joinder satisfies section 1332's requirements and *later adding claims* not within original federal jurisdiction against other defendants who have intervened or been joined on a supplemental basis." House Report to Judicial Improvements Act of 1990, p. 29.

b. **Excluded claims and parties:** Here are the claims that, according to §1367(b), should *not* get the benefit of supplemental jurisdiction in cases where the core claim is founded solely on diversity:

   i. **Claims against third-party defendants:** Claims made by a plaintiff against a *third-party defendant*, pursuant to Rule 14(a), are excluded from supplemental jurisdiction.

   Example: Review the facts of *Owens Equipment v. Kroger, supra*. Recall that P sued D, and D brought a third-party claim against X, asserting that if D was liable to P, X was liable to D. P and X were citizens of the same state. Section 1367(b) follows the approach of *Owens Equipment*: P does not get supplemental jurisdiction for her claim against X. Since that claim is not supported by diversity, P cannot sue X in federal court at all, and must bring a separate state-court action against X. (But D's claim against X, and any claim X might have against P arising out of the same transaction or occurrence, *do* get the benefits of supplemental jurisdiction.)

ii. Compulsory joinder: Rule 19(a) covers the joinder of "persons to be *joined if feasible*." Neither a claim *against* such a person, nor a claim *by* that person, comes within the supplemental jurisdiction in a diversity-only case.

Example 1: Certain stock in D Corp. is shown, on the records of D, as belonging jointly to P and to X. P and X are both Arizona residents. D is a citizen of California. P brings an action against D to compel D to issue stock certificates showing P as the sole owner. P's action is founded solely on diversity of citizenship (i.e., it involves no federal question). D asserts that X is a necessary party, who must be joined if feasible under Rule 19. But §1367(b) says that X's joinder under Rule 19 does not fall within the court's supplemental jurisdiction. Since the claim by P against X does not independently meet federal subject matter jurisdictional requirements (both P and X are citizens of the same state), X cannot be joined. The court must decide whether the entire action should be dismissed because of X's absence, or whether the action can be permitted to go forward without X. (The factors that the court should consider in deciding which of these two courses to follow are set out in 19(b).)

Example 2: Same facts as prior example. Now, however, assume that X is a citizen of California, not Arizona. Suppose that D wants X brought into the action as, in effect, a co-plaintiff, on the theory that otherwise D may be left with inconsistent obligations (ordered in the present action to convey the stock to P, and ordered in a subsequent suit brought by X to convey the stock to X). Rule 19(a) allows the absent person to be brought in as an "involuntary plaintiff." Apparently, there is *not* supplemental jurisdiction for X's "involuntary" claim against D, because §1367(b) denies supplemental jurisdiction for "claims by persons proposed to be joined as plaintiffs under Rule 19. …" (But in this situation, D could probably use statutory interpleader instead, which requires only diversity between some two claimants. See *infra*, p. 394.)

iii. Rule 20 joinder of defendants: Supplemental jurisdiction also does not apply in diversity-only cases for claims by plaintiffs against parties *"permissively" joined as defendants* pursuant to Rule 20. (Rule 20 allows multiple people to be joined as defendants if any right to relief is "asserted against them jointly, severally, or in the alternative, with respect to or arising out of the same transaction, occurrence, or series of transactions or occurrences and ... any question of law or fact common to all defendants will arise in the action.")

Example: P, a pedestrian, is hit by a car driven by D1. As P is lying on the sidewalk, D2, a doctor, negligently gives him first aid, slightly worsening his condition. P is a citizen of New York; D1 is a citizen of Connecticut and D2 is a citizen of New Jersey. P brings a diversity action against D1, and then joins D2 as a second defendant, pursuant to Rule 20's "permissive joinder" provision. P's claim against D1 is for $200,000. P's claim against D2 is for $20,000 (reflecting the fact that D2 only slightly worsened P's condition). P's claim against D2 does *not* fall within the court's supplemental jurisdiction, because §1367(b) bars diversity-only claims "by plaintiffs against persons made parties under Rule … 20." Therefore, P's claim against D2 must be dropped, because it does not meet the $75,000 amount in controversy requirement. (Remember that supplemental jurisdiction, where it applies, overcomes lack of amount in controversy as well as lack of diversity.)

> **(1) Claims by Rule 20 plaintiffs not excluded:** But what about the situation where an outsider comes into the action as a Rule 20 permissive co-***plaintiff***, rather than co-defendant? Here, §1367(b) does *not* bar supplemental jurisdiction. See *infra*, p. 149.

iv. Intervention: Claims by prospective plaintiffs who try to ***intervene*** under Rule 24 do *not* get the benefit of supplemental jurisdiction.

c. Claims still allowed: Despite the above examples, there remain a number of diversity-only situations in which supplemental jurisdiction *does* apply. These situations appear to include:

i. Compulsory counterclaims: Rule 13(a) *compulsory counterclaims*;

ii. Additional parties to compulsory counterclaims: Rule 13(h) joinder of ***additional parties to compulsory counterclaims***;

iii. Multiple plaintiffs joined under Rule 20: *Multiple plaintiffs* who join together under Rule 20's *"permissive joinder"* provision. (Supplemental jurisdiction applies for amount-in-controversy purposes, but does not apply so as to remove the requirement of complete diversity; see *Exxon Mobil Corp. v. Allapattah Services, Inc.*, 125 S.Ct. 2611 (2005), discussed *infra*, p. 150.)

iv. Class action plaintiffs: Joinder of plaintiffs for Rule 23 ***class actions based on diversity.*** (That is, if one or more named plaintiffs meet diversity and amount in controversy requirements, the unnamed plaintiffs ***don't*** need to meet these requirements, because they fall within the court's supplemental jurisdiction. Again, see *Exxon Mobil Corp. v. Allapattah Services, Inc.*, 125 S.Ct. 2611 (2005), discussed *infra*, p. 150.)

v. Cross-claims: Rule 13(g) *cross-claims* (i.e., claims by one defendant against another);

vi. Impleader: Rule 14 *impleader* of ***third-party defendants*** (for claims by and against third-party plaintiffs, and claims by third-party defendants, but *not* claims by the original plaintiff against third-party defendants).

Here are some examples of these situations in which supplemental jurisdiction *will* apply:

> **Example 1 (compulsory counterclaim):** P, a citizen of New York, brings a diversity-only suit against D, a citizen of New Jersey. The claim is for $100,000. D may bring a Rule 13(a) compulsory counterclaim (i.e., a counterclaim arising out of the same transaction or occurrence) against P for $10,000 — supplemental jurisdiction applies, so D's claim does not independently have to meet the amount in controversy requirement.

Example 2 (additional parties to compulsory counterclaim): Same facts as above. Now, assume that D's counterclaim alleges that in the same episode that P is suing on, D was injured not only by P but also by Y. Y is a New Jersey citizen. D may bring Y in as a Rule 13(h) additional defendant to D's compulsory counterclaim against P, because supplemental jurisdiction applies and obviates the need for diversity as between D and Y.

Example 3 (multiple plaintiffs joined under Rule 20): P1 and P2, both citizens of New York, joining together as co-plaintiffs under Rule 20, bring a diversity-only suit against D, a citizen of New Jersey. P1's claim is worth $100,000, and P2's claim is worth no more than $50,000. The two claims arise out of the same transaction or occurrence. The action may proceed — supplemental jurisdiction allows P2 to ride P1's coattails, for amount-in-controversy purposes.[5] See *Exxon Mobil Corp. v. Allapattah Services, Inc.*, discussed *infra*, p. 150.

Example 4 (members of plaintiff class in class action): In a Rule 23 diversity-only class action, the named plaintiff class members are P1, a citizen of New York with a claim for $100,000 and P2, a citizen of Pennsylvania with a claim for $90,000. The defendants are D1 (a citizen of New Jersey) and D2 (a citizen of California). Because all named plaintiffs (a) meet the amount in controversy requirement and (b) are diverse with all defendants, the class action may go forward even though it includes unnamed class members whose claims are not individually worth in excess of $75,000, and who are citizens of New Jersey and/or California. Again, see *Exxon Mobil Corp. v. Allapattah Services, Inc.*, discussed *infra*, p. 150.

Example 5 (impleader claim): P, a citizen of California, sues D, a retailer located in Arizona, claiming that a product sold to P by D was defective and injured P. The suit is based solely on diversity, and meets the amount in controversy requirement. D then brings a Rule 14 impleader claim against X, the manufacturer of the item, contending that if D owes damages to P, X must indemnify D. X is a citizen of Arizona. D's suit against X is within the court's supplemental jurisdiction, so the lack of diversity as between D and X makes no difference.

4. **Aggregation to satisfy the amount in controversy (the *Allapattah* case):** For   years after the enactment of § 1367, the greatest unanswered question was whether, in a diversity case, plaintiffs who ***did not individually meet the amount in controversy requirement*** could use supplemental jurisdiction to join together permissively with one or more plaintiffs who did meet the requirement. Various federal Courts of Appeals split on the issue. Finally, the Supreme Court answered this question ***affirmatively*** by a 5-4 vote in ***Exxon Mobil Corp. v. Allapattah Services, Inc.***, 125 S.Ct. 2611 (2005). *Allapattah* lets one plaintiff ride another's coattails as to amount-in-controversy in two scenarios: (1) the plaintiffs ***join permissively under FRCP 20***; and (2) the plaintiffs are ***members of a plaintiff class action under FRCP 23***.

---

5. But supplemental jurisdiction does *not* dispense with the requirement of **complete diversity** in this multiple-plaintiffs-under-Rule-20 scenario. So if P1 was a citizen of New York, P2 a citizen of New Jersey, and D a citizen of New Jersey, supplemental jurisdiction would not allow P2's claim to remain in the suit. See *infra*, p. 153.

a. Facts: *Allapattah* actually involved two separate cases that were consolidated before the Supreme Court. The fact patterns of the two cases posed the jurisdictional-amount issue squarely.

[1] In *Allapattah* itself, 10,000 Exxon dealers brought a diversity-only class action against Exxon, claiming that Exxon had overcharged them for fuel. Since it was clear that at least some members of the class had a claim for the jurisdictional amount ($75,000), the issue was whether other dealers whose claims did not meet this amount could remain part of the class.

[2] In the other case, *Ortega*, one of the plaintiffs was a nine year-old girl who had been severely injured when she sliced her finger on a tuna can made by D (so her diversity-based product-liability claim met the amount in controversy requirement); the question was whether her family members, with claims worth less than $75,000 for items like emotional distress and medical expenses, could join with her as co-plaintiffs under FRCP 20.

i. All other jurisdictional elements satisfied: In both of the underlying cases, it was clear that amount in controversy posed the only problem — all other requirements for supplemental jurisdiction (e.g., the presence of complete diversity, and the sharing of a single Article III "case or controversy" across the multiple plaintiffs) were satisfied. So the case boiled down to this question: given that § 1367(a) applies to "any civil action of which the district courts have original jurisdiction," does a case in which ***at least one plaintiff satisfies*** the amount in controversy requirement ***count*** as a "civil action of which the [court has] original jurisdiction" if there are other plaintiffs in the filing who don't meet that requirement?

b. Holding: Justice Kennedy, writing for himself and four other justices, said that the answer was *yes*: "When the well-pleaded complaint contains ***at least one claim that satisfies the amount-in-controversy requirement***, and there are no other relevant jurisdictional defects, the district court ... has original jurisdiction over that claim."

Kennedy continued, "The presence of other claims in the complaint, over which the district court may lack original jurisdiction, is of no moment. If the court has original jurisdiction over a ***single claim in the complaint***, it ***has original jurisdiction*** over a 'civil action' within the meaning of § 1367(a), even if the civil action over which it has jurisdiction comprises fewer claims than were included in the complaint."

(1) "Indivisibility theory" rejected: In reaching this conclusion about how § 1367(a) should be interpreted, the majority rejected the so-called *"indivisibility theory,"* under which the district court would be deemed to have "original jurisdiction" over a "civil action" only if the court had original jurisdiction over ***every claim*** in the complaint (so that all claims in the complaint must stand or fall as a single indivisible 'civil action'). To the majority, the indivisibility theory was inconsistent with the very notion of supplemental jurisdiction.

(2) "Contamination theory" rejected: The majority also rejected the broad form of the *"contamination theory,"* by which the inclusion of a claim or party falling outside the district court's original jurisdiction "somehow contaminates every other claim in the complaint, depriving the court of original jurisdiction over any of these claims[.]" The majority conceded that the contamination theory might have merit when used to justify the requirement of ***complete diversity***, because "the presence of nondiverse parties on both sides of a lawsuit eliminates the justification for providing a federal forum." But the contamination theory, the majority said, makes little sense with respect to the ***amount-in-controversy*** requirement, because that requirement is designed to ensure that the dispute is sufficiently ***important to justify a federal-court forum***, and "the presence of a claim that falls short of the minimum amount in controversy ***does nothing to reduce the importance*** of the claims that do meet this requirement."

c. **Dissent:**   Four justices ***dissented*** in *Allapattah*. The main dissent was by Justice Ginsburg (who, by the way, was a professor of Civil Procedure before she was originally appointed to the federal bench). The dissent conceded that the majority's reading of § 1367 was "plausible." But the dissent preferred an alternative reading.

   i. **Nature of the alternative reading:**   Under the dissent's reading, we should first look at the action as filed, and determine whether, under § *1332*, each plaintiff or class member independently satisfies the amount in controversy requirement. Any party who does not satisfy this requirement must be ***dismissed before we even get to*** the question of whether § 1367(a) applies, under this reading.

      (1) **Preserves ancillary and pendent jurisdiction:**   One reason Justice Ginsburg preferred this alternative reading was that it would mostly preserve the judge-made doctrines of ***pendent*** and ***ancillary*** jurisdiction (see *supra*, pp. 142-145). Under the alternative reading, § 1367 was intended by Congress essentially as a codification of these two doctrines, except insofar as the section expressly overruled the result in *Finley v. U.S.*, 490 U.S. 545 (1989), by reversing that case's refusal to allow additional parties to be brought in to defend against pendent state-law claims. (Everyone, including the majority, agreed that reversing the result in *Finley* was the main objective of Congress when it passed § 1367).

      (2) **"Resolved in favor of continuity":**   Ginsburg conceded that § 1367's "enigmatic text defies flawless interpretation." But, she concluded, her narrow reading was better than the majority's, because it did not "attribute to Congress a ***jurisdictional enlargement broader than the one to which the legislators adverted,"*** and because it followed the sound principle that "close questions of [statutory] construction should be resolved ***in favor of continuity and against change.***"

d. **Significance:**   *Allapattah* is actually a quite ***narrow*** piece of statutory interpretation. It establishes merely that Rule 20 co-plaintiffs and Rule 23 unnamed plaintiff class members can use supplemental jurisdiction to get around amount-in-controversy problems in diversity-only cases, as long as one Rule 20 co-plaintiff or one Rule 23 named class member does meet the jurisdictional amount.

i. **Does not dispense with complete diversity:** Significantly, *Allapattah* clearly does *not* allow the use of supplemental jurisdiction to dispense with the need for *complete diversity* in cases involving the *permissive joinder of multiple plaintiffs* under Rule 20. Cf. Y, 2006 Supp., p. 212, n. 2(a). This result is indicated by the majority's *partial endorsement* of the "contamination theory": "The contamination theory ... can make some sense in the *special context* of the complete diversity requirement because the presence of nondiverse parties on both sides of a lawsuit *eliminates the justification for providing a federal forum.*"

Example: P1, a citizen of Illinois, and P2, a citizen of Indiana, join as co-plaintiffs under Rule 20 to sue D, a citizen of Indiana, in diversity. Assume that the claims of P1 and P2 are closely related. It's clear from *Allapattah* that although that case would allow P2 to use supplemental jurisdiction to avoid having to meet the amount in controversy requirement (as long as P1 met it), supplemental jurisdiction does *not* obviate the need for complete diversity in Rule 20 joinder actions. Therefore, since at least one plaintiff (P2) is a citizen of the same state as at least one defendant (D), the action cannot go forward as long as P2 remains in the case.

5. **Discretionary rejection of supplemental jurisdiction:** So far, we have examined when a claim is or is not covered by the court's supplemental jurisdiction. But merely because a claim is within the court's supplemental jurisdiction does not mean that the court *must* hear that claim. Section 1367(c) provides four reasons for which a court "may *decline to exercise* supplemental jurisdiction" that exists:

   (1) The claim raises a novel or complex issue of State law,

   (2) The claim substantially predominates over the claim or claims over which [the district court] has original jurisdiction, or

   (3) The district court has dismissed all claims over which it has original jurisdiction,

   (4) In exceptional circumstances, there are other compelling reasons for declining jurisdiction.

   a. **Dismissal of other claims:** The most important of these reasons for "abstention" is probably (3), "the district court has dismissed all claims over which it has original jurisdiction." One especially important factor is likely to be the *time* — in terms of the suit's progress — at which the original claim is dismissed. The later dismissal occurs, the less likely the court is to exercise its discretion to decline to hear the remaining, supplemental claim.

   Example: Consider the facts of *Finley, supra,* p. 144 — P sues D1 (the U.S.) in federal court, under the Federal Tort Claims Act, for failing to provide adequate runway lights, and thus causing P's husband's death in a plane crash. Then, P amends her complaint to include state-law negligence claims against D2 and D3 (a city and a private company) whose negligence she alleges to have contributed to the accident. P is a citizen of the same state as D2 and D3, and there is no federal question claim against those two defendants. If, before the case has gone to trial and in fact before there has been very much discovery, the court grants a 12(b)(6) dismissal of the claim against D1, the court will probably exercise its discretion to decline to hear the claims against

D2 and D3. But if the claim against D1 is only dismissed after discovery and after P has put on her case at trial (i.e., the dismissal is made pursuant to a Rule 50 motion for "judgment as a matter of law"), then the court will probably hear the remainder of the case against D2 and D3 anyway — here, considerations of judicial economy, and fairness to P, probably dictate that she be allowed to continue with her state-law claims rather than having to litigate them from scratch in state court.

b. Must fall into 1 of the 4 classes in order for the court to dismiss: Just how much discretion does the court have to throw out a supplemental claim while hearing the other claim(s) over which it has original jurisdiction? Unless the court expressly finds that the supplemental claims falls into one of the four classes mentioned in §1367(c), probably it *must keep the claim*, even though it thinks that judicial economy would be better served by dismissing it. See, e.g., *Executive Software North America, Inc. v. United States District Court*, 24 F.3d 1545 (9th Cir. 1994), concluding that "By use of the word 'shall,' the statute [§1367(c)] makes clear that if power is conferred under section 1367(a), and its exercise is not prohibited by section 1367(b), a court can decline to assert supplemental jurisdiction over a pendent claim *only if one of the four categories specifically enumerated in section 1367(c) applies.*"

   i.   The "exceptional circumstances" catch-all: Of course, the fourth category is a "catch-all," covering "exceptional circumstances" where "there are other compelling reasons for declining jurisdiction." So this gives the court some flexibility in justifying a decision to throw out the supplemental claim. But if *Executive Software* is right, the court has to carefully justify a dismissal based on the catch-all — it can't just reason, for example, "this supplemental claim isn't the sort that the federal courts should hear."

6. No effect on personal jurisdiction: The application of the supplemental jurisdiction doctrine does *not* eliminate the requirement of *jurisdiction over the parties*, nor does it eliminate the requirements of service of process. It speaks solely to the question of *subject matter jurisdiction*.

   a. Used with 100-mile bulge: Much of the time, the supplemental jurisdiction doctrine is applied in the kinds of multiparty cases in which, according to Rule 4(k)(1)(B), service in the *100-mile bulge* area may be used. (See *supra*, p. 70.)

7. Venue not required: At least under case law decided before the codification of §1367, courts held that where "ancillary" jurisdiction (one of the precursors to supplemental jurisdiction) applied, *venue* requirements did not have to be satisfied with respect to each party. Wr., pp. 39-40. Presumably the same theory will apply in cases involving supplemental jurisdiction under §1367. (The venue requirements are treated *supra*, p. 103.)

   Example: P is a resident of the Northern District of Illinois. D is a resident of the Southern District of New York. X is a resident of the District of Rhode Island. P brings a federal court diversity-only action against D in the Southern District of New York. The events involved in the suit did not occur in New York. D impleads X, using the New York state long arm to do so (as allowed by Rule 4(k)(1)(A)). Without relief from the venue requirements, the Southern District of New York probably wouldn't qualify — it's not located in a state where all defendants reside (§1391(a)(1)), at least if we assume, as we probably should, that X is a "defendant." Nor is the S.D.N.Y. a district in which a "substantial part" of the events at issue occurred (§1391(a)(2)). But the fact that supplemental jurisdiction applies to impleader claims, and the further (probable) fact that supplemental jurisdiction eliminates the need for the additional party to satisfy venue requirements, allows the action to go forward in S.D.N.Y.

Quiz Yourself on

SUPPLEMENTAL JURISDICTION

27. P and D are competing furniture stores. Each is operated in the form of a corporation headquartered in Georgia (and incorporated in Georgia); both stores serve the same small town. P has sued D in federal district court for the Middle District of Georgia. P makes two claims: (1) that certain advertising and marketing practices engaged in by D are a violation of the federal antitrust statutes; and (2) that those same practices are a violation of a Georgia statute prohibiting "unfair competition." Each claim involves more than $100,000. D moves to dismiss claim (2) on the grounds that federal subject matter jurisdiction is lacking over it.

    (a) What doctrine determines the validity of D's motion? _____

    (b) Should D's motion be granted? _____

28. Paula, a pedestrian, was seriously injured when a mail truck owned by the U.S. and driven by Dexter (a post office employee), hit her while she was crossing the street. Paula reasonably believed that both the U.S. and Dexter may be liable to her. Applicable statutes and court decisions interpreting those statutes indicate that a suit against the U.S. under the Federal Tort Claims Act may only be brought in federal court. Therefore, Paula sued both the U.S. and Dexter in federal district court for Nevada. Both Paula and Dexter are citizens of Nevada. Paula's claim is for more than $200,000 against each of the defendants. Paula's claim against the U.S. is based on the Federal Tort Claims Act; her claim against Dexter is based on a state-law theory of negligence. Dexter has moved to have the claim against him dismissed for lack of subject matter jurisdiction. Should Dexter's motion be granted? _____

29. P and D were both injured (P more seriously than D) when a car driven by P collided with a car driven by D. P is a citizen of Oklahoma; D is a citizen of Kansas. P has sued D in federal district court for the District of Kansas, asserting a claim whose amount in controversy is $100,000. D, who sustained only a few scratches and some damage to his car, has counterclaimed against P for $12,000. P moves to dismiss D's claim for lack of subject matter jurisdiction.

    (a) What doctrine determines whether D's claim should be dismissed? _____

    (b) Should P's motion be granted? _____

30. Same facts as prior question. Now, however, assume that there was a third car involved in the collision, driven by Xavier, a citizen of Kansas. P has not filed suit against Xavier, only against D. But D has concluded that both P and Xavier were at fault and were responsible for his injuries. Therefore, he has joined Xavier as an additional party (defendant) to the counterclaim which he is making against P; he seeks $12,000 against each of P and Xavier. If Xavier moves to dismiss the claim against him for lack of federal subject matter jurisdiction, should the court grant his motion? _____

31. P is a citizen of Washington. D is a citizen of Oregon. P has sued D for negligence, arising out of an auto accident in which a car driven by D collided with a car driven by P. The amount at stake for P is $100,000.

This suit has been brought in federal court for the District of Oregon. D has taken advantage of the pending suit to file a counterclaim against P for breach of a contract which the two had signed several years ago (before the auto accident). D has added Wanda as a defendant to this counterclaim, on the grounds that Wanda induced P to breach the contract with D. Wanda is a citizen of Oregon. D's counterclaim plausibly seeks $200,000 in damages from each of P and Wanda. Wanda moves to dismiss D's claim against her on the grounds that the court lacks subject matter jurisdiction over it. Should the court grant Wanda's motion? _____

32. Pedro, a pedestrian, was hit and injured in New Jersey by a car owned by Denise, and driven by her employee, Ted. Pedro (a citizen of New York) has sued Denise (a citizen of New Jersey) in federal district court for the Southern District of New York; his claim is for $100,000. Ted is a Pennsylvania resident, but Pedro has not bothered joining him (because he believes Ted is judgment-proof.) Pedro began the action by serving Denise pursuant to the New York long-arm. Denise (knowing, as Pedro does not, that Ted has a small nest egg) has brought a third-party claim against Ted, in which she asserts that if she is forced to pay anything to Pedro, Ted owes that amount to her. Denise has served Ted, claiming authority of the New York long-arm. Ted has no connection with New York, but Denise has substantial connections with New York. Ted now moves to dismiss, on the grounds that the New York federal court has no personal jurisdiction over him. Should Ted's motion be granted? _____

33. Patricia, a citizen of New York, ate dinner one night at a restaurant operated in New York by David, a citizen of Connecticut. For dessert, Patricia had an apple pie bought by David from Terry, a New York citizen who is in the business of baking and selling pies to restaurants. Patricia became violently ill shortly thereafter, and tests indicated that the pie contained botulism. After months of hospitalization, Patricia commenced a product liability action in New York federal district court against David. Her claim is for $100,000.

David then impleaded Terry as a third-party defendant pursuant to Federal Rule 14, asserting that if he is liable to Patricia, Terry is liable to him. (This represents a correct statement by David of the applicable substantive rule in a product liability action brought against a restaurateur who makes a claim over against his supplier.) Patricia then made a product liability claim against Terry for $100,000, as allowed by Federal Rule 14. Terry now moves to dismiss Patricia's claim against her for lack of subject matter jurisdiction. Should Terry's motion be granted? _____

Answers

27. (a) Supplemental Jurisdiction.

(b) No, probably. This fact pattern is a classic illustration of what was formerly known as pendent jurisdiction, and is now covered under the doctrine of *supplemental* jurisdiction. Supplemental jurisdiction, codified in 28 U.S.C. §1367, provides that in cases where "the district courts have original jurisdiction [over a federal question], the district court shall have supplemental jurisdiction over all other claims that are so related to claims in the action within such original jurisdiction that they form part of the same case or controversy under Article III. ..." Supplemental jurisdiction applies to additional claims between the same two parties, as well as to "pendent parties" (third parties brought into the suit who are under the federal court's jurisdiction), provided that both claims derive from a *common nucleus of operative fact* (a requirement implied by the statute's reference to "Article III case or controversy").

Here, the federal court would not ordinarily have jurisdiction over the state unfair competition claim, because that claim apparently does not present a federal question, and there is no diversity between the parties (since both are citizens of Georgia). But since the antitrust claim presents a federal question, and since the practices that are being relied on by D to support that federal claim are the same as the practices that are alleged to violate the state statute, both claims derive from a "common nucleus of operative fact," and P would ordinarily be expected to try them all in one suit. The federal court would still be free to use its *discretion* under §1367(c) to decline to hear the state-law claim, but on these facts it probably would hear the claim (since considerations of judicial economy and convenience militate in favor of hearing both claims).

28. **No.** Paula's second claim falls within the supplemental jurisdiction of the court, as it involves a "common nucleus of operative fact" and Paula would normally try them both in the same proceeding. See 28 U.S.C. §1367. Before 1990 (and the enactment of §1367), the Supreme Court's decision in Finley v. U.S., 490 U.S. 545 (1989), meant that the doctrine of pendent jurisdiction did not offer Paula the right to bring in "pendent parties" unless Congress had expressly stated in the applicable statute (here the FTCA) that it would allow pendent parties.

However, when Congress in 1990 codified the doctrines of pendent and ancillary jurisdiction, one of the most important changes made was to specifically overrule *Finley* and **allow "pendent parties"** in federal question cases, as indicated by the last sentence of §1367(a) — "Such supplemental jurisdiction shall include claims that involve the joinder or intervention of additional parties."

29. **(a) Supplemental jurisdiction.** Where the plaintiff has a valid diversity claim against the defendant, the doctrine of *supplemental jurisdiction* often allows additional claims or parties to be brought into the litigation, even though the additional claim or party does not satisfy the requirement of diversity or the amount in controversy requirement ($75,000) applied in diversity actions.

(b) No. Supplemental jurisdiction (formerly known as ancillary jurisdiction in this context) will always encompass a defendant's compulsory counterclaim. According to Federal Rule 13(a), a counterclaim is compulsory "if the claim (A) arises out of the transaction or occurrence that is the subject matter of the opposing party's claim; and (B) does not require adding another party over whom the court cannot acquire jurisdiction." By this test, D's counterclaim against P was a compulsory one, since both claims arose out of the same auto accident. Accordingly, the court will hear the counterclaim as part of its supplemental jurisdiction, even though that counterclaim does not independently meet the amount in controversy requirement for diversity suits.

30. **No.** Just as the federal courts virtually always allow supplemental jurisdiction over a compulsory counterclaim, so they also allow supplemental jurisdiction over an additional party to a compulsory counterclaim. Consequently, the fact that Xavier is a citizen of the same state as D (thus technically preventing complete diversity from existing) will be disregarded by the court. Although 28 U.S.C. §1367(b) does restrict certain types of joinder when the original claim is based on diversity, these restrictions do not apply to claims by defendants, nor do they apply to Rule 13 counterclaims.

31. **Yes.** D's claim against P is a *permissive* counterclaim (Rule 13(b)), since it does not arise out of the transaction or occurrence that is the subject matter of the plaintiff's claim. Because this permissive counterclaim and the original claim do not derive from a common nucleus of operative fact, the counterclaim does not satisfy the standard of 28 U.S.C. §1367, and it will **not** fall under a court's supplemental jurisdiction. For the same reason, D's claim against Wanda does not fall under supplemental jurisdiction. Therefore, D's claim must independently meet the federal subject matter jurisdictional requirements — that is, there must be either diversity or a federal question, and any applicable amount in controversy requirement must be satisfied. Since there is no federal question, and since D and Wanda are citizens of the same state (Oregon), the federal subject matter jurisdictional requirements are not satisfied, and Wanda is entitled to

dismissal.

32. Yes. A Rule 14 third-party claim brought by a third-party plaintiff (the defendant in the main action) against a third-party defendant is always considered to be within the supplemental jurisdiction of the court. 28 U.S.C. §1367. However, the fact that supplemental jurisdiction will encompass the third-party claim against Ted under §1367 does not mean that the requirements of *personal* jurisdiction don't have to be satisfied as to Ted. For the third-party claim against Ted to be heard by the New York federal court, it must still be the case that Ted has minimum contacts with New York, which the facts say he does not.

33. Yes. Terry is a third-party defendant. A claim by the original plaintiff against the third-party defendant does not fall within the court's supplemental jurisdiction, so it must have independent jurisdictional grounds. Although there is now a federal statute, 28 U.S.C. §1367, codifying what was once called "ancillary jurisdiction," §1367(b) still excludes certain claims made *by plaintiffs* when the original claim is based on diversity. By specifically precluding claims by plaintiffs against persons made parties under Rule 14, §1367(b) preserves the result of *Owen Equipment & Erection Co. v. Kroger*, 437 U.S. 365 (1978), and thus excludes Patricia's claims against Terry. In the absence of a federal question and in the absence of supplemental jurisdiction, Patricia and Terry must be citizens of different states, which they are not. Consequently, the court has no jurisdiction over Patricia's claim against Terry, and it must be dismissed.

Observe that there is a good rationale for denying supplemental treatment to Patricia's claim against Terry: Patricia would not have been able to institute an initial suit against both David and Terry, because of the lack of diversity between Patricia and Terry; it seems improper to allow Patricia to do indirectly (by dropping Terry from the initial suit, waiting for David to implead Terry as he will surely do, then making a third-party claim against Terry) what she may not do directly.

VII. REMOVAL OF CASES TO THE FEDERAL COURTS

A. **General right to remove:** Generally, any action brought in *state court* of which the federal courts *would have had original jurisdiction* may be *removed* by the defendant to federal district court.

  1. **Limitation:** The most important limitation on this is that in *diversity* cases, the action is removable *only if no defendant is a citizen of the state in which the action was brought*. (28 U.S.C. §1441(b))

B. **Removal statute:** The right of removal is statutory, and is not mentioned in the Constitution. Wr., 223. The basic removal statute is 28 U.S.C. §1441. That statute provides in brief:

  1. **Where suit goes:** When a case is removed, it passes *"to the district court of the United States for the district and division embracing the place where [the state] action is pending."* Only cases which could *originally have been brought in the federal courts* may be removed. §1441(a).

  2. **Federal question cases:** In *federal question* cases (of which by hypothesis the federal courts would have had original jurisdiction), the case may be removed by defendant(s) *regardless of citizenship or residence* of the parties. (§1441(b)).

3. **Diversity:** In *diversity* cases, the action may generally be removed only if *no* properly joined and served *defendant* is a *citizen of the state in which the action is pending*. (§1441(b)).

   a. **Class actions:** One exception to this rule barring removal if any defendant is a citizen of the forum state is that in most state-court *class actions*, removal is allowed even if one or more defendants are citizens of the state where the action was originally filed. See 28 U.S.C. § 1453(b).

4. **Illustrations:** Following are some examples of the practical operation of the removal statute.

   Example 1: P, a Massachusetts citizen, sues D, a Connecticut citizen, in Massachusetts state court. The only basis for jurisdiction is diversity. D may remove (to the Massachusetts Federal District Court), because he is not a citizen of the state where the action was brought.

   Example 2: Same facts as above, except that P's suit is brought in *Connecticut* state court. D may not remove, because he is a citizen of the state where the action is pending.

   Example 3: Same facts as Example 2, except that the suit is for federal trademark infringement. D may remove, even though he is a citizen of the state where the action is pending, because the citizenship of the defendant is irrelevant in cases where a federal question is present.

5. **Removal of multiple claims:** Whenever a "*separate and independent claim* or cause of action, within the [court's federal question] jurisdiction ..., is joined with one or more otherwise non-removable claims, the *entire case* may be removed and the district court may determine all issues therein. ..." (§1441(c)).

C. **Diversity and amount rules applicable:** Since removability is based on the existence of original federal jurisdiction, the usual principles governing the existence of a federal question or of diversity, and those governing the jurisdictional amount, apply. (For instance, diversity must be "complete" except in certain specified kinds of cases, such as interpleader suits and class actions involving more than $5 million.) Cf. Wr., 224.

1. **Anomaly:** Using the same test for original and removal jurisdiction produces the strange result that in a case where there is no diversity, "a defendant can remove a case where the plaintiff relies on federal law for his claim, though the plaintiff is perfectly willing to entrust his federal claim to a state court, but neither party can take the case to federal court where the defendant sets up federal law as a defense to a nonfederal claim by plaintiff." Wr., 224.

   Example: In the *Louisville & Nashville v. Mottley* situation (*supra*, p. 121), the railroad could not have removed from state court even though its answer was based on a federal question claim.

D. **Removal not allowed by plaintiff:** Only a *defendant*, not a plaintiff defending a counterclaim, may remove.

1. ***Shamrock* case:** Thus where a plaintiff brought a state court suit (which happened to be for more than the federal jurisdictional amount, and against a defendant as to whom there would have been diversity), and then tried to remove when confronted by a counterclaim, the removal was not allowed. *Shamrock Oil & Gas Corp. v. Sheets*, 313 U.S. 100 (1941).

E. **Certain kinds of cases not removable:** Removal is not allowed in certain kinds of cases, even though original federal jurisdiction would have existed. This limitation reflects Congress' desire to give certain kinds of plaintiffs an ***absolute choice of forum***, which cannot be frustrated by defendant's removal.

1. **Examples:** Two important examples of non-removable actions are suits under the ***Federal Employers' Liability Act*** (personal injury suits against railroads) and suits under state workers' compensation laws. See 28 U.S.C. §1445. Wr., 228, fn. 30.

F. **Original state-court jurisdiction not required:** Until 1988, the federal courts were — paradoxically — permitted to exercise removal jurisdiction only if the state court in which the action was originally pending had jurisdiction. But that year, this limitation was removed by 28 U.S.C. §1441(e). Therefore, today *the fact that the state court did not have jurisdiction does not prevent the defendant from removing to federal court.*

>   **Example:** P sues D in Rhode Island state court, alleging that a novel published by D has violated P's copyright in a novel P wrote. Because the federal courts have exclusive jurisdiction over copyright cases (see 28 U.S.C. §1338(a)), the Rhode Island state court does not have jurisdiction over the case. Under 28 U.S.C. §1441(e), D may remove the case to the federal court for the District of Rhode Island. (Prior to 1988, D would not have been able to remove at all, because only cases of which the state court had proper jurisdiction could be removed, an absurdity that Congress finally did away with. See Wr., 226.)

G. **Pleadings not pierced:** The right of removal is generally decided *from the face of the pleadings*. The jurisdictional allegations of *plaintiff's complaint* control.

1. **As of when evaluated:** The jurisdictional allegations are viewed *as of the time the notice of removal is filed.*

>   **Example:** A sues B to recover accrued installments on an installment contract. The action may not be removed if the amount due on the date of removal did not satisfy the jurisdictional amount requirements, even though additional installments that have accrued *after* removal make the amount sufficient. Wr., 201-02.

a. **Change in status:** A case not removable when commenced may sometimes later become removable. For instance, if plaintiff has ***amended his complaint*** to change the nature of his cause of action, so as to make it a federal question, or if he has dropped a party whose presence prevented diversity, the case may then be removed. Plaintiff cannot, however, take action to *defeat* federal jurisdiction after the case has been properly removed. Wr., 229.

b. **Exception for diversity cases:** *Diversity cases present an exception to the rule that removability is determined as of the time when the notice of removal is filed.* In diversity cases, diversity must exist *at the time of filing the original action,* as well as at the time of notice of removal (unless plaintiff has dropped a party who had destroyed diversity).

    i.   **Rationale:**   The purpose of this limitation is to prevent the defendant from acquiring a new domicile after commencement of the suit, and then removing on the basis of diversity. But as noted above, if plaintiff drops a non-diverse party, and diversity exists with respect to the remaining parties, the action may be removed. Wr., 231.

2. **Plaintiff controls his claim:**   Plaintiff is *"master of his claim"*; if he chooses not to assert a federal claim, even though one is available to him, the defendant may not remove. Wr., 230.

H. **Removal of multiple claims:**   Suppose P asserts against D in state court two claims, one of which could be removed if sued upon alone, and the other of which could not be removed if sued upon alone. May the entire case be removed by D?

  1. **§1441(c):**   28 U.S.C. §1441(c) makes the answer "yes," at least sometimes. Section 1441(c) provides that "whenever a separate and independent claim or cause of action within the [federal question] jurisdiction … is joined with one or more otherwise non-removable claims or causes of action, the entire case may be removed and the district court may determine all issues therein, or, in its discretion, may remand all matters in which State law predominates."

    a. **Not available in diversity cases:**   An important aspect of §1441(c) is that it ***does not apply at all to diversity cases***.

    Example: P is a citizen of Kentucky. D1 is a citizen of Ohio. P brings a state-law contract claim against D1 in Michigan state court. P joins (under the liberal joinder rules of Michigan) an unrelated tort claim that P has against D1 and D2; D2 is a Kentucky citizen. Even though there is complete diversity for P's contract claim against D1, D1 and D2 can't remove, and the entire case must stay in state court. This is true even if the sole reason P added the tort claim against D1 and D2 was to prevent D1 from removing the contract claim.

      i.   **Tactic for plaintiff:**   The unavailability of §1441(c) in diversity cases means that a plaintiff who wants to defeat diversity has a potent weapon: as long as some additional claim can be found that will bring in a non-diverse party, and the joinder rules of the state are liberal enough to allow that claim to be joined, the plaintiff can defeat diversity.

    b. **Federal question cases:**   Section 1441(c) does apply to allow removal of the entire controversy where one of the "separate and independent" claims is based on *federal question* jurisdiction.

    Example: P and D1 are both citizens of Kentucky. P brings an action in Kentucky state court asserting that D1 has violated the federal antitrust laws. P adds to that claim a claim against both D1 and D2 (D2 is a citizen of Kentucky) asserting that D1 and D2 have acted in a way that violates Kentucky unfair competition laws. There is, of course, no independent federal jurisdiction over P's state-law claim against D1 and D2. But §1441(c) will allow D1 and D2 to remove to federal court anyway, assuming that the judge concludes that the antitrust claim is "separate and independent" from the state unfair competition claim.

i.   Probably unnecessary: However, §1441(c) is probably ***unnecessary*** in most of the very federal-question situations where it is usable. It will almost always be the case that the court's §1367 "supplemental" jurisdiction (of the sort that, before 1990, was referred to as "pendent" jurisdiction) will apply; if so, §1441(c) does not need to be used at all.

Example: Consider the facts of the prior example. If P brought both of his claims (antitrust and state unfair competition) in a federal action, the court would almost certainly conclude that the state claim fell within the supplemental ("pendent" under the old language) jurisdiction of the federal court. See *supra*, p. 142. Therefore, §1441*(a)* will be all that is needed for removal, since that section says that "any civil action … of which the district courts of the United States have original jurisdiction, may be removed. …"

ii.   Completely unrelated claims: Of course, if the state-law claim was ***completely unrelated*** to the federal-question claim, then there would not be supplemental/pendent jurisdiction, and §1441(c) might seem to be both applicable and useful. But in this situation, it is not clear that as a ***constitutional*** matter, the court could hear the state-law case anyway (since the constitutional basis for supplemental jurisdiction is that the two claims arise from a "common nucleus of operative fact," as *UMW v. Gibbs*, *supra*, p. 143, puts it).

c.   Remand: If §1441(c) does apply, and the entire case is removed to federal court, the federal judge is not necessarily required to hear the entire matter. Observe that by the last clause of §1441(c), the district court "may determine all issues therein, or in its discretion, may ***remand all matters*** in which ***State law predominates***." So in those relatively rare instance where a defendant actually relies on §1441(c), plaintiff may score a partial victory by getting the state claim sent back to state court. This would probably then mean that defendant would have to defend two separate actions, one federal and one state, which might be even worse for defendant than having the whole case remain in state court.

i.   Remand even the federal claim: In fact, some courts and commentators have held that the federal judge, after determining that removal is proper, may remand ***all claims*** — even the properly-removed federal claim — if state law predominates in the whole controversy.

I.   Remand: If the federal judge concludes that the removal did not satisfy the statutory requirements, he must ***remand*** the case to the state court from which it came. For instance, if in a diversity case it turns out that one or more of the defendants was a citizen of the state in which the suit was commenced, the federal judge must send the case back to the state court where it was commenced. §1447(c).

1.   Discretion to remand: The federal court also has ***discretion*** to remand to the state courts if a federal trial of the case would be jurisdictionally proper but unwise. This is most likely to happen if a federal question claim and a ***supplemental*** state claim are both removed, and the federal claim is ***dismissed before trial***. *Carnegie-Mellon Univ. v. Cohill*, 484 U.S. 343 (1988).

> **Note:** The principle that the federal court has discretion to decline to hear the supplemental state claim if the federal claim has been dismissed before trial is now codified in 28 U.S.C. §1367(c)(3). See *supra*, p. 153. (§1367(c)(3) apparently contemplates that the federal judge will dismiss the action, rather than remanding it to the state court, in this event.)

   a. Not appealable: By the way, the federal judge's decision to remand the removed case back to state court is generally ***not appealable.*** See 28 U.S.C. §1447(d).

J. Waiver: The defendant may be held to have ***waived*** his right of removal if he takes extensive action on the merits in state court. But federal judges have usually been ***reluctant*** to find such a waiver, even in cases where the defendant did such things as taking depositions in the state suit. Wr., 232.

K. Mechanics of removal: (see 28 U.S.C. §§1446-50)

   1. Filing: Defendant must usually file for removal within 30 days of the time he receives service of the complaint.

   2. Where filed: Defendant files by submitting to the district court a "notice of removal," setting out the facts that entitle him to remove.

   3. Stay: Once the notice has been filed, the state court may take no further proceedings until and unless the district court finds that no removal jurisdiction exists, and remands to the state court.

   4. *All defendants* except purely nominal ones must normally ***join*** in the notice of removal.

   a. Exceptions: But there are a few exceptions to this "all defendants must sign" rule (e.g., defendants in cases invoking §1441(c) who are not involved in the "separate and independent" claim, and defendants in certain class actions).

   > **Note:** Certain aspects of removal jurisdiction are handled in other sections. See, for example, the Sections on Amount in Controversy, Devices to Destroy Diversity, and Venue in Federal Actions.

Quiz Yourself on

REMOVAL OF CASES TO THE FEDERAL COURTS

34. P is a citizen of Ohio. D is a citizen of Kentucky. P has brought suit in the Ohio state courts, asserting that D drove his car negligently, thereby injuring P. P has incurred $65,000 of medical bills, plus significant pain and suffering. If P prevails at all, the likely award will be at least $120,000. Nonetheless, in the state court action P seeks only $65,000. (P is aware that under Ohio law, the jury is not limited to the sum demanded in the complaint.) D has filed a timely notice of removal with the federal district court for Ohio. P has made a timely motion to have the case remanded to the Ohio state courts due to the federal court's lack of removal jurisdiction. Should P's motion for remand be granted? _____

35. P is an individual who is a citizen of Pennsylvania. D is a corporation with its principal place of business in New Jersey, but incorporated in Delaware. P has sued D in the New Jersey state courts for breach of contract. P's claim seeks $100,000. D has filed a prompt notice of removal with the federal district court for New Jersey. P has moved to have the case remanded to the New Jersey state courts, on the grounds that removal was improper. Should P's motion be granted? _____

36. P is a citizen of Arizona. D is a citizen of New Mexico. P has sued D in the New Mexico state courts for violation of a federally-registered trademark held by P. Suits alleging violation of the federal trademark laws may be brought in either state or federal court. D has filed a timely petition removing the case to federal court for the District of New Mexico. P moves to have the case dismissed for lack of subject matter jurisdiction. Should P's motion be granted? _____

37. P, a citizen of North Carolina, has brought a state-law products liability suit against D1, D2, and D3, all citizens of South Carolina. P's suit has been brought in the North Carolina state courts. $1 million is at stake. D1 and D2 have signed and filed a notice of removal with the Eastern District of North Carolina (embracing the area where the state courthouse handling P's suit is located). D3 does not care whether the suit is removed or not, and has not signed the notice of removal. P moves to have the case remanded for lack of subject matter jurisdiction. Should P's motion be granted? _____

Answers

34. Yes. The federal courts only have removal jurisdiction of a case which could have been brought as an original action in the federal courts. For this purpose, "could have been brought" includes all requirements of federal subject matter jurisdiction, including any applicable amount in controversy requirement. Since P's claim could only have been brought as a diversity action (no federal question is present), that claim must be for more than $75,000 to satisfy the amount in controversy requirement. P is deemed to be **master of her complaint**, and if she seeks less than $75,000, that is dispositive even though her claim could quite properly have been for more than the jurisdictional amount. So the federal judge, as in any situation where removal is not proper, should remand the case to state court.

35. Yes. The most important single fact to remember about federal removal jurisdiction is that where a case is based solely on diversity, the defendant **may not remove if he is a citizen of the state where the action is pending**. (This restricts removal and diversity cases to situations in which the defendant would suffer from having to litigate "away" rather than "at home" if removal were not allowed.) Since a corporation is deemed to be a citizen of the state where it has its principal place of business as well as the state where it is incorporated, D is deemed a citizen of both New Jersey and Delaware, and may therefore not remove an action pending in the New Jersey courts.

36. No. Where the plaintiff's claim raises a federal question, the defendant may remove even though the state court suit is pending in the state of which the defendant is a citizen. This is the principal difference between removal jurisdiction in federal-question actions and removal in diversity suits (where a defendant may not remove if the suit is pending in his home state, as shown by the prior question).

37. Yes. Where there are multiple defendants, **all** defendants, not just a majority, must sign the notice of removal. See Wr., p. 242.

Exam Tips on
SUBJECT MATTER JURISDICTION

In any fact pattern involving a federal suit, you must check to make sure that the requirements of subject matter jurisdiction are satisfied. Here are some particular things to check for:

☛ First, check to see whether *diversity* can serve as the basis for subject matter jurisdiction. [122-130]

☞ Most important of all, make sure diversity is *complete.* Professors love to make fact patterns that include "incomplete" diversity (e.g., P1 from NY, P2 from CA, D1 from MA and D2 from CA). Remember that the requirement of complete diversity means that *no plaintiff may be a citizen of the same state as any defendant.* [122]

☞ Also, remember that a *corporation* is deemed to be a citizen of *both* the state where it is incorporated, and the state where it has its *principal place of business*, so no opposing party can be a citizen of *either* of these states.

☞ Keep in mind that a corporation's "principal place of business" is determined by the *"nerve center"* test: it's generally the *corporate headquarters* (not the place where the corporation does the most daily business). [128]

☞ Make sure the *amount in controversy* requirement is satisfied. More than *$75,000* must be at stake. [138-140]

☞ Professors frequently test *aggregation* issues. [139-140] You can spot such an issue when you see either: (1) several claims totalling more than $75,000, with no single claim equalling $75,000; or (2) one (or more) claims exceeding $75,000, plus one (or more) claims for less than $75,000. The rules on aggregation are too tricky to summarize here, but in general: (1) a P may combine several claims against a single D to get to $75,000; (2) a P may not bring in an additional D against whom all claims total less than $75,000; and (3) multiple P's can't combine their claims against a single D if no P has a claim for more than $75,000, but if one P *does* have a claim for more than $75,000, under supplemental jurisdiction other Ps whose claims are for less than $75,000 *can* join, because of the *Allapattah* case.

☛ Whether there's diversity or not, check on whether there's a *federal question* present. The existence of a federal question means, of course, that the case can go forward even if there's no diversity. [131-133]

☞ Remember that a "federal question" is one "arising under the Constitution, laws or treaties of the United States." Usually, your fact pattern will involve a constitutional issue or a federal statute if the professor is trying to see whether you can spot a federal question. [132]

☞ In general, look only to P's *claim*, not D's possible defenses, to determine whether there's a federal question. [132]

☞ But in rare cases where resolving P's state-law claim requires *interpreting federal law*, and there is a strong federal interest in having a *uniform interpretation* of that federal law (e.g., interpretation of an IRS statute), then the case might be found to raise a federal question anyway. [133]

☞ You don't have to worry about the amount in controversy if a federal question is present.

☛ Once you've determined that your fact pattern contains a valid diversity claim between two or more parties, or a valid federal question claim, be on the lookout for applications of *supplemental jurisdiction* ("SJ"). Professors love to create patterns that have SJ lurking in them, because SJ can be well hidden. [142-155]

☞ If the "core" (basic) claim in your fact pattern involves a *federal question*, remember that SJ lets *state-law claims* be added to the suit. So anytime a P wants to assert both a federal-statutory claim and a state-law (perhaps common-law) claim, and there is not diversity between P and D, "Think SJ". [142-146]

☞ Also, recall that SJ lets *additional parties* be added to the state-law claim. So look for patterns where P has both federal and state-law claims against D1, and state-law-only claims against D2; if P is a citizen of the same state as either D1 or D2, SJ is the way that the entire suit can go forward. [143, 146-154].

☞ If the "core" claim is state-law-only, but is supported by *diversity*, look to see whether SJ is available to cover *new claims* or *new parties* that would otherwise destroy diversity or would fail to satisfy amount-in-controversy.

☞ These types of situations are *covered* by SJ: (1) compulsory counterclaims; (2) joinder of additional parties to compulsory counterclaims; (3) cross-claims; (4) impleader claims by third-party plaintiffs (TPP's) against third-party defendants (TPD's); (5) any claims by TPP's or TPD's against anyone.

☞ These types of situations are *not covered* by SJ: (1) claims by a P against a TPD; (2) claims by a P against a person who is to be "joined if feasible"; (3) claims by a P against multiple Ds; and (4) claims by would-be intervenors who want to enter on the Plaintiff side of the suit.

☞ If you can't remember all this, just remember the rule of *"defensive posture"*: in a diversity case, SJ helps only those in a defensive posture. So SJ applies to additional claims by defendants (including TPDs and TPPs), but *not* to additional claims asserted by plaintiffs. [144]

☞ Remember that SJ *never affects* the requirements of *personal* jurisdiction. So if a D (even a TPD) does not have minimum contacts with the forum state, the fact that the claim is of a type to which SJ applies is not enough to allow D to be joined.

☛ Whenever your pattern involves a D who is sued in *state* court, and you're asked about the options available to D, consider *removal* of the suit to the federal courts. In general, any action brought in state court which P could have brought in federal court may be removed. [158-163]

☞ But remember that in a *diversity* case (not in federal question cases), there's a key additional requirement: the case may be removed only if *no D is a citizen of the state in which the action is pending.* Professors love to test on this exception, because it's easy to slip into the fact pattern and easy for the student to miss.

☞ And remember that a *corporation* is a citizen of *both* its state of *incorporation* and the state where it has its *principal place of business* (generally defined as the company's *headquarters*).

CHAPTER 4

PLEADING

ChapterScope

This Chapter covers pleading, the process by which the parties to a litigation spell out their claims and defenses. The emphasis in this chapter is on the pleading provisions of the *Federal Rules*. These exemplify the modern, non-technical approach to pleading, and have served as the model for the pleading provisions of many states. The most important concepts in this Chapter are:

- **Two types:** In most instances, there are only two types of pleadings in a federal action. These are the *complaint* and the *answer*. The complaint is the document by which the plaintiff begins the case. The answer is the defendant's response to the complaint.

  - ❏ **Reply:** In some circumstances, there will be a third document, called the *reply*. The reply is, in effect, an "answer to the answer." Most often, a reply is allowable if the answer contains a *counterclaim* (in which case a reply is *required*).

- **Elements of complaint:** There are three essential elements which a complaint must have:

  - ❏ **Jurisdiction:** A short and plain statement of the grounds upon which the court's *jurisdiction* depends;

  - ❏ **Statement of the claim:** A *short and plain statement of the claim* showing that the pleader is entitled to relief; and

  - ❏ **Relief:** A demand for judgment for the *relief* (e.g., money damages, injunction, etc.) which the pleader seeks.

- **Defenses against validity of complaint:** Either in the *answer*, or by separate *motion*, defendant may attack the validity of the complaint in a number of respects. Grounds for attack include lack of *jurisdiction*, insufficiency of *service of process*, and failure to *state a claim upon which relief may be granted*.

- **Affirmative defenses:** There are certain defenses which must be *explicitly pleaded* in the *answer*, if D is to raise them at trial. These are so-called *"affirmative defenses."* (Examples: *contributory negligence*, *fraud*, *res judicata*, *statute of limitations*, and *illegality*.)

- **Counterclaim:** In addition to defenses, if D has a claim against P, he may (in all cases) and must (in some cases) plead that claim as a *counterclaim*. If the counterclaim is one which D is *required* to plead, it is called a *compulsory* counterclaim. If it is one which D has the option of pleading or not, it is called a *permissive* counterclaim. A counterclaim is compulsory if it "arises out of the transaction or occurrence that is the subject matter of the [plaintiff's] claim."

- **Variance of proof from pleading:** The Federal Rules allow substantial *deviation* of the proof at trial from the pleadings, so long as the variance does not seriously prejudice the other side.

I.   HISTORY AND GENERAL PRINCIPLES

A. Three forms: Pleading evolved through three major forms:

1. *common law*, which is of largely historical interest;

2. *codes*, which are still in effect in a number of states; and

3. *the Federal Rules*, which are imitated in an increasing majority of jurisdictions.

B. Three purposes: Each of these three forms of pleading was or is characterized by a distinct overall purpose:

1. **Common law:** The object of pleading at *common law* was to *formulate the issues for trial.*

2. **Codes:** Pleading under the *codes* was/is designed to *reveal the underlying facts on which the claim rested.*

3. **Federal Rules:** The primary purpose of *federal* pleading is to *give notice* of the claim (or defense) to the adversary, so that he may make effective *discovery* requests and *trial preparation.*

II.   MODERN FEDERAL PLEADING GENERALLY

A. Purpose: The guiding principle of pleading under the Federal Rules is that the pleadings should give *notice* to all parties of the nature of the lawsuit, sufficient to allow the other parties to make *pre-trial and trial preparation.*

1. **Functions of pleadings revised:** At common law, and to some extent under the Codes, pleadings served a number of functions: (1) stating the facts underlying the case; (2) formulating the issues for trial; (3) weeding out sham claims; and (4) notifying the parties so that they could prepare for trial. The first three of these functions are not performed primarily by the pleadings under the Federal Rules:

   a. **Fact stating:** The setting out of the facts underlying the claim is now mainly accomplished by the use of extensive *discovery* procedures, which compel each side to state the facts of the case as it believes them to be. (But some recitation of the factual allegations must still be done by the complaint, or else the complaint may be dismissed for failure to state a claim.)

   b. **Definition of issues:** Issues are mainly defined through discovery, and also through the *pre-trial conference* — Rule 16 provides for such a conference to consider, among other things, "simplifying the issues."

   c. **Sham claims:** Meritless claims are now disposed of primarily through *summary judgment* under Rule 56. This is a more effective means of rejecting unmerited claims, since not only affidavits, but also all the fruits of discovery, may be introduced at the hearing on the summary judgment motion.

2. **Notice-giving:** Therefore, the main function left to be performed by the pleadings is that of giving enough *notice* to the defendant that he can understand the basic nature of the claim, and start to prepare a defense. Cf. Wr., 468.

B. General principles: Here are some of the general principles behind federal pleading:

1. **No "theory of pleadings":** The Federal Rules do not require, as many Codes do, that the plaintiff confine himself to one particular *"theory of the pleadings."* If plaintiff is entitled to relief, he is not to be thrown out of court because his lawyer chose an incorrect legal theory when drafting the pleadings. The ease with which pleadings may be amended, even during trial (see *infra*, pp. 193-198) is one indication of the abandonment of the "theory of the pleadings" requirement.

2. **Substantial justice:** The pleadings are to be "construed so as to *do justice*." Rule 8(e). This replaces the common law principle that the pleadings are to be construed "most strongly against the pleader." Wr., 471.

3. **Dismissal:** The complaint can be dismissed for "failure to state a claim on which relief may be granted" (Rule 12(b)(6)). But it's relatively difficult for the defendant to satisfy this standard (though not as hard as it was before two Supreme Court decisions dating from 2007 and 2009). If the court, after assuming that all factual allegations in the complaint are true, cannot *"plausibly infer"* that the defendant is liable, the court will dismiss the complaint for failure to state a claim. For more about dismissals for failure to state a claim, including this "plausibility" rule, see *infra*, pp. 179-186.

C. Mechanics of pleadings:

1. **Kinds of pleadings:** In most instances, only two pleadings, a *complaint* and an *answer*, are allowed under the federal system. This represents a change from the common law system, in which the parties traded pleadings *ad infinitum*, until a single issue for trial was formulated.

   a. **Reply:** A *reply*, which is an "answer to the answer," is allowable in two circumstances: (Rule 7(a))

      i. where the answer contains a *counterclaim* which is identified as such (in which case a reply is required); or

      ii. by *order* of the court.

      Note: Where the answer contains a counterclaim, the reply must address itself solely to the allegations of the counterclaim, and must not discuss the defensive allegations contained in the answer. Wr., 456.

2. **Verification of pleadings:** Whereas the Codes often required that the pleadings be *verified*, i.e., *sworn to*, Rule 11 states that the pleadings need not be verified unless this is required by statute or rule.

   a. **Where verification required:** The Federal Rules requiring verification in certain circumstances include:

      i. Rule 23.1, dealing with *stockholders' derivative suits;*

      ii. Rule 27(a), allowing the taking of certain *depositions before an action has been commenced;* and

    iii. Rule 65(b), permitting ***temporary*** restraining orders on a verified complaint showing that the petitioner will suffer "immediate and irreparable injury, loss or damage" if the restraining order is not granted.

3. **Attorney must not file frivolous pleading (Rule 11):** The non-lawyer commonly thinks that "you can say anything you want in a lawsuit." But in fact, at least in federal suits, it is the lawyer's job to make sure that a pleading (or any other paper submitted to the court) is ***not frivolous***, and not issued to ***harass*** or ***delay*** the adversary. Rule 11 imposes this requirement, and provides that a lawyer who fails in this duty may be ***fined*** or otherwise ***sanctioned***.

    a. **Lawyer's obligation:** The pleader herself does ***not*** need to swear to the pleading in most instances. But the pleader's ***lawyer*** must sign the pleading, and is responsible for its contents in some important ways. When the lawyer files a pleading, the lawyer thereby "***certifies*** that to the best of the [lawyer's] knowledge, information, and belief, formed after an ***inquiry reasonable under the circumstances***, —

    (1) the pleading "is not being presented for any ***improper purpose***, such as to ***harass,*** cause ***unnecessary delay,*** or needlessly ***increase the cost*** of litigation";

    (2) "the claims, defenses, and other legal contentions are ***warranted by existing law*** or by a ***nonfrivolous argument for extending, modifying, or reversing*** existing law or for establishing new law";

    (3) "the factual contentions have ***evidentiary support***, or if specifically so identified, will likely have evidentiary support after a reasonable opportunity for further investigation or discovery"; and

    (4) "the ***denials*** of factual contentions are ***warranted on the evidence*** or, if specifically so identified, are reasonably based on belief or a lack of information."

    See generally Rule 11(b).

    b. **Purpose of rule:** Rule 11 applies to all papers filed with the court, whether these are complaints, answers, motions, etc. But the main real-world consequence of the rule has been to deter lawyers for ***plaintiffs*** from asserting claims that have no basis in law or fact, and to prevent them from bringing to a multi-party action peripheral defendants (the "join 'em all" strategy).

        i. **Important litigation area:** Since Rule 11 was strengthened in 1983 in order to better deter delay and other abuses, litigation seeking or opposing Rule 11 sanctions has grown into one of the most important aspects of federal practice.

    c. **Nature of sanctions:** Rule 11 allows the court to impose a number of ***sanctions*** on lawyers or parties who violate the rule. Sanctions can include non-monetary measures such as ***censuring*** the offending lawyer, ***striking*** the offending pleading, etc. See 1993 Advisory Committee Notes to Rule 11(c).

        i. **Monetary sanctions:** The most common sanction, however, is a monetary ***fine***. Any monetary penalty is normally be paid ***to the court***, and will be paid to the other party only if "warranted for effective deterrence." Rule 11(c)(4). This of course deprives the party who is complaining of a Rule 11 violation of much of the financial incentive for doing so, probably reducing the number of Rule 11 motions.

   ii. Discretionary: Rule 11 sanctions are ***discretionary*** with the court: if the court concludes that Rule 11 has been violated, it "***may*** impose an appropriate sanction. …"

d. What is "reasonable inquiry": The lawyer must make *"reasonable inquiry"* before signing the pleading. What constitutes "reasonable inquiry" will, of course, vary from case to case. If the claim is one which, if true, should logically be supported by evidence already available to the plaintiff, the plaintiff's lawyer probably cannot blindly accept the client's word for what happened, and must at least question the client about his story. But if the only likely evidence in support of the proposed claim lies with the defendant, plaintiff's lawyer probably may sign the complaint without detailed inquiry, on the theory that she can obtain evidence through discovery after filing the action (though under Rule 11(b)(3), the factual contentions for which there is a lack of present evidence must be "specifically so identified" in the pleading.)

   i. Duty not to reaffirm bad pleading: Suppose a lawyer makes a "reasonable inquiry" before filing the pleading, then ***later learns*** that the pleading is not meritorious. Must the lawyer ***withdraw*** the pleading or face sanctions? The answer is ***"yes."*** Under Rule 11(b), the certifications being made by the lawyer are triggered not only by the signing, filing, and submitting of a document, but also by the lawyer's ***"later advocating"*** that document. The Advisory Committee's notes to Rule 11 illustrate the "later advocating" rule by saying that if an attorney ***orally insists*** on preserving a claim or defense during a ***pretrial conference***, he should be viewed as "presenting to the court" that contention and can be sanctioned if, based on his present (as opposed to original) state of knowledge, he is using it to delay or harass or it is without basis in existing law, etc.

   Note: Observe that this "later advocating" rule is likely to have at least as much, maybe more, impact on ***defendants*** as on plaintiffs — a defendant who denies a claim based on lack of knowledge or information sufficient to form a belief as to the claim's truth (see Rule 8(b)), for instance, may not continue to assert the defense if developments since his filing of an answer show him that the claim has substantial merit.

   ii. Bad faith not required: Also, sanctions can be awarded without a showing that the lawyer (or the party signing the pleading) behaved in ***bad faith***. If the lawyer honestly believes that the complaint is true, but a reasonable person would have made inquiries that would have shown the complaint to be false, sanctions may be imposed. See *Business Guides, Inc. v. Chromatic Communications Enterprises, Inc.*, 498 U.S. 533 (1991), holding that this "objective standard of reasonable inquiry" applies.

e. Procedure for invoking Rule 11: Normally, proceedings to impose a sanction for violation of Rule 11 will come about because the opposing party has made a ***motion*** to impose the sanctions. But the court may also impose sanctions on its own initiative. Rule 11(c)(1)(B).

i.   **"Safe harbor" provision:** Under 11(c)(2), the party seeking sanctions serves a motion on the other party, but is not allowed to ***file*** the motion with the court "if the challenged paper, claim, or defense ... is ***withdrawn*** or appropriately corrected within 21 days after service." In other words, an offending party gets a 21-day ***"safe-harbor"*** in which to withdraw or correct any bad pleading, and if he does so, there can be no sanctions no matter how outrageous the original misconduct.

f.   **Sanctions on signer's firm:**   What happens if the lawyer purports to sign the pleadings on behalf of her law firm (e.g., "Janet Jones, on behalf of Smith, Brown & Jones, P.C.")? May Rule 11 sanctions be awarded against the entire law firm?

    i.   **Joint responsibility:** Rule 11(c)(1) makes the answer ***"yes."*** The Rule says that "[a]bsent exceptional circumstances, a law firm must be held ***jointly responsible*** for a violation committed by its partner, associate, or employee."

g.   **Sanctions against party:**   Normally, the ***pleader herself*** does ***not sign*** the pleadings. But even without signing the pleadings, the pleader can be ***liable*** for Rule 11 sanctions if the court finds that the party, not just the lawyer, was responsible for the Rule 11 violations (as where the pleader lies to her lawyer, leading the lawyer to believe that a claim or defense has merit when it does not.) See Rule 11(c)(1) (court may impose sanctions upon "a party that violated [Rule 11] or is responsible for the violation.")

    i.   **Party signs:** If the pleader ***does*** sign the pleadings (either without being required to, or because the situation is one of the rare ones requiring such a signature, such as where verification is required, or where the party is not represented by counsel) then the pleader is treated essentially like a lawyer for Rule 11 purposes. *Business Guides, Inc. v. Chromatic Communications Enterprises, Inc.*, 498 U.S. 533 (1991).

h.   **Applicable where case voluntarily dismissed:**   A standard technique among some over-aggressive litigators is to file a complaint first, then investigate. Such litigators may reason, "If my post-filing investigation shows that the complaint has no chance of winning, I can always take a voluntary dismissal under Rule 41(a)(1)(i), and there won't be any pending action in which the court can award Rule 11 sanctions against me." However, as a result of a Supreme Court decision, this strategy will not work. In *Cooter & Gell v. Hartmarx Corp.*, 496 U.S. 384 (1990), the Court held that even where the complaint has already been ***voluntarily dismissed*** by P, the court retains jurisdiction to award Rule 11 sanctions, including attorney's fees, if it finds that the complaint was filed without reasonable inquiry.

i.   **Applicability to discovery abuses:**   Rule 11 is ***inapplicable*** to ***discovery*** abuses. Therefore, the special discovery-specific sanctions contained in Rules 26 through 37 are the only ones used in the discovery context. See Rule 11(d).

j.   **Court has inherent sanction power apart from Rule:**   Federal courts also have ***"inherent power"*** to sanction conduct that is in contempt of the court, whether or not this conduct is covered by Rule 11. That is, where a litigant abuses the judicial process, the court may use its general power to punish contempt in order to punish the litigant by fines or other sanctions, without using the procedures of Rule 11 at all. This is true even if the type of conduct being punished consists of the filing of harassing pleadings or motions (which would make Rule 11 sanctions applicable). *Chambers v. NASCO*, 501 U.S. 32 (1991).

4. **Pleading in the alternative:** The pleader, whether he is plaintiff or defendant, may plead "*in the alternative*." That is, by Rule 8(d), "A party may set out 2 or more statements of a claim or defense alternately or hypothetically[.]" This rule also provides that "[a] party may state as many separate claims or defenses as it has, regardless of consistency."

   Example: P performed certain work for D, for which he has not been paid. P can allege in one count that the work was done under a valid written contract, and that the measure of damages includes lost profits. P can then also allege, in a second count, that if the contract was not valid, P rendered value to D, and is thus entitled to recover in *quantum meruit* for the value of his performance. The two theories are obviously inconsistent, and are in fact phrased in the alternative. Such alternative pleading is allowed by Rule 8(d).

III. THE COMPLAINT

A. **Definition of complaint:** The complaint is the initial pleading in a lawsuit, and is filed by the plaintiff.

1. **Commencement of action:** The action is deemed to have been "commenced" by the filing of the complaint with the court. See Rule 3.

   a. **Effect on statute of limitations:** In diversity cases, this filing, although "commencing" the action, does not satisfy or toll a state statute of limitations requiring actual service of process. Federal courts in diversity cases are required to follow the statute of limitations in the state where they sit. See *Guaranty Trust v. York*, *infra* p. 261, and *Ragan v. Merchants Transfer & Warehouse Co.*, *infra*, p. 261.

B. **Elements of complaint:** Rule 8(a) sets out three essential elements which a complaint must contain:

1. **Jurisdiction:** "a short and plain statement of the grounds for the court's *jurisdiction*";

2. **Statement of claim:** "a short and plain *statement of the claim* showing that the pleader is *entitled to relief*";

3. **Relief:** "a demand for the *relief* sought[.]"

   Note: The three elements above required by Rule 8(a) apply not only to a plaintiff's original complaint, but also to a defendant's *counterclaim*, to any party's *third-party claim*, and to any party's *cross-claim*. The nature of these other kinds of claims will be treated in the chapter on Multi-Party and Multi-Claim Litigation.

C. **Jurisdictional allegation:** The requirement that the complaint contain jurisdictional allegations stems from the U.S. Constitution's limitation of the subject matter jurisdiction of the federal courts. The requirements of federal subject matter jurisdiction are treated in the previous chapter.

1. **Diversity suit:**   In a diversity suit, the jurisdictional allegation might read as follows: "Jurisdiction is founded upon diversity of citizenship, plaintiff being a citizen of State A and defendant being a citizen of State B. The amount in controversy, exclusive of interest and court costs, is in excess of $75,000."

2. **Federal question:**   If the plaintiff asserts federal question jurisdiction, a reference is normally made to the federal statute or constitutional provision relied upon.

D. **Degree of specificity required:**   Rule 8(a)'s requirement of a *"short and plain statement of the claim showing that the pleader is entitled to relief"* has generally been construed so as to place *relatively few technical requirements on the pleader*. The level of factual detail required has not been high; gaps in the facts are usually remedied through *discovery* or other pre-trial procedures.

1. **Rationale:**   One of the reasons for not insisting on extreme specificity in pleadings is that when a complaint is dismissed for failure to plead a valid cause of action, the plaintiff normally has the right to *amend* the pleading. Therefore, the dismissal-plus-repleading may have the effect of teaching P's lawyer how to plead better, but often it will not eliminate any lawsuits.

2. **Complaint must support a "plausible" inference of liability:**   But as the result of a pair of Supreme Court cases from 2007 and 2009 (*Bell Atlantic v. Twombly* and *Ashcroft v. Iqbal*), the federal district courts *do* have the right to dismiss a claim for failing to satisfy Rule 8(a) if, taking all the complaint's factual allegations as true, the court cannot *"plausibly" infer* that the defendant is liable. This is an important change to how Rule 8(a) has been interpreted, and is discussed extensively *infra*, pp. 179-187.

3. **Conclusory statement not enough:** The pleader must state at least the basic facts of his claim, and may not simply *recite his legal conclusion* that he is entitled to relief.

    Example: Suppose that P sues his employer, D, for racial discrimination. P's complaint states solely that "D has discriminated against me on the basis of my race." The complaint does not say what form the discrimination took (e.g., firing vs. denial of promotion), and does not recite what P's race is. This complaint is so completely conclusory — so lacking in even the basic facts surrounding the transaction at issue — that the court will almost certainly dismiss it for failure to state a valid claim.

E. **Single or separate counts:**   Rule 10(b) provides that each individual claim should be set forth in a *separate count*, and that the counts should in turn be broken into numbered paragraphs, each of which is limited to the statement of a "single set of circumstances."

F. **Demand for judgment:**   Under Rule 8(a), each complaint (as well as each counterclaim and cross-claim) must contain "a demand for the relief sought."

1. **Contents:**   Generally, this demand for relief (sometimes called the *"prayer")*, will be for one or more of the following three things:

    a. *money damages;*

    b. *injunctive* or other equitable relief;

    c. a *declaratory judgment* as to the parties' rights and liabilities.

2. **Wrong relief requested:** If the trial makes it clear that the demand for relief was inappropriate, the court must nonetheless grant "the relief to which each party is entitled, even if the party has not demanded that relief in its pleadings." Rule 54(c).

   a. **Default judgment:** But this rule does not apply to *default judgments*, i.e., judgments entered against a defendant who never answers the complaint. Rule 54(c) states that "a judgment by default shall not be different in kind from or exceed in amount that prayed for in the demand for judgment."

G. **Special matters:** In addition to the general requirement of a "short and plain statement of the claim" imposed by Rule 8(a), certain *"special matters"* must be pleaded with *particularity* if they are to be raised at trial. These "special matters" are ones notice of which is thought to be necessary in order for the opponent to be able to prepare for trial. They are typically claims which the adversary will *not be expecting* unless his attention is specifically called to them.

   1. **Catalogue of matters:** These special matters, which are listed in Rule 9, include the following:

      a. any denial of any party's *legal capacity* to sue or be sued (9(a));

      b. the circumstances giving rise to any allegation of *fraud or mistake* (9(b));

      c. any denial of the performance or occurrence of a *condition precedent (9(c));*

      d. the existence of *official documents* and *acts or judgments*, on which the pleader plans to rely (9(d) and (e), respectively);

      e. material facts of *time* and *place* (9(f));

      f. *special damages* (9(g));

      g. certain aspects of *admiralty and maritime* jurisdiction (9(h)).

   2. **Effect of failure to plead special matter:** Plaintiff's failure to specially plead one of the items listed in Rule 9 may prevent him from recovering at all, or from recovering particular items of damage.

      Example: P brings an action against D for false arrest and imprisonment. His complaint does not contain any allegation of "special damages." At trial, P testifies that as a result of the false imprisonment, P missed a chance to bid to buy a building. P further testifies that had he been able to bid, he would have submitted the winning bid, and would have made a large profit by reselling the building later after the market rose. Because P did not plead special damages, he will not be able to recover for any items of loss which are not considered to be natural consequences of D's tort. Therefore, P will only be entitled to recover nominal damages for the false imprisonment itself; he will not be able to recover the lost profits from not buying the building.

   3. **If item not listed in Rule 9, no heightened pleading required:** If a particular matter is *not* listed in Rule 9, its exclusion means that the court may *not* require the party to plead that matter with great particularity. *Leatherman v. Tarrant County Narcotics Intelligence & Coordination Unit*, 507 U.S. 163 (1993).

      Example: P sues D, a governmental body, under 42 U.S.C. §1983, alleging that D has violated P's rights "under color of law." *Held*, since §1983 actions are not listed in

Rule 9, a §1983 complaint does not need to plead with particularity, and merely needs to contain a "short and plain statement of the claim." *Leatherman, supra.*

Note: However, the post-*Leatherman* case of *Ashcroft v. Iqbal, infra*, p. 181, seems to mean that even matters not listed in Rule 9 must be pleaded with some degree of specificity rather than in a completely "conclusory" fashion.

IV. MOTIONS AGAINST THE COMPLAINT

A. **Motions generally:** Motions are met throughout litigation. Typically, they are contained in papers that are separate from the pleadings. They may be heard orally, or submitted to the court on briefs, from one or both sides. They may be heard and/or decided separately from the merits of the case, or on certain occasions heard at the time of trial and disposed of then. They typically relate to a particular point of law. The following discussion concerns one broad category of motions, those made by a defendant asserting the ***invalidity of the plaintiff's claim or pleading.***

1. **Defenses which may be raised in motion:** Certain defenses may be raised either in the answer, or by motion. These defenses are listed in Rule 12(b):

   a. lack of ***jurisdiction over the subject matter***;

   b. lack of ***jurisdiction over the person***;

   c. improper ***venue***;

   d. insufficiency of ***process***;

   e. insufficiency of ***service of process***;

   f. failure to ***state a claim upon which relief may be granted***, see *infra*, p. 179; or

   g. failure to ***join a necessary party*** under Rule 19, see *infra*, p. 348.

2. **Time to move:** The time period in which each of these motions must be made varies.

   a. The defenses listed in (b) through (e) above must generally be made ***before trial;*** the precise time requirements are set out in Rule 12(h)(1).

   b. Defenses (f) and (g) may be made ***at any time*** before and during the trial. See Rule 12(h)(2).

   c. The defense of lack of subject matter jurisdiction may be made ***even after the trial***, and may be raised by the trial or appeals court if neither party raises it. See Rule 12(h)(3).

3. **Based solely on pleadings:** The motions referred to in Rule 12(b) are directed ***solely at the pleadings***, and must be decided solely by reference to them. If either party raises contentions or introduces evidence not contained in the pleadings, the motion is treated as a motion for summary judgment under Rule 56, and not as a Rule 12 motion. See Rules 12(b), 12(c), and 12(d). See the discussion of summary judgment, *infra*, p. 288.

   Example: P sues D on a contract. D signs an affidavit that the contract was never put in writing, and contends that the contract is therefore unenforceable under the statute of frauds. Even though D makes his motion in the form of a 12(b)(6) motion to dismiss for failure to state a claim on which relief may be granted, the motion must be treated as a Rule 56 motion for summary judgment, since items outside the pleading (e.g., the affidavit) have been introduced by the motion. Under the provisions of Rule 56, P will have a chance to produce affidavits and any relevant discovery to show that the contract was written, as well as the chance to argue that no writing was required.

B. 12(b)(6) motion to dismiss for failure to state claim: If the defendant believes that the plaintiff's complaint does not state a legally sufficient claim, he can make a Rule 12(b)(6) motion to dismiss for *"failure to state a claim upon which relief can be granted."* Under recent Supreme Court decisions, the motion can succeed by demonstrating that even if every fact asserted in the complaint is taken as true, no recovery is *"plausible"* under *any legal theory.*

> **Example:** P, a former patient in D Hospital, a state hospital, brings a federal diversity tort malpractice action against the hospital. A state statute provides that sovereign immunity is a bar to state hospitals being held liable in tort. D's 12(b)(6) motion to dismiss should try to demonstrate that even if every fact asserted in the complaint is taken as true, sovereign immunity makes any recovery, on any theory, either legally impossible or "implausible." If D can show this, the federal trial judge will grant the dismissal motion, without even allowing P to proceed to discovery.

1. **Standard for granting:** This "plausibility" standard has only been the standard for deciding 12(b)(6) dismissal motions *since 2007.* A 2007 case (*Bell Atlantic v. Twombly*) introduced the plausibility standard, and a 2009 case (*Ashcroft v. Iqbal*) then interpreted and expanded it. The result of the two cases is that federal judges now seem to have significantly *more latitude to dismiss a complaint at the pleading stage* than they had had previously. These two cases represent one of the most important developments in federal civil procedure law in decades, so we will discuss them in detail.

2. **Historical standard for granting:** Prior to 2007, the standard for granting a 12(b)(6) motion was *extremely demanding*, as the result of statement in *Conley v. Gibson*, 355 U.S. 41 (1957). In *Conley*, the Court said that the 12(b)(6) motion must not be granted "unless it appears *beyond doubt* that the plaintiff can prove *no set of facts in support of his claim* which would entitle him to relief."

   a. **Mechanical standard:** This was essentially a *mechanical* standard: the defendant could succeed in getting the complaint dismissed on a 12(b)(6) motion only if she could show — as a *logical matter* rather than as a matter of real-world possibilities — that even if the plaintiff proved every fact asserted in the complaint, no legal theory would allow the plaintiff to win.

   b. **Difficult to satisfy:** The *Conley* standard was so hard to satisfy that defendants rarely prevailed with 12(b)(6) dismissal motions.

3. ***Twombly* "plausibility" standard:** But in a surprising 2007 decision, the Supreme Court *overturned* this stringent "can prove no set of facts" standard of *Conley*. In ***Bell Atlantic Corp. v. Twombly***, 127 S.Ct. 1955 (2007), the Court said that the *Conley* "prove no set of facts" standard had *"earned its retirement."* The Court set an *easier* standard, that a 12(b)(6) motion should now be granted if the complaint does not suggest the existence of

a specific set of facts that, if true, would make it *"plausible"* to *infer that the defendant is liable.*

a. **Facts of *Twombly*:** *Twombly* was an antitrust class action, alleging violations of §1 of a federal statute called the Sherman Antitrust Act. The plaintiff class consisted of telephone subscribers who sued the major telephone companies (the "Baby Bells"), alleging that the Baby Bells had conspired to maintain monopolies by two means: (1) inhibiting the growth of local phone companies, i.e., non-Baby Bells; and (2) having each Baby Bell refrain from entering any market dominated by another Baby Bell.

    i. **No direct evidence:** The plaintiffs had no *direct* evidence that the defendant Baby Bells had ever made any forbidden "agreement" to restrain trade, without which no Sherman Act claim can succeed. Therefore, the plaintiffs did not plead any facts directly alleging any particular agreement (e.g., that defendants X and Y had agreed to some specified uncompetitive action.)

    ii. **Inferences from "parallel conduct":** Instead, the plaintiffs relied on *indirect* evidence, by alleging that the Baby Bells had engaged in particular instances of *"parallel business behavior* that *suggest* an agreement." The plaintiffs claimed that the Baby Bells had all behaved in similar ways (e.g., by not attempting to compete in each other's local markets), and asserted that this parallel behavior was circumstantial evidence that the Bells had made a forbidden agreement to restrain trade.

b. **Court finds complaint insufficient:** By a 7-2 vote, the Supreme Court concluded that the complaint *must be dismissed* under 12(b)(6) as failing to state a claim on which relief may be granted.

    i. **"Formulaic recitation" not enough:** The majority opinion, by Justice Souter, said that to survive a 12(b)(6) motion, a complaint must have *"more than labels and conclusions,"* and "a *formulaic recitation of the elements* of a cause of action will not do." The factual allegations in the complaint must be "enough to raise a right to relief *above the speculative level."*

    ii. **"Plausible grounds" required:** Souter then proceeded to apply these "general standards" to the more specific context of a claim brought under §1 of the Sherman Act. Such a claim "requires a complaint with enough factual matter (taken as true) to suggest that *an agreement* [to monopolize] *was made*. ... Asking for *plausible grounds* to infer an agreement *does not impose a probability requirement* at the pleading stage; it simply calls for enough facts to *raise a reasonable expectation* that *discovery will reveal* evidence of illegal agreement." But a mere "allegation of parallel conduct and a bare assertion of conspiracy will *not suffice*."

    iii. **Application to §1 claim:** Souter then concluded that the complaint did *not* meet this requirement of stating a "plausible" claim that there had been an agreement. The only factual allegations were of "conscious parallelism" (i.e., each firm's conscious decision to do what the others were doing). And, Souter said, conscious parallelism did not conclusively prove — even though it might be circumstantial *evidence of* — an illegal agreement.

(1) Rationale: Souter reasoned that the parallel conduct that was alleged in the complaint was *just as well explained* by the fact that each Baby Bell defendant had independently decided that the conduct being pursued by all (e.g., staying out of each others' territories) was in that defendant's own economic interest. The Court was not requiring "heightened fact pleading of specifics," Souter said, merely requiring the pleading of "enough facts to state a claim to relief that is *plausible on its face.*" Here, because the plaintiffs had not "*nudged their claims across the line from conceivable to plausible,*" the complaint had to be dismissed under 12(b)(6).

4. **"Plausibility" test given extra teeth (*Ashcroft v. Iqbal*):** Two years after *Twombly*, the Court significantly **broadened** the *Twombly* holding, in *Ashcroft v. Iqbal*, 129 S.Ct. 1937 (2009), a 5-4 decision. In *Iqbal*, the Court made it *easier* for defendants to get complaints dismissed at the pleading stage. The Court did this mainly by:

[1] making it clear that the *Twombly* requirement of a *"plausible"* inference of liability now applies to motions to dismiss in *all* federal-court civil suits, *not just antitrust matters*; and

[2] instructing the federal trial court hearing a dismissal motion to "draw on its *judicial experience and common sense*" in deciding whether the complaint indeed justifies a plausible inference of liability.

a. **Facts of *Iqbal*:** In *Iqbal*, P (Javaid Iqbal) was a Pakistani Muslim who was arrested in the U.S. after the 9/11 attacks. He sought to hold the U.S. Attorney General and the Director of the FBI personally liable for violating his constitutional rights on account of what he said was their policy of singling out Muslim men for extra-harsh conditions of imprisonment based solely on their race and religion.

i. **P's arrest and imprisonment:** P was arrested in November 2001 on immigration identity-fraud charges. The arrest was part of a massive FBI investigation into the 9/11 attacks, and into terrorism in general. 762 of the thousands of people questioned in the investigation were held on immigration charges, and of these, 184 — including P — were deemed to be of "high interest" to the investigation. These 184 high-interest people were housed in the maximum-security unit of a New York City prison. In the maximum-security unit, P alleged, he and all other prisoners were kept in lockdown 23 hours a day. He alleged that he was kicked, punched, subjected to repeated strip and body-cavity searches, and otherwise mistreated.[1]

ii. **Suit:** P's civil suit named a wide range of federal employees, including individual correction officers. But the part of the complaint that came before the Supreme Court involved just two defendants: John Ashcroft, who at the time was the U.S. Attorney General, and Robert Mueller, the director of the FBI (we'll refer to the two men jointly as "the Ds"). The suit claimed that the federal prison system had adopted a policy of holding post-September-11th detainees in highly-restrictive confinement until they were "cleared" by the FBI. It also claimed that Ashcroft

---

1. P later pleaded guilty to immigration fraud, served additional prison time, and was deported to his native Pakistan. From Pakistan, he then filed the federal civil suit that led to the Supreme Court's *Iqbal* opinion.

was the *"principal architect"* of this policy, and that Mueller was *"instrumental"* in carrying it out. The policy of harsh confinement was, P alleged, *based solely on P's religion, race and/or national origin*, and the Ds *knew of and approved* this impermissible purpose.

    iii. The issue: Ashcroft and Mueller seem to have conceded for purposes of the litigation that anyone who treated P worse during his imprisonment solely on account of his race, religion, or national origin would be civilly liable for violating P's constitutional rights. The issue was whether the complaint made allegations about Ashcroft's and Mueller's *own* behavior and motive that were sufficient to *tie them* to the claimed unconstitutional conduct. (We'll discuss later, in the treament of the majority opinion, why this was this issue.)

b. Majority: A five-Justice majority, in an opinion by Justice Kennedy, *agreed* with Ashcroft and Mueller that their 12(b)(6) motion to dismiss should be *granted*, because the allegations against the two defendants did not tie them to the claimed unconstitutional behavior with enough specificity to satisfy *Twombly*'s *"plausibility"* test.

    i. Substantive standard for liability: Kennedy pointed out that under the substantive law governing liability of government officials for violating constitutional rights, D was required to plead enough factual matter not only to show that Ashcroft and Mueller adopted and carried out harsh detention policies, but also to show that they did so for the *purpose* of discriminating on account of race, religion, or national origin, not for a neutral purpose like conducting an investigation. Futhermore, it would not be enough for P to plead that the Ds merely had *knowledge* of their *subordinates'* discriminatory purpose — Ashcroft and Mueller must be shown to *themselves* have had an intent to discriminate on race or another of the forbidden grounds. (There doesn't seem to have been disagreement by any of the Justices on this point about what the substantive law required.)

    ii. Limits on the "accept as true" rule: Kennedy then described how a federal district court judge should go about deciding any motion to dismiss on the pleadings. There was a "tenet that a court must *accept as true* all of the allegations contained in a complaint[.]" But, he said, this tenet was subject to two important *limitations*:

        [1] First, any pure *"legal conclusion"* that was not *supported by factual allegations* could be *ignored*. *"Threadbare recitals* of the *elements of a cause of action*, supported by mere *conclusory statements*, do not suffice."

        [2] Second, the complaint must state a *"plausible claim"* for relief. Determining whether there was a statement of a plausible claim was a *"context-specific task* that requires the reviewing court to draw on its *judicial experience and common sense.*" If the facts alleged in the complaint do not permit the court to infer more than "the *mere possibility* of misconduct," *that's not enough*. FRCP 8(a)(2) requires "a short and plain statement of the claim *showing* that the pleader is entitled to relief," and if the facts just permit an inference of the "mere possibility" of wrongdoing, *that doesn't constitute a "showing,"* Kennedy said.

iii. Application of test: Kennedy then evaluated P's complaint against these limitations, and found it ***insufficient***, because P had not "nudged his claims ... across the line from conceivable to plausible."

(1) Mere legal conclusions disregarded: Kennedy first identified the allegations of the complaint that he said were ***not entitled to be assumed to be true*** because they were ***mere legal conclusions.*** This category included the allegation that Ashcroft and Mueller "***knew of, condoned,*** and willfully and maliciously ***agreed*** to subject [P]" to the harsh detention conditions "as a matter of ***policy,*** solely on account of [his] region, race, and or national origin and for no legitimate penological interest." The category also included allegations that Ashcroft was the ***"principal architect"*** of the discriminatory detention policy, and that Mueller was "instrumental" in adopting and executing it. All of these were ***"bare assertions,"*** a ***"formulaic recitation of the elements"*** of a claim. Therefore, like the allegation in *Twombley* that the defendants had engaged in a conspiracy, these allegations were ***not entitled to be presumed to be true.***

(2) Distinguished from "fanciful" problem: Kennedy emphasized that with respect to these allegations that he found to be legal conclusions, it was *not* their "extravagantly *fanciful* nature" that was causing them to be ineligible for the presumption of truth, it was their ***"conclusory nature."***

(3) Plausibility: Kennedy then focused on what he identified as the truly ***factual*** allegations of the complaint, as opposed to the statements that he found to be just legal conclusions. Those factual allegations would be assumed to be true, but the complaint could avoid dismissal only if those allegations, taken as a whole, ***"plausibly suggest an entitlement to relief."*** He concluded that the allegations here did not rise to this level.

(4) Factual allegations don't meet the "plausibility" test: Kennedy summarized the main truly-factual allegations as being that (1) the FBI under Mueller "arrested and detained thousands of Arab Muslim men ... as part of its investigation of the events of September 11"; and (2) Ashcroft and Mueller had approved "the policy of holding post-September-11th detainees in highly restrictive conditions of confinement until they were 'cleared' by the FBI[.]" It was true, Kennedy said, that these allegations were "***consistent with*** [Ashcroft and Mueller's] purposefully designating detainees 'of high interest' because of their race religion or national origin." But, he continued, "[g]iven the ***more likely explanations"*** — like a *bona fide* pursuit of national security — the allegations did not ***plausibly establish*** this purpose.[2] Since the factual allegations did not, even taken together, plausibly establish the required forbidden purpose, the complaint had to be dismissed for failure to state a claim to relief.

(5) Ps' other arguments rejected: Kennedy quickly rejected two other arguments made by P:

---

2. Notice that this reference to ***"more likely explanations"*** seems to introduce a ***probability*** component into the analysis of whether the plaintiff's inference that the defendant is liable is a plausible one.

[1] P argued that the *Twombly* "plausibility" requirement should be applied **only in antitrust disputes**. But Kennedy answered that *Twombly* supplies the pleading standard "for **all** civil actions" in federal court, including discrimination suits like the one in *Iqbal*.

[2] P also argued that pleadings should be **less strictly scrutinized** where the trial court was willing (as it apparently was in *Iqbal*) to **restrict discovery** as much as possible. P contended that the main benefits to Ashcroft and Mueller from the qualified immunity doctrine (if they were entitled to it) — the benefit of not having to **undergo intrusive discovery** — **wouldn't be jeopardized** if the suit were permitted to go forward with only very **limited** ("cabined") discovery. But Kennedy **rejected** this argument, too, saying that where a complaint is deficient under Rule 8, the plaintiff is **"not entitled to discovery, cabined or otherwise."**

c. **Dissent:** The four liberal Justices **dissented**. The main dissent was by Justice Souter, who had written the majority opinion in *Twombly* but who thought that *Twombly* was being misapplied here. (Souter's dissent was joined by Stevens, Ginsburg and Breyer.)

Souter did not seem to disagree with the majority's starting point that under *Twombly*, P's complaint could survive only if it made a "plausible" claim to relief. But Souter disagreed about whether the complaint here *satisfied* that standard: he argued that the majority, in deciding that the complaint did not state a plausible claim, **incorrectly disregarded many of the complaint's statements**, and therefore reached the wrong conclusion.

i. **Underlying liability standard:** Souter pointed out that if P could show that Ashcroft and Mueller **knew** that their subordinates were classifying Muslim men as being of "high interest" **solely on the grounds** of their race, not their possible terrorist status, and could also show that the two men were **deliberately indifferent** to this conduct, then the two would not be immune, and would have direct liability for violating P's constitutional rights. (The majority didn't seem to disagree with this assessment.) So the question was whether the complaint, taken as a whole, "plausibly" asserted that Ashcroft and Mueller had the requisite knowledge and indifference.

ii. **Enough factual detail:** Souter believed that the complaint had **enough factual detail** to meet this requirement that the allegations of knowledge and deliberate indifference be plausible. He argued that *Twombly* doesn't require that the factual allegations be "probably true" — under *Twombly,* he said, the court must accept the factual allegations as true **"no matter how skeptical the court may be,"** subject only to the court's right to disregard allegations that are "sufficiently **fantastic to defy reality as we know it**: claims about **little green men**, or the **plaintiff's recent trip to Pluto**, or experiences in **time travel**."

iii. **"Principal architect" and "instrumental" allegations:** Souter's main disagreement was with Kennedy's assertion that certain allegations in the complaint should be completely disregarded as mere **"naked legal conclusions."** The majority had put into this category virtually all of the allegations purporting to connect Ashcroft and Mueller to their subordinates' decision to classify Muslim men as being of high interest solely on the grounds of race rather than for *bona fide* security issues. But Souter pointed out that the complaint alleged that Ashcroft was the ***"principal architect"*** of the discriminatory policy, that Mueller was ***"instrumental"*** in adopting and executing the policy, and that both men "knew of, condoned, and willfully and maliciously agreed" to subject P to harsh conditions on account of impermissible racial or ethic reasons.

    iv. **Rationale:** To Souter, these allegations ***should not be disregarded as mere conclusions of law***, because they were ***far more detailed*** than the very general allegations of conspiracy found insufficient in *Twombly*. The allegations here, when they were all ***taken together*** and put in a ***single context***, accused the two men of ***knowing about and condoning*** a ***"particular, discrete, discriminatory policy detailed in the complaint."*** This level of detail tying the two men to their subordinates' conduct was, for Souter, more than sufficiently factual and detailed to meet the *Twombly* requirement that the complaint state a plausible claim to relief.

d. **Criticism of *Iqbal*:** Commentators have been almost uniformly ***critical*** of the result and reasoning in *Iqbal*. Here are the main criticisms:

    [1] In those cases where ***only the defendant has access*** to critical information, the majority opinion ***puts the plaintiff in a Catch-22,*** by requiring her to ***plead detailed factual information*** but not giving her ***discovery*** to find that information. As one writer has put it, plaintiffs in such cases — including many civil rights plaintiffs — "cannot state a claim because they do not have access to documents or witnesses they believe exist; and they cannot get access to those documents or witnesses without stating a claim." Kilaru, 62 Stan. L. Rev. 905, 927 (2010).

    [2] When *Iqbal* tells federal trial judges to evaluate the complaint's plausibility by "draw[ing] on [the judge's] ***judicial experience and common sense***," the Supreme Court is confering on trial judges ***"virtually unbridled discretion"*** to decide whether the complaint can proceed to discovery. Miller, 60 Duke L.J. 1, 22 (2010). As one law professor put it, *Iqbal* "licenses ***highly subjective judgments*** [and] is a ***blank check*** for federal judges to ***get rid of cases they disfavor."*** Burbank, quoted in *N.Y. Times*, July 21, 2009, p. A10.

    [3] Finally, *Iqbal* is ***confusing and hard-to-apply***, especially given that it applies to such an early, ***pre-evidentiary*** stage of the litigation. By requiring the plaintiff to show that liability is "plausible," the case has imposed an "unavoidably ***probabilistic standard.***" Clermont & Yeazell, 95 Iowa L. R. 821, 833 (2010). This use of probabilities means that the standard for deciding 12(b)(6) motions against the complaint is now as a practical matter virtually ***identical to the standard for deciding motions for summary judgment motions*** under Rule 56 (under which the motion will be granted only if there is no genuine dispute as to any material fact; see *infra*, p. 288). But letting the trial judge assess probabilities at the complaint stage, as opposed to at the post-discovery summary-judgment stage, is unwise and unfair, because the judge is "weigh[ing] likelihood ***without any evidential basis*** and with scant procedural protections[.]" Clermont & Yeazell,

supra, at 833-34.

5. **12(b)(6) dismissal motions after *Twombly* and *Iqbal*:**   Here's a summary of how 12(b)(6) motions against the complaint will now apparently work in federal civil litigation, in light of *Twombly* and *Iqbal*:

[1] **"Plausible" liability required:** Rule 8(a), by requiring a "short and plain statement of the claim showing that the pleader is entitled to relief," means that the complaint must contain factual allegations that lead to a *"plausible" inference* that the defendant is liable to the plaintiff. If the defendant can show that there is no plausible inference of liability to be drawn from the facts alleged in the complaint, the defendant is entitled to a 12(b)(6) dismissal at the *beginning of the case*.

[2] **"Legal conclusions" disregarded:** In deciding whether the inference of liability is plausible, it's still the case (as it was pre-*Twombly*) that the court must *assume* that *factual* allegations are *true*. But now, the assumption of truth will be given only to factual allegations that have some degree of *detail*, not those that the court finds to be really just *"legal conclusions"* or *"formulaic recitation[s]"* of the elements of the claim. So only these non-conclusory allegations will be counted in measuring the overall plausibility of plaintiff's assertion that the defendant is liable to him.

[3] **"Judicial experience and common sense" to be used:** After the district court has disregarded all conclusory allegations, and is deciding whether the remaining truly factual allegations support a plausible inference of liability, the court must "draw on its *judicial experience and common sense.*" If, taking the factual allegations as true, there is only a *"mere possibility"* that the defendant has engaged in wrongdoing subjecting him to liability, and there are *"more likely explanations"* that would not lead to liability, then apparently the complaint *flunks the "plausibility" requirement*, and must be dismissed. So the judge must apparently make some sort of assessment of the *"probabilities"* that the defendant will turn out to be liable (since the existence of "more likely" explanations that, if true, won't result in liability will be fatal to the complaint).

[4] **Where P lacks personal knowledge:** The "plausibility" standard will generally make the *most difference* where plaintiff alleges facts as to which he *doesn't have personal knowledge*, and as to which the defendants are in *sole control* of the *relevant records or testimony*. Cases trying to hold *supervisors* liable for violations of *civil rights laws* or *employment discrimination laws* are good illustrations.

[5] **D relieved from discovery:** When the plausibility requirement makes a difference, the main way it will do so is that D gets *spared from having to undergo discovery.* That is, P's case gets dismissed before he gets to examine D's files or take depositions. Pre-*Iqbal*, defendants faced by factually-weak but logically-coherent complaints generally had to undergo discovery and then make a motion for summary judgment (*infra*, p. 288), which would be granted if the defendant could show that after examining the record post-discovery, there was no genuine dispute as to a material fact. Now, the defendant has a much better chance to knock the case out of the box at the pleading stage, thereby not just saving time and money, but also *reducing* the *pressure to settle* on terms favorable to the plaintiff.

[6] **"Smoking gun" never uncovered:** If there simply never *was* any discoverable evidence that would have established the defendant's liability, the defendant's advantage from *Iqbal* will merely be to avoid the cost and time of discovery in a case that the defendant would have won anyway before trial on a post-discovery motion for summary judgment. But in cases where there exist documents or witnesses under the defendant's control that would show liability (e.g., a *"smoking gun"* document), but plaintiff can't learn of or get access to them without discovery, *Iqbal* may well be highly "outcome-determinative," transforming what would have been a *victory* (or a favorable *settlement*) for the plaintiff into an *outright loss* early in the case.

6. **Amendment following dismissal:** If the complaint is dismissed under 12(b)(6), the court will almost always *give the plaintiff an opportunity to replead.* If *more than 21 days* have passed from the time the defendant made its 12(b)(6) motion, Rule 15(a)(2) says that to amend, the plaintiff needs either "the opposing party's *written consent* or the court's *leave.*" And 21 days will normally have passed in this situation (since the court would likely have needed this long to grant the dismissal motion). But 15(a)(2) goes on to say that where leave of the court is required, "The court should *freely give leave* when justice so requires"; when the court has granted a 12(b)(6) dismissal, ordinarily the court will conclude that justice requires giving the plaintiff another chance. (Amendment of the pleadings is discussed further *infra*, p. 193.)

C. **Motion for judgment on the pleadings:** A Rule 12(b)(6) motion to dismiss is generally made *before* the defendant files his answer. *After* the defendant files his answer, and the pleadings are complete, defendant can challenge the sufficiency of the complaint by a *Rule 12(c) motion for judgment on the pleadings.*

1. **Substance:** The *substance* of a Rule 12(c) motion is *exactly the same* as that of a 12(b)(6) motion, except that the former is made only after the pleadings are completed, while the latter can be made as soon as the complaint is served.

D. **Motion for more definite statement:** If the complaint is "so *vague or ambiguous* that [the defendant] cannot reasonably prepare a response," Rule 12(e) lets the defendant move for a *more definite statement*. If the motion is granted, the plaintiff will be required to replead his complaint in a more detailed or clearer manner. If the motion is not granted, the denial is not appealable and the defendant must file his responsive pleading.

1. **Plaintiff's motion:** The plaintiff also may make a similar motion with respect to the defendant's counterclaim.

2. **Courts reluctant to grant:** Motions for a more definite statement are not readily granted by the courts, since discovery is always available to tell the defendant more about the plaintiff's contentions.

   a. **Test for granting:** The test for whether a motion for a more definite statement should be granted is not whether plaintiff's complaint gives defendant enough information about the claim to go to trial, but merely whether it gives the defendant *enough information from which to draft his answer*, and to *commence discovery*.

E. Motion to strike: Rule 12(f) allows matter which is "redundant, immaterial, impertinent, or scandalous …" to be *stricken* from a pleading. Such material can be stricken from any kind of pleading, whether a complaint, answer, counterclaim, or other pleading.

    1. Reluctance to grant: Most courts are reluctant to strike material from a pleading. Most judges feel that the pleader should be given an opportunity to show on the merits that the material in question is founded in fact, and is not immaterial, scandalous or otherwise violative of Rule 12(f).

    2. Pruning: If a pleading is grossly complicated, and Rule 8(d)'s requirement of "simple, concise and direct" averments is clearly violated, the court may sometimes *"prune"* the pleading without affecting its substance.

    3. Prejudicial material: If the pleading contains material which is *prejudicial* to the other side, it may sometimes be stricken.

        a. Where pleadings shown to jury: In cases tried to a jury, the trial judge does not usually allow the jurors to see the pleadings. For this reason, there is little danger that material in the pleadings will be prejudicial to the other side, and material will generally not be stricken. But in those few jurisdictions where the pleadings are shown or read to the jury, the striking of material on the grounds of possible prejudice is not uncommon.

Quiz Yourself on

PLEADING GENERALLY, THE COMPLAINT AND MOTIONS AGAINST IT

38. One day, Paul called Larry, a lawyer whom Paul had never met. Paul said to Larry, "Larry, I've been in a terrible car accident. I was a passenger in a car driven by Dave. Dave ran a stop sign, plowed into another car, and I was badly injured. I've been in the hospital for two months, I've got severe lower back damage, and the doctors say I'll never be able to work again. I'd like to sue Dave." Larry accepted the truth of Paul's statements, asked only a few questions about how the accident occurred, and then prepared a complaint stating that Paul had been permanently injured, had lost the ability ever to work again, and was entitled to $1 million in damages. Who, if anyone, must sign this complaint before it is served on Dave in a federal court action based on diversity? _____

39. Same facts as prior question. Assume that Larry honestly and in good faith believed everything that Paul told him. Larry did not ask for a copy of the police report. The actual police report showed that the driver was Dennis, not Dave. The case then went to trial. At trial, it turned out that Dennis, not Dave, was the driver, and that the suit was just Paul's attempt to find a "deeper pocket" to sue, since Dennis was judgment-proof. It also turned out at trial that Paul had only minor injuries, and had already been back at work at the time he made the telephone call to Larry. Dave has now finally won the case, but only after spending $10,000 in attorney's fees to defend the case. What, if any, action should Dave's lawyer take now that Dave has prevailed at trial? _____

40. P was injured in an automobile accident when his car was hit by a car driven by D. P has brought a negligence suit in federal court for the district in which P resides. The complaint states that P is a citizen of New York and that D is a citizen of New Jersey. The complaint also recites the facts of the collision, asserts that D was negligent, and asserts that P has suffered serious injuries (in an amount not specified). Nothing else in the complaint refers to any dollar amount. Is P's complaint a sufficient one?

41. P and D entered into a contract. The contract turned out to be very unfavorable to P. P has uncovered evidence suggesting that D misrepresented certain major facts about the proposed contractual arrangement in order to induce P to enter into the contract. Therefore, P has brought a federal court action, based on diversity, against D. P's complaint recites the date and general subject matter of the contract, and then states, "D fraudulently induced P to enter into this contract." On account of this fraud, P asks the court to grant the equitable relief of rescinding the contract.

(a) Putting aside the correctness of the complaint's jurisdictional allegations and the adequacy of its demand for judgment, does the complaint satisfy the pleading requirements of the Federal Rules?

(b) In light of your answer to (a), what procedural steps should D take? _____

42. P, an individual, brought a federal diversity action for libel against D, a television station. Before filing an answer, D made a timely motion under Federal Rule 12(b)(6) for dismissal for failure to state a claim upon which relief can be granted. The motion was served on P on April 1. The essence of D's motion was that under applicable substantive law, a statement made over the airwaves by a television station cannot be libel, and is at most slander. The federal judge agreed with D, and on June 1 ordered P's claim dismissed. Now, on May 1, P wishes to amend his pleading to allege slander rather than libel. Assuming that D doesn't consent, must P get the court's permission to amend his pleading in this manner?

Answers

38. Larry. Federal Rule 11, first sentence, provides that "every pleading ... must be signed by at least one attorney of record in the attorney's name. ... "

39. Move for Rule 11 sanctions against Paul and/or Larry. Rule 11 states that "by presenting [a pleading] to the court ... an attorney or unrepresented party certifies that to the best of the person's knowledge, information, and belief, formed after an *inquiry reasonable under the circumstances* ... (3) the factual contentions have *evidentiary support*." The rule goes on to say that if there is a violation, "the court may impose an appropriate sanction." Possible sanctions include "an order to pay a penalty into court."

Although Larry acted in good faith in signing the pleading, he almost certainly did not have a belief, made after a "reasonable inquiry," that there was evidentiary support for the proposition that Dave was the driver. For instance, reasonable inquiry would probably have included getting a copy of the police report, which would have led Larry to realize that Dennis, not Dave, should be the defendant. Assuming that the court agrees that Larry acted without making reasonable inquiries, the court could award sanctions against either Larry or Paul. Since Paul is the more guilty of the two (his wrongdoing was deliberate), the court will almost certainly award sanctions against Paul, and possibly against Larry as well. The court should probably order Paul and/or Larry to pay Dave the $10,000 that Dave has spent in attorney's fees defending the suit.

40. No. Observe that nothing in the complaint states that P has been injured to the extent of more than $75,000. Since the case is brought in diversity, the $75,000 amount in controversy requirement must be met. A federal court complaint is required to include "a short and plain statement of the grounds upon which the court's jurisdiction depends. ..." Federal Rule 8(a)(1). This is interpreted to require, in the case of a diversity suit, a statement that more than $75,000 is at stake. Consequently, P must amend her complaint to state something like, "As the result of D's negligence, P has suffered injuries aggregating more than $75,000."

41. **(a) No.** Federal Rule 9 sets out certain matters that must be pleaded in extra detail, called "special matters." One of these is fraud, as detailed in Rule 9(b): "In alleging fraud or mistake, a party must state with particularity the circumstances constituting fraud or mistake." P's conclusory statement that D fraudulently induced him to enter into the contract (without a statement of what the fraudulent misrepresentations were, or how D knew that these representations were false) seems not to satisfy this requirement of particularity.

(b) Make a Rule 12(e) motion for more definite statement. If this motions fails, then at the least, D would be entitled in discovery to probe the details of how P thinks D behaved fraudulently.

42. **Yes.** Rule 15(a)(1) says that a party may amend a pleading a single time by right, but only only where (1) the amendment is made within *21 days* after the party originally served the pleading; or (2) in a case where a responsive pleading is required, the amendment comes within 21 days after *service of that responsive pleading*, or within 21 days after the responder served a *motion* under Rule 12(b), (3) or (f), whichever of these 21-day periods occurs *earlier*. So once D made his April 1 motion, that event started P's 21-day amendment-of-right clock ticking. After April 21, P could amend only with either D's written permission, or leave from the court. Rule 15(a)(2). (But 15(a)(2) says that "the court should freely give leave when justice so requires." In all probability, the court will conclude that justice requires that P be given a chance to amend here, since P could not necessarily have foreseen, when drafting the complaint, that a broadcast statement would be held to constitute "slander" rather than "libel" under state law.)

V.   THE ANSWER

A. **The answer generally:**   The defendant's response to the plaintiff's complaint is called an answer. Just as the plaintiff, in his complaint, must make a "short and plain statement of the claim," so the defendant in his answer must "state in short and plain terms [his] defenses to each claim asserted against [him] and admit or deny the allegations asserted against [him]." Rule 8(b).

   1. **Answer to counterclaim:**   The language of Rule 8(b), quoted above, applies not only to a defendant's answer to a plaintiff's claim, but also to a plaintiff's answer to a defendant's counterclaim, to the answer of a third-party defendant to a third-party claim, and other such pleadings.

   2. **Liberal rules:**   The liberal rules of pleading, described above with respect to the complaint, are equally applicable to the answer. Thus answers, like complaints, must be "so construed as to do substantial justice."

   3. **Alternative pleading:**   Defenses, like claims, may be pleaded in the *alternative*. The defendant may even make defenses which are incompatible with each other.

> **Example:** In a breach of contract suit brought by P, D can in count 1 of his answer state that no contract ever existed, and in count 2 state that if such a contract did exist, it was breached by P, not D.

B. Denials: The defendant will seldom wish to concede, in his answer, the truth of all of the plaintiff's allegations. He is, therefore, permitted to make various kinds of *denials*, depending on how much of the plaintiff's complaint he wishes to deny, and on the state of his knowledge regarding the truth of the plaintiff's claims.

1. **Where not denied:** Averments in a complaint, other than those concerning the *amount of damage*, are deemed admitted if *not denied* in the answer. See Rule 8(b)(6).

2. **Kinds of denials:** There are five kinds of denials in federal practice, four of which are set out in Rule 8(b), and the fifth of which is a judge-made extrapolation from Rule 11.

   a. **General denial:** Rule 8(b)(3) permits the defendant to say that he denies *all of the allegations* in plaintiff's complaint. This is a *"general denial."* 8(b)(3) restricts the general denial to situations where the defendant "intends in good faith to contest *all of the plaintiff's allegations* — including the complaint's jurisdictional grounds[.]" The rule goes on to say that "A party that does not intend to deny all the allegations must either specifically deny designated allegations or generally deny all except those specifically admitted."

   So unless the defendant is prepared to contest *every single allegation* in the complaint, one of the other types of denials listed below (e.g., specific denial or qualified denial) must be used rather than general denial. See, e.g., *Zielinski v. Philadelphia Piers, Inc.*, 139 F.Supp. 408 (E.D. Pa. 1956) (penalizing a defendant who improperly used a general denial when the defendant was really only contesting only one aspect of the complaint).

   b. **Specific denial:** A denial may be made of all the allegations of a specific paragraph or averment of the complaint. This is a *"specific* denial."

   c. **Qualified denial:** A denial may be made of a particular portion of a particular allegation. This is a *"qualified* denial."

   d. **Denial of knowledge or information (DKI):** Defendant may "deny *knowledge or information*" if he does not have knowledge or information sufficient to form a belief as to the truth of plaintiff's complaint. This has the effect of a full denial, and is subject to the requirement of good faith.

   e. **Denial based on information and belief:** The "denial based on *information and belief*" is not specifically set forth in 8(b). The courts have allowed a defendant without *first-hand knowledge*, but with enough information to believe in good faith that the complaint is false, to deny it on that ground. This kind of denial is usually used by *large corporate defendants*, on whom the burden of obtaining information may be great.

C. Signed by defendant's attorney: The answer must be *signed* by the defendant's lawyer. Rule 11 requires that every pleading be signed by an attorney representing the pleader, and provides that by presenting the pleading to the court, the attorney "certifies that to the best of the [attorney's] knowledge, information, and belief, formed after an *inquiry reasonable under the circumstances,*" the pleading is, among other things, "*warranted* by existing law or by a nonfrivolous argument for extending, modifying, or reversing existing law or for establishing new law," and that any denials are "warranted on the evidence, or if specifically so identified, are reasonably based on belief or a lack of information." See *supra*, p. 172, for more about Rule 11.

1. **Theoretical good faith requirement:**   This "reasonable inquiry" requirement in theory at least prevents the defendant's attorney from denying allegations which he knows to be truthful, and from denying knowledge or information about the allegation if he knows it to be truthful. If the lawyer violates Rule 11, sanctions may be used by the court. See *supra*, p. 172.

D. Affirmative defenses: Rule 8(c) lists 18 specific defenses which must be explicitly pleaded in the answer, if the defendant is to raise them at trial. Among the more important of these *"affirmative defenses"* are contributory negligence, fraud, *res judicata*, statute of limitations, and illegality.

1. **Test for affirmative defense:**   In addition to the 18 items specifically listed in Rule 8(c), that Rule requires the defendant to plead affirmatively "any avoidance or affirmative defense." The essential criterion for deciding whether a defense is an affirmative one is roughly as follows: *any new matter or issue not embraced by the complaint should be pleaded as an affirmative defense.*

2. **Rationale:**   The justification for requiring the pleading of affirmative defenses derives from the notice-giving function of pleadings in federal practice. Affirmative defenses are those which the plaintiff may not be anticipating. This is so because they involve new issues not contained in the complaint. Therefore, the defendant must plead these new matters in order to put the plaintiff on his guard.

   a. **Facts within defendant's knowledge:**   Furthermore, affirmative defenses often involve facts that are peculiarly within the *defendant's knowledge*. For this reason as well, it seems fair to put the burden upon the defendant, rather than the plaintiff, to allege these factual matters. See, e.g., *Gomez v. Toledo*, 446 U.S. 635 (1980), in which P sued D, a public official, for damages under §1983 of the Civil Rights Act. A public official's qualified immunity from damages liability was held to be an affirmative defense, and therefore up to D to plead, because it "depends on facts peculiarly within the knowledge and control of the defendant" (e.g., his good faith belief that his conduct was lawful, based upon "state or local law, advice of counsel, administrative practice, or some other factor of which the official alone is aware").

3. **Amendment:**   A defendant who has neglected to plead an affirmative defense may use Rule 15(a)'s liberal amendment mechanism. In most instances, 15(a) gives the defendant 21 days from the service of the original answer in which to amend. After that, leave of court is necessary, but "[t]he court should freely give leave when justice so requires." Even in the early stages of trial, when pleading may be presumed to be completed, leave to plead an affirmative defense will almost invariably be granted.

E. Counterclaims: In addition to defenses, if the defendant has a claim against the plaintiff, he may, in all cases, and must, in some cases, plead that claim as a *counterclaim*. If the counterclaim is one which the defendant is required to plead, it is called a *compulsory* counterclaim. If it is one which the defendant has the option of pleading or not, it is called a *permissive* counterclaim. Counterclaims, which are treated by Federal Rule 13, are discussed more extensively *infra*, p. 337.

VI. TIME FOR VARIOUS PLEADINGS

A. Timetable: The timetable for various pleading steps is given by Rule 12(a), and is as follows:

1. **Complaint:** Filing of the complaint will normally occur before it is served. Service must then normally occur within 120 days (Rule 4(m)).

2. **Answer:** The *answer* must be served within *21 days* after service of the complaint, except that:

   a. **Different state rule:** If the plaintiff has served the defendant *out of state*, by using the long arm statute of the state where the district court sits (as allowed by Rule 4(k)(1)(A) — see *supra*, p. 70), the time to answer allowed under that state rule governs (typically a longer period).

   b. **Rule 12 motion:** If defendant makes a Rule 12 motion against the complaint, and loses, he has 14 days after the court denies the motion to answer. (If he wins, the plaintiff will usually replead.)

   c. **60 days if D waives formal service:** Under a 1993 amendment to Rule 12, if the defendant agrees to the plaintiff's request for *waiver of formal service* of the summons, then the defendant gets *60 days*, rather than 20 days, to answer. See Rule 12(a)(1)(A)(ii). The time runs from the date the request for waiver was sent by the plaintiff. This additional time is meant as an incentive to the defendant to accept "service by mail" in lieu of formal service. See *supra*, p. 73.

3. **Reply to counterclaim:** If the answer contains a *counterclaim*, the plaintiff must serve his *reply* within *21 days* after the service of the answer.

VII. AMENDMENT OF THE PLEADINGS

A. Liberal policy: Rule 15 sets forth an extremely liberal policy on the amendment of pleadings.

B. Amendment as of right: A pleading may be amended once *as a matter of course* (i.e., *without leave* of court) in the following circumstances:

   [1] Amendment of right is *always* allowed if it occurs within *21 days* after the pleader *served the original pleading*. Rule 15(a)(1)(A).

   [2] In those cases in which a *responsive pleading* is required, amendment of right is *also* allowed even if it happens more than 21 days after the original pleading was served, as long as the amendment happens within 21 days following the earlier of (a) service of the *responsive pleading*; or (b) service of the other side's *motion* under Rule 12(b), (e), or (f). Rule 15(a)(1)(B).

1. **More time:** Point [2] above means that in the case of a *complaint* (which requires a "responsive pleading"), the plaintiff can amend of right at any time until 21 days after the defendant has served either an answer or a 12(b), (e) or (f) motion, *no matter how long has elapsed* since the plaintiff served the original complaint.

2. **Response not required:** Point [1] above means that if the pleading is one to which a responsive pleading is *not* required (e.g., an *answer,* which does not require a response unless it contains a *counterclaim*), then the pleading may be amended of right only within *21 days* after it is served.

C. **Amendment by leave of court:** If the requirements for amendment as of course are not met, the pleading may be amended only by *leave of court,* or by *consent of the other side.*

  1. **Leave freely given:** Rule 15(a)(2) says that "the court should *freely* give leave [to amend] when *justice so requires*."

    a. **"Actual prejudice" usually required:** Normally, leave to amend should be denied only if it would cause *actual prejudice* to the other party.

      Example: P, who has been injured using a water slide, brings a personal injury action against D. D initially admits that it manufactured the slide. More than a year after this admission (and after the statute of limitations has apparently passed on any personal injury claim by P arising out of this accident), D discovers that it did not manufacture the slide, and moves to amend its answer to deny manufacture. The trial judge allows the amendment, a jury finds that D did not manufacture the slide, and P appeals the judge's grant of the amendment.

      Held, the trial court did not abuse its discretion in allowing D to amend. Leave to amend will generally be denied only where granting it would result in actual prejudice to the other party, and the burden is on that other party to show such prejudice. Here, P did not show such prejudice, since he did not establish that if D were allowed to amend, D would prevail on the factual issue of manufacture of the slide; nor did P demonstrate that he would not be able to sue other parties because of the statute of limitations. Since disallowing the amendment would have been clearly prejudicial to D, and since there was no evidence that D's delay in moving to amend was motivated by bad faith, the trial court's ruling was not an abuse of discretion. *Beeck v. Aquaslide 'N' Dive Corp.*, 562 F.2d 537 (8th Cir. 1977).

      i. **Belated amendment:** Despite the rule that actual prejudice must generally be shown for an amendment to be denied, "a busy court does not abuse its discretion if it protects itself from being imposed on by the presentation of theories seriatim, and may deny a belated application to amend that makes a *drastic change* in the case in the absence of some good reason why the amendment is offered at a late stage." Wr. 459.

    b. **Amendment at trial:** In addition to the general principle that leave to amend should be freely given if justice requires (see Rule 15(a)(2)), amendment is generally allowed at trial when the evidence is objected to as being outside the scope of the pleadings. See Rule 15(b). See also the discussion of variance, below.

D. **Relation back:** Where a pleading has been amended, if the claim or defenses asserted in the amended pleading "arose out of the conduct, transaction or occurrence set out — or attempted to be set out — in the original pleading," the amendment *relates back* to the date of the original pleading. Rule 15(c)(1)(B).

1. **Utility:** The utility of this provision is in meeting ***statutes of limitation*** that have run between the filing of the original complaint and the amendment. Without such a provision, a plaintiff whose original complaint met the statute of limitations might find himself barred by the statute, even though his amended pleading was only slightly different from the original one, and even though the defendant had received fair notice of the general nature of the plaintiff's claim before the statute of limitations had run. Wr., 459-60.

2. **When action is deemed "commenced":** According to Rule 3, an action is deemed commenced as of the date on which the complaint is filed. In federal question cases, it is to this date that the amendment presumably relates back. In ***diversity cases***, by contrast, it will sometimes be the case that state law recognizes a different date (e.g., the date on which the complaint is ***served*** on the defendant) as being the commencement of the action for statute of limitations purposes. In this situation, it is probably the state commencement date, not the date of filing, to which the amendment of the pleading relates back. *Cf. Ragan v. Merchants Transfer and Warehouse Co, infra*, p. 261.

3. **Easier state "relation back" rule followed:** In a ***diversity*** case, the pleader gets the benefit of any more ***liberal state rule*** for deciding whether the amended complaint relates closely enough to the original complaint to qualify for relation back, if such a rule exists. In fact, the pleader gets the choice of the federal "same transaction or occurrence" standard or the state standard, whichever is more favorable. That's because FRCP 15(c)(1)(A) allows relation back if "the law that provides the applicable statute of limitations allows relation back."

4. **What's a single "conduct, transaction, or occurrence":** The "relation back" doctrine under 15(c) only applies where the pleading as amended "arose out of the ***[same] conduct, transaction, or occurrence***" as that set forth in the original pleading. Courts have generally taken a fairly ***narrow*** view of when the newly-pleaded material and the originally leaded matter arose from the same "conduct, transaction, or occurrence."

   a. **Mere change of theory:** When what's amended is simply the ***claim*** or ***theory***, not the underlying facts that are asserted in support of the claim, the court will typically find that the "same conduct, transaction or occurrence" requirement is ***satisfied***.

   b. **Change of facts:** But where the ***underlying facts*** needed to sustain the new pleading are materially ***different*** from those needed to sustain the original complaint, the court is likely to find that the "same conduct, transaction or occurrence" standard is not met.

   c. **Whether D is placed on "notice":** Courts often phrase the issue in terms of ***notice***: if the defendant reading the original complaint would not be placed "on notice" of the essence of what will later be claimed in the amended complaint, then the two complaints ***don't*** involve the same conduct, transaction or occurrence, and relation back won't apply.

      Example: P consults D, a doctor, about a blockage of her carotid artery. D advises surgery, and warns her about the risks of it. P signs a consent form. The operation goes badly. On the last day before the statute of limitations runs, P sues D in federal court, alleging solely that D violated state informed-consent requirements by not telling her about an alternative theory. P later amends her complaint to allege that D was negligent in the way he performed the surgery and the post-operative case. D claims that the amendment does not relate back.

Held, for D. The allegations in P's original complaint contained nothing that would have put D on notice that the new claims of negligence might be asserted. The original complaint focused on D's actions before P decided to have the surgery, whereas the amended complaint focused on D's actions during and after the surgery. So the amended complaint does not involve the same "conduct, transaction or occurrence" as the original complaint, and the amended complaint therefore does not "relate back" to the original filing. Consequently, P's amended complaint is time-barred. *Moore v. Baker*, 898 F.2d 1129 (11th Cir. 1993).

5. **Change of party:** Suppose that the amendment to a pleading *changes the party* against whom the claim is asserted. In this situation, the amendment "relates back" only if, in addition to the "same transaction or occurrence" rule discussed above, it is the case that "within the period provided by Rule 4(m) for serving the summons and complaint, the party to be brought in by amendment (i) received such notice of the action that it will *not be prejudiced in defending* on the merits; and (ii) *knew* or *should have known* that the action would have been *brought against it*, but for a *mistake* concerning the *proper party's identity*." Rule 15(c)(1)(C).

    a. **Two scenarios:** There are two different scenarios — each involving a mistake by the plaintiff about the identity of the proper party — in which Rule 15(c)(1)(C)'s relation-back doctrine will protect the plaintiff. In discussing each of these, we'll refer to the sole defendant against whom P initially (and mistakenly) files suit as "D1," and to the "correct" defendant whom P serves after the statute of limitations has run as "D2."

        i. **P does not know of D2's existence:** The first scenario is where P, at the time the complaint is originally filed, knows *only* of the existence of D1, not D2. Assume that P serves D1 within the limitations period, but by the time P learns that the correct defendant is D2, the limitations period has elapsed. P can bring an amended suit that substitutes D2, as long as two conditions are met:

            [1] before the time for proper service against D2 expired, D2 *"knew or should have known* that the action *would have been brought* against" D2 had P not made a *"mistake concerning the proper party's identity,"* and

            [2] D2 got sufficient notice that she won't be *prejudiced* in defending the action.

        Example: *Sizzle* magazine runs a story that P believes libels him. P believes (whether reasonably or not) that the corporate owner of the magazine is Sizzle Corp. P's lawyer therefore drafts a federal diversity complaint naming "Sizzle Corp." as the sole defendant, and serves it at the physical address shown in the magazine as the publisher's address. The suit is filed and served on March 30, just before the one-year state statute of limitations would have run on April 1. It turns out that there is no Sizzle Corp., and that the magazine is owned by "Gossip Corp." (which P had never heard of prior to the filing of the suit). Gossip Corp's CEO learns of the suit on April 10, when the complaint is forwarded to him by the editor-in-chief of the magazine. On December 1, shortly after learning that the owner is Gossip Corp., P amends the complaint to drop Sizzle Corp. and substitute Gossip Corp., and that same day serves Gossip Corp.

The amendment "relates back" to March 30 (preventing Gossip from claiming the benefit of the statute of limitations), as long as it was the case that by July 30 (the end of the 120-day maximum post-filing period set in FRCP 4(m) for making service), Gossip Corp. either learned or should have learned that the suit existed and that P would have sued Gossip had he known that Gossip was the magazine's owner. And the facts tell us that Gossip knew these facts long before July 30 (i.e., by April 10). So the suit is not time-barred.

ii. **P knows of D2's existence, but thinks D1 is correct party:** The second scenario occurs where, at the time the original complaint is filed and served, P *knows of both D1's and D'2s existence*, but (mistakenly) believes that D1 is the proper party, so she brings suit only against D1. As the result of a 2010 Supreme Court case, here, too, P *gets the benefit* of the relation-back doctrine as long as D2 learns or should have learned, within the statute-of-limitations-period-plus-120-days, that the suit has been filed and that D2 is the correct party. *Krupski v. Costa Crociere S.p.A.*, 130 S.Ct. 2485 (2010).

(1) **P's awareness of D2 doesn't hurt P:** So under *Krupski*, it doesn't make any difference that P, at the time she originally filed suit against D1, was aware of D2's existence, as long as P believed that the correct party to sue was D1, not D2.

(2) **Needless delay by P in amending doesn't hurt:** In fact, under *Krupski* P gets the benefit of relation back even if P, after learning that the suit should be against D2, *needlessly delays making the amendment* (as long as D2's ability to defend itself is not prejudiced by the delay).

Example: On Feb. 21, 2007, P trips and falls while on board the cruise ship Costa Magica. Her ticket identifies the carrier as "Costa Crociere," an Italian corporation. The ticket lists "Costa Cruise Lines N.V." as the sales and marketing agent for the cruise and as the "issuer" of the ticket. The ticket includes Costa Cruise Lines' south Florida address, says that any lawsuit for more than $75,000 must be filed in federal court for the Southern District of Florida, and sets a one-year statute of limitations on any accident claim. On Feb. 1, 2008 (i.e., three weeks before the statute of limitations will run), P brings a diversity action for negligence against only Costa Cruise Lines. During the next several months, Costa Cruise Lines repeatedly tells P's lawyer that the owner/operator of the vessel, and thus the only proper defendant, is Costa Crociere. P eventually files an amended lawsuit against Costa Crociere, and serves Costa Crociere on Aug. 21, 2008 (i.e., more than 120 days after the original statute of limitations would have run). Costa Crociere argues that relation back should not apply because P could see from the face of the ticket that Costa Crociere was the owner of the vessel; Crociere argues that Rule 15(c)(1)(C)(ii)'s reference to a "mistake concerning the proper party's identity" should not cover a plaintiff's deliberate decision not to sue a party whose identity the plaintiff knew of before the statute of limitations had run.

Held, for P: relation back applies, preventing P's claim from being time-barred. Rule 15(c)(1)(C)(ii) asks "what the prospective *defendant* knew or should have known during the Rule 4(m) period [i.e., the 120-day period that starts after the statute of limitations ran], not what the *plaintiff* knew or should have known at the time of filing her original complaint." Since the complaint made it clear that P meant to sue whichever company owned and operated the ship on which she was injured, Costa Crociere knew or should have known, within less than 120 days after the running of the one-year limitations period, that it, not Costa Cruise Lines, was the party P intended to sue. That's all that matters. (And P's delay in amending once P learned that Crociere was the proper party doesn't matter.) *Krupski v. Costa Crociere S.p.A.*, *supra*.

VIII. VARIANCE OF PROOF FROM PLEADINGS

A. **Common law and Code rules:** At common law, and under the Codes, a party was generally *barred* from proving material which he had not pleaded. If the court allowed such a *variance* of the proof from the pleadings, judgment was frequently reversed on appeal.

B. **Federal practice:** The Federal Rules are quite tolerant of deviation of proof from pleadings, so long as the variance does not unduly prejudice the other side.

1. **Tolerance:** The federal policy of tolerance toward variance is demonstrated by Rule 15(b), which provides that "If, at trial, a party objects that evidence is not within the issues raised in the pleadings, the court may permit the pleadings to be amended. The court *should freely permit an amendment* when doing so will *aid in presenting the merits* and the objecting party fails to satisfy the court that the evidence would *prejudice* that party's action or defense on the merits." 15(b) then provides that "The court may grant a *continuance* to enable the objecting party to meet the evidence."

2. **Effect:** The effect of Rule 15(b) is that an objection at trial that proffered evidence is outside the scope of the pleadings will seldom be sustained. The objecting party's best chance is to show that the omission of the issue from the adversary's pleading was *intentional*, and was designed to lead the objecting party into *wasted preparation*.

   a. **Objection after trial:** If the variance is not objected to until *after* the trial, the objection is even less likely to be successful. The reason for this is that, by Rule 15(b), "When issues not raised by the pleadings are tried by express or implied consent of the parties, they shall be treated in all respects as if they had been raised in the pleadings." The objecting party's failure to speak up during the trial will generally be held to be an *implied consent* to trial of the issue, and the issue will be treated as if it had been originally pleaded.

      Example: P's complaint does not allege special damages. At trial, P introduces evidence of such special damages. D does not object that such evidence is beyond the scope of the pleadings, and in fact cross-examines P's witness as to the special damages. D has *waived his right* to contend that special damages are not allowable when not pleaded. By his cross-examination, D has impliedly consented to the trial of the special damages issue, and Rule 15(b) applies.

   b. **Evidence on two issues:** But if evidence is relevant to two issues, only one of which is pleaded, the adversary's failure to object to the evidence does not amount to an implied consent to trial of the issue not contained in the pleadings.

Example: P sues D on a breach of contract claim, but does not make a *quantum meruit* claim. P introduces evidence at trial that he substantially performed the contract, and D produces evidence that there was not substantial performance. After trial, P argues in his brief that he is entitled to recover in *quantum meruit*, despite the absence of such a claim in his complaint. He contends that D introduced evidence on the substantial performance question, a question relevant to *quantum meruit*, and that D has therefore impliedly consented to the trial of the *quantum meruit* issue. P's argument should **not** succeed, because D's evidence on substantial performance was also relevant to the contract claim, and D has therefore not impliedly consented to trial of the *quantum meruit* claim.

Quiz Yourself on

THE ANSWER, TIMING, AMENDMENTS AND VARIANCE

43. P brought a federal diversity action against D, alleging that D breached an oral agreement to employ P for a five-year period. D, in his answer, denied each and every allegation of P, as permitted by Federal Rule 8(b). In what respect, if any, could D's answer have been improved? _____

44. P began a diversity suit against D by filing a complaint with the court on July 1. Service was made upon D on July 5. (D was served within the state in which the action is pending.) Assuming that D has not made any motion against the complaint, what is the last day upon which D may serve his answer? _____

45. On July 1, P filed with the federal court a complaint alleging that D violated a particular patent belonging to P; the complaint alleged that D imported a certain machine into the United States on a particular day, thereby committing the patent violation. According to federal trademark statutes, P's time for commencing the action expired on July 5. On July 10, P made personal service of the complaint upon D. On July 25, P, after realizing that it had cited the wrong patent number in its complaint, served upon D an amended complaint listing the correct patent number. All other aspects of the complaint are the same. Is P's amended complaint time-barred? _____

46. Pedestrian was severely injured when a car driven by Driver and owned by Owner struck him. Under state law, vehicle owners are vicariously liable for the negligent driving of those to whom they lend their vehicle. Pedestrian brought a diversity action alleging negligence; the complaint was filed on July 1, and listed Driver as the sole defendant. The complaint (mistakenly) asserted that Driver was the owner of the vehicle. According to applicable state law, the statute of limitations would be satisfied only if Pedestrian commenced the action no later than July 5; under state law, the filing of a complaint with the court is deemed to commence the action (as it is under Federal Rule 3). On July 10, Pedestrian made personal service upon Driver. That same day, Driver gave a copy of the suit to Owner, saying, "I'm surprised they didn't realize that you were the vehicle owner; obviously if they had, they'd have brought you into the suit too." On July 11, Owner turned the complaint over to his insurer, saying, "I'm assuming that they'll eventually name me as co-defendant once they realize I own the car." On Nov. 15, Pedestrian filed an amended complaint listing Owner as a co-defendant on a vicarious-liability theory. On Nov. 16, this complaint was served on both Driver and Owner. Owner now moves to dismiss the amended complaint as being time-barred, at least as against him. Should Owner's motion be granted? _____

47. P, while standing on the sidewalk, was injured when a car driven by Driver and manufactured by Carco suddenly swerved in the street and struck her. P brought a federal court diversity action against Carco. Her complaint asserted that Carco had produced a dangerously defective product, and that Carco is strictly liable for P's injuries. At trial, P offered evidence that Carco was negligent in not ascertaining that the design of the car produced a significant likelihood of a sudden swerve to the right. Carco's lawyer did not object to this proof of negligence. The judge (the case was tried to a judge rather than to a jury) found that strict product liability does not apply to injuries caused to a bystander such as P, but also found that Carco is liable to P because of Carco's negligence in designing the car. Carco now moves to have the trial judge's verdict set aside, on the grounds that it is based upon a claim (negligence) that was not contained in P's complaint. How should the trial judge respond to this motion? _____

Answers

43. **By asserting the affirmative defense of Statute of Frauds.** Rule 8(c) states that a party must "affirmatively state" a number of defenses, including Statute of Frauds. A defendant who does not specifically plead an affirmative defense may be held at trial to have waived the right to present evidence on that defense.

44. **July 25.** Even though the case is deemed commenced by filing the complaint with the court (see Federal Rule 3), D's time to answer does not start to run until he receives service. Under Rule 12(a)(1)(A)(i), D generally has 21 days from receipt of summons and complaint within which to answer.

45. **No.** First, understand that in cases in which the Plaintiff's claim arises under the federal Constitution or a federal statute (i.e., federal-question cases), the action is deemed commenced, for statute of limitations purposes, by the filing of a complaint with the court. (Rule 3.) (In a diversity suit, state law determines what constitutes the commencement of the action for statute of limitations purposes.) Therefore, at least as to P's original complaint, P satisfied the statute of limitations by filing before July 5, even though service was not made on D until after this date.

    Second, when P served the amended complaint on July 25, P got the benefit of Rule 15(c)(1), which provides that "an amendment to a pleading relates back to the date of the original pleading when ... (B) the amendment asserts a claim or defense that arose out of the conduct, transaction or occurrence set out — or attempted to be set out — in the original pleading," The same transaction (importation of a particular machine violating P's patents) is charged in both complaints, despite the fact that the patent number changed. Therefore, the amended complaint relates back to the original July 1 complaint filing, and is timely.

46. **No.** If there is a change of party, relation back (see previous question) may still help the plaintiff. But for the amended complaint to relate back in this changed-party situation, the plaintiff must pass three obstacles: (1) the claim must arise out of the same conduct, transaction or occurrence as the original complaint; (2) before the time for service of the summons and complaint has expired, the new defendant must have "received such notice of the action that it will not be prejudiced in defending on the merits"; and (3) before the time for serving the complaint and summons has expired, it must be the case that the new defendant "knew or should have known that the action would have been brought against it, but for a mistake concerning the proper party's identity." Federal Rule 15(c)(1)(C)(ii). Since requirement (1) is clearly satisfied, the issue is whether (2) and (3) are.

    According to Rule 4(m), the time limit for service of the summons and complaint is 120 days after the complaint is filed (i.e., by Oct. 31). Since prior to Oct. 31 (indeed, by July 10), Owner knew that but for a mistake about the vehicle's ownership, Owner would have been joined in the lawsuit, requirement (3) is satisfied. There is no indication that the delay in service on Owner has prejudiced his ability to mount a defense (indeed, the fact that he immediately turned over the complaint to his insurer indicates just the contrary), so requirement (2) is satisfied, as well. Therefore, the action is not time-barred and Owner's motion should not be granted. See *Krupski v. Costa Crociere S.p.A.*, 130 S.Ct. 2485 (2010) (p. 197).

47. **Deny it.** The first sentence of Rule 15(b) provides that "when an issue not raised by the pleadings is tried by the parties' express or implied consent, it must be treated in all respects as if raised in the pleadings." When Carco remained silent in the face of P's presentation of evidence on negligence, Carco was implicitly consenting to the trial of this issue, so the court will treat the case as if the complaint alleged negligence by Carco.

Exam Tips *on*
PLEADING

Be alert to Pleadings issues whenever the fact pattern gives you information about either (1) *when* a pleading was served or filed (whether it's a complaint, answer or reply), or (2) the *contents* of the pleading. Here are some particular things to check for:

☛ If the pleading you are given is a federal complaint, make sure that it contains the requisite *jurisdictional* allegations. [175] Professors sometimes give you the text of a complaint, and expect you to notice that the jurisdictional allegations are missing. If so, state that D can move to dismiss for lack of jurisdiction (since the burden is on P to make the jurisdictional allegations explicitly.)

☛ Again in a federal complaint, make sure that any *"special matter"* is pleaded with *particularity*. If it is not, have the defendant make a motion for a more definite statement. [177-178]

☞ Thus be on the lookout for allegations of *fraud*, *mistake*, etc., that are stated conclusorally. Also, if the complaint claims damages that are in fact *"special" damages* (i.e., ones which would not normally be expected to flow from the kind of injury P is claiming), make sure these special damages are pleaded in detail. For instance, damages for intangible torts like slander and false imprisonment, or consequential damages in contracts cases, will often be "special."

☛ Remember that pleading in the *alternative* is *allowable* under the FRCP (and in most states), so don't fall for assertions that a complaint should be dismissed because the allegations are inconsistent or mutually exclusive. [175]

☛ Scrutinize any *motions* made by D, to determine whether the rules governing motions have been satisfied. For instance, a Rule 12(b)(6) motion for "failure to state a claim upon which relief can be granted" must be made *before* D answers (though after the answer, D can move under 12(c) for "judgment on the pleadings.")[178-188]

☞ Keep in mind that in deciding a 12(b)(6) motion, the court must *assume* that all factual allegations are *true*. If, when the court does this, the court thinks it's not *"plausible"* for P to recover under any theory, the complaint should be dismissed for failure to state a claim. (So it's not enough that the judge thinks that P is very unlikely to be able to *prove* the allegations contained in the complaint; the question is whether liability is legally plausible *assuming* that the alleged facts are all true.) Cite to *Ashcroft v. Iqbal* on this point. [179]

☞ But also remember that statements in the complaint that just recite *"legal conclusions"* rather than factual allegations *aren't* assumed to be true, and get disregarded when the court is deciding the 12(b)(6) motion. (Again, cite to *Ashcroft v. Iqbal*.) [183]

☛ If the pattern indicates that at trial D has tried to prove facts that amount to an *affirmative defense*, check back to make sure that the answer contained the affirmative defense. This applies to defenses like contributory negligence, fraud, res judicata, statute of limitations and illegality. If the trial is already well along before this failure-to-plead surfaces, have P move to dismiss the affirmative defense, or in the alternative to postpone the trial while P prepares to rebut the affirmative defense. [192-192]

☛ Be alert to whether pleadings are served and filed in a *timely* manner. [193-193] In a federal suit:

☞ D has *21 days* after service to answer, but if he has been served out of state by use of the state's long-arm, any *longer* period to answer allowed by that long-arm controls.

☞ If D *waives* formal service, then he gets *60 days* from the date the request for waiver was sent to him by P.

☞ If the answer contains a *counterclaim*, P gets *21 days* after service to reply.

☛ Know when *amendment* is allowed of right, and when it must be granted by leave of court. For instance, P gets to amend once by right prior to D's service of an answer. [193-194]

☛ If there seems to be a question whether a statute of limitations (S/L) is satisfied, and the complaint was originally served before expiration of the S/L, but amended after expiration, look for a *"relation back"* issue. [194-198]. In general, the amended complaint "relates back" to the date the action was originally commenced.

☞ If the amendment *changes the identity of the defendant*, then be sure that during the original time for service under the statute of limitations, the newly-named defendant *knew or should have known* that it (not the originally-named defendant) was the party P would have sued but for P's mistake about who was the proper party. [197]

CHAPTER 5

DISCOVERY AND PRETRIAL CONFERENCE

Introductory Note: The main emphasis of this chapter is on the discovery procedures set forth in the *Federal Rules*. More states have adopted the Federal Rules for discovery than have adopted any other set of provisions of the Federal Rules, and these provisions give a good indication of the trends of modern discovery. The federal procedures for conducting pretrial conferences are also discussed.

ChapterScope

This Chapter covers discovery, the process by which each party to a litigation reveals to her adversaries facts, documents, and other aspects of her claims or defenses. The emphasis in this chapter, as noted, is on the discovery provisions of the Federal Rules. The most important concepts in this Chapter are:

- **Forms of discovery:** Discovery under the Federal Rules includes six main types:

  - *Automatic disclosure*, in which each party must disclose in writing the names of occurrence witnesses, facts about documents, etc., early on in the litigation without a request from the other side.

  - *Depositions*, in which a lawyer asks questions to a party or to a non-party witness. (Usually depositions are *oral*, i.e., both questions and answers are spoken and recorded.)

  - *Interrogatories* addressed to a party. An interrogatory is a set of written questions, which is also answered in writing.

  - Requests to *inspect* documents or property;

  - Requests for *admission* of facts;

  - Requests for physical or mental *examination*.

- **Scope generally:** FRCP 26(b), which applies to all forms of discovery, provides that the parties "may obtain discovery regarding *any nonprivileged matter that is relevant to any party's claim or defense*[.]" So the two principal requirements for discoverability of material are that it is: (1) *not privileged*; and (2) *relevant* to the subject matter of the suit.

- **Relevant but inadmissible:** To be discoverable, it is *not required* that the information necessarily be *admissible*.

- **Privilege:** Only material which is *not privileged* may be discovered.

- **Trial preparation immunity:** Certain immunity from discovery is given to the *materials prepared by counsel for trial purposes*, and to the *opinions of experts* whom counsel has consulted in trial preparation. This immunity is often referred to as *"work-product"* immunity.

  - **Qualified immunity:** *"Qualified"* immunity is given to documents prepared *"in anticipation of litigation"* or for trial, by a party or that party's *representative*.

❑ **Absolute immunity:** *"Absolute"* immunity from discovery is given to the *"mental impressions, conclusions, opinions, or legal theories* of an attorney or other representative of a party concerning the litigation."

■ **Use at trial:** The rules for determining whether the fruits of discovery can be *introduced at trial* vary depending on the type of discovery.

❑ **Easily admissible:** Interrogatory answers, admissions and the results of physical and mental examinations are almost always admissible.

❑ **Depositions:** Answers to deposition questions are sometimes admissible, but a multi-part test must be applied to each answer to determine its admissibility.

I.   GENERAL PRINCIPLES

A. Liberalization: The Federal Rules which cover discovery represent a great *liberalization* of the older common law and Code discovery provisions.

B. Forms: Discovery under the Federal Rules takes several forms:

1. *Automatic disclosure*, furnished by one side to the other early on in the litigation;

2. *Depositions*, taken from both written and oral questions;

3. *Interrogatories* addressed to a party;

4. Requests to *inspect* documents or property;

5. Requests for *admission* of facts;

6. Requests for physical or mental *examination*.

C. Scope: *Any relevant material which is not privileged may be discovered.*

D. Objectives: The basic objectives of federal discovery are:

1. **Evidence not later obtainable:**   To obtain evidence that might *not be obtainable at the time of trial.*

   a. **When used:**   This is especially the case with respect to the testimony of individuals who are *ill, old, or about to leave the jurisdiction.*

2. **Issue formulation:**   To *isolate and narrow the issues for trial.*

3. **New leads:**   To obtain information about the *existence of additional evidence* that may be admissible at the trial, and to obtain *leads* that will allow the discovering party to find further evidence on his own.

   a. **Rationale:**   The uncovering of material through discovery leads to more just trials, because *unfair surprise* is reduced. Hopefully the trial will become a contest that is in part a search for truth, and not solely a battle of wits between opposing counsel, with victory going to the more agile.

4. **Automatic disclosure:**   The traditional federal approach to discovery assumed that discovery would almost *never be self-executing*. That is, a party had to *request* a particular

type of discovery, as to a particular issue, from her adversary. But in 1993, the FRCP were amended by adding a new provision, Rule 26(a), which calls for ***automatic disclosure*** of certain items by each party to the other early in the litigation, without any request needed from the adversary. This wide-sweeping change is discussed extensively *infra*, p. 217.

II. SCOPE OF DISCOVERY

A. Scope covered by Rule 26(b): Rule 26(b), which applies to all forms of discovery, provides generally that the parties "may obtain discovery regarding ***any nonprivileged matter*** that is ***relevant to any party's claim or defense*** — including the existence, description, nature, custody, condition and location of any ***documents*** or other tangible things and the identity and location of ***persons who know of any discoverable matter.***"

B. General scheme: Determining whether material falls within the scope of discovery can be accomplished by a seven question process to which each potentially discoverable item should be subjected:

1. *Is the material subject to the "Initial Disclosure" provisions of Rule 26(a)(1), or the "Pretrial Disclosure" provisions of Rule 26(a)(3)?*

   a. If so, it is discoverable regardless of the answer to the following questions.

   b. If not, go to step 2.

2. *Is the material **relevant** to the subject matter involved in the pending action?*

   a. If so, go to step 3.

   b. If not, discovery will not be allowed.

3. *Will the material be **admissible at trial**?*

   a. If so, go to step 4.

   b. If not, discovery will not be allowed unless the information sought appears ***reasonably calculated to lead to the discovery of admissible evidence.*** If so, go to step 4.

4. *Is the information sought **privileged**?*

   a. If the information is privileged, it is not discoverable, unless the privilege is waived.

   b. If the material is not privileged, go to step 5.

5. *Is the information outside of the **work product immunity**?*

   a. If so, go to step 6.

   b. If the material is within the ***qualified*** work product immunity, discovery is allowed only if there is a showing of ***substantial need*** of the material, and an ***inability to acquire it by other means*** without undue hardship. If the showing can be made, go to step 6.

   c. If the material falls under the ***absolute*** work product immunity (covering ***counsel's mental impressions***) it is generally not discoverable at all.

6. *Is the material composed of facts and/or opinions held by **experts**?*

a. If so, discovery may or may not be allowed depending on the factors discussed in the section on Discovery Concerning Experts, *infra*, p. 213.

b. If not, go to 7.

7. *Is the material sought for the purpose of discovering whether the other party has evidence designed to **impeach** the discovering party's credibility?*

a. If so, the material may or may not be discoverable depending on the factors discussed in the section on Impeachment Material, *infra*, p. 215.

b. If this point has been reached without the material having been disqualified for discovery, it is probably discoverable.

C. Relevance: Rule 26(b)(1) requires that the information sought be *"relevant to any party's claim or defense."*

1. Admissibility irrelevant: If information is "relevant to [any] claim or defense," it can be discovered even though the information would not itself be *admissible.* As 26(b)(1) puts it, "Relevant information *need not be admissible at the trial* if the discovery appears *reasonably calculated to lead to the discovery* of admissible evidence."

> **Example:** P's suit claims that he was denied a promotion by his employer D, on account of P's race. During the deposition of W, P's co-worker, P's lawyer asks, "Do you know why P didn't get the promotion?" W answers, "X [a co-worker of P and W] told me it was because the boss said didn't like black people." W's statement probably won't be admissible (because of the rule against hearsay). But since the statement is "relevant to the claim ... of [a] party," and because reasonably likely to lead to admissible evidence (e.g., X's testimony, or the boss' testimony), it's the proper subject of discovery. Therefore, D's lawyer, defending the deposition, may not object to the question on grounds of the inadmissibility of the answer.

a. Three categories of relevant-but-inadmissible information: In fact, there are at least *three kinds* of *inadmissible* information which meet the relevancy standard of 26(b)(1) and which therefore may be discovered:

i. Leads: material which will serve as a *lead* to admissible evidence (see the above Example for an illustration);

ii. Legal theories: material relating to *legal theories* on which the responding party expects to rely at trial; Rule 33(a)(2) allows any interrogatory that "relates to … the application of law to fact. …"

iii. Witnesses: the identity and whereabouts of any *witness* who is thought to have discoverable information. See Rule 26(b)(1). Not only is the testimony of such a witness relevant, but it is also not privileged, and is outside the work-product immunity rule. Wr., 584.

D. Privilege: Rule 26(b)(1) allows discovery "regarding any *nonprivileged* matter[.]"

1. Test: Material is privileged against discovery if it would be protected against disclosure *at trial*. In other words, if a person who has knowledge or who has a document could refuse to relate or produce it at trial on the grounds that he was protected by a privilege, such as the attorney-client privilege, that knowledge or document may not be the subject of discovery.

2. **Who may assert:** An attempt to obtain discovery of privileged material may be resisted only by the ***person who could assert the privilege at trial.***

> **Example:** In a tort case, P sues D1 and D2 for conversion of his property. P asks D1 questions relating to the alleged theft at D1's deposition. D1 knows the answer, and is willing to respond, but D2's lawyer objects on the grounds that the questions may violate D1's privilege against self-incrimination. The existence of the privilege does not bar the deposition questioning, since the privilege, in order to block discovery, must be asserted by the person whom the privilege protects, D1.

3. **Test in federal cases:** In federal cases, the existence of privileges is determined under Federal Rule of Evidence 501. That Rule provides basically that with respect to a claim or defense "as to which state law supplies the rule of decision," state law of privileges shall be looked to.

   a. **Other federal cases:** As to matters where state law does not supply the rule of decision, the court shall apply "the principles of the common law as they may be interpreted by the courts of the United States in t light of reason and experience."

   b. **Difficult distinction:** The distinction between state and federal claims or defenses is often a difficult one, and is to be determined by reference to the body of case law stemming out of *Erie v. Tompkins.* See *Byrd v. Blue Ridge Rural Electric Cooperative, infra*, p. 262.

E. **Trial preparation immunity:** Certain immunity from discovery is given to the ***materials prepared by counsel for trial purposes***, and to the ***opinions of experts*** that counsel has consulted in trial preparation. This immunity is granted by Rule 26(b)(3) (material) and 26(b)(4) (expert opinions). This immunity is often referred to as ***"work-product"*** immunity, since it is the lawyer's work-product which is in question.

1. **Conflict:** The work-product immunity rule represents an attempt to reconcile the basic conflict between the ***purpose of discovery*** (i.e., extensive pre-trial ***issue formulation*** and ***fact-revelation***) and the ***adversary model*** (i.e., truth through lawyerly combat at trial.) A widely defined work-product immunity would thwart the aims of discovery; a too narrowly-defined immunity rule might lead to the situation where lawyers either kept everything in their heads, or failed to prepare and investigate, knowing that they would have to turn over the fruits of their labor to their adversaries.

2. **Distinction:** The ***work-product immunity*** must be distinguished from the ***attorney-client privilege***. The attorney-client privilege governs only confidences made ***by the client to the lawyer***, and allows these to be protected against discovery. It does not extend to materials that the attorney has acquired and ***passed on*** to the client; nor does it cover communications which were made for purposes other than the communication of legal advice. The work-product immunity, on the other hand, governs ***all preparation for trial done by the lawyer***, or by any other representative of the party.

3. **Absolute or qualified:** The work-product immunity in a particular instance may be either ***qualified*** or ***absolute***.

a. Absolute immunity: Documents containing the ***subjective thoughts (legal theories, conclusions, opinions, mental impressions)*** of a party's lawyer or other representative are given what is usually called ***"absolute"*** immunity from discovery, an immunity which is almost impossible to overcome.

b. Qualified immunity: All other documents prepared for litigation purposes by either a party or his representative (e.g., notes taken on what prospective witnesses said when interviewed) are only given ***"qualified"*** immunity. This immunity may be overcome by a strong showing that the discovering party has a ***substantial need*** for the materials, and that their equivalent is ***not available through other means.***

4. *Hickman v. Taylor:* The leading case discussing the work-product immunity is ***Hickman v. Taylor***, 329 U.S. 495 (1947).

a. Facts: The general facts of *Hickman:*

    i. The tug "J.M. Taylor" sank while towing a car float across a river, drowning most of the crew-members (including plaintiff's decedent).

    ii. Counsel for the tug owners interviewed each survivor privately and obtained signed statements from each.

    iii. Plaintiff requested that the tug owner's lawyer "attach exact copies of all statements [by the survivors] if in writing, and if oral, set forth in detail the exact provisions of such oral statements or reports."

    iv. Objection: The lawyer refused the discovery request on the grounds that it called for "privileged matter obtained in preparation for litigation," and was an "attempt to obtain indirectly counsel's private files." He argued that answering such a request "would involve practically turning over not only the complete files, but also the telephone records, and, almost, the thoughts of counsel."

b. Holding: The Supreme Court held the discovery request to be ***improper*** because it violated the trial-preparation or "work-product" immunity of defendant's counsel.

    i. But not within attorney-client privilege: The Court found, however, that the material sought was ***not*** within the attorney-client privilege (as distinguished from the work-product immunity). The Court implied that the scope of a privilege in discovery was equivalent to that of the privilege at trial. Since the latter only covers communications from client to lawyer, the privilege was not applicable here.

c. Absolute vs. qualified immunity: The Court held that the attorney's ***mental impressions*** (i.e., his recollections of what witnesses had told him in oral statements) were ***absolutely privileged***. But existing transcriptions of the interviews and signed statements were only ***qualifiedly*** privileged.

    i. Rationale for qualified privilege: With respect to qualifiedly privileged material, "the general policy against invading the privacy of an attorney's course of preparation is so well recognized and so essential to an orderly working of our system of legal procedure that a burden rests on the one who would invade that privacy to establish ***adequate reasons*** to justify production … [of the material sought to be discovered.]"

ii. Where other sources available: If the discovering party can obtain the desired qualifiedly privileged information *elsewhere*, he has *not* met the burden of showing the kind of special circumstances required to overcome a qualified privilege. In *Hickman*, direct interviews with the witnesses by the plaintiff himself would have yielded substantially the information sought through discovery.

iii. Absolute privilege: With respect to the absolutely privileged *mental impressions of counsel*, "forcing an attorney to repeat or write out all that witnesses have told him and to deliver the account to his adversary gives rise to grave dangers of *inaccuracy and untrustworthiness*. … The standards of the [legal] profession would thereby suffer." Therefore, discovery of such absolutely privileged mental impressions will be possible only in *exceptionally rare* circumstances. Such circumstances are, in the *Hickman* analysis, presumably much rarer than those sufficing for the discovery of qualifiedly privileged material, for which merely "adequate reasons" are required by *Hickman*.

5. **Rules not adequate:** After *Hickman* was decided, the Supreme Court chose to develop the work-product rule suggested by that case on a case-by-case basis, rather than by amendment to the Federal Rules. The areas of confusion which resulted were numerous.

6. **Revision of Rules:** The FRCP rules relating to trial preparation (or "work-product") material are now covered by Rule 26(b)(3), which roughly codifies *Hickman v. Taylor*, maintaining the distinction between qualified and absolute immunity.

7. **Qualified immunity:** Qualified immunity is given by 26(b)(3)(A). That rule begins by saying:

> "Ordinarily, a party *may not discover* documents and tangible things that are *prepared in anticipation of litigation or for trial by or for another party* or its *representative* (including the other party's attorney, consultant, surety, indemnitor, insurer, or agent)."

But the rule goes on to give an *exception* (i.e., to make the immunity *qualified* rather than absolute):

"But, subject to Rule 26(b)(4), those materials *may* be discovered if:

(i) they are otherwise discoverable under Rule 26(b)(1); and

(ii) the party shows that it has *substantial need for the materials* to prepare its case and *cannot, without undue hardship*, obtain their *substantial equivalent by other means.*"

a. **Non-legal representatives:** As you can see from the quoted material, the qualified immunity given by Rule 26(b)(3)(A) applies to trial preparation materials produced not only by a party's lawyer, but by *any other representative* of the party, and even by the party himself.

b. **Test for hardship:** In determining whether the party seeking discovery of qualifiedly privileged material "*cannot, without undue hardship*, obtain their *substantial equivalent by other means,*" here are some of the factors the court is likely to consider:

> **i.** the *cost* of obtaining the desired information through means other than discovery of the qualifiedly privileged material;
>
> **ii.** the *finances* of the party seeking discovery;
>
> **iii.** if what's sought is a transcript of a witness's statement, the *hostility* of the witness to the discovering party.

Example: Suppose that after an accident involving a train run by D Railway, D's insurance company interviews members of the train crew, and writes down their statements. P, an injured passenger, seeks a copy of the crew's statements, and is met with the objection that this material is covered by a qualified work-product immunity.

A court would probably hold that the transcripts of the crew's statements are similar to the transcripts sought in *Hickman,* which the Supreme Court found to be qualifiedly privileged. If so, P could overcome this qualified privilege by showing that the crew is likely to be *hostile* to any attempt by P's lawyer to interview them directly, because the crew members do not want to displease their boss, D Railway. By such a showing, P will have demonstrated that he is unable to obtain the "substantial equivalent" of the statements without "undue hardship."

8. Absolute immunity: In addition to the qualified work-product immunity discussed above, Rule 26(b)(3)(B) also provides for what is sometimes called *"absolute"* immunity. The rule states that even where the required showing has been made to overcome qualified immunity, "the court ... must *protect against disclosure of the mental impressions, conclusions, opinions, or legal theories of a party's attorney or other representative concerning the litigation."*

Example: Suppose that in the insurance claims report described in *Rackers*, *supra*, the claims agent has written his impressions of who he thinks was at fault in the accident. The court will allow discovery of the portion of the report containing the skid measurements since this material is qualifiedly privileged material as to which the necessary showing of need has been made. But discovery will not be allowed of the portion containing the agent's conclusions about liability, since these conclusions fall under the absolute immunity given to "mental impressions, conclusions, opinions, or legal theories of a party's attorney or other representative concerning the litigation." To permit the discovery of such conclusions would be to permit the plaintiff to benefit from the agent's expertise, and would undermine the adversarial nature of the litigation process.

a. May not be "absolute":   As noted, the immunity against disclosure given for "mental impressions, conclusions [etc.]" is sometimes referred to as "absolute" immunity. However, it is not clear that this immunity is truly absolute. What is clear is that at the very least a *substantially stronger showing of need* must be made in order to discover such mental impressions, conclusions, etc. than must be made to overcome the ordinary qualified work-product immunity.

Example: D, a corporation, conducts an investigation to determine whether any of its officials have made illegal bribes to foreign officials. D's legal department conducts interviews with company officials, and the lawyers take notes; the lawyers also write memos about the case. In a tax proceeding, the government seeks discovery of the notes and memos. D argues that disclosure should not be required because (apart from the attorney-client privilege) the materials reveal the attorneys' mental processes.

Held, by the Supreme Court, for D. The documents "reveal the attorneys' mental processes in evaluating the communications [between employees and company lawyers]. … [S]uch work product cannot be disclosed simply on a showing of substantial need and inability to obtain the equivalent without undue hardship. While we are not prepared at this juncture to say that such material is always protected by the work-product rule, we think a far stronger showing of necessity and unavailability by other means than was made by the Government … would be necessary to compel disclosure." *Upjohn Co. v. U.S.*, 449 U.S. 383 (1981).

Note: *Upjohn* seems to establish that an attorney's handwritten notes on a meeting, interview, etc. will fall within the "absolute" protection given to attorneys' "mental impressions, conclusions. …" The lawyer in such a position is not a mere stenographer; he is making judgments about what is important (and thus worth writing down) and what is not. He is also choosing the language in which to express concepts, and these language choices themselves may reflect "mental impressions, conclusions, opinions, or legal theories. …"

b. **Discovery of legal claims or defenses:** Although the discovery of documents containing conclusions of law is barred by the "absolute" work-product immunity rule, there is nothing to prevent the discovering party from directly asking, in an *interrogatory* or *request to admit*, what the other party's *legal claims or defenses* in the case are.

   i. **Interrogatory:** Rule 33(a)(2) thus provides that "An interrogatory is not objectionable merely because it asks for an opinion or contention that relates to fact or the *application of law to fact*[.]".

   ii. **Request to admit:** A request for admission, made under Rule 16, may similarly relate to "the application of law to fact." See Rule 36(a)(1)(A).

   iii. **Pure conclusions of law:** However, even in the interrogatory or request to admit, the discovering party may only ask about matters that involve *both facts and law*, not about matters that involve *only* legal theories.

c. **Difficult distinction:** It is sometimes difficult to distinguish between the rules applying to documents, which may be subject to the work-product immunity rule, and those applying to concepts not reduced to paper, which are usually not subject to this immunity. Pre-existing documents containing the legal theories, opinions, and conclusions of counsel, are given "absolute" work-product immunity. Interrogatory questions asking for legal/factual theories and conclusions by the witness, on the other hand, are not protected.

d. **Attorney's document selection:** Suppose that out of many thousands of documents that are potentially relevant to a litigation, a lawyer for one of the parties *focuses on certain ones*, and uses them to prepare the case (perhaps by reviewing them with prospective witnesses). May the other party obtain discovery as to which documents his opponent has singled out for this special review? Probably not — the selection and compilation of documents by counsel in preparation for pre-trial discovery would likely fall within the highly-protected category of opinion work product, since the selection would undoubtedly reveal key aspect's of the attorney's theory of the case.

e. **Status in subsequent litigation:**   Material entitled to absolute work-product immunity in one litigation will also generally have that status in *subsequent litigation*.

9. **Statements by witnesses:**   If a party makes a *statement* to another party or that other party's lawyer or representative, the maker of the statement may obtain a *copy* of his statement *without being required to overcome the work-product immunity.* Rule 26(b)(3)(C) says that "Any party or other person may, on request and without the required showing, obtain the person's own previous statement about the action or its subject matter."

   a. **Effect:**   Thus a party who makes a statement can obtain a copy of that statement without showing that he has substantial need of it, or that he is unable to obtain its equivalent by other means.

      i. **Right to depose first:**   Although a party is automatically entitled to obtain his own statement, many federal courts allow the party in possession of a statement made by an opposing party to *depose* the maker of the statement before turning it over to him. The purpose of this deposition is to prevent the maker of the statement from doctoring his deposition testimony to accord with the statement if the statement is false.

   b. **Non-party:**   A person who is *not* a party may, like a party, automatically obtain a copy of any statement concerning the action that he made previously. See Rule 26(b)(3)(C). This automatic right to receive one's own statement applies even if there is evidence that the maker is friendly to the party opposing the party that took his statement, and will turn it over to that opposing party.

   c. **Non-maker's right to obtain:**   But a party to an action may obtain from his opponent the statement of a *non-party witness* only if the qualified work-product immunity is *overcome*.

10. **Names of witnesses:**   Rule 26(b)(1) allows discovery of *"the identity and location of persons who know of any discoverable matter."*

   a. **Eye-witnesses:**   This category includes persons who were *eye-witnesses* to the events of the lawsuit, sometimes called "occurrence witnesses."

      i. **Disclosure now automatic:**   In fact, a party is now required to *automatically* disclose (even without a specific request from the adversary) the name, address and phone number of any person possessing information that the disclosing party *"may use to support its claims or defenses."* FRCP 26(a)(1)(A)(i). This provision is discussed further *infra*, p. 217.

      Example: P sues D in diversity for negligence arising out of a car accident in which a car driven by D hit P, a pedestrian. Assume that P has found a witness, W, who saw the accident, and P plans to call W at trial to testify that W ran a red light. Under Rule 26(a)(1)(A)(i), P must automatically disclose to D, during the pre-trial stage, W's name and address, or be foreclosed from offering W's testimony at trial.

b. Experts to be called at trial: The identity of ***experts who will be called at trial*** is discoverable in the same way as are the names and locations of occurrence witnesses. See Rule 26(a)(2)(A). Discovery of the names of such experts will allow all parties to present a full case, based on all relevant expert opinions.

   i. Mandatory disclosure: As with occurrence witness, the identity of experts who will be called at trial is subject to ***mandatory, automatic*** disclosure under Rule 26. See Rule 26(a)(2)(A), discussed further *infra*, p. 219.

c. Experts not to be called at trial: Usually courts will *not* allow discovery concerning the identity and whereabouts of experts who have been retained by a party but who will ***not be called at trial***. See *infra*, p. 214.

F. Discovery concerning experts: The basic rule dealing with ***experts***, Rule 26(b)(4), treats those experts to be used at trial in Section A of the Rule, and those not expected to be called in Section B. However, it is more useful to break the subject down even further. The classification below depends not only upon whether the experts will be used at trial, but also upon whether they were retained by opposing counsel, and upon whether they have personal knowledge of actual events relevant to the case.

   1. Classes of experts: The following classes of experts are each considered separately below:

   a.   experts who will be ***called at trial***;

   b.   experts who have been ***retained by counsel***, but who will ***not be called at trial***;

   c.   experts who have ***not been retained***, and who will ***not be called at trial***;

   d.   *participant* experts; and

   e.   *parties* who are themselves experts.

   2. Experts to be called at trial: It is comparatively easy to get discovery concerning experts who the other party expects to ***call at trial***.

   a. Identity: First, a party must furnish a list ***identifying*** "any witness it may use at trial to present evidence under [FRE] 702, 703 or 705" (i.e., the expert-testimony rules). Rule 26(a)(2)(A). This list must be supplied ***automatically***, i.e., even without a request from the other side. Normally this disclosure must occur at least 90 days prior to trial. Rule 26(a)(2)(D).

   b. Report: Second, the party who intends to call an expert witness must have the expert ***prepare*** and sign a ***report*** containing:

   i.   all of the expert's ***opinions***, and the basis for them;

   ii.   the ***facts*** or ***data*** considered by the expert in forming the opinion;

   iii.   any ***exhibits*** to be used by her;

   iv.   her ***qualifications*** (including a list of all publications authored by her within the preceding ten years);

v. the *compensation* she is receiving; and

vi. a listing of any *other cases* in which she has testified as an expert within the preceding 4 years.

See Rule 26(a)(2)(B), discussed further *infra*, p. 219.

So regardless of what report an expert to be called for trial has already prepared for the calling party's own use (a report that may be protected by the work-product immunity rules), the expert must normally also prepare a special "discovery" report just for purposes of complying with the mandatory disclosure provisions of 26(a)(2)(B).

Note: The parties can *stipulate* not to require this report, and the court can *order* that it need not be produced. But even in that event, under 26(1)(2)(C) (added in 2010), the party who expects to use the expert at trial must disclose in writing the *"subject matter"* on which the witness will present expert testimony, and a "*summary* of the *facts and opinions*" to which she is expected to testify.

c. **Employee as expert:** The written report described above is not just required from *independent* experts retained by a party. Such a report must also be supplied by an expert who is already an *employee* of the party, if his *regular duties* involve giving expert testimony. (For instance, in a product liability suit against an automobile manufacturer, the head design engineer employed by the company would come under this provision, if in past suits he had been frequently designated to give this type of testimony by the manufacturer).

d. **Deposition of expert:** A party also has the right to take the *deposition* of the other side's expert-to-be-called-at-trial. See Rule 26(b)(4)(A). However, the deposition may not take place until the other side has furnished the mandatory report by the expert (described above). Also, the party taking the deposition must normally pay a *"reasonable fee"* to the expert for the time spent preparing for and undergoing the deposition. Rule 26(b)(4)(C).

3. **Experts retained by counsel, but not to be called at trial:** Rule 26(b)(4)(D) makes it quite difficult to obtain discovery of an expert who has been retained by the other side, but who will *not* be called at trial.

a. **Physician's report:** Discovery of a *physician's report* made pursuant to a Rule 35 physical examination may be discovered as provided in 35(b), whose provisions are discussed below.

b. **Other reports:** Facts or opinions held by any other retained expert who will *not be called at trial*, as well as reports procured from such experts in anticipation of litigation, may be discovered only "on a showing of *exceptional circumstances* under which it is impracticable for the party to obtain facts or opinions on the same subject by other means." See Rule 26(b)(4)(D)(ii).

i. **Only one expert available:** One situation in which discovery under the "exceptional circumstances" provision of 26(b)(4)(D)(ii) might be allowed is where there is only *one expert available* in the field, and where the side resisting discovery has retained him for the sole purpose of keeping him out of the discovering party's hands, without intending to call him at trial.

c. **Rationale:** There are two main reasons for distinguishing between discovery of experts to be called at trial, and discovery of those not to be called:

    i. **Parasitism:** Generally, a party will use at trial only those experts favorable to him, and will not use those who will not be helpful. If non-trial experts were routinely subject to discovery, opposing counsel would be induced to simply sit back and *let the other side do all the work* of finding out the expert's opinion. This is the problem of *"parasitism."*

    ii. **Inhibition:** If non-trial experts were easily subject to discovery, full preparation for trial might be *inhibited*. A party might be reluctant to consult with an expert prior to trial when there was a good chance that the expert would express an opinion contrary to the party's interest, and then become available through discovery to the other side.

4. **Unretained experts not to be called at trial:** There is virtually no way to discover the opinions of an expert who was *consulted, but not retained*, by the other side.

    Example: An expert's opinion is asked by one party, who then decides not to call him, since his opinion is unfavorable. The other party cannot obtain discovery of this expert's opinions. The Advisory Committee Note on Rule 26(b)(4)(D) states that that rule "precludes discovery against experts who were informally consulted in preparation for trial, but not retained or specially employed."

5. **Participant experts:** Rule 26(b)(4)(D) "does not address itself to the expert whose information was not acquired in preparation for trial but rather because he was *an actor or viewer* with respect to transactions or occurrences that are part of the subject matter of the lawsuit. Such an expert should be treated as an ordinary witness." Advisory Committee Note to Rule 26(b)(4). Such *participant* experts are apparently to be treated as ordinary witnesses, whether or not they have been retained by the opposing side. They may therefore be deposed with respect to the occurrences which they witnessed.

G. **Impeachment material:** A party may wish to discover what *impeaching information* the adversary has obtained about the discovering party's own testimony, or the testimony of the moving party's witnesses. This information will *not normally be discoverable*.

1. **No automatic initial or pre-trial discovery:** The main categories of information that a party must automatically disclose early in the case (see *infra*, p. 217) *exclude items* that the disclosing party plans to use *solely for impeachment.* Thus 26(a)(1)(A)(i) says that the names, addresses and phone numbers of each individual "likely to have discoverable information ... that the disclosing party may use to support its claims or defenses" must be automatically disclosed, but adds the proviso, "unless the use would be *solely for impeachment*." The same is true under 26(a)(1)(B)(ii), requiring disclosure of all "*documents, electronically stored information and tangible things*."

    a. **Pre-trial disclosures:** Similarly, this "impeachment only" information need not be disclosed *just before trial*, as part of the disclosure of the names of witnesses who are expected to be called at trial, and the identification of each document which the party expects to offer as a trial exhibit. See FRCP 26(a)(3).

Example: P brings a diversity action against D for injuries P sustained while driving a car that collided with D's car. P asserts that he is now totally disabled as a result of the collision. D has hired a private investigator to research whether P is in fact totally disabled. The private eye has made a videotape of P playing golf, and has also interviewed W, P's next-door neighbor, who says that he sees P ride a bicycle all the time. If D is content to use the tape and W's testimony for impeachment purposes only, D need not disclose to P in advance of the trial either a description of the tape, or the name and address of W.

Note: Notice that this "impeachment only" escape hatch may put the disclosing party to an uncomfortable choice. For instance, on the facts of the above example, if D fails to disclose the tape or W's identity, D will lose the ability to offer either as substantive evidence on the issue of damages — each will have to come in solely for its impeachment value. On the other hand, if D does make disclosure of these items, the surprise value — the chance to expose P at trial as a liar — is likely to be lost. So D's lawyer will have to make a tradeoff either way.

2. **Court-ordered disclosure:** Even where a party plans to use particular evidence only for its impeachment value, it's possible that the court could specifically *order* that party to disclose it. That's because FRCP 26(b)(1) says that "For *good cause*, the court may *order discovery* of *any matter relevant to the subject matter* involved in the action." So in theory, a party could make a motion asking for the court to order the other party to disclose, say, "any impeaching matter expected to be used at trial." However, in view of the new policy now embedded in Rule 26(a) that impeachment-only material should not have to be automatically disclosed, a court is unlikely to find that there is the required "good cause" for ordering such disclosure.

H. **Insurance agreements:** Under Rule 26(a)(1)(A)(iv), a party may obtain discovery of the existence and contents of "any *insurance agreement* under which an insurance business may be liable to satisfy all or part of a possible judgment in the action or to indemnify or reimburse for payments made to satisfy the judgment."

1. **Automatic discovery:** This discovery of the existence and contents of insurance policies is automatic. The discovering party does *not* have to show that the policy is *relevant* to the lawsuit, as long as he shows that the insurer may be liable for some possible judgment that might be entered in the action. In fact, under Rule 26(a)(1)(A)(iv), information about insurance coverage has to be disclosed by the party having the coverage early on in the suit, and without even a request for it from the adversary. This provision is discussed further *infra*, p. 219.

2. **Not necessarily admissible:** The fact that information concerning the insurance agreement is discoverable does not imply that it is admissible in evidence at trial. In fact, under the Federal Rules of Evidence, such information is not admissible, since the existence of insurance is not relevant to the issue of liability in most cases.

3. **General financial condition:**   The general *financial condition* of a party, other than its insurance policies, is *not discoverable* under the insurance contract provision of 26(a)(1)((A)(iv).

    a. **Use of general provision:**   Under some circumstances, financial status would seem to be discoverable under the broad provisions of 26(b)(1). For instance, if a store burns down, the store-owner's financial condition would be relevant in a suit against him for fraud by his insurance company. Discovery would therefore seem reasonably likely to lead to admissible evidence of motive, and would presumably be allowed.

        i. **Lawyer-client arrangements:** But questions designed to elicit the financial arrangements made between the *plaintiff and his lawyer* (e.g., the presence or absence of a *contingent fee*) are likely to be found *irrelevant* to the suit, and therefore not the proper subject of discovery.

I. **Mandatory disclosure:**   Various kinds of disclosure are *automatic* and *mandatory*. There are three types of mandatory disclosure now imposed by Rule 26: (1) automatic disclosure early in the case, before discovery has begun; (2) automatic disclosure later in the case of proposed expert testimony; and (3) automatic disclosure just before trial of witnesses and exhibits expected to be used at trial. We consider each of these in turn.

1. **Automatic pre-discovery disclosure:**   Probably the most important of the mandatory-disclosure types is the one embodied in Rule 26(a)(1). Under that Rule, "a party must, *without awaiting a discovery request*, provide to the other parties …" various types of information *early in the case*.[1]

    a. **Four categories:**   The information which must be automatically provided early on in the lawsuit falls into *four categories*. Let's consider each in turn.

        i. **Witnesses:** Automatic disclosure is required of the identity of certain prospective *witnesses*:

            "The name and, if known, the address and telephone number of *each individual* likely to have *discoverable information* — along with the *subjects* of that information — that the disclosing party may use to support its claims or defenses, unless the use would be *solely for impeachment*." (26(a)(1)(A)(i)).

            So a party must identify all *"occurrence witnesses"* whose information the disclosing party *expects to use in the case,* but *not* occurrence witnesses whose information *won't* be used by the disclosing party.

            Example: P, an employee of D, sues D in federal court for racial discrimination, on the theory that D's refusal to promote P was based on the fact that P is an African American. D has interviewed two of its employees in connection with the suit, with the following results: (1) W, P's friend and co-worker, tells the investigator that P's work was always very good, and that in W's judgment P would have gotten the promotion except for the fact that the decision was made by X, P's boss,

---

1. There are a few kinds of routine cases in which these mandatory-disclosure provisions *don't apply* (e.g., civil suits brought *pro se* by prisoners; suits by the U.S. to collect on guaranteed student loans, etc.). See Rule 26(a)(1)(E). But the vast majority of ordinary civil suits are covered.

who dislikes blacks; (2) X, P's boss, says that P did terrible work on a particular project, and that that was the sole reason why X did not promote P. Neither witness tells the investigatory anything else that's relevant to the case. D's lawyers have decided that they will probably use (either at trial and/or in dismissal motions) X's testimony, but that they will not in any event use W's testimony, since it wouldn't help their case.

Under Rule 26(a)(1)(A)(i), D must automatically, and without a discovery request from P, disclose to D W's name and address, and the "subjects" on which W has information that D "may use to support its claims or defenses." (The "subject" would probably be listed as "the reasons for P's non-promotion.") But D need *not* disclose the identity of X, because X does not have any "discoverable information that [D] may use to support its claims or defenses."

ii. **Documents and tangible things:** Automatic disclosure is also required of *documents* and other tangible items that a party plans to use. A party must disclose:

> a *copy* — or a *description* by *category and location* — of all *documents*, *electrically stored information*, and *tangible things* that the disclosing party has in its possession, custody, or control and *may use to support its claims or defenses*, unless the use would be *solely for impeachment*." (26(a)(1)(A))(ii).)

Notice that documents or other tangibles that *won't be used in the case* by the disclosing party (or that she'll use only for impeachment) *don't* have to be automatically disclosed.

Example: Assume the same race-discrimination employment lawsuit as in the prior example. Now, D has located two documents relevant to the case: (1) an employee evaluation prepared by X (P's boss) stating that X is not promoting P because P's work on the recent project was bad; and (2) a confidential memo written by X to D's Human Resources director, stating that "P is a little bit arrogant, as I've found many college-educated blacks to be." Since D wants to use item (1) in the case, it will have to automatically furnish P with a copy or description of that item. But since D obviously doesn't want to use item (2) in the case, it doesn't have to disclose to P that item (2) even exists. Of course, P can still *request* the document under some other discovery provision (e.g., a Rule 34 document production request; see *infra*, p. 231), but P won't get a "heads up" from D that this smoking-gun document exists.

iii. **Damages:** A party who is seeking *damages* must disclose the basis for those damages:

> "[Automatic disclosure must be made of] a *computation* of each category of *damages* claimed by the disclosing party — who must also make available for inspection and copying as under Rule 34 the documents or other evidentiary material, *unless privileged* or *protected* from disclosure, on which each computation is based, including materials bearing on the nature and extent of injuries suffered." (26(a)(1)(A)(iii)).

iv. **Insurance:** Finally, a party (typically a defendant) must disclose any *insurance policies* that would apply in the case of a judgment in the case:

"For inspection and copying as under Rule 34 [there must be disclosure of] any *insurance* agreement under which an insurance business may be *liable to satisfy all or part of a possible judgment* or to indemnify or reimburse for payments made to satisfy the judgment." (26(a)(1)(A)(iv)).

b. **Merely need to describe documents:** Observe that when it comes to *documents*, 26(a)(1)(A)(ii) gives the defendant a *choice* between furnishing copies of the documents themselves, or just a "*description* by category and location" of the documents. Where there will be a large number of documents, the defendant will find normally it cheaper and easier to furnish merely the description rather than the documents themselves.

c. **No change in scope:** Probably every item listed in the above four categories would have had to be disclosed, upon suitable request, under the pre-1993 federal discovery rules. To cite one example, insurance agreements already had to be disclosed under old 26(b)(2). So the significance of post-1993 26(a) lies in the fact that: (1) the new provision requires disclosure *even in the absence of any request* by the other side for the information; and (2) the disclosure must come quite *early* on in the suit (as is discussed immediately below).

d. **Timing:** The automatic pre-discovery disclosure will ordinarily take place quite *early* in the case. The disclosures must ordinarily be made no more than 14 days after the parties hold a discovery-related meeting required by 26(f); this meeting must take place at least 21 days before a "scheduling conference" with the judge takes place, as required by Rule 16(b). The scheduling conference will normally have to occur within 90 days of when the defendant either answers or makes a Rule 12 motion. The net result of all these inter-related timetables is that the pre-discovery disclosures will ordinarily be due no later than *85 days after the defendant first moves or answers.* See Advisory Committee's Notes to Rule 26(a)(1). Indeed, one of the criticisms of the automatic disclosure scheme of 26(a)(1) is that it forces the parties to spend lots of effort on disclosure very early on in the case, even though the case may well have settled without the need of disclosure had more time been given.

2. **Disclosure of expert testimony:** Apart from the early mandatory disclosures required by paragraph 26(a)(1), 26(a)(2) requires each side to make disclosures regarding any *expert* who will be called at trial.

   a. **Types of disclosure:** The things that must be disclosed regarding any witness are:

      i. **Names of witnesses:** The *name* of the expert witness. 26(a)(2)(A).

      ii. **Report:** For any expert who is "*retained* or *specially employed* to provide expert testimony …," the party who will call that witness must furnish a *written report* prepared and signed by the witness. 26(a)(2)(B). See *supra*, p. 213, for a description of what this report must contain.

3. **Trial witnesses and exhibits:** Rule 26 also calls for automatic disclosure concerning *non-expert witnesses and exhibits* to be used at trial. Under 26(a)(3), the party must supply the name of each witness who may be presented at trial (separately identifying those whom the party "expects" to call at trial from those whom the party "may call if the need arises"). Also, each witness whose testimony is to be presented by means of their deposi-

tion must be identified, and each document or other exhibit to be introduced must be furnished to the other side. These disclosures are normally to be made at least 30 days before trial; the information must also be filed with the court.

4. **Exclusion at trial:** The court may punish a party who fails to comply with mandatory disclosure by preventing that party from *offering certain evidence*, or proving certain claims or defenses. In fact, 37(c)(1) makes this sanction *mandatory* in many instances: "If a party fails to provide information or identify a witness as required by Rule 26(a) or (e) [the various types of mandatory disclosure summarized above, plus the duty to supplement, described below], the party is *not allowed to use that information or witness* to supply evidence on a *motion, at a hearing, or at a trial,* unless the failure was *substantially justified or is harmless*." (This sanction is in addition to other more traditional sanctions such as the award of attorneys fees.)

J. **Duty to supplement:** Suppose a party makes a disclosure that is accurate when made, but later discovers that the disclosure is no longer accurate. Or suppose the party is honestly mistaken about some fact at the time of disclosure, but then learns of her mistake. In either of these situations, must the party *amend* or *supplement* her disclosure?

1. **Present law:** The answer is that there *is* (as the result of the 1993 amendments to Rule 26) a significant *duty to supplement one's prior disclosures*:

   a. **Automatic disclosures:** First, any mandatory automatic disclosure required under 26(a) (i.e., all the material discussed in section I. above) must be supplemented or corrected "in a timely manner if the party *learns* that in some material respect the disclosure or response is *incomplete or incorrect* and if the additional or corrective information has not otherwise been made known to the other parties during the discovery process or in writing." 26(e)(1)(A).

      Example: P is suing D regarding an auto accident in which P was injured. As part of the mandatory disclosures required by Rule 26(a)(1)(A)(i), P gives D a list of persons that witnessed the accident, and that have knowledge that P may want to introduce at trial. Three months later, P learns, through work done by a private detective hired by P's lawyer, that X, a person not on this list, in fact saw the accident. If P wants to be able to use X's testimony at trial, P must promptly disclose to D X's existence.

   b. **Expert:** Second, a party must supplement any disclosure made by that party's *expert(s)* who will be called at trial. So if the expert changes any opinion or other aspect expressed in the expert's report (see *supra*, p. 213), the party sponsoring that expert must disclose the change.

   c. **Interrogatory and requests:** Third, a party has a similar broad duty to supplement with respect to a response to an *interrogatory*, a request for *production*, or a request for *admission*. Rule 26(e)(1).

K. **Privilege log:** Suppose a party realizes that certain documents come within the other party's discovery request, or within the scope of mandatory disclosure under Rule 26(a)(1)(A)(ii), but the party also believes that the documents are immune from discovery because they are either *privileged* or *attorney work-product*. Does the party have to disclose to her adversary the fact that such a claim of non-discoverability is being made, or may the party just keep silent, fail to disclose the documents, and hope for the best?

1. **Change of law:** The answer is that the party ***must disclose*** the fact that a claim of non-discoverability is being made. Rule 26(b)(5), provides:

> "When a party withholds information otherwise discoverable by claiming that the information is privileged or subject to protection as trial-preparation material, the party must:
> (i) ***expressly*** make the claim; and
> (ii) ***describe*** the nature of the documents, communications, or tangible things not produced or disclosed — and do so in a manner that, without revealing information itself privileged or protected, will enable other parties to assess the claim."

Thus, a party must in effect compile a ***"privilege log"*** and show it to the other party. The latter can then, if he disagrees with the claim of privilege, litigate the issue.

L. Required meetings: Rule 26(f) requires the parties to ***meet*** to "consider the nature and basis of their claims and defenses and the possibilities for promptly settling or resolving the case," as well as to make or arrange for the mandatory pre-discovery disclosures required by 26(a)(1), and to schedule other discovery. This meeting must take place at least 21 days before a scheduling conference with the judge occurs, so that the meeting will generally occur within the first two or at most three months of the case.

Quiz Yourself on
SCOPE OF DISCOVERY

48. P was injured in an auto accident involving a car driven by D. P's lawyer deposed D. During this deposition, the fact emerged that D stood by the car after the accident, and watched while W, an eyewitness to the accident, gave a statement to the police. P's lawyer asked D during the deposition, "What was the substance of W's statement to the police about what occurred?" D's lawyer objected on the grounds that any answer would be hearsay, and instructs D not to answer. (Assume that it would indeed be hearsay for D to testify at trial regarding W's statement.) P now moves for an order compelling D to answer this question. Should the court grant the order sought by P? _____

49. P brought a federal court diversity action against D. P's claim was that D willfully breached a contract with P. D raised the defense that the contract is unenforceable due to the Statute of Frauds. During a deposition of D conducted by P's lawyer, L, L ascertained that D had consulted with his own lawyer, X, before signing the contract. L then asked D, "Did you discuss with X the enforceability of the contract before you signed it?" D objected to the question on the grounds of attorney-client privilege. (This matter would indeed be privileged under the law of the state where the district court sits, if the question were asked of D at trial.) P now moves to compel D to answer the question. Should the court grant P's motion, and issue an order compelling an answer? _____

50. P was injured in an automobile accident involving a car driven by D. P brought a federal diversity suit against D on a negligence theory. After commencement of the suit, D's lawyer, L, conducted an interview with an eyewitness to the accident, W. L wrote down those aspects of W's account of the accident that seemed most interesting to L. P's lawyer, after learning about this interview, submitted to D a Rule 34 Request for Production of Documents, requesting "any notes taken by L of any interviews with W." D and L refused to comply, so P made a motion to compel discovery. Should the court grant P's motion to com-

pel production of the notes? _____

51. P and D were involved in an automobile accident. P sued D in federal court based on diversity; the suit alleges that D behaved negligently. Shortly after the accident and before P filed his lawsuit, P furnished a statement to D's insurance company, at the insurer's request. At the time of the interview, P was not given a copy of the statement (which was in the form of a tape recording that was later transcribed). P's lawyer now submits, pursuant to Federal Rule 34, a request that D give P a copy of the transcript of P's statement. Is D obligated to give P a copy of this statement, assuming that P makes no showing of special need for this statement? _____

52. P, driving one car, was injured by a collision with a car driven by D. (P believes that the accident occurred because D went through a stop sign.) P sued D for negligence in federal court based on diversity. P's lawyer hired an expert accident reconstructionist, Rufus T. Firefly, to: (1) examine the skid marks, the damage to the two automobiles, and any other physical evidence of how fast each car was going at the time of the accident; and (2) determine whether this speed proves that D definitely did not stop at the stop sign. As a result of his investigation, Firefly has formed an opinion that D definitely did not stop at the stop sign. P plans to call Firefly to testify at trial to this effect.

(a) How, if at all, can D learn that P will be calling Firefly at trial? _____

(b) How, if at all, can D get details of what Firefly will say at trial? _____

(c) Assume that D has learned of Firefly's identity and the fact that he will be called to testify at trial about the results of his investigation. If D wishes to take the deposition of Firefly to hear in detail Firefly's conclusions about what caused the accident, is D entitled to do so? If so, when? _____

53. P (the U.S. government) has brought a federal-court antitrust action against D (Macrosoft, a large software company), contending that D has illegally monopolized certain software markets. One of P's key allegations is that D incorporated a free browser into the latest version of D's operating system, Macrosoft Doors, so as to illegally extend D's operating-system monopoly into the browser market. D is in possession of two documents that bear directly on P's claim: (1) a market research report prepared for D before the government filed suit, which recites that D's share of the operating-system market is 48%; and (2) a confidential email written by D's vice-president to its chairman, saying, "Let's put the browser into the operating system at no extra charge to customers, to make sure no competitors can get a foothold in the browser market." D expects to present item (1) as part of its case if the suit goes to trial, but does not expect to use item (2) as part of its case. No discovery request has been served by P. The parties have had a pre-trial meeting as required by FRCP 26(f). What, if anything, must D now disclose to P concerning documents (1) and (2)? _____

54. In a federal court action for antitrust, P, a corporation, claimed that D's predatory conduct had caused X to terminate a contract with P that was valuable to P. In a set of interrogatories, D asked P to state when and how the alleged interference by D with the P-X contract had occurred. P, in a set of answers signed by Prexy, P's president, responded that the interference had been in the form of a phone call by D's chairman, Charm, to X, on Sept. 15, 1989, in which Charm told X that P was preparing to breach the contract. Subsequent to the filing of this interrogatory answer, Prexy has learned that the conversation between Charm and X was a face-to-face one, and that it took place on Sept. 18, not Sept. 15. What obligation, if any, does P have to amend its interrogatory answer? _____

55. D, a plastic surgeon, performed cosmetic surgery on P's face to reduce the size of her chin. P was mildly displeased with the results, and found a lawyer, L, willing to bring a malpractice action (in federal court based on diversity) against D. L has commenced the action, and now would like to know whether D is covered by malpractice insurance for any verdict that P might recover here. L would also like to know the limits of the policy, if one does exist. How may L get this information? _____

Answers

48. Yes. Even though it is true that the answer would consist solely of hearsay material, which would be inadmissible at trial, Rule 26(b)(1) states that the information sought in discovery "need not be admissible at the trial if the discovery appears reasonably calculated to lead to the discovery of admissible evidence." Here, D's answer to the question will at least tell P whether it is worthwhile to conduct discovery of W (which may in turn produce admissible evidence), and may lead to admissible evidence in other not easily foreseen ways. Therefore, the court will almost certainly hold that the defendant must answer the question.

49. No. According to Federal Rule 26(b)(1), first sentence, parties may obtain discovery "regarding any ***non-privileged*** matter that is relevant to any party's claim or defense[.]" In diversity actions the rules of privilege are those of the state whose substantive law controls the action. The facts tell us that according to state law here, the question asked by L would require D to divulge information protected by the attorney-client privilege. Therefore, the court will not order D to answer the question.

50. No. The notes clearly fall within the ***work-product immunity*** of Federal Rule 26(b)(3). In fact, the notes probably come within the "***absolute***" protection given by 26(b)(3)(B), under which, if the court orders discovery of materials prepared in anticipation of litigation or for trial, the court "must protect against disclosure of the mental impressions, conclusions, opinions, or legal theories of a party's attorney or other representative concerning the litigation[.]" Since L has written down only what he thinks is important, his notes of necessity contain his "mental impressions" and probably his "opinions." Therefore, the court is almost certain to reject discovery of those notes even if P needs them very badly (e.g., because W has died).

51. Yes. Rule 26(b)(3)(C) provides that even though a party's statement made to the other party is technically work product, it is still discoverable: "Any party or other person may, on request and without the required showing [of special need], obtain the person's own previous statement about the action or its subject matter." So P is entitled to the transcript even without any showing of special need.

52. (a) D need not do anything; P has an obligation to automatically disclose this information. Under Rule 26(a)(2)(A), "A party shall disclose to other parties the identity of any person who may be used at trial to present [expert] evidence. ..." This disclosure is "automatic," in the sense that the adversary does not have to ask for it. The disclosure must be made at least 90 days before trial; Rule 26(a)(2)(D).

(b) Again, D need not do anything; P has an obligation to provide a report prepared by Firefly. Under 26(a)(2)(B), the party preparing to call a retained expert must automatically provide to the other party "a written report — prepared and signed by the [expert] witness." The report must contain "a complete statement of all opinions the witness will express and the basis and reasons for them," as well as the data relied on, any exhibits to be used, the witness' qualifications and publications, the compensation to be paid the witness for testifying, and even a list of all cases in which the witness has testified as an expert in the previous four years. *Id.*

(c) Yes, after the report is provided. FRCP 26(b)(4)(A) says that a party may "depose any person who has been identified as an expert whose opinions may be presented at trial." The rule goes on to specify that where a report is to be provided by the expert, as Firefly would have to do here (see (b) above), the deposition may not be conducted until after the report has been provided.

53. **D must furnish a copy or description of item (1), but need not disclose the existence of item (2).** Under FRCP 26(a)(1)(A), "a party must, without awaiting a discovery request, provide to the other parties: ... (ii) a copy — or a description by category and location — of *all documents*, electrically stored information, and tangible things that the disclosing party has in its possession, custody, or control and *may use to support its claims or defenses*, unless the use would be solely for impeachment[.]" So D must automatically furnish P with furnish a copy or description of item (1) (the market-research report), since D plans to introduce that as part of its substantive case at trial. (If D doesn't do this, the court must exclude the document from evidence, under Rule 37(c).) But D does not have to automatically furnish a copy or description of item (2) (the email), since D does not plan to use that document in its case. If P submits a valid discovery request that would call for disclosure of the email's existence (e.g., a Rule 34 document-production request calling for "all documents or files in D's possession referring to D's decision to incorporate a free browser in D's operating system"), then D *would* have to produce the email — but D has no obligation to disclose the email automatically, as it does with the items it plans to use in its case.

54. **P must amend its response unless the error has already been called to D's attention.** Under Rule 26(e)(1), "A party who has made a disclosure under Rule 26(a) — or who has responded to an interrogatory, request for production, or request for admission — must *supplement or correct* its disclosure or response: (A) in a timely manner if the party learns that in some material respect the disclosure or response is incomplete or incorrect, and if the additional or corrective information has not otherwise been made known to the other parties during the discovery process or in writing[.]" Since P has now learned that its answer was materially incorrect (the place and date of this key conversation would surely be material), P must file an amended response, so long as D has not learned of the error in some other way.

55. **L does not need to do anything; D's lawyer must disclose this information automatically.** Automatic disclosure regarding liability insurance is mandatory. Under Rule 26(a)(1)(A), "[A] party must, without awaiting a discovery request, provide to the other parties: … (iv) for inspection and copying as under Rule 34, *any insurance agreement* under which an insurance business *may be liable to satisfy all or part of a possible judgment* in the action or to indemnify or reimburse for payments made to satisfy the judgment." This mandatory disclosure must occur early on in the case.

III. METHODS OF DISCOVERY

A. **General characteristics:** The various forms of discovery (including *depositions, interrogatories* and *requests to produce documents*) are set out in Rules 30, 31, 33, 34, and 36. With the exception of Rule 35 requests for physical examination (discussed below), each of these forms has several important characteristics common to all. Among these common attributes are the following:

1. **Extrajudicial:** Each of these modes of discovery is designed to operate *extrajudicially*, that is, without the intervention of the court. It is only where one party refuses to comply fully with the other's discovery request that the court intervenes.

2. **Scope:** The scope of discovery, as discussed above, is the same for all of these forms of discovery. In general, the material sought to be discovered by any of these modes must simply be relevant to the subject matter of the lawsuit, and unprivileged.

3. **Signature required:** Every request for discovery of any type, and any response or objection to discovery, must be *signed* by the lawyer preparing it. Rule 26(g).

    a. **Certification:** The signature constitutes a certification by the lawyer that the request, response or objection is consistent with the Federal Rules, is not imposed for the purpose of harassing the adversary, causing unnecessary delay or needless increase in the cost of litigation, or other improper purpose, and that it is not "unreasonable nor unduly burdensome or expensive, considering the needs of the case, prior discovery in the case, the amount in controversy, and the importance of the issues at stake in the action." Rule 26(g), including 26(g)(1)(B)(iii).

    b. **Sanctions:** If the court later finds that the certification was false, it may issue sanctions, including an order to pay the "reasonable expenses, including reasonable attorney's fees," caused by the violation. Rule 26(g)(3).

4. **Court orders:** Upon motion by a person from whom any of these forms of discovery is sought, the court may make any order necessary to protect the discoveree from undue annoyance, embarrassment, or harassment. Such an order, called a *protective order*, may limit the scope, terms, method, or use of discovery. See Rule 26(c); see also Wr., 599-605.

B. Persons affected: There are differences among the forms of discovery with respect to the *persons from whom discovery may be taken.*

1. **Depositions:** Depositions upon oral (Rule 30) or written (Rule 31) questions can be held of *either party, or of non-parties* who are thought to have information relevant to the case. In a deposition, the responses are given orally.

2. **Other forms:** The other forms of discovery, by contrast, interrogatories (Rule 33), requests to produce or inspect tangible property (Rule 34) and requests for admissions (Rule 36) can be addressed *only to parties*, not to non-party witnesses.

C. Times usable: Before 1993, there was no limit to the *number of times* a particular method of discovery could be used, or a person discovered.

1. **Amendments:** But the 1993 amendments to the FRCP added some *"presumptive limits"* to the number of times certain discovery devices may be used. Unless the court orders otherwise, or the parties so stipulate, each side is limited to *10 depositions* and *25 interrogatories* (not *sets* of interrogatories, but individual interrogatory questions). See Rules 30(a)(2)(A) and 33(a), discussed *infra*, p. 228 and p. 230, respectively. Also, there's a presumptive rule that a particular person's deposition may be taken only once, and for a maximum of 7 hours. See Rule 30(d)(1), discussed *infra*, p. 228.

2. **Protection against abuse:** Also, rule 26(b)(2) explicitly directs the court to limit the *"frequency or extent of discovery,"* under certain circumstances. Among the situations in which the court must limit discovery are where: (1) the discovery sought is "unreasonably *cumulative* or *duplicative*," or can be "obtained from *some other source* that is more convenient, less burdensome, or less expensive"; (2) the party seeking the discovery has already had, through prior discovery in the case, *"ample opportunity"* to obtain the infor-

mation; and (3) the "***burden or expense*** of the proposed discovery ***outweighs its likely benefit***, considering the needs of the case, the amount in controversy, ***the parties' resources***, the importance of the issues at stake in the action, and the importance of the discovery in resolving the issues."

    a. Rationale: These provisions for eliminating the abuse of discovery are directed at two main situations: (1) where a lawyer tries to force a favorable settlement by driving up the litigation costs of his less-affluent adversary; and (2) where the lawyer fears that if he loses and is shown to have missed a fact which might have been discoverable, he may be sued for malpractice. See Advisory Committee's comments to 1983 amendment of Rule 26.

D. Oral depositions (Rule 30): After the beginning of an action any party may take the ***oral testimony*** of any person (party or non-party) thought to have information within the scope of discovery, by asking oral questions. This is a "an deposition."

  1. Leave not required: Except for a few situations (e.g., depositions to be taken within 30 days after service of the complaint), leave of the court is ***not required***. (Rule 30(a)(2)).

  2. Notice: The deposing party must give ***reasonable notice not only to the deponent, but also to every other party*** in the action. Notice should state the time, place, and person to be deposed. (Rule 30(b)(1)).

    a. No subpoena for party: If a ***party*** is to be deposed, a ***subpoena*** is not used, because non-compliance with the notice can be followed up by the discovering party with motions to compel discovery or impose sanctions under Rule 37.

    b. Subpoena for non-party optional: If a ***non-party*** is to be deposed, then the discovering party may subpoena the person to attend. The price of using a subpoena rather than a simple request is that the party must (1) pay witness fees; and (2) risk antagonizing the deponent. However, if no subpoena is used, the deponent cannot be compelled to attend. If he does not attend, the deposing party may have to pay the costs set forth in Rule 30(g).

      i. Range of subpoena: If the discovering party decides to use a subpoena, that subpoena is valid only if it requires the deposition to be held at a place within a 100-mile radius of "the place where [the deponent] resides, is employed or regularly transacts business in person. ..." Rule 45(c)(3)(A)(ii).

    c. Answers by corporation: Where the deponent named in the notice or subpoena is a corporation or partnership, the onus falls upon the business to ***appoint*** an appropriate person to answer the questions. Rules 30(b)(6), 31(a)(4).

  3. Documents: If the deponent is a party, Rule 30(b)(2) provides that the discovering party may attach a Rule 34 ***request to produce*** to the notice to the party. If the deponent is a non-party, the discovering party must serve the non-party with a subpoena *duces tecum* (since Rule 34 applies only to parties.)

  4. Mechanics of deposition: Typically the deposition is held in a lawyer's office with every party (and often non-party deponents) represented by counsel. The deponent is sworn, interrogated by counsel for the discovering party, and possibly cross-examined by the other parties' counsel. Rule 30(c)(1) provides that "the examination and cross-examination of a deponent [shall] proceed as they would at trial under the Federal Rules of Evidence."

a. **Presiding officer:** A presiding officer appointed by the court must be present unless the parties stipulate, as they usually do, that his presence is waived. (In fact, most of the mechanics of discovery can be varied by agreement of the parties — see Rule 29).

b. **Transcription:** The depositions so taken are then transcribed, and read and signed by the deponent. Under certain circumstances described below, these depositions may then be introduced as evidence at trial.

c. **Method of recording:** Traditionally, depositions were recorded manually by a stenographer (court reporter) who was present at the deposition, and who then transcribed his notes. But *sound*, or *sound-and-video*, are now the preferred recording methods.

   i. **Party's option:** Under Rule 30(b)(3)(A), "The party who notices the deposition must state in the notice the method for recording the testimony. Unless the court orders otherwise, testimony may be recorded by *audio, audiovisual, or stenographic means.* The noticing party bears the recording costs. Any party may arrange to transcribe a deposition."

   So the party ordering the deposition can arrange to have it recorded by audio tape recorder, or video recorder; either of these is likely to be significantly cheaper than the use of a court reporter. (But whatever method is chosen by the person conducting the deposition, another party may arrange for a different method to be used as well. Thus, if the plaintiff notices a deposition to be conducted by audio tape recording, the defense may order a stenographic record as well, but the defense will then have to pay for the stenography.)

   ii. **Transcript for testimony to be introduced at trial:** If a non-stenographic (e.g., video or audio recording) method is used, the party may use that non-stenographic version *at trial*. Rule 32(c). However, in that event the party must also *prepare a transcript*, and must give the transcript in advance of trial to the other parties (Rule 26(a)(3)(B)) and to the court (Rule 32(c)).

   iii. **Preference for non-stenographic version:** Rule 32 shows a *preference* for video or audio recording as opposed to stenographic reporting, in the case of a *jury trial*: "On any party's request, deposition testimony offered in a jury trial for any purpose other than impeachment must be presented in *nontranscript form*, if available, unless the court for good cause orders otherwise." Rule 32(c). So a party who notices a deposition and specifies that it should be recorded in video or audio form takes the risk that his adversary can require that this version (rather than the dryer stenographic version) be introduced in the jury trial.

5. **Coaching by lawyer:** Suppose the lawyer conducting a deposition asks a question that the deponent and the lawyer "defending" the deposition (i.e., the deponent's lawyer) don't expect. A crafty defending lawyer will often *coach* the deponent, by making a spurious objection that intentionally includes extraneous information suggesting to the deponent how the question should be answered. Rule 30 tries to prevent this type of coaching: "An

objection must be stated concisely in a non-argumentative and ***nonsuggestive*** manner." Rule 30(c)(2).

6. **Presumptive limit of 10:** Each "side" (plaintiff and defense) is ***limited*** to a total of ***10 depositions***, unless the adversary agrees to more or the court issues an order allowing more. See Rule 30(a)(2)(A). In a multi-party situation, this limit applies to all of the plaintiffs, or all of the defendants, taken as a whole; therefore, there are likely to be disputes among co-parties about how the 10 deposition opportunities should be used.

7. **Limit of 7 hours and one day:** There is a second, very important presumptive limit on depositions: Unless the court orders (or the parties agree) otherwise, no person's deposition shall last more than "one day of seven hours." Rule 30(d)(1). So if, say, D wants to depose P for 20 hours over 3 days, D will have to convince the court that the extra time is "needed to fairly examine the deponent" (though if such extra time is indeed needed, the court "must" allow it). *Id.*

8. **Party may take statements under oath without complying with deposition rules:** Not every question-and-answer session conducted by a party under oath is a deposition. Therefore, a party or his lawyer may ***interview non-party witnesses*** under oath, and with a stenographer present, ***without having to comply*** with the rules for depositions. This means, for instance, that the other party doesn't have to be invited, no notice of the proceedings has to be given to the opponent, and the opponent doesn't get to cross-examine the witness. Of course, transcripts of these examinations won't be admissible as evidence under situations where true depositions would be admissible (see *infra*, p. 244), so the lawyer doing the interviewing gives up some important rights by not treating the interview as a deposition. But there's no reason why a lawyer can't use this non-deposition technique for ***fact-gathering*** purposes.

E. **Depositions upon written questions:** After the beginning of an action, any party may take the oral responses to ***questions written prior to the deposition***, of any person (party or non-party) thought to have discoverable information. Rule 31.

1. **Distant non-party witnesses:** The main utility of Rule 31 depositions on written questions is for deposing ***distant non-party witnesses*** who cannot be served with Rule 33 interrogatories (since these are limited to parties). The discovering party's counsel is saved the expense of the journey.

2. **Similarity:** Deposition upon written questions is similar to deposition upon oral questions in all respects, except that a list of questions to be asked at the deposition is sent to the presiding officer, who then poses them to the deponent.

3. **Lack of flexibility:** The major disadvantage of depositions upon written questions is that the discovering party has much less flexibility, because he obviously does not have the ability to rephrase a question based upon the response to an earlier question. For this reason, depositions upon written questions have been little used in the federal system, except for distant witnesses.

4. **Cross-examination:** Copies of the questions to be asked are sent not only to the presiding officer who will pose them, but also to the other parties. These other parties may in

turn serve ***written cross-questions***, which will be posed by the presiding officer to the witness after the questions of the initial discovering party. See Rule 31(a)(5).

> **Note:** During the course of a deposition, whether upon oral or written questions, either the deponent or a party may ***object*** to a particular question as being outside the scope of discovery. The presiding officer or the stenographer then notes the objection upon the transcript. Although the objecting party has the right to ***suspend the deposition*** for the time needed to make a Rule 30(d)(3) motion to terminate or limit the deposition, generally the parties save up all their objections and go to the judge for rulings on all of them at the same time. Objections to deposition questions will be considered further in the treatment of abuse and sanctions relating to discovery generally, below.

F. Interrogatories to the parties: An interrogatory is a set of ***written questions*** to be answered in writing by the person to whom they are addressed. Interrogatories may be addressed ***only to a party***. Rule 33(a).

1. **Under oath:** Answers to interrogatories are made under oath by the party, usually in close consultation with his counsel.

   a. **Who signs:** Answers are signed by the person making them, but objections to questions are signed by the attorney.

   b. **Objection:** If the interrogatory question is objected to (e.g., on the grounds that the question is outside the scope of Rule 26(b)(1)), the discoveree does not answer the question until the objection is ruled on by the court.

2. **Answer in records:** Where the answer to the interrogatory is in ***business records*** accessible only to the party served, it is a sufficient answer to the interrogatory for the deponent to ***specify which records*** contain the answers and to afford the discovering party an opportunity to ***examine the records*** and ascertain the answer. (Rule 33(d)). This procedure enables the party served to ***shift the cost*** of ascertaining the answer from himself to the discovering party.

   a. **Burden of searching records:** The court will generally only allow this type of "answer" where the record examination burden is about equal for both parties. If the discoveree's familiarity with the records would enable him to find the answer more easily than the discoveror could, the burden will generally remain on the former.

   b. **Electronically stored information:** Often, the discoveree will possess the information in ***"electronically stored"*** (i.e., ***computer***) form. If so, and if the burden of searching the computer records would be about equal for the discovering party and the discoveree, the discoveree may simply ***give the discovering party access to the computer file.*** See Rule 33(c) (allowing the discoveree to answer by providing the discovering party an opportunity to examine, inter alia, "electronically stored information" in the possession of the discoveree). But to make the burden about equal, the discoveree may need to "provide some combination of ***technical support***, information on application software, or other assistance." ACN to 2006 Amendment to Rule 33.

   c. **Harassment:** If the discoveror's request seems to be a harassment of the discoveree, the court may prevent discovery, or may shift costs under Rule 37(d).

3. **Limit of 25 questions:** Each party is limited to *25 interrogatory questions* directed to any other party, unless the parties stipulate otherwise or the court orders otherwise. Rule 33(a).

   a. **What is a "question":** Furthermore, a party cannot get around this limit by clever drafting, since each "discrete subpart" of a question counts as though it were a separate question, if it seeks information about a "discrete separate subject". Advisory Committee Notes to 1993 Amendments to Rule 33(a).

G. Requests for admission (Rule 36):   A party may serve upon any other party (but not upon non-parties) a written request for the *admission, for the purposes of the pending action only, of the truth of any matters within the scope of Rule 26(b). The statements the admission of whose genuineness may be requested include statements or opinions of fact*, or of the application of law to fact. An admission of the *genuineness of any documents* described in the request may also be sought. Wr., 636-39.

1. **Utility:**   A request for an admission is not used primarily to obtain information, but to *narrow the disputed issues* and remove the necessity of *proving at trial* the fact whose admission is sought.

2. **Answers and objections to requests to admit:**   If the party does not answer the request to admit at all within 30 days after its service (except that a defendant has at least 45 days after service of the complaint in which to answer), the matter is taken as *admitted.*

   a. **Answer:**   The party may answer by:

      i. *admitting* the truth of the matter;

      ii. *denying* the matter in whole or in part (there is a specific requirement of *good faith* with respect to qualified admissions or partial denials — Rule 36(a)(4); or

      iii. setting forth the *reasons why he cannot truthfully admit or deny* the matter. *Lack of information* is not an acceptable reason for this, unless the party states that he has made reasonable inquiries and does not have enough information to admit or deny honestly.

   b. **Triable issue:**   It is *not* grounds for objection to a request to admit that the discoveree feels that the matter is a *genuine issue for trial*. However, a party can object on the ground that the question encompasses too many issues, some of which the party can admit and others which cannot be admitted.

   c. **Sufficiency of the objection:**   If the answering party has objected to a request, the requesting party may move to determine the sufficiency of the objection. He may also move to determine the sufficiency of the answers which have been given. Rule 36(a)(6).

3. **Expenses for failure to admit:**   If a party fails to admit the truth of any matter requested for admission under Rule 36(a), and if the party making the request *proves* the truth of the matter at trial, the court upon motion by the discovering party may require the party who refused to admit to pay *reasonable expenses sustained by the movant in proving the matter*. (Rule 37(c)(2)). These expenses may not be levied if (1) the request to admit was successfully objected to; (2) the admission sought was not of substantial importance; (3) the

party who failed to admit had reasonable grounds to think he might prevail on the issue at trial; or (4) there was other good reason for the failure to admit.

    a. Rule 37(b)(2) sanctions not applicable: The sanctions and orders of Rule 37(b)(2) (contempt, striking of pleadings, etc.) do *not* apply to requests to admit, since to do so would in effect infringe upon the party's right to his day in court by coercing him into making involuntary admissions. Of course, even the 37(c)(2) imposition of costs is coercive to a certain extent, but probably to a lesser one than, for example, a contempt citation.

4. Effect at trial: If a party makes an admission under Rule 36, the matter is ***conclusively established at trial***, unless the court grants a motion to withdraw or amend the admission. The court may permit the admission to be ***withdrawn or amended*** only if two conditions are met:

    a. Presentation of merits: withdrawal or amendment "would promote the presentation of the merits of the action"; *and*

    b. Lack of prejudice: the court is "not persuaded that it would ***prejudice*** the requesting party in maintaining or defending the action on the merits."

See Rule 36(b).

H. Requests to produce documents and to inspect land: A party may, by Rule 34, require any other party to ***produce documents, electronically stored information,*** and ***tangible things***. Thus any papers, computer files, photographs, and objects relevant to the subject matter of the case may be obtained by the discovering party from any other party, but ***not from a non-party***.

1. Inspection of land: Rule 34 also allows a party to demand the right to inspect, photograph, and survey any *land* within the control of another party.

2. No requirement of "good cause": It is not necessary for the party seeking production or inspection to demonstrate "good cause" for his request. Therefore, the scope of discovery under Rule 34 is the same as for interrogatories and depositions. The material must simply meet the test of Rule 26(b)(1), i.e., it must be not privileged and relevant to the subject matter of the pending action.

3. Party's control: A party may be required to produce only those documents and other objects which are in his ***"possession, custody or control"***. Rule 34(a). If the party who is requested to produce a document does not have actual possession of it, but is legally entitled to obtain possession or a copy, the request must be honored. Therefore, a party cannot escape discovery by turning the document or object over to his attorney, or to a third person. See Wright, p. 585.

4. "Electronically stored information" (i.e., computer files): Rule 34's reference to ***"electronically stored information"*** means that ***computer files*** are now discoverable on the same basis as paper documents.

    a. Same footing as paper documents: The reference to electronically stored information was added in 2006, to "confirm that discovery of electronically stored information ***stands on equal footing*** with discovery of paper documents." ACN to 2006 Amendments to Rule 34.

b. Right to specify form for the data: The requesting party can specify the *"form or forms"* in which the electronic data is to be produced. Rule 34(b)(1)(C). (For instance, the requesting party might ask for "email and word-processed files, supplied in their original format.")

   i. Where no request: If the requesting party does not specify the desired format, the responding party can choose between producing the information "in a form ... in which it is *ordinarily maintained*" or "in a *reasonably usable* form[.]" Rule 34(b)(2)(E)(ii). If the responding party elects the "reasonably usable" approach, that party may need to supply not only a computer file, but "some reasonable amount of *technical support*, information on application software, or other reasonable assistance to enable the requesting party to use the information." ACN to 2006 Amendment to Rule 34.

c. "Metadata": An increasingly important question is whether one party can get discovery of so-called *"metadata"* about the electronically-stored documents being produced by the other. The term "metadata" covers a variety of information that "puts a given document *in context*." Y (2010 Supp.), p. 431. The metadata for a document might include the *date* on which it was created, details of *changes* made to it during the course of successive drafts, who *created* it, who was *cc'd* on it, and the like. Sometimes the metadata is stored *in the document itself* but not visible on a standard printout; at other times, the metadata is kept *separately* from the document.

   i. No consensus yet: There is no consensus yet on whether and when the party who has possession of a discoverable document must also produce the metadata for it. The subject is not yet explicitly covered in the Federal Rules. Here are some observations about how early federal cases have handled the issue:

   [1] If the metadata for a document is *shown to be relevant* to the particular issues in the case, the court is *likely* to order that the metadata be produced along with the document.

   Example: Suppose that in a case in which P is trying to hold D, an organization, liable for conduct by low-level employees, an issue under the substantive law is whether the higher-ups in the organization knew about the low-level conduct. If P asks for metadata showing, as to each document dealing with the low-level conduct, what persons within the organization were cc'd on the document and when, the court is likely to order that this information be produced, since it is directly relevant to an issue in the case.

   [2] If producing the metadata and matching it up to the underlying documents would constitute a *significant burden* for the producing party, the court may well use its *cost-shifting discretion* under Rule 26(b)(2)(B) (discussed *infra*, p. 233) by ordering that the party requesting the data *pay* for all or part of the incremental cost of producing it.

   [3] The court is likely to be more sympathetic to metadata requests that are made *at the same time* the underlying documents are requested, than to a request made *after* the producer has already produced the documents themselves. So litigants should generally include, as part of their standard document-produc-

tion requests, a request for specified types of metadata about any documents that are being asked for.

For a case illustrating the above tendencies, see *Aguilar v. Immigration & Customs Enforcement Div.*, 2008 WL 5062700 (S.D.N.Y. 2008).

d. Cost of production: Discovery of electronically stored information often raises the issue of who should *bear the costs* of finding and producing the information.

    i. Presumption that responding party bears costs: Our discussion of this topic should start by noting that the federal discovery rules contain an embedded *presumption* — applicable to all discovery, not just electronically stored materials — that the *discoveree*, not the party requesting discovery, must ordinarily bear the cost of that discovery.

    ii. Cost shifting at court's discretion: However, the trial court has discretion to *shift* this cost burden partly or fully to the requesting party in an appropriate case. See, e.g., *Oppenheimer Fund v. Sanders*, 437 U.S. 340 (1978): "The presumption is that the responding party must bear the expense of complying with discovery requests, but [it] may invoke the district court's discretion under Rule 26(c) to grant orders protecting [it] from 'undue burden or expense' in doing so, including orders conditioning discovery on the *requesting party's payment of the costs of discovery.*"

    iii. Rule 26(b)(2)(B) allows relief: Rule 26 was amended in 2006 to deal with the special cost issues of discovering electronically-stored information. 26(b)(2)(B) now says that "A party need not provide discovery of electronically stored information from sources that the party identifies as *not reasonably accessible because of undue burden or cost.*" If the parties disagree about whether cost considerations make the requested data not readily accessible — and therefore about whether to condition discovery of this data on the requesting party's willingness to pay those costs — the court will resolve the issue by considering, among other things:

    [1] whether the discovery can be obtained from "*some other source* that is more convenient, less burdensome, or less expensive" (26(b)(2)(C)(i)) and

    [2] whether the "burden or *expense* of the proposed discovery *outweighs its likely benefit*, considering the *needs* of the case, the *amount in controversy*, the *parties' resources*, the *importance of the issues* at stake in the action, and the importance of the discovery in resolving the issues." (26(b)(2)(C)(iii)).

(The quoted language in both [1] and [2] applies to all contested discovery, not just discovery of electronically stored information.)

    iv. Cost-shifting for inaccessible data: A court order shifting some or all of the cost to the requesting party is especially *likely* in those cases involving discovery of *"offline"* computer files, such as *computer backup tapes.* In deciding whether to order cost-shifting, the court will balance the costs of finding, restoring and searching the backup tapes with the likely "payoff" from doing so.

(1) Use of sampling: Often, it will not be clear to the parties in advance of the discovery how much searching the backup data would cost, or how fruitful that searching would be. Courts often deal with this uncertainty by ordering that a *sampling* process be used, under which a few designated backup tapes are searched to see how expensive and fruitful the process is; only after that sampling does the court decide whether or how the costs should be shifted.

Example: P sues D, a large Wall Street firm, for sex discrimination and retaliation. P seeks all e-mails relating to P's job performance over a several-year period. D searches its readily-accessible (i.e., currently-online) e-mail records and produces 100 pages of emails. It states that any additional e-mails that ever existed about P reside only on a series of 94 different backup tapes, and that these can be restored and searched only at a cost of $300,000. D seeks a ruling that because of this heavy cost, P is either not entitled to this backup data at all, or must pay the full cost of retrieving it.

Held, back up tapes are a relatively "inaccessible" method of storage, as to which the court will consider cost-shifting. (By contrast, emails stored on optical discs are sufficiently "near-line" that D must bear the full cost of searching such discs, with the court unwilling to even consider cost-shifting.) However, before the court will actually order cost-shifting, D must retrieve and search any five backup tapes specified by P, and the court will make its cost-shifting decision based on a cost/benefit analysis of the results of producing these five samples. *Zubulake v. UBS Warburg LLC*, 217 F.R.D. 309 (S.D.N.Y. 2003).

Note: After the sampling was done in *Zubulake*, the trial court decided that, because the discovery was quite successful in producing relevant emails that had not been previously produced by D, P should be required to pay only 25% of the cost of restoring the full set of backup tapes, and none of the costs of having a lawyer or paralegal for D review the tapes prior to production.

5. **May be addressed only to a party:** Rule 34 requests to produce, like Rule 33 interrogatories, can be addressed *only to parties*.

    a. **Use of subpoena against non-parties:** Since non-parties cannot be made the subject of a Rule 34 request to produce, the only way to force a non-party to produce documents is to serve a *subpoena duces tecum* upon him, pursuant to Rule 45. (See Rule 34(c), providing that the Rule 45 subpoena procedure may be used for non-parties.) If the non-party fails to comply with such a subpoena, he is subject to a citation for contempt of court, pursuant to Rule 45(e).

I. Physical and mental examinations (Rule 35): When the mental or physical condition of a party (but *not non-parties*) or of a person in the custody or under the legal control of a party (e.g., a ward), is *in controversy*, the court in which the action is pending may order the party to submit to a *physical or mental examination* by a physician or other examiner, or to produce for examination the person under his custody or legal control. The order may be made only on motion; *good cause* must be shown, and *notice* must be given to the person to be examined and to all other parties.

1. **Difference from other discovery:** There are two important differences between Rule 35 orders for examination and the other discovery devices discussed above:

   a. **Motion required:** Rule 35 does not operate *extrajudicially*; the discovering party must make a motion showing good cause. The other discovery devices can be initiated by the parties themselves.

      i. **Agreement:** If the parties agree by themselves to allow a physical examination of one of them, Rule 35 does not come into play at all, and the court is never involved. This often happens where the parties are interested in an out-of-court settlement.

      ii. **Good cause:** Generally, good cause can be shown where the information can be acquired through no other means, and is relevant to the issues expected to be tried.

   b. **Controversy:** Rule 35 requires that the mental or physical condition of the party be *in controversy*. This means that the scope of discovery under Rule 35 is somewhat narrower than that governing the other modes of discovery under Rule 26(b), where the material simply has to be relevant to the *subject matter* in the pending action, and not *necessarily related to an actual issue in controversy* at trial.

      i. **Not formality:** The Supreme Court in *Schlagenhauf v. Holder*, 379 U.S. 104 (1964), emphasized that the "good cause" and "in controversy" requirements were not mere formalities, but "require an affirmative showing by the movant that each condition as to which the exam is sought is really and genuinely in controversy and that good cause exists for ordering each particular exam." In some cases, however, the pleadings alone may meet these requirements — this would be the case, for example, where plaintiff alleges personal injury in a negligence action.

      ii. **Interest in privacy:** The chief reason for the closer judicial supervision and narrower scope of Rule 35 examinations is the growing public, judicial, and constitutional concern for the right to privacy.

   c. **Rule 35 valid under Enabling Act:** In *Sibbach v. Wilson*, 312 U.S. 1 (1941), the Supreme Court held that Rule 35 was *valid* under the Rules Enabling Act of 1934. The Court held that although the right to be free of a compulsory physical examination might be a substan*tial* right, the right was not substan*tive* in the sense of the Enabling Act. Therefore, the Rule was upheld. (See the fuller discussion of *Sibbach*, *infra*, p. 260). See also *Schlagenhauf v. Holder*, *supra*, similarly upholding Rule 35.

2. **Reports of examiner:** Rule 35(b) allows discovery of the *actual medical report* produced through a Rule 35 examination. This is an important exception to the rule that expert's reports are not generally discoverable.

   a. **Who may receive:** *A party against whom an order is made* under Rule 35(a), or the *person examined*, may request and have delivered from the party causing the exam to be made, a copy of a written report of the examiner detailing his findings.

   b. **Other examinations:** After delivery of the report, the party who caused the examination is entitled on request to receive from the party against whom the order was made a report of any other examination made for the same condition at the requestee's behest.

    c. **Waiver of objection:** By requesting and obtaining a report of the examination ordered or by deposing the examiner, the party examined *waives any privilege* he may have in that action or any other involving the same controversy, regarding testimony about *all examinations* of the same condition. (Rule 35(b)(4)).

    d. **Where examination made by agreement:** (a), (b), and (c) above apply also to an examination made by agreement of the parties without court intervention, unless the agreement expressly provides otherwise.

Quiz Yourself on
METHODS OF DISCOVERY

56. P brought a federal court action against D in connection with an automobile accident. P learned that the accident was personally observed by W. P served upon W a set of interrogatories asking W to describe the accident as he saw it. Must W answer the interrogatories? _____

57. P brought a diversity-based negligence action against D in federal district court for the Southern District of New York. One of the witnesses to the accident in question was W (who is not a party). W is an individual who was visiting in New York at the time of the accident, but who resides in the Southern District of Florida. P's lawyer wished to take W's deposition, but P's lawyer did not wish to travel to Florida to do so. Consequently, P served upon W at W's residence in Miami a notice of deposition, together with a notice stating that W's reasonable travel and lodging expenses for a trip to New York (where the deposition was to be held) would be paid by P. W has indicated that she will not submit to any deposition unless subpoenaed to do so. If P is ready to bear W's travel and lodging expenses to New York, may W be subpoenaed to appear in New York for her deposition? _____

58. P and D were involved in an automobile accident. P sued D for negligence in federal court, based on diversity. P discovered the existence of a police report, issued by the police department of the City of Langdell (where the accident occurred). P served upon that police department a Rule 34 Request to Produce Documents, listing the police report as the document to be produced. Assuming that the City of Langdell is within the district where the action is pending, must the police department comply with the request? _____

59. P was hit by an automobile driven by D. P brought a federal diversity action against D alleging negligence. P claimed that he suffered serious whiplash in the accident, and that he has been physically disabled from working. D's lawyer had doubts about whether P was as severely disabled as he claims. Therefore, D's lawyer served upon P a notice to undergo physical examination, which stated, "Please present yourself at any time within the next two weeks at the office of Dr. John Smith, who will conduct a physical examination of you to determine the degree of your disability." Must P comply with this request? _____

Answers

56. No. Only *parties* may be served with, and required to respond to, interrogatories. See Federal Rule 33(a). If a party wishes to get discovery from a non-party witness, this must usually be done by taking the witness' deposition.

57. No. Federal Rule 45(c)(3)(A)(ii), which protects persons subject to subpoenas, states that a court shall quash a subpoena if it "requires a person who is [not] a party ... to travel more than 100 miles from where the person resides, is employed, or regularly transacts business in person[.]" Since a 1,300-mile trip from Miami to New York goes far beyond the 100 miles ordinarily contemplated for a subpoena, it is highly unlikely that a court would uphold the necessary subpoena. (But if P's lawyer is willing to travel to Miami to conduct the deposition, the lawyer can serve the subpoena for deposition on W at W's residence. And, by the way, that's true even if P's lawyer is not admitted to practice in Florida — see Rule 45(a)(3)(B), authorizing an attorney as an officer of the court to issue a subpoena for a deposition in another district, "if the attorney is authorized to practice in the court where the action is pending.")

58. No. A Rule 34 request to produce documents may be served *only on a party*. To compel the police department to deliver the report, P must cause the clerk of the court to issue a subpoena duces tecum on the department, pursuant to Rule 45(b).

59. No. Unlike nearly all the other discovery tools, the right to require another party to undergo a physical examination may be accomplished only by *obtaining a court order*. According to Rule 35(a), if the mental or physical condition of a party is "in controversy," the court where the action is pending may order that party to submit to a physical or mental examination. The order may only be made upon a showing of "good cause." Here, if D makes a motion to have P subjected to a physical examination, the court will almost certainly grant D's motion, since P's physical condition is clearly in controversy, and there is no other good way to ascertain the truth of P's claim of disability.

IV. ORDERS AND SANCTIONS

A. **General availability of sanctions:** Several types of orders and sanctions are available to the parties to enforce the discovery process. The type of sanction applied by the court depends both upon the *seriousness* of the violation, and whether a prior court order *compelling discovery* has been administered. Wr., 639-44.

B. **Abuse of discovery:** A party may sometimes use discovery in such a way as to harass his adversaries as, for example, by scheduling depositions for inconvenient places, or by requesting that the discoveree reveal trade secrets. There are two distinct ways in which the discoveree may resist such abuse: (1) he may simply object to a particular request, whether it is in the form of a deposition, an interrogatory, or a request to produce; or (2) he may seek a Rule 26(c) *protective order.*

1. **Objection:** An objection may be raised to a discovery request in the same way that a question at trial may be objected to. The usual ground for such an objection is that it is not within the scope of discovery under Rule 26(b)(1), or that it is privileged.

    a. **Interrogatory objection:** An objection to an interrogatory question is written down, and must be signed by the attorney making it. See Rule 33(b)(4) and (5).

        i. **Burdensome interrogatories:** Where objections are raised to interrogatory questions, the court will normally evaluate each of the challenged questions. But if they are extremely voluminous, the court may simply conclude that the entire set of questions is burdensome and sustain the objections as a whole, relieving the interrogee from having to respond.

b. Request to admit: An objection to a request to admit may be signed by either the party or his lawyer. The objection must state the grounds for the objection. See Rule 36(a)(5).

c. Deposition: If an objection is made to a deposition question, the stenographer simply notes the objection, the question is usually not answered, and the deposition continues. All of the objections are then usually disposed of at once by the judge.

2. **Protective order:** A party or other person against whom discovery is sought may, instead of raising a particular objection, seek a judicial order known as a *"protective order,"* pursuant to Rule 26(c). Such a protective order generally deals with a much broader range of material than does a simple objection. Whereas an objection generally relates to a single question, a protective order may be issued to prohibit an entire line of questioning, the use of a particular form of discovery, or the examination of a particular witness. Rule 26(c) allows the judge to make "an order to protect a party or person from annoyance, embarrassment, oppression, or undue burden or expense. ..." Certain specific reasons for concluding that a discovery request is unduly burdensome or expensive are now supplied in Rule 26(b)(2)(c) (e.g., the information is available from some other, more convenient, source).

   a. Where sought: A party may always seek a protective order from the court in which the action is *pending*. Furthermore, in the case of a deposition, the protective order may be sought from the court in the district where the deposition is to be taken as well as in the district where the action is pending. See Rule 26(c).

   Example: P sues D in the Southern District of New York. P deposes X, a competitor of D and a stranger to the action, in Los Angeles. X may seek a protective order from either the Southern District of New York, or the Central District of California.

   b. Kinds of orders: Rule 26(c) lists eight particular kinds of protective orders which a judge may issue in order to protect a party from embarrassment or oppression. Among the more important possibilities are the following:

   i. he may order that discovery or disclosure *not be had at all;*

   ii. he may order that it be held only at a *certain time or place;*

   iii. he may order that a *method* of discovery other than that sought by the discovering party be used;

   iv. he may *restrict the scope* of discovery or disclosure (e.g., by prohibiting questions about certain subject areas);

   v. he may order that a deposition be *sealed*, and opened only by court order; or

   vi. he may limit or altogether bar the revealing of *trade secrets or other commercial information.*

   c. Prohibition of public disclosure: As the above listing indicates, one of the common functions of a protective order is to allow trade secrets or other information to be discovered, but then to *bar the public disclosure* of the information by the discovering litigant. Discovering parties faced with such anti-disclosure orders have sometimes argued that the orders violate their *First Amendment right of free speech*. However, the Supreme Court has made it clear that only rarely will a protective order barring disclosure violate the First Amendment. The Court laid down the rules for evaluating such free speech claims in *Seattle Times Co. v. Rhinehart*, 467 U.S. 20 (1984).

i. ***Seattle Times* test:** Under the Court's test in *Seattle Times*, a protective order barring disclosure of discovered materials will ***not violate*** the First Amendment if it meets the following criteria: (1) there is a showing of ***"good cause,"*** as is required of any protective order by Federal Rule 26(c); (2) the order is limited to the context of ***pretrial*** discovery in ***civil*** cases (so that anti-disclosure orders in criminal cases are not necessarily immune from free speech claims, and so that material ***introduced at trial*** may not normally be ordered concealed); and (3) the order does not bar the dissemination of the discovered information if it is also ***independently gained from other, non-discovery, sources.***

ii. **Disclosure allowed where no "good cause" shown:** Conversely, if the party opposing disclosure does ***not*** show "good cause" for keeping the discovered materials secret, Rule 26(c) implies, and most courts have held, that the court must ***permit*** public disclosure of that material. And even if the court bars pre-trial disclosure to guarantee a fair trial, it may (perhaps must) allow that disclosure once the trial passes and the need for secrecy no longer exists.

Example: Suppose the Ps bring a tort suit against D, a cigarette manufacturer, alleging that D fraudulently advertised that its cigarettes were safe. Suppose further that the Ps get discovery of D's internal work-papers, which show knowledge by D that the cigarettes are dangerous, but which also contain D's trade secrets. The trial court might issue a protective order preventing the Ps (or their counsel) from disclosing any of the contents of these work papers except as evidence during the trial. Or, the court might make the protective order applicable only up until the trial (to prevent unfair bias against D), and then rescind or limit the order once the trial was over, so that the press or other litigants can then read the work-papers.

d. **Use in deposition:** If a protective order under Rule 26(c) is to be sought in the case of a deposition, the order is generally sought before the deposition is conducted. If, however, a deposition is commenced and is being conducted "in bad faith or in a manner that unreasonably annoys, embarrasses or oppresses the deponent or party," any party or the deponent may go to the judge on a ***motion to terminate or limit examination*** under Rule 30(d)(3). The judge may either terminate the deposition completely, or limit the "scope and manner" of the deposition just as he could do under Rule 26(c).

C. **Compelling discovery:** A party seeking discovery may seek an ***order compelling discovery*** under Rule 37(a). Such an order is sought when the discoveree ***refuses***, in the first instance, to divulge the requested information. Thus just as a discoveree may seek court protection against an unfair discovery request, so a person seeking discovery may enlist the court's help when the discoveree refuses to comply.

1. **From whom sought:** If the discovering party wishes to compel ***another party*** to grant discovery, he can seek an order compelling discovery from the ***court in which the action is pending.***

a. **Deposition:** If the form of discovery is a *deposition*, the party seeking discovery from another party may seek an order compelling discovery *either* in the court where the action is pending or in the court in the district where the deposition is being taken.

b. **Non-party deposition:** If the order that is being sought is an order to compel discovery from a *non-party deponent*, the order *must* be sought from the court in the district where the *deposition is being taken.*

2. **When available:** An order to compel discovery may be granted if the discoveree fails to do any of the following things:

a. answer a *written or oral deposition* question under Rules 30 or 31;

b. answer an *interrogatory* submitted under Rule 33;

c. allow a *request for inspection* or a *request to produce documents*, under Rule 34; or

d. *designate an officer* to answer deposition questions as required by Rules 30(b)(6) or 31(a)(4), if the discoveree is a *corporation.*

Note: The Federal Rules use the word "failure" throughout the enforcement and sanction sections of the discovery provisions to denote both *intentional* and *innocent* non-compliances with the rules and/or court-orders. However, since the court has wide *discretion* in applying sanctions, the innocence or guilt of the delinquent party is usually taken into account.

3. **Failure to answer deposition question:** If a deponent fails to answer a question in oral deposition, the discovering party can choose either to adjourn the examination in order to seek an order compelling discovery, or go on to other questions, and seek the order to compel at the end of the examination.

4. **Partial response:** The discovering party may seek an order to compel discovery not only if the discoveree refuses to answer a question entirely, but also if he makes *"an evasive or incomplete answer"*; such an evasive answer is to be treated as a failure to answer. See Rule 37(a)(4).

5. **Sanctions:** If an order compelling discovery is obtained and the discoveree still refuses to divulge the information, certain Rule 37(b) *sanctions*, discussed below, may be imposed by the court.

D. **Sanctions:** Rule 37(b) provides a number of *sanctions* against parties who behave unreasonably during discovery.

1. **Financial sanctions:** If a discovering party seeks an order compelling discovery under Rule 37(a), and the court grants the order, the court may require the discoveree to pay to the discovering party the *reasonable expenses* he incurred in obtaining the order compelling discovery.

a. **Lawyers' fees:** The expenses of procuring such an order may include the *cost of the lawyer's time* in making the motion for the order, and the damages suffered by the party in having the litigation delayed until the order was procured. But the costs of conducting the *discovery itself* (e.g., the cost of taking the deposition) may *not* be awarded under Rule 37(a).

b. Exceptions: The court ***must*** grant the successful discovering party his expenses of procuring the order unless it finds either: (i) that the opposition to the discovering party's motion was ***"substantially justified;"*** (ii) that the party seeking the expenses failed to make a ***good faith effort*** to resolve the dispute ***without court intervention***; or (iii) that "other circumstances make an award of expenses ***unjust***." See Rule 37(a)(5)(A).

c. Expenses following denial: Conversely, if a Rule 37 motion for an order compelling discovery is ***denied***, the court may award expenses to the ***discoveree***. Again, these expenses may include ***attorneys' fees***, and must be awarded unless the court finds that the discovering party's motion was substantially justified or that there are other circumstances which make an award of expenses to the discoveree unjust. Rule 37(a)(5)(B).

d. Expenses after protective order: If the ***discoveree*** seeks a Rule 26(c) ***protective order*** against discovery, the court may similarly award expenses to the winner, under the same standards as those set out in Rule 37(a)(5) and summarized in (a) through (c) above. See Rule 26(c)(3).

e. Refusal to admit: A party who ***refuses to admit*** on a matter which is later proved at trial may be required to pay ***his adversary's cost of proving the matter***. Rule 37(c).

2. Other sanctions: If the discoveree does not furnish the discovery requested of him by the discoveror, the first step the latter must generally take to force disclosure is to seek a Rule 37(a) order compelling discovery. If he obtains such an order, and the discoveree ***persists in his refusal*** to grant discovery, then Rule 37(b)(2) allows the court a choice of coercive sanctions. The court may take the following actions, among others:

a. Facts established: It may order that "the matters regarding which the order was made or any other designated facts shall be taken to be ***established*** for the purposes of the action in accordance with the claim of the party obtaining the order".

   i. Personal jurisdiction: Even ***personal jurisdiction*** over the defendant may be taken to be established, if the defendant refuses to comply with a court order requiring him to furnish discovery of facts related to the existence of such jurisdiction. *Insurance Corp. of Ireland v. Compagnie des Bauxites de Guinee*, 456 U.S. 694 (1982).

b. Claims or defenses barred: The court may prevent the disobedient party from ***making certain claims or defenses*** in the case, or prevent him from introducing certain matters in evidence.

c. Entry of judgment: The court may ***dismiss the action***, or enter a ***default judgment***, or ***strike*** any portion of the pleadings.

   i. Drastic sanctions: However, these sanctions of dismissal/default judgment are the most ***drastic*** ones in the trial judge's arsenal, and even where the judge is convinced that there has been a major breach of discovery rules, she will use these sanctions only if others are inadequate. For instance, in *Coca-Cola Bottling Co. v. Coca-Cola Co.*, 110 F.R.D. 363 (D.Del. 1986), Coca-Cola flatly refused to comply with a court order compelling it to produce its secret formula. Even though the refusal was an unambiguous, intentional and serious breach of the discovery rules, the court refused to enter a default judgment against Coke (and instead ordered that most facts as to which the documents would be relevant should be taken as established against Coke, a lesser sanction described above).

d.   Contempt: Lastly, the court may hold the disobedient party in ***contempt of court.***

e.   Mandatory sanctions for failure to disclose: The above sanctions are all essentially discretionary with the court. But another part of Rule 37 imposes ***mandatory*** sanctions for a party's failure to comply with the automatic ***early disclosure*** provisions of Rule 26(a) (see supra, p. 217) or with the ***duty-to-supplement*** obligations of 26(e)(1) (see *supra*, p. 220). Under 37(c)(1), "If a party fails to ***provide information or identify a witness*** as required by Rule 26(a) or (e), the party is ***not allowed to use*** that information or witness to ***supply evidence on a motion, at a hearing, or at a trial***, unless the failure was ***substantially justified or is harmless***."

Example: Suppose D fails, at the outset of the case, to list X as a person having knowledge of an event pertaining to the suit. Under 37(c)(1), the court is required to prevent D from calling X to testify unless D had substantial justification or the failure was harmless (as it might be if P already knew about X or learned about X's existence later on during discovery.)

3.   Wilfulness usually required: Rule 37(b) does not say anything about the ***degree of culpability*** necessary before the various sanction measures may be used. Generally, courts have not used sanctions — at least the more serious ones, such as dismissal or contempt — except on a showing that the offender has *wilfully*, rather than merely negligently, failed to follow the discovery rules. But courts have sometimes allowed some sort of sanction even for non-wilful violations.

a.   Gross negligence suffices: Courts have sometimes distinguished between "ordinary" negligence and "gross" negligence. For instance, in *Cine Forty-Second Street Theatre Corp. v. Allied Artists*, 602 F.2d 1062 (2d Cir. 1979), the Second Circuit held that a severe sanction (the preclusion of the discoveree's right to introduce evidence on matters that were the subject of the discovery order) was appropriate where the discoveree's failure to comply with the discovery order was ***grossly negligent.***

4.   Which court may issue: The sanctions listed in subsections (a), (b), and (c) of paragraph 2 above may be applied only by the court in which the action is pending, and not by the court in which the deposition was held, if it was held outside of the district of the lawsuit. See Rule 37(b)(2).

a.   Refusal to obey other judge: These sanctions by the judge of the case may, however, be in response to the discoveree's refusal to obey an order compelling discovery made by the judge where the deposition was taken.

b.   Contempt: Either the judge of the case or the judge where the deposition was taken may hold the discoveree in ***contempt*** for refusing to obey an order compelling discovery. See Rules 37(b)(1) and 37(b)(2)(A)(vii).

5.   Physical exam: Where the order which has been disobeyed is a Rule 35(a) order to submit to a ***physical or mental examination***, the sanctions outlined above are applicable, except that the disobedient party may ***not be held in contempt of court***. See Rule 37(b)(2)(A)(vii). This exception was apparently the product of a concern that it might be unconstitutional to imprison a party for refusing to submit to an examination of his person.

6. **Where allowed:** The sanctions listed in (2) above may be used in the following situations:

   a. in the case of ***refusal to answer deposition questions;***

   b. against a ***party*** who ***fails to attend*** his own deposition;

   c. against one who ***fails to answer interrogatories***; and

   d. against one who ***fails to answer a request for inspection.***

   Note: A party who does any of these things may ***not*** defend himself on the ground that the discovery sought is ***objectionable***, unless the discoveree has previously applied for a Rule 26(c) protective order.

7. **Sanctions prior to issuance of order:** As noted, sanctions (other than the costs of making a motion) may generally be imposed only where the discoveror has procured an order compelling discovery, and this order has been disobeyed. But there are a few exceptions: where a party ***fails to attend his own deposition*** called by an opposing party, ***fails to answer interrogatories***, or ***fails to answer a request for inspection***, these violations generally occur before an order to compel discovery has been made, and are the only kinds of violations for which sanctions are meted out ***prior to the issuing of an order compelling discovery***. Rule 37(d).

   a. **Failure must be complete:** The violations referred to in the previous paragraph are deemed to have occurred only where the party ***completely*** fails to respond to discovery. If he responds to discovery with an objection, the discovering party will have to make a motion for an order to compel discovery, rather than seeking the stronger sanctions of Rule 37(d). Then, if the order compelling discovery is disobeyed, the Rule 37(d) sanctions will become available.

V. USE OF DISCOVERY RESULTS AT TRIAL

A. **Use of results generally:** Once a party has obtained information through discovery, he may wish to put that information into ***evidence*** at the trial. Yet the introduction of discovery results may sometimes conflict with the rules of evidence, particularly since inadmissible material is sometimes discoverable.

B. **Rules on use:** To deal with such conflicts, certain rules with respect to the admissibility of various forms of discovery at trial have been set forth in the Federal Rules of Civil Procedure.

C. **Rule 34 requests to produce:** Documents and reports which have been obtained through ***Rule 34 requests to produce*** pose little problem, because their admissibility does not depend on the unavailability at trial of the person who created them (as the admissibility of the depositions of non-party witnesses does — see *infra*). The admissibility of such tangibles is determined ***without regard*** to the fact that these items were obtained through discovery. They will therefore be admissible unless their contents constitute prejudicial, hearsay, or other objectionable material.

D. Depositions: The admissibility of *depositions* is determined through a *two-part* test, *both* parts of which must be satisfied:

1. **Test 1:**   First, it must be determined whether the deposition statement sought to be introduced would be admissible *if the deponent were giving live testimony*. If not, the statement is automatically *inadmissible*. See Rule 32(a)(1)(B).

    Example: At his deposition, the deponent states, "X told me that D went through the red light." The deponent would probably not be permitted to make that statement on behalf of P at the trial of P's civil suit against D for auto negligence, because of the hearsay rule. Since the statement would not be admissible if made at trial, the deposition testimony is not admissible.

2. **Test 2:**   Use of a deposition statement, rather than live testimony, is itself a form of hearsay. Therefore, even if the testimony would be admissible if given live, it will be allowed in its deposition form only if it falls within one of the four following categories, which are in effect exceptions to the hearsay rule:

    a. **Adverse party:**   The deposition of an *adverse party*, or of a *director or officer* of an adverse *corporate* party, may be admitted for *any purpose at all.* See Rule 32(a)(3).

    b. **Impeachment:**   The deposition of any witness, *party or non-party*, may be used to *impeach the witness' credibility*; see Rule 32(a)(2).

       Example: In an automobile accident case brought in diversity by P against D, W, a witness friendly to P, takes the stand. W testifies that the accident happened when D drove through a red light. In cross-examination, D's lawyer introduces a transcript of W's testimony from a deposition taken during the case. In the transcript, W admits having once falsified a job application. Even though W is not a party, this deposition testimony is admissible, because it is used to impeach W's credibility.

    c. **Use for substantive purposes where conflicts with trial testimony:**   Deposition testimony that *conflicts* with a witness' trial testimony may be used even for *substantive* purposes. This result is not contained directly in the Federal Rules, but is instead incorporated from the Federal Rules of Evidence. FRE 801(d)(1) allows admission of a witness' out-of-court statement if "the declarant testifies at the trial or hearing and is subject to cross-examination concerning the statement, and the statement is (a) inconsistent with the declarant's testimony, and was given under oath … in a deposition. …" FRCP 32(a)(1) then allows use of "any deposition … for any … purpose permitted by the Federal Rules of Evidence."

       Example: P brings a diversity action against D for automobile negligence. During D's case, D calls to the stand W, a non-party witness, who testifies that D was blameless and that P caused the accident by failing to stop at a stop sign. P's lawyer, in cross-examination of W, introduces W's deposition testimony, in which W said that P did stop at the stop sign in question. This statement from the deposition — that P stopped — is admissible as *substantive* evidence of whether P stopped at the stop sign.

d.   Other circumstances: The deposition of any person, party or non-party, can be used for any purpose if any one of the following *"deponent unavailable"* conditions exists:

　　i.   the deponent is *dead*;

　　ii.   the deponent is *100 or more miles from the trial* (and the absence is not due to the conduct of the party introducing the deposition);

　　iii.   the deponent is *too ill* to testify;

　　iv.   the deponent is *not obtainable by subpoena*; or

　　v.   there are *exceptional circumstances* that make it desirable to dispense with the deponent's live testimony.

　　See Rule 32(a)(4).

e.   Sometimes not allowed: The above four categories are not all-inclusive — there remain circumstances where a deposition may *not* be used. For instance, a party may ordinarily not introduce her own deposition to buttress her case. Nor may a party normally introduce the deposition of a witness for substantive purposes, or to bolster that witness' credibility, if the witness is testifying at trial or is available to testify at trial. (But F.R.E. 801(d)(1)(b) makes an exception where the deposition or other out-of-court statement is "consistent with the declarant's testimony and is offered to rebut an express or implied charge against the declarant of recent fabrication or improper influence or motive. …")

Example 1 (Deponent is party): P brings a diversity suit against D, arising out of an auto accident. In a deposition taken during the course of the suit, P testifies that D went through a red light. At trial, P may not introduce his own deposition for any purpose, because the situation does not fall within any of the special cases described above (e.g., use by an adverse party, use to impeach, a deponent unavailable to testify, etc.) However, if D's lawyer expressly or impliedly charges at trial that P has recently changed his story (e.g., by asking P on cross-examination, "Isn't this the first time you've said that D went through a red light?"), P may now use his deposition to rebut this charge of recent fabrication.

Example 2 (Use of non-party witness' deposition): P sues D in diversity relating to an automobile accident. D takes the deposition of W, who was in P's car and who is friendly to P. In that deposition, W testifies that D went through a red light. At trial, P elects not to call W as a witness, even though W is available, because P thinks W has shifty eyes and may be perceived by the jury as being untruthful. P may not introduce W's deposition testimony on the red-light issue, because that testimony does not fall within any of the exceptions discussed above. The fact that the deposition was taken by D, and that D had a right to cross-examine at the time, is irrelevant. (But if W was now *unavailable*, because she was, for instance, ill, or located more than 100 miles away from the trial for reasons not due to P's conduct, P could use the deposition in lieu of W's live testimony.)

3.   Partial offering: If only *part* of a deposition is offered into evidence by a party, an adverse party may introduce *any other parts* of the deposition which in *fairness* ought to be considered with the part introduced. See Rule 32(a)(6). This rule of fairness will almost always require that if only part of a particular deposition answer is offered by one party, the rest of the answer may be read in by any other party.

E. **Interrogatories:**   The *interrogatory answer* of a party can be used by an *adverse party* for *any purpose*, including substantive as well as impeaching purposes. Since interrogatories may be addressed only to the parties, the rule allowing an interrogatory answer to be introduced by a party against the respondent is the same as the rule allowing the use of a deposition given by an adverse party. See Rule 33(c).

1. **Not binding:**   Statements made in *depositions* and *interrogatories* are *not irrefutably binding* upon the maker. He may contradict them in court, and the trier of fact will weigh all relevant evidence in determining the issue. Of course, the credibility of a party who changes his story will suffer, but he is not legally bound by his interrogatory answer.

    Example: A party states in his deposition that a particular fact is so, "to the best of his recollection." After the deposition, he checks his records, and finds that he was mistaken. At trial, he may assert that his deposition answer was erroneous, and he will not be bound by that answer. The jury will, however, be entitled to conclude that the party's explanation of his change of response lacks credibility.

F. **Admissions:**   *Admissions* obtained under Rule 36 are held to *conclusively establish* the matter admitted, except for an occasional right of rebuttal or amendment granted by Rule 36(b); see *supra*, p. 231.

G. **Physical and mental examinations:**   The results of *physical and mental examinations* made under Rule 35 are almost always *admissible at trial*. Since such examinations are only conducted after a court has found that the physical or mental condition of the party to be examined is in controversy, the requirement of relevance has virtually always been satisfied. Only if the legal theories underlying the lawsuit have changed between the time of the examination and the time at which its results are to be introduced, might the examination be irrelevant.

1. **Waiver as to report:**   The admissibility of the report is rendered even more probable by the fact that *if the examined party requests and obtains a report of the examiner*, that party is held to *waive any privilege* (e.g., doctor/patient) he may have in that action or in "any other action involving the same controversy," concerning "testimony about all examinations of the same condition." See Rule 35(b)(4). Since in most cases, the examined party will request a copy of the physician's report, the question of admissibility never even arises.

H. **Use in subsequent proceedings:**   The above discussion relates to use of discovery materials in the action during which they were acquired. A separate issue is whether these results are usable in *subsequent actions*.

1. **Depositions:**   If a *deposition* meets the above requirements for admissibility with respect to the action pursuant to which it was given, it may also be admissible in a subsequent proceeding. In federal civil trials, the admissibility of a deposition from a prior proceeding is governed by a combination of the FRCP and the Federal Rules of Evidence.

a. **Adverse party:** A *party's* own deposition may be admitted *against him* for any purpose at all, even if it comes from a prior proceeding. See FRE 801(d)(2)(A); FRCP 32(a)(8).

    Example: P believes that she has been injured by a prescription drug she has taken. She believes that the drug was manufactured by D1 and thus sues D1. She gives a deposition in that action, in which she says that her symptoms did not begin until 1985. P loses that suit. P then sues D2, another drug manufacturer, on a similar claim. In this trial, D2 may introduce, against P, P's deposition from the P-D1 case, just as D1 could have introduced that deposition in the original action — this is because FRCP 32(a)(1) allows use of a deposition "for any … purpose permitted by Federal Rules of Evidence," and FRE 801(d)(2) makes a party's own statement non-hearsay (and thus admissible) if offered against that party. (FRE 801(d)(2) is not limited to statements made during the course of the present proceeding.)

b. **Impeachment:** Similarly, the deposition of any witness, *party or non-party*, may be used to *impeach* that witness' credibility, even though the deposition was taken in a prior action. See FRE 801(d)(1)(A).

c. **Deponent unavailable:** The tricky question comes when the deponent in the first action is not a party to the current action, and is not a witness either. In this situation, the Federal Rules of Evidence try to guarantee that the deposition will be used only if this is *fair* to the party against whom the deposition is offered. Under FRE 804(b)(1), the deposition may only be offered if *both* of the following conditions are satisfied: (1) the deponent is now *unavailable* to give testimony (e.g., W is dead, not available by subpoena, or otherwise unavailable for the reasons summarized on p. 245 *supra*); and (2) the party against whom the deposition is now sought to be admitted, or that party's *"predecessor in interest,"* had the opportunity to *cross-examine* the deponent at the time of the earlier deposition.

    i. **Significance:** Requirement (2) means that if the deposition is not offered against a person who was a *party* to the earlier action, then at least a person who was *similarly situated* to the person now opposing the deposition's use (in terms of posture in the suit and incentive to cross-examine) must have been present at the deposition.

        Example: P sues D1, a drug manufacturer, alleging that a drug manufactured by D1 injured P when she took it. D1 takes the deposition of W, P's mother, during which W says that P took the drug only during the year 1985. P then loses the suit against D1, because the jury believes that the drug was not made by D1. W dies. P now brings an action against D2, a manufacturer of a similar drug, alleging that in fact it was D2 who made the drug in question. P seeks to introduce W's deposition testimony to prove that P took the drug in 1985 (not, as D2 is now asserting, 1984, before D2 was producing the type of drug in question).

        Unless the court in the P-D2 action is convinced that D1 was *situated similarly* to D2 — in the sense that D1 was motivated to cross-examine W in the same way as D2 would have been — the court will *not* allow the deposition to be used against D2. This is because D2 is in effect deprived of its opportunity to cross-examine W and to show that she may be mistaken about the date. So if the year of P's ingestion was not an issue in the first suit, and was not in fact the subject of cross-examination by D1 during the deposition, P will probably be unable to use the deposition now against D2. (In terms of FRE 804(b)(1), the issue is whether D1 is D2's "predecessor in interest.")

2. **Admissions:**   Rule 36 explicitly states that *admissions* are for the purposes of the ***pending action only***. Admissions, unlike interrogatory or deposition answers, thus cannot be used against the admitting party in any other proceeding.

3. **Medical report:**   The courts have not agreed on whether a **medical report** obtained under Rule 35 is generally admissible in subsequent proceedings. However, if the examinee requests a copy of the report, he waives any claim of privilege in any action "involving the same controversy." See Rule 35(b)(4). In that case, the report is admissible if relevant to the subsequent controversy.

Quiz Yourself on

ORDERS AND SANCTIONS; USE OF DISCOVERY RESULTS AT TRIAL

60. P and D are each corporations engaged in the pharmaceutical business; they compete with each other. P has brought a federal patent infringement suit against D, and has added to it a pendent state claim alleging that D, by hiring a former employee of P, effectively stole certain trade secrets belonging to P. During the discovery phase, P has served upon D a Rule 34 document production request seeking documents containing details of certain secret manufacturing processes used by D, so that P can determine whether these are derived from P's own trade secrets. D is afraid that if it complies, two bad results may occur: (1) P may use the information, including the trade secrets, to compete with D; and (2) P may disclose those trade secrets to the world, thus stripping D's competitive advantage. What should D do to deal with these problems? _____

61. P brought a product liability suit (based on diversity) against D. D is a corporation. P served D with a notice of deposition, which stated that D or its representative would be asked questions concerning how the product in question was designed. D designated Smith to be deposed on its behalf. Smith was D's Director of Product Safety at the time the product in question was designed, but had since left D's employ. Now, at trial, P seeks to introduce in evidence answers given by Smith in the deposition. The answers are offered for substantive purposes, and are offered even though Smith is available to testify at trial. Are the deposition answers admissible under these circumstances? _____

62. P and D were involved in an auto accident while each was driving a car. P brought a diversity action against D for negligence. D took the deposition of W, a bystander who observed the accident. W is available (indeed eager) to testify at trial, but neither party has called her. D now offers a portion of W's deposition testimony as evidence. Will this testimony be admitted if objected to by P? _____

63. Same facts as prior question. Now, however, assume that W was called to the stand by P and gave live testimony. D now seeks to offer into evidence portions of W's deposition testimony which would cast doubt upon the accuracy of W's statements made at trial. Is this deposition material admissible? _____

64. Cars driven by P and D were in an accident. P sued D in federal court for negligence. During the discovery process, P served upon D an interrogatory containing the following question: "State what, if anything,

you told the police officer investigating the accident regarding whether you stopped at the stop sign located at the corner of Main and 21st Street just before the accident." D submitted the following response to this question: "I told the police officer that I did not stop at the stop sign."

(a) Suppose that at trial, D does not take the stand. May P introduce D's interrogatory statement for the purpose of proving that D did not in fact stop at the stop sign? _____

(b) Assume that at trial, (i) D testifies that he did stop at the stop sign; and (ii) P is permitted to introduce the interrogatory answer to impeach D's testimony. Will a properly-instructed jury be permitted to conclude that D stopped at the stop sign? _____

Answers

60. **Seek a protective order limiting how the information can be used.** Federal Rule 26(c) allows the federal court to issue, on motion by a party from whom discovery is sought, a protective order protecting the requesting party from annoyance, embarrassment, oppression, etc. One of the steps the court can order is "that a trade secret or other confidential research, development, or commercial information not be revealed or be revealed only in a specified way." Rule 26(c)(1)(G). D should seek an order that the information sought be used by P only for purposes of the litigation, that it not be used in P's business operations, and that it not be disclosed to any third parties. The Supreme Court has held that such an anti-disclosure protective order will generally not violate the First Amendment free speech rights of the other party (here, P). See *Seattle Times Co. v. Rhinehart* 467 U.S. 20 (1984).

61. **Yes.** Federal Rule 32(a)(3) states, "An adverse party may use for any purpose the deposition of a party or anyone who, when deposed, was the party's officer, director, managing agent, or designee under Rule 30(b)(6) or 31(a)(4)." Here, at the time of deposition, Smith was a person designated under Rule 30(b)(6) (by which the deposing party serves a notice of deposition on the corporation without naming an individual, and the corporation designates the person to answer the questions). Therefore, Smith's answers can be used against D even though Smith was no longer in D's employ at the time of the deposition. This is true even if Smith is available to testify at trial.

62. **No.** A non-party deponent's deposition testimony may be admitted for substantive purposes only under narrowly-defined circumstances, relating to the witness' unavailability to give live testimony. See Federal Rule 32(a)(4).

63. **Yes.** "Any party may use a deposition to **contradict or impeach** the testimony given by the deponent as a witness, or for any other purpose allowed by the Federal Rules of Evidence." Federal Rule 32(a)(2). The use here is for impeachment, so it's covered by 32(a)(2).

64. **(a) Yes.** Federal Rule 33(c) states that "an answer to an interrogatory may be used to the extent allowed by the Federal Rules of Evidence." Since an interrogatory may only be addressed to a party, and since by Federal Rule of Evidence 801(d)(2)(A), a party's statement is not classified as hearsay and is admissible against him for any purpose, an interrogatory answer will always be admissible against the party who made it. Therefore, D's interrogatory answer may be used substantively against him.

(b) Yes. Although a party's interrogatory answer is always admissible against him (whether for substantive or impeachment purposes), that answer is not "binding" on him. That is, the party who has given the interrogatory answer is always free at trial to state that his answer was wrong, and it is up to the jury to decide whether to believe what the defendant says at trial or what he said in the interrogatory. (Contrast this with the response to a Rule 36 request to admit, which *is* binding on the party making the admission.)

VI. PRETRIAL CONFERENCE

A. Pretrial conference generally: Many states, and the federal system, give the judge authority to conduct a ***pretrial conference***. Typically, the judge will use such a conference to simplify or formulate the issues in the case, to keep the case moving, to identify witnesses to be presented at trial, and perhaps to facilitate a ***settlement***. See Federal Rule 16(a) and 16(c).

1. **Scheduling:** Rule 16, although it leaves to the discretion of the judge whether to conduct a pretrial conference, ***requires*** in most cases that the judge issue a ***"scheduling order"*** within 120 days after filing of the complaint. This scheduling order must set a time limit for joinder of additional parties, amendment of the pleadings, filing of motions, and completion of discovery. Rule 16(b).

2. **Pretrial order:** If a pretrial conference is held, the judge must then enter a ***pretrial order*** reciting the actions taken in the conference. Such an order might summarize admissions of fact made by the lawyers, list the witnesses to be presented, narrow the issues to be litigated (perhaps by eliminating "frivolous claims or defenses"), etc. Rule 16(c), (e). This pretrial order is ***binding*** during the rest of the litigation, unless the court modifies it; but if the order is issued following the ***final*** pretrial conference, it may be modified ***"only to prevent manifest injustice."*** Rule 16(e).

3. **Sanctions:** If a party or his lawyer fails to participate in the pretrial conference, fails to do so "in good faith," or fails to comply with the scheduling or pretrial order, the judge may apply whatever ***sanctions*** are "just." Rule 16(f). 16(f) gives the trial judge explicit authority to use the sanctions imposed in Rule 37(b)(2)(A)(ii)-(vii) for failure to comply with discovery orders (striking of claims or defenses, barring of the submission of matters into evidence, dismissal of the action, issuance of a contempt citation, etc.)

   a. **Promoting settlement:** One of the key functions of the pretrial conference is to ***promote settlement***. Some judges, anxious to clear their dockets, use "persuasion" that verges on coercion in trying to bring about a settlement. If the judge goes too far in trying to get the parties to settle, she may find herself reversed on appeal.

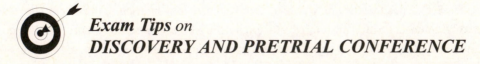

Exam Tips on
DISCOVERY AND PRETRIAL CONFERENCE

The good news about Discovery on exams is that you'll almost always be able to recognize that you are indeed dealing with a discovery issue — you'll be told about a deposition, a request for document production, etc. The bad news is that discovery issues are extremely technical and based on the precise working of the FRCP — you can't rely on general reasoning or on "On the one hand, on the other hand …" analysis. Here are some particular things to check for:[2]

☛ Be alert to ***privileges.*** [206, 220] Remember that information protected by a privilege may not be subjected to discovery. Also, remember that on federal-question issues, federal common law determines what is privileged, but on state-law issues, state law of privilege controls.

☞ Be alert to *work-product immunity* issues. Any time one litigant seeks from the other information that was prepared in anticipation of litigation, either the qualified or the absolute w.p. immunity will apply. So be on the lookout for attempts to get a lawyer's notes or memos, an investigator's report, etc. [207-212]

   ☞ Be sure to distinguish between *qualified* and *absolute* immunity. The latter applies only to *"mental impressions, conclusions, opinions or legal theories."* So documents that are entirely fact-based (e.g., what caused the accident?) will generally get merely qualified protection. If the immunity is qualified, it can be overcome by a showing of "substantial need" and an inability to obtain the equivalent materials without "undue hardship." [207-212]

   ☞ Before you conclude that something is w.p., make sure it was "prepared in anticipation of litigation." Even a document written by or to a lawyer won't be w.p. if it wasn't prepared at least partly in anticipation of litigation (so that, for instance, a document prepared to comply with a statute or government regulation won't be covered, though it might be covered by attorney-client privilege).

   ☞ Remember that documents prepared by a *non-lawyer* (e.g., a private investigator) who is assisting in preparing for litigation will be covered.

   ☞ If the document in question was prepared by an *expert*, special rules governing experts (discussed below), not the work-product immunity rules, apply.

☞ Remember that if a person (whether party or non-party) makes a statement concerning the litigation to a party, the maker of the *statement* may automatically get a copy, *supra* p. 212. This rule overrides any work product immunity.

☞ Remember that names of *"occurrence witnesses"* are automatically discoverable. [212]

☞ Keep in mind that special rules apply to *experts.* [213-215] Professors love to test this area. If a party plans to call an expert at trial, the party must have the expert prepare and sign a *report* containing his opinions and other information; the report is automatically given to the other side.

☞ Look out for any *"automatic"* disclosure duties. Thus parties must now disclose automatically (i.e., *without a specific request* from the other side), early in the case:

   ☞ *Names and addresses* of each person having discoverable information that the disclosing party plans to *use in its substantive case*; and

   ☞ Copies or descriptions of all *documents* and tangible things that the disclosing party plans to *use in its substantive case*. [217-221]

☞ Always keep in mind the distinction between parties and non-parties. For instance, an *interrogatory* can only be addressed to a *party*; disclosure relating to non-parties must occur

---

2. In most of this discussion, we're assuming that your exam question is to be answered by reference to the FRCP.

through *depositions*. [224-234]

☞ Also, beware of the limits on the use of subpoenas for depositions. A subpoena to force a non-party to be deposed must set the deposition for no more than *100 miles* from the deponent's residence or place of business, *supra* p. 245.

☛ Remember that *medical exams* are even more limited: only a party may be forced to undergo an exam, and then only if the party's condition is *in controversy* and the discovering party convinces the court that there is *good cause* for the exam. [234]

☛ Professors like to test the *admissibility* of discovery results at trial. [243-248] Use of *deposition* transcripts is the most-frequently-tested area. Use the two-part test:

☞ First, ask whether the deposition statement would be admissible if the deponent were giving *live testimony*.

☞ Second, make sure the statement falls into one of these *four categories*: (i) it was made by an *adverse party*, or by an officer or director of an adverse corporate party (in which case it is admissible for any purpose); (ii) it is used to *impeach* the deponent's credibility while the deponent is testifying (in which case it doesn't matter whether the deponent is a party); (iii) it *conflicts* with the deponent's trial testimony, if the interests of the deponent and the questioner are adverse (in which case it may even be used for substantive purposes); or (iv) various circumstances make the deponent *unavailable* to testify at trial (e.g., she is dead, or is located 100 or miles from the trial site).

CHAPTER 6

ASCERTAINING APPLICABLE LAW

ChapterScope

This chapter is concerned with how federal and state courts determine what law to follow. For instance, in a diversity case, is the federal judge required to apply the law of the state in which she sits, or is she free to decide on her own, following other federal cases, what the law should be? In a state case involving a subject of federal concern (e.g., U.S. government bonds), to what extent is the state court obligated to apply principles formulated in federal cases?

The bulk of this chapter is concerned with the choice of law in *diversity* cases. The choice of law in federal question cases, and in state cases involving matters of federal interest, is treated at the end of the chapter.

Key concepts in this Chapter are:

- ◼ ***Erie v. Tompkins:*** Under *Erie Railroad v. Tompkins,* in *diversity* cases the federal courts must apply ***state judge-made law*** ("common law") on any ***substantive*** issue where there is no federal statute on point.

    - ❏ **"Forum shopping":** A key reason for this rule is to prevent ***"forum shopping."*** "Forum shopping" occurs where a plaintiff chooses between federal and state court based on which system is more favorable to her substantive case. Applying state substantive law in federal diversity cases thus removes the benefits of forum shopping.

- ◼ **Determining state law:** When the federal court tries to apply state law, the standard is, ***How would the state's highest court determine the issue if the case arose today?***

    - ❏ The federal court must also apply state law governing ***conflict of laws***. In other words, the conflict of laws rules of the state ***where the federal court sits*** must be followed.

- ◼ **Procedure/substance distinction:** *Erie v. Tompkins* says that state common law controls in "substantive" matters. But federal rules and policies generally control on matters that are essentially "procedural." It is thus vital to distinguish between ***procedure and substance.*** As to procedural issues:

    - ❏ **Federal Rules take precedence:** *Erie* is only applicable where there is no controlling federal statute. Since the Federal Rules of Civil Procedure are adopted pursuant to a congressional statute, ***the FRCP take precedence over state policy when applicable***.

    - ❏ **Federal statute on point:** Similarly, where there is a federal procedural ***statute*** (as distinct from a Federal Rule) that is directly on point, that statute will ***control*** over any state law or policy, even though this may promote "forum shopping."

    - ❏ **Case not covered by a Federal Rule or statute:** If the issue at hand is ***not*** covered by anything in the FRCP or in a federal statute, but the issue is nonetheless arguably "procedural," the federal court ***balances*** the state and federal policies against each other. ***Where the state interest in having its policy followed is fairly weak, and the federal interest strong, the court is likely to hold that the federal procedural policy should be followed.***

■ **Federal question cases:** In *federal question* cases, *federal common law, not state common law, usually applies*.

I. NATURE OF PROBLEM

A. Concurrent jurisdiction: The jurisdiction of federal courts is, in most cases, *concurrent* with that of the state courts. That is, a particular controversy that is litigable in federal court may also, in most situations, be brought in state court. Since the decision whether to use state or federal court is left to the litigants, it becomes important to know whether these two courts will apply the same legal principles.

     1. Who chooses: Where jurisdiction of a particular claim is concurrent, the plaintiff makes the initial decision whether to use state or federal court. If he chooses state court, the defendant may sometimes remove the action to federal court.

     2. Choosing favorable forum: If jurisdiction in a particular situation is concurrent, and the state courts would apply rules of law different from those which would be applied by the federal court, the plaintiff, and in situations where removal is possible, the defendant, will have an incentive to *choose the court more favorable to his case.*

         a. Forum-shopping: This process of selecting the more favorable court is generally called *"forum-shopping."* The undesirability of forum-shopping plays a large role in the cases discussed throughout this chapter.

II. THE *ERIE* DECISION AND OTHER FUNDAMENTALS

A. Rules of Decision Act: The Rules of Decision Act, 28 U.S.C. §1652, states that in civil actions, the federal courts must apply the "law of the *several states*, except where the Constitution or treaties of the United States or Acts of Congress otherwise require or provide." This Act has been in effect (with occasional changes of terminology) since 1789; (Wr., 369). Its interpretation, however, has changed drastically with the decision in *Erie Railroad v. Tompkins*, discussed extensively below.

     1. Interpretation: The Rules of Decision Act, together with Article VI of the Constitution, means and *has always been taken to mean* that the federal *Constitution, treaties*, and constitutional *Acts of Congress* always take precedence, where relevant, over all *state* provisions. *This rule applies to proceedings in federal and state courts alike.*

     2. State statutes: The Act has also *always* been taken to mean that in the absence of controlling federal provisions, the federal courts will be bound to follow *state constitutions and statutes.*

     3. Dispute about common law: There has been much dispute, however, about what law the federal courts should apply where there is *no controlling constitutional or statutory provision*, federal *or* state; that is, where the "law" in question is the so-called *"common," or judge-made, law.*

a. ***Swift v. Tyson:***   For many years the definitive Supreme Court opinion on the subject was contained in ***Swift v. Tyson***, 16 Pet. (41 U.S.) 1 (1842). There, the Court held that:

    i.   the federal courts were bound by state court opinions which construed the state's ***constitution or statutes***, or which pertained to ***real estate*** or other essentially ***local***, immobile matters;

    ii.   in all other questions, such as "general commercial law" (which was what was at issue in *Swift*) the federal courts were free to evolve their ***own common law*** irrespective of what state courts were doing. In other words, the phrase "laws of the several states" in the Rules of Decision Act ***did not encompass "general" common law.***

b. ***Swift* in disfavor:**   During the first decades of the last century, the *Swift* doctrine gradually fell into disfavor.

    i.   **Ideal theory rejected:**   The legal philosophy which seemed to justify *Swift* — the view that the common law was an ***ideal entity*** which judges could not "create" but only try to ***"discover"*** — had been rejected by the best legal minds. Wr., 371-72. This "ideal entity" theory formed the foundation of the *Swift v. Tyson* doctrine; it was because judges do not "make" law but only "discover" the true common law that the federal courts should be free to engage in their own search for that truth. When legal writers began to express the view that judges "make" common law in much the same way that legislatures make statutory law, common law came to be seen as a "law of the state" just as statutes are laws of the state. *Swift's* distinction between statutory and common law therefore had less meaning.

    ii.   **Forum-shopping:**   On a more pragmatic plane, the practice of ***"forum-shopping"*** was becoming notorious. "Forum-shopping" was the process by which a party tried to maneuver into a federal court in order to evade a state body of law that he found unfavorable, or into a state court to avoid the application of unfavorable federal common-law principles. The party (often the plaintiff, but sometimes the defendant using his right to remove to federal court) was said to be "shopping" for the most favorable forum in which to try his claim.

        (1) **Discrimination against citizens:**   Forum-shopping often allowed ***non-citizens*** to ***gain an advantage*** against ***citizens of the state where the federal court sat***.

           Example: Assume that in 1935, P, an Ohio resident, wants to bring a tort action against D, a Kansas resident. The relevant events took place in Kansas. Assume that Kansas judge-made tort law would be favorable to D, but that the federal courts in Kansas, if left to their own devices, would apply federal common-law tort principles favorable to P.

           The doctrine of *Swift v. Tyson* would give P the choice between federal or state court in Kansas. Therefore, P can select federal court and profit at D's expense. So even though the litigation is taking place within Kansas, P, the non-Kansan, will get an advantage over D, the Kansan.

4. ***Erie v. Tompkins:***   Then, in perhaps the most famous Civil Procedure decision of all time, the Court rejected the core holding in *Swift v. Tyson*. The decision was ***Erie Railroad v. Tompkins***, 304 U.S. 64 (1938). There, the Court held that when the Rules of Decision Act required federal courts in diversity to apply "laws of the several states," this phrase ***included a state's common law,*** not just its constitutional and statutory provisions. Therefore, a federal court sitting in diversity would normally ***have to apply state common law principles,*** and was not free to apply "federal common law."

   a. **Facts of *Erie*:**   Here are the facts of *Erie*:

      i. **Subject of suit:**   The suit was brought by a Pennsylvania citizen, for damages sustained as a result of being struck while walking along the railroad's right of way in Pennsylvania, by "something … projecting" from a moving railroad car.

      ii. **Suit in New York:**   The railroad was incorporated in New York, so plaintiff Tompkins filed suit in a federal district court there.

      iii. **Pennsylvania common-law rule:**   Pennsylvania common law favored the railroad, holding that it had no duty or liability toward people walking along the right of way (these being deemed "trespassers") unless its negligence was "wanton or willful."

      iv. **General federal common law used by District Court:**   The federal court in New York, following *Swift*, decided to interpret general common law on its own, and found against the railroad.

   b. **Supreme Court's holding in *Erie*:**   The Supreme Court reversed, in an opinion by Brandeis. The opinion said that ***the Rules of Decision Act applies to common law*** as well as to constitutional and statutory provisions. The *Swift* doctrine was held ***unconstitutional***, as it allowed the federal courts to ***make*** law in areas where the power to do so had never been granted to the federal government by the Constitution. The Court made three distinct arguments:

      i. **Historical evidence:**   First, the Court claimed that new evidence had been produced demonstrating that the Rules of Decision Act was ***intended by its authors*** to include state common law.

      ii. **Discrimination:**   Second, the practical results of *Swift v. Tyson* were undesirable: "*Swift v. Tyson* introduced ***grave discrimination by non-citizens against citizens***. It made rights enjoyed under the unwritten 'general law' vary according to whether enforcement was sought in the state or federal court; and the privilege of selecting the court in which the right should be determined was conferred upon the non-citizen." In other words, the *Swift* doctrine gave the non-citizen the ability to ***"forum-shop"*** for the forum most favorable to him.

      Note: The requirements of jurisdiction, venue, and removal, taken together, produce the result that it is generally the ***non-citizen*** of the forum state who chooses whether state or federal court will serve as the forum.

      iii. **Unconstitutional:**   Discrimination against citizens by itself would not have been enough to induce the Court to abandon *Swift*; "but the ***unconstitutionality*** of the course pursued … compels us to do so. … ***There is no federal general common law. Congress has no power to declare substantive rules of common law applicable in a state***, whether they be local in their nature or 'general,' be they commercial law or a part of the law of torts. And no clause in the Constitution purports to confer such a power upon the federal courts."

c. **Concurrence:** Justice Reed, concurring, argued that the case should be decided solely on the grounds that the *Swift* interpretation of the Rules of Decision Act was erroneous, without discussing the constitutionality of the *Swift* view. Reed stated that he was "not at all sure whether, in the absence of federal statutory direction, federal courts would be [constitutionally] compelled to follow state decisions."

d. **Constitutional basis confusing:** Whether Brandeis was saying that the holding in *Erie* was ***required*** by the U.S. ***Constitution*** has never been clear. In any event, the Supreme Court's subsequent interpretations of *Erie* have tended to focus on the ***policy*** considerations expressed in the decision (e.g., the policy against forum-shopping) more than on its constitutional basis. Cf. *Guaranty Trust v. York* (*infra*, p. 261), where the Court stated that "*Erie* expressed a ***policy*** that touches vitally the proper distribution of judicial powers between State and federal courts." Wr., 382-83.

5. **Certain federal common law matters remain:** Just as under *Swift* there was still a binding state common law in matters closely related to state sovereignty, such as real estate, similarly under *Erie* there remains a federal common law in matters ***related to clear federal questions***. See *infra*, p. 274.

> **Example:** An example of federal common law, related to a federal question case, was given in a decision made by the Supreme Court the same day as *Erie*; the apportionment of the waters of an ***interstate stream*** was held to be a matter of federal, not state, common law. Wr., 411-12. It is only ***general*** federal common law that was held not to exist by the *Erie* decision.

B. **Federal procedural law:** The Rules of Decision Act, *Swift*, and *Erie*, all have to do with ***substantive*** law. Federal ***procedure*** has a separate history:

1. **Conformity Act:** Before 1934, under the Conformity Act of 1872, 28 U.S.C. §724, a federal court had to apply the ***procedures of the courts of the state in which it was sitting***, if no federal statute governed. And, typically, there *was* no federal statute that governed most procedural matters.

2. **Enabling Act:** Then, in 1934, the Congress passed an "Enabling Act," 28 U.S.C. §2072, which allowed the Supreme Court to "prescribe, by general rules … the forms of process, writs, pleadings, and motions, and the ***practice and procedure in civil actions*** at law" for the federal courts.

a. **Substantive rights not affected:** The Enabling Act provided that the rules so enacted must not ***"abridge, enlarge, nor modify the substantive rights of any litigant."***

b. **Federal Rules:** Pursuant to the Enabling Act, the Court ***promulgated the Federal Rules of Civil Procedure*** in the same 1938 term in which it handed down the *Erie* decision.

i.   **Still the source of authority:** The Enabling Act remains today the ***statutory authority*** under which the Supreme Court promulgates the FRCP, the Federal Rules of Evidence, and other procedural rules for the federal courts. As we'll see later, this means that the wording and intent of the Enabling Act remain highly important when the federal courts determine the meaning and constitutionality of federal rules of procedure. See, e.g., *Hanna v. Plumer, infra*, p. 263, the main Supreme Court decision on how to determine whether a Federal Rule of Civil Procedure is valid under the Enabling Act.

III. *ERIE* PROBLEMS

A. **Ascertaining state law:**   If the federal courts are to apply the "laws of the various states," they must be able to determine what these "laws" are. Statutes and constitutions are relatively easy to look up, but the determination of "case law" presents special problems. Perhaps no holding on point by the highest state court exists; or perhaps there is a holding which any reasonable observer would regard as obsolete and subject to change as soon as the court in question has a chance to reconsider.

1.   **Intermediate-court decisions:**   If there is no holding by the highest state court, the federal court looking for a state law to apply should apply any available ***intermediate-court*** decision, unless there is persuasive information indicating that the highest court of the state would not follow that intermediate-court decision.

   a.   **Lower-court cases:**   Federal courts are not bound by ***minor, unreported***, state court decisions, although these decisions can be given some weight. Wr. 393.

   b.   **Where no court has spoken:**   If no court in the state has ever considered the issue of law in question, the practice of other states, and the position of the Restatements and other authorities, may be consulted. But the issue is still ***what the state's highest court would do*** if confronted with the question, ***not*** what the federal court thinks is the proper holding. Wr., 396-97.

2.   **State decision obsolete:**   Where there exists an ***old*** determination of state law by the highest state court, it is open to the federal courts to conclude that the state court would decide otherwise if confronted with the present case, and that therefore ***the old ruling is not binding.*** *Bernhardt v. Polygraphic Co. of America*, 350 U.S. 198 (1956). Wr., 393-94.

3.   **Certification:**   In some states, questions of law may be "certified" to the highest court in the state. In such cases, a federal court in doubt as to what the state "law" is can simply ask the state courts. Other states, however, will not allow this; their courts can only decide questions actually in controversy before them. F,K&C, p. 245.

4.   **Change to conform with new state decision:**   Under *Erie*, it is ***never too late*** to change a federal decision in order to conform with a new pronouncement of state law, until the ***final appeal*** has been disposed of. A federal appellate court must rely on a new decision of a state's highest court even if handed down ***after*** the federal district court action was completed. Wr., 394.

a. **De novo review by appellate court:** Also, the federal appellate court must make its **own de novo determination** about what state law would provide — the appellate court should not give deference to the federal trial judge's determination on this issue (deference that would be given, for instance, to factual findings by the trial judge — see *infra*, p. 322). See *Salve Regina College v. Russell*, 499 U.S. 225 (1991).

5. **Substantive rules found in rules on appellate procedure:** "Substantive" state-law rules can be found in strange places, including occasionally a state's law on how and when **appeals courts** should review trial proceedings. For instance, if a state statute requires that an appellate court must follow a certain rule in deciding whether to **overturn the results of a jury trial**, this statute may have so much "substance" embedded in it that the federal courts must follow the rule as closely as they can. And that's true even if this may lead to a lack of uniformity in the federal system.

> **Example:** A New York state statute says that a New York appellate court must reverse a jury award for being "excessive" if the award "deviates materially from what would be reasonable compensation." *Held*, this is a "manifestly substantive" policy that must, therefore, be respected by a New York federal court sittting in diversity. So the federal court must apply the New York standard, and order a new trial if the verdict deviates materially from what would be reasonable compensation. *Gasperini v. Center for Humanities, Inc.*, 518 U.S. 415 (1996).

B. **Conflict of laws:** The Rule of Decision Act does not specify **which** state's law is controlling if, for example, the state in which a federal court is sitting is different from the state where the cause of action arose, and the laws of the two states (*lex fori* and *lex loci delicti* respectively) happen to differ.

1. **Swift rule:** Under *Swift v. Tyson*, a question of this sort was a "matter of general jurisprudence" and it was therefore up to the federal court to decide which state's law to apply, if one or both states had statutes covering the matter. If there were no state statutes, then of course the federal court did not have to refer to state law at all, unless the action were local.

2. **Erie rule:** But under *Erie*, the federal court should ask itself **which state's law would be applied by the courts of the state where the federal court sits**. In other words, the **conflict of laws rules** of the state where the federal court sits must be followed. **Klaxon Co. v. Stentor Electric Mfg. Co.**, 313 U.S. 487 (1941). If this were not the case, the Court said in *Klaxon*, "the accident of diversity would constantly disturb equal administration of justice in coordinate state and federal courts sitting side by side. ..."

C. **Burden of proof:** The federal court must also follow the **rules governing the allocation of the burden of proof** in force in the state where it is sitting. *Palmer v. Hoffman*, 318 U.S. 109 (1943).

> **Example:** Suppose that the hypothetical state of Ames has an unusual policy governing the allocation of the burden of proof in products liability cases. Under this unusual approach, once P has shown some evidence that she was harmed in some way by a product manufactured by D, it is up to D to come forward with evidence sufficient to make it more probable than not that D's product was not "defective." (This is in con-

trast to the rule applied in all other states that the burden of proving a defect is on P.) A federal district court sitting in Ames, in a diversity products liability suit, must follow the Ames rule, and must require D to prove non-defectiveness. This is true even if the federal court believes that the Ames policy is completely illogical and misguided.

D. Procedure/substance problems: The most difficult set of *Erie* problems is that which arises out of the distinction between *"procedural"* and *"substantive"* matters. State common law, under *Erie*, is controlling in "substantive" matters, but "procedure" in federal courts is regulated by the Federal Rules, promulgated by the Supreme Court in the same 1938 term as the *Erie* decision was handed down. Here's a summary of how *Erie* and the Federal Rules interact:

1. **Federal Rules always take precedence:** *Erie* is only applicable where there is *no controlling federal statute.* Since the Federal Rules were adopted pursuant to a valid statute (the Enabling Act), the Rules take precedence over state policy according to the Rules of Decision Act. *Erie doctrine is thus irrelevant to this supremacy of the Federal Rules.* But as we'll see (*infra*, p. 263), it took the Supreme Court until 1965's *Hanna v. Plumer* decision to reach this conclusion.

2. **Rule's validity under Enabling Act:** The only question, in deciding whether a Federal Rule takes precedence over a conflicting state policy, is *whether that Rule is valid under the Enabling Act*. To be valid, a Rule must:

   a. fit into the list in the first sentence of the Enabling Act ("forms of process, writs, pleadings, and motions, and the practice and procedure in civil actions at law") *and*

   b. *not "abridge, enlarge, nor modify* the substantive rights of any litigant." The reference to "substantive rights" was intended to include rights created by both state and federal law.

3. **Little protection of state substantive interests:** In the early years after the 1934 adoption of the Enabling Act, the Supreme Court interpreted the Act in a way that gave state substantive principles *practically no protection* against being altered by the Federal Rules. That was true even though the Enabling Act said that the Rules couldn't *"abridge, enlarge [or] modify"* any litigant's substantive right — the Court simply interpreted the term "substantive right" in an exceptionally *narrow* way.

   a. *Sibbach v. Wilson*: For instance, in *Sibbach v. Wilson*, 312 U.S. 1 (1941), the Supreme Court found that a state policy *forbidding compulsory physical examinations* did *not involve a "substantive right*." The Court therefore held that Federal Rule 35, allowing such examinations to be ordered, was not invalid under the Enabling Act.

4. **Reliance on *Erie* to construe Rules:** Since state-created substantive rights found little protection in *Sibbach's* narrow construction of the "no modification of substantive rights" provision of the Enabling Act, the Court came to rely instead directly on *Erie* doctrine to determine the scope and validity of the Federal Rules. Although no Rule was ever actually found to be unenforceable as against the state common law because of *Erie*, the *scope* of many Rules was limited by a kind of *Erie* analysis. Cf. *Ragan v. Merchants Transfer*, discussed *infra*, p. 261. The use of *Erie* for testing the validity and scope of the Federal Rules

was aided by the Supreme Court's decision in ***Guaranty Trust Co. v. York***, 326 U.S. 99 (1945).

a. *Guaranty Trust*: *Guaranty Trust* involved the applicability of a ***state statute of limitations*** to a right of action arising under state law, but tried in federal court.

    i. Federal courts must follow state statute of limitations: The *Guaranty* opinion, by Frankfurter, first rearticulated the "realist" view of common law as something made by men, not discovered by them. He then held that this realist view, in the context of *Erie*, required that the federal courts obey the state statute of limitations.

    ii. *Erie* applies to equitable rights: Even though the right sought to be enforced in federal court in *Guaranty* was essentially ***equitable***, and the state statute of limitations applied only to actions at ***law***, the state statute still had to be respected. The basis of this holding seems to be that the state action, which would have been one at law, and not at equity, was barred by the statute, and that the federal court must therefore ***not give it longer life.***

    iii. Meaning of "procedure": Even though a statute of limitations might be "procedural" ***in some uses of the word***, for the purposes of *Erie* doctrine it was substantive. "[T]he question is not whether a statute of limitations is deemed a matter of 'procedure' in some sense. The question is whether such a statute concerns merely the manner and the means by which a right to recover, as recognized by the State, is enforced, or whether such statutory limitation is a ***matter of substance*** in the aspect that alone is relevant to our problem, namely ***does it significantly affect the result of a litigation for a federal court to disregard a law of a State that would be controlling in an action upon the same claim by the same parties in a State court?***"

    iv. Outcome-determinative test: A statute of limitations was substantive by the above definition — it affected the result of the litigation in the sense that the plaintiff could not sue ***at all*** in state court; he had at least a chance of winning in the federal court if the statute were ignored. The test of affecting the result of the litigation came to be known as the ***"outcome-determinative"*** test.

5. Outcome-determination and the Federal Rules: In *Guaranty Trust*, no Federal Rule was involved at all. In later cases, however, the outcome-determinative test did come to affect how the Federal Rules were interpreted.

a. *Ragan v. Merchants Transfer*: For instance, in *Ragan v. Merchants Transfer and Warehouse Co.*, 337 U.S. 530 (1949), the issue was not whether a state statute of limitations was applicable at all, but ***whether it was satisfied by the mere filing of the complaint with the court*** within the designated period, or on the other hand, required ***service on the defendant*** within the period. The state law held the latter, but Federal Rule 3 says that "a civil action is commenced by filing a complaint with the Court." The Supreme Court held that the ***state rule was controlling*** and had to be followed.

b. *Ragan* still valid law: Much later, *Ragan v. Merchants Transfer* was expressly held ***still to be valid law***, in *Walker v. Armco Steel Corp.*, 446 U.S. 740 (1980). It remains the case today that in a diversity action, the federal court must follow state law (not Federal Rule 3) in determining when an action is "commenced" for the purpose of satisfying the **statute of limitations.**

    i.   **Rationale:** The Court in *Walker* reasoned that *Hanna v. Plumer* (see *infra*, p. 263) does not apply to the "when is the action commenced?" question, because Federal Rule 3 **simply does not speak to the issue** of when a state statute of limitations is tolled. Rather, the Court said, Rule 3's statement that a civil action is commenced by the filing of the complaint is merely designed to give a starting point for the **measurement** of various time periods in the federal suit. Since there is **no conflict** between Rule 3 and the state law on tolling, the Court stated, a conventional *Erie* analysis must be done. As *Ragan* had concluded, **state law** should clearly be chosen on this question.[1]

6. ***Byrd v. Blue Ridge:*** But eventually, in ***Byrd v. Blue Ridge Rural Electric Coop., Inc.***, 356 U.S. 525 (1958), the Court began to **retreat from its complete acceptance of the "outcome-determinative" test.**

    a.   **Facts:** Plaintiff sued for negligence in a federal court in South Carolina. The defense argued that the plaintiff was a "statutory employee" of the defendant, rather than an independent contractor, and that therefore workmen's compensation benefits were his sole remedy.

    b.   **Decision by judge:** Under a South Carolina decision, the question whether plaintiff was a "statutory employee," rather than an independent contractor, was to be determined by the **judge**, not the **jury.**

    c.   **Holding:** The Supreme Court held that the **federal policy** of having factual matters decided by a jury, not the state approach of having the judge decide the issue, must be followed. The Court reasoned as follows:

        i.   **Outcome-determinative:** On one hand, the state policy **might** be outcome-determinative, and therefore **"in the absence of other considerations,"** the federal courts should follow it.

        ii.   **Federal policy:** On the other hand, the **federal policy** requiring jury trial of such "factual" issues was a very strong one and could **override the state policy**. "It cannot be gainsaid that there is a strong federal policy against allowing state rules to disrupt the judge-jury relationship in the federal courts."

        iii.   **Weak state interest:** Also, the **state interest** in having the trial judge decide the question of employee status did not seem to be a strong one; it was **"not a rule intended to be bound up with the definition of the rights and obligations of the parties."**

---

1. A 2010 case shows that it's still true that where there is **no conflict** between the relevant federal rule and a state substantive policy, a conventional *Erie* analysis must be done. See *Shady Grove Orthopedic v. Allstate*, discussed *infra*, p. 265. In *Shady Grove* itself, the Court split 5-4 on the issue of whether there *was* in fact a conflict between the federal rule in question and the state policy. But all members of the Court seem to have agreed that *if* there had been no conflict (in other words, if the federal rule hadn't been addressed to the same point as the state policy), then *Erie* analysis, not *Hanna*-type "Is the Rule valid?" analysis, would have been needed.

iv. **Probability of outcome-determination:**   In any case, the decision between judge- and jury-adjudication was *less likely* to "determine" the outcome of the suit than would be a choice, say, between an already expired state statute of limitations and no statute of limitations at all. The decision here *might* influence the outcome, but it was less likely to make a decisive difference than in most of the other cases where the Court had applied outcome-determination.

d. **Effect of *Byrd*:**   The overall importance of *Byrd* is that it showed that state decisions that are basically procedural (though they may, of course, *affect* substantive rights) are *not necessarily controlling even if they are outcome-determinative*. The federal interest in the proper maintenance of the federal judiciary has to be given some respect, and controls if the federal policy is significantly stronger than the state policy. The test seems to be one of rough "*balancing*."

e. ***Forum non conveniens:***   The *Byrd* rationale means that federal policies on when a case should be dismissed for *forum non conveniens* should be followed, rather than state policies, even though the choice of policies may be outcome determinative.

7. ***Hanna v. Plumer:* *Hanna v. Plumer*, 380 U.S. 460 (1965), *removed the Federal Rules of Civil Procedure entirely from the scope of the Erie decision,* as to any issue on which the Rule is found to be on point.**

a. **Facts:**   In *Hanna*, Plaintiff filed a diversity suit in federal court in Massachusetts, serving process on the wife of the defendant-executor, according to Rule 4(d)(1) (now 4(e)(2)), by leaving copies of the summons and complaint with her at his dwelling-place. Defendant claimed that this service conflicted with a Massachusetts statute making special provision for service upon the executor of an estate, and that the court must therefore find that service was improper because it would have been improper in a Massachusetts suit on the same claim.

b. **Holding:**   But the Supreme Court disagreed with the defendant, and found that Rule 4(d)(1) was to be given effect. The Court held that Rule 4(d)(1) was "in harmony with the Enabling Act," and that Rules thus valid are *not overridden by state policies or laws. Erie* doctrine is *not controlling,* the Court said, when a valid Federal Rule that *speaks to the issue in question* is in conflict with state common-law policy.

i. **Rationale:**   To hold otherwise, the Court argued, would be to render the Federal Rules *unworkable.* "Thus, though a court, in measuring a Federal Rule against the standards contained in the Enabling Act and the Constitution, need not wholly blind itself to the degree to which the Rule makes the character and result of the federal litigation stray from the course it would follow in state courts [the Court then cited *Sibbach*], it cannot be forgotten that *the Erie rule*, and the [outcome-determinative test] suggested in [*Guarantee Trust v.*] *York*, were created to *serve another purpose altogether.* To hold that a Federal Rule of Civil Procedure must *cease to function* whenever it *alters the mode of enforcing state-created rights* would be to *disembowel* either the Constitution's grant of power over federal procedure or Congress' attempt to exercise that power in the Enabling Act."

c. **Rejection of outcome-determination:**   The Court further claimed that *even in the absence of a Federal Rule* applicable to the question before it, state policy on service to executors might *still* not control. " 'Outcome-determination' analysis was never intended to serve as a talisman. ... ***The 'outcome-determination' test ... cannot be read without reference to the twin aims of the Erie rule: discouragement of forum-shopping and avoidance of inequitable administration of the laws.***"

i.   No forum-shopping in *Hanna*:   In *Hanna*, the Court noted, it was almost inconceivable that plaintiff chose the federal, rather than state, forum, merely because the manner of service of process was slightly different. Thus, no forum-shopping considerations were really involved.

ii.   No discrimination: Neither was discrimination against residents really at issue: "It is difficult to argue that permitting service of defendant's wife to take the place of in-hand service of defendant himself alters the mode of enforcement of state-created rights in a fashion sufficiently 'substantial' to raise the sort of equal protection problems to which the *Erie* opinion alluded."

d.   Harlan's concurrence: Justice Harlan, in a very well-known concurrence, proposed a new test for determining when state law should be deferred to:

i.   Stricter test of Federal Rule: A Federal Rule should not be automatically deferred to, Harlan argued. The majority had held that a Rule was constitutionally valid when it "regulate[d] matters which though falling within the uncertain area between substance and procedure, are rationally capable of classification as either." Harlan answered that "[s]o long as a reasonable man could characterize any duly adopted federal rule as 'procedural,' the Court, unless I misapprehend what it said, would have it apply ***no matter how seriously it frustrated a State's substantive regulation of the primary conduct and affairs of its citizens***. ... Whereas the unadulterated outcome and forum-shopping tests may err too far toward honoring state rules, I submit that the Court's 'arguably procedural, ergo constitutional' test moves too fast and far in the other direction."

ii.   Primary decision test: Harlan's test would thus "inquire ... if the choice of rule would substantially affect those ***primary decisions respecting human conduct*** which our constitutional system leaves to state regulation." If it would, state law must be applied even in the face of a Federal Rule to the contrary. Harlan cited *Ragan* and the present case as examples where the state rule did ***not*** substantially affect primary decisions, but rather affected only behavior ***after the cause of action arose***. He cited a different case, however, as an example of a state rule that *did* in fact regulate primary human conduct: a statute requiring plaintiffs in stockholder derivative suits to ***post a bond*** "was meant to inhibit small stockholders from instituting 'strike suits,' and thus it was designed and could be expected to have a substantial impact on ***private primary activity***."

e.   Validity of rule: *Hanna v. Plumer* does not by itself immunize a Federal Rule against being found to be invalid under the Rules Enabling Act. It remains today the case that a Federal Rule must not "abridge, enlarge or modify any substantive right[.]" But the standard for judging the validity of a Rule is ***far more forgiving*** than the standard for determining whether a federal policy not embodied in a Rule abridges a state-created substantive right. "Rules which ***incidentally*** affect litigants' substantive rights do not violate this provision if ***reasonably necessary*** to maintain the ***integrity of that system*** of rules." *Burlington Northern Railroad Co. v. Woods*, 467 U.S. 1230 (1987). Furthermore, because any proposed Rule is scrutinized and approved by an Advisory Committee, a federal Judicial Conference, and the Supreme Court, plus subjected to a possible Congressional veto, any Rule that passes through this process is entitled to ***"presumptive validity."*** *Id.*

    i.   **No Federal Rule found invalid:** In fact, ***no Federal Rule has ever been found invalid under the Rules Enabling Act.*** Cf. Wr., 430.

    ii. **Narrow construction to avoid Enabling Act violation:** Indeed, the Supreme Court has sometimes gone out of its way to ***interpret federal rules narrowly***, so that they will ***not*** be found to abridge any litigant's substantive rights and thus not be invalid under the Rules Enabling Act.

8. **Conflict must exist:** *Hanna v. Plumer* applies — and thus both allows and requires the federal court to disregard a state law and follow a Federal Rule — only if there is a ***conflict*** between the two.

    a. **No conflict found:** It will sometimes be the case that a Federal Rule and a state rule cover similar ground but are found ***not*** to be in conflict. That is, the court may decide that the federal rule is addressed to a ***different issue*** than the state provision. In that "no real conflict" scenario, the court must ***conduct a conventional Erie/Byrd analysis***, balancing the state and federal interests against each other.

    b. **Disagreement about existence of conflict:** Federal judges sitting in diversity will not always ***agree*** about whether a given Federal Rule ***conflicts*** with a given state rule or policy (in which case the Federal Rule applies and displaces the state rule, assuming as will virtually always be the case that the Federal Rule is valid under the Enabling Act) or ***doesn't conflict*** (in which case the court must normally apply the state rule if that rule strongly reflects the state's substantive policies). For instance, in an important 2010 case, ***Shady Grove Orthopedic Assoc. v. Allstate Ins. Co.***, 130 S.Ct. 1431 (2010), the Court split 5-4 on whether a conflict existed, with five Justices believing that there was indeed a conflict, so that the state policy must be disregarded.

        i. **Fragmented opinion:** *Shady Grove* was a badly fragmented holding, with different 5-4 majorities standing for different propositions, as we'll see below. The case is worth analyzing in detail even though doing that will take a good deal of time and space.

        ii. **The possible conflict:** The case involved a possible conflict between FRCP 23's requirements for maintaining a ***class action*** (see *infra*, p. 356) and a New York statute that prohibited any suit to ***recover a penalty or statutory damages*** from proceeding as a class action, except in certain narrow circumstances.

           (1) FRCP 23: Federal 23(a) sets out four requirements (e.g., numerosity; see *infra*, p. 357) that every federal-court class action must meet. FRCP 23(b) then says that a class action "may be maintained" if all the requirements of 23(a) are met, as long as the suit falls into one of three categories specified in 23(b) (categories that don't matter for our purposes here). Rule 23 applies to class actions based solely on diversity, as well as to those based on a federal question.

(2) NY §901(b): The New York statute was §901 of the state's "Civil Practice Law and Rules" (CPLR), the basic New York statute governing the rules for litigation. Section 901(a) closely echoes FRCP 23(a)'s requirements for class actions. But the legislature added §901(b), which has no counterpart in federal law. 901(b) says that if a suit is brought "to recover a *penalty* or a *minimum measure of recovery*," the suit *"may not be maintained as a class action,"* unless a statute expressly allows a class action suit to be brought to recover the penalty or minimum damages.[2]

iii. **Facts:** Here's how the suit arose: Shady Grove Orthopedics provided medical care to Sonia Galvez after she had a car accident. In return, Galvez assigned her rights to insurance benefits under a policy she had with D (Allstate). A special New York statute requires that insurance companies pay such claims (or deny them) within 30 days, and also provides for *statutory interest* at 2% per month on any claim that is paid late. Shady Grove filed a claim, which D paid; but D's payment was made later than the 30-day limit, and without the statutory interest.

(1) Class action in diversity: Shady Grove brought a diversity-only class action suit in New York federal court, seeking the unpaid interest. The overdue interest on Shady Grove's individual claim came to only about $500, far below the $75,000 amount in controversy requirement for individual diversity actions (see *supra*, p. 138). There were no federal question claims in the case. Therefore, the only way Shady Grove could satisfy the amount in controversy, and thus maintain its suit, was if the suit could go forward as a class action.[3] So Shady Grove sought relief not just for itself but on behalf of a class defined as everyone to whom D owed interest under the 2%-per-month New York provision.

(2) Suit dismissed: The lower federal courts held that Shady Grove's claim must be dismissed for lack of subject matter jurisdiction. These courts believed that there was no conflict between FRCP 23 and the New York statute, because they were designed to deal with different issues. Therefore, these courts held that the New York "no class action suits for penalties" rule could and should be applied, depriving the federal courts of the right to hear the case as a class action.

iv. **Reversed by U.S. Supreme Court:** But the Supreme Court *reversed*, allowing Shady Grove's class action suit to go forward. Five members of the court believed

---

2. The statute doesn't expressly limit itself to suits brought in New York State; it says simply that a class-action suit for a penalty or statutory damages "shall not be maintained." It's not clear whether the legislators were intentionally trying to apply the provision to federal-court actions based on state law, or were instead simply not focusing on how the statute would apply anywhere but in the New York State courts.

3. The usual rule against aggregating the claims of multiple plaintiffs to meet the amount in controversy requirement is relaxed in diversity class actions, as long as the claims put together are for $5 million or more. See 28 U.S.C. §1332(d)(2), part of the Class Action Fairness Act, discussed *supra*, p. 140 and *infra*, p. 370.

that there *was indeed a conflict* between Federal Rule 23 and the New York statute. Consequently, as long as Rule 23 did not violate the Enabling Act, that Rule would *displace state law* and would thus permit the suit to go forward as a diversity class action. And these five justices believed that *Rule 23 was valid* under the Enabling Act.

(1) Dissent: The four other members of the Court, in *dissent*, believed that (1) there was *no actual conflict* between Federal Rule 23 and the New York statute; and (2) Rule 23 should be interpreted to *honor* the New York "no class actions for penalties" rule, because the New York rule, though contained in a procedural statute, *embodied a substantive policy entitled to deference* under *Erie*.

v. **Fragmentation:** Actually, the opinions in *Shady Grove* were more *fragmented* than the above summary suggests. There were *three* opinions:

[1] Five members of Court, in an opinion by Justice Scalia, agreed that there *was a conflict* between Federal Rule 23 and the New York provision, and that Rule 23 allowed the class action to go forward even though it could not have been brought in the New York courts.

[2] But one of those five Justices, Stevens, although he concurred in the above result, did not agree with all of Scalia's reasoning. Stevens agreed with the dissenters on an important issue, about *what test* should be used to determine the existence of a conflict.

[3] The four remaining members, in a dissent by Justice Ginsburg, agreed with the lower courts that (1) there was *no conflict* between the federal rule and the New York provision, and (2) the suit should therefore not be permitted to go forward as a federal class action because this would *violate a state substantive policy*. Justice Stevens did not agree with either of these two propositions, but he did agree with the dissenters (and disagreed with the four justices led by Scalia) on the *test* that should be used for determining whether there is a conflict between the federal rule and a state rule.

So neither the four-Justice bloc led by Scalia nor the four-Justice bloc led by Ginsburg had a complete victory — each enlisted Justice Stevens as a fifth vote for one or more important propositions. There was an unusual alignment, which featured Roberts and Scalia opposing Alito, and Sotomayor opposing Ginsburg.

vi. **Scalia's opinion:** Justice Scalia concluded that Rule 23 *directly conflicted* with the New York no-penalties-in-class-actions statute, and therefore displaced the New York statute. On this point, he spoke for five Justices.

(1) Summary of decision-tree: Scalia explained that under the Court's "framework" for assessing conflicts between federal rules and state laws, "We must first determine whether Rule 23 *answers the question* in dispute. ... *If it does it governs* — New York's law notwithstanding — unless it *exceeds statutory authorization*[.] ... *We do not wade into Erie's murky waters unless the federal rule is inapplicable or invalid*" (citing *Hanna v. Plumer*).

(2) Rule 23 applies: Scalia then concluded that on the key issue of whether the plaintiffs could maintain a federal class action on these facts, FRCP 23 ***provided an answer***. The rules said that a class action ***"may be maintained"*** if the requirements of 23(a) (numerosity, etc.) are satisfied, and if the case fits into one of the three categories described in 23(b). Therefore, he said, Rule 23 "creates a ***categorical rule*** entitling a plaintiff whose suit meets the specified criteria to pursue his claim as a class action." Since the New York statute said that the case couldn't go forward as a class action, and Rule 23 said that it could, the two were in ***direct conflict***, and the state rule prohibiting a class action on these facts could not be given effect in the federal court.

(3) "Purpose" ignored: Scalia acknowledged that the New York Legislature's ***purpose*** in enacting §901(b) was to limit monetary remedies awarded in class-action proceedings, a substantive purpose. But to Scalia, the state's ***purpose*** (and the fact that that purpose was ***substantive***) ***were irrelevant*** — since the ***"clear text"*** of the New York statute was to prevent a plaintiff from even starting a class action seeking penalties, and since FRCP 23 allowed such a class action, the two were in conflict, and the Federal Rule had to prevail.

(4) The state-by-state variation problem: Scalia argued that if a state's legislative purpose mattered in determining whether state and federal rules conflicted, then "one State statute could ***survive pre-emption*** (and accordingly affect the procedures in federal court) while another State's identical law would ***not***, merely because its authors had ***different aspirations***." Furthermore, he said, district judges would often be required to conduct complex ***investigations*** into often-unclear state legislative history.

(5) Validity of Rule 23: Given that FRCP 23 and the New York statute were in direct conflict, the only way the policy embodied in the state statute could be given effect by the federal court was if Rule 23 violated the Enabling Act's requirement that a federal rule shall not "abridge, enlarge or modify any substantive right." For Scalia (joined on this point only by ***three*** other Justices), *Sibbach v. Wilson* (*supra*, p. 260) had long-since established ***how to answer*** the question of whether a Rule violated the Enabling Act: "the validity of a federal rule depends ***entirely*** upon ***whether it regulates procedure*** ... if it does, it is authorized by [the Enabling Act] and is ***valid in all jurisdictions***, with respect to all claims, ***regardless of its incidental effect on state-created rights***." He conceded that *Sibbach* may have been a clumsy interpretation of the Enabling Act. But, he said, *stare decisis* dictated that *Sibbach* not be overruled without a "special justification," and that justification hadn't adequately been shown in this case.

(6) Forum-shopping: Finally, Scalia, joined by the same three Justices, acknowledged that keeping the federal court door open to diversity class actions that could not have been brought in state court would inevitably produce ***forum shopping***. But, he said, "[A] ***federal rule governing procedure*** is ***valid*** whether or not it ***alters the outcome of the case in a way that induces forum shopping.***"

vii. Stevens' concurrence: Justice Stevens concurred in part with Justice Scalia, and concurred with the result: that Federal Rule 23 was in *direct conflict* with the New York rule here, and must therefore displace the New York rule as long as Rule 23 was valid under the Enabling Act. And he agreed with Scalia that Rule 23 — even when interpreted in a way that would knock out the New York rule — was *indeed valid* under the Enabling Act. So on these overall points, Stevens supplied the necessary fifth vote.

    (1) Disagreement with Scalia: But Stevens disagreed with Scalia about *how to determine* whether a given Federal Rule violates the Enabling Act when the Rule is applied in the context of a particular state substantive provision. As noted, Scalia believed that as long as the Federal Rule "regulates procedure," that was the *end of the matter* — the Rule was valid, no matter how much it interfered with some state substantive right. But Stevens thought that this reading ignored the Enabling Act's command that no federal rule "abridge, enlarge or modify *any* substantive right." Even if a given federal rule "regulates procedure," if the rule "displaces a state rule that is 'procedural' in the ordinary sense of the term ... but [that is] sufficiently *interwoven* with the scope of a *substantive right or remed*y, there *would be an Enabling Act problem*, and the federal rule would have to give way." So on this point, Stevens agreed with Ginsburg's dissent (which we'll discuss below), not Scalia's 4-Justice opinion.

    (2) Disagreement with Ginsburg: But Stevens disagreed with Ginsburg's belief that the present case *amounted* to such a conflict between a federal rule and a state's substantive right or remedy. For him, the New York statute was a classically procedural rule, comparable to a state rule setting filing fees or deadlines for submitting briefs — it was *not deeply bound up with any substantive right* that the Enabling Act protected from abridgment.

viii. Ginsburg's dissent: Justice Ginsburg (joined by Kennedy, Breyer, and Alito) dissented not only on the result, but on the threshold issue of whether this was a case that should be governed by *Erie* principles or instead the validity of the federal rule under the Enabling Act. Ginsburg believed that (1) Rule 23 and the New York rule were *directed at different issues*, and were therefore *not in conflict*; (2) New York intended to *pursue important substantive policies* in its rule; and (3) this was therefore a classic *Erie*-type issue, in which the federal rule must be applied in a way that *would allow the state substantive policy to prevail.* That meant that the federal courts shouldn't hear the case as a class action, since the state courts wouldn't hear it as one.

ix. Significance of *Shady Grove*: *Shady Grove* is a badly fragmented decision, but here's what it seems to establish:

    (1) FRCP 23 is valid, and controls: At the narrowest level, *Shady Grove* establishes that Federal Rule 23 is *valid* under the Rules Enabling Act, and is the *exclusive determinant* of when a federal diversity class action may be brought. If an action satisfies all the requirements of Rule 23, any state procedural provision that says that the particular claim could *not* be brought in state court (or, for that matter, in federal court) *may not be honored* by the federal court. And that's true even though the state provision is ***extremely outcome determinative***, as was the state rule in *Shady Grove*, which said that no class action for statutory damages could be brought. (The Scalia bloc plus Stevens represented five votes for everything stated in this paragraph.)

(2) Effect of conflict: More generally, *Shady Grove* confirms that if a Federal Rule of Civil Procedure and a state law deal with the ***same issue*** in ***conflicting ways***, then the federal rule will ***apply*** (and ***displace*** the state provision) as long as the federal rule is ***valid under the Enabling Act.*** And that's true even though applying the federal rule will ***promote a large degree of forum-shopping***. This central holding of *Hanna v. Plumer* remains unchanged by *Shady Grove*, and, indeed, no member of the *Shady Grove* Court believed otherwise. (But *Shady Grove* itself illustrates that the Court may be badly split about *whether* a conflict *really exists* on a particular set of facts.)

(3) Still no FRCP found to violate Enabling Act: Once it's clear that there is a conflict between the federal and state rule, the validity of the federal rule under the Enabling Act must be checked. But it remains the case, after *Shady Grove*, that ***no federal rule has ever been held to violate the Enabling Act.***

(4) Judging validity under Enabling Act: A majority of the Court (the four dissenters plus Stevens) believes that the fact that a federal rule ***"regulates procedure"*** does ***not automatically mean that the rule governing is valid under the Enabling Act.*** The Enabling Act forbids a federal rule from modifying or abridging a state substantive right. And this Enabling Act prohibition means that even a federal rule that regulates procedure, if it ***squarely conflicts*** with a state substantive rule, must ***not be applied in a way that displaces the state rule.*** (But no member of the Court seemed to believe that Rule 23 violates the Enabling Act; they just disagreed about how to ***reach the conclusion*** that it didn't violate it.)

(5) Consulting state purpose: Proposition [4] above means that for a majority (the dissenters plus Stevens), to determine whether a federal procedural rule is valid under the Enabling Act, looking at state legislative ***purpose*** in enacting even an apparently-procedural rule will sometimes be ***necessary***. For if the state, in enacting a basically procedural rule, was ***intending to set the contours of a substantive right***, and had a significant interest in doing so, then for these five Justices the federal rule may have to be ***interpreted in such a way that does not displace the state rule.*** (But only the four dissenters believed that New York was clearly pursuing a substantive policy; Stevens thought that New York was making a "classically procedural calibration," so that the federal rule could be applied in a way that would displace state law without thereby violating the Enabling Act.)

x. Analysis tip: Even after *Shady Grove*, if you have to analyze a federal procedural rule that directly ***conflicts with a state rule*** that is essentially ***"procedural,"*** you should conclude that the federal rule is ***valid*** and must be applied. And that's true even though applying the federal rule will displace state law in an outcome-determinative way, unless applying the federal rule clearly "modifies or abridges" a state substantive right, something that will virtually *never* be found to occur.

9. **Conflict between congressional statute and state policy:** So far, we have assumed that the federal-state conflict is either between a federal policy and a state statute or policy (the standard *Erie* situation), or between one of the Federal Rules and a state statute or policy (the *Hanna v. Plumer* situation). But there is at least one other interesting type of federal-state conflict: that between a *federal statute* directly enacted by Congress, and a state policy or statute. If a valid congressionally-enacted procedural statute outside of the Federal Rules conflicts with a state law or policy, the federal statute will control *even though this may promote forum shopping.* Cf. *Stewart Organization, Inc. v. Ricoh Corp.*, 487 U.S. 22 (1988).

Quiz Yourself on
ERIE *PROBLEMS*

65. P has brought a negligence action against D (based on diversity) in federal district court for the District of Iowa. P's complaint alleges that P was a social guest in D's house, that P fell when a wooden step on a stairway inside the house broke, and that had D used ordinary reasonable care in keeping his house safe, he would have discovered the danger and avoided it. (The complaint does not claim that D knew of the defect, merely that a reasonable person in D's position would have learned of the defect and fixed it.) A five-year-old decision of the Iowa Supreme Court holds that a social guest is only a "licensee," not an "invitee," and that a property owner owes a licensee no duty of inspection. A number of courts in other states have in the last few years abolished the licensee/invitee distinction, and have held that a property owner owes a duty of reasonable inspection to a licensee as well as an invitee. The federal district judge in whose court P's action is pending believes that these newer decisions represent the much better view. However, there is no evidence that the Iowa Supreme Court would change its attitude on this issue, since the court has on more recent occasions rejected other chances to expand tort liability. Should the federal judge impose upon D the duty of making reasonable inspection of his premises? _____

66. Same basic fact pattern as the prior question. Now, however, assume that the only Iowa case on the issue of whether a property owner owes a duty of inspection to a licensee is a 50-year-old decision by the Iowa Supreme Court, in which the court refused to impose any such duty of inspection. Since the courts of most states that have considered the matter within the past five years have rejected the traditional rule and imposed a duty of inspection on behalf of a licensee, the federal judge believes that the Iowa Supreme Court would probably follow this modern trend if it heard the case today. Should the federal court impose a duty of inspection on D? _____

67. P has sued D in federal district court for the Central District of California. The suit is based on diversity (since P is a citizen of California and D is a citizen of Arizona). P claims that D negligently drove an automobile, thus injuring P in an accident. The accident took place in Arizona. Under California state court decisions, any suit brought in the California state courts arising out of an auto accident is to be decided under California law if the plaintiff is a California resident, even if the accident took place in another state. This California approach is a minority and old-fashioned one; nearly every other state applies the rule of "lex locus delicti," whereby in auto accident cases the law of the state where the accident took place is the law that is used. The federal judge hearing the P-D suit believes that the majority "lex locus

delicti" approach is the much sounder one. In the P-D suit the issue arises whether California state substantive law (under which contributory negligence is not a defense) or Arizona law (under which contributory negligence is still a defense) should be applied. The federal judge hearing the case believes that the California law (no contributory negligence defense) is the better approach. Which state's substantive law of negligence, California's or Arizona's, should be applied by the federal judge? _____

68. The state of Acme, in order to reduce health insurance costs, enacted a statute capping damages in any action for medical malpractice brought in the Acme state courts at $1 MM of compensatory damages, and zero punitive damages. P, a citizen of Beta, had a knee replacement done by D, a surgeon living in Acme; the operation was done in Acme. Due to D's gross negligence during the operation, the replacement failed and had to be replaced. P has now brought a diversity malpractice suit against D in Acme federal district court, seeking $1 MM of compensatory damages and $500,000 of punitive damages. Assume that federal courts, when they are free to make their own decision, typically award punitive damages in tort actions if the court believes that the defendant behaved with gross negligence and that the award of punitive damages will have a useful deterrent effect. If the federal court, after trial, believes that these conditions have been satisfied, may the court award P $100,000 in punitive damages? _____

69. P has sued D in diversity in federal court for the Northern District of Georgia. P seeks to assert against D a tort claim relating to an accident, as well as a breach of contract claim arising from a prior business relationship between P and D, having nothing to do with the accident. Under a Georgia statute, a tort claim may not be joined with a contract claim against the same defendant in state court, if the two claims relate to different transactions. However, joinder of unrelated contract and tort claims against a single defendant is expressly allowed by FRCP 18(a). In the federal action, may P join his contract and tort claims against D in a single action? _____

70. P and D signed a contract whereby P was to perform personal services for D. Almost immediately, it became clear to P that D was not living up to his part of the bargain, with respect to the duties that P was to be given. However, P tried to work things out with D for a long time (reasonable conduct by P in the circumstances), and therefore took no legal action for more than two years. He then brought a diversity action against D in federal district court for the District of Kansas, the state in which the contract was signed and was being performed. Under Kansas law, any action (whether legal or equitable) related to performance of a contract must be brought within two years of the performance or non-performance complained of. P does not seek damages in his federal suit; instead, he seeks to have the contract declared rescinded on account of D's nonperformance.

The federal courts have traditionally regarded actions to rescind a contract as being primarily equitable, and they apply the equitable doctrine of laches rather than any strict statute of limitations doctrine when the action is primarily equitable. Thus under general federal principles, P's suit will not be time-barred so long as P has acted within a "reasonable" period of time considering the circumstances. Should the federal court for the District of Kansas regard P's action as time-barred? _____

71. P has brought a diversity suit against D in federal district court for Montana; the suit alleges negligence. In both the Montana state trial courts and the federal district court of Montana, the applicable rules provide for a six-person jury. By Montana statute, the verdict in a civil case needs to be by only a 5/6's majority. The state rule allowing a 5/6's majority was adopted to reduce the number of hung juries and re-trials, thus reducing court congestion. By a long-standing federal policy a federal civil jury must reach a unanimous verdict. (There is no federal statute or Rule of Civil Procedure which directly requires unanimity.) Should the federal district judge recognize a verdict on which five out of the six jurors agree?

_____

Answers

65. No. This is a classic *Erie* situation. There is neither a state nor a federal statute on the matter. State common law creates the right being sued upon. Therefore, the federal court in diversity ***must apply the common law (judge-made law) of the state where the federal court sits***, and may not apply the federal judge's own opinion of what a desirable rule would be. Since all the evidence is that the Iowa Supreme Court would not impose any duty of inspection on D here, the federal court may not impose any such duty either.

66. Yes. Again, the only issue is what the highest court of the state where the federal court sits would do if it heard the issue *today*. Since the facts indicate that the Iowa Supreme Court would probably overturn its 50-year-old ruling today, the federal court is not bound by that old ruling, and is instead required to behave as it thinks the Iowa court would behave today, by imposing the duty on D.

67. California's. In deciding an *Erie* case, the federal judge must apply the law of the state where the federal court sits. This principle includes the forum state's ***conflict-of-laws principles*** as well as its substantive principles. Therefore, the federal judge must apply California's conflicts rules. Since California's conflicts rules would make California rather than Arizona law applicable, the court must follow California's substantive rules as well. One way to remember this is to apply the general principle that the federal court must ***reach the same underlying decision*** as the court of the state where the federal judge sits. (Observe that if California would apply Arizona law, then the task for the federal judge is not to apply what it thinks Arizona's state courts would decide, but rather, to apply what it thinks California's courts would think that Arizona's laws are!) See *Klaxon Co. v. Stentor Electric Mfg. Co.*, 313 U.S. 487 (1941).

68. No. There is no federal rule or statute on point, and the case is a diversity suit based solely on state law. Therefore, conventional *Erie* analysis applies: if the state interest is essentially substantive, then the federal court must apply state law, unless there are very strong federal procedural interests in not doing so. Here, although the state statute has a small procedural aspect (it refers to what should happen in litigation in the Acme courts), the state is pursuing a heavily-substantive interest: Acme is mainly trying to affect how much money malpractice plaintiffs can recover. Furthermore, the choice of federal or state law is highly outcome-determinative; P has a shot at large punitive damages (and uncapped compensatory damages) if federal common law principles apply, but no shot at punitive damages (and a $1 MM compensatory cap) if state law applies. Because of this highly outcome-determinative aspect of the choice, out-of-state patients in P's situation will have a strong incentive to forum-shop (by suing in diversity) if federal common law is to be applied. On the other side of the balance, there is no strong federal procedural interest (such as an interest in national uniformity of procedures) that will be negatively affected by following state law. So this is an easy case: the heavily substantive, and heavily outcome-determinative, state law imposing damage caps must be applied. See, e.g., *Gasperini v. Center for Humanities*, 518 U.S. 415 (1996) (*supra* p. 259): "A statutory cap on damages would supply substantive law for *Erie* purposes."

69. Yes. This is an instance in which the federal policy is embodied in a Federal Rule of Civil Procedure that is exactly on point, and that is in direct conflict with the relevant state rule. In situations involving such a direct conflict, *Erie* doctrine (and the avoidance of forum shopping) does not apply at all. Instead, the sole question is ***whether the federal rule is a valid one***. See *Hanna v. Plumer*, 380 U.S. 460 (1965) and *Shady Grove Orthopedic Assoc. v. Allstate Ins. Co.*, 130 S.Ct. 1431 (2010). Since no Federal Rule of Civil Procedure has ever been found invalid under the Rules Enabling Act (i.e., no rule has ever been found to violate the Enabling Act's ban on the abridgement or enlargement of a litigant's substantive rights), Rule 18(a)'s rule of permissive joinder is certainly valid. Therefore, the federal court must follow Rule 18(a), and must disregard the policy behind the conflicting state rule. See *Har-Pen Truck Lines, Inc. v. Mills*, 378 F.2d 705 (5th Cir. 1967).

70. **Yes.** In diversity suits, the federal court must ***apply the state-law statute of limitations***. Even though a statute of limitations has a "procedural" aspect, the choice of statute of limitations is heavily outcome-determinative. For example, here P will be allowed to maintain his suit if the federal laches approach is used, but will not be allowed to maintain suit at all if the state statute of limitations is used — the choice of law, therefore, is ***completely*** outcome determinative. The doctrine that state statutes of limitations control in diversity actions is the central holding of one of the most important *Erie* cases of all, *Guaranty Trust Co. v. York*, 326 U.S. 99 (1945).

71. **No.** Here, as in the previous question, we have a conflict between a federal policy not embodied specifically in a Federal Rule, and a state policy or statute. Therefore, we must balance the two. The state interest here is relatively weak, and is in any event not thwarted by following the federal policy (since the number of hung juries and thus re-trials in state court will probably not be increased if the federal court has a hung jury). Conversely, the federal policy is a long-standing and apparently strong one — it is related to the Seventh Amendment's policy of giving maximum weight to the jury system, for instance. Similarly, there is a strong federal interest in having a treatment of the unanimity issue that is the same from one federal courtroom to another. Also, the choice of law is quite unlikely to be outcome determinative — it is hard to say, for instance, whether having a less-than-unanimous jury verdict would help P or D, since it is unclear who would get five but not six votes. And the choice of law is unlikely to promote forum shopping — it is hard to imagine that P will sue in state rather than federal court because juries in the former don't have to be unanimous.

All in all, the federal interests seem so much stronger than the state interests, and the risk of forum shopping so small, that the court will probably decide to follow the federal policy requiring unanimity. See, e.g., *Masino v. Outboard Marine Corp.*, 652 F.2d 330 (3d Cir. 1981), in which the court so decided.

IV. FEDERAL COMMON LAW

A. **Federal common law still exists:** Even though the *Erie* case makes it clear that there is no *general* federal common law, there are still *particular instances* in which federal common law is applied. That is, there are instances in which the federal court is free to disregard state law in making judicial interpretations.

    1. **Federal question cases:** Most such instances arise in cases in which federal jurisdiction is founded on something other than diversity, such as *federal question cases*, cases in which the U.S. is a party, cases between a state and citizens of another state, or admiralty cases.

    2. **General rule:** In most federal question cases, federal common law, not state common law, applies.

        a. **Statutory construction:** When the precise meaning of a federal statute is at issue, the federal court is of course free to follow federal decisions, and to ignore state constructions of the statute. This is not really even federal "common law" so much as pure statutory interpretation.

b. **Right to ignore state precedents:** Even if the statute serving as the basis for federal question jurisdiction does not treat a particular problem at all, the federal court will still, in many instances, be free to disregard state decisions on point.

Example: A check issued by the W.P.A., a federal agency, is stolen from the payee; an endorsement is forged, and the check is cashed by Clearfield Trust. *Held*, in a suit between Clearfield Trust and the Federal Reserve about whether there was timely notice of the forgery, federal, not state, common law must be consulted. "The issuance of commercial paper by the United States is on a vast scale and transactions in that paper from issuance to payment will commonly occur in several states. The application of state law, even without the conflict of laws rules of the forum, would subject the rights and duties of the United States to exceptional uncertainty. It would lead to great diversity in results by making identical transactions subject to the vagaries of the laws of the several states. The desirability of a uniform rule is plain." Thus all federal courts may follow each other's cases as precedent, so that a uniform body of law regarding federal commercial paper will emerge. *Clearfield Trust Co. v. United States*, 318 U.S. 363 (1943).

c. **U.S. as party:** In the great majority of cases in which the *U.S.* is a *party*, federal common law will be applied, as it was in *Clearfield, supra.*

d. **Private litigants:** Where a federal question case is between two *private litigants*, federal common law will usually, but not always, be applied to the federal question issues. If a particular issue in such a case is not one with which the federal courts have *expertise*, state law may be *deferred to.*

Example: The federal copyright act gives certain rights to the "children" of the original copyright owner. Suppose a federal case involves the issue of whether an illegitimate (and never acknowledged) child of the original copyright owner is his "child" for copyright purposes. Since the federal courts do not have expertise in deciding issues of who is a "child," the federal court would probably look to state law on the question of whether the illegitimate child was a child for federal copyright-law purposes.

Note: The federal court construing a federal question claim is always free to follow state law if it feels that this course is desirable. An example of this is the common situation of a federal statute which creates a right of action without setting a limit on the *time* within which such action shall be brought (e.g., Rule 10(b)(5) under the federal securities laws).

"The usual rule in such situations is to apply whatever statute of limitations the state has for analogous suits. If the case were subject to the *Erie* doctrine, then the state limitations doctrine would have to be applied in its full force. The *Erie* doctrine does not apply, and the federal court has much more freedom, where the state rule has merely been absorbed as the relevant federal rule." Wr., 418-19. Here the federal court is *permitted, but not required,* to follow state law if it thinks it wise to do so. *Id.*

B. **Federal common law in diversity cases:** Federal common law is in some instances applied even where the basis for federal jurisdiction is *diversity.*

1. **Defense based on federal law:**   This may be the case, for instance, where plaintiff's claim does not raise issues of federal law, but a claim by the ***defendant*** does.

> **Example:** A patent owner sues his licensee, in a diversity action, for unpaid royalties. The licensee raises the defense that the patents are invalid under the federal patent statutes. The validity of the defense will be determined by resort to federal case law, not state case law.

2. **Balancing test:**   In determining whether to apply federal common law in diversity cases whose subject matter bears some relation to a federal statute, courts employ roughly the same kind of balancing between state and federal interests as was used in *Byrd v. Blue Ridge.*

C. **Federal common law in state courts:**   Federal jurisdiction with respect to most federal question claims is concurrent with state jurisdiction. If concurrent jurisdiction exists with respect to a particular claim, and the suit is brought in ***state court***, federal common law applies there if it would apply in federal court.

1. **Binding on state court:**   Thus in the kinds of cases described in the preceding sections, a state court would be compelled to apply earlier federal precedents, and to ignore state decisions, just as a federal court would. Wr., 416.

2. **Procedural questions:**   The application of federal common law to state court suits on federally-created rights may even extend to certain "procedural" matters.

> **Example:** The Ps bring an FELA (Federal Employer's Liability Act) suit against D, a railroad, in Ohio state court. (The FELA is a federal statute giving injured railroad employees the right to sue the railroad for personal injury damages in state court.) D defends on the grounds that the Ps have previously signed a release of all claims against D. The Ps assert that D committed fraud in obtaining the release, and that the fraud should vitiate the release. Under Ohio procedural law, the existence of fraud is to be determined by the judge. Under federal case law, all fact-based aspects of an FELA claim (including the existence of fraud as to a release) are to be determined by the jury.
>
> *Held* (by the U.S. Supreme Court), federal law is binding on the judge/jury allocation, so the issue of fraud should have been heard by the jury. The federal right to a jury trial on all factual matters is "part and parcel of the remedy" offered by the FELA, and cannot be overridden by a "mere local rule of procedure." *Dice v. Akron, Canton & Youngstown R.R.*, 342 U.S. 359 (1952).

   a. **Impact on federal policies:**   This does not mean that federal procedure must be followed in every state case dealing with federally-created claims, but simply that local procedure must give way if it ***substantially infringes on a federal policy.***

3. **Effect of prior diversity-court judgment:**   One illustration of how federal common law can be binding on a state court arises when a federal court sitting in diversity issues a judgment, and a state court must later decide what *res judicata* (see *infra*, p. 416) effect that earlier judgment should be given. As a result of the Supreme Court's 2001 decision in *Semtek Int'l Inc. v. Lockheed Martin Corp.*, 531 U.S. 497 (2001) (discussed more fully *infra*, p. 446), federal common law says that the diversity judgment should have whatever "preclusive" effect (i.e., effect on later suits involving the same party or parties) that a sim-

interests by giving heavy weight to:

☞ whether the choice of which policy to follow is heavily ***outcome-determinative***. (If so, lean towards choosing the state rule.)

☞ whether using the federal policy is likely to induce the plaintiff to ***forum-shop,*** i.e., to choose between state and federal court based on whose law is more favorable to her. (If so, lean towards choosing the state rule.)

☞ whether using the state rule is likely to ***thwart an important federal policy*** governing the procedures to be used in federal trials. (If so, lean towards choosing the federal rule.) [262]

☛ Some of the common situations that *are* true Erie problems are:

☞ whether to follow the state ***statute of limitations*** where there is no applicable Congressionally-enacted S/L (*yes*, because the choice of S/L is heavily outcome-determinative, and important federal procedural policies aren't implicated) [261]

☞ whether to follow the state ***conflict-of-law***s provision (*yes*, for the same reason) [259]

☞ whether to follow the state allocation of the ***burden of proof*** (*yes*) [259]

☞ whether to follow a state ***cap on damages*** for the type of claim in question (yes)

☞ whether to follow the state rules allocating issues between ***judge and jury*** (*no*, because this is not heavily outcome-determinative, and will not induce forum shopping) [262]

☛ If you do decide that *Erie* applies, remember that the issue is ***what the state's highest court would do now*** if it heard the issue fresh. (Thus the fact that there is a precedent on the books from some time ago does not bind the federal court, if it thinks that the states highest court would overrule that precedent today.) [258-259]

☛ Consult the flow chart on p. 277.

CHAPTER 7

TRIAL PROCEDURE

ChapterScope

This Chapter examines the mechanics of trials, both jury and non-jury. The most important concepts in this Chapter are:

■ **Two meanings of "burden of proof":** There are two kinds of *"burden of proof"* which a party may have to bear. Assuming that the issue is called *A*:

❏ **Burden of production:** The party bears the "burden of *production*" if the following is true: unless the party produces *some* evidence that *A* exists, the judge must *direct the jury* to find that *A* does not exist.

❏ **Burden of persuasion:** The party bears the "burden of *persuasion*" if the following is true: at the close of the evidence, if the jury cannot decide whether *A* exists or not, the jury must find that *A* does not exist.

■ **"Preponderance" standard generally:** The usual standard of proof in civil actions is the *"preponderance of the evidence"* standard. A proposition is proved by a preponderance of the evidence if the jury is convinced that it is *"more likely than not"* that the proposition is true.

■ **Summary judgment:** If one party can show that there is *no "genuine dispute of material fact"* in the lawsuit, and that she is "entitled to judgment as a matter of law," she can win the case without going to trial. Such a victory without trial is called a *"summary judgment."*

■ **Trial without jury:** A case will be tried without a jury if *either* of the two following conditions exists: (1) *No right to a jury trial* exists; or (2) *All parties* have *waived* the right to a jury trial.

❏ **Appellate review:** When a case is tried to the judge (who thus acts as fact-finder), the trial judge's findings of fact will be set aside on appeal only if they are *"clearly erroneous."*

■ **Jury trials:**

❏ **Unanimity:** The verdict of a *federal* civil jury must be *unanimous*, unless the parties stipulate otherwise. FRCP 48. But most states allow a *less-than-unanimous* civil jury verdict.

❏ **Jury selection:** The process by which the jury is selected is called the *"voir dire."* Any juror who is shown through the voir dire to be biased or connected to the case must be dismissed upon motion by a party (dismissal *"for cause"*). In addition to the jurors dismissed for cause, each party may dismiss a certain number of other prospective jurors *without showing cause* for their dismissal (*"peremptory challenges"*).

■ **Directed verdict:** In both state and federal trials, either party may move for a *directed verdict*. Such a verdict *takes the case away from the jury, and determines the outcome as a matter of law*. (In federal trials, the phrase "directed verdict" is no longer used — instead, a party moves for "judgment as a matter of law.")

❏ **Standard for granting:** Generally, the court will direct a verdict if the evidence is such that *reasonable people could not differ* as to the result.

■ **New trial:** The trial court, in both state and federal courts, may grant a *new trial*.

❏ **Harmless error:** A new trial may not be granted except for errors in the trial which are serious enough that they affect the substantial rights of the parties. FRCP 61. This is the so-called *"harmless error"* doctrine.

■ **JNOV:** Most states allow the judge to set aside the jury's verdict, and enter judgment for the verdict-loser. This is called a Judgment Notwithstanding the Verdict, or *JNOV*. In federal practice, the device is called *"judgment as a matter of law"* (JML).

■ **Constitutional right to jury trial:** The Seventh Amendment provides that "in suits at *common law* … the right of *trial by jury* shall be preserved." This means that there is a federal jury trial right as to "legal" claims.

❏ **No state application:** The Seventh Amendment does not apply to *state* trials, only federal ones. So states may abolish jury trials in some or all civil cases.

❏ **Equitable claim:** Even in a federal case, there is no jury trial right as to *"equitable"* claims (e.g., a claim for injunction).

I. BURDEN OF PROOF

A. Two meanings of "burden of proof": To say that a party bears the "burden of proof" with respect to a particular issue, A, can mean either of two very different things:

1. **Burden of production:** It can mean that unless he produces *some* evidence that A exists, the judge must direct the jury to find that A does not exist. The party in such a situation is said to bear the "burden of *production*." James & Hazard, p. 340.

2. **Burden of persuasion:** Or, it can mean that if at the close of the evidence, the jury cannot decide whether A exists or not, it must find that A does not exist. The party seeking to prove A in this situation is said to bear the "burden of *persuasion*," or the risk of non-persuasion. James & Hazard, p. 314.

B. Factors in allocation: The allocation of both burdens to one side or the other depends on many factors — there is no simple test. Among the factors considered are (1) who has "the better *access* to the fact in question", and (2) who is alleging something that "*departs from what would be expected* in the light of ordinary human experience." James & Hazard, p. 324.

1. **Both burdens not always on same party:** The burden of production is not necessarily placed on the same party as the burden of persuasion. F,K&C, pp. 673-74. Indeed, the burden of production may itself shift throughout the course of the trial.

> **Example:** A trial consists of only one issue, A, which P asserts and D denies. P starts out bearing initially the burden of producing some evidence of A. If he produces just enough evidence so that the judge finds that a reasonable jury *might* find that A exists, P has met his burden of *production*. If P produces so much evidence that he is, in the absence of evidence from D, entitled to a directed verdict, P has *shifted* the burden of production to D. If D now produces evidence, he can either make a jury issue of A (in

which case neither P nor D bears the production burden anymore) or he can produce enough evidence so that P must once more meet the production burden, or suffer a directed verdict against him. See the diagram in F,K&C, p. 672.

C. What meets burden: In general, a party has met his burden of *production* on an issue, A, if he has given enough evidence to *send that issue to the jury*. He has met his burden of *persuasion* with respect to A if he has produced enough evidence to lead the jury "to believe that the existence of [A] is *more probable than its non-existence*." J & H (3d ed.), pp. 316-17. Or as the persuasion burden idea is often put, a party bearing that burden with respect to proving A's existence must demonstrate "by a *preponderance of the evidence*" that A exists. *Id.* at 243.

II. PRESUMPTIONS

A. Definition: A presumption, in the sense of the word relevant here, is a "convention that when a designated basic fact exists, another fact, called the presumed fact, *must* be taken to exist in the absence of adequate rebuttal." F,K&C, p. 680-81. We shall refer to the designated basic fact as *B* and the fact presumed from *B*'s existence as *P*.

B. Assumptions for discussion: Assume in the following that the only disputed fact in a case is P, and that existence of the basic fact, *B*, is agreed to by both sides. Assume also that there is a statutory or common law presumption that where *B* exists, *P* exists. Plaintiff seeks to prove the existence of *P*. Assume that if there were no presumption, plaintiff would bear the *burden of persuading* the jury that *P* exists.

1. Burden of production: If no evidence is offered at all as to *P*, but *B* exists beyond dispute, plaintiff is entitled to a *directed verdict*. The party against whom the presumption is directed (in this case the defendant) bears the initial burden of producing evidence of non-*P*. If he produces no evidence, he suffers a directed verdict.

2. Burden of persuasion: If defendant offers enough evidence of non-*P* that a reasonable jury might find non-*P*, it is clear that he has met his production burden. *But who bears the burden of persuasion*? Courts and commentators are in complete dispute about whether the presumption of *P* from *B* changes the allocation of the persuasion burden from where it would be if no presumption existed. Three important different positions exist:

a. "Bursting bubble" approach: Under the so-called *"bursting bubble"* approach, the presumption affects *only* the production burden. Once the party bearing the burden (in our ongoing hypothetical, the defendant) satisfies that burden by producing evidence of non-*P*, and the case goes to the jury, the persuasion burden is allocated *exactly as if there were no presumption* — in this case, on the plaintiff. This approach is called the "bursting bubble" approach because once evidence tending to show the non-existence of the presumed fact is introduced, the presumption bursts like a bubble.

i. Federal Rules of Evidence: This "bursting bubble" approach is used by the *Federal Rules of Evidence* in civil suits. Under FRE 301, "A presumption imposes on the party against whom it is directed the burden of going forward with evidence to rebut or meet the presumption, but *does not shift to such party the burden of proof in the sense of the risk of non-persuasion*, which remains throughout the trial upon the party on whom it was originally cast." (But FRE 302 provides that if **state law** provides the rule of decision as to the claim or defense to which the presumed fact relates, the law of that state will determine the effect of the presumption. Thus if the presumed fact relates to a claim or defense under which **Erie principles** (*supra*, p. 258) require that state law be followed, state law will also determine whether the presumption can shift the burden of non-persuasion.)

   b. Uniform Rules of Evidence approach: A second approach is exemplified by the Uniform Rules of Evidence:

      i. Rational connection: If there is a **rational connection** between *B* and *P*, the existence of the presumption places the burden of persuasion as to *P* on the party against whom the presumption is directed — in this case, defendant.

      ii. No rational connection: If there is no logical or rational connection between *B* and *P*, the persuasion burden is unaffected by the existence of the presumption, the same as in the Thayer approach.

   c. Originally-proposed Federal Rules of Evidence approach: The Federal Rules of Evidence as they were originally proposed to the Supreme Court (but not as finally enacted; see *supra*, Paragraph 2(a)(i)) took a third position. They gave a presumption the effect of ***completely shifting the burden of persuasion***. That is, the mere existence of the presumption placed the burden of persuasion as to *P* on the party against whom the presumption was directed. In other words, this approach treated **all** presumptions, logical or not, the way the Uniform Rules treated logical presumptions.

   Example of the three approaches: A statute states that where a railroad locomotive causes damage, there is a presumption that the railroad was negligent. *B* = damage by locomotive. *P* = railroad's negligence. The railroad offers enough evidence of its own due care to send the case to the jury (but not enough to obtain a directed verdict). The three approaches would work as follows:

     Federal Rules of Evidence: The presumption has no effect on the persuasion burden. Therefore, plaintiff must affirmatively convince the jury that the railroad was negligent.

     Uniform Rules: There is no logical connection between the fact of damage by a locomotive, and the negligence of the railroad — some other cause could explain the damage just as easily. Therefore, the persuasion burden is placed on plaintiff.

     Originally-proposed Federal Evidence Rules: Existence of the presumption against the railroad places the burden of persuasion on it. It must therefore affirmatively convince the jury that it exercised due care.

III. PREPONDERANCE OF THE EVIDENCE

A. Definition of preponderance: The usual standard of proof in civil actions is the ***preponderance*** standard. A proposition is proved by a preponderance of the evidence if the jury is convinced that it is ***"more likely than not"*** that the proposition is true.

1. **Utility:** The preponderance standard is a measure of how much evidence the party bearing the ***burden of persuasion*** as to an issue must present in order to meet that burden. "If … the burden is upon a party to prove a specified fact by the preponderance of the evidence, … this means that [the jury] must find that the fact does not exist unless the evidence convinces them that its existence is more probable than its non-existence." F,K&C, p. 687.

B. Test for measuring probability: How is a jury to evaluate whether the existence of a fact is more "probable" than not? It is sometimes said that it is "not enough that ***mathematically*** the chances somewhat favor a proposition to be proved." *Sargent v. Massachusetts Accident Co.*, 29 N.E.2d 825 (Mass. 1940). Thus, "the fact that colored automobiles made in the current year outnumber black ones would not warrant a finding that an undescribed automobile of the current year is colored and not black." *Id.* As the idea is put, the belief in the truth of the proposition must be ***"actual,"*** not ***"speculative."***

C. Adversary's denials: A party who has the burden of proving a fact by a preponderance of the evidence may ***not rely solely on the jury's disbelief of his adversary's denials of that fact.*** The party who bears the burden must offer some affirmative evidence in support of the fact.

> **Example:** Assume that P, a pedestrian, while crossing the street in mid-block, is struck by a car driven by D. P sues D for negligence. In P's testimony, P says nothing about how D was driving at the time of the collision. P then calls D as a hostile witness. D asserts, "I drove within the speed limit, and was careful in every way." P offers no other evidence bearing on whether D drove carefully.
>
> The trial judge should direct a verdict in favor of D at the close of P's evidence — P has not borne his burden of proving D's negligence by a preponderance of the evidence, and the mere possibility that the jury may disbelieve D's statement that he drove carefully does not constitute the requisite evidence of D's lack of due care.

1. **Rationale:** There is a good reason for this doctrine. If it were otherwise, a party could never successfully ***appeal*** a judge's ***refusal to direct a verdict.*** (On the facts of the above example, for instance, if the trial judge refused to direct a verdict for D, D could not successfully appeal.) For no matter how overwhelming in the trial record was the evidence for the party seeking the directed verdict, and no matter how non-existent the evidence for the other side, an appeals court would still have to conclude that "a reasonable jury might have disbelieved all the witnesses, based on their demeanor, which we cannot evaluate on appeal. Therefore, the trial judge rightly sent the case to the jury." See *Dyer v. MacDougall*, 201 F.2d 265 (2d Cir. 1952). See also, James & Hazard, p. 362, n. 27.

Quiz Yourself on

BURDEN OF PROOF, PRESUMPTIONS AND PREPONDERANCE OF EVIDENCE

72. D, driving her car, struck and injured P, a pedestrian. P sued D in the courts of the state of Ames, which follows the Federal Rules of Civil Procedure and the Federal Rules of Evidence. P's suit charged that D drove negligently. The substantive law of the state of Ames imposes on P both the burden of production as to negligence and the burden of persuasion (by a preponderance of the evidence) on this issue. The case was tried to a jury. As part of P's case, P showed that shortly after the accident, D was stopped by the police, asked to take a breathalyzer exam, and refused to do so. According to the substantive law of Ames,

refusal to take a breathalyzer upon request by the police gives rise to a presumption of intoxication (which under state law is a form of negligence when the person is the driver). During his case, P came up with no evidence of D's negligence other than the refusal to take a breathalyzer exam. At the close of P's case, D made a motion for a directed verdict, based on P's failure to prove negligence. Should the trial judge grant D's motion? _____

73. Same facts as prior question. Now, however, assume that the trial judge allowed the case to go forward, and D came up with some evidence indicating that she was not in fact intoxicated despite her refusal to take the breathalyzer exam. At the close of D's case, the judge instructed the jury as follows: "Under our law, the defendant's refusal to take a breathalyzer exam when asked to do so by the police gives rise to a presumption of intoxication. If you find that D refused to take the breathalyzer, then you must find that D was intoxicated unless D persuades you by a preponderance of the evidence that she was not intoxicated." Are the judge's instructions appropriate? _____

Answers

72. The trial judge should grant D's motion for directed verdict only if the judge believes that P has not carried his burden of production, that is, his burden of producing some credible evidence (evidence that might be believed by a reasonable jury) that D behaved negligently. The presumption (failure to take a breathalyzer equals intoxication and thus negligence) is enough to get P past this burden of production — by proving that D did not take the breathalyzer (the basic fact), P will be deemed to have met the burden of producing evidence that D was negligent (the presumed fact). Unless D comes up with credible evidence of her non-negligence, the court will in fact have to instruct the jury at the end of D's case that it should find for P on this issue.

73. **No.** Under the "bursting bubble" approach to presumptions imposed by Federal Rule of Evidence 301, "a presumption imposes on the party against whom it is directed the burden of going forward with evidence to rebut or meet the presumption, but does not shift to such party the burden of proof in the sense of the risk of non-persuasion, which remains throughout the trial upon the party on whom it was originally cast." Thus although the presumption "refusal to take breathalyzer equals intoxication" meant that once P showed such refusal, the burden of *production* as to intoxication shifted to D (see answer to prior question), this presumption did not help P get rid of the burden of *persuasion*. At the end of the trial, just as at the beginning, the burden remained on P to show by a preponderance of the evidence that D was in fact intoxicated. Thus if the jury believed that there was exactly a 50% chance that D was intoxicated, P loses, just as if there had been no presumption at all. To the extent that the judge's instructions indicate that D loses where the jury is completely undecided, those instructions are wrong.

IV. ADJUDICATION WITHOUT TRIAL

A. **Trial sometimes unnecessary:**   Not all cases end in a full-scale trial. For instance, as was stated in the chapter on Pleading, a complaint can sometimes be dismissed under Rule 12(b)(6), for failure to state a claim upon which relief can be granted.

　　1. **Other means of disposition:**   Treated in this section are some of the other means by which a case may be disposed of *without* a full-scale trial with both parties presenting evidence.

B. Voluntary dismissal by plaintiff: A plaintiff in federal court may *voluntarily dismiss* his complaint *without prejudice* any time *before the defendant serves an answer or moves for summary judgment*. The plaintiff may do this without leave of court. The fact that the dismissal is "without prejudice" means that he may *bring the suit again*. See Rule 41(a)(1).

1. **Only one dismissal:**   Only the *first* dismissal of a claim is without prejudice. If a plaintiff has already once before dismissed a claim in either state or federal court, his second dismissal operates as an *"adjudication on the merits,"* i.e., he is barred from bringing the claim a third time by *res judicata* just as if the claim had been fully litigated and decided against him. See Rule 41(a)(1). This is sometimes called the *"two dismissal"* rule.

2. **After answer or motion:**   After the defendant has answered or moved for summary judgment, plaintiff may voluntarily dismiss only with the court's approval, and on the court's terms. See Rule 41(a)(2).

3. **Payment of expenses:**   If a claim has been voluntarily dismissed once before, the second time it is brought the court can order that the plaintiff pay the *court costs* of the first action before allowing the second one to go forward. See Rule 41(d).

C. Involuntary dismissal: The plaintiff's claim may also be *involuntarily* dismissed, by court order.

1. **Grounds:**   An involuntary dismissal under Rule 41(b) may be ordered by the court, on motion, for:

    a. **Failure to prosecute:**   failure to *prosecute* (failure of complainant to pursue the action);

    b. **Disobedience:**   failure of complainant to *obey court orders* (e.g., discovery or pretrial conference orders);

    c. **Other:**   any of the reasons listed as defenses in Rule 12(b).

2. **With prejudice:**   Normally an involuntary dismissal is *with prejudice*, and thus has the effect of an adjudication on the merits, unless the dismissing court states otherwise. Rule 41(b). *Exceptions* to this general rule (i.e., situations in which the dismissal is not with prejudice if the dismissing court is silent on the issue) are dismissals for:

    a. *lack of jurisdiction* (of both the *parties* and the *subject matter*, and for *insufficient service);*

    b. improper *venue*; and

    c. *failure to join an indispensable party* under Rule 19.

        See Rule 41(b).

3. **Judgment on partial findings:**   If the plaintiff puts on her case and fails to show that she is entitled to relief, the judge can dismiss the case before the defendant puts on his case.

    a. **Non-jury case:**   In a *non-jury* case, if the plaintiff does not prove facts entitling her to relief, the defendant can make a motion for *"judgment on partial findings,"* pursuant to FRCP 52(c). The judge makes the findings of fact as if the case had been fully tried, since by hypothesis the plaintiff has been given a chance to establish all facts which she needs to sustain her case and has failed to do so.

    b. Jury case: In a *jury* case, defendant's motion at the close of plaintiff's case is called a motion "for judgment as a matter of law," a topic treated *infra*, p. 299.

D. Summary judgment: If one party can show that there is *no "genuine dispute as to any material fact"* in the lawsuit, and that he is "entitled to judgment as a matter of law," he can win the case without going to trial. Such a victory without trial is called *"summary judgment,"* and is provided for by Rule 56.

    1. Court goes behind pleadings: In deciding a motion for summary judgment, the court will go *"behind the pleadings."* That is, even if it appears from the pleadings that the parties are in dispute on some material issue of fact, the summary judgment motion should be granted if the movant can show that the disputed factual issues presented by the pleadings are *illusory.*

    2. How shown: The movant (the person seeking summary judgment) can show the lack of a genuine issue of fact by two main means:

        a. Affidavits: First, he may submit *affidavits*.

            i. Contents of affidavits: These affidavits must recite only matters as to which the affiant has *personal knowledge*, must state only matters which would be *admissible at trial*, and must "show that the affiant ... is competent to testify on the matters stated." See Rule 56(c)(4).

        b. Discovery materials: Second, he may submit the fruits of *discovery* (e.g., depositions, interrogatory answers, etc.), no matter which side they were obtained from. See Rule 56(c)(1)(A).

    3. Showing by movant: Regardless of who will have the burden of persuasion on an issue at trial, the *movant* bears the initial burden of *production* on that issue. That is, as part of his summary judgment papers, he bears the burden of coming forward with information that "clearly establishes that there is no factual dispute regarding the matter upon which summary judgment is sought." F,K&M, p. 444.

        a. How to do this: Normally, the movant will, as noted, do this by presenting affidavits, depositions, etc. However, the Supreme Court has made it clear that at least in those situations in which the responding party will bear the burden of *persuasion* at trial, the movant will not necessarily have to come up with affidavits, depositions, or other evidentiary materials. Instead, he may be entitled to summary judgment merely by showing that *the existing record contains no evidence that the other side* (which will bear the burden of persuasion at trial) *will be able to prove an essential element of its case. Celotex Corp. v. Catrett*, 477 U.S. 317 (1986).

            i. Facts of *Celotex*: The facts of *Celotex* indicate how this can happen. P claimed to have been injured by exposure to asbestos manufactured by D. After discovery, D moved for summary judgment on the grounds that there was no evidence in the record that any of D's products caused the injury, an issue on which P would clearly have the burden of persuasion at trial. D did not produce affidavits, depositions, or any other independent information in support of the proposition that its products were *not* the ones that caused P's injury — it simply pointed out to the court that P had no evidence implicating D's products.

    ii. Holding: The Supreme Court held that in this situation, summary judgment could properly be given for D. "We find no express or implied requirement in Rule 56 that the moving party support its motion with affidavits or other similar materials negating the opponent's claim."

    iii. How shown: But the Federal Rules have been amended since *Celotex*, to make the job of the party moving for summary judgment somewhat harder. Today, the moving party must do *more* than merely *state* in a conclusory fashion that there is no evidence for an essential element of the other party's claim. Under present Rule 56, the moving party must *review* all affidavits, depositions, and other parts of the record, and must *explain to the court in some detail* why these materials fail to establish the existence of an element that the non-movant will be required to prove. See Rule 56(c)(1)(A).

    (1) Admissibility issue: Alternatively, the movant can show that, whatever the contents of the record, the non-movant won't be able to come up with *admissible* evidence of a fact that the latter will be required to prove at trial. Rule 56(c)(1)(B).) So if the record contains only, say, inadmissible hearsay evidence establishing some element of the non-movant's case, and the movant can show that no admissible evidence of that element is available to the non-movant, that showing will suffice under 56(c)(1)(B).

4. Opposition: The party *opposing* the summary judgment motion may also submit affidavits, depositions, and other materials, which must meet the same standards as those prescribed for materials submitted by the movant. See Rule 56(c)(1)(A) and (B).

    a. Opponent can't rest on pleadings: If the affidavits of the movant show that there is no genuine material dispute for trial, the opposing party cannot avoid summary judgment merely by *repeating his pleadings' denial* of the allegations of the movant's affidavits. Instead, the non-movant who wants to claim that a fact asserted by the movant to be not-disputed really *is* disputed will have to either:

    [1] *point to specific places in the record* (such as depositions, documents, admissions, etc.) showing that the fact in question is disputed, or else

    [2] demonstrate that the movant won't be able to produce *admissible evidence* to establish the fact.

Rule 56(c)(1)(A) and (B) (added in 2010).

Example: P sues D on a promissory note. P's claim states that the note was validly executed by D. D's answer denies that D signed the note. P moves for a Rule 56 summary judgment, and submits an affidavit by X stating that X saw D sign the note.

    D cannot avoid summary judgment by merely repeating his answer's general denial of the signature. He must do something more. For instance, D can point to something in the record that establishes a genuine dispute about whether he signed (e.g., an affidavit or deposition testimony — even if only his own — asserting that the signature is a forgery, or that it was obtained by duress, etc.). Or, he can show that P won't be able to come up with any admissible evidence at trial that D really signed. But D can't just rest on his pleadings in which he denied signing. Cf. Rule 56(c)(1)(A) and (B).

5. **Payment of costs:**   If the court decides, at any time, that affidavits presented for or against a summary judgment motion were made "in bad faith or solely for delay," the trial judge must order the party who submitted the affidavits to pay to the other side the *costs* of presenting opposing affidavits, including attorney's fees. The court may also hold the offending party or attorney in contempt of court. See Rule 56(h).

6. **Partial summary judgment:**   Summary judgment may be granted with respect to *certain claims* in a lawsuit even when it is not granted with respect to all claims. Rule 56(a). If this occurs, the court may order the entry of judgment on the claims as to which summary judgment has been granted if there is "no just reason for delay" in the entry of judgment. See Rule 54(b). This is called *partial summary judgment*. The losing party may then *appeal* the partial summary judgment, while the undisposed-of claims are being tried. (For more about appeals from orders granting partial summary judgment, see *infra*, p. 324.)

    a. **Order establishing individual fact:**   Furthermore, the court might grant partial summary judgment as to one or more *particular facts* that don't collectively resolve an entire claim. Thus the court might issue summary judgment on the issue of *liability alone*, if a genuine issue concerning damages remains. See Rule 56(g) (allowing the court to enter "an order stating any material fact — including an item of damages or other relief — that is not genuinely in dispute and treating the fact as established in the case").

        i. **Interlocutory:** This type of "partial" summary judgment is "interlocutory" in nature, since it doesn't fully resolve the entirety of even one claim. It is therefore normally *not immediately appealable*. See, e.g., *Liberty Mutual Insurance Co. v. Wetzel*, 424 U.S. 737 (1976) (also discussed *infra*, p. 325).

Quiz Yourself on
ADJUDICATION WITHOUT TRIAL

74. P has brought a medical malpractice suit against D in federal court based on diversity. P's complaint asserts that D performed an operation upon P to reduce the size of P's nose, and that the results were disastrous. The complaint asserts that the operation took place on October 13, 1988. D has moved for summary judgment pursuant to Rule 56, and has submitted in support of that motion an affidavit stating that he was not in the U.S. on October 13, 1988. D's moving papers give much additional information, all of which tends to indicate that D could not have performed the operation on the date P said D performed it (e.g., an affidavit from D's travel agent stating that D was in the south of France that day, as well as charges on D's phone bill showing calls made from the south of France to D's office on that date).P, in opposition to D's motion, has submitted an affidavit that furnishes a couple of details about the alleged operation (e.g., "On October 13, 1988, I went to D's offices at 456 Main Street. D was a brown haired man of about 50 years of age who wore glasses, and he performed the surgery on me.") P has not submitted any other information in opposition to D's motion. In reviewing these moving papers, the federal judge concludes that there is about a 90% chance that P is either honestly mistaken or is lying when she

asserts that D performed the operation on her on that date. Should the federal judge grant D's motion for summary judgment? _____

Answer

74. No. Federal Rule 56(c) states that the motion for summary judgment may be rendered only if all the materials submitted by both parties "show that there is no genuine dispute as to any material fact. ..." It is not enough that the judge concludes that the moving party is very likely to win at trial — the judge must conclude that *as a matter of law* all issues must be decided in favor of the movant, before the judge may grant summary judgment. Here, there is some chance (although admittedly not a very good chance) that P will be able to come up with more evidence that D really did perform the operation on the day stated, or will be able to show that D's evidence was fraudulent. Alternatively, P may be able to show that D performed the operation on a different day. Since the issue of whether D performed the operation is very fact-bound, and there seems to be an honest dispute, the court should deny D's motion even though it appears very probable that D will prevail at trial.

V.   TRIALS WITHOUT A JURY

- **A. When tried to court:**   A case will be tried without a jury if one of the two following conditions exists:

  1. *no right to a jury trial* exists, or

  2. all parties have *waived* the right to jury trial.

     Note: The circumstances under which a right to jury trial exists are discussed *infra*, p. 308.

- **B. Effect:**   If there is no jury, the trial judge serves as both the *finder of fact* and the decider of law.

- **C. Evidence rules:**   The rules of evidence followed by the judge (in federal trials, the Federal Rules of Evidence) are officially the same in non-jury trials as in jury trials. However, in practice, judges tend to *relax the rules* more when there is no jury present which could be prejudiced by the admission of evidence of dubious reliability.

- **D. Findings of fact:**   If an action is tried without a jury, Rule 52 requires the trial court to *"find the facts specially* and [to] state its conclusions of law separately[.]"* This means that the trial judge must *set forth the facts* as she finds them with some *particularity*, and must in a separate section of her opinion state the law which she believes disposes of the case.

  1. **Where separate findings required:**   The separate findings of fact and conclusions of law required by Rule 52 are obligatory not only in cases which are fully tried, but also in the following circumstances:

     a. where requests for interlocutory *injunctions* are made, whether they are granted or denied; and

b. where *"judgment on partial findings"* is given pursuant to Rule 52(c). Thus if, at the end of plaintiff's case, the trial judge believes that plaintiff has not carried his burden of proof, the judge may throw plaintiff's case out without even hearing the defendant's case; if the judge does this, Rule 52(c) requires her to make separate findings of fact and conclusions of law.

2. Where separate findings not required: The trial judge is *not* obligated to make findings of fact and conclusions of law pursuant to the disposition of any kind of *motion* except one under 52(c).

   a. Summary judgment: Thus the *grant* or *denial* of a Rule 56 motion for *summary judgment* or of a Rule 12(b)(6) motion for dismissal for *failure to state a claim* need not be accompanied by findings of fact and conclusions of law.

3. Judgment on partial findings: The trial judge is encouraged to conduct a *"mini-trial"* of just one issue, if the judge thinks that the party carrying the burden of proof on that issue may not be able to satisfy it, and that issue is dispositive of a claim or the whole case. If the judge then finds against the party bearing the burden of proof, the judge issues a *"judgment on partial findings."* See Rule 52(c).

   a. Rationale: The Advisory Committee Note to Rule 52 says that "If the court in considering a motion for summary judgment under Rule 56(b) determines from the discovery materials that a crucial fact may be quickly resolved at trial, it may (pursuant to Rule 42(b)) order trial of that issue, hear the evidence and enter judgment in conformity with the requirements of Rule 52(a). The availability of this course should eliminate any temptation by the court to shortcut the process of trial by entering summary judgment on Rule 56 despite doubts about the availability of essential proof."

   Example: Suppose that P sues D for automobile negligence in diversity. D pleads the 3-year statute of limitations. Because of D's defense, the key issue quickly becomes the date on which the accident occurred, and on this the parties come up with conflicting, and credible, affidavits. The trial judge should not try the whole case, since the trial may be unnecessary if the statute of limitations issue is resolved against P. Conversely, the trial judge should not stretch to find against P on summary judgment, if there is some chance that P will prevail on the limitations issue. Instead, the trial judge should conduct a "mini-trial," at which only evidence bearing on the date of the accident is examined. If P fails to prove that the accident occurred less than three years before the suit was filed, the trial judge should render judgment against P based on the partial findings concerning the accident date. The judge must issue findings of fact and conclusions of law about the accident date and the statute of limitations, but need not try the rest of the case.

E. Appellate review of factual findings from bench trials: If the loser of a non-jury trial appeals, the appellate court will be *reluctant to second-guess* the trial judge's findings of fact. In the federal system, the trial judge's findings of fact will be set aside only if they are *"clearly erroneous."* See FRCP 52(a). Appellate review of findings of fact in bench trials is covered later in this chapter as part of our general discussion of appeals; see p. 322 *infra*.

_____

Quiz Yourself on

TRIALS WITHOUT A JURY

75. P sued D in federal district court for employment discrimination. The case was tried to a judge. Both sides put on their case. The judge announced from the bench that she would decide the case within several weeks. After four weeks, the judge issued a written opinion, which read in its entirety as follows: "The judge finds for D, on the grounds that while P has proven that D did not hire P, P has not proven that this refusal was on account of D's race, as required by the federal civil rights statute under which P brought suit." The judge has not issued any other statements or documents in connection with the case. Has the judge complied with applicable procedural requirements? _____

76. P brought a federal suit against D for negligence relating to an automobile accident in which P was injured. The suit was based on diversity. The essence of P's claim was that D went through an intersection while the light was red, striking P's car. The case was tried without a jury. At trial, P presented a witness, W, who testified to having seen D go through the intersection when the light was red against D. P himself also testified that the light was green for him (and thus red for D) when D entered the intersection. The only witness or other evidence on behalf of D was D's own testimony, in which D asserted that the light was yellow when D passed through the intersection. The trial judge found in favor of D. The judge's findings of fact, after summarizing the testimony given by each of the witnesses, stated, "Although the only apparently objective witness supports P's account, I find that D's testimony was more credible, and I therefore conclude that the light was yellow at the time D entered the intersection. Accordingly, I find that D did not act negligently, and is therefore not liable."

P appealed the case to the Court of Appeals. The three-judge panel hearing the appeal has concluded, after reading the entire trial transcript, that there is a 70% or so chance that the light was red against D at the time D entered the intersection. The only issue on the appeal is whether the trial judge's finding of fact as to the color of light was a correct one. Should the appeals court affirm the lower court judgment?

_____

_____

Answers

75. No. Federal Rule 52(a) provides that "In an action tried on the facts without a jury ... the court must find the facts specially and state its conclusions of law separately." The judge has almost certainly failed to find the facts "specially" — this word indicates that the judge must state the facts with some particularity, so that a reviewing court will know whether the judge has conducted the trial in an adequate way and has reached a verdict in accord with the weight of the evidence. At a minimum, the judge should have summarized the evidence of intentional discrimination produced by P (if any), and should have described why she did not find this evidence sufficient. If P were to appeal this case, the appellate court would probably remand it to the district court for an opinion that recites the facts and conclusions of law much more specifically.

76. Yes. One of the most important sentences in the entire Federal Rules of Civil Procedure is in Rule 52(a): "Findings of fact, whether based on oral or other evidence, must not be set aside unless ***clearly erroneous***, and the reviewing court must give due regard to the trial court's opportunity to ***judge the witnesses' credibility.***" Here, each witness' testimony is internally consistent, and there are no documents that contradict any witness' story. Therefore, the case boils down completely to whether one believes P and W on the one hand, or D on the other. This is the very sort of credibility determination that the Federal Rules leave to the trial court. Thus even though the appellate court believes that there is a 70% chance that the trial judge made an error, the appellate court should not reverse or even order a new trial. (The main rationale for this deference to the trial judge's findings, especially on matters of credibility, is that the trial judge can *see* things in court that are not apparent from the trial transcript. For instance, both P and W may have appeared to be evasive, pausing a long time before answering questions, failing to look the questioner in the eye, etc.; by contrast, D might have appeared to be a quite straight shooter whose demeanor strongly suggested honesty.)

VI. THE JURY

A. Seventh Amendment: The Seventh Amendment to the U.S. Constitution provides that "in suits at common law … the right of trial by jury shall be preserved. …" As we discuss more fully *infra*, p. 308, this Amendment applies to *federal trials*, but does not apply to state trials.

B. Number of jurors: Traditionally, juries have been composed of 12 members. But the Seventh Amendment is no longer construed to require, even in federal civil cases, that the jury be composed of 12 members.

1. **Six-person jury:** The Federal Rules provide that a federal jury must have *six or more* members participating in the verdict. FRCP 48 provides that "A jury must initially have at least 6 and no more than 12 members[.]" Normally, the court will seat *more* than six jurors, so that even after illness of one or more jurors, at least six will be left to render the verdict. (Since 1991, federal juries no longer include "alternates." See *infra*, p. 295.)

   a. **Too few remaining:** If the jury dwindles to fewer than six members by the time of deliberations and verdict, a *mistrial* must be declared unless the parties both agree to continue. See FRCP 48, last sentence ("unless the parties stipulate otherwise, the verdict must ... be returned by a jury of at least 6 members").

2. **State trials:** The number of jurors in *state* trials varies from state to state.

C. Unanimity: The verdict of a federal civil jury is still required to be *unanimous*, unless the parties stipulate otherwise. Rule 48. (But it is not clear whether unanimity in federal civil suits is required by the Seventh Amendment. See F,K&M, p. 530; Wr., p. 671, n. 5.)

1. **States:** More than half of the states allow a less-than-unanimous civil verdict. F,K&C, p. 739.

   a. **New York:** For example, in New York, a civil verdict is reached when five of the six jurors agree on it. CPLR, §4113.

D. Jury selection: The process by which the jury is selected is called the *"voir dire."* In most states the *voir dire* consists of oral questions by both sides' counsel to the prospective jurors. These questions are designed to discover whether a potential juror is biased, and whether he has connections with a party or with a prospective witness. See Rule 47(a).

1. **Dismissal of juror:** Any juror who is shown through the *voir dire* to be biased or connected to the case must be dismissed upon motion by a party. When a juror is dismissed for such bias or connections, his dismissal is said to be *"for cause."* There is no limit to

the number of motions, or "challenges," that may be made to have jurors dismissed for cause.

2. **Challenges without cause:** In addition to the jurors dismissed for cause, each party may dismiss a certain number of other prospective jurors, ***without showing cause*** for their dismissal.

    a. **Peremptory challenges:** The right to dismiss a juror without cause is called a ***"peremptory challenge."***

    b. **Federal practice:** In federal civil trials, each party receives ***three*** peremptory challenges. See 28 U.S.C. §1870.

3. **Balanced pool:** The Seventh Amendment requires that the jury, and the pool from which it is drawn, must be roughly ***representative of the overall community***. As Wright has stated, "the jury must be an impartial cross-section of the community, without systematic and intentional exclusion of any economic, social, religious, racial, political or geographical group." Wr., 671.

4. **Alternates:** After the members of the jury have been selected, in most states the court may order the selection of up to six ***alternates***.

    a. **Not used in federal practice:** Under ***federal*** practice, alternates are ***no longer used***, since the Rules were amended in 1991. The use of alternate jurors was rejected in 1991 "because of the burden it places on alternates who are required to listen to the evidence but denied the satisfaction of participating in its evaluation." Advisory Committee Notes to Rule 47. See FRCP 48, which now provides that "each juror must ***participate*** in the verdict unless excused under Rule 47(c)." (Although six jurors is the minimum number needed for a federal verdict, the judge typically seats additional ones to allow for attrition due to sickness, etc.)

    b. **Minority approach:** In a few jurisdictions, more than the required number of jurors are selected to sit in the jury box, and only after the case has been presented are some of them chosen to be jurors and the rest dismissed as alternates. This procedure avoids the danger that persons who know they are merely alternates will not pay attention during the trial.

E. **Instructions:** The judge must ***instruct the jury*** as to the law relevant to their finding of fact.

    Example: If plaintiff sues for negligence, the judge must instruct the jury that they should find for the plaintiff if the defendant's conduct was not that of a reasonable man, and was the "proximate cause" of the plaintiff's injuries.

1. **Judge's right to comment:** In federal courts, and in some but not all states, the judge retains the right to comment on the quality and weight of the evidence, Wr., 673.

2. **Requests to charge:** At the close of evidence, any party may file "written requests for the jury instructions it wants the court to give." Rule 51(a)(1).

3. **Objections:** In order to raise the inadequacy of the instructions on appeal, a party must make an objection to them ***before the jury retires***. In other words, he must give the trial judge a chance to reconsider, and to correct his mistake. This objection must be specific enough to allow the judge to see what is wrong and to correct it.

a. Where no objection made: The court also has the right to reconsider its instructions to see if they contain *plain error*, even though no objection was timely made. See Rule 51(d)(2). But this power is rarely exercised.

F. Juror misconduct: A jury verdict may be set aside, and a ***new trial*** ordered, for certain kinds of jury misconduct. These include subjecting themselves to ***outside influence*** (as by talking to a party, or by taking an unauthorized view of the scene of an accident), and concealing a ***bias*** or prejudice on *voir dire.*

1. Impeachment: The traditional rule, still followed in most states, has been that the jury may not ***impeach its own verdict***. That is, a verdict will not be set aside because of a juror's testimony of his own or another juror's misconduct. A verdict, on this view, will only be set aside on evidence offered by a third party ("such as from persons having seen the transaction through a window"; F,K&C, p. 744 fn. 5).

2. Federal Rules of Evidence: The Federal Rules of Evidence have modified this principle slightly for federal trials. Under Rule 606(b), the general principle is stated that "A juror may not testify as to any matter or statement occurring during the course of the jury's deliberations or to the effect of anything upon his or any other juror's mind or emotions as influencing him to assent to or dissent from the verdict … or concerning his mental processes in connection therewith. …"

    a. Exception for extraneous information: However, that same Rule makes one exception: a juror may "testify on the question whether ***extraneous prejudicial information*** was improperly brought to the jury's attention or whether any ***outside influence*** was improperly brought to bear upon any juror." Thus a juror could testify that he or a fellow juror ***read a newspaper article*** about the case, or was bribed by one of the parties. But he would not be allowed to testify that he didn't really agree with the verdict but just went along with the others, or that he and/or the others failed to heed the judge's instructions.

3. Bias discovered after trial: Suppose that after the trial, one of the lawyers discovers that a juror ***failed to disclose*** information during *voir dire* that would have indicated possible bias. The lawyer may make a ***motion for a new trial*** (*infra*, p. 302). At least in federal litigation, the Supreme Court has held that the lawyer must show the following in order to prevail on a new trial motion: (1) that the juror "failed to ***answer honestly*** a ***material question***" during the *voir dire*; and (2) that a correct response "would have provided a valid basis for a challenge for ***cause***." *McDonough Power Equipment, Inc. v. Greenwood,* 464 U.S. 548 (1984).

    a. Inadvertent error: Under this standard, if the juror fails to disclose information because he ***innocently misunderstands*** the question, the new trial motion should not be granted.

    b. Discretion of trial court: In any event, a new trial motion based on subsequently-discovered bias, like new trial motions in general, is "committed to the ***discretion*** of the [trial] court" under the Federal Rules. See *McDonough, supra.* Therefore, if the district court denies the motion, it will only rarely be overturned on appeal.

Quiz Yourself on
THE JURY

77. P has sued D in a diversity action brought in the federal court for the District of Iowa. According to properly-adopted local court rules for the Iowa District Court, a civil jury shall consist of six members. P's claim against D was tried before a six-person jury, and the jury split 5-1 in favor of P. No aspects of the jury trial procedure have been agreed upon between the parties. May a verdict be entered in favor of P?

_____

78. Same facts as prior question. Now, however, assume that before the trial, P and D signed a stipulation providing that any verdict reached by four or more of the six jurors shall be taken as the verdict of the entire jury. The jury split by 4-2 in P's favor. Should the judge enter a verdict in favor of P?

_____

79. P sued D in federal court for the District of Colorado. The suit, which was based on diversity, alleged that D negligently injured P in an automobile accident. At the close of D's case, the judge instructed the jury that under Colorado law of comparative negligence (applicable here because of *Erie* doctrine) any contributory negligence by P would not bar P from recovery. However, the judge omitted to point out, as requested by D, that under Colorado law if P's fault was greater than D's, P may not recover at all. D's lawyer made no comment on the judge's jury instructions. The jury found in favor of P. On appeal, D now asserts that the trial judge's failure to give the requested "P more negligent than D" instruction constitutes reversible error. Assuming that the appellate court agrees that the judge's instruction was erroneous, should the appellate court affirm the verdict? _____

Answers

77. No. The six-person jury is allowable; see *Colgrove v. Battin*, 413 U.S. 149 (1973) (holding that a six-person jury does not violate the Seventh Amendment right to jury trial in civil cases, and allowing such a jury where provided by local court rules). But it *is* required in federal civil trials that the verdict be *unanimous*. See FRCP 48, which states, "Unless the parties stipulate otherwise, the verdict must be unanimous[.]" Since P and D did not stipulate that a less-than-unanimous verdict would suffice, the trial must be treated as a "hung jury" and the case retried.

78. Yes. Federal Rule 48 expressly allows a stipulation of the parties regarding what majority shall control. See the language quoted in the answer to the prior question.

79. Yes, probably. Federal Rule 51(d)(1) provides that "A party may assign as error: (A) an error in an instruction actually given, if that party properly objected; or (B) a failure to give an instruction, if that party properly requested it and — unless the court rejected the request in a definitive ruling on the record — *also properly objected*." As you can see from the italicized phrase, a request for a particular instruction, made before the judge gives his instructions, is not a substitute for an after-the-instruction objection. Therefore, by the strict language of Rule 51, D waived his right to an instruction on this point by failing to object before the jury retired. There is some chance that the appellate court might conclude that this error was "plain error" which should be reversed despite the lack of an objection; however, most appellate courts in the federal system are reluctant to reverse even for plain error in instructions, on the theory that this wastes judicial resources (since a new trial is necessary, whereas with a timely objection the judge might have corrected his mistake and obtained a properly-instructed jury verdict the first time around).

VII. CHALLENGING THE JUDGE FOR BIAS

A. Judicial bias generally: The trial judge has a great deal of power. This is obviously true in bench trials. But it's also true in jury trials, where the judge makes many important procedural decisions, such as decisions about the admissibility of evidence or the instructions to be given to the jury. And judges, being human, are sometimes *biased* — or give the appearance of bias — for or against one of the litigants. Therefore, both federal and state systems try to protect the litigants against judicial bias. In general, systems do this by giving a litigant a chance to ask the judge to *"recuse" (i.e., disqualify) herself* from the case where there is a danger of bias.

B. The federal recusal statute: In federal litigation, the problem of judicial bias is handled by two statututory provisions, 28 U.S.C. §§ 144 and 455.

    1. For cause only: The federal system permits a litigant to challenge a judge only for *cause* (in §144) — unlike some states, such as *California*, the federal system does *not* give litigants any *"peremptory"* challenges analogous to those given as to jurors (see *supra*, p. 295). Y, p. 583.

    2. Grounds for recusal: 28 U.S.C. §455 specifies the circumstances under which there is cause for a judge to recuse herself. Section 455 recognizes *two main categories* in which recusal is required:

        a. Broad provision: The first is a *broad*, but *vague*, category: "Any justice, judge, or magistrate of the United States *shall* disqualify himself in any proceeding in which his *impartiality might reasonably be questioned."* 28 U.S.C. §455(a). So this is an "*appearance*-of-bias" standard — if the facts are such that it would *look to an observer* as though the judge might well be biased for or against one party, the judge must recuse himself even if he *subjectively* (and reasonably) *believes* that he can in fact be perfectly fair to both sides. (But the parties may agree to *waive* any danger of bias under this general provision.)

        b. Narrow provisions: 28 U.S.C. §455(b) then contains a number of narrow, *specific* categories requiring recusal. Unlike the vague "appearance of bias" category covered by §455(a), the parties are *not free to waive* the conflict in a situation covered by §455(b). Some of the specific categories requiring recusal under §455(b) include:

        [1] that the judge has "*personal knowledge* of disputed *evidentiary facts*" that will be involved in the suit;

        [2] that the judge served as a "*lawyer* in the *matter in controversy*" when he was in private practice, or was *associated* with a lawyer who served in that matter while the two practiced law together;

        [3] that when the judge "served in *governmental employment*," he "*expressed an opinion* concerning the *merits* of the *particular case*";

        [4] that the judge or a member of his immediate family "has a *financial interest* in the

subject matter in controversy or in a *party* to the proceeding." This provision, by the way, is interpreted exceptionally *stringently*: for instance, if the judge owns even *$1 of stock* in a company that is a party, the judge must recuse himself.

C. **Bias great enough to violate due process:** In extreme circumstances, a judge's *refusal* to recuse himself for bias, or apparent bias, may constitute a violation of a litigant's *federal constitutional right to due process*. The Supreme Court found such a due process violation to have occurred in a celebrated 2009 case involving large *campaign expenditures* by one litigant on behalf of a candidate for a judgeship, where the judge won election and then heard the case. See *Caperton v. A.T. Massey Coal Co., Inc.*, 129 S.Ct. 2252 (2009).

1. **Facts:** In *Caperton*, plaintiffs were small mining companies who claimed that D, a much larger mining company, had improperly driven them out of business. The Ps obtained a $50 million damage award from a West Virginia jury. D appealed to the West Virginia Supreme Court. While the appeal was pending, the CEO of D spent $3 million in independent campaign expenditures in what turned out to be a successful attempt to have a sitting justice of that court replaced by Brent Benjamin. (This sum was more than all others contributed to Benjamin's campaign, and three times the amount spent by Benjamin's own campaign committee.) When the appeal came before the court, Benjamin refused to recuse himself; he then voted with a 3-2 majority that threw out the $50 million verdict against D. The Ps claimed that Benjamin's refusal to recuse himself violated their federal constitutional due process rights.

2. **Holding:** By a 5-4 Vote, the U.S. Supreme Court agreed with the Ps that Benjamin's refusal to recuse himself had violated their constitutional due process rights. The majority held that due process could be violated not just by proof of "*actual* bias," but also by a "*serious risk* of actual bias ... based on *objective and reasonable perceptions*[.]"

   a. **Application to facts:** The majority then articulated one of the situations in which a serious risk of bias will be deemed to exist: where "a person with a *personal stake* in a particular case had a *significant and disproportionate influence* in *placing the judge on the case* by *raising funds* or *directing the judge's election campaign* when the case was *pending or imminent*." The majority said that this would happen only in "*rare cases*," but that the present case was one of those rare "*extreme*" situations.

   b. **Significance:** So as a result of *Caperton*, civil litigants have a federal constitutional due process right not to have their case litigated in front of a judge who poses a serious risk of actual bias. Cases where the apparent bias is great enough to rise to the level of a due process violation will probably be rare. But in states where judges are *elected* (there were 39 such states at the time of *Caperton*), it may well be enough that a litigant has made large campaign contributions or expenditures for or against one candidate, at a time when that candidate was likely to soon hear the litigant's case.

VIII. DIRECTED VERDICT / JUDGMENT AS A MATTER OF LAW

A. **Effect:**   In both state and federal trials, either party may move for a *directed verdict*. Such a verdict *takes the case away from the jury, and determines the outcome as a matter of law*. (In federal trials, the party now moves for "judgment as a matter of law" rather than the more traditional "directed verdict." FRCP 50. We will continue to speak generally of "directed verdicts," but use the federal phrase "judgment as a matter of law" when speaking specifically of federal practice.)

1. **Federal trials:**   In federal trials, a party may move for *"judgment as a matter of law"* after the other party "has been *fully heard* on an issue. ..." FRCP 50(a)(1). Generally, this means that the defendant may move for a directed verdict at the *close of plaintiff's case*. Either party may move for directed verdict after *both sides* have rested.

B. **Standard for granting directed verdict:**   As a general rule, "the court has the power to direct a verdict if the evidence is such that *reasonable [persons] could not differ* as to the result." Wr., 672.

1. **Federal standard:**   Federal Rule 50 articulates a standard for granting *"judgment as a matter of law"* (the federal term combining directed verdict and JNOV): "If a party has been fully heard on an issue during a jury trial and the court finds that *a reasonable jury would not have a legally sufficient evidentiary basis to find for the party on that issue*, the court may: (A) resolve the issue against the party; and (B) grant a motion for judgment as a matter of law against the party on a claim or defense that, under the controlling law, can be maintained or defeated only with a favorable finding on that issue." Rule 50(a)(1).

> **Example:** P is an inventor who has invented a two-deck VCR, which can be used to make copies of video tapes. P brings suit against D1 and D2, the two largest VCR manufacturers, asserting that they conspired to block her from manufacturing and selling her invention. In P's direct case, she shows that D1 and D2 both refused to manufacture her invention, but shows no evidence whatsoever that the Ds conferred with each other, or tried to influence any other manufacturer not to make P's device. At the close of P's case, the federal trial judge, either on his own motion or on a motion by D, should order judgment as a matter of law against P. That is, the trial judge should conclude that no reasonable jury could, based on the evidence produced by P, find that the asserted conspiracy existed.

2. **Distinction:**   Some courts have distinguished between the amount of evidence needed to direct a verdict *against* the party bearing the burden of persuasion, and that needed to direct a verdict in *favor* of that party.

   a. **Stronger showing where burden against movant:**   Clearly, a party seeking a directed verdict must make a stronger showing of evidence if he bears the burden of persuasion. But it is difficult to formulate a clear conceptual distinction between the two degrees of evidence required.

C. *Erie* **effect of directed verdict standards:**   The Supreme Court has never decided whether the degree of evidence needed to issue a judgment as a matter of law in a diversity case is controlled by state or federal law. F,K&C, pp. 695-96. Most federal courts have followed what they perceive to be federal law.

D. **Use of JNOV:**   A judge's grant of a directed verdict, thus taking the case from the jury, may be reversed on appeal. This will necessitate a new trial, and the original jury's work will be wasted. For this reason, most judges "reserve decision" on a directed verdict motion until after the jury has reached a verdict; the motion is then treated as one for a judgment notwithstanding the verdict (JNOV). This procedure is described more fully *infra*, p. 306. (Federal Rule 50 now obliterates the difference between directed verdict and JNOV — both concepts are combined to "judgment as a matter of law.")

Quiz Yourself on
DIRECTED VERDICT; JUDGMENT AS A MATTER OF LAW

80. P has brought a diversity-based contract action against D in federal court. The sole issue in the case is whether D in fact signed the document that P has proffered as "the contract." At trial, the only witnesses were P and D. P testified that D signed the contract. D testified that he did not sign the contract. No documentary evidence was produced (except for the alleged contract document itself). After both sides rested, the judge instructed the jury, and the jury found in favor of P. D has now moved for judgment as a matter of law (after having complied with any procedural prerequisites for this motion). In considering the j.m.l. motion, the trial judge has a fairly strong belief that D told the truth and that P lied; however, the judge also recognizes that if P's testimony is believed rather than D's, P should win the case. The judge has also concluded that a person would not be completely irrational in concluding that it was D, rather than P, who had lied. Should the judge grant the j.m.l. motion? _____

81. P brought a negligence action against D in federal court, based on diversity. At the close of P's case, D immediately presented his first and only witness, and at no time made any motions. The jury found in favor of P. D then made a motion for j.m.l. Assuming that the trial judge agrees with D's contention that a reasonable jury could not possibly have found in favor of P, should the trial judge grant D's j.m.l. motion? _____

Answers

80. **No.** When a judge decides a j.m.l. motion (as when she decides a motion for directed verdict), the judge's job is not to substitute herself for the jury. Instead, her task is to decide whether a reasonable juror could possibly find in favor of the non-movant; if the answer to this is "yes," the j.m.l. or directed verdict must be denied. Where the non-movant (here, P) presents testimony which if believed is adequate to make out a claim, the judge will rarely grant the motion even though the judge believes the contradicting testimony supporting the movant. On the other hand, if the trial judge believed that P's testimony was so implausible, so internally self-contradictory, or so completely contradicted by other evidence that no rational juror could believe it, then it would be proper for the judge to grant the motion.

81. **No.** Rule 50(a)(2) says that a j.m.l. motion may be made "at any time before the case is submitted to the jury." 50(b) then says that any j.m.l. motion made after trial must be a "renewed motion," i.e., a *repeat of a motion made before* the case was submitted to the jury. See Adv. Comm. Notes to 2006 Amendment to Rule 50 ("Because the Rule 50(b) motion [i.e., the post-verdict motion] is only a renewal of the preverdict motion, it can be granted only on grounds advanced in the preverdict motion.") Since on our facts, D never moved for j.m.l. before the case went to the jury, he has waived his right to seek a j.m.l. now (post-trial). This means that the most D can get, either from the trial judge or on appeal, is a new trial, not an entry of judgment in his favor.

IX. SPECIAL VERDICT AND INTERROGATORIES

A. Special verdict: A special verdict is a *specific finding of fact*, as opposed to a general verdict, which merely grants victory to one side or the other.

B. Permitted by Federal Rules: Rule 49(a) allows a court at its discretion to order a special verdict "in the form of a *special written finding* on each issue of fact." This procedure is not used very often. (But state-court trials often make use of special verdicts.)

    1. Judge's omission of issue: If the judge fails to submit a question on a specific issue of fact when he gives his list of special verdict questions to the jury, the parties waive their right to a jury trial on that issue if they do not object before the jury retires. Rule 49(a).

C. General verdict with interrogatories: The judge may, instead of requiring a special verdict, require a general verdict supported by interrogatories as to specific findings of fact. Rule 49(b).

    1. Where consistent: If these facts are consistent with the verdict, the verdict is entered.

    2. Where inconsistent: If the findings of fact are inconsistent with the verdict, the judge may either enter a judgment consistent with the interrogatory answers, ignoring the jury's verdict, or he may order a new trial.

    3. Return to jury: If the answers are inconsistent with *each other*, the judge must send the case back to the jury for further deliberation.

X. NEW TRIAL

A. Judge's discretion: The trial court in both state and federal courts generally has wide discretion to grant a motion for a *new trial*, since such a motion runs less of a risk of abridging the Seventh Amendment than does a directed verdict or a JNOV.

B. Federal new trials: The Federal Rules set different standards for granting new trials in jury and non-jury cases.

    1. Grounds for new jury trial: Where there has been a jury trial, the judge may order a new trial "for any reason for which a new trial has [before 1938] been granted in an action *at law*" in federal court. Rule 59(a)(1).

    2. Grounds for new non-jury trial: Where the action was tried without a jury, a new trial may be granted for any of the reasons an *equity court* would have granted rehearing. Rule 59(a)(2).

        a. Evidence rulings in non-jury trials: Judges conducting non-jury trials typically err on the side of admitting *too much*, rather than too little, evidence. This approach certainly lowers the risk that the judge will be reversed on appeal. That's because it is highly unusual for a new trial to be ordered, even on appeal, because of the *admission* of incompetent evidence by a judge sitting without a jury. Conversely, a judge who excludes evidence in a bench trial that an appellate court later finds admissible can easily be overturned.

3. **Harmless error:** A new trial may *not* be granted for *"harmless error,"* that is, an error that does not affect the "substantial rights" of the party seeking the new trial. So, for instance, the judge's error admitting or excluding evidence won't be grounds for a new trial if the judge believes that the error didn't affect the outcome of the case. This result comes from Rule 61, which says:

> "Unless *justice requires otherwise*, *no error* in admitting or excluding evidence — or any other error by the court or a party — is *ground* for granting a *new trial*, for *setting aside a verdict*, or for vacating, modifying, or otherwise disturbing a judgment or order. At every stage of the proceeding, the court *must disregard all errors and defects that do not affect any party's substantial rights.*

4. **Objection required:** For most types of error at the trial court level (e.g., the erroneous admission or exclusion of evidence), the party injured by the error must make a *timely objection*, in order to preserve the right to cite that error on appeal as a ground for a new trial. For more about the need to make an objection in order to preserve an issue for appeal, see *infra*, p. 320.

5. **\Grounds for new trial:** Some of the more common grounds for granting a new trial are: (1) judicial error; (2) prejudicial conduct by party, witness or counsel; (3) juror misconduct; (4) verdict against the weight of the evidence; (5) excessive or inadequate verdict; and (6) newly discovered evidence. We consider each of these immediately below. (The discussion that follows assumes that the new trial motion is addressed to the trial judge. However, the appellate court can order a new trial on essentially the same grounds.)

C. **New trial so judge can correct own error:** The trial judge may order a new trial because of what the judge has concluded were *her own errors* committed during the trial. This is especially likely to occur in jury trials, where the judge believes that her errors have tainted the jury's verdict. "The trial judge may thereby correct its own errors in much the same way that an appellate court does." James & Hazard, p. 383.

1. **Examples:** Thus, the trial judge may grant a new trial where she is convinced that she has improperly charged the jury, or where she believes that she has improperly excluded or admitted evidence.

D. **New trial for prejudicial conduct by party, witness or counsel:** If a *party*, *witness*, or *counsel conducts herself improperly*, so that there is a substantial risk that an unfair verdict has resulted, the trial judge may grant a new trial.

> **Example:** In the closing argument of a tort suit brought for battery, P's lawyer repeatedly — and after being warned not to do so by the judge — calls D racially derogatory names. The jury awards large damages against D. If the judge believes that these remarks so prejudiced the jury that D didn't receive a fair trial, the judge may order a new trial.

E. **New trial for jury misconduct:** A new trial may under some circumstances be granted where there is evidence that the jury behaved improperly. The criteria for granting a new trial based on this are discussed *supra*, p. 296.

F. New trial where verdict against the weight of the evidence: Most jurisdictions allow the trial judge to set aside a verdict as *"against the weight of the evidence."* States vary in the standard for doing so.

1. **Unlimited discretion:** A *minority* of courts give the trial judge virtually ***unlimited discretion*** in deciding whether to grant a new trial on this ground. If he grants a new trial, he will not be reversed for abuse of discretion "where there is *any evidence* which would support a judgment in favor of the moving party."

2. **Strict test:** A different minority of courts are extremely strict about when a new trial may be granted. In these courts, the judge may *not* order a new trial if "on the evidence as presented and under the pleadings, the ***jury could reasonably have found in accordance*** with the verdict as rendered." This boils down to virtually the same test that is sometimes used in determining whether to allow a directed verdict. J & H (3d ed.), pp. 385-86. See *supra*, p. 300.

3. **Federal standard:** The *federal courts,* and some state courts, have taken a ***middle position***. The judge does not have unlimited discretion, but neither is he as restricted as on a motion for directed verdict. According to the classic formulation of the federal test, the judge must on motion order a new trial "if he is of the opinion that the verdict is against the ***clear weight*** of the evidence, or is based upon evidence which is *false*, or will result in a miscarriage of justice, ***even though there may be substantial evidence which would prevent the direction of a verdict." Aetna Casualty & Surety v. Yeatts***, 122 F.2d 350 (1941). See also James & Hazard, p. 393.

    a. **No substitution of judgment:** The federal test emphasizes that the judge must ***not substitute his own judgment*** for that of the jury on matters of credibility of testimony and weight of evidence, unless the verdict is so obviously against the general trend of the evidence "that the court can clearly see that [the jury] has acted under some mistake, or from some improper motive, bias, or feeling." James & Hazard, 320. ***It is not enough that the judge merely disagrees with the verdict, and would vote otherwise if he were a juror.***

        i. **Granting of JML and new trial distinguished:** A new trial may be granted, under the federal test, even if there is substantial evidence to support the verdict (e.g., new trial because of excessive verdict or verdict against the weight of the evidence.) A motion for "judgment as a matter of law" (JML), on the other hand, may *not* be granted under such circumstances. (In the federal system, JML is the modern term for both the JNOV and directed verdict motions. *Supra*, p. 300.)

G. New trial where verdict is excessive or inadequate: Where the damages allowable in an action are *fixed* as a *matter of law*, or are liquidated (e.g., an insurance policy with an upper amount), a verdict in *excess* of this sum may be set aside as being wrong as a matter of law. James & Hazard, p. 394. Similarly, a verdict which gives plaintiff *less* than he is allowed by law, given that he is entitled to recovery, may be set aside.

1. **Where excess is matter of discretion:** But where the damages are set according to the jury's *discretion*, as in the case of personal torts, trial judges are more hesitant to set aside a verdict as *excessive*. However, if the damages are completely out of line, the judge may order a new trial. Since the judge's power to do so dates back well beyond the enactment

of the Bill of Rights, the Seventh Amendment is not in danger of violation — that Amendment allows re-examination of facts tried by jury "according to the rules of the common law."

2. **Inadequate:** Where the verdict is *inadequate*, but not fixed by law (as in a nominal recovery for a very serious tort injury), the judge also has some power to order a new trial. Where it is apparent that the inadequacy of the verdict is due to the jury's mixing of issues of liability and damages, courts differ. Some invariably set aside the verdict, on the grounds that as a matter of law, the jury must consider the two issues separately. Other courts allow such compromises to stand. James & Hazard, p. 394.

H. *Remittitur* and *Additur*: A judge may find the jury's verdict excessive or inadequate, but may wish to avoid, if possible, ordering a new trial. This is particularly the case where he is confident that the jury has decided the issue of liability properly, but has miscalculated the damages. He may therefore ***conditionally order a new trial***, the new trial to occur ***unless the plaintiff agrees to a reduction*** of the damages to a specified amount (***remittitur***), or (where the damages are inadequate), the new trial to occur ***unless the defendant consents to a raising*** of the damages (***additur).***

1. **Validity:** The validity of the ***remittitur*** in federal practice is today firmly established. James & Hazard, 396. The ***additur***, however, has been found by the U.S. Supreme Court to be in ***violation of the Seventh Amendment***, and is therefore ***not allowed in federal trials.*** (The Seventh Amendment has not been applied to state trials). ***Dimick v. Schiedt***, 293 U.S. 474 (1935).

2. **Allowed in many state trials:** Some *states allow* the trial judge to use the additur. States are free to do this, because the Seventh Amendment (the basis for the Supreme Court's *Dimick* decision banning the additur in federal trials), does not apply to state trials.

3. **Amount of *remittitur*:** The usual test for determining the amount of the *remittitur* is that it should reduce the verdict only to the ***highest amount that the jury could properly have awarded***. James & Hazard, p. 401. This seems to be established as the federal rule. *Id.* at 402, n. 52.

4. **Not appealable:** If the plaintiff accepts the *remittitur*, he may not thereafter ***appeal*** the trial court's *remittitur* order. *Donovan v. Penn Shipping Co.*, 429 U.S. 648 (1977).

I. Partial new trial on damages: It is sometimes apparent from the jury's verdict that they have reached an acceptable conclusion as to one issue, but an incorrect decision as to another. This most typically occurs with respect to the separate issues of liability and *damages* — the trial judge finds the jury's conclusion that defendant is liable perfectly reasonable, but feels that the damages are either inadequate or excessive. Rather than using the *remittitur* or *additur*, he may grant a new trial ***on the issue of damages only***.

J. New trial for newly discovered evidence: *Four criteria* must generally be met before a judge will grant a motion for a new trial because of ***newly discovered evidence***. (F,K&C, pp. 778-79).

    [1] **New discovery:** The evidence must clearly have been ***discovered since the end*** of the trial;

    [2] **Diligence:** The movant must demonstrate that he was "reasonably ***diligent***" in his

search for evidence prior to and during trial, and that he *could not reasonably have found* the evidence in question *before* the trial's end;

[3] **Materiality:** The evidence must be *material* (not just cumulative or impeaching), and "of such character that on a new trial such evidence will probably produce a different result"; and

[4] **Injustice:** In addition to the above criteria, "[a]s a practical matter the motion is usually denied unless the trial judge has an abiding feeling that *injustice* has plainly resulted." F,K&C, pp. 779-80.

K. **Appealability of new trial order:** An order for a new trial is normally *not appealable*, at least in the federal system, because it is not a *final judgment*. James & Hazard, p. 41. A party who wishes to raise on appeal the granting of a new trial must wait until the new trial has been carried out, and has yielded a final judgment. He may then appeal from the final judgment, and raise as an issue the new trial order. (For more about when and how this "final judgment rule" applies, see *infra*, p. 323.)

Quiz Yourself on
NEW TRIAL

82. P has brought a diversity-based product liability action against D in federal court. The jury has awarded damages (compensatory only) of $3 million, a sum which the trial judge believes to be at least twice what a reasonable damage award would be. However, the judge agrees with the jury's finding that D should be liable. The judge does not want to waste the litigants' and court's time by ordering a new trial. What should the judge do? _____

Answer

82. **Grant a remittitur.** That is, the judge should conditionally order a new trial — the new trial will occur unless P agrees to a reduction of the damages to an amount set by the court, probably $1.5 million. It will then be up to P whether to accept this "deal" or not. If P accepts, he may not appeal the remittitur thereafter, and must be content with the $1.5 million. If P declines the remittitur, he must go through a new trial, which he may lose entirely.

XI. JUDGMENT NOTWITHSTANDING VERDICT (JNOV) / JUDGMENT AS A MATTER OF LAW (JML)

A. **Dilemma:** A judge who is requested to direct a verdict is in a dilemma. If he grants the directed verdict, the appeals court may find that he erred, and a whole new trial will be necessary, wasting the original jury's work. But if he denies the motion, he may be sending a case to the jury that should be decided as a matter of law, and he risks being overturned on appeal.

1. **Use of JNOV:** Many judges avoid this problem by *reserving judgment* on a motion for a directed verdict, and submitting the case to the jury. Then if the jury decides against the movant, the judge can evaluate the legal sufficiency of the evidence on a motion for *judgment notwithstanding the verdict* (judgment *"non obstante veredicto"* in Latin, or

JNOV). A JNOV results in the entry of **judgment for the party who lost the verdict;** it is a finding that the verdict had **no sufficient legal basis.**

    a. **Rationale:** The use of the JNOV avoids the need for a second trial if the appellate court holds, contrary to the trial court, that the evidence was not sufficient to take the case from the jury. The jury's verdict can simply be reinstated.

2. **Federal Rules change term:** In federal practice, the concept of JNOV no longer exists. Under a 1991 amendment to FRCP 50, the trial judge, even after the jury's verdict, grants **"judgment as a matter of law,"** rather than a JNOV. See FRCP 50(b).

    a. **Practice unchanged:** The underlying practice remains unchanged. Most importantly, the party seeking judgment as a matter of law must make a **motion** for that judgment **before the case is submitted to the jury.** The moving party must "specify the judgment sought and **the law and facts** that entitle the movant to the judgment." Rule 50(a)(2). Then, the judge submits the case to the jury, and waits for its verdict. Now, assume verdict goes against the movant. Assume further that the movant **renews** the motion after the verdict (as she must do under Rule 50(b), second sentence, if the judge is to reconsider the motion). If the judge agrees with the movant that no reasonable jury could have found against the movant, then the judge may effectively overturn the jury's verdict by granting judgment as a matter of law.

    Example: P brings an employment discrimination action against his former employer, D, alleging racial discrimination. The suit is brought in federal court. After both sides have presented their evidence, D believes that P has not made an evidentiary showing that would enable a reasonable jury to find that D discriminated against P on the basis of race. Before the case goes to the jury, D should make a "motion for judgment as a matter of law," pursuant to FRCP 50(a).

        Even if the judge agrees that no jury could find in P's favor on the core issue of whether there was racial discrimination against P, the judge will probably **reserve decision** on D's motion, and submit the case to the jury anyway. If the jury finds in favor of P, and the judge believes that the jury could not reasonably have done so, then the judge will belatedly grant judgment as a matter of law (or, alternatively, order a new trial). See FRCP 50(b). If D failed to make the judgment-as-a-matter-of-law motion before the case went to the jury, then the judge would *not* be authorized to grant the judgment as a matter of law. See FRCP 50(b). (The reason for requiring a motion before the case is sent to the jury is "to assure the responding party an opportunity to cure any deficiency in that party's proof that may have been overlooked. …" Advisory Committee Notes to FRCP 50.)

3. **Applicable to defenses:** JNOV (or, under federal practice, Judgment as a Matter of Law) is usually entered on a claim. But some jurisdictions permit JNOV/JML to be entered on a **defense** as well. Thus, under FRCP 50(a), the court is authorized to issue JML on a defense, either for or against the party asserting the defense.

    Example: P brings a federal court diversity action against D for battery, alleging that D shot him. D raises a Rule 8(c) affirmative defense, claiming that the shooting was in self-defense. Under Rule 50(a), if the judge concludes that no reasonable jury could find for D on the self-defense defense, the judge can prevent that defense from being submitted to the jury.

B. Combined new trial and JML motions: In federal practice, a motion for judgment as a matter of law (JML) may be *combined* with one for a new trial. Rule 50(b).

    1. Conditional ruling: Then, if the judge grants the JML motion, she must also *rule conditionally* on the new trial motion. Later, if the JML order is reversed on appeal, and the trial judge has conditionally *granted* the new trial motion, the new trial occurs *automatically*, unless the appeals court specifies otherwise. Rule 50(c)(1).

        a. Effect of denial of new trial motion: If the trial judge conditionally *denies* the new trial motion, then the *original verdict is reinstated* if the grant of JML is overturned on appeal.

    2. Utility: This provision for conditional ruling *saves time*, because the appeals court is not obliged to remand for a determination of whether to award a new trial.

XII. CONSTITUTIONAL RIGHT TO JURY TRIAL

A. Seventh Amendment: The Seventh Amendment provides that "in suits at *common law* … the *right of trial by jury* shall be *preserved*. …"

    1. No state application: This provision clearly applies to *federal* trials. It has *never been held applicable to state trials*. We shall consider only the right to jury trial in federal actions in this section.

    2. Federal Rule protection: Federal Rule 38(a) provides that "the right of trial by jury as declared in the Seventh Amendment to the Constitution — or as provided by a federal statute — is preserved to the parties inviolate."

        a. Party must demand: This right is not self-executing. A party who wishes a jury trial on a particular issue must file a *demand* therefor to the other parties within 14 days after the service of the last pleading directed to that issue. (Rule 38(b)).

    3. Distinguished from equitable claim: But there is no jury trial as to "equitable" claims (e.g., a claim for injunction). The legal/equitable distinction is discussed further below.

    4. "Preserving" the right of jury trial in suits "at common law": Notice that the Seventh Amendment says that the right of jury trial "shall be *preserved*." In other words, the drafters of that amendment were continuing a right that already existed, at the time the Amendment was adopted in 1791. Notice further that the Amendment applies only to "suits at *common law*." These two phrases ("...be preserved" and "at common law") mean, in essence, that *only if the suit is one that would or could have been a suit "at common law" in 1791 will there be a right to jury trial.*

B. Modern statutes and procedural devices, and their effect on the jury-trial right: Two trends — the expansion of modern statutes, and the rise of modern multi-party, multi-claim litigation — have complicated the issue of when a party has a right to a jury trial.

    1. Pre-merger simplicity: Before the merger of law and equity, litigation at law was generally restricted to single-action cases demanding single remedies. Furthermore, most of those single-action cases were based on common (judge-made), rather than statutory, law. It was thus usually simple to determine whether a cause of action was "at common law," and therefore merited a jury trial as provided by the Seventh Amendment, or whether the action was equitable, and did not qualify for jury trial.

2. **Modern trends complicate this:** But two modern trends have greatly complicated the problem of deciding when there is a right to jury trial:

   a. **Modern statutes:** First, there are *far more statutes* in existence now than there were in 1791. And those statutes frequently confer remedies that are different from the remedies that would have been available for a similar wrong in 1791.

   b. **Multi-party problems:** Second, litigation today is *procedurally far more complex* than it was in 1791. For example, any given case is much more likely to involve multiple parties, multiple claims, multiple configurations (e.g., P sues D1 and D2; D1 counterclaims against P, but also cross-claims against D2, and impleads X — see generally Chap. 8). This type of modern multi-party, multi-claim litigation makes it very difficult at times to determine what is equitable and what is legal, and therefore to figure out to what cases and issues the right of jury trial applies.

3. **Various problems:** We consider below three main problems that the modern explosion of statutes and procedural devices has raised:

   [1] What happens when a case contains *both legal and equitable claims*, and some factual issues are common to both the legal and the equitable claims? (See Par. C below for the answer.)

   [2] How does the court determine *whether a particular claim is legal or equitable*? The problem arises mainly when the claim is based on a *statute* that has no precise analogue in pre-1791 law. (See Par. D, p. 311 *infra*, for the answer.)

   [3] What is the effect of a *procedural device that didn't exist "at common law"* at the time the Seventh Amendment was enacted? (See Par. E, p. 313 *infra*, for the answer.)

C. **Mixed legal and equitable claims:** Modern cases often contain *both legal and equitable claims*. When this happens, often there are *factual issues that are common* to both sorts of claims. What happens to the right of jury trial when this occurs?

   1. **Distinct issues:** It may be the case that some of the claims in a specific lawsuit are legal, and some are equitable, but that the issues of fact involved are particular to each claim. There is then no problem in trying the equitable claims to the judge, and the legal claims to the jury — neither interferes with the other, and the order of hearing can be determined by considerations of judicial efficiency, since there are no common factual issues.

   2. **Issue of fact common to legal and equitable claim:** But where an *issue of fact is common to a legal and to an equitable claim*, problems arise. If the equitable claim is tried first, the judge's findings of fact will be *binding on the jury* which subsequently tries the legal claim, by the doctrine of "law of the case." Yet the case may be such that it is inefficient to try the legal claim first. For instance, if a party wishes to have a contract reformed for mutual mistake, and then to recover for breach of the reformed contract, it makes little sense to try the legal recovery issue before trying the equitable reformation issue.

3. ***Beacon Theatres:*** The principal Supreme Court case dealing with this problem of "issues of fact common to both legal and equitable claims" is ***Beacon Theatres v. Westover***, 359 U.S. 500 (1959). The case stands for the proposition that where there are both legal and equitable claims in the same case, the trial judge must ordinarily ***try the legal claims first*** (to the jury), so as to preserve the right of jury trial as to those claims.

   a. **The facts:** The facts of *Beacon Theatres* were as follows:

      i. Plaintiff Fox Theaters had certain contracts with movie distributors allowing it exclusive showing rights to films. A competitor, Beacon Theatres, threatened Fox with an antitrust suit, claiming that the contracts were in restraint of trade.

      ii. Fox sought both an injunction preventing Beacon from instituting the antitrust suits, and also a declaratory judgment that its contracts with the distributors did not violate the antitrust laws.

      iii. Beacon counterclaimed that the contracts were indeed in violation of the antitrust laws, and sought treble damages. It demanded a ***jury trial*** on the factual issues presented by its counterclaim.

   b. **Lower court's holding:** The district court held that even though certain factual issues were common to both Fox's claim and Beacon's counterclaim, it would hear Fox's claim for equitable relief first. The appeals court affirmed.

   c. **Supreme Court's reversal:** The Supreme Court held that the judge had ***no authority to hear the equitable claim first***, against Beacon's wishes. To allow it to do so might "operate either by way of *res judicata* or collateral estoppel so as to conclude both parties with respect [to the issues involved in] the subsequent trial of the treble damage claim."

      i. **Summary of holding:** Thus *Beacon* stands for the proposition that ***where there are both legal and equitable claims in the same case***, the trial judge must ordinarily ***try the legal claims first***, so as to ensure the right of jury trial as to those claims (unless, of course, there has been a waiver of the jury trial right).

      ii. **Legal claim rarely triable second:** The Court in *Beacon* did not absolutely forbid, in all situations, the trial of equitable claims before legal ones. But it held that only if the party asserting the equitable claims would be ***irreparably harmed*** by having these claims delayed till after hearing of the legal claims, could the court hear the equitable claims first (assuming that issues of fact common to the legal and equitable claims were involved.)

      iii. **No problem in *Beacon*:** This rare situation clearly did ***not*** exist in *Beacon* itself. The status quo could have been temporarily preserved by a temporary injunction preventing Beacon from starting other antitrust suits during the trial; this injunction would not have resolved any important fact issues. Then, the underlying issues germane to Beacon's counterclaim (e.g., the issue of whether the distributor contracts violated the antitrust law) could have been tried by a jury. If the jury found that there was no antitrust violation, then a permanent injunction could have been issued by the trial court against further suits by Beacon, and a declaratory judgment could have been entered. In summary, the Federal Rules gave the trial judge in *Beacon*, as in nearly all cases, enough flexibility to ensure that equitable rights were preserved even though issues germane to a legal claim were tried first.

D. Deciding whether a particular statutory claim is legal or equitable: Putting aside the problem of mixed legal and equitable claims, how is a court to determine whether a particular claim is legal or equitable? The issue arises mainly in the case of claims based on a *statute* that *didn't exist* — or even have a close analogue — in pre-1791 law.

1. **Two-part test:** The Supreme Court has articulated a *two-part test* for deciding whether a claim based on a modern statute is legal or equitable:

   ❏ First, "we compare the *statutory action* to the 18th-century actions brought in the courts of England prior to the merger of the courts of law and equity."

   ❏ Second, "we examine the *remedy* sought and determine whether it is legal or equitable in nature."

   Tull v. U.S., 481 U.S. 412 (1987). The Court has consistently held that the second of these inquiries — concerning the nature of the remedy sought — is the more important. *Id.*

2. **Application in *Tull*:** *Tull* itself provides a good illustration of how the two-part test works.

   a. **Facts:** In *Tull*, the federal government sued D for millions of dollars for violating the Clean Water Act. D asked for a jury trial, but the trial court denied the request. The government got a judgment of $325,000 after the bench trial.

   b. **Holding:** The Supreme Court held that D was *entitled* to a jury trial on the issue of liability.

      i. **First part not dispositive:** As to the first part of the test — nature of the statutory action — the Court conceded that the Clean Water Act had some resemblance to an 18th century action to abate a public nuisance, which was equitable.

      ii. **Second part more important:** But the second part was the more important one, the Court said. And on that part — nature of the relief sought — the answer was unequivocally *"legal."* That is, the government was seeking a *civil penalty*, for the purpose of punishing D, and that type of relief had always been legal rather than equitable.

      iii. **Court may fix amount:** However, the Court concluded, D had no right to a jury trial on the issue of the *amount* of the penalty, once liability was determined. The issue was whether the right to a jury trial on amount of the civil penalty was "fundamental[ly] … inherent in and of the essence of the system of trial by jury"; the Court concluded that it was not.

3. **Damages usually legal:** A post-*Tull* case illustrates that a claim for *compensatory damages* will be *legal* except in rare cases. That case is *Chauffeurs, Teamsters and Helpers Local 391 v. Terry*, 494 U.S. 558 (1990), a case involving breach of a union's duty of representation.

   a. **Facts:** The Ps in *Terry* were union truck drivers who asserted that D (the union) had violated its duty of fairly representing them in their dealings with their employer regarding seniority. The Ps sought money damages to compensate them for the wages and benefits they would have received had the Union not breached that duty of representation.

b. Right to jury found: The Court found that the Ps were entitled to a jury trial on their claim. Again, the Court applied the two-part test of *Tull*, and again the Court found that the second part of the test (nature of relief sought) was the more important.

    i. Statutory action: On the first part (nature of the statutory action), there was no action in 18th Century England that was truly comparable to a suit for breach of a union's duty of representation. Therefore, the Court had to find the most analogous action that existed. However, this inquiry was complicated by the fact that the Ps, to win, would have had to prove two separate statutory violations, by two different entities:

        (1) First, the Ps would have had to have shown they had a valid claim against the *employer* under a federal statute, § 301 of the Labor Management Relations Act, for violating a collective bargaining agreement;

        (2) Then, the Ps would have had to show that the *union* violated a separate statute requiring a union to *represent its members fairly* in connection with the collective agreement.

    The first part (the § 301 violation) was comparable to a breach of contract claim, and was thus legal. But the second part (breach of the union's duty of representation) was most comparable to an action by a trust beneficiary against a trustee for breach of fiduciary duty — in 18th-Century England, this was an equitable action. So the nature of the statutory action was ambiguous.

    ii. Nature of relief sought: On the more important issue — nature of the relief sought — the answer was clearly *"legal."* The only relief sought by the Ps was *compensatory damages*, to make up for the wages and benefits they would have received had the Union done its duty properly. And, the Court said, this was a classic action for money damages, "the traditional form of relief offered in courts of law."

        (1) Not restitutionary: The Court conceded that there was one instance in which "damages" could be equitable: where they were *"restitutionary,"* i.e., awarded to force the defendant to *disgorge a benefit* that it received unjustly. For instance, an employee's action against an *employer* for backpay would fall into this equitable category, because the employer unjustly kept the employee's wages. But here, even though the action was in a sense for "backpay," the Ps were not seeking money wrongfully kept by the union. Therefore, the relief they sought fell within the *usual rule that money damages are legal*, not within the exception saying that restitutionary damages are equitable.

c. Significance: So *Terry* establishes that a *claim for compensatory damages* will be *legal*, except in the unusual case where it seeks restitution of a benefit unjustly kept by the defendant (as in a suit for backpay against an employer).

4. **Construction of written documents is best done by judges:** Occasionally, the two-part test used in *Tull* and *Terry* won't give a clear answer about whether the claim in question is best treated as legal or equitable based on pre-1791 jurisprudence. When this happens, the Court will consider (at least sometimes) "the *relative interpretive skills of judges and juries*[.]" *Markman v. Westview Instruments, Inc.*, 517 U.S. 370 (1996). For instance, in *Markman* itself the Court performed a "functional analysis" of the relative skills of judges and juries, and concluded that *judges are the better decisionmaker* when the *"construction of written instruments"* is at issue. Consequently, the Court found no right of jury trial as to the written-instrument-dependent question at issue there, involving patents.

E. **Procedural devices and the expansion of legal claims:** Several Supreme Court cases demonstrate that as *new procedural devices* have proliferated, these devices have *expanded the types of claims and cases that will be legal.*

1. **Explanation:** To understand why this is so, first remember that equitable relief — for instance, an injunction or order of specific performance — will be available *only where legal relief would be inadequate.* As newer procedures have broadened the results that can be obtained in what are essentially suits for legal relief, a wrong for which equity would formerly have been the remedy (because legal relief was inadequate) might well now become a wrong for which legal relief is adequate (making equitable relief unnecessary and thus unavailable).

2. *Dairy Queen:* The older case of *Dairy Queen v. Wood*, 369 U.S. 469 (1962), illustrates how this expansion of the scope of legal relief may happen.

   a. **Facts:** The facts of *Dairy Queen* were as follows:

      i. **Licensing:** D had been licensed by P to use the latter's "Dairy Queen" trademark. The terms of the contract provided that D make certain payments for the use of the trademark.

      ii. **Plaintiff's claims:** D fell behind in payment, and P sought two kinds of relief: (1) an injunction preventing D from further use of the trademark, and (2) an "accounting" to determine the amount owed by D, and a judgment for that amount.

      iii. **D's jury trial motions:** D moved for jury trial on the accounting demand, arguing that since it was a demand for a money judgment, it was clearly legal, not equitable.

      iv. **Plaintiff's response:** P countered that the demand was equitable, since it asked not for damages but for an "accounting."

   b. **Supreme Court allows jury trial:** The Supreme Court held that a jury trial *must be allowed on the claim for accounting.* No matter whether the claim was for damages for trademark infringement, or for the sum owed under the contract (it was not clear which was being sought), the claim was definitely *legal*.

      i. **Nature of claim not determined by pleadings:** First, the use of the word "accounting" in the complaint did not make the claim equitable — "the constitutional right of trial by jury *cannot be made to depend on the choice of words used in the pleadings.*"

    ii. Legal relief not inadequate: More importantly, the claim could have been equitable *only if no adequate legal remedy was available.* Where a money judgment is sought, the only reason legal relief might be inadequate is because the accounts between the parties are so complicated that a jury cannot understand them. But now that special masters were available under Rule 53(b) to assist the jury in understanding such complicated matters, it certainly could not be said that legal relief was inadequate.

    iii. Equity constricted, law enlarged: So procedural innovations at law — like the ability here to use a special master to assist the jury — can *constrict the scope of equity*, and therefore *increase the right of jury trial.*

3. Other procedural devices: Post-*Dairy Queen* decisions have demonstrated that other procedural devices can involve a right to jury trial, even though the device was historically available only in equity. Examples are *class actions* (see *infra*, p. 355), *shareholder's derivative actions*, and *interpleader* suits (*infra*, p. 392). As the Supreme Court has said, *"nothing now turns upon … the procedural devices by which the parties happen to come before the court." Ross v. Bernhard*, 392 U.S. 531 (1970)

F. Limitations on jury trial right: In several special situations the courts have considered whether there is a right to jury trial:

1. Declaratory judgment: Recall that the plaintiff in *Beacon, supra,* p. 310, sought, among other things, a *declaratory judgment* that the distributor contracts were valid. Unlike a suit for injunction, a suit for declaratory judgment is, by itself, *neither legal nor equitable*. Moore's Manual, §22.01[6]. Instead, it is the *underlying issues* which control whether there is a right to a jury trial in a declaratory judgment suit.

    a. Contract action: Thus suppose an action were brought to obtain a declaratory judgment that a particular contract was valid. The facts underlying a counterclaim raised by the defendant might determine the extent to which there was a right to a jury trial: facts suggesting the right to *have the contract reformed* would not be triable before a jury (since reformation is equitable), but facts showing that there *was a contract*, and that it was *breached by one side*, would be triable before a jury (since actions for breach of contract are legal.)

2. Complex case: In a footnote to *Ross v. Bernhard, supra,* the Supreme Court indicated that one factor to be considered in determining whether there was a right to jury trial is "the *practical abilities and limitations of juries." Therefore, it may be that there are some cases that are *so complex* that their mere complexity makes them unsuitable for jury trial. However, while courts and commentators have hinted at this possibility, few if any cases have ever actually found that the case in question dictated a complexity exception to the right of jury trial. The argument for a "complexity exception" to the Seventh Amendment is strongest in *securities and antitrust* cases, because of the large numbers of claims, and huge numbers of documents, that are often involved in such cases.

    a. Courts of Appeal are split: The federal courts of appeal are *split* about whether a case can be so exceedingly complex that there should be no right to jury trial. Compare, e.g., *In re Japanese Electronic Products Antitrust Litigation*, 631 F.2d 1069 (3d Cir. 1980) (holding that if a case is too complex for jurors to decide by rational means, a jury trial would violate the Due Process Clause of the Fifth Amendment, but not deciding whether the particular case there met this condition) with *In re U.S. Financial Securities Litigation*, 609 F.2d 411 (9th Cir. 1979) (rejecting a "complexity exception" to the Seventh Amendment even though the case would have required the factfinder to read over 100,000 pages during a two-year trial).

b. No Supreme Court case on point: The Supreme Court has never decided whether there should be such a "complexity exception" to the right to jury trial.

Quiz Yourself on

CONSTITUTIONAL RIGHT TO JURY TRIAL

83. P has sued D for negligence in Colorado state court. A recently-enacted Colorado statute provides, "In any civil suit in which the amount in controversy is less than $10,000, the case shall be tried before a judge sitting without a jury." P's claim is for $9,000. P asserts that the statute, insofar as it deprives him of the right to have his claim tried before a jury, violates the Seventh Amendment. Is P's contention correct?

_____

84. On July 1, P served on D a summons and complaint for a federal district court action alleging breach of contract. On July 15, D served an answer on P. There were no pleadings after the answer. At no time did P make a demand for a jury trial. On September 1, shortly before the case was to be tried, D served upon P a demand that the case be tried before a jury. Is D entitled to a jury trial? _____

85. P has brought a federal trademark infringement action against D. P seeks two types of relief: (1) an injunction prohibiting D from further violating P's trademark; and (2) money damages for the past violations. D seeks a jury trial on any issues for which he has a jury trial right.

   (a) On which, if either, of the two claims does D have a jury trial right? _____

   (b) What rule should the court follow with respect to the order in which the issues should be tried?

_____

86. Insurer wrote a $100,000 policy on the life of X. X, who owned the policy, notified Insurer that the beneficiary should be W, X's wife. Two years later, just before X died, he wrote to Insurer, "I wish to change the beneficiary from W to S, my son." After X's death, both W and S made a claim to the policy proceeds (W's claim was on the basis that X was not mentally competent at the time he purported to change the beneficiary). Insurer instituted a Rule 22 interpleader action in federal court, with W and S as the defendants. Insurer and S were content to have the case heard by a judge, but W demanded a jury trial. Is W entitled to a jury trial on the issue of whether she is the proper beneficiary? _____

Answer

83. **No.** The Seventh Amendment is one of the few Bill of Rights provisions that has never been "incorporated" into the 14th Amendment's due process guarantees. Therefore, the Seventh Amendment applies only to federal, not state, civil trials. A state is free to deny juries entirely in civil trials if it wishes.

84. **No.** According to Federal Rule 38(b), "On any issue triable of right by a jury, a party may demand a jury trial by: (1) serving the other parties with a written demand — which may be included in a pleading — no later than *14 days after the last pleading directed to the issue* is served; and (2) filing the demand [with the court.]" This means that the last time D could demand a jury trial was 10 days after he served his

answer, or July 25. After that, he waived his right, and only in very exceptional cases will the court relieve him from this waiver.

85. **(a) Only the damages claim.** Federal Rule 38(a) gives the right of jury trial "as declared by the Seventh Amendment to the Constitution." That Amendment applies only to suits "at common law." Therefore, there is only a right to a jury trial (unless Congress specifically otherwise provides) where the suit is one which is "legal" rather than "equitable." An injunction suit is always regarded as "equitable," so there is no right to a jury trial on an injunction claim. A claim for damages, by contrast, is virtually always "legal," so it does carry with it a right to a jury trial.

(b) The court should try the damages claim first. If the court tries the injunction claim (without a jury) first, this will probably bind the jury when the jury hears the damages claim later, because of the doctrine of "law of the case." Yet if the jury is not given comparatively free rein in deciding the damages claim, D's right to a jury trial is violated. Therefore, even though it may be somewhat inefficient, the federal judge should try the damages claim first, then the injunction claim, if there are significant issues in common between the two. (There are almost certainly such common issues here, e.g., the issue of whether P's trademark is valid and whether D has in fact infringed it.) See *Beacon Theatres v. Westover*, 359 U.S. 500 (1959).

86. **Yes.** The issue is whether the action is legal or equitable. It may well be that prior to the enactment of the Federal Rules of Civil Procedure in 1938, interpleader was regarded as an equitable action. But today, the court determines whether a claim is equitable or legal not by reference to the procedural device by which the parties come before the court (here, interpleader) but rather, by reference to the **underlying claim**. Here, the underlying issue is basically an issue of contract law (was X competent to change the policy beneficiary?), and such a contract-law issue will almost always be legal rather than equitable. Since the underlying issue is legal, each party has the right to demand a jury trial as to that issue (and if one party so demands, there will be a jury trial even though the other parties do not want one). See *Ross v. Bernhard*, 396 U.S. 531 (1970) (for determining whether the claim is legal or equitable, "nothing now turns upon … the procedural devices by which the parties happen to come before the court").

XIII. REMEDIES

A. **Introduction:** At this point, we're going to say a few things about "remedies," that is, the *types of relief* that the court awards to successful litigants.

B. **Damages generally:** The primary form of judicial relief is *money damages*. Indeed, the vast majority of the cases we've looked at so far in this outline are suits for money damages. We consider here the two major types of damages, compensatory and punitive.

C. **Compensatory damages:** The usual form of money damages is *"compensatory"* damages. Compensatory damages attempt to make the plaintiff *"whole"* for the damage she has suffered as the result of the defendant's wrongdoing. For instance, in a contract action, the usual form of damages for breach is a form of compensatory damages called "expectation" damages — the sum of money needed to put the plaintiff in the position she would have been in had the contract been fulfilled.

D. Punitive damages: A second form of damages is *"punitive"* damages. Punitive damages, as the name implies, are used to *"punish"* the defendant for extreme wrongdoing. Punitive damages are rare in contract suits, but are somewhat common in tort suits, especially those involving serious personal injuries.

1. **Due process limits:** For our present purposes, we're interested in one particular sub-issue relating to punitive damages: to what extent is a court's freedom to award punitive damages curtailed by the federal constitutional requirement that each litigant (including each defendant) be given *"due process* of law"? The answer, which has only started to become clear in the 1990s, is that the due process clause imposes real limits on the awarding of punitive damages. Here's a brief summary of what we can say at this point:

   a. **"Grossly excessive" standard:** An award will violate due process if it is *"grossly excessive."* *BMW of North America v. Gore*, 517 U.S. 559 (1996).

   b. **Appellate review required:** A state must give the defendant *appellate review* of the amount of any punitive award.

   c. **Ratio of actual to punitive:** One of the most important factors in whether an award of punitive damages violates due process is the *ratio* of the *punitive damages* to the *actual damages.* The Court's latest word about the permissible ratios (as of mid-2006) is that *"few awards* [significantly] exceeding a *single-digit ratio* between punitive and compensatory damages ... will satisfy due process." *State Farm Mut. Automobile Insur. Co. v. Campbell*, 123 S.Ct. 1513 (2003).

      i. *BMW v. Gore:* For instance, in one of the two cases in which the Supreme Court has found that a punitive damages award was so excessive that it violated the defendant's due process right, the court attached a lot of weight to the fact that the punitive award to P was *500 times* the amount of his actual harm as determined by the jury. *BMW of North America, supra.*

         (1) **Facts:** In the *BMW* case, P proved that D, a car manufacturer, had sold him as "new" (and for full price) a car that had in fact been repainted due to acid-rain damage. The jury found that such a car was worth $4,000 less than a truly new car (even though P did not discover the repainting until an expert happened to examine it for unrelated reasons). But the jury also awarded $4 million of punitive damages, which the Alabama appellate courts reduced to $2 million.

         (2) **Holding:** The Supreme Court, by a 5-4 vote, concluded that even this $2 million award violated D's due process rights. The extreme ratio of actual damages to punitive damages was one factor in the majority's analysis. Another was that D's conduct was *not especially reprehensible* (e.g., there was no trickery or deceit, just basic non-disclosure). A last factor was that the punitive damages assessed were vastly greater than the civil or criminal penalties that could have been imposed (under either Alabama law or the law of other states) for similar conduct. All in all, the award was "grossly excessive."

      ii. *State Farm* case: Similarly, in a 2003 case the Court found that a punitive damages award of $145 million (*145 times* the $1 million compensatory award) violated the defendant's due process rights. *State Farm Mut. Automobile Insur. Co. v. Campbell, supra.*

(1) Facts: In *State Farm*, D (an insurance company) refused to settle a case in Utah against P (the policy holder) for the policy limits, even though there was (the Supreme Court later concluded) a "near-certain probability that by taking the case to trial, a judgment in excess of the policy limits would be awarded." The Ps suffered emotional distress from facing a judgment of $136,000 in excess of the policy limit (though D ultimately paid this whole sum before the P-vs.-D suit, thus sparing P from actual financial loss.) The trial court in the P-vs.-D suit allowed in evidence of 20 years worth of assorted alleged wrongdoing by D in states other than Utah, most of which had nothing to do with the refusal-to-pay-valid-claims practice at issue in the case itself.

(2) Ratio too high: As noted, in striking the award the Court relied heavily on the fact that there was a 145-to-1 ratio between punitive and compensatory damages, far higher than the single-digit ratios that the Court said would usually be the appropriate limit.

(3) Irrelevant wrongdoing: But the Court also objected to the trial court's consideration of evidence of other wrongdoing that *"had nothing to do with"* the type of refusal-to-settle wrongdoing at issue in the case itself. One of the key factors in the due process analysis is the *reprehensibility* of the defendant's conduct, and, the Court said, only conduct that is *"similar* to that which harmed [the plaintiffs]" may be considered in determining reprehensibility.

E. Equitable remedies: Money damages are the "usual" form of relief in civil actions. Historically, money damages come from the system of "law" rather than the system of "equity." (See *supra*, p. 1 for more about the distinction between law and equity.) But occasionally, the appropriate form of relief is *"equitable"* rather than "legal."

1. Two forms of equitable relief: There are two main types of equitable relief: (1) *injunctions*; and (2) *orders of specific performance*.

a. Injunctions: An *injunction* is an order of the court *prohibiting* a party from doing something.

Example: P, an author, claims that D, a publisher, is distributing a book that violates P's copyrights. If P can establish that this is true, the court will "enjoin" D from making any further distribution of the book. That is, the court will issue an order telling D not to distribute. If D violates the order, D will be in contempt of court, and can be fined or sent to prison.

b. Specific performance: A decree of *specific performance* is a decree ordering a party to *do something* affirmative, typically, to *comply with a contract.*

Example: P and D have a contract under which D is to supply all of P's requirements for uranium to be used in P's nuclear power generation plant for a 10-year period. D violates the contract by refusing to deliver. The court may well issue a decree of specific performance against D, ordering that D comply with the contract by delivering the required amount of uranium (as opposed to just paying damages for uranium not delivered). If D doesn't comply, D will be in contempt of court, and can be fined or (if an individual) sent to jail.

    c. **Legal remedy inadequate:** A full discussion of the circumstances in which a court will award equitable relief is beyond the scope of this book. For now, just know that the most important single principle about equitable relief is this: the court may only award equitable relief if legal relief (i.e., an award of money damages) is *inadequate in the circumstances*.

    Example: Return to the prior example, about uranium supplies. If the court can compute with reasonable precision how much uranium P will need over the remainder of the contract, and what the market price will be over that period, the court can (and will) make P whole by awarding him damages. But if (as is probable) P doesn't know exactly what his requirements for uranium will be (because he doesn't know how much power he'll need to generate), and/or it isn't knowable what the market price of uranium will be during the future course of the contract, then an award of damages isn't "adequate." (Sure, the court could make a guess about what the market price would be, but that estimate may turn out to be badly wrong in either direction.) Only after determining that damages won't be adequate may the court award the equitable remedy of an order that D specifically perform the contract.

XIV. APPEALS

    A. **Appeals generally:** In both federal and state litigation, the party who loses at trial generally has the right to *appeal* the adverse judgment.

        1. **Not constitutional right:** The Supreme Court has never held that the loser in a civil case has the *constitutional right* to make an appeal. Y, p. 633.

        2. **Virtually all jurisdictions allow:** However, both the federal system and virtually all state-court systems make it relatively easy to take at least one appeal from most civil judgments.

            a. **Intermediate appeals courts:** In the federal system, and in most states, there are *two possible levels* of appellate review. The first level is an *"intermediate"* court, which hears appeals directly from the trial court. In the federal system, appeals from the federal district courts are heard by the "U.S. Courts of Appeal." For more about the setup of the federal court system, see *supra*, p. 2. See also Y, p. 51.

            b. **Highest court:** Then, in both the federal system and in most states, there is a *highest* appeals court, which has the *power* — but typically *not the obligation* — to hear appeals *from the intermediate appeals courts.* In the federal system, this is of course the U.S. Supreme Court, whose powers include the right to hear appeals from the U.S. Courts of Appeal. In most state-court systems, there is a state "supreme court,"[1] which

---

1. State-court naming conventions vary. In New York, for instance, each of the general-jurisdiction trial courts is (confusingly) called the "Supreme Court," the intermediate appeals courts are called the "Appellate Division, *n*th Department," and the highest court is called the "Court of Appeals."

typically has discretion about which civil appeals to hear from that state's intermediate appeals courts.

    i.   **Supreme Court's jurisdiction over state-court appeals:**   The U.S. Supreme Court does *not* have general jurisdiction to hear appeals from all *state-court cases.* As a constitutional matter, only cases that *raise an issue of federal law* — in fact, only ones raising a federal issue whose resolution was *necessary* for arriving at the state court judgment — may be heard on appeal by the Supreme Court.

        Example: Suppose the California Supreme Court, interpreting California tort law, decides in a car-accident case that P is entitled to recover compensatory damages against D. Assuming (as seems likely) that no federal constitutional or statutory issue is posed by the case, the U.S. Supreme Court does not have constitutional authority to review the California Supreme Court's decision. That's true even if the Supreme Court believes that the decision is an incorrect application of state law, or that the decision is unwise as a matter of public policy.

B. **The scope of appellate review:** The function of American appeals courts is *not* to ensure that the trial court made no errors. Allowing appeals courts to review, as part of a free-ranging search for error, everything that happens in the trial court would be very expensive, and would unduly prolong litigation. Therefore, both federal and state systems have various procedural rules that significantly limit *what issues* may be grounds for reversal.

    1. **Requirements for an issue to be reviewed:** Here are the three major procedural limits on what *types of issues* will be reviewed on appeal, and on whether the appellate court will reverse on account of those issues:

        [1]   The loser must *preserve the issue* during the trial-court proceeding (typically by making an *"objection"*), and must then raise the issue properly on appeal.

        [2]   If the issue is one of *fact*, the appellate court will typically give *great deference* to the trial court's handling of the matter, and is much less likely to reverse than for an error of *law.*

        [3]   The appeals court will not reverse where it finds that the error was *"harmless."*

    Let's look briefly at each of these three limits.

    a. **Preserving the issue and raising it properly on appeal:** A party must be careful to (1) *preserve the issue* during the trial-court proceedings, and to (2) *raise the issue properly* during the appeal.

        i.   **Objection:** The requirement that the issue be preserved means that both during *pretrial* proceedings, and during the trial itself (if there is one), the party must make sure that (1) any error that is later to be the subject of an appeal *is reflected on the trial court record*; and (2) the trial court is *made aware* that that party is dissatisfied with the court's handling of the issue. Typically, this means that the party who hopes to raise issue X on appeal must make an *"objection"* to the trial court's handling of X, and must state on the record her *grounds* for that objection.

            (1) FRCP 46: Thus in federal trials, FRCP 46 says that for any ruling or order that's made or denied, the party must *"state* the action that it wants the court to take or *objects* to, along with the *grounds* for the request or objection." If the party doesn't do this, that contention is deemed *waived* on appeal. Notice the requirement that the *grounds* be stated; the idea is to "avoid situations in which a litigant can *'sandbag'* the trial court — by vaguely expressing an objection, then proceeding through the rest of the trial, hoping to win on the merits but thinking it has 'banked' an appellate reversal in case of a loss." Y, p. 630. (But Rule 46 *abandons* the common-law requirement that the party must make a formal *"exception"* to the ruling in order to preserve it for appeal.)

ii. **Raising on appeal:** The appellant must also properly *raise the issue* during the appeal itself. This means that only the issues that are *presented in the parties' briefs* — and as to which the relevant part of the *trial court record* is brought to the appellate court's attention — will be considered on appeal. F,K&M (3d), p. 620. So, for instance, a party cannot *during oral argument* raise an issue that was not previously presented in the briefs.

b. **Deference to trial court:** Even assuming that the error was properly preserved for appeal, the appeals court will *not* necessarily make its own *"de novo"* (i.e., *from-the-ground-up*) determination of whether the trial court and/or jury got it right. The appellate court will usually make a closer scrutiny of decisions of *law* than of findings of *fact*, and will typically give a somewhat closer (though not all-that-close) review to factual findings by a judge sitting *without a jury* than to the factual basis for a jury verdict.

i. **Questions of law:** If the issue is a *pure question of law*, the appeals court typically decides the issue *from scratch* — it *does not give deference* to the trial court's ruling. F,K&M (3d Ed.) p. 621.

Example: Suppose the case is a federal age-discrimination-in-employment suit, brought by a plaintiff who was 39 at the time of the alleged discrimination. The trial judge instructs the jury that any plaintiff who was over the age of 35 at the time of the discrimination can potentially recover under the relevant statute.

The correctness of this instruction presents a pure issue of law. Therefore, the federal Court of Appeals will decide the issue from scratch — it will not give deference to the trial court's reasoning about how the statute should be interpreted. If the appeals court believes that the statute should be interpreted to allow recovery only by those who are over 40, it will automatically apply this view (and reverse if the error was non-harmless).

ii. **Factual basis for jury verdicts:** When the issue involves solely findings of *fact*, and those findings were made by a *jury*, appellate courts are *very reluctant* to reverse and thereby second-guess the jury.

(1) **State courts:** In *state-court* systems, the legislature generally gives the state's appellate courts the *power* to reverse a civil jury verdict as being *"against the weight of the evidence."* However, state courts exercise this power only rarely, limiting reversal to cases where it is *very clear* to the reviewing court that the jury got it wrong.

(2) Federal courts: Appellate reversals of jury findings of fact are even rarer in the *federal-court* system, for federal *constitutional* reasons. The *"re-examination clause"* of the *Seventh Amendment* says that "no fact, tried by a jury, shall be *otherwise re-examined* in any Court of the United States, than *according to the rules of common law.*" The Supreme Court has indicated that the re-examination clause limits the power of federal appeals courts to reverse the factual findings of juries. See *Gasperini v. Center for Humanities*, Inc., 518 U.S. 415 (1996) (other aspects of which are discussed *supra*, p. 259). See also Y, p. 661. A federal appeals court will generally overturn a jury verdict because of what it perceives as fact-finding error only if there is a virtually *complete absence of proof* on some material issue (so it's not enough that the appellate court thinks that the jury's verdict is against the weight of the evidence). See F,K&M (3d Ed.), pp. 624-25.

iii. Facts found by judge in bench trial: Appellate courts conduct a somewhat more probing review of factfinding by *judges* in *bench* trials, i.e., ones conducted *without a jury*. Here, too, however, appeals courts typically give *significant deference* to the trial court.

(1) FRCP 52(a)(6) "clearly erroneous" standard: This deference is *required* in *federal trials* by FRCP 52(a)(6). That Rule says that, in appeals from bench trials, "Findings of fact, whether based on *oral or other evidence*, must *not be set aside* unless *clearly erroneous*, and the reviewing court must give *due regard* to the *trial court's opportunity to judge the witnesses' credibility.*"

Note: As to *oral* testimony, this rule makes obvious sense: the trial judge is watching the witness, and can see her demeanor (e.g., whether she seems forthcoming or evasive), an ability that the appeals court does not have. But Rule 52(a)(6) also covers *written* evidence (documents), where the trial court's advantage in judging credibility does not exist; so the "clearly erroneous" standard applies to such documentary evidence. Why?

As the Supreme Court held in a case that led to the amendment of 52(a) to cover documentary evidence, "The trial judge's major role is the determination of fact, and with experience in fulfilling that role comes *expertise*. Duplication of the trial judge's effort in the Court of Appeals would very likely contribute only negligibly to the accuracy of fact determination at a *huge cost* in diversion of judicial resources." *Anderson v. Bessemer City*, 470 U.S. 564 (1985). As the Court said in *Anderson*, "the trial on the merits should be 'the *main event*,' rather than a *'tryout on the road.'*" That policy means that the federal appeals courts should defer to the trial judge even as to the factual conclusions to be drawn from documents.

c. "Harmless error" doctrine: Even if the issue is properly preserved for the appeal, and the appeals court concludes that trial judge made a mistake, the appeals court will not necessarily reverse. That's because all appellate courts apply some version of the *"harmless error"* doctrine, whereby the results in the trial court will be reversed only if the appeals court believes that there is a substantial chance that the error *made a difference to the outcome*.

i. **Federal standard:** In federal cases, the harmless error doctrine is imposed by statute, 28 U.S.C. §2111. That provision says that the appellate court must conduct its review of the record "without regard to errors or defects which ***do not affect the substantial rights*** of the parties."

Example: P brings a federal diversity action against D for making what P claims was a defective product that injured P. In a jury trial, P puts on no proof that the product was defective. D offers testimony from Expert 1, which is properly admitted, that the product was not defective. D also offers an affidavit to the same effect from Expert 2, which the trial court allows, but which is in fact inadmissible because it is hearsay not within any exception. The jury finds for D. P appeals.

If, as seems likely, the appeals court concludes that even without considering the inadmissible affidavit D has offered so much unrebutted evidence of the product's non-defectiveness that a rational jury could not have found for P, the appeals court will affirm. That is, the appeals court will conclude that the trial judge's error of law in admitting the affidavit was "harmless error," because P was extremely unlikely to win the case even if the affidavit had been excluded. Cf. *Harnden v. Jayco, Inc.,* 496 F.3d 579 (6th Cir. 2007) (similar though not identical facts).

C. **The "final judgment" rule, and exceptions to it:** We turn now to the issue of ***when*** a losing party will be permitted to file an appeal. The only really important issues bearing on this "when" question are (1) whether something called the ***"final judgment rule"*** applies; and (2) if the rule does apply, whether it has been satisfied.

1. **The rule in general:** The federal system, and the vast majority of state systems, apply some form of the ***final judgment rule.*** While the precise parameters of the rule vary from jurisdiction to jurisdiction, the basic concept is that an appeal is allowed "only after ***all the issues*** involved in [the suit] have been ***finally determined by the trial court.***" F,K&M (3d Ed.), p. 600.

   a. **Suit, not just issue, must be finally determined:** So even if a particular ***issue*** in the case has been finally determined, the loser on that issue cannot generally take an immediate appeal. At least in the standard two-party scenario,[2] the final judgment rule means that ordinarily the loser on one or more issues cannot take an appeal until the ***entire case has been finished at the trial-court level***, and a judgment in the case has been entered. *Id.* at p. 601.

      i. **"Interlocutory" appeals:** As a matter of nomenclature, an appeal that is taken when no final judgment has yet been entered is called an ***"interlocutory"*** appeal.

      ii. **Rationale:** The final judgment rule reflects a ***cost-benefit analysis.*** If we ***allow*** interlocutory appeals, the cost is that there has been an ***"unnecessary extra appeal*** if the trial judge turns out to have been ***correct.***" Y, p. 639. But if we ***don't allow*** interlocutory appeals, the cost is "an ***unnecessary*** or an ***unnecessarily long trial*** if the trial judge turns out to have been ***wrong.***" *Id.* at p. 640. The decision of most court systems to apply the final judgment rule is based on two main underlying facts: (1) trial judges are ***reversed far less frequently than they are affirmed***, and

---

2. For multi-party scenarios, see p. 326 *infra*.

(2) final judgments in many cases are ***not even appealed***. Taken together, these facts mean that the risks posed by unnecessary interlocutory appeals are probably greater than the risks presented by allowing trials to go forward that would have been (properly) eliminated by allowing such appeals. *Id.*

b. **Federal statute (28 U.S.C. §1291):** The ***federal*** court system ***applies*** the final judgment rule in a fairly rigorous way. 28 U.S.C. §1291 says that except in a few special situations covered by other statutory provisions, the U.S. Courts of Appeal shall only have jurisdiction over "***final decisions*** of the district courts." Because Congress drafted this provision so that it deprives the federal Courts of Appeal of ***jurisdiction*** to hear an appeal in a case in which no final judgment has been rendered, the Courts of Appeal do not generally have the ***power*** to relax the rule in a particular case even though they think that hearing an interlocutory appeal would serve some important interest, unless one of the special statutory exceptions (discussed *infra*, pp. 326 and 329) to the federal final judgment rule applies.

i. **Partial summary judgment not enough:** For instance, in the federal system a grant of ***partial summary judgment*** — in which, say, the district court finds for the plaintiff on liability but has not yet decided on damages or other relief — does not constitute a final judgment, and cannot yet be appealed by the defendant. If the Court of Appeals hears such an appeal, it is acting without jurisdiction, even though both parties may want the court to hear the appeal immediately.

Example: The Ps, who work for D (a large insurance company), sue D in federal court for employment discrimination, contending that D's insurance benefits and maternity-leave regulations discriminate against female employees. The Ps ask for various forms of relief, including an injunction, damages and attorneys fees. The district court finds initially that D's policies violate federal law, and it issues a ruling "direct[ing] that final judgment be entered in favor of [Ps]" on the issue of liability. But the judge denies any injunction against continuation of these practices, and does not yet decide on damages or attorneys fees. D takes an appeal from the finding of liability, arguing that the appeal is timely under the final judgment rule because the trial judge has ordered that "final judgment" be entered on the liability issue. The Court of Appeals agrees that the final judgment rule has been satisfied. The case then goes to the U.S. Supreme Court (with, apparently, both sides wanting that Court to decide on the merits of the liability issue).

Held, by the Supreme Court: the case should not have been appealed even to the Court of Appeals, because the final judgment was not in fact satisfied. If there had truly been *multiple claims* in the case, and one of those claims had been reduced to a final judgment, then the special multi-claim provisions of FRCP 54(b) (discussed *infra*, p. 326) might have allowed an immediate appeal of the final judgment on that one claim. But here, the Ps asserted a single legal theory (that D's policies violated a particular provision of federal employment law), and argued that this theory applied to a single set of facts. This meant that the Ps were making only a single "claim." And that single claim had not been finally disposed of, since some (indeed all) of the types of relief that the Ps had requested remain undecided. It's true that the Ps asked for *multiple forms of relief* pursuant to that one claim, but a grant of partial summary judgment on liability alone (which is effectively what the trial court did here) does not constitute a final judgment within the meaning of 28 U.S.C. §1291, even if the trial court calls what it did a "final judgment."

There are two escape hatches to the final-judgment rule, but neither applies here. First, there is a provision (28 U.S.C. §1292(<u>a</u>), discussed *infra*, p. 329) by which a grant or denial of an *injunction* may be immediately appealed; but even if what the trial court did here were deemed to be a denial of an injunction, that would have allowed only the *Ps* to appeal, and the appellant here was D (which wasn't the loser on the injunction issue, and therefore couldn't appeal on that issue). Second, there is also a provision (28 U.S.C. §1292(<u>b</u>), discussed *infra*, p. 326) allowing the district court to *certify a question* for interlocutory appeal when the issue is very important. But the district court did not make such a certification here (and even if it had, the Court of Appeals would have had to formally agree in its discretion to hear the appeal, which is not how the appeals court proceeded here — it heard the appeal because it thought it *had to* under the final-judgment rule, not because it was accepting a certification request). "Were we to sustain the procedure followed here, we would condone a practice whereby a district court in virtually any case ... might render an interlocutory decision on the issue of liability ..., and the defendant would thereupon be permitted to appeal ... without satisfying any of the requirements that Congress carefully set forth." ***Liberty Mutual Insur. Co. v. Wetzel***, 424 U.S. 737 (1976).

c. **State-court exceptions:** The *states* are, whenever they wish, free to decide not to impose the final-judgment rule. A few states in fact allow interlocutory appeals where the federal system would not. Most famously, in **New York**, a very broad range of interlocutory appeals is allowed.

2. **When is a judgment "final":** If an appeal is not permitted except from a "final" judgment, it will often be important to know exactly **when** a final judgment has occurred. Answering this "when" question will often be needed in order to decide whether an appeal is "too early" (as in *Liberty Mutual v. Wetzel*, supra). But the answer can also be important in cases where the appeal is arguably "too late," because all systems impose post-judgment appeals deadlines after which the loser can no longer appeal.

a. **FRCP 58:** In the federal system, FRCP 58 tries to reduce ambiguity by setting out a bright-line standard for determining whether and when a judgment has been reached. In most instances, FRCP 58 says that the judgment "must be set out in a ***separate document***." The purpose of the separate-document requirement is to prevent a litigant from having to worry that something buried in a judge-authored document not labelled a judgment might be held after the fact to be one. The judgment is generally deemed to be ***"entered"*** — thus ***starting the time to appeal*** — when the clerk of the court places the judgment into the ***"civil docket"*** kept in each district for case-tracking purposes. FRCP 58(c)(2).

i. **Time limit:** In ordinary federal civil cases (those not involving the U.S. government), the appellant must ***file a notice of appeal*** with the district clerk ***within 30 days*** after the judgment or order being appealed from was entered. Fed. R. App. Proc. 4(a).

3. **Multi-claim and multi-party federal litigations (FRCP 54(b)):** The final judgment rule poses special problems where the case involves either *multiple claims or multiple parties.* In federal litigation, FRCP 54(b) may allow for an appeal when there is a final judgment on one claim but other claims in the same suit remain. 54(b) says that if the suit involves multiple claims or multiple parties, "the [trial] court may *direct entry* of a final judgment as to one or more, but fewer than all, claims or parties *only if the court expressly determines* that there is *no just reason for delay.*" So if the court does *not* "expressly determine[] that there is no just reason for delay," there can be no appeal as long as some claim, by some party, remains to be completed. 54(b) is thus a special procedure that lets the trial judge in effect *allow an immediate appeal* of the final judgment on just one claim. This special procedure is, in practice, reserved for the *"infrequent harsh case."* F,K&M (3d Ed.), p. 606

   a. **Multiple defendants:** Let's consider how appeals would work in a federal case in which one plaintiff, P, brings claims against *multiple defendants* (say D1 and D2), and all claims arise from a single series of related transactions.

      Example: Assume that both Ds move for summary judgment, and the trial judge grants the motion as to D1 but denies it as to D2. Even if judgment is entered in favor of D1 — dismissing him completely from the case — P normally cannot appeal that decision yet. P must try the case against D2 alone, and only then appeal the dismissal of D1. This means that even if P can later persuade the appeals court that the trial judge was wrong to dismiss D1, P will have had to try two separate cases involving overlapping facts.

      But if P can persuade the trial judge to "*expressly determine* that there is *no just cause for delay*" (FRCP 54(b)) in entering the judgment in favor of D1, then P will be able to *immediately appeal* that judgment, without having to first try the case against D2. In that scenario, if P gets the dismissal reversed on appeal, he can try the claims against D1 and D2 together.

   b. **Multiple claims by P against the sole D:** Now, consider the federal-litigation situation in which there is a *single* plaintiff (P) and a *single* defendant (D), but P has *two claims* against D, each on a different legal theory. Here, too, the same principle applies as in the multi-party situation: if the district court grants partial summary judgment to D *dismissing one of the claims*, P must *try the other claim* without first appealing the dismissal, unless P can persuade the court to invoke Rule 54(b) and "expressly determine[] that there is no just cause for delay."

4. **Certifying the issue:** Another path by which an appeal may be taken in a federal-court action before the entire case has been concluded is the *"certification"* method. 28 U.S.C. §1292(b) sometimes allows an interlocutory appeal of an otherwise-unappealable district court order if the judge who rendered the order certifies that order for an immediate appeal. But this certification method requires that *both* the trial court and the court of appeals *approve* the interlocutory appeal:

   [1] The trial judge has to specifically state in writing in his order (a) that the order involves a *"controlling question of law"*; (b) that on that question, there is *"substantial ground for difference of opinion"*; and (c) that an immediate appeal "may *mate-*

rially advance the ultimate termination" of the litigation. *Id.*

[2] Then, *within 10 days* after the district court's order is entered, the party wishing to appeal the order must ask the court of appeals to hear the appeal. *Id.*

[3] Finally, the Court of Appeals "may ... *in its discretion* ... permit [the] appeal to be taken[.]" *Id.* So if the Court of Appeals does not want to hear the appeal of the certified question, it doesn't have to, and it doesn't need to give a reason for refusing.

> **Note:** *Liberty Mutual Insur. v. Wetzel, supra,* p. 325, is a good illustration of the type of fact pattern in which this "certification" method might have been used. After the district court issued a partial summary judgment in favor of P on the issue of liability, D could have asked the court to certify the liability issue under 28 U.S.C. §1292(b). Then, the Court of Appeals would have had discretion to hear the appeal. (The problem in *Wetzel* itself was that the trial judge did not make the formal certification that's required by §1292(b), so that section was never triggered; therefore, there was no opportunity for the Court of Appeals to use its discretion — it simply didn't have jurisdiction over the appeal.)

5. **The "collateral issue" exception:** There is one more important exception to the final judgment rule in federal litigation, a judge-made rather than statutory exception. This is the so-called *"collateral order"* doctrine. This doctrine holds that even where some part of the case remains unresolved, an order may be immediately appealed if it "*finally determine[s]* claims of right *separable from, and collateral to,* rights asserted in the action, [that] are *too important* to be denied review and too *independent of the cause itself* to require that [an appeal] be deferred until the whole case is adjudicated." *Lauro Lines s.r.l. v. Chasser,* 490 U.S. 495 (1989) (quoting *Cohen v. Beneficial Indus. Loan Corp.,* 337 U.S. 541 (1949)).

   a. **3 requirements:** The Supreme Court has held that the collateral order doctrine allows for an immediate appeal only if the order satisfies *three requirements*:

   [1] the order must *"conclusively determine* the disputed question";

   [2] the order must "resolve an *important issue completely separate from the merits* of the action"; and

   [3] the order must "be *effectively unreviewable* on appeal from a final judgment."

   Lauro Lines, supra.

   b. **"Effectively unreviewable":** The third of these requirements — that the order would be *"effectively unreviewable"* if the loser were force to wait until a final overall judgment in the case before appealing — is the requirement that is most often at issue. (This requirement is sometimes called the requirement of *"practical finality."* But we'll use the term "effectively reviewable" here.)

      i. **Judged based on "entire category":** When the federal court is deciding whether the order is "effectively reviewable," the court is to decide the issue based on what the impact of denying immediate review will be on the *entire category* of which the claim is a part, not on the impact that will occur on the *particular litigant* who is trying to appeal. *Mohawk Industries, Inc. v. Carpenter,* 130 S.Ct. 599 (2009).

So, for instance, if the issue is whether denial of a government official's claim of **absolute immunity** is "effectively reviewable," the court will decide the issue based on the impact of allowing or disallowing review for the **entire category of absolute-immunity claims by public officials,** not by how much of a burden would be placed on the particular official seeking an appeal in the present case.

ii. **Delay damage must be incurable:** Furthermore, it's **not enough** that delaying review will **somewhat diminish** the value of the right. Permitting "piecemeal" prejudgment appeals "undermines **efficient judicial administration.**" *Mohawk Industries, supra.* Therefore, it's not enough that the underlying interest be one that's important — only where delaying the review will "**so imperil** [that] interest as to **justify the cost** of allowing immediate appeal of the **entire class**" of order, will the court apply the collateral order rule. Thus if an eventual reversal on appeal would **cure much of the damage** from an incorrect order, the fact that the party who was required to wait has been *somewhat* damaged by the delay won't be enough. *Id.*

Example: P, a former employee of D, sues D in federal court for employment discrimination. In discovery, P seeks various documents that D contends are protected by the attorney-client privilege. The trial court rules that D has waived the privilege, and that D must therefore produce the documents. D attempts to take an immediate appeal to the Court of Appeals, on the theory that the trial court's rejection of its claim of privilege is immediately reviewable under the collateral order doctrine. The Court of Appeals rules that the collateral order doctrine does not apply, and D appeals again, to the Supreme Court.

Held, for P: the collateral order doctrine does not apply to disclosure orders that reject a claim of attorney-client privilege, so the appeal of such an order must wait until after the trial is completed. The collateral order doctrine applies only where the right in question is "effectively unreviewable" during the ultimate appeal from the final judgment in the case. And the issue of effective-reviewability is to be decided based on the "entire category" to which the claim relates, in this case orders compelling the discovery of materials claimed to be protected by the attorney-client privilege. Postjudgment appeals of such privilege rulings "generally suffice to protect the rights of litigants and assure the vitality of the attorney-client privilege." That's because appellate courts can remedy improper disclosure "the same way they remedy a host of other erroneous evidentiary rulings: by vacating an adverse judgment and **remanding for a new trial**[.]" *Mohawk Industries, Inc. v. Carpenter, supra.*

iii. **Categories that don't qualify:** There are only a *few* categories where the "effectively unreviewable" standard is *satisfied*. So for most types of rulings, the loser cannot make an interlocutory appeal under the collateral order doctrine. Here are some examples of categories where the court has ruled that an interlocutory appeal is *not* permitted:

[1] Orders **denying or allowing** the **introduction of evidence**.

[2] Orders compelling **disclosure of materials** that one party claims are **privileged** (as in the attorney-client privilege situation in *Mohawk, supra*).

[3] Orders denying a party's attempt to have the case **tried somewhere else** on the basis of a **forum-selection clause** in a contract (see *Lauro Lines s.r.l. v. Chasser*, 490 U.S. 495 (1989)).

[4] Orders granting or denying a party's attempt to have the other party's **lawyer disqualified on account of a conflict**.

[5] Orders **denying class action status** (see *infra*, p. 371).[3]

iv. **Categories that qualify:** There are only a very **small number of categories** that the Supreme Court has found to **qualify** for immediate appeal under the collateral order doctrine. Here are the most important ones:

[1] Rulings where a **government official** asserts a **qualified or absolute immunity** from suit, and the trial court denies the motion as a **matter of law**. Cf. *Nixon v. Fitzgerald*, 457 U.S. 731 (1982).

[2] Rulings where the court **refuses to dismiss** an action against a **governmental entity** which has asserted **Eleventh Amendment immunity** from federal-court suit.

[3] Rulings where the (federal) court **declines to apply a state law** requiring that the plaintiff in a **shareholders-derivative action post a bond**.

See Y, p. 649. As the first two categories illustrate, an immediate appeal is most likely to be allowed where the loser has made a claim of **immunity** from being required to **stand trial at all** — if the court perceives that the interest in question is truly an interest in not having to stand trial at all, the court is likely to conclude that the denial of the right cannot be "effectively reviewed" after the party has been forced to stand trial.

6. **Orders involving the grant or denial of an injunction:** In federal litigation, there is a special provision making it easy to take an interlocutory appeal from a decision granting or denying an **injunction**. 28 U.S.C. §1292(a)(1) allows for an immediate appeal of a federal district court order "**granting**, continuing, **modifying**, **refusing** or dissolving **injunctions**, or **refusing to dissolve or modify** injunctions[.]"

Example: The Ps claim that D is running an intentionally-segregated school system in violation of the Ps' constitutional rights. The Ps seek both damages and an injunction against continuation of the segregation. If the court *denies* the injunction, the Ps may take an immediate appeal from this denial, even though D's liability, and the Ps' right to damages, have not yet been resolved. Similarly, if the court *grants* the injunction, D may take an immediate appeal (even though here, too, liability and damages have not yet been decided).

---

3. But FRCP 23(f) gives the Court of Appeals jurisdiction to hear an interlocutory appeal from an order granting or denying class action status; however, this is at the *discretion* of the Court of Appeals, not a right possessed by the party who lost the certification decision.

Quiz Yourself on
APPEALS

87. P, a 50-year-old married executive previously employed by D, a corporation, brings a federal diversity action against D. The suit claims that D breached their employment contract by firing P for posting on Facebook a photo of P at a party. In the photo, P is shown holding a bottle of whiskey, and has his arm around a woman, X, who appears to be a teenager; P has captioned the photo, "Isn't she a babe?" At the ensuing bench trial, both sides agree that the only relevant clause in the contract is one allowing termination for an "act of moral turpitude," a term that is not defined in the document. P testifies that (1) X was a family friend with whom P had no inappropriate relationship, criminal or otherwise; (2) the parties intended "moral turpitude" to cover only conduct that would be both criminal and reflective of serious immorality; and (3) nothing in the photo would suggest to a reasonable observer that P was behaving with moral turpitude. D's CEO testifies that the parties intended "moral turpitude" to include non-criminal acts reflecting a serious error of moral judgment, and that a reasonable observer who saw the photo and who knew that P was married to someone other than X would believe that P was showing poor moral judgment. The trial judge, in an opinion upholding the firing, concludes that as a factual matter D has proved a violation of the moral-turpitude clause. P has appealed to the U.S. Court of Appeals, arguing that, as shown by the trial testimony, his conduct did not constitute a violation of the clause.

(a) What standard should the appeals court use in deciding whether the trial judge was correct in concluding that P violated the contract? _____

(b) When the court applies the standard you listed in (a), should the court affirm or reverse the trial judge's verdict? _____

88. P, an author, brings a federal court action against D, a publisher, claiming that a book published by D violates P's copyrights. The parties agree to have the case tried without a jury. The trial judge decides to hear the case in two stages, liability and then (if there is a finding of liability) damages. After discovery is complete, the judge grants partial summary judgment in favor of P under FRCP 56, on the grounds that there is no genuine dispute about whether D violated P's copyrights. The judge now proposes to hear testimony on the issue of damages. Before testimony begins, and with the consent of P, D files a notice of appeal contending that the judge improperly ordered summary judgment on the liability issue. What should the court of appeals do?

Answers

87. (a) Whether the judge's finding of a violation was "clearly erroneous." FRCP 52(a)(6) says that in bench trials (i.e., trials without a jury), "Findings of fact, whether based on oral or other evidence, must not be set aside unless **clearly erroneous**, and the reviewing court must give **due regard** to the **trial court's opportunity to judge the witnesses' credibility**." The trial court's findings here are essentially about factual matters, including what the parties meant by the ambiguous term "moral turpitude" and how a reasonable observer would have interpreted the photo. So the "clearly erroneous" standard is the standard the appeals court must apply.

(b) **Affirm.** Since the appeal essentially turns on issues of fact, P can win only by showing that the trial court's determination on these issues was clearly erroneous. P and D's CEO gave conflicting on-point testimony on the issues. Therefore, their relative credibility as witnesses was an important part of the trial judge's findings of fact. Because of the importance of witness credibility here, the challenged findings do not meet the hard-to-satisfy requirement that they be "clearly erroneous," and the appeals court must affirm. And that's true even if the appeals judges think that they would probably have reached a different conclusion had they been trying the case.

88. **Dismiss the appeal for lack of jurisdiction.** The federal courts, like those of most states, impose the "final judgment rule." Under 28 U.S.C. §1291, the U.S. Courts of Appeals only have jurisdiction over "final decisions of the district courts." Normally, the federal district judge is not deemed to have made a "final decision" for purposes of §1291 until the judge has entered a "final judgment" in the entire case. The issuance of an order of partial summary judgment here was not a final judgment, since the entire case has not been disposed of. There are some exceptions to the final judgment rule in federal litigation (e.g., the "collateral order" exception), but these exceptions are narrow, and none of them comes close to applying here. Therefore, the Court of Appeals cannot hear the appeal even if it wants to, because it lacks jurisdiction. And the lack of jurisdiction is not waivable by the agreement of the parties, so P's consent to the interlocutory appeal doesn't make any difference. See *Liberty Mutual Insur. Co. v. Wetzel* (*supra*, pp. 324-325).

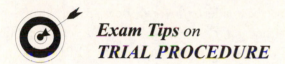

Exam Tips on
TRIAL PROCEDURE

Trial Procedure covers a welter of disparate issues. The professor will often be able to hide the issues from you by having the litigants state their requests and objectives cursorily and without much reasoning (e.g., "D moves for summary judgment"). Because you have to figure out what the reasoning could have been, issue-spotting can be unusually difficult in the trial context.

☛ Keep in mind the distinction between the burden of *"production"* and the burden of *"persuasion,"* — don't use the ambiguous phrase "burden of proof." [282-283]

   ☞ If the facts involve a *presumption*, remember these rules: the party against whom the presumption is directed bears the burden of *production* (if he produces no evidence to rebut the presumption, he suffers a directed verdict or judgment as a matter of law). But in the federal system and most states, the presumption has no effect on the burden of *persuasion* — once the production burden is met, the presumption disappears (*"bursting bubble"*). This is the most frequently-tested aspect of burden of proof / presumptions. [283]

☛ Where a party moves for *summary judgment*, remember the applicable standard: the movant wins only if there is *no "genuine dispute of material fact."* Typically, the facts will *not satisfy* this requirement, and you should conclude that s.j. is not appropriate. For instance, often there will be a genuine dispute of material fact remaining either because:

   ☞ there is a dispositive issue as to which you may feel that one party is highly likely to prevail at trial, but the issue still turns on the *credibility* of the witnesses, or

   ☞ there are *multiple* sub-issues (one of which may be non-obvious), and although there's no genuine factual question as to some part(s), there *is* an issue as to one (probably a non-obvious) part. [288-290]

☛ If the case is *tried to a judge*, and is then *appealed*, be careful to distinguish between fact-based arguments for reversal and law-based ones. Remember that on appeal, the court is extremely *limited* in its ability to reverse for *fact-finding* errors: "Findings of fact, whether based on oral or other evidence, must not be set aside unless *clearly erroneous*, and the reviewing court must give due regard to the trial court's opportunity to judge the witnesses' *credibility*." FRCP 52(a)(6). Normally you should conclude that the appeals court can't reverse, since the prof. probably can't make a fact-finding error seem egregious in a brief question without tipping off the "clearly erroneous" issue. [321-322]

☛ When the case is tried to a jury, be on the lookout for non-unanimity. In the federal system, the verdict must be *unanimous* unless the parties stipulate otherwise (and in the typical fact-pattern, they don't so stipulate). [294]

☛ If a party moves for *judgment as a matter of law* (in the federal system) or directed verdict / JNOV (some states), two points are most vital to remember [299-301]:

☞ The standard is essentially *whether reasonable jurors could differ* as to the result — if they could, the court shouldn't grant JML/directed verdict/JNOV.

☞ The motion (whatever it's called) must be made *before the jury retires*. Profs. frequently have the jury retire without either party's making a directed verdict motion, then have the verdict loser move for JML — it's too late by then. See FRCP 50(a)(2); 50(b).

☛ Professors frequently test on *juror misconduct*. The most important rule to remember is that generally, "the jury *may not impeach its own verdict*." That is, the verdict won't be set aside because of a juror's testimony about his own or another juror's misconduct — only evidence from a *third party* will suffice. [296]

☞ But under the FRCP, there is a limited *exception* — a juror may testify about whether *extraneous prejudicial information* was brought to the jury's attention, or whether any *outside influence* was improperly brought to bear. But a juror can't testify about how the jury conducted its deliberations, so that testimony that, say, the jurors ignored the judge's instructions will still not be allowed under the FRCP.

☛ Fact patterns often involve a party's efforts to obtain a new trial, either from the trial judge or on appeal. Some of the reasons for which the court (either the trial judge or the appellate court) can grant a new trial are [302-305]:

☞ Improper conduct by a *party*, *witness* or *counsel*

☞ *Jury* misconduct (see above)

☞ *Judicial error* (e.g., the judge charges the jury incorrectly)

☞ *Verdict against the weight of the evidence*. (In the federal system, the verdict must be against the "*clear* weight" of the evidence, but a new trial can be granted even if there is substantial evidence supporting the verdict, which would be enough to prevent the issuance of Judgment as a Matter of Law.)

☞ Verdict *excessive* or *inadequate*

Note: Remember that to be grounds for a new trial, the error must "affect any party's substantial rights." FRCP 61. This is the *"harmless error"* doctrine. Whenever your fact pattern suggests to you that one of the above grounds for new trial exists, be sure to mention the possibility that the error might be "harmless" unless it's clear that it's not. [303]

☛ Instead of a new trial, state courts usually allow the judge to order a *remittitur* (new trial to occur unless the victorious plaintiff accepts a lower amount specified by the judge) or *additur* (new trial to occur unless the defendant agrees to pay a higher amount). But in federal trials, only remittitur is allowed — *additur has been held to violate the constitutional right to jury trial.* This last point is frequently tested. [305]

☛ Many essay questions involve the *constitutional right to jury trial*. [308-315] Here are the most important (and frequently-tested) points:

☞ The 7th Amendment (right to jury trial in civil cases) applies only to *federal*, not state, trials.

☞ The 7th Amendment applies only to *"legal,"* not *"equitable,"* issues. [308]

☞ Therefore, you must be on the lookout for claims or defenses that are equitable in nature, so you can point out that there's no right to jury trial on these. Thus attempts to procure an *injunction*, to *rescind* a contract, to receive an *accounting*, or to *reform* a contract for *mistake*, would all be claims for which there is no right to jury trial.

☞ A suit for *money damages* will almost always be "legal." The one exception is where the suit seeks money as restitution for a benefit unjustly held by the defendant (e.g., suit against an employer for backpay which P says he would have earned had the employer not discriminated).

☞ If a case contains *both* legal and equitable claims, and there is an issue of fact common to both, the court must usually allow the *legal claims to be tried first* (to the jury). This is the single most frequently-tested aspect of right-to-jury-trial. You should cite to *Beacon Theatres v. Westover* if this "which claims to try first" issue arises. [310]

☞ In deciding whether something is legal or equitable, remember that it's not the procedural device by which the issue comes before the court, but the nature of the underlying claim, that counts. For instance, a declaratory judgment suit can be either legal or equitable, depending on the underlying issue.

☛ If the exam facts involve a suit that is being *appealed*, make sure that any applicable *final judgment* rule was obeyed. So in *federal* litigation, for instance, if at the time of the loser's appeal the *entire case* hadn't yet been resolved at the trial level, the court of appeals *won't have jurisdiction* unless some exception to the final judgment rule (e.g., the *"collateral order"* doctrine) applies. [323]

Example: If the judge in a federal suit gives partial summary judgment to P on liability but hasn't decided the damages so far, D can't yet appeal.

CHAPTER 8

MULTI-PARTY AND MULTI-CLAIM LITIGATION

ChapterScope

This Chapter examines various devices that either enlarge the number of claims between the existing parties to a litigation, or bring new parties into the litigation. Again, the emphasis is on the devices available under the Federal Rules. The most important concepts in this Chapter are:

■ **Counterclaims:** A *"counterclaim"* is a claim *by a defendant against a plaintiff*. The Federal Rules provide for both *"permissive"* and *"compulsory"* counterclaims. FRCP 13.

❏ **Compulsory counterclaim:** If D's counterclaim arises out of the *same transaction or occurrence* as P's claim, it is a *"compulsory"* counterclaim. If D does not assert her compulsory counterclaim, she will *lose* that claim in any future litigation.

❏ **Permissive:** Any claim that does *not* arise out of the same transaction or occurrence as P's claim is a *"permissive"* counterclaim. D does not lose her counterclaim in future litigation if she declines to assert it in the first suit.

■ **Joinder of claims:** Under the device of *"joinder of claims,"* once a party has made a claim against some other party, he may then make *any other claim he wishes against that party*. FRCP 18(a).

■ **Joinder of parties:** Under the device of *"joinder of parties,"* multiple plaintiffs may join together, or a plaintiff may sue multiple defendants.

❏ **Permissive joinder by plaintiffs:** Joinder done at the *discretion* of the plaintiff(s) is called *"permissive"* joinder. FRCP 20. Multiple plaintiffs may (but need not) join together in an action if they satisfy two tests (1) their claims for relief must arise from a *single "transaction, occurrence, or series of transactions or occurrences,"* and (2) there is a *question of law or fact common to all plaintiffs* which will arise in the action.

❏ **Permissive joinder of defendants:** If one or more plaintiffs have a claim against *multiple defendants*, these defendants may be joined based on the same two tests as plaintiff-joinder. That is, claims against the co-defendants must: (a) arise from a *single "transaction, occurrence, or series of transactions or occurrences"*; and (b) contain a *common question* of law or fact.

❏ **Compulsory joinder:** There are certain situations in which additional parties *must* be joined, assuming the requirements of jurisdiction can be met. Such joinder is called *"compulsory"* joinder. The basic idea is that a party must be joined if it would be *uneconomical* or *unfair* to litigate a claim without her. FRCP 19. (There are two sub-classes involving compulsory joinder: *"necessary"* parties and *"indispensable"* parties. Necessary parties must be joined where possible, but the action can go on without them if joinder is made impossible by jurisdictional problems; indispensable parties are ones so vital that the action must be dismissed if they cannot be joined.)

■ **Class action:** The *class action* is a procedure whereby a single person or small group of co-parties may *represent* a larger group, or *"class,"* of persons sharing a *common interest*. FRCP 23.

❏ **Binding on absentees:** The results of a class action are generally *binding on the absent members*. Therefore, all kinds of procedural rules exist to make sure that these absentees receive *due process* (e.g., they must receive notice of the action, and notice of any proposed settlement).

❏ **Defendant class:** The class may be composed *either* of plaintiffs or defendants. The vast majority of the time, the class will be composed of *plaintiffs*.

■ **Intervention:** By the doctrine of *"intervention,"* certain persons who are not initially part of a lawsuit may enter the suit *on their own initiative*. The person who intervenes is called an "intervenor." FRCP 24.

❏ **"Of right" vs. "permissive":** Intervention can be "of right" or "permissive". "Of right" means that no permission of the court is required; "permissive" means that the court has discretion whether to allow the intervention or not.

■ **Interpleader:** The device of *interpleader* allows a party who owes something to one of two or more other persons, but is not sure whom, to force the other parties to argue out their claims among themselves. The technique is designed to allow the "stakeholder" to avoid being made to pay the same claim twice.

■ **Impleader:** Under the device of *impleader*, a defendant who believes that a third person is *liable to him* for all or part of the plaintiff's claim against the defendant may *"implead"* such a person as a *"third-party defendant" ("TPD")*. FRCP 14(a). The defendant who is making the third-party impleader claims is called the *third-party plaintiff* ("TPP").

❏ **Additional claims:** Once a TPD has been impleaded, she may make *claims of her own*, including counterclaims against the TPP (either permissive or compulsory), cross-claims against any other TPDs, etc.

■ **Cross-claims:** A claim by a party against a *co-party* is called a *"cross-claim."* A cross-claim is made only against a party who is on the *same side* of an already-existing claim (e.g., a claim by one co-defendant against another, or by one co-plaintiff against another).

■ **Jurisdiction and venue:** When dealing with any of these multi-claim and multi-party devices, it's vital to examine the requirements of *personal jurisdiction*, *subject matter jurisdiction* and *venue*. The doctrine of *supplemental jurisdiction* will often (but not always) be available to negate the need for an additional party or claim to independently meet the requirements of federal subject matter jurisdiction.

I.   BACKGROUND

A. Common law: At common law, the prevailing policy was to prohibit any sort of action other than one involving a single plaintiff and a single defendant. Also, a lawsuit was generally limited to a single legal theory, or cause of action.

B. Equity: The courts of equity, however, were willing to entertain more complex sorts of actions, since they used no juries and all their proceedings were in writing. Many of the maneuvers to be discussed in this section had their origin in the willingness of equity courts, as contrasted with common law courts, to hear all possible aspects of a case at once.

1. **Merger:** The merger of law and equity, as represented by the Federal Rules and by the present rules of most states, resulted in the incorporation of multi-party, multi-claim suits into the unitary civil action.

   > **Note:** The material in this chapter treats a number of devices which bring new parties into the action. These devices include ***compulsory and permissive joinder, class actions, intervention, interpleader***, and ***third-party complaints***. Before these joinder-of-party devices are considered, however, two devices which do not bring new parties to the lawsuit, but which enlarge the number of claims between the existing parties, are treated. These devices are the ***counterclaim***, and Rule 18(a) ***joinder of claims.***

II. COUNTERCLAIMS

A. Generally: Suppose the defendant has what he thinks is a valid cause of action against the plaintiff. May he bring this into the original suit, or must he file a separate action of his own?

1. **Common law:** At common law, there were two devices, both quite limited, by which a defendant could bring a claim against the plaintiff:

   a. ***recoupment***, in which he could assert claims arising from the same transaction as the original complaint, but only for the purpose of reducing or cancelling out the plaintiff's recovery. That is, he could ***not*** win an ***affirmative recovery.***

   b. ***set-off***, which was not limited to the "same transaction," but which had to be for liquidated damages or arise out of a contract or judgment. Like recoupment, set-off did not allow an affirmative recovery. See F,K&C, p. 569.

2. **Codes:** The codes, in general, combine these remedies into the "counterclaim." A typical code provision permits assertion as a counterclaim of any claim "arising out of the contract or transaction set forth in the complaint as the foundation of plaintiff's claim, or connected with the subject of the actions." F,K&C, p. 570. On such a counterclaim, however, there is the possibility of an affirmative recovery.

   a. **State practice:** A number of states still follow the code rule that only claims related to the plaintiff's claim may be asserted by the defendant as counterclaims. Most states, however, follow the more liberal federal procedure, described in the following paragraphs.

B. Federal Rules: The Federal Rules, in order to promote judicial economy, have gone beyond the codes with respect to counterclaims. Rule 13 provides for both ***"permissive"*** and ***"compulsory"*** counterclaims.

1. **Permissive counterclaim:** Rule 13(b) allows assertion as a counterclaim at the defendant's ***discretion*** of "any claim that is ***not compulsory.***" We'll see shortly below what makes a claim compulsory. But for now, the important thing is that ***no claim is too far***

removed from the subject of the plaintiff's claim to be allowed as a counterclaim. (Exceptions are indicated in Rule 13(d), and in the "presence of third parties" clause of 13(a), but these are minimal.)

2. **Compulsory counterclaim:** A claim will be *"compulsory"* under 13(a) if it meets two requirements:

> [1] It "arises out of the *transaction or occurrence that is the subject matter of the opposing party's claim* …," and

> [2] it "does *not require adding another party* over whom the court *cannot acquire jurisdiction."*

a. **Failure to state compulsory counterclaim:** The penalty for failing to state such a compulsory counterclaim is *loss of the claim in future litigation*. That is, if a compulsory counterclaim is not asserted, a later suit on that claim by the present defendant will be precluded by the rules of *res judicata*. This consequence is discussed further *infra*, p. 340.

b. **Exceptions:** Rule 13 lists certain claims that are *not compulsory* even though they are within the same "transaction or occurrence" as the plaintiff's claim. These include:

> [1] a claim which "was the *subject of another pending action*" at the time the present action was commenced (Rule 13(a)(2)(A)); and

> [2] a claim in which the suit against defendant is *in rem* or *quasi in rem* (assuming that the defendant is not making any other counterclaim in the action) (Rule 13(a)(2)(B)).

Note: The reason for exception [2] above — i.e., for why a counterclaim is not compulsory if the claim against the defendant is *quasi in rem* or *in rem* — is as follows: *Quasi in rem* and *in rem* suits do not subject the defendant to personal liability; he can defend such a suit without risking anything more than the property which is under attachment. If a counterclaim by him against the plaintiff were compulsory, the defendant would be put to the harsh choice between: (1) losing his claim forever through failure to assert it, or (2) making his claim and thereby subjecting himself to unlimited personal liability. (According to most courts, personal liability results if a defendant makes a claim of his own.) Therefore, Rule 13(a)(2)(B) gives the defendant a chance to avoid unlimited liability and at the same time preserve his claim for a separate suit.

c. **Must be asserted in defendant's pleading:** If the defendant's counterclaim is a compulsory one, it must be brought in the defendant's *pleading*. See Rule 13(a).

> i. **Dismissal of action before D files answer:** If an action is *dismissed* before it reaches the point where defendant must file an answer, then no compulsory counterclaim ever comes into existence.

d. **Default by plaintiff:** If the defendant has asserted a counterclaim (whether compulsory or permissive), and the plaintiff neglects either to serve a reply or to move against the counterclaim, a *default judgment* may be entered against the plaintiff on the counterclaim. See Rule 55(d).

C. "Transaction or occurrence": A counterclaim is compulsory, under Rule 13(a), only if it arose out of the *same "transaction or occurrence"* as the plaintiff's claim. The meaning of the term "transaction or occurrence" is therefore of substantial importance. The courts have not agreed on a precise formula for determining what constitutes a "transaction or occurrence."

1. **Logical relation:** The most accepted verbal formula is that a claim arises out of the same "transaction or occurrence that is the subject matter of [P's] claim" (and is therefore a compulsory, rather than permissive, counterclaim) if it is *"logically related"* to P's claim. This is the test advocated by Wr., p. 567.

   a. **"But for" cause:** The tort-law notion of a *"but for"* cause may be relevant. That is, if the counterclaim would not have arisen but for the events which gave rise to the main claim (or vice versa), the court is somewhat more likely to find the requisite "logical relation" between the two, and therefore to find that the counterclaim is compulsory.

2. **Rule of thumb:** Many courts, in deciding whether a counterclaim meets the "transaction or occurrence" test, are especially interested in whether there is a substantial amount of *evidence* that bears upon both the claim and the counterclaim, and which would therefore have to be considered twice if the counterclaim were not allowed (or, under the Federal Rules, if the defendant were allowed to keep it in reserve for another action, and chose to do so.)

D. Counterclaims by third parties

1. **Any party may make:** A counterclaim may be made by *any party* against "an opposing party." Rule 13(a), 13(b). The test for distinguishing between "compulsory" and "permissive" counterclaims in this context is the same as in the case of the single defendant counterclaiming against the single plaintiff.

   a. **Third-party defendant:** Thus a third-party defendant (see discussion of third-party Practice, *infra*, p. 399) may counterclaim against either the original defendant, or against the original plaintiff. (In the latter case, a claim by the plaintiff against the third-party defendant must first have been made.)

   b. **Plaintiff's counterclaim:** A plaintiff may have a counterclaim to a counterclaim. This "counter-counterclaim" will even be compulsory, if it arises from the same transaction or occurrence as the defendant's counterclaim. (This is true even if the defendant's counterclaim is itself permissive rather than compulsory.) The defendant's counterclaim is a "claim" under Rule 8(a), so any claim by any other "opposing party", arising out of the same transaction or occurrence, is a compulsory counterclaim under Rule 13(a).

   c. **New parties:** *New parties* to a counterclaim can be brought into a suit, as long as the joinder test of either Rule 19 or Rule 20 is satisfied. Rule 13(h).

   Example: D's counterclaim against P requires for its just adjudication the joinder of a third party, X, as a defendant to the counterclaim. X may be joined under Rule 19(a) if to do so would not destroy diversity, and if personal jurisdiction over X may be obtained. Here, diversity is no problem, since the general rule is that a compulsory counterclaim need meet no independent subject matter jurisdictional requirements, since such a counterclaim is within a court's *supplemental jurisdiction*. But *personal* jurisdiction may be a problem — if service cannot be made on X, D's counterclaim is *not* considered compulsory, no matter what its relationship to P's claim. (Rule 13(a)).

    d. Cross-claims: A claim by a party against a *co-party* (someone joined *with* him as a co-defendant, co-plaintiff, or co-third-party) is a *cross-claim*, not a counterclaim. Cross-claims are *never compulsory*, and are discussed *infra*, at p. 406.

E. Failure to raise a compulsory counterclaim

1. Barred: Generally, a party who fails to assert a compulsory counterclaim in a federal action is then *forever barred* from suing on that claim in another federal action. Wr., 567.

    a. Basis unclear: It is not clear whether the basis for this rule is a general principle of "*res judicata*," or whether the bar is simply an implied provision of Rule 13.

    b. Lenient: In cases of *hardship*, where a party was not at the time of the first suit *aware* that he had a compulsory counterclaim, the federal courts have been lenient in waiving the bar against subsequent assertion of the claim in a new action. That might happen, for instance, where the defense of an alleged tortfeasor is handled by his insurance company, and the tortfeasor himself only later discovers what turns out to be a compulsory counterclaim.

2. State court: There has been dispute about whether a *state* court may entertain a claim that should have been asserted as a compulsory counterclaim in an earlier *federal* action. *Most state courts have barred such claims*. Wr., 568-69.

3. First suit in state court, second in federal: Where a claim should have been asserted as a counterclaim in a state court, and was not, it is possible that a *federal court* would dismiss it when brought as a separate action. But few if any federal courts have explicitly decided this question.

F. Jurisdictional requirements for counterclaims

1. Supplemental jurisdiction: A *compulsory* counterclaim to a federal action is within the federal court's *supplemental jurisdiction*, and requires *no independent subject matter jurisdictional grounds*. Wr., 572-73.

    Example: A, a N.Y. resident, sues B, a Massachusetts resident. B has a compulsory counterclaim against A for less than $75,000. The counterclaim is also against C, a Massachusetts resident not yet in the action, who is required for "just adjudication" as this term is used in Rule 19. B's counterclaim falls within the court's supplemental jurisdiction, and thus diversity is not affected, and the jurisdictional amount does not have to be satisfied.

    Note: The concept of *supplemental jurisdiction* (formerly called "ancillary" jurisdiction in this context) is of the utmost importance to multi-claim litigation. Without it, the modern complex federal action would be virtually impossible. In reading this chapter, the reader should carefully observe to which joinder devices the supplemental doctrine applies, and thus for which parties and claims no independent subject matter jurisdictional grounds are required. See *supra*, p. 142.

2. **Permissive counterclaims not supplemental:** A permissive counterclaim is probably *not* within a court's supplemental jurisdiction, and must therefore satisfy the requirements of federal subject matter jurisdiction. Thus a permissive counterclaim may not be used to join a third party who is of the same citizenship as the party asserting the counterclaim against him. Similarly, it is generally held that a permissive counterclaim must *independently exceed the amount in controversy requirement*. Wr., 572-73.

G. **Pleading of counterclaims:** The party raising a counterclaim is, for the purpose of that claim, a "plaintiff" and his opponent a "defendant," whatever their positions are in the litigation as a whole. The rules of pleading relevant to the counterclaim correspond substantially to those for an ordinary plaintiff's claim, and an ordinary defendant's response. See Rule 8(a).

H. **Statutes of limitations for counterclaims:** Assertion of a counterclaim often raises issues concerning the *statute of limitations*.

1. **State rule:** If P's complaint is timely, but D's counterclaim would be barred by the statute of limitations if sued on alone, may D assert the counterclaim? The most common rule in *state* courts follows common-law precedent: counterclaims arising from the *same transaction* as P's claim may be asserted as *defenses against any timely claim, but may not yield an affirmative recovery*. A counterclaim *not* arising from the transaction on which P sues must generally be timely on its own.

2. **Federal diversity cases:** Where the case is a *federal* one based on *diversity*, D's right to bring an arguably time-barred counterclaim will depend in part on whether the statute of limitations ran before or after plaintiff brought the case:

   a. **Time-barred when P sued:** If D's counterclaim was *already time-barred* at the time P sued, few if any federal courts will allow D to assert the counterclaim as a means of making an affirmative recovery.

      i. **Allowed as defense:** However, a court might allow the "counterclaim" to be used as a *defense*, in the sense that it could reduce P's recovery but not yield an affirmative recovery for D. The court is far more likely to allow this limited use if the "counterclaim" is one that would be *compulsory* (related to the subject matter of P's complaint) than if it is one that would be "permissive."

   b. **Time-barred after P sues:** If the statute of limitations on the counterclaim ran *after* P commenced the suit, but before D asserted his counterclaim, D has a much better chance of getting the court to hear the counterclaim. Wright argues that "the counterclaim ought to be allowed for all purposes." Wr., p. 572.

3. **Federal question cases:** Suppose now that the case is a *federal question* case. Where the main claim and the counterclaim are based on federal rights rather than state-created ones, state law on the statute of limitations issue becomes irrelevant. As in the diversity situation, if D's counterclaim was time barred before P sued, the federal courts will almost certainly not allow D to sue. If the counterclaim became time-barred after P commenced the action, federal courts are split. Most do *not* permit the counterclaim, even as a means of reducing P's recovery. See Wright, pp. 534-35.

Quiz Yourself on

COUNTERCLAIMS

89. P and D were each seriously injured when a car driven by P collided with a car driven by D. P sued D in federal district court on a negligence theory; the case was based on diversity. D submitted a general denial as his answer. The jury found in favor of D. D has now brought a separate federal diversity-based action against P relating to the same accident; D's suit asserts that P's negligence caused the accident. Will D's suit be permitted to go to trial? _____

90. Pedestrian was injured when she was struck by a delivery van driven by Worker. The van was owned by Boss, and was being driven by Worker as part of the job that Worker did for Boss. Pedestrian brought a federal court diversity-based action against Boss alleging that Worker drove negligently and that Boss was liable for that negligence under the doctrine of respondeat superior. Boss impleaded Worker as a third-party defendant under Federal Rule 14(a), on the theory that if Boss was liable to Pedestrian based on respondeat superior, Worker must indemnify Boss. The jury found against Pedestrian and thus in favor of Boss. Worker has now commenced a new federal action, alleging that Boss knowingly gave Worker a defective van to drive, thus preventing Worker from stopping, and contributing to injuries suffered by Worker in the same accident in which Pedestrian was injured. Should Worker's suit against Boss be allowed to go forward? _____

91. In Connecticut, a car driven by Alan collided with a car owned by Bob but driven by Carol. Bob has sued Alan for negligence in Connecticut federal district court; the case is based on diversity. Bob's claim is for $100,000. Alan and Carol are citizens of Massachusetts; Bob is a citizen of Connecticut. The Connecticut long arm allows out-of-state mail service on anyone who is involved in an accident which takes place inside the state. Now, Alan wishes to make a counterclaim (relating to the same accident) against Bob; Alan's claim is such that Carol must be made a co-defendant if it is feasible to do so (see FRCP 19(a)). Alan's claim is for $20,000 against Bob, and would be for another $20,000 against Carol if she is joined.

(a) May Alan bring a counterclaim against Bob and Carol together? _____

(b) If Alan does not bring his counterclaim against Bob or Carol, may he bring a later state-court suit against them both? (Ignore jurisdictional problems with this second suit.) _____

92. P has brought a tort action against D, arising out of an automobile accident. The case is pending in federal district court. The case is based on diversity, and P's claim is for $100,000. D now seeks to assert a counterclaim against P; the counterclaim is for $30,000, and alleges that P breached a contract with D entered into before (and unconnected with) the automobile accident.

(a) Is D's counterclaim compulsory? _____

(b) May D bring that counterclaim? _____

Answers

89. No. Since D's present claim arises out of the "same transaction or occurrence" that was the subject of P's claim in the first suit, D's claim was a ***compulsory*** counterclaim in the first action. That is, D was required to assert that claim as a Rule 13(a) compulsory counterclaim in the first action, or face losing it. Since D did not do so, he will be barred from bringing the claim as a separate suit now (even though the result in the first trial indicates that D is probably correct in asserting that the accident was caused by P's negligence).

90. No. The rule that compulsory counterclaims must be asserted in the initial action or waived applies not only to defendants, but to any other parties. Thus Federal Rule 13(a) does not refer to defendants specifically, but instead to any "pleading" by any "pleader" — the pleader is required to raise any claim against "any opposing party" if that claim arises out of the same transaction or occurrence that is the subject matter of the opposing party's claim. Since Worker's claim against Boss for injuries results from the same transaction or occurrence (the accident with Pedestrian) as Boss's third-party claim against Worker, Worker must assert his claim as a counterclaim against Boss, or lose it. Since he did not so assert it, he will be found to have waived it.

91. (a) Yes. Compulsory counterclaims fall within the ***supplemental jurisdiction*** of the court under 28 U.S.C. §1367. Since Alan's counterclaim arises out of the same transaction or occurrence as Bob's claim, Alan's counterclaim is compulsory and will satisfy the "same case or controversy" requirement of §1367. Since §1367(b), which excludes certain types of claims in diversity actions, does not mention counterclaims, Alan's claim will fall within supplemental jurisdiction, and it will not matter that Carol and Alan, opposing parties, are citizens of the same state. Nor does it matter that Alan's claim totals less than $75,000. (The supplemental jurisdiction statute, where it applies, obviates the need to meet the usual requirements of subject matter jurisdiction, such as complete diversity and amount in controversy.)

(b) No. Alan's federal-court counterclaim was compulsory, so by not asserting it he lost it. If Alan had not been able to get ***personal*** jurisdiction over Carol, his counterclaim against Bob would not have been compulsory, because Rule 13(a)(1)(B) says that a counterclaim is compulsory only if it "does not require adding another party over whom the court cannot acquire jurisdiction." But since Carol had minimum contacts with Connecticut, and Connecticut had a long arm authorizing service out-of-state on Carol, jurisdiction was not a problem. The supplemental jurisdiction statute would have taken care of any subject matter jurisdictional problem. Therefore, Alan's claim was an ordinary compulsory counterclaim, even though it needs for just adjudication the presence of a third person not previously a party to the action. Since a state court will normally bar a claim that would have been a compulsory counterclaim in an earlier federal action, Alan will be barred.

92. (a) No. Since the two claims arise out of different transactions or occurrences, the counterclaim is permissive.

(b) No. Permissive counterclaims do not fall within the court's supplemental jurisdiction, because by definition they do not derive from a "common nucleus of operative fact." They must therefore satisfy the requirements of federal subject matter jurisdiction independently of the main claim. Consequently, most courts hold that a permissive counterclaim must independently exceed the amount-in-controversy requirement (i.e., the counterclaim cannot be aggregated with the main claim), which in diversity cases is $75,000.

III. JOINDER OF CLAIMS

A. Joinder of claims generally: Rule 18(a) provides that "[a] party asserting a claim, counterclaim, cross-claim, or third-party claim, may join, as independent or alternative claims, as many claims as it has against an opposing party."

1. **Rule:**   In other words, *once a party has made a claim against some other party*, he may then make *any other claim he wishes against that party*. Wr., 564.

> **Example:** P sues D, claiming that D intentionally assaulted and battered him. Rule 18(a) allows P to join to this assault and battery claim a claim that D owes P money on a contract entirely unrelated to the alleged tort.

2. **Never required:**   Joinder of claims is *never required* by Rule 18(a), but is left at the claimant's option. However, the rules of *res judicata*, particularly the rule against splitting a cause of action, will often as a practical matter induce the claimant to join claims. See *infra*, p. 418.

> **Example:** P is involved in a car collision with D, and suffers both personal injury and damage to his car. If P were to sue only for the bodily injury, the rule against splitting a cause of action might result in his losing his claim for property damage, whether he wins or loses the bodily injury suit.

3. **Subject matter jurisdiction not affected:**   Rule 18(a) *does not affect the requirements of subject matter jurisdiction*, which must be *independently satisfied* by the joined claim. That is, *supplemental* jurisdiction does not apply to a claim joined with another under Rule 18(a).

> **Example:** P sues D. D counterclaims against P, and brings in X as a co-defendant to his counterclaim, allowed by Rule 13(h). D may join to his claim against X any other claim against X that he cares to assert, but there must be diversity between D and X, or a federal question raised between them.

   a. **Not usually restrictive:**   As a practical matter, however, the subject matter jurisdiction requirements will not usually impede the use of Rule 18(a). Wr., 562.

   i. **Diversity:**   Diversity is not affected generally by Rule 18(a) joinder of claims. This is because no new parties are added when the Rule is used.

   ii. **Amount in controversy:**   *Aggregation* of the claims is possible to satisfy the *jurisdictional amount;* aggregation of all claims by a given plaintiff against a given defendant is allowed. See *supra*, p. 139.

   iii. **Supplemental jurisdiction:**   However, if the initial claim against a particular defendant is itself possible only because of the court's *supplemental jurisdiction*, there may be jurisdictional problems with joinder of other claims. For instance, in the above example, suppose that D's claim against X is worth less than $75,000, and is allowed only because the counterclaim was compulsory and therefore within the court's supplemental jurisdiction. An additional claim against X, which together with the counterclaim does not aggregate to $75,000, is not joinable under Rule 18(a).

   iv. **Federal question claim:**   Similarly, if the original claim against a particular defendant was a *federal question* claim, a non-federal claim could not be joined to it under 18(a), unless either diversity exists, or the two claims are closely related so that the doctrine of supplemental jurisdiction (formerly called "pendent" jurisdiction in this context) applies. See *supra*, p. 142.

IV. JOINDER OF PARTIES

A. Reason for joinder: If every lawsuit were limited to the trial of one claim by one plaintiff against one defendant, much wasteful, repetitious litigation might ensue. For instance, if several persons share the same claim against one potential defendant, or if a particular person has a claim against several potential defendants, it would be highly inefficient to break up the litigation into several pieces, each consisting of one plaintiff, one defendant, and one claim.

   1. Rules 19 and 20: Therefore, Rules 19 and 20 provide for the bringing in of multiple plaintiffs or defendants in certain circumstances, in federal actions. Most states have similar joinder provisions.

   2. Two kinds of joinder: Two kinds of joinder of parties are provided by the Federal Rules: (a) *permissive joinder* (Rule 20), and (b) *compulsory joinder* (Rule 19). Each is considered separately below.

   3. Multiple plaintiffs or defendants: Each of these two kinds of joinder can apply to *either multiple plaintiffs or multiple defendants.*

B. Permissive joinder: Rule 20 allows plaintiff in certain circumstances (a) to join other *plaintiffs* with himself, or (b) to make several parties *co-defendants* to his claim.

   1. At plaintiff's option: If the requirements for Rule 20 joinder are met, it is completely at the option of the *plaintiff* (or plaintiffs) whether to use this device or not. For this reason, Rule 20 joinder is known as *"permissive"* joinder, as distinguished from Rule 19 "compulsory" joinder.

   2. Requirements: Plaintiffs may join together in an action if they satisfy two tests:

      a. Single transaction or occurrence: Their claims for relief must arise from a *single* *"transaction, occurrence, or series of transactions or occurrences;"* and

      b. Common questions: There must be a question of *law or fact common to all plaintiffs* which will arise in the action. See Rule 20(a).

   3. Test: The test for determining whether all claims arise from a single "transaction or occurrence" is approximately the same as for determining whether a counterclaim is compulsory. (See *supra,* p. 339.) Thus the "logical relation" and "common evidence" tests have been suggested for determining whether all claims in question arise from the same transaction or occurrence, and may therefore be subject to permissive joinder.

   4. Common question must be substantial: The "common question of law or fact" must be of *substantial importance* to all the claims. The existence of other questions *not shared* by all plaintiffs does *not*, however, bar joinder.

      Example: A car driven by Driver and containing Passenger is hit from the rear by Taxicab. Driver and Passenger can join together as plaintiffs in a suit against Taxicab, even though the damages suffered by the two plaintiffs are not the same, and even though contributory negligence may be an issue with respect to Driver's claim but not as to Passenger's. The "common question of law or fact" is the negligence of Taxicab. Wr., 503-04.

5. **Each plaintiff must be voluntary:**   A person can be brought in as co-plaintiff under Rule 20 only if he so *agrees*. A potential plaintiff who does not want to be part of the suit cannot normally be forced to be. Under limited circumstances, however, he can be made an "involuntary plaintiff" under Rule 19(a).

6. **Joinder of defendants:**   *Defendants*, as well as plaintiffs, may be joined under Rule 20, if the claims against them satisfy the same two-pronged test as for plaintiff-joinder. Rule 20(a). That is, claims against the co-defendants must: (a) arise from a single "transaction, occurrence, or series of transactions or occurrences," and (b) contain a common question of law or fact.

   a. **At plaintiff's option:**   Joinder of multiple defendants is at the option of the plaintiff or plaintiffs.

7. **Judicial discretion:**   Once joinder of plaintiffs or defendants has occurred, the court under Rule 20(b) has considerable discretion in arranging the proceedings so as not to cause undue inconvenience or prejudice to any party (e.g., *separate trials*).

C. **Use in multi-plaintiff product liability cases:** Plaintiffs' tort lawyers have often tried to use plaintiff-joinder in *"mass product liability"* cases, especially where the lawyers have been unsuccessful in getting a *class action* certified (see *infra*, p. 355). For instance, multiple people who say they've been injured by cigarettes might join together to sue tobacco companies in diversity on a product-liability theory.

   1. **Advantages to plaintiffs:** There are several potential advantages to the plaintiffs (and their lawyers) from such joinder: the plaintiffs' litigation costs may be reduced; the proof entered on behalf of one plaintiff may work to the benefit of other plaintiffs; and the defendants may feel more pressure to settle because the case is bigger (and perhaps more highly-publicized).

   2. **May not meet "single transaction" standard:** However, defense counsel have often been successful in persuading the trial judge that the *"single transaction*, occurrence or series of transactions or occurrences" standard is *not met*.

      Example: Three plaintiffs, all former smokers with lung cancer, join together to sue the country's major cigarette manufacturers and two tobacco industry trade organizations, alleging fraud and civil conspiracy to commit fraud. The Ds move to sever the claims into three separate actions. *Held*, for the Ds, because the Ps' claims do not arise from the same transaction or series of transactions as required by Rule 20. For instance, the Ps started smoking at different ages, they bought different brands, they quit for different reasons and under different circumstances, and industry advertising reached them through different channels and with varying degrees of success. Also, causation issues (did the smoking cause the illness?) are not the same for all the cases. *Insolia v. Philip Morris, Inc.*, 186 F.R.D. 547 (E.D. Wisc. 1999).

D. **Jurisdiction in permissive joinder cases:**   Permissive joinder under Rule 20 may raise problems of *personal jurisdiction, diversity*, and *venue.*

   1. *In personam* **jurisdiction:**   Where joinder of defendants is involved, the requirements of *in personam* jurisdiction must be met with regard to *each defendant individually*. This means that:

a. **Service:** Each defendant must be *personally served.*

b. **Contacts:** Each defendant must individually fall within the *in personam* jurisdictional limits of the court (e.g., by having *"minimum contacts"*).

c. **Long-arm limits:** Since federal courts in diversity suits follow the *long-arm of the state in which they sit*, certain defendants may be out of joinder range even though personal jurisdiction could be constitutionally exercised over them. See *supra*, p. 73.

Note: The requirements of personal jurisdiction must be met with respect not only to permissive-joinder defendants, but with respect to *any* defendant, no matter under what device he is brought into the action. Thus defendants to *impleader* and *interpleader* actions, and parties brought in to *defend against counterclaims*, must all be subject to the personal jurisdiction of the court.

Two devices, however, neither of which applies to Rule 20 joinder, are sometimes available to make personal jurisdiction more easily obtained. First, the 100-mile bulge provision of Rule 4(k)(1)(B) makes service easier in certain multi-party cases, particularly impleader cases. See *supra*, p. 70. Secondly, nationwide service of process is allowed by federal statute in certain interpleader cases. In Rule 20 cases, however, the ordinary rules of personal jurisdiction apply.

2. **Subject matter jurisdiction:** In addition to the requirements of personal jurisdiction over defendants outlined above, all parties (whether plaintiffs or defendants) joined under Rule 20 must meet federal *subject matter jurisdiction* requirements. *Supplemental jurisdiction generally does not apply* to Rule 20 joinder of *multiple defendants*; it only partially applies to Rule 20 joinder of *multiple plaintiffs*. See 28 U.S.C. §1367(b), discussed *supra*, p. 148. Therefore, these subject matter jurisdiction requirements often prove fatal to Rule 20 joinder.

a. **Complete diversity:** If the action is brought as a diversity action, the diversity must be *complete*, as 28 U.S.C. §1332 has always been construed. That is, no state may be represented on both sides of an action.

Example: In an action where no federal question is present, there are 12 plaintiffs, 11 from Connecticut and one from New York, and 12 defendants, 11 from New Jersey and one from New York. On these facts there is no diversity, because complete diversity is required. Thus one of the New Yorkers must be dropped if the action is to proceed in federal court. And supplemental jurisdiction (see *supra*, p. 142) does not apply so as to remove the complete-diversity requirement; see "Note" following the *Allapattah* Example, *infra*, p. 348.

b. **Aggregation where one P meets the amount:** Multiple plaintiffs are *permitted* to *aggregate* their claims to meet the jurisdictional amount, *if at least one plaintiff meets the amount.* The Supreme Court held in *Exxon Mobil Corp. v. Allapattah Services, Inc.*, 125 S.Ct. 2611 (2005) that supplemental jurisdiction applies to this situation. See *supra*, p. 150.

Example: P1 is a nine-year-old girl who has been severely injured when she sliced her finger on a tuna can made by D; her claim is for more than $75,000. P2, P3, etc. are members of P1's immediate family, who have claims for less than $75,000 for items like emotional distress and medical expenses.

Held, P2, P3, etc., may join with P1 as co-plaintiffs under FRCP 20. As long as one plaintiff meets the jurisdictional amounts, additional co-plaintiffs may join the suit under Rule 20 even though their individual claims don't meet the amount, because supplemental jurisdiction applies. *Exxon Mobil Corp. v. Allapattah Services, Inc., supra.*

Note: In the Rule 20 scenario, supplemental jurisdiction applies only to the amount in controversy, *not the requirement of complete diversity.* So if, on the facts of *Allapattah*, any one of the Ps was a citizen of the same state as D, the suit could not go forward.

   i.   **Each defendant must meet:**   Where the Rule 20 joinder involves *multiple defendants*, it is quite clear that supplemental jurisdiction does *not* apply, so that *each defendant* must have claims against him equal to the jurisdictional amount. See 28 U.S.C. § 1367(b).

   Example: P1 has a diversity claim for $80,000 against D1, and a diversity claim for $15,000 against D2 that is closely related to the claim against D1. Supplemental jurisdiction does not apply. Therefore, P1's claim against D2 must be dropped from the suit, since it does not independently meet the amount-in-controversy requirement.

3. **Venue:**   In addition to the requirements of personal and subject matter jurisdiction, Rule 20 joinder must satisfy applicable *venue* requirements. In a case in which there are co-defendants who reside in different states, the easiest way to satisfy the venue requirements will be by bringing suit in a district in which a substantial part of the *events* giving rise to the claim occurred. (Such "place of events" venue is available in both diversity and federal question cases.) See 28 U.S.C. §1391(a) and (b), discussed *supra*, p. 103.

E. **Compulsory joinder (Rule 19):**   The joinder discussed above is completely at the option of the plaintiff or plaintiffs. For this reason, it is called "permissive" joinder. In some circumstances, however, it would be uneconomical or unfair to litigate a claim between two parties without at the same time bringing in other claims and parties. Therefore, Rule 19(a) sets forth certain situations in which additional parties *must* be joined, if the requirements of jurisdiction are met. This Rule 19 joinder is said to be *"compulsory."*

1. **Two categories:**   Rule 19(b) goes further, and sets forth situations in which, if joinder is not possible for jurisdictional reasons, the entire action must be dropped.

   a. **"Necessary" parties:**   Parties whose joinder, if possible, is required by Rule 19(a), are called *"necessary"* parties.

   b. **"Indispensable" parties:**   Parties who are so vital that if their joinder is impossible, the whole action must be dropped, are called *"indispensable" parties.* See Rule 19(b).

2. **Distinguishing "necessary" from "indispensable":**   How does the court determine, then, whether a party is merely "necessary" (to be joined if possible), or truly "indispensable" (so that the whole action must be dropped if joinder is not possible)? The standard for distinguishing between these two classes is laid out in Rule 19.

a. **"Necessary":** Rule 19 first describes those parties who must be joined if (1) service can be validly made on them, and (2) their joinder would not destroy diversity. These are *"necessary"* parties (though Rule 19 does not actually use that term.) To be a "necessary" party, a person must meet one of the following two tests:

   i. **Incomplete relief:** "in that person's absence, the court cannot accord complete relief among existing parties." (19(a)(1)(A)) *or*

   ii. **Impaired interest:** a judgment in the person's absence will either (1) as a practical matter impair an interest the person has, or (2) impose on some of the existing parties "double, multiple, or otherwise inconsistent obligations." (19(a)(1)(B)).

b. **"Indispensable":** Assuming that the absentee meets the test of (i) or (ii) above, the court then determines whether that absentee is *"indispensable"* (though Rule 19 does not actually use this term either) — so vital that the action should be discontinued if joinder is not possible. In determining indispensability, the court is to consider the following additional factors, all laid out in Rule 19(b):

   i. **Prejudice:** the extent of *prejudice* to the absentee, or to those already parties;

   ii. **Framing of judgment:** the possibility of *framing the judgment* so as to mitigate *such* prejudice;

   iii. **Adequacy of remedy:** the adequacy of the *remedy* that can be granted in his *absence*;

   iv. **Result of dismissal:** whether the *plaintiff* will have an *adequate remedy* if the action is *dismissed*.

c. **Illustration of "indispensable":** Here is a good illustration of an absentee who is truly "indispensable," and in whose absence the action must be dismissed:

Example: P brings a federal-court diversity suit against D, a bank holding some stock. P alleges that although the stock is registered solely in the name of X, P and X in fact co-own the stock. P and D are citizens of different states, but X is a citizen of the same state as P. X thus cannot be joined as a co-defendant, because his presence would destroy diversity. The issue is whether X is "necessary" or "indispensable."

Held: First, X is definitely a person who must be joined if feasible under Rule 19(a), because his absence will expose D to the risk of double obligation — a judgment that P owns the stock will not bind X, who can later sue D for the whole value of the stock. Second, X is in fact "indispensable" — his presence is so important that the suit must be dismissed rather than proceed in X's absence. *Haas v. Jefferson Bank*, 442 F.2d 394 (5th Cir. 1971).

3. **Jurisdictional obstacles:** In determining whether joinder is jurisdictionally possible, and thus whether it is 19(a) or 19(b) which applies, personal jurisdiction, subject matter jurisdiction, and venue, must all be examined.

   a. **Variety of difficulties:** There are thus several different reasons why the joinder of a particular party might be impossible. In the case of a potential defendant, these reasons might include:

    i. his presence would ***destroy diversity***, since he is a citizen of the same state as one plaintiff, and there is no federal question. (That's what happened in *Haas*, *supra*.)

    ii. the claim against him does not meet the ***amount in controversy*** requirement; or

    iii. he is beyond the personal jurisdiction of the court, because the ***local long-arm*** would not reach him (since the local long-arm is what is relied on in diversity suits — see *supra*, p. 74.)

b. **Supplemental jurisdiction:** If a person who is sought to be joined as a defendant under Rule 19(a) is not diverse with all plaintiffs, or if the claim against her does not meet the amount in controversy requirement, the doctrine of ***supplemental jurisdiction*** does ***not*** apply to overcome these defects. Therefore, joinder will not be allowed in this situation.

    i. **Clarified by 1990 statute:** This result became clear in 1990, when Congress enacted 28 U.S.C. §1367. That section creates "supplemental" jurisdiction (combining the prior judge-made concepts of "ancillary" and "pendent" jurisdiction). §1367 further provides, in subsection (b), that in diversity cases there will not be supplemental jurisdiction "over claims by plaintiffs against persons made parties under Rule … 19 …, or over claims by persons proposed to be joined as plaintiffs under Rule 19. …"

    ii. **Significance:** So no matter how badly an absent prospective defendant is needed for carrying out the litigation in a sensible manner, if that defendant is not diverse with all plaintiffs (or if the claim against that defendant does not meet the jurisdictional amount), Rule 19(a) joinder may not occur.

4. ***Provident Tradesmen's:*** *Provident Tradesmen's Bank and Trust Co. v. Patterson*, 390 U.S. 102 (1968), illustrates the kind of fact pattern in which the absentee is at least "necessary," and perhaps "indispensable."

  a. **Facts:** The facts of *Provident* were as follows:

    i. The litigation arose from a traffic accident in which a car belonging to Dutcher and driven by Cionci collided with a truck. Cionci and one of his passengers, Lynch, were killed.

    ii. Provident Bank, the administrator of the estate of Lynch, the dead passenger, sued Cionci, the driver. The suit was settled for $50,000 which was never paid, due to the insolvency of Cionci's estate.

    iii. Dutcher, the owner, had an insurance policy that had a limit of $100,000 per accident. Provident sued for a declaratory judgment to the effect that Dutcher had given Cionci permission to use the car, and that therefore the insurance policy covered the accident and the $50,000 judgment.

    iv. The defendants in Provident's declaratory judgment suit were Cionci's estate, and Dutcher's insurance company. Dutcher was not joined as a defendant, since his presence would have destroyed diversity.

    v. **Lower court holding:** Judgment was given for Provident, and Dutcher's insurers appealed. Dutcher's indispensability as a defendant was never raised at trial or on appeal, but the Court of Appeals, on its own initiative, held that Dutcher was an ***indispensable party*** to the action, and that the judgment must be thrown out because of his absence.

b. Absence not fatal: The Supreme Court held that under Rule 19(b), Dutcher's absence was not fatal, particularly since the trial had already been carried out.

i. Absence possibly prejudicial: The Court acknowledged that Dutcher's absence might have been prejudicial to him, a possible reason for dismissal listed in 19(b). The possible prejudice was due to the fact that other suits arising from the same accident might be brought against Dutcher by other injured parties. Dutcher therefore had an interest in having it held that he had not given Cionci permission, and that the insurance policy did not cover the accident. That way, the $100,000 from the policy would all be available, in case future suits should decide the issue of permission against Dutcher, and grant judgments against him as the lender of the car.

ii. But prejudice unlikely: But the Court found that this possibility of future judgments was very unlikely, since the only suits on this accident which were not barred by the statute of limitations were two suits which had lain dormant in state court for ten years, and which seemed unlikely to be resumed. Also, Dutcher might be able to relitigate in these suits the permission issue — since he was not a party to the first suit, he could argue that he was not bound by the finding that permission had been given. The Court noted the possibility that Dutcher might be held to have ***waived the right to intervene as of right*** under Rule 24(a)(2). But the Court declined to decide whether the failure to intervene did in fact constitute such a waiver.

iii. Judgment not thrown out: All things considered, the Court concluded, the possibility of prejudice to Dutcher was not sufficiently great that the judgment should be ***thrown out***, even though that possibility might have been enough to result in dismissal at the beginning of the suit. The case was remanded to the Court of Appeals, with orders that the judgment be adjusted to protect Dutcher's interests.

iv. Remand: On remand, the Third Circuit (411 F.2d 88 (1969)) directed the trial court to amend its judgment so as to protect Dutcher's interests, by enjoining any payment out of the insurance fund until Dutcher had had the opportunity to litigate his assertion that the fund did not cover Cionci. Presumably this suit would be against Cionci for declaratory judgment.

Quiz Yourself on

JOINDER OF CLAIMS AND JOINDER OF PARTIES

93. P brought, in federal court, an action against D for violation of P's federally-registered copyrights. (The suit alleged that D plagiarized language in a novel written by P.) Before D's time to answer ran, P amended his suit to add a second claim, that D libelled P by calling P a "dishonest writer." The alleged libel has nothing to do with the alleged copyright violation. Putting aside questions of personal and subject matter jurisdiction, is P entitled, procedurally, to add this second claim to his action? _____

94. Same basic fact pattern as prior question. Now, however, assume that P and D are citizens of the same state. Assume also that both the copyright claim and the libel claim are for more than $75,000. May the federal court hear the libel claim? _____

95. P and D were both injured in a car accident, when the cars driven by each collided. P brought a federal court diversity action against D for negligence, seeking $100,000 of damages. D brought a counterclaim against P for negligence (relating to the same accident) in that same action; D joined to that counterclaim a second person, X (the owner of the car driven by P). D claimed that P and X each owed $30,000 on D's counterclaim. D then joined a second claim against X, for breach of contract, in an unrelated transaction; this claim was for $15,000. P is a citizen of Alabama, D is a citizen of Georgia, and X is a citizen of Florida.

    (a) May the court hear D's claim against X for damages from the car accident? _____

    (b) May the court hear D's claim against X for breach of contract? _____

96. P, a motion picture company, is the owner of the "Richie Rat" cartoon character. Because of Richie Rat's enormous popularity, a number of small entrepreneurs produce teeshirts, sweatshirts, dolls, and other objects with the Richie Rat character on them, without authorization from P. P has brought a federal district court action against D1 and D2, alleging federal copyright violation. D1 and D2 have no connection with each other or with P, except that P claims that D1 has put Richie Rat on a series of teeshirts, and that D2 has put the character on a series of dolls, both without authorization. Is P justified in joining D1 and D2 in a single action? _____

97. P1 and P2 were both passengers in a twin-engine aircraft owned and operated by D1 (a commuter airline) and manufactured by D2. Both P1 and P2 were seriously injured when the plane caught fire while landing. P1 and P2 are both citizens of New York. D1 is incorporated in Delware and has its principal place of business in New York. D2 is both incorporated in, and has its principal place of business in, Kansas. P1 and P2 have brought a single federal court diversity action, in which D1 is charged with negligent inspection and operation, and D2 is charged with strict products liability. P1 and P2 each meet the amount in controversy requirement. Is the joinder of all parties proper? _____

98. X, shortly before dying, signed a contract in which he promised to leave P $100,000 in his will, in consideration for services performed for him by P. X then died, and his will did not mention P. P has brought a federal court diversity action against D1 (X's estate), seeking to enforce this contract to make a will. P's suit does not list as defendants D2 and D3 (X's children, who are his beneficiaries under the will). Neither P nor D1 seems troubled by the absence from the suit of D2 and D3. Assuming that D2 and D3 can be subjected to the personal jurisdiction of the federal court, and that they are not citizens of the same state as P, what if any action should the federal judge hearing the suit take? _____

99. X, a wealthy citizen of New York, in 1980 gave possession of a valuable Van Gogh painting to P, a museum located in Florida. X assured P that she wanted P to have the painting forever, and that this would be confirmed in X's will. In 1990, X died. X's will left all of X's property (including, specifically, the Van Gogh) to Y, X's daughter, who is a citizen of Florida. (Y has no contacts with New York.) P has brought a diversity suit against D (X's estate) in New York federal district court, seeking a judgment that the 1980 transfer of possession of the Van Gogh to P was a completed gift, and that the painting now belongs to P. (X's estate is deemed a citizen of New York.) P has not joined Y as a co-defendant, because Y's presence

would destroy diversity of citizenship and because the court could not get personal jurisdiction over Y. Y is afraid that if the action proceeds without her, and P wins, P may sell the painting, lend it to a museum outside the U.S., or otherwise put the painting beyond Y's reach. Assuming that there is no way for Y to become part of the pending action, should the New York federal district court dismiss the action on account of Y's absence? _____

100. Same facts as the prior question. Now, however, assume that Y, because of regular business dealings with New York, has such minimum contacts with the state of New York as to make it constitutional for Y to be subjected to the personal jurisdiction of the New York courts (and, by extension, to the personal jurisdiction of the New York federal district court sitting in diversity). Also, the New York long-arm would reach Y in a New York state-court action. Should the New York federal court order Y to be joined, order the action to go on without Y, or dismiss the action because Y cannot be joined? _____

Answers

93. Yes. Federal Rule 18(a) provides, "A party asserting a claim … may join, as independent or alternative claims, as many claims as it has against an opposing party." Since P and D are opposing parties based on P's initial copyright claim, P has the right to add whatever claims against D he wishes, even if these other claims have nothing to do with the original copyright claim.

94. Probably not. Since P and D are citizens of the same state, there is no diversity jurisdiction. This is not a problem for the copyright claim, since that is founded upon federal law. But the libel claim is based upon state law. If the libel claim were closely related to the copyright claim (e.g., both related to the same transaction or occurrence), the libel claim could be heard together with the copyright claim under the doctrine of supplemental (formerly pendent) jurisdiction. The supplemental jurisdiction statute, 28 U.S.C. §1367, allows parties to join claims that are so related as to form part of the "same case or controversy" in the same suit. But since the two claims have nothing to do with each other, supplemental jurisdiction does not apply here. Therefore, there is no federal subject matter jurisdiction over the libel claim, and it cannot be heard by the federal court.

95. (a) Yes. D's claim against X for the car accident is a compulsory counterclaim. (That is, D's claim against P is a garden-variety compulsory counterclaim, and X is an additional party to that counterclaim joined pursuant to Rule 13(h).) Compulsory counterclaims, and the joinder of additional parties to compulsory counterclaims, fall within the court's supplemental jurisdiction under 28 U.S.C. §1367 because they concern a "common nucleus of operative fact." Consequently, it does not matter that D's claim against X fails by itself to meet the amount in controversy requirement; supplemental jurisdiction obviates the need for the usual diversity jurisdiction in this case. (In fact, it wouldn't even matter that D and X were citizens of the same state.)

(b) No. This second claim by D against X is allowed procedurally only because of Rule 18(a)'s joinder of claims provision (which allows any party, not just the plaintiff, to join additional claims against an opposing party who is already in the action). But Rule 18(a) joinder of claims does not fall within the court's supplemental jurisdiction unless the claims are so related as to form part of the same case or controversy (the "common nucleus of operative fact" standard). We are told that the breach of contract claim is based on an unrelated transaction. Since it does not fall under supplemental jurisdiction, the unrelated claim must independently meet federal subject matter jurisdictional requirements. Because D's second claim against X is not for more than $75,000, that second claim cannot be heard.

96. No, probably. The circumstances under which a plaintiff may join two or more defendants are governed by Federal Rule 20(a)(2)'s "permissive joinder" provision: "Persons … may be joined in one action as defendants if: (A) any right to relief is asserted against them jointly, severally, or in the alternative with respect to or arising out of the same transaction, occurrence, or series of transactions or occurrences; *and* (B) any question of law or fact common to all defendants will arise in the action."

Here, there is a good chance that P could meet the second of these tests (common question of law or fact), since identical questions as to what constitutes federal copyright infringement, or whether Richie Rat is copyrightable, are likely to be involved in the case against D1 and D2. But the first test — that all claims involve the "same transaction, occurrence, or series of transactions or occurrences …" — probably is not satisfied. It is true that the transactions are roughly similar, but they are not the *same*. Just as a plaintiff probably cannot join in one federal action all defendants who owe him money where each defendant is liable under a separate contract, so it is probably the case that P cannot join independent copyright violators.

97. **No.** In general, multiple plaintiffs may join together, and may join multiple defendants, provided that (1) the claims arise out of the "same transaction, occurrence, or series of transactions or occurrences" and (2) there is at least one question of law or fact in common. FRCP 20. Since all claims involve a single occurrence (the accident) and a single question of law or fact (who caused that accident?), this two-part test is easily satisfied.

However, the ***usual requirements of subject matter matter jurisdiction*** (as well as personal jurisdiction) ***apply to joinder of parties.*** Since D1 has its principal place of business in New York, it is deemed to be a citizen of New York (as well as of Delaware, its state of incorporation.) This means that there is not the required complete diversity of citizenship (i.e., it is not the case that no plaintiff is a citizen of the same state as any defendant.) Since the action involves no federal question, and there is no diversity, the action could go forward as pleaded only if supplemental jurisdiction somehow eliminated the requirement of complete diversity. But the supplemental jurisdiction statute, 28 U.S.C. §1367, states in subsection (b) that in diversity actions the district courts shall ***not*** have supplemental jurisdiction over claims by plaintiffs (like P1 and P2) against persons made parties under Rule 20 (such as D1) if the result would be inconsistent with the requirements of diversity. Because §1367 does not apply in this case, each claim and each party must independently meet federal subject matter jurisdictional requirements. Consequently, D1 will have to be dropped from the action (though the action may proceed as a suit by P1 and P2 against D2).

98. **Order that D2 and D3 be joined as defendants.** Federal Rule 19(a) provides that if any of the three criteria stated there are satisfied by a person who not currently a party to the action, that person must be joined if feasible. One of these criteria is that the person "claims an interest relating to the subject of the action and is so situated that disposing of the action in the person's absence may … as a practical matter impair or impede the person's ability to protect the interest. …" If D2 is not made a party to the action, and P prevails against the estate, then the estate will pay out the $100,000 to P immediately. In a strictly legal sense, D2's legal rights cannot be affected by a suit to which D2 is not a party — D2 is free to sue P and/or D1, and to re-litigate the issue of whether the contract to make a will was enforceable. But as a *practical* matter, D2's interest will be impaired — D1 will already have laid out the money to P, and it will be harder for D2 to get this money back (since the estate will no longer have the money and P may spend it immediately) than if D2 were a party to the original P-D1 suit. The same analysis is true of D3. Therefore, even though neither P nor D1 moves to have D2 and D3 joined to the action, the court should on its own order that they be joined since joinder is (by the hypothesized facts) available.

99. **Yes, probably.** Y is clearly a person who should be joined if feasible (Federal Rule 19(a)), but the facts

make it clear that it is not "feasible" to join Y. Therefore, we have to look at Rule 19(b) to determine whether Y's presence is so indispensable that it is better to dismiss the action entirely than to proceed in Y's absence. Rule 19(b) lists four factors to be considered by the court on this issue of indispensability. One of these factors is "the extent to which a judgment rendered in the person's absence might prejudice the person or the existing parties." On this factor, Y's claim to have the action dismissed is very strong — a judgment entered in P's favor (especially since P already has possession) might make it very difficult indeed for Y to ever get her own day in court, since P might sell the property, lend it abroad, or otherwise effectively put it outside the court's jurisdiction.

Another factor also cuts in Y's favor — "whether the plaintiff would have an adequate remedy if the action were dismissed for non-joinder." Since P and Y are both Florida residents, and D (the estate) owns property currently located in Florida, it is almost certain that the Florida courts would have jurisdiction over an action by P against D and Y jointly; therefore, P would have an adequate remedy if the federal judge dismissed for non-joinder.

Cutting the other way is still another factor listed in Rule 19(b): "the extent to which any prejudice could be lessened or avoided by: (A) protective provisions in the judgment[.]" That is, the federal court could find in favor of P, but could simultaneously instruct P to hold the painting without disposing of it for, say, one year to permit Y to bring a separate action. However, this method only avoids prejudice by allowing a complete re-litigation of the merits, a very wasteful approach.

So putting it all together, the court will probably conclude that it is better to dismiss the action (and let P bring a Florida state court action or D bring a federal statutory interpleader action joining both P and Y) than to let the action proceed in Y's absence. See *Haas v. Jefferson Bank*, 442 F.2d 394 (5th Cir. 1971), finding the absentee to be an indispensable party, on analogous facts.

100. **Dismiss the action because Y cannot be joined.** Y's minimum contacts with New York take care of the problem of personal jurisdiction over her. But the problem of lack of diversity persists. Before 1991, there was some chance that the federal court might have applied ancillary jurisdiction to this situation (which would have the effect that complete diversity as between Y and P would not be needed). But the supplemental jurisdiction statute enacted that year, 28 U.S.C. §1367, would *definitely not* allow jurisdiction in this case, thus preserving the policy established in *Owen Equipment v. Kroger*, 437 U.S. 365 (1978). *Kroger* only granted supplemental-type jurisdiction to parties in a *defensive* posture. Similarly, §1367(b) specifically excludes claims by plaintiffs against persons joined under Rule 19 if the result would destroy diversity. All Rule 19 parties, whether indispensable or not, must therefore each meet the usual subject matter jurisdiction requirements.

V. CLASS ACTIONS

A. Background

1. **Definition:**   The class action is a procedure whereby a single person or small group of co-parties may *represent* a larger group, or "*class*," of persons sharing a *common interest*. It may be used where joinder of all the potential co-parties is not feasible, either because the class is simply too *large* (numbering possibly in the millions) or because of insuperable difficulties of personal jurisdiction, venue, or diversity.

a. **Jurisdiction:**   In the class action, ***only the representative(s)*** must satisfy the requirements of personal jurisdiction, subject matter jurisdiction, and venue. As to jurisdictional amount, see *infra*, p. 370.

2. **Due process:**   One factor tending to limit the use of the class action is the necessity of insuring ***due process*** to the "represented" members. If a class action is to be of any use in curtailing massive litigation, its results must be ***binding on the absent members***; therefore steps have to be taken so that these absentees are not deprived of their day in court. See *infra*, pp. 367-369, for guarantees found in the Federal Rule governing class actions.

3. **Federal and state:**   The class action is available in ***both the federal courts and in most state courts.*** Our discussion focuses on the *federal* class action, the requirements for which are set out in Federal Rule 23.

4. **Defendant class:**   In federal practice, as well as in states which permit class actions, the class may be either plaintiffs or defendants. The vast majority of the time, the class will be composed of plaintiffs. However, defendant class suits, in which the class is designated by the plaintiff, have been brought.

> **Example:** A patentee alleges that numerous persons have infringed his patent. He brings suit against the class of all persons alleged to have committed acts of infringement, and he names only a few of these class members to be "representatives" of the class, for purposes of defending the suit. If he can persuade the court that these representatives will do an adequate job of presenting a defense applicable to the other, unnamed, infringers, and meets all the other requirements of Rule 23, the court may allow the suit to proceed as a class action against the defendant class.

5. **Certification as class:** At some point before trial, a federal court must ***"certify"*** the action, i.e., affirmatively determine that it meets the requirements of FRCP 23. If the judge rejects certification, the action must proceed as a normal action involving only the named parties, or not proceed at all.

a. **"Putative" designation:** Until certification has occurred, the action is called a ***"putative"*** class action.

b. **Usually desired by plaintiffs:** Normally, it is the named ***plaintiffs*** (or at least their lawyer(s)) that wish to proceed as a class action, and the defendant(s) typically oppose class certification. But sometimes the reverse is true — the defendant(s) want to turn one or more individual suits into a class action in which absent plaintiff class members will be bound. Certification is discussed *infra*, p. 356.

B. **Rule 23 generally:**   The Federal Rules give extensive guidance as to when and how the class action device is to be used in federal courts. Virtually everything the FRCP have to say about class actions is contained in Rule 23.

1. **Rule 23:**   Rule 23(a) states four ***prerequisites*** that must be met before there is ***any possibility*** that a case may proceed as a class action:

a. **Size:**   The class must be ***so large*** that "***joinder*** of all members is ***impracticable***";

b. **Common questions:**   There must be ***"questions of law or fact common to the class"***;

c. Typical claims: The claims or defenses of the representatives must be *"typical"* of those of the class;

d. Representation: The representatives must *"fairly and adequately protect the interests of the class."*

2. **Three categories:** In addition, once these prerequisites are met, a class action will still not be allowed unless the action fits into **one of three categories**. These categories are represented by 23(b)(1), 23(b)(2), and 23(b)(3), each of which is treated in a separate section beginning with (D) below.

C. Rule 23(a)'s prerequisites for class actions Here is an overview of the important issues concerning the four Rule 23(a) prerequisites applicable to *any* class action:

1. **Size:** The class must be *"so numerous* that joinder of all members is **impracticable**." Rule 23(a)(1). This is the requirement of *"numerosity."*

   a. No consensus: No consensus has emerged as to **how large** the class must be in order to satisfy the requirement that using the alternate method, joinder of all members as co-plaintiffs (*supra*, p. 343), would be "impracticable." A class of only 25 members has been held large enough, and one of 350 held not large enough. Wr., 510.

2. **"Common questions":** The requirement that there be "questions of **law or fact common to the class**" (23(a)(2)) has become **much more important** than it had been, due to a 2011 decision in *Wal-Mart v. Dukes*, 131 S.Ct. 2541 (2011). Therefore, we discuss this "commonality" requirement, and *Wal-Mart*, separately at some length *infra*, Par. 4, p. 358.

3. **"Typical claims":** The "claims or defenses" of the *representatives* (i.e., the named class members) must be "*typical* of the claims or defenses **of the class**." (Rule 23(a)(3).) This requirement — called *"typicality"* — means that the class representatives must in some sense "*stand ... in the same shoes* as the **average class member**." Y (8th), p. 878. Or as the idea has been put, there must be enough of an **overlap** between the types of claims held by the representatives and those held by the class members that the representatives will *"feel the pain"* of the members. G,P&R, p. 703.

   Example: Suppose that a putative class action is brought in which the plaintiff class consists of every individual who has ever been exposed to an asbestos product made by any of dozens of defendants. The class is defined by the plaintiffs' lawyer to include not only people who have already become sick or died from their asbestos exposure, but also a greater number of people whose asbestos exposure has *not yet* caused them to have symptoms of sickness but may do so in the future. Suppose further that there are only three named representatives, and all three have already developed serious illnesses from apparent asbestos exposure.

   There's likely to be a sharp conflict between the remedies desired by the named plaintiffs (e.g., high compensation for already-developed sickness) and the remedies desired by those non-representative class members who have been exposed to asbestos but not yet become sick (e.g., periodic health examinations paid for by the defendants). Therefore, there's a good chance that a court deciding whether to certify the class will hold that the typicality requirement is *not satisfied* — the type of harm suffered by the named representatives is so different from the type of harm suffered by the many unnamed plaintiffs that the named representatives don't really stand in the shoes of the unnamed ones.[1]

    a. **Blends with "adequate representation":** In practice, the requirement of typicality blends with the requirement that the representatives will "*fairly and adequately protect the interests* of the class" (imposed by 23(a)(4), discussed immediately below in Par. 4, and further in Par. E, p. 361). Thus on the facts of the above asbestos-exposure example, the fact that all named plaintiffs have already gotten sick whereas not all rank-and-file members have done so would suggest not just that the named members do not have "typical" claims, but also that these named representatives *will not adequately represent* the many absent non-representative class members who have not yet gotten sick.

4. **Fair representation:** The final requirement imposed by Rule 23(a) is that the representatives "will *fairly and adequately protect the interests* of the class." 23(a)(4). This requirement is commonly called the requirement of *"adequacy"* or *"adequate representation."* (For more about the adequacy requirement, see *infra*, p. 361.)

D. **"Common questions of law or fact" (*Wal-Mart* case):** Of the four pre-requisites for class actions set by Rule 23(a), the one that as of this writing (2014) is most likely to be in dispute is 23(a)(2)'s requirement that there be *"questions of law or fact common to the class."* Prior to 2011, this "commonality" requirement was interpreted in a way that was easily satisfied by most class-action complaints.

But in *Wal-Mart Stores, Inc. v. Duke*, 131 S.Ct. 2541 (2011),[2] the Supreme Court construed the commonality prerequisite in a way that tends to make the requirement *hard or impossible to satisfy* in many types of cases, especially in *employment discrimination cases* against large employers as well as in *mass- toxic-exposure* tort cases.

1. **Facts of *Wal-Mart*:** In *Wal-Mart*, the named plaintiffs were three female employees of the defendant (the Wal-Mart store chain) who worked in various local stores owned by Wal-Mart. These named plaintiffs brought a class-action for employment discrimination on behalf of a class of *all 1.5 million female employees* of 3,500 Wal-Mart stores located in all 50 states.

    a. **Granting of discretion to managers:** The suit claimed that Wal-Mart had given each store manager in the U.S. (nearly all of them male) *wide discretion* over pay and promotion practices at the manager's local store, and that these individual managers exercised that discretion in a way that had a *disparate impact* on women. The Ps[3] did not

---

1. The facts of this example are suggested by those of *Amchem Products, Inc., v. Windsor*, 117 S. Ct. 2231 (1997), discussed *infra*, p. 376. There, the Supreme Court, in denying the certification of a class for settlement purposes, relied mainly on problems of "adequacy of representation" rather than typicality. But the non-overlapping of interests that the *Amchem* Court viewed as indicating inadequacy of representation — the conflicting interests of the named plaintiff class members who had already become ill, versus the interests of the many unnamed class members who had been exposed to the defendants' asbestos-laden products but not yet become ill — would also indicate a lack of typicality.

2. The case is also discussed *infra*, p. 364.

3. I'll refer to all class members as being "the Ps" — in other words, the proposed class of named and unnamed Ps consisted of *every female who worked for Wal-Mart anywhere in the U.S.* during the relevant years.

assert that Wal-Mart had an explicit corporate policy to treat female workers less favorably. Instead, the Ps claimed that company's *system of giving discretion* to individual store managers was *itself* a form of discrimination — the store managers had a "corporate culture" of discrimination, and the company's decision to give each manager discretion over pay and promotion decisions therefore turned every woman at the company into a victim of what the Ps called a "common discriminatory practice."

2. **No "common question":** Every member of the Supreme Court agreed that the ***case should never have been certified as a class action.*** But for our present purposes, what's more important is that a five-justice majority — in an opinion by Justice Scalia — held that not even the threshold requirement of ***"questions of law or fact common to the class"*** had been satisfied.

   a. **Violation of same law not enough:** Scalia said that the commonality requirement was ***not*** satisfied merely by the fact that all of the class members (i.e., all of the 1.5 million female employees) had suffered a ***violation of the same law*** (the statute barring employment discrimination based on gender). Instead, he said, ***two sub-requirements*** had to be met for commonality:

      [1] Every plaintiff's claim must "depend upon a ***common contention*** — for example, the assertion of discriminatory bias on the part of the ***same supervisor***[,]" *and*

      [2] "That common contention ... must be of such a nature that it is ***capable of class-wide resolution*** — which means that ***determination of its truth or falsity*** will ***resolve*** an issue that is ***central to the validity of each one of the claims in one stroke.***"

   b. **Proof, not allegation:** Furthermore, Scalia said, the four prerequisites of Rule 23 — including commonality — do not impose a "mere ***pleading*** standard." Instead, the party seeking class certification must ***"be prepared to <u>prove</u>"*** each prerequisite. The trial judge, before deciding to certify the class, must conduct a ***"rigorous analysis"*** of the plaintiffs' potential proof as to each prerequisite, an analysis that will "unfortunately" often "***overlap with the merits*** of the plaintiff's underlying claim."

   c. **Consequence:** Scalia was thus saying that before a federal trial judge may certify a class action, the "common questions of law or fact" requirement means that the judge must be satisfied, after "rigorous analysis," that the plaintiffs are prepared to demonstrate affirmatively at trial all of the following:

      [1] that there is at least one ***"common contention"*** of law or fact

      [2] whose ***"truth or falsity"*** will

      [3] resolve ***"in one stroke"***

      [4] an ***issue*** that is ***"central to the validity of each one of the claims."***

      This Scalia formulation seems to impose a new and ***much tougher standard*** for commonality than the Court had ever applied in pre-*Wal-Mart* class actions.

   d. **Application to facts:** Scalia concluded that the plaintiffs' employment-discrimination claim here did ***not*** satisfy the combined requirements for commonality. In any Title VII case, he said, the key issue is "the ***reason*** for a particular employment decision."

But here, the 1.5 million class members wanted to sue about *"literally millions of employment decisions at once."* There was, he said, *no single common contention the resolution of which was central to all of these claims*. The only crucial question for each plaintiff was *"Why was I disfavored?"*

    i.   **Needs proof of "specific employment practice":**   To satisfy commonality, Scalia continued, the Ps would have to prove that Wal-Mart followed a *"specific employment practice"* in regard to *each class member*. And the grant of *discretion to each store manager* to make individual employment decisions was *not* itself a "specific employment practice." So the plaintiffs had not carried their burden of coming forward with some evidence that they would be able to prove at trial that there existed a *single question or contention* the answer to which would *resolve every class member's individual claim of discrimination.*

3. **Significance:** *Wal-Mart*'s new standard for judging the existence of commonality will probably make it very difficult for class actions to proceed where there are many plaintiffs, and where the viability of each plaintiff's claim *depends mostly on the individual facts of that plaintiff's experience*.

    a.   **Employment-discrimination claims:** So most large *employment-discrimination claims* will fail to be certified under the *Wal-Mart* commonality requirement. That's because, as in *Wal-Mart* itself, each class member would have to make separate proof of the defendant's *discriminatory intent* as to that member — the fact that D discriminated in the terms of employment against *P1* would not tend to resolve the issue of whether D discriminated against *P2*.

    b.   **Mass toxic-exposure cases:** Similarly, in many *mass toxic-tort cases* — e.g., cases where each P claims exposure to a toxin placed by D into the *atmosphere or the water supply* — each plaintiff's claim will likely require individualized proof that she herself was *exposed* to the defendant's product. The need for this individualized proof of exposure will likely prevent the plaintiffs as a group from being found to have met the showing of a common question that will resolve *"in one stroke"* an *issue* that is *"central to the validity of each one of the claims"* (as *Wal-Mart* requires).

    Example: Consider the facts of our asbestos-exposure example (p. 357). Even apart from the typicality and representation issues, there's probably no common question of law or fact that would satisfy the *Wal-Mart* standard. After all, no class member could recover without proof that he or she was exposed to asbestos in a product made by the defendant. And the existence of exposure is inevitably a plaintiff-by-plaintiff question.

    So a court applying the *Wal-Mart* standard would probably conclude that even a smaller class action than the one in our example (e.g., one in which the only members are people alleging that they *got sick* from exposure to an asbestos-containing product made by D) does not satisfy commonality. If so, such an action could not be brought in federal court.[4]

---

4. So the class action of all people who were allegedly sickened by exposure to D's asbestos materials would likely have to be brought in *state* court, in a state that does not impose a commonality requirement (or at least not the demanding form of commonality imposed by the Supreme Court in *Wal-Mart*).

E. "Fair and adequate" representation of class: Recall that one of the four requirements imposed by Rule 23(a) is *"adequacy of representation"* — the court must be satisfied that the representatives "will *fairly and adequately protect the interests* of the class." Rule 23(a)(4).

1. **Class members versus lawyers for class:** Courts differ as to which participants should be most closely scrutinized for adequacy of representation: some look mostly at the adequacy of the *named class members*, and others at the adequacy of the *lawyers* representing the class. Y (8th), p. 879.

2. **Avoidance of conflicts:** Recall that the main function of the adequacy requirement is to ensure that there are no major *conflicts* between the interests of the representatives and the interests of the unnamed class members.

   a. **Reps have separate lawsuits:** A key reason why the trial court might find an inadequacy of representation is that some of the named representatives have *separate individual pending or potential lawsuits* against the defendant, and the court believes that the representatives' *"real reason* for pursuing the class action [is] to *gain leverage for their own case." Id.*

      Example: Consider the facts of the asbestos-exposure example on p. 357. Recall that all named plaintiffs have already gotten sick but not all rank-and-file members have done so. Let's assume that each named plaintiff is currently litigating a separate "individual" claim against one or more of the defendant manufacturers (the "Ds"), in which the plaintiff is seeking large compensatory damages for her present illnesses. Let's also assume that each of the individual suits is being handled by the same lawyer, Larry, who's representing the class members in the class action. And finally, let's assume that the unnamed rank-and-file class members who have not yet gotten sick are mainly interested in (1) having the Ds pay for these members' annual physical exams to spot possible symptoms; and (2) avoiding a situation in which the already-injured plaintiffs get such large judgments that the Ds are bankrupted so as to be unable to satisfy any later claims by the not-yet-sick unnamed members.

      On these facts, there is a very good chance that the court will hold that the requirement of adequacy of representation is *not* satisfied. That is, there's a good chance that the court will conclude that the already-sick named representatives (and their lawyer, Larry) will be so focused on obtaining large immediate payments for those already sick that they will neglect the conflicting objectives of the not-yet-sick unnamed members. Cf. *Amchem Products, Inc., v. Windsor*, 117 S. Ct. 2231 (1997).

   b. **Separate sub-classes:** Adequacy problems like the ones in the above example — where different groups of plaintiffs have different incentives — can sometimes be overcome if the suit designates *multiple "sub-classes" of plaintiffs,* and has *separate named representatives and lawyers* for each sub-class.

      Example: Suppose that in the above asbestos-exposure Example, plaintiffs' lawyers had taken the trouble at the beginning of the case to designate a "Subclass 1" consisting only of already-injured plaintiffs, and a separate "Subclass 2" of exposure-only plaintiffs. If the two sub-classes each had its own named representatives and its own non-overlapping lawyers, the court would be much less likely to find a fatal inadequacy of representation, than in the situation in which already-injured and not-yet-injured-but-exposed plaintiffs are grouped together in a single class with a single set of lawyers.

That is, the court might well certify the action and let it go forward, in the belief that by the time of any later proposed settlement, the separate lawyers for the Subclass 2 (exposure-only) plaintiffs would bargain with the lawyers for the Subclass 1 (already-injured) ones to minimize the chance that there wouldn't be sufficient settlement funds left to later compensate those Subclass 2 plaintiffs who eventually got sick post-settlement.

F. 23(b)(1) actions: In addition to the prerequisites of Rule 23(a), a class action will not be permitted unless the case fits into one of the *three categories* of Rule 23(b).

The first of these categories, *23(b)(1)*, applies to a fairly *narrow* group of situations that are similar to the circumstances requiring the *joinder of necessary parties* under Rule 19 (see *supra*, p. 348).

1. Test for 23(b)(1):   A class action is allowed under Rule 23(b)(1) if individual actions by or against members of the class would create a risk of either:

a. *inconsistent decisions* that would establish *incompatible standards of conduct* for the party opposing the class; Rule 23(b)(1)(A); or

b.   the *impairment of the interests* of members of the class who are not actually a party to the individual actions; Rule 23(b)(1)(B).

2. Typical cases: The risk of inconsistent standards is illustrated by Example (a) below; the risk that individual actions would impair the interests of members of the proposed class is illustrated by Example (b):

Example (a): A number of taxpayers wish to have a municipal bond issue declared invalid, and others wish to have the terms of the issue changed. If the taxpayers bring individual actions, the municipality may as the result of one suit be required to refrain from floating the bond issue altogether, but as the result of another suit merely be forced to limit the size of the issue, or to change the prospectus. There would thus be a risk that the municipality would be forced to observe incompatible standards of conduct, if individual actions were required. A court would therefore hold that this fact situation met the requirement of Rule 23(b)(1)(A), and would allow a class action, providing that 23(a) had been satisfied. See the Advisory Committee's Notes to present Rule 23(b)(1), Clause A.

Example (b): Members of an association wish to prevent a financial reorganization of the association. If one member sues individually and loses, the reorganization will proceed, since its validity will have been determined by a court. The reorganization's effect will thus spread to all the other members who wished to prevent it, without these others having had their day in court. A court would therefore hold that the requirement of 23(b)(1)(B) is satisfied and a class action would be permitted. See Advisory Committee's Notes to present Rule 23(b)(1), Clause B.

Note: If individual suits are brought instead of a class action, a person who is not present at one of the individual suits can never be *legally* bound by that suit. (The principles of *res judicata* prevent a person from being adversely bound by a judgment in a suit to which he was not a party.) Clause B of Rule 23(b)(1) is directed to the *practical*, rather than the *legal*, effects of an adverse judgment on an absentee. In Example (b) above, for instance, the reorganization might be vindicated by the first individual suit, and other association members would for practical purposes be too late to stop it, even though they would not be legally barred from doing so.

3. **No opting out:** A key aspect of the Rule 23(b)(1) type of class action (in contrast to the more common 23(b)(3) action, discussed below) is that members of the 23(b)(1) class *may not "opt out"* of the class, and will therefore *necessarily be bound* by the disposition. See Rule 23(c)(3).

4. **Mass tort claims:** The 23(b)(1) device has sometimes been used for the joint litigation of *mass tort claims*. Typically, these efforts have involved 23(b)(1)(B), on the theory that if there is no class certification, individual plaintiffs whose cases are not among the first tried may find their interests impaired, especially with respect to the recovery of *damages* from a defendant with *limited financial resources.* The topic is more extensively discussed *infra*, p. 383.

G. **23(b)(2) actions:** The second category of Rule 23(b) actions is specified in 23(b)(2). Rule 23(b)(2) allows the use of a class action if "the party opposing the class has acted or refused to act on *grounds that apply generally to the class*, so that final *injunctive* relief or corresponding *declaratory* relief is appropriate respecting the class as a whole[.]"

1. **Civil rights cases:** The main utility of Rule 23(b)(2) tends to be for *civil rights cases*, where discrimination against a whole class is alleged, and an *injunction* prohibiting further discrimination is sought.

> **Example:** Suppose that Broker Corp., a financial brokerage corporation, has hundreds of employees. Several black employees of Broker (the "named Ps") bring suit alleging that as a matter of corporate policy, whenever an opening for a supervisory-level position opens up Broker's president consciously awards the position to a current white employee rather than a current black employee of comparable or better skills; the named Ps say that they are among the black employees who have been passed over for promotion in favor of less-qualified whites. The named Ps seek certification of a class consisting of all black employees of Broker who will in the future seek promotion to supervisor. The only relief the Ps seek is (1) a declaration by the court that Broker has in the past as a matter of corporate policy discriminated against black applicants for supervisor; and (2) an injunction against Broker from discriminating in this way in the future.
>
> This is an appropriate case for certification as a (b)(2) class action. That's because what the named plaintiffs are alleging is that Broker, by discriminating against current black employees for promotion, has "acted ... on grounds that *apply generally to the class*" (all black employees who seek promotion). Furthermore, if as a result of the action the court declares that Broker has previously intentionally discriminated against black applicants for promotion, and enjoins Broker from doing so in the future, the declaratory relief and injunction will automatically be relief that is "appropriate" as to

the "class as a whole" (any black employee seeking promotion). (But if the relief sought also included ***back pay***, then as the result of *Wal-Mart v. Dukes*, discussed immediately below, a 26(b)(2) class-action would ***not*** be appropriate.)

2. **Equitable relief:** Notice that 23(b)(2) requires, in essence, that the wrong of which the defendant is accused have been a ***class-wide*** wrong, and that "final ***injunctive*** relief or corresponding ***declaratory*** relief" must be "appropriate respecting the ***class as a whole***." So it's clear that a b(2) claim must not only allege a class-wide wrong, but seek a ***class-wide equitable remedy*** (an injunction and/or declaratory judgment that would run in favor of the entire class).

3. **Seeking of money damages:** Suppose an employment discrimination suit seeks not only an injunction against further discrimination against plaintiff class members, but also an award of ***back pay*** to restore each class member to the financial position he or she would have been in had there been no discrimination. (Such an award of back pay is authorized by Title VII, the federal anti-employment-discrimination statute.) Notice that since the appropriate amount of back pay depends on when (or even whether) the discriminatory action occurred (longer-ago requires more back pay to make P whole now), the back-pay aspect will require a ***separate, individualized, determination*** for each class member. Does this need for individualized back-pay findings automatically make the action ***unsuitable*** for (b)(2) certification?

   a. ***Wal-Mart* rejects (b)(2) suits for back-pay:** The Supreme Court, in ***Wal-Mart Stores, Inc. v. Duke***, 131 S.Ct. 2541 (2011), ***has answered "yes"*** to this important question. (The case is also discussed *supra*, p. 358.) So as the result of *Wal-Mart*, if the amount of ***back pay*** would ***vary*** from member to member, the mere ***request*** for it ***rules out (b)(2) certification***, even if the back-pay being sought is viewed as ***"subordinate"*** to the class members' main goal of getting an injunction against further discrimination.

      i. **Facts of *Wal-Mart*:** Recall that in *Wal-Mart*, the claim was that all class members (i.e., all 1.5 million female employees of Wal-Mart) had been discriminated against by the company, by virtue of the company's grant of excess discretion to local store managers over the pay and promotion of employees of that store. The complaint sought back pay for each class member, in addition to a declaratory judgment (that the company had discriminated in the past) and an injunction (against future discrimination). To award any given plaintiff (call her "P1") back pay, the trial court would have had to compute the proper amount of that back pay, which would depend on such class-member-specific data as the *date* of any discrimination, *how long* P1 worked after the discrimination, etc.

      ii. **New rule by majority:** The plaintiffs had argued that as long as the money claims (like the back pay claims here) ***did not "predominate"*** over the claims for injunctive and declaratory relief, the fact that the plaintiffs asserted some ***"incidental"*** money claims did not disqualify the action from (b)(2) status. But five members of the Supreme Court sharply ***disagreed:*** "[W]e think it clear that ***individualized monetary claims belong in Rule 23(b)(3)***[,]" not (b)(2).

iii. Rationale: In so holding, the majority noted several procedural aspects that these justices believed collectively make (b)(2) an improper category for individualized money claims:

(1) No notice right: First, members of a (b)(2) class don't have to be given **notice** of the claim, as do class members of the more common (b)(3) actions (see *infra*, p. 367). This is because the drafters of Rule 23 had in mind cases (like civil rights cases) seeking only **class-wide relief**, and notice to class members would not be needed where the only relief would be a class-wide one (e.g., an injunction that would cause the defendant to change her behavior as to *all* class members). This lack of a right of absentees to receive notice was, the majority said, inconsistent with allowing individualized money claims.

(2) No opt-out right: Similarly, members of a (b)(2) class don't have a right to **opt out** of the class, as (b)(3) class members do — again, the drafters assumed that opting out would not be practicable for any member, since all members would be getting the same relief. This right of opt out, too, was inconsistent with allowing individualized money claims.

(3) Bad incentives: Finally, the majority was worried that the plaintiffs' proposed "predominance" test (monetary claims to be allowed as long as they won't predominate) would **incentivize** class representatives to **jeopardize the monetary claims of absent members**. For instance, the named representatives might decide (as they apparently did here in *Wal-Mart*) to assert only back-pay monetary claims, not any claims for "compensatory" damages; such a decision to drop compensatory claims would help ensure that individualized claims would not "predominate," and would thus help the class get (b)(2) certification. But because absent non-named plaintiffs couldn't opt out (and wouldn't even receive notice), the trial or settlement of the (b)(2) action might, under the rules of former adjudication (see *infra*, p. 416), cause absent plaintiff class members to lose the ability to litigate, in a **separate later action**, possibly-valid claims for compensatory damages.

iv. Significance: So *Wal-Mart* appears to mean that if the plaintiff class seeks **any monetary relief that requires individualized fact-finding** — even if the trial court believes that this monetary relief is **"subordinate"** to the class-wide injunctive or declaratory relief also being sought — the case is **automatically disqualified from being certified as a (b)(2) action**.

(1) Why it matters: Why does this rule forbidding (b)(2) status where individualized damages are sought even *matter*? After all, as we'll see immediately below, cases seeking relief that requires individualized findings may still qualify under the 23(b)**(3)** category, for cases in which questions of law or fact common to the class **"predominate"** over "any questions affecting only individual members[.]" So why, for instance, did the named plaintiffs (or their lawyers) in *Wal-Mart* fight so hard for certification under (b)(2) instead of (b)(3)?

(2) **"Superiority" doesn't matter under (b)(2):** The answer is that when the court is considering whether to grant (b)(2) status, the court is *not* instructed to consider whether trying the case as a class action is *superior* to some other procedural method (e.g., consolidated individual suits), or even whether the class action format is *practical* for the type of claim being asserted. But in a (b)(3) action, as we'll see in a moment, the court must find that the class action *is* "*superior* to other available methods for fairly and efficiently adjudicating the controversy." And pre-*Wal-Mart* cases have established that where class members have claims that vary from plaintiff to plaintiff with regard to damages (or even liability), a (b)(3) action will usually *not* be "superior" to other available methods, like multiple single-plaintiff suits, class actions involving smaller and more tightly-defined classes, etc.

(3) **Future of this type of case:** So *Wal-Mart* probably means that in **mass employment-discrimination cases**, plaintiffs' lawyers will have to choose between seeking only injunctive and declaratory relief (in which case any court-awarded **attorneys fees** are likely to be **small**, and the plaintiffs' lawyers' bargaining position in post-certification settlement negotiations likely to be weak), and *not bringing a federal class action at all.*

4. **"Commonality" and "typicality" requirements:** Keep in mind that the class in a 23(b)(2) suit, like those in (b)(1) and (b)(3) suits, must still satisfy the "commonality," "typicality," and "adequate representation" requirements of Rule 23(a) (*supra*, p. 356).

> **Example:** Recall the facts of *Wal-Mart, supra.* Even if the plaintiff representatives there had not been seeking back pay, those representatives would have had to convince the trial court that they could *adequately represent* the absent class members, and that the Supreme Court's recent tougher test for *"commonality"* (whether there is at least one contention whose disposition will resolve an issue central to each plaintiff's claim) was satisfied. As I discuss *supra*, p. 358, in *Wal-Mart* the plaintiffs were *not* able to meet the requirement for showing commonality, even apart from the issue of whether their inclusion of monetary claims was fatal to (b)(2) status.

5. **No opting out:** Members of a 23(b)(2) class, like those who belong to a 23(b)(1) class, *may not "opt out"* of the class. See Rule 23(c)(3).

H. **23(b)(3) actions:** The final type of class action, and the most common, is provided for by Rule *23(b)(3)*.

1. **Two requirements:** Rule 23(b)(3) allows a class action if the court makes *two findings*:

a. **Common questions:** "that the questions of law or fact *common* to class members *predominate* over any questions affecting only individual members"; and

b. **Superior method:** "that a class action is *superior to other available methods* for fairly and efficiently adjudicating the controversy."

2. **Most popular form:** This is the famous "b(3)" class action, into which category have fallen "the great bulk of reported cases in which class actions have been allowed under the revised rule." Wr., 517. This is so in part because the requirements imposed by b(3) are less restrictive than those imposed by b(1) and b(2).

3. **Factors:** To aid the court in determining whether a class action is *"superior"* to other forms of adjudication, and whether common questions predominate, Rule 23(b)(3) lists four factors to be considered:

   a. **Interest in individual control:** "the class members' interests" in *individually controlling* the prosecution or defense of separate actions";

   b. **Existing litigation:** "the extent and nature of any litigation concerning the controversy *already begun* by or against class members";

   c. **Concentration in one forum:** "the desirability or undesirability of *concentrating the litigation* of the claims in the *particular forum"*;

   d. **Difficulties of management:** "the likely difficulties in *managing* a class action."

4. **Securities cases:** Rule 23(b)(3) class actions have been found particularly useful in *securities fraud* cases, where it is impractical for most investors who have been harmed to sue individually, since the amount lost is often too small to justify the costs of a suit. It has also frequently been used in *antitrust* cases.

5. **Mass tort claims:** Some litigants have tried to use section b(3) for *mass tort actions*, such as *airline crashes* and mass drug-related *product liability* suits. But in general, courts have been slower to allow the use of (b)(3) than they have been to permit (b)(1) actions, in the mass tort context. See *infra*, p. 383.

I. **Requirement of notice:** The members of a class, other than the representatives, do not necessarily know that the suit has been commenced. Therefore, the court will normally require that these class members be given *notice* of the fact that the suit is pending.

1. **When required:** The Federal Rules explicitly require the giving of notice of the suit only where it is a 23(b)(3) class action. Rule 23(c)(2)(B) requires the giving of "the best notice that is practicable under the circumstances" to all b(3) class members.

   a. **Individual notice:** Individual notice, almost always by mail, must be given to all those class members whose names and addresses can be obtained *"through reasonable effort,"* even if the class numbers in the millions. Cf. Rule 23(c)(2)(B), first sentence.

   b. **Cost borne by named plaintiffs:** The named plaintiff(s) must *pay the cost* of mail notice to each such member in a b(3) suit. If they don't do so, the class action must be *dismissed*. See *Eisen v. Carlisle & Jacquelin,* 417 U.S. 156 (1974).

2. **Contents of notice:** The notice provided for in Rule 23(c)(2) must advise the class member of a number of facts, including that:

   a. **Right of exclusion:** the court will *exclude* him from the class if he so requests, so that the judgment will not affect him;

   b. **Binding effect:** the judgment will affect him, whether it is favorable or not, unless he excludes himself; and

   c. **Right to lawyer:** if he does not exclude himself, he may *appear, with a lawyer*, in the class suit.

3. **b(1) and b(2) actions:** In *(b)(1)* and *(b)(2)* actions, the court *"may"* (but is not required to) order that "appropriate notice" be given to the class. FRCP 23(c)(2)(A). "Appropriate notice" will not necessarily be individual notice, such as mail notice — it may instead be *mass notice* such as by newspaper or Website publication.

4. **Cost of identifying class members:** *Eisen, supra,* established that the plaintiff must bear the cost of *notifying* the class members, but did not address the question of who should bear the cost of *identifying* them. In ***Oppenheimer Fund v. Sanders***, 437 U.S. 340 (1978), the Supreme Court held that in most circumstances, this burden must also be borne by the named *plaintiff.*

    a. **Facts:** In *Oppenheimer*, the proposed class consisted of all persons who had held shares in the Oppenheimer Investment Fund during certain years. Because this group did not match the group of present shareholders of the Fund, it was estimated that it would cost about $16,000 to compile a list of class members. This work could not be done directly by the defendant, but would have to be done by the Fund's Transfer Agent (which keeps records of the company's shareholders).

    b. **Holding:** The Supreme Court held that since the cost of the compilation would be about the same whether the work was paid for by the plaintiff or the defendant, the plaintiff must pay. The Court indicated, however, that if the cost had been *"insubstantial"*, or if the task had been one the defendant would have had to do during the ordinary course of its business, the cost might be placed on the defendant.

J. **Binding effect of class action decision:** Judgment in a Rule 23(b)(3) class action is *binding*, whether it is *for or against* the class, on all those whom the court finds to be members of the class. Rule 23(c)(3).

1. **Exclusion:** However, any person has the right to *exclude himself* from the class in a b(3) action, if he notifies the court to that effect prior to a date specified in the notice of the action sent to him. 23(c)(2)(A). One of the reasons for which notice to all known members of the class must be sent is to give each member the chance to "*opt out*," and to bring his own suit.

    a. **Consequence of exclusion:** A person who excludes himself from the action will not be bound by an adverse judgment. But conversely, he may not *assert collateral estoppel* in his own action, if the judgment turns out to be favorable to the class. Wr., p. 520.

    b. **b(1) and b(2) actions:** By contrast, absent class members in Rule *23(b)(1) and b(2)* actions do *not* have the right to "opt out" of the class and bring their own suits.

        i. **b(1):** To allow exclusion in b(1) cases would give rise to exactly the kind of inconsistent adjudication that the Rule is designed to prevent.

        ii. **b(2):** Similarly, opting out of a b(2) action would make no sense, since the declaratory or injunctive relief to which b(2) addresses itself generally applies to the whole class.

            Example: A restaurant enjoined from discriminating would hardly make a point of continuing to discriminate against those class members who excluded themselves from the class suit. Thus there is no reason to permit members of the class to opt out of the 23(b)(2) class suit.

2. **Minimum contacts not required:** An absent plaintiff who does not "opt out" will be bound by the decision, ***even if he lacked "minimum contacts" with the forum state*** (and thus could not have been bound had he been a *defendant*). The Supreme Court so held in *Phillips Petroleum Co. v. Shutts*, 472 U.S. 797 (1985), discussed more extensively *supra*, p. 49.

    a. **Due process problem:** As noted above, absent class members in a b(1) or b(2) action apparently do not have the right to "opt out" of the class and bring their own suits. Where a plaintiff does not have minimum contacts with the forum state, ***and*** is not permitted to opt out because the action is a b(1) or b(2) action, the absent member could plausibly argue that his ***due process*** rights have been infringed. It is not clear whether a federal court that refuses to allow an absentee plaintiff to opt out of a b(1) or b(2) action, where the absentee lacks minimum contacts with the state where the federal court sits, has violated due process — this issue is discussed further *infra*, p. 384, in the context of mass tort litigation.

K. Subject-matter jurisdiction issues: Federal class actions can sometimes raise questions of *subject matter jurisdiction*.

1. **Federal question cases:** Where the plaintiffs' claims are based on a ***federal question***, there are no significant subject-matter jurisdiction issues. Diversity of citizenship, of course, does not matter. And there is no amount in controversy requirement. So nationwide class actions based upon federal causes of action are quite easy to bring, even where each claim is for a small amount.

    Example: Named plaintiffs seek certification of a class action against XYZ Corp., with the class consisting of all persons who bought stock in XYZ during a particular three-year period. XYZ is a citizen of Delaware, and the unnamed plaintiffs are citizens of all 50 states, including Delaware. The suit alleges that XYZ violated federal securities laws in its financial reporting. No individual class member's claim is for more than $5,000, and many claims are for less than $100. Nonetheless, there are no subject-matter jurisdiction problems that will impede the action, because: (1) diversity is not required (since the securities-law claims are federal-question claims); and (2) there is no amount in controversy requirement (again because the claims raise federal questions).

2. **Diversity cases:** On the other hand, a federal class action in which all claims are based *solely on diversity* does face very meaningful subject-matter jurisdiction problems, principally related to amount in controversy.

    a. **Diversity:** In determining whether the required *"complete diversity"* exists, there will rarely be a problem. That's because the Supreme Court has long held that ***only the citizenship of the class representatives***, not the citizenship of the unnamed class members, counts. So as long as none of the named representatives is a citizen of the same state as any defendant, there is no diversity problem. And, since the lawyer for the plaintiff class gets to decide who the named representatives will be, the lawyer can easily assure that no representative is a citizen of the same state as any defendant. Cf. Y, p. 818.

b.   Amount in controversy: By contrast, diversity class actions raise issues regarding the *amount in controversy* requirement.

    i.   At least one named member meets amount: If *at least one named class member satisfies* the jurisdictional amount, other class members can be part of the action even though their claim is for less than this amount. This result is due to the doctrine of *"supplemental jurisdiction"* (28 U.S.C. § 1367; see *supra*, p. 142). Under supplemental jurisdiction, if one plaintiff has a valid diversity (or, for that matter, federal-question) claim against a defendant, other plaintiffs with closely-related claims may be brought into the action even if they don't separately satisfy subject-matter-jurisdictional requirements. In *Exxon Mobil Corp. v. Allapattah Services, Inc.*, 125 S.Ct. 2611 (2005) (discussed extensively *supra*, p. 150), the Supreme Court held that supplemental jurisdiction applies in the diversity-based class action context, thus allowing the action to go forward as long as at least one class member meets the jurisdictional amount.

    Example: 10,000 Exxon dealers bring a diversity-only class action against Exxon, claiming that Exxon has overcharged them for fuel. It is clear that at least some members of the class have a claim for the jurisdictional amount ($75,000), but many other class members' claims are for less than the $75,000 amount. *Held*, the dealers whose claims do not meet this amount may remain part of the class — as long as at least one named class member meets the jurisdictional amount, supplemental jurisdiction applies to the claims of the other class members, no matter how small those claims. *Exxon Mobil Corp. v. Allapattah Services, Inc., supra.*

    ii.   Named members can't aggregate: On the other hand, nothing in § 1367 or in *Allapattah* changes the rule that *at least one named class member must independently meet the jurisdictional amount.* So unless the plaintiff's lawyer can find at least one named claimant with $75,000 at stake, the diversity class action cannot go forward. In other words, several named class members, each having a claim of less than $75,000, *cannot "aggregate" their claims* to get over the $75,000 minimum. In "small claims" types of actions (e.g., ones involving, say, allegations that D has made small overcharges against many thousands of class members), this rule means that federal class actions based on state-law claims are virtually dead (unless the action involves at least $5 million in total and falls under the Class Action Fairness Act of 2005, discussed immediately below). Cf. Y, p. 818 (federal class actions based on state securities-law claims are not viable).

    iii. $5 million at stake: In 2005, Congress decided that certain types of class actions are so major that they ought to be *"federalized."* Therefore, in the *Class Action Fairness Act of 2005* ("CAFA"), Congress said that a class action can go forward if: (a) there is minimal diversity (at least one plaintiff is diverse with at least one defendant); and (b) there is *at least $5 million in controversy in the aggregate,* even if *no class member's claim is for more than $75,000.*[5] See 28 U.S.C. § 1332(d)(2).

Example: A class action is filed in Missouri federal district court in which the Ps are taxpayers who used D (H&R Blockhead Inc., a citizen solely of Missouri) to prepare their tax returns, and who took out "Refund Anticipation Loans" (RALs) from D, secured by their anticipated tax refunds. The Ps' claims are based on the theory that the RALs violated the consumer-fraud and usury laws of each plaintiff's home state. There are 20,000 members of the proposed class, none of whose claim is worth more than $10,000. The total amount in controversy is $100 million.

As long as at least one plaintiff class member is a citizen of a state other than Missouri (D's state of citizenship), the action can go forward even though no plaintiff separately meets the usual $75,000 amount in controversy. That's because the fact that more than $5 million is at stake overall brings the case within CAFA.

L. Determination that no valid class action exists: Rule 23(c)(1) provides that "at an early practicable time" following the filing of a class action, the court must "determine by order whether to *certify* the action as a class action." "Certifying" the class means to decide that a class action is appropriate. The certification requirement applies to Rule b(1) and b(2) suits as well as to those brought under b(3).

1. **Consequence of denial:** If the court finds that no class action is possible, the suit may be continued by the "representatives," but with *no res judicata* effect for or against the absent would-be class members.

2. **Sub-class:** Alternatively, the suit may be continued by a *sub-class* of the original class. In that event, no *res judicata* effect extends to those original class members not included in the new sub-class.

3. **No right to appeal:** If the trial court finds that the action should not proceed as a class action, this finding is not a *final judgment*, and consequently an *immediate appeal generally may not be taken.* The named plaintiffs have to try the case as a non-class action (or with a smaller class), and only on appeal from the judgment on the merits can the correctness of the trial court's refusal to certify the class be reviewed. For more about the general rule that appeals may not be taken until there is a final judgment, see *supra*, p. 323.

   a. **Some relief from Rule 23(f):** But plaintiffs who have had their class status denied might get some *relief*, thanks to FRCP 23(f). Under Rule 23(f), a Court of Appeals has *discretion* to *permit an interlocutory appeal* from a district court's decision either to grant or deny class certification. So if the district court says "no" to the plaintiffs' request for class status, they at least have a fighting chance of getting their appeal heard right away.

      i. **Help for defendants, too:** Notice that present 23(f) may help defendants, too, sometimes — if the district court *grants* class status, the defense may be able to

---

5. The CAFA statute instructs the district court not to exercise its jurisdiction under this provision if the action is not sufficiently "national" in scope according to criteria set forth in the statute (e.g., jurisdiction is not to be exercised if more than two-thirds of the proposed plaintiff class members, and the primary defendants, are citizens of the state in which the action was filed). See 28 U.S.C. § 1332(d)(4).

persuade the Court of Appeals to hear an interlocutory appeal on this grant, and then have it overturned before undergoing a class trial.

M. Waiver of the right to bring class action: An increasingly important issue is whether a party to a contract may agree in advance to *waive* her right to bring a class action if litigation should ensue. The issue typically arises where the contract contains a boilerplate clause stating that all disputes will be subject to one-plaintiff-at-a-time *arbitration*. The general principle is that such waivers are *valid*, and will be *enforced*.

1. **Adhesion contracts containing waivers on class actions:** A large corporation often makes many nearly-identical *"adhesion" contracts* with large numbers of consumers or employees. An adhesion contract is one in which the individual party on one side (e.g., a consumer or a prospective employee contracting with the other, typically larger, party) does not have enough *bargaining power* to insist on changes to the boilerplate drafted by the other party's lawyers.

   a. **Desire for waiver of class-action right:** Most large corporations typically want to *avoid* in advance the possibility that the corporation's counter-parties in the contract (e.g., individual consumers or employees) will *join together* in a class action against the corporation. Therefore, large corporations now frequently insist that each of their many small-scale consumer or employment agreements contain a clause under which the customer or employee agrees to *waive* in advance her right to be part of a class-action suit against the corporation should there be a later contractual dispute.

   b. **Arbitration agreement:** Typically, the large corporation does this by:

      [1] inserting an *"arbitration clause"* into the boilerplate customer or employee agreement, under which all disputes will be *privately arbitrated* instead of subjected to court-based litigation; and

      [2] providing in that arbitration clause that any such arbitration will be limited to adjudicating the rights of *the single consumer or employee.* In other words, increasingly the arbitration clauses demanded by large potential corporate defendants forbid both class action lawsuits and *"class arbitrations."*

   c. **Nature of arbitration:** In an arbitration, a private person (usually a lawyer) is appointed to hear and decide the dispute. Arbitration is sometimes thought of as "litigation lite" — it usually includes *limited discovery*, *abbreviated presentation* of *evidence*, and a written decision by the arbitrator that frequently does not include any *statement of reasoning*. Y (8th Ed.), p. 575. Typically, the arbitration agreement prevents either party from *appealing* either the legal or factual conclusions made by the arbitrator.

      i. **Quicker and more final:** All of these attributes mean that a decision is likely to be both *quicker* and *more final* in an arbitration than in a lawsuit.

   d. **Purpose of typical arbitration clause:** From the perspective of the corporation inserting the arbitration clause into its standard small-scale contracts, the desired (and actual) effect of the clause is to make it *economically near-impossible* for the consumer or employee party to *litigate any dispute under the agreement*. That's so mainly because the *amount at stake* in any arbitration conforming to the clause will typically be *too small for any rational lawyer to handle,* even if the statute under which the case is brought allows the award of reasonable attorney's fees to the prevailing plaintiff. As the dissenters put it in a Supreme Court arbitration case about a plaintiff family whose claim involved $30.22, "What rational lawyer would have signed on to represent the [family] in litigation for the possibility of fees stemming from a $30.22 claim?" *AT&T Mobility LLC v. Concepcion,* 131 S.Ct. 1740 (2011) (dissent by Breyer).

Example: Assume that PhoneCo offers wireless cellphone service to millions of customers for an average of less than $100 per customer per month. PhoneCo realizes that few if any lawyers will find it economical to bring a contingent-fee suit on behalf of a single consumer should the consumer have a contract dispute with PhoneCo. On the other hand, since all of PhoneCo's customer agreements are substantially identical, a *plaintiff's class action lawyer* might find it very economically attractive to bring a class action suit (or a class-based arbitration) on behalf of, say, all of PhoneCo's millions of customers, alleging that the company has breached a given provision of the customer agreements.

To avoid the risks of being subjected to a well-funded class action of this sort, PhoneCo would be well-advised (from a purely-legal perspective, anyway) to insert into its boilerplate contracts a provision requiring that any dispute under the contract be subjected to private arbitration administered by, say, the American Arbitration Association. Such a clause will also likely state that the customer agrees that arbitration shall involve *only the individual parties* to the particular agreement in question (i.e., that there will be no "class arbitrations" permitted under clause).

As long as the relevant courts will *enforce* this arbitration clause — a subject we discuss immediately below — PhoneCo's use of the clause in its standard agreement will effectively *immunize it* from any breach-of-contract class actions or group-arbitrations brought by its customers. It will be nearly impossible for any individual consumer to afford to pay a lawyer to sue PhoneCo, or for any lawyer to take the solo-plaintiff's case on a contingent-fee or court-awarded-fee basis. Furthermore, any single-customer arbitration award will have limited power to damage PhoneCo, either in terms of the size of the award or the creation of a bad legal precedent (since arbitration awards generally have no precedential or collateral-estoppel [see *infra,* p. 427] effect).

2. **Enforceability of arbitration agreements generally:** The general policy of American courts, both state and federal, is to *enforce arbitration agreements.*

a. **Federal "FAA" statute:** In fact, a federal statute dating back to 1925, the *Federal Arbitration Act (FAA),* essentially *compels* both state and federal courts to *enforce as drafted any arbitration* clause that is part of any transaction "involving commerce," which today includes virtually all arbitration clauses. M,R,S&P, p. 114.

i. **Consequence:** So even if a state-court judge were inclined to believe that forcing an individual claimant into mandatory "bilateral" arbitration[6] rather than, say, class arbitration is an unfair limitation of remedy, the FAA will typically *nullify* the judge's authority to offer the escape-route of either a judicial trial or a class arbitration to a party who has signed a standard bilateral-arbitration-only clause.

The FAA is said to *"preempt"* the state's right to refuse to enforce the arbitration clause as drafted.

ii. **The "savings" clause of the FAA:** However, the FAA contains a so-called *"savings"* clause (§2 of the Act). That savings clause says that the FAA does *not* prevent either party to an arbitration clause from asserting any general state-law grounds allowing "for the *revocation* of any contract." Thus any general *defense* that state law would recognize as sufficient to allow a party to *avoid a "contract"* — defenses like lack of consideration, mistake, duress, fraud, and (of particular importance) *"unconscionability"* — may in theory be used by the plaintiff to avoid a bilateral-arbitration clause that would otherwise be enforceable under the FAA's main provision. But as we'll see shortly below, the Supreme Court has taken a *narrow view* of when the state-law defense of unconscionability may be used by a plaintiff to avoid an agreement to arbitrate.

3. **Unconscionability and bans on class arbitrations:** As you have learned or will learn in your *Contracts* course, most states refuse to enforce a contractual provision that the court considers to be *"unconscionable."* The idea is that a court may, and often will, refuse to enforce a provision of a contract that is *deeply unfair* and that stems directly from the parties' *greatly-unequal bargaining power.*

a. **Suit alleging unconscionability of arbitration clause:** Some plaintiffs who have signed bilateral-arbitration clauses have tried to escape the clause by use of the unconscionability doctrine. That is, the plaintiff (who wants to bring a class action, or at least a class arbitration, rather than be content with her contractual obligation to arbitrate her own claim one-on-one), brings a breach-of-contract suit in which she argues that the mandatory-bilateral-arbitration clause is unconscionable under state law and thus unenforceable. Can the plaintiff successfully argue that her unconscionability defense falls within the FAA's "savings" clause, thus giving the court authority to *refuse enforcement* of the mandatory-bilateral-arbitration provision as the FAA's main provision would normally require?

b. **Ban is enforceable (*AT&T Mobility v. Concepcion*):** The answer is, essentially, *"no"* — the Supreme Court has decided that a state-law-based defense that a particular type of arbitration clause is unconscionable does not trigger the FAA's "savings" clause. Therefore, the main parts of the FAA apply, and typically *preempt* any state rule of law that would treat a bilateral-arbitration clause (i.e., a no-class-arbitration clause) as being unconscionable and thus unenforceable. That's the holding of *AT&T Mobility LLC v. Concepcion*, 131 S.Ct. 1740 (2011). We'll refer to the case as *Concepcion*.

i. **Facts:** In *Concepcion*, the Ps (a couple named Concepcion) purchased a cell phone service plan from D (AT&T), which advertised free phones as part of the

---

6. "Bilateral" arbitration means arbitration that is *limited to the two basic parties* to the agreement that includes the arbitration clause. As noted in Par. (1)(b)[2] above, arbitration clauses drafted by large companies typically demand bilateral arbitration, in the sense that they not only require arbitration of all disputes, but prohibit either party from requesting "class arbitration," in which the arbitration claims of multiple plaintiffs are heard together (the arbitration equivalent of a judicial class action).

plan. The Ps were not charged for the phones, but were charged $30.22 in sales tax based on the phones' retail value. Although the cellphone plan contained a mandatory bilateral-arbitration clause, the Ps nonetheless brought a conventional suit against D in federal district court for the Southern District of California. Their suit was later consolidated into a putative class action alleging various acts of fraud by D in cellphone marketing, including the Concepcions' claim that D had committed fraud by charging sales tax on phones that had been advertised as free. D then moved to have the Concepcions' part of the case dismissed, and replaced by one-on-one arbitration as required under the Concepcions' original contract with D.

ii. **D's motion for arbitration denied below:** But the federal district court *denied* D's motion, on the grounds that: (1) the California courts would regard this particular mandatory-bilateral-arbitration clause as being unconscionable; and therefore (2) the FAA's "savings" clause (see *supra*, p. 374) applied, in a way that took the case out of the FAA's main "enforce arbitration clauses as drafted" rule. Consequently, the Concepcions had the right to insist that any arbitration should be a class arbitration (something that D didn't want, any more than it wanted to face a standard judicial class action).

iii. **FAA pre-empts state doctrine of unconscionability:** But by a 5-4 vote, the Supreme Court decided that Congress, in enacting the FAA, had never intended to recognize state-law doctrines treating bilateral arbitration as unconscionable as being the sort of contract-avoidance defense that would trigger the FAA's "savings" clause.

(1) **Rationale:** The majority in *Concepcion* reasoned that the FAA's "principal purpose," in the eyes of the Congress that enacted it, was to *"ensur[e] that private arbitration agreements are enforced according to their terms."* California's use of the unconscionability doctrine would fundamentally alter the parties' agreement about arbitration, by letting consumers force corporate defendants into the much-less attractive (for the defendant) format of class arbitration. Since California's use of unconscionability would interfere with the main pro-arbitration purposes of the FAA, that use was *pre-empted*.

(2) **Federal court must follow:** The FAA's preemption of state doctrines of unconscionability meant, in turn, that the federal district court in *Concepcion*, too, was required to disregard state doctrines of unconscionability, and instead to obey the FAA's general rule enforcing arbitration clauses as drafted.

(3) **Congress has right to change:** But keep in mind that Congress is free at any time to *reverse* the effect of *Concepcion* by *modifying* the FAA so as clarify that the statute's "savings" clause *is* triggered by a court's finding that the arbitration clause as written would be unconscionable under state law. And, indeed, there have been attempts in Congress post-*Concepcion* to amend the statute in this way, though these attempts have not come close to success as of this writing.

N. Settlements: Any *settlement of a class action* must be *approved by the court*. FRCP 23(e), 1st sentence. This requirement is not consistent with the general rule that parties to an action are free to settle or end their case. The purpose of the approval requirement is principally to ensure that the **interests of the absent class members** are **adequately protected**. (For instance, the court will want to be sure that the defendants are not "buying off" the plaintiffs' contingent fee lawyers, at the expense of the plaintiff class members.)

1. **Notice requirement:**   In addition, at least if a class has already been certified, "**notice** in a reasonable manner" of a **proposed settlement** must also be given to "all class members who would be bound by the proposal." Rule 23(e)(1).

    a. **Court approval before certification of class:**   Suppose, however, that some or all of the named plaintiffs wish to settle the case **before** the class has been certified; is notice to the "putative" class members necessary? The answer is **"no"** — only notice to the named class representatives, not to the unnamed members, is required before settlement of a putative class action that will never be certified. See ACN to 2003 Amendments to Rule 23(e)(1).

2. **Financial condition:**   Some courts have held that the **financial condition of the defendant** may be taken into account in determining whether the settlement is fair. For example, a settlement that otherwise seems small might be approved if the defendant is in a weak financial condition.

3. **Settlement-only class actions:** Sometimes, a class is certified **"for settlement purposes only."** This is a way of giving the parties — especially the defendants — a method of disposing of all claims on a particular subject, even claims that have not yet ripened, held by persons who may not yet even have been injured.

    a. **Danger of collusion:** Such settlement-only uses of the class action device are controversial, because they may be motivated by **collusion** between the lawyers for the plaintiffs and the defense lawyers, and because they may short-change the future plaintiffs.

        Example: In *Amchem Products, Inc., v. Windsor*, 117 S. Ct. 2231 (1997), the class was a massive one, consisting of everyone who had ever been exposed to an asbestos product made by any of 20 defendants. Class members included not only those who were already sick or dead, but also those who were asymptomatic (including many who did not even know that they had been exposed or that they might become sick in the future). In the course of a single day the parties filed a complaint, an answer, a proposed class certification, and a proposed settlement. The settlement would have bound the not-yet-sick members, with only very limited opt-out rights. The settlement was attractive to the defendants, because it allowed them to limit, in one fell swoop, all claims by anyone they had ever injured.

        But the Supreme Court held that the class should never have been certified at all; therefore, the court had no power to approve a settlement. (See *infra*, p. 380). The Court relied heavily on the fact that the not-yet-sick plaintiffs were not adequately represented.

    b. **Must meet regular rules:** Settlement-only classes must **meet the same basic requirements** as class actions that will be tried. *Amchem, supra*. Thus the trial court cannot certify the class (a prerequisite to approving the settlement) unless the court finds that

Table 8-2
CLASS ACTIONS

Type of Class Action	Requirements	Examples	Notice	Opt-Out Options	Effect on Future Actions by Same P
23(b)(1)	Individual actions by or against the class would create: (a) *inconsistent decisions* forcing an opponent of the class to observe incompatible standards; *or* (b) *impairment of the interests* of members of the class who are not actually a party to the individual actions	(1) A number of taxpayers wish to have a municipal bond issue declared invalid, and others wish to have the terms of the issue changed. If taxpayers bring individual suits, the municipality may be forced to observe incompatible standards concerning the bonds. See R. 23(b)(1), Clause A. (2) Members of an association wish to prevent a financial reorganization of the association. If one member sues individually and loses, the reorg. will proceed. The reorg.'s effect will thus spread to members who wished to prevent it. See R. 23(b)(1), Clause B. (3) *Mass-tort* cases: If individual suits are brought, plaintiffs with early suits may bankrupt the defendant, leaving nothing for the latter plaintiffs. Examples: airline crashes; asbestos cases; IUD and breast-implant suits.	Court "may" (but is not required to) direct *"appropriate notice"* to the class. FRCP 23(c)(2)(A). This will not necessarily be individual (e.g., mail) notice — it may instead be mass notice such as by newspaper or Website publication.	Class members may *not* opt out. (However, if an absent member lacked minimum contacts with the state where the federal court sits, the absentee might be able to claim that binding her violated her due process rights.)	Since no one may opt out, *all* class members are *bound* by the disposition. See Rule 23(c)(3).
23(b)(2)	The party opposing the class has acted or refused to act on grounds generally applicable to the class.	*Civil rights* cases, where discrimination against the whole class is alleged, and an injunction prohibiting further discrimination is sought.	Same as for (b)(1) actions.	Same as for (b)(1) actions.	Same as for (b)(1) actions.
23(b)(3)	The court makes two findings: (1) *Common questions* of law or fact *predominate* over any questions affecting only individual members. (2) The class action is *superior* to other available methods for fair and efficient adjudication of the controversy.	This is the most common type of class action. (1) Often used in *securities fraud* cases (it's impractical for most investors who've been harmed to sue individually, bec. the amount lost is too small to justify the cost of a suit.) (2) *Antitrust* cases (consumers who've been injured by anti-competitive conduct, such as price-fixing). (3) Occasionally, *mass-tort* cases (but (b)(1) is more common in the tort context, especially where there's a danger the defendant will be bankrupted by individual suits.)	*Best notice practicable* under the circumstances" must be given to all class members. Rule 23(c)(2)(B). This means *individual* notice (e.g., by mail) to all class member whose names can be obtained with reasonable certainty. *Id.* The named plaintiffs must front the cost. If they can't or won't, class action must be dismissed. *Eisen.*	Class members have the *right to opt out*. Rule 23(c)(2).	The judgment will affect each class member (whether favorable to the member or not), *unless the member opted out.*

the named parties will fairly protect the interests of all class members, that (in the case of a b(3) action) common questions of law and fact predominate, etc.

    i. **Management of action not considered:** However, the fact that the action is being immediately settled does have a bearing on one class action requirement: 23(b)(3)(D)'s command that the court consider "the likely difficulties in managing [the] class action" may be dispensed with, since there won't be any true "action" to "manage." *Amchem, supra.*

O. **Attorneys' fees:** If the class is victorious (or receives a settlement), courts often award *reasonable attorneys' fees* to the class' lawyers. These fees are generally added to the sum awarded, and serve as an incentive to the bringing of actions where no single class member could afford to hire a lawyer. The granting of attorneys' fees thus encourages a kind of "private enforcement" against legal wrongs which the government does not have the resources to police itself.

    1. *Alyeska Pipeline* **case:** In suits brought under *federal statutes*, attorneys' fees may be awarded *only if a federal statute so provides*. See *Alyeska Pipeline Service Co. v. Wilderness Society*, 421 U.S. 240 (1975). Congress has passed such statutes for a few kinds of federal actions. For instance, attorney's fees have been allowed by Congress in a wide range of *civil rights* cases; see 42 U.S.C. §1988.

    2. **Court supervision of fees:** Most class actions that result in the award of attorneys fees are *settled* rather than litigated to their conclusion. Even in the case of a settlement, however, courts exercise substantial authority to approve or disapprove of the amount of attorneys fees agreed upon between the parties. In fact, courts closely scrutinize such agreements, for fear that the defendant will "buy off" the plaintiffs' lawyers, enriching those lawyers at the expense of the members of the plaintiff class.

P. **Mass tort cases:** So-called *"mass tort"* cases have become an increasingly important aspect of modern litigation. Starting in the late 1980s, the federal diversity class action has begun to be an important way of dealing with mass tort problems. Therefore, it is worth exploring in some detail how federal courts have handled some of the problems in using federal class action procedures to deal with these kinds of cases.

    1. **Definition of "mass tort":** To begin with, what do we mean by *"mass tort"*? In reality, there are two different kinds of situations covered by the term. These sub-types are often referred to as "mass accidents" and "mass product liability" respectively.

        a. **"Mass accident" suits:** In a *"mass accident,"* a large number of persons are injured as the result of a *single accident*. Examples of such accidents include an *airplane crash*, the collapse of a building, or the explosion of a factory accompanied by the release of toxic substances (e.g., Bhopal).

        b. **"Mass product liability" cases:** A *"mass product liability"* case arises out of the sale of a *defective product* to thousands of buyers, who are thereby injured. Whereas even a very large "mass accident" case tends to involve a few thousand claimants, a mass product liability "case" can involve hundreds of thousands of people. Examples of products which have given rise to mass product liability scenarios include *asbestos*,

IUDs such as the Dalkon Shield, prescription drugs such as DES (to prevent miscarriages) and medical devices such as breast implants or heart valves.

2. **The problem to be solved:** Both mass accident and mass product liability scenarios are hard for the conventional "bilateral" (two-party) traditional tort litigation model to handle. In the traditional model, an individual litigant, represented by a lawyer for whom that claim presents a unique set of facts (and with the client's approval on such matters as pleading, discovery tactics, trial tactics and settling), builds a case from scratch. Discovery, trial, appeal, and/or settlement negotiations are all conducted as if no other case has presented closely-similar issues, and as if there were no opportunities for economies of scale in the litigation process.

a. **Mass torts overwhelm the system:** This traditional model works very poorly, if at all, in the mass tort situation. Consider the problems of *asbestos* litigation, for instance. Let's examine a somewhat typical, mostly hypothetical, asbestos litigation.

i. **Facts:** Suppose that our particular plaintiff, P, was a shipyard worker who was exposed to the substance while working in a government shipyard during WWII. P has now contracted mesothelioma, a uniformly fatal form of cancer. P is one of 3,000 workers who all worked in the same Navy shipyard during the same period, all of whom have contracted diseases which they believe to be due to their asbestos exposure. D is the principal, but not sole, manufacturer of the asbestos to which P and his co-workers were exposed.

ii. **Discovery and trial:** Now, observe what is likely to happen if P conducts his case according to the traditional two-party tort litigation model, and following traditional tort doctrine. P will need to carry out discovery, as well as a trial, in which P will try to establish: (1) that D was one of the manufacturers of the asbestos to which P and his co-workers were exposed; (2) that D knew at the time of manufacture that asbestos was defective and dangerous, but concealed this information from P and his co-workers; (3) that asbestos is in fact defective and dangerous; (4) that P's condition of mesothelioma (a universally fatal cancer which hundreds or thousands of the co-workers have also contracted) is frequently caused by asbestos exposure, and almost never caused by exposure to any other kind of substance; and (5) that in addition to compensatory damages, D's conduct is so outrageous that punitive damages ought to be awarded to P.

iii. **Difficulties:** Obviously, discovering and proving all these facts is a tremendously time-consuming business, not only for P and his lawyer, but for D, for other potential co-defendants (such as other manufacturers who may also have made asbestos to which P was exposed), and for the court system as a whole. If 5,000 workers each insist on conducting extensive discovery and then having a full-dress trial on their claim, the transaction costs will be enormous, and the court system may well be paralyzed (as has indeed happened in those federal judicial districts where many asbestos claimants live).

iv. **Common issues:** At the same time, many of the issues listed above for P's suit are probably *common* to many or all of the similarly-situated plaintiffs: whether asbestos is indeed defective and dangerous; whether D manufactured it; whether the workers at a particular place were exposed to it; whether D knew of the dangers at a particular moment; whether a particular disease such as mesothelioma is always caused by asbestos; whether D's conduct in concealing its knowledge and selling the product anyway was so outrageous as to justify punitive damages, etc. Clearly a way of litigating these issues *once* or a few times, rather than thousands of times, seems sensible both economically, and in terms of expediting compensation to those who have been injured in a way that deserves redress.

3. **Suitability of class actions, generally:** The federal class action, on its face, seems like a potentially good way of handling these problems. A class action could be certified for the purpose of disposing of the common questions of fact (e.g., defectiveness) while reserving for separate actions the individualized questions (e.g., causation and damages). But the federal courts have been slow to allow the class action procedure of Rule 23 to be used in this way.

   a. **Advisory Committee Notes:** Much of courts' initial reluctance to allow class actions in mass tort cases stems from the original Advisory Committee Notes, written in 1966, to the present version of the FRCP 23. These Notes state that "a 'mass accident' resulting in injuries to numerous persons is ordinarily *not appropriate* for a class action because of the likelihood that significant questions, not only of damages but liability, would be present, *affecting the individuals in different ways.* In these circumstances, an action conducted nominally as a class action would degenerate in practice into multiple law suits separately tried."

   b. **Single-accident cases:** In mass-tort cases involving a *single "mass disaster"* or a single *"course of conduct"* by one defendant, a number of courts have *allowed* class certification. Cases involving a single *explosion*, or involving *toxic exposure* on account of one course of conduct (e.g., dumping) by a single defendant, fall into this category.

   c. **Product liability suits:** But most of the argument has been about whether federal class actions are suitable for *product liability* cases. Here, most federal courts have held that the federal class action is *not* suitable. In fact, in most instances the courts have held that the class action device may *not* be used even for the *limited purpose* of deciding such core "all or nothing" issues as: Was D negligent? or Was D's product "dangerously defective"?

4. **The Supreme Court's *Amchem* asbestos-liability decision:** A 1997 Supreme Court decision illustrates how mass tort claims will often be unsuitable for class action status. In *Amchem Products, Inc. v. Windsor*, 117 S. Ct. 2231 (1997), the court held that a massive class action, in which the plaintiffs were all individuals who had pending or future claims that they had been injured by exposure to asbestos made by the defendants, should never have been certified.

   a. **Class:** The class in *Amchem* consisted of hundreds of thousands or even millions (no precise count was possible) of people who had been exposed to asbestos products made by any one of 20 defendants. The plaintiff class included not only those who already had symptoms of illness, but also those who were asymptomatic but might become sick in the future. This latter category included people who did not yet even know that they were in danger.

b. Certified for settlement only: The class was certified "for settlement only." (See *supra*, p. 376.) That is, lawyers for the plaintiff class and for the defendants got together and filed a complaint, an answer, a proposed class certification and a proposed settlement, all in the space of a single day. The trial court agreed to certify the class, and approved the settlement.

c. Certification struck down: But the Supreme Court held that the class should never have been certified. The two main reasons relied on by the court were:

    i. No predominance of common questions: First, Rule 23(b)(3)'s requirement that *common questions of law or fact predominate* over questions affecting only individual members, was not met. The trial court had relied upon two factors in finding commonality: (1) the fact that all class members had been exposed to asbestos; and (2) the fact that all class members had an interest in receiving prompt and fair compensation for their claims. But the Court found that these factors did not suffice (and, indeed, that the interest in getting fair and prompt compensation via a settlement was not even *relevant* on the issue of commonality.) Non-common factors predominated, the Court found: (1) claimants had been exposed to different products, for different amounts of time, in different ways, over different periods; (2) some claimants were already physically ill, while others had no symptoms at all or minor ones; and (3) each claimant had a different history of cigarette smoking, complicating causation analysis.

    ii. Inadequate representation: Second, there was a representation problem: the class did not meet Rule 23(a)(4)'s requirement that the named parties "will *fairly and adequately protect the interests* of the class." The class members had sharply varying incentives, yet each named party purported to act on behalf of the "single giant class" rather than on behalf of a discreet sub-class. For instance, the currently-injured plaintiffs wanted generous immediate payments, whereas the exposure-only plaintiffs most cared about a large, inflation-protected fund for the future; there was no structure to ensure that both groups were adequately represented.

    iii. Notice problem: The Court also observed that there was a big "notice" problem: there was no good way to give notice to every class member, including such subgroups as family members of asbestos-exposed workers, who might themselves become sick in the future from second-hand exposure, or who might have loss-of-consortium claims. The Court didn't rely on the notice problems, because it had already knocked the class out for the two reasons discussed above; but it signalled that notice would be a problem in future suits involving class members whose claims had not yet ripened.

5. Factors: All in all, it's very hard to get (and keep on appeal) federal class action status for a mass-tort suit, where the suit relates not to a single "accident" but to people who are exposed to a faulty product at different times and different circumstances. Here are some of the factors that courts consider in deciding whether to allow certification in such product-liability actions:

a. **State-by-state law variations:** In the typical diversity case in which there are class members from every or nearly every state, the fact that the federal court would some-how have to come to grips with the ***differing laws of 50 states*** weighs heavily ***against*** class status.

b. **Centrality of single issue:** Where one issue is truly ***"central"*** to the case, the court is ***most likely*** to allow class status. Thus in cases where every P was exposed at essen-tially the same time under the same circumstances, and the only issue apart from dam-ages is the nature of D's conduct, the chances for certification are highest. Single-explosion and single-dumping cases are examples. At the other end of the spectrum, where there are multiple Ds, and each sells different products to Ps at different times and under different circumstances (e.g., with differing warnings), the odds for class status are the lowest. This was the case, for instance, in *Amchem, supra*.

c. **Size of typical claim:** The ***larger each individual claim***, the ***less likely*** the court is to allow class status. More precisely, if each individual claim is big enough that it would be feasible, economically speaking, to ***bring it as a separate suit***, class status is not likely to be "superior" to other alternatives. So where each P has suffered serious physical injuries, this cuts against class status.

d. **Novelty of claim:** Where the plaintiff's claim is ***"novel,"*** certification is ***unlikely***, because the court won't want to let the future of a whole industry turn on whether one jury likes the claim. Instead, a series of actions heard by multiple juries and judges will probably be viewed as being the best way to get a "baseline" for whether there is liability, for how much a successful claim is worth, etc.

e. **Closing off of "future" plaintiffs:** Where the action binds class members who ***haven't yet suffered physical injuries***, certification is ***unlikely*** to be found to be fair to those class members. This is especially true where the same set of lawyers simultane-ously represents presently-ill (and fully identified) class members and unidentified "futures" plaintiffs, since there's a great risk that the presently-ill members and the lawyers will "sell out" the "futures" plaintiffs, who aren't really "on the scene" to speak for themselves. This was a key consideration in *Amchem, supra*.

f. **Limited fund:** Where there are so many thousands of claimants, and such valid and large claims, that there is reason to believe that the defendant(s) will be ***insolvent*** before the last claimant has recovered, certification is ***more likely***. That's because the court can make this a 23(b)(1) "mandatory" class action (in which, usually, ***no opt-out*** is allowed), on the theory that what's involved is a ***"limited fund."*** See *infra*, p. 383, for more about the "limited fund" rationale for mass-tort claims.

g. **Partial certification, limited to certain issues:** The odds for certification are better where what's proposed is a class-wide trial limited to ***certain issues***. See FRCP 23(c)(4), allowing this. For instance, in most product-liability suits where the trial court has certified a class, the court has done so only on the issue of ***liability*** (or the partial issue of whether the Ds were "negligent," or whether the product was "danger-ously defective"), while leaving such issues as damages, comparative negligence or proximate cause for second-phase suits by one plaintiff at a time. (See *infra*, p. 384, for more about partial certification). But even where the trial court takes this approach, the appeals court may well find that the certification was improper.

6. **A limited fund as a rationale for a mass-tort class action:** Recall that under Rule 23(b)(1)(B), a "mandatory" (i.e., non-opt-out) class action can be certified if individual actions would "substantially impair or impede [absent class members'] ability to protect their interests[.]" Where there is just a *limited fund* available to pay claims, and later claimants might receive their judgments only after the fund has been exhausted, courts have sometimes held that this requirement of impairment of the interests of absent members is satisfied, so that the case can be certified as a (b)(1) action.

    a. **Punitive damages:** Where early claimants seek *punitive* damages, the case for (b)(1)(B) certification is especially strong. The size of a punitive damage award bears no foreseeable relation to the size of a compensatory damage award, so that *just a few very successful early punitive-damage claimants can wipe out a small or mid-sized defendant.* (This is what happened, for instance, in the early litigation involving A.H. Robins Corp. and its Dalkon Shield IUD.) Also, the outrageousness of the defendant's conduct is usually a "common" factor (as opposed to the questions bearing on causality and compensatory damages), making the class action vehicle especially suitable.

    b. **The *Ortiz* case:** The Supreme Court has so far (as of mid-2014) decided only one major case involving a mass tort class action certified on a (b)(1) "limited fund" theory. That case, ***Ortiz v. Fibreboard Corp.**, 527 U.S. 814 (1999), suggests that it will generally be *difficult* to get judicial approval of (b)(1) limited-fund settlements.

        i.   **Facts:** The settlement in *Ortiz* would have settled all *not-yet-filed* (as of the time of settlement) asbestos claims against Fibreboard (D), in return for the setting up of a $1.5 billion trust fund, mostly from D's insurers. All claims that had already been filed against D prior to the settlement, including about 45,000 that had already settled and 53,000 that were pending, were *excluded* from the settlement (and would therefore *not be limited* by the settlement). And D was permitted to keep nearly all of its own net worth rather than contributing it to the fund.

            (1) **Existing claimants favored:** So the settlement advocated by the plaintiffs' lawyers in *Ortiz* was *much less favorable to future claimants* than to claimants whose claims had already been filed against and/or settled by D (claims which were therefore not covered by the settlement at issue).

        ii. **Conditions:** The Supreme Court rejected the proposed settlement in *Ortiz,* out of concern that it unfairly disfavored future not-yet-identified plaintiffs. The case indicates that for a mass tort case to be to be properly certified and settled under a (b)(1) limited-fund theory, the settlement will probably have to *satisfy three requirements*:

            (1) **Limited fund must be insufficient:** First, it will have to be apparent that the total of the aggregate claims is *clearly greater* than the limited fund.

            (2) **Whole fund must be used:** Second, the *whole of the fund* will have to be *devoted to the claims* (not set aside for other purposes, such as *preserving the value of stockholder equity* in the defendant corporation); and

(3) Equitable treatment among claimants: Finally, the claimants will have to be treated *"equitably among themselves,"* i.e., no sub-class (e.g., present claimants) can be *unfairly favored* over another sub-class (e.g., future claimants).

iii. Significance: *Ortiz* demonstrates that the use of a mandatory limited-fund (b)(1) settlement in mass tort cases will be just as difficult to get past a reviewing court as opt-out (b)(3) settlements have proved to be in cases like *Amchem*.

c.   **Opting out:**   Recall that the major difference between a b(1) and b(3) action is that in the latter, claimants must clearly be given the right to opt out, whereas in the former, no specific requirement in FRCP 23 requires an opt-out. However, there may well be *due process* problems with certifying an action as a b(1) action and disallowing absent claimants the right to opt out.

7.   **Amount in controversy:**   Nearly all mass tort actions are brought as diversity, rather than federal question, cases (since they are based upon state tort law). Such diversity-based class actions face can amount-in-controversy problems. But under *Exxon Mobil Corp. v. Allapattah Services, Inc.*, as long as *one member* of the plaintiff class of tort claimants has a claim worth *more than $75,000*, others with claims for *less than $75,000* may *join* as class plaintiffs. See *supra*, p. 370.

a.   **One big claim required:** But if there is *no single claimant* with a claim worth more than $75,000, the amount in controversy requirement will *block* the diversity-based tort class action. (The Class Action Fairness Act of 2005 creates an exception for certain cases with more than $5 million at stake, even where no single claim is worth $75,000. See *supra*, p. 370.)

8.   **Partial certification:**   In considering the use of a class action in a mass tort case, keep in mind the possibility of *partial* class certification, that is, certification as to a *single issue*. This is expressly allowed by Rule 23(c)(4). Thus certification will frequently be appropriate as to *liability*, or at least portions of liability (e.g., was the product "defective"?) even where it is not appropriate for damages. If the court grants a partial certification along these lines, then there will be a single trial on the certified issues. Each claimant would then have her own conventional trial or hearing on the non-class issues, such as damages (assuming that the class action was decided favorably to the class on the certified issues.)

9.   **Other techniques:**   In addition to the class action, courts have begun to use other special techniques for dealing with mass tort cases. Here are two important ones:

a.   **Consolidation for pretrial proceedings:**   Cases from across the nation may be *consolidated* into a single district, for *pretrial* purposes. Under this approach, authorized by 28 U.S.C. §1407, the Judicial Panel on Multidistrict Litigation (consisting of seven circuit and district judges from around the country) can order all related cases pending nationwide to be transferred to a single district for pretrial proceedings. The district judge who receives the cases coordinates *discovery* and, possibly, settlement discussions. The cases are then sent back to their original districts for trial.

b.   **Aggregation and sampling:**   In mass tort cases, there will be important issues that are *not* common to the entire group of victims. Most dramatically, *damages* will typically vary greatly from claimant to claimant. If a full-dress trial has to be had on the damages issue, then much of the benefits from class action certification will be lost. A few courts have dealt with this problem by the method of *"aggregation and sampling."* Under this procedure, for each type of injury or for each relatively narrow fact setting, a few *"representative"* claimants try their cases before a jury. The results of these "test cases" are then *averaged out*, and each of the claimants who did not have an individual trial gets the average verdict attributable to his group.

    i. **Due process:** Probably this technique of "sampling and aggregation" is permissible in terms of *due process* only if the plaintiff *voluntarily* agrees to participate.

Quiz Yourself on
CLASS ACTIONS

101. A cooperative located in the City of Langdell has 16 apartments, and thus 16 shareholders. The members of the co-op wish to bring a federal court securities action against the prior owner of the building; the suit would allege that the prior landlord created a false prospectus (concealing defects in the building's structure known to him), and then sold shares in the corporation holding title to the building, in violation of a federal securities law provision. Each of the 16 members has a claim worth in excess of $100,000. The co-op members would like to bring their suit as a class action. Are they likely to be able to do so?

———————————

102. P1 and P2 are individuals whose applications to live in a particular federally-subsidized housing project were rejected by D, the state agency that administers the project. P1 and P2 brought a federal action alleging that D's refusal to furnish them with a statement of reasons for their rejection constituted a deprivation of their right to due process, in violation of a federal civil rights statute. P1 and P2 now seek to certify as a plaintiff class all individuals whose applications for this project were rejected where the rejection was not accompanied by a statement of reasons. They seek a declaratory judgment that D violated the civil rights of each class member, and an injunction against further violations. (They don't seek damages.) The identities of the would-be class members can be compiled quite readily from the records of D; there are approximately 700 such individuals. Assuming that the trial judge believes that the lawyers for P1 and P2, and P1 and P2 themselves, can adequately represent the interests of the 700 absent members, should the judge permit the action to go forward as a class action? If so, under what subdivision of Rule 23(b)?

———————————

103. Same basic fact pattern as prior question. Assuming that the federal judge certifies the plaintiff class as requested by P1 and P2, must P1 and P2 pay for notice to all 700 absent class members?

———————————

104. D operates a chemical plant in the Town of Pound. Late one night, an explosion occurred in the plant, and a cloud of toxic gas was released. The cloud drifted for several miles before dispersing, and hundreds of people appeared to be injured by it in various ways. One year after the explosion, P1, a resident of Pound who claimed to have been seriously injured by his exposure to the toxic cloud, filed suit against D for violation of federal environmental protection statutes. P1, as sole named plaintiff, seeks certification of a class consisting of all individuals residing within five miles of the plant who were or may have been injured by the toxic substance released. The suit seeks compensatory damages on behalf of each class member. Should class certification be granted? If so, under what subdivision of Rule 23(b)?

———————————

105. P1 instituted a federal class action against D. D is a large investment banking firm, and P1's suit alleged that D broke federal securities laws when it sold stock on behalf of Z Corporation. D and Z are both Delaware corporations with their principal place of business in New York. The suit took place in New York federal district court. The court certified as a class all persons who purchased Z Corp. stock during a certain time period. One of these individuals was X, a California resident with no significant contacts with either Delaware or New York. X ignored the notice telling him he had the right to opt out. The class action was decided in favor of D. X then instituted his own individual suit against D in California federal district court. D now argues that X should be bound by the prior class action results. X points out in rebuttal that he, X, had no minimum contacts with New York, and argues that he should not be bound by the results in the New York class action suit given this lack of minimum contacts. Is X's contention correct?

_____

106. P1 and P2 have instituted a federal suit against D, a large bank that issues many credit cards. The suit contends that credit cards issued by D were misleadingly advertised, in violation of the law of New York (the state where the federal action is pending). P1's claim is for $80,000 and P2's claim is for $90,000. P1 and P2 are both citizens of New Jersey. D is a citizen of New York. No federal question is present. P1 and P2 seek certification of a class consisting of all those who ordered credit cards from D in reliance on the misleading advertising, regardless of the amount of damage suffered by that person. (All these others have damages of at most $20,000 each.) Assuming that the requirements of Federal Rule 23(a) and 23(b)(3) are satisfied, should the court grant certification of the proposed class? _____

107. Biff is the publisher of Biff's Notes, a series of study aids sold to college and high school students. Each year, Biff's acquires about one million new customers for its study aids, which cost an average of $3 each. P, a college student who is a customer of Biff's Notes, brought a federal antitrust suit against Biff, accusing him of price fixing, predatory tactics, and other Congressionally-forbidden tactics to maintain a dominant share of the study aid market. P has asked the court to certify a class consisting of all customers who have bought any study aids from Biff during the last four years. (Of the approximately four million Biff's customers during this period, the names and addresses of about 800,000 are identifiable by Biff's from its records, because they have sent in a card requesting free updates.) The court has certified this class under Rule 23(b)(3).

(a) Which, if any, of these customers must receive individualized notice of the pendency of the class action? _____

(b) Assuming that at least some customers must receive such notice, who must pay for it?

_____

(c) What if anything can the person who must pay for notice pursuant to (b) do to reduce the cost?

_____

108. Same facts as prior question. Assume that after the court has certified the action as a class action, P's lawyer and the lawyers for Biff work out a proposed settlement, by which a $1 discount coupon will be sent to each identifiable class member, and Biff's will reduce its prices by 10% for the next two years. What procedural steps, if any, must be taken? _____

_____

Answers

101. No. One of the requirements for a federal class action, according to Rule 23(a)(1), is that the class be "so *numerous* that joinder of all members is impracticable. ..." Sixteen is such a small number that it is hard to see why the individual co-op members cannot simply join together as co-plaintiffs under Rule 20(a).

Twenty-five seems to be about the smallest group that has been granted class action status.

102. Yes, under Rule 23(b)(2). First, a proposed class action must meet the four requirements of Rule 23(a): numerosity, common questions of law or fact, typicality of claims or defenses, and adequate representation. Seven hundred members seems sufficiently numerous. There are certainly questions of law or fact common to the class — for instance, each class member's claim presents the issue of whether due process is owed to a rejected housing applicant. The claims of P1 and P2 seem quite typical of the claims of other class members, since all are rejected applicants claiming a due process right. Finally, the facts tell us to assume that there is adequate representation.

Now that Rule 23(a) is satisfied, we must still find some subdivision of Rule 23(b) that is satisfied. The most likely candidate is (b)(2): "The party opposing the class has acted or refused to act on grounds that apply generally to the class, so that final injunctive relief or corresponding declaratory relief is appropriate respecting the class as a whole. ..." Here, the plaintiffs are seeking a declaratory judgment that due process is owed to a housing applicant, and an injunction against denying due process to future applicants. Since D is apparently treating all rejected applicants the same way (by not giving them a statement of reasons for the rejection, or other trappings of due process), the "generally applicable to the class" requirement seems satisfied.

103. No. In a (b)(1) or (b)(2) class action, notice is not required by Rule 23 (in contrast to (b)(3) actions). Instead, Rule 23(c)(2)(A) leaves it up to the discretion of the judge whether to order notice to some or all members of a (b)(2) class action. The reason for this is that if the suit is successful, it will result in an injunction or declaratory judgment applicable to *all* members of the class, whether notified or not, and class members will not be able to opt out, so that no good would probably come of class-wide notice. On these facts, it is unlikely that the judge will order notice given to each individual (though the judge might order publication notice, or notice sent to a small sample).

104. Unclear, but probably not. Even assuming that the four requirements of 23(a) can be satisfied, P's only chance of certification would be as a (b)(3) action. (A Rule 23(b)(1) action is out, because there is no risk of inconsistent or varying adjudications, or prejudice to the absentees — even if D was ordered to pay damages to P and not to some absentee, or vice versa, there would be no inconsistency or prejudice. Similarly, (b)(2) is out, because the suit does not seek declaratory or injunctive relief.)

For a (b)(3) action to be certified, the court must find that "questions of law or fact common to the class members predominate over any questions affecting only individual members." This requirement seems not to be met here: while there is a common question of liability, the more interesting and time-consuming questions will probably relate to causation (given that a particular class member was sick or injured, was this because of the toxic cloud?) and damages, issues which are not common. In general, mass-toxic-exposure cases do not meet the "common questions predominate" requirement. See, e.g., *Amchem Products, Inc. v. Windsor*, 117 S.Ct. 2231 (1997), finding that a mass-asbestos-exposure case did not meet this requirement. Similarly, it is unclear that the court should conclude that "a class action is superior to other available methods for fairly and efficiently adjudicating the controversy," as required by Rule 23(b)(3).

Lastly, in all class actions (not just (b)(3) actions), the court must find that the named parties "will fairly and adequately protect the interests of the class." Rule 23(a)(4). Again, it's questionable whether P1 — who claims to have been actually injured physically — can adequately represent all absent members (e.g., those that have suffered exposure but have not yet have suffered visible injury). Cf. *Amchem Products, supra* (lack of adequate representation found in mass-asbestos-exposure case).

104. No. In *Phillips Petroleum Co. v. Shutts*, 472 U.S. 797 (1985), the Supreme Court held that an "absent" member of the plaintiff class (i.e., one who does not participate in the suit, but who also does not opt out) will nonetheless be bound by the results of the case, even if the absent member does not have minimum contacts with the state where the class action is pending. Thus even though X had absolutely no contacts with New York, where the class action took place, he is bound by the results since he did not opt out.

106. Yes. The Supreme Court once held that *each member* of a federal class action founded on diversity of citizenship must *independently* meet the amount in controversy requirement (now $75,000). See *Zahn v. International Paper Co.*, 414 U.S. 291 (1973). That is, according to *Zahn* it was not enough that the named plaintiffs each meet the jurisdictional amount.

But the 1990 supplemental jurisdiction statute, 28 U.S.C. §1367, changed this analysis. According to *Exxon Mobil Corp. v. Allapattah Services, Inc.*, 125 S.Ct. 2611 (2005), as long as the named members of the class each have claims that satisfy the amount in controversy requirement, the supplemental jurisdiction statute is to be read so as to permit non-named persons with claims for less than that amount to be part of the plaintiff class. So the action will be certified even though the unnamed members don't independently have claims exceeding $75,000.

107. (a) All 800,000 identifiable members. Individual notice must be given (usually by mail) to any class member who can be "identified through reasonable effort." *Eisen v. Carlisle & Jacquelin*, 417 U.S. 156 (1974). Thus the 800,000 customers whose names and addresses are on file at Biff's offices must each be sent notice by mail. This is true even though the average Biff's Notes costs $3, and thus even though the cost of notice is large, if not prohibitive, compared with the possible recovery. Additionally, the court may order publication notice to reach the approximately 3,200,000 customers whose names are not on file.

(b) P must pay the entire cost. This is true even if the court concludes that P would probably prevail at trial, and even if the court concludes that the cost of notice is so great relative to P's possible recovery that imposing the cost of notice on P will effectively kill the action.

(c) P could define a sub-class, and give notice only to that class. For instance, P could restrict his suit only to those who bought during the most recent year, or only to those who bought more than a certain quantity of books, or to those who bought only certain titles. The advantage would be that P's costs of notice diminish. The disadvantage, of course, would be that any recovery would be reduced, and the fees awarded by the court to P's lawyer in the event of victory would be correspondingly reduced.

108. **Notice of the proposed settlement to absent class members, and judicial approval of the settlement.** Rule 23(e) provides that "The claims, issues, or defenses of a certified class may be *settled* ... only with the *court's approval*. The following procedures apply to a proposed settlement ... : (1) The court must direct *notice in a reasonable manner* to all class members who would be bound by the proposal." In the case of a large class, each member of which has very small claims, the court will probably not order notice by mail to anyone, but will instead probably permit publication notice. In deciding whether to approve the settlement, the court will consider principally whether it is fair to the absent class members (since there is a danger that P's lawyer and Biff will collude, by agreeing to pay P's lawyer a large amount and paying smaller damages to class members than would be appropriate based on the strength of P's case).

VI. INTERVENTION

A. **Intervention generally:** Rule 24 allows certain persons who are not initially part of a lawsuit to enter the suit **on their own initiative**. Such an entry is called "intervention," and the person who intervenes is called an "intervenor".

1. **Two forms:** Rule 24 recognizes two forms of intervention:

   a. **"intervention of right";** see Rule 24(a), and

   b. **"permissive intervention";** see Rule 24(b).

2. **Distinction:** Where the intervenor is permitted to intervene "of right," no leave of court is required for his entry into the case. Where the facts are such that only "permissive" intervention is possible, it is left to the court's discretion whether to allow intervention.

B. **Intervention as of right**

1. **Who may intervene as of right:** A stranger to an existing action has an automatic **right** of intervention, under Rule 24(a), if he meets all of the following criteria:

   a. **Interest in subject matter:** He must "claim an interest relating to the **property or transaction** that is the **subject** of the action;"

   b. **Impaired interest:** He must be "so situated that disposing of the action may as a **practical matter impair or impede the movant's ability to protect its interest";** and

   c. **Inadequate representation:** He must show that this interest is not **"adequately represent[ed]"** by existing parties.

2. **Statute:** If the outsider cannot meet the criteria of (1) above, he may nonetheless automatically intervene under Rule 24(a) if a federal **statute** gives him such a right.

   a. **Intervention by U.S.:** Of the federal statutes giving certain outsiders the right to intervene, the most common are those which allow the **U.S.** to intervene. Of this latter group of statutes, the most important is 28 U.S.C. §2403, which allows federal intervention of right in actions involving the **constitutionality of an act of Congress.**

3. **Practical impairment:** Rule 24(a)'s reference to the outsider's ability to protect his interest is not concerned with the danger that the non-party will be legally bound by a judgment entered in his absence; the principles of *res judicata* prevent this. As a **practical** matter, however, his interest may be compromised.

   Example: Company A has a subsidiary, Gas Company. A is sued by the government for antitrust violations, and as a settlement agrees to divest itself of Gas Company. Company X, which distributes natural gas, depends solely on Gas Company for its supply. It fears that its supply will be interrupted because of the divestiture, and seeks to intervene as of right in the antitrust suit, and prevent the settlement.

   Held (by the Supreme Court), X's interests are not adequately represented by the existing parties, since all of these parties want the settlement. Although X would not be bound in any legal sense by the settlement agreement, X's supply of gas would effectively be cut off by the divestiture. Therefore, X has a right to intervene without leave of court. *Cascade Natural Gas Corp. v. El Paso Natural Gas Co.*, 386 U.S. 129 (1967).

Note: The *Cascade* case has been given very limited effect in subsequent cases, which have tended to require a stronger showing of interest and inadequate representation before allowing intervention of right.

4. *Stare decisis* **effect:**   Rule 24(a) has occasionally even been stretched to the point of requiring the intervention of right of a party who is interested in the litigation only because it may set an *adverse precedent* whose *stare decisis* effect may later hamper him.

5. **Comparison to necessary joinder:**   The criteria which allow a person to intervene as of right are the same as those which require that he be *"joined if feasible"* under Rule 19(a)(1)(B)(i). As the Advisory Committee's Notes to Rule 24(a) put it, "where, upon motion of a party in an action, an absentee should be joined so that he may protect his interest which as a practical matter may be substantially impaired by the disposition of the action, he ought to have a right to intervene in the action on his own motion."

6. **Jurisdiction:**   Independent *subject matter* jurisdictional grounds are *required* for an intervention of right in a diversity case. In other words, such intervention does *not* fall within the court's *supplemental* jurisdiction. See *supra*, p. 149.

    Example: A, a citizen of New York, and B, a citizen of California, have closely related interests that they would like to assert in a diversity suit against D, a citizen of New York. If A and B join as plaintiffs from the outset, they will of course not have complete diversity as against D. Now, suppose that B sues D by himself, and A seeks to intervene as of right. Because there is no diversity as between A and D, A's intervention will not be allowed. See 28 U.S.C. §1367(b).

    a. **Tightening:**   This represents a tightening of the law, compared to federal practice prior to 1990. Before Congress codified supplemental jurisdiction in 28 U.S.C. §1367, the case law generally held that intervention of right fell within the court's ancillary jurisdiction; thus on pre-1990 law, A would have been able to intervene as of right in the above example.

C. **Permissive intervention:**   A person who has a "claim or defense" involving a *"common question of law or fact"* with a pending action may be allowed to intervene at the *discretion of the court*. See Rule 24(b). Such intervention, since it requires the court's permission, is called *"permissive intervention."*

1. **Discretion:**   Since the granting of permissive intervention is left to the trial court's discretion, the trial court's decision, whichever way it goes, is *unlikely to be reversed on appeal*. Since appeal of a refusal to allow permissive intervention is seldom fruitful, most appeals concerning intervention therefore relate to Rule 24(a) intervention of right.

2. **Jurisdiction:**   An outsider given permission to intervene in a diversity case under Rule 24(b) must meet federal *subject matter jurisdictional* requirements independently (as in the intervention-of-right situation). See 28 U.S.C. §1367(b).

Quiz Yourself on
INTERVENTION

109. P and X were passengers aboard an airplane owned and operated by D. The plane caught fire while landing, and P and X were both seriously injured. P filed a diversity suit against D in federal district court for the Southern District of Michigan, arguing that D flew the plane in a negligent manner. X now plans a separate suit against D. Before filing that suit, X has learned that P and he are both planning to use the same expert witness at trial, Edward, who will testify that D's pilot did not land the plane in accordance with the manufacturer's instructions. X's lawyer fears that if P tries his suit first, and does not properly prepare Edward for testimony, Edward will be seriously attacked in cross-examination, and will be a less useful witness in X's own later action against D. In this situation, what tactical step should X consider?

_____

110. Same facts as prior question. Assume that P is a citizen of Michigan, D is a citizen of Ohio, and X is a citizen of Ohio. Will the tactic you suggested in your answer to the prior question still work?

_____

111. Same facts as prior question. Now, however, assume that the federal district court rules that X is entitled to intervene as of right in the action. Does X's presence in the action satisfy the requirements of federal subject matter jurisdiction? _____

112. The United States government (represented by the Justice Department) has brought a federal court suit against the Ames Board of Education, charging that Ames is administering its public schools in a racially discriminatory manner. The essence of the complaint is that intra-district boundaries are being intentionally drawn on racial lines, and that predominantly-black schools within Ames are receiving fewer resources than predominantly-white schools. P is the parent of a black Ames public school student, who wishes to intervene as of right in the action, as a co-plaintiff. Should such intervention be granted?

_____

Answers

109. Seek the court's permission to intervene under Federal Rule 24(b). Since X's proposed claim and P's existing action have a "common question of law or fact," X can move the Michigan federal court for leave to intervene as a co-plaintiff in P's suit. Clearly there is one major question of law/fact that the two claims have in common: whether D flew the plane in a negligent manner. The fact that there is also at least one non-common question of fact (each plaintiff's damages) should be irrelevant. It will be up to the district court's discretion whether to allow the intervention. (The requirements for intervention of right under Rule 24(a) do not seem to be satisfied — X is not really "so situated that disposing of the [main] action may as a practical matter impair or impede [X's] ability to protect its interest …," since X ought to be able to find a different expert witness, or to improve Edward's testimony even if he gives poor testimony in P's action.)

111. No. The action is in diversity, which means that there must be complete diversity (no plaintiff from the same state as any defendant). If X's motion for permissive intervention is allowed, X will be treated as a plaintiff. Since he will then be a citizen of the same state (Ohio) as D, diversity will be ruined. Supplemental jurisdiction would not apply for permissive intervention — 28 U.S.C §1367(b) provides that intervenors under Rule 24 must meet jurisdictional requirements for diversity actions and cannot rely on the court's supplemental jurisdiction. The statute thus treats permissive intervenors in the same way as the judge-made "ancillary" doctrine did.

111. No. The supplemental jurisdiction statute makes no distinction between intervention as of right and permissive intervention. 28 U.S.C. §1367(b) clearly states that persons seeking to intervene under Rule 24 will not be allowed if their presence would destroy diversity (as it would here).

112. Yes, probably. For a person to be entitled to intervention as of right, Rule 24(a) requires that the applicant claim "an interest relating to the property or transaction that is the subject of the action, and [be] so situated that the disposing of the action may as a practical matter impair or impede the [applicant's] ability to protect its interest, unless existing parties adequately represent that interest." P certainly has an interest relating to the same transaction as the main action: the procedure by which Ames draws district boundaries and administers its schools. There is also a danger to P that his ability to bring a successful action in the future might be compromised by a poor result in the U.S.'s action — if the Justice Department does a lackluster job and loses the case (e.g., the court finds that there was no racially discriminatory intent on Ames' part), a subsequent court is unlikely to permit the issue of intentional discrimination to be completely relitigated (even though the rules of collateral estoppel do not formally bind P, since P was an absentee to the U.S.-Ames original action).

The toughest question is whether "existing parties adequately represent [the applicant's] interest" — either the U.S. or Ames can make a plausible argument that the Justice Department is adequate to represent P's interests. But P can argue in turn that the U.S. government may be pursuing other interests (e.g., a desire to settle such suits in return for partial relief, rather than litigating them to the fullest extent to get complete compliance with the law), and that P's interests are therefore not completely congruent with the U.S.'s.

On balance, the court will probably rule that P is entitled to intervene as of right (and will almost certainly at least allow P to intervene permissively). See *Smuck v. Hobson*, 408 F.2d 175 (D.C. Cir. 1969), allowing parents to intervene as of right in a similar litigation.

VII. INTERPLEADER

A. **Definition:** Interpleader is a technique whereby a party who owes something to one of two or more other persons, but isn't sure which, may force them to argue out their claims among themselves before coming to sue him. It is designed to ***prevent the party from being made to pay the same claim twice.***

> **Example:** X and Y both claim a bank account at Bank. Y alleges that it was assigned to him by X; X denies the assignment, claiming that a document Y offers as evidence was a forgery. Y demands the money from Bank.
>
> If there were no interpleader, Bank could not avoid the possibility of having to pay both X and Y:
>
> (1) If Bank chose to pay Y, X could come in with his own demand, sue, and prove his allegation of forgery. Bank has to pay X, and practical factors may prevent it from getting the amount back from Y.
>
> (2) Bank could refuse to pay Y in the first place, let Y sue, and then raise the issue of forgery. But if Y wins, and Bank pays, this result is in no way binding on X, who

may still sue Bank, allege the forgery and, free of any estoppel, win. Bank not only has paid twice; it is worse off than in (1), since it is now legally impossible for it to get back the money from Y, who is armed with a judgment which is binding on Bank, though not on X.

Interpleader allows Bank to avoid this dilemma, by forcing X and Y to litigate between themselves as to the ownership of the account. Bank need pay only the winner.

1. **Federal and state:** Interpleader is allowed in both the federal courts and most state courts, in situations where it is necessary to prevent double liability.

2. **Federal practice:** In federal practice, two sorts of interpleader are allowed:

   a. *"statutory interpleader"* pursuant to 28 U.S.C. §1335, and

   b. *"rule interpleader"* permitted by Federal Rule of Civil Procedure 22. Both of these forms are discussed below. The chief differences between them concern personal and subject matter jurisdiction.

B. **Need for jurisdiction over both claimants:** Interpleader only works well if the court has *jurisdiction* over both (or all) claimants. If one or more claimants are absent from the proceedings, then the whole purpose of an interpleader — to relieve the stakeholder of the possibility of having to pay the same claim twice — is likely to be thwarted, since the absentee will not be bound and can bring her own suit later. An early Supreme Court case, *New York Life Insurance Co. v. Dunlevy*, 241 U.S. 518 (1916), illustrates how this may happen.

   1. **Facts:** The facts of *Dunlevy* were as follows:

      a. Gould, and his daughter Ms. Dunlevy, were at the outset both residents of Pennsylvania. Gould held a life insurance policy, the surrender value of which was $2,479. Ms. Dunlevy claimed that her father had assigned the policy to her.

      b. Boggs and Buhl held a valid personal judgment against Ms. Dunlevy. They sued in Pennsylvania state court to garnish the policy, which Ms. Dunlevy claimed to own. Gould, however, denied the assignment, and claimed the money owed under the policy for himself. Meanwhile, Ms. Dunlevy had moved to California.

      c. New York Life, the insurer on the policy, wanted the Pennsylvania court to establish which of the parties, Gould, Ms. Dunlevy or Boggs and Buhl (through their claim against Dunlevy), had the valid claim on the policy. The insurer therefore moved for interpleader. The Pennsylvania court was not able to obtain *in personam* jurisdiction over Ms. Dunlevy in California, due to the fact that Pennsylvania, like most states at the time, had no long-arm statute. Therefore, although Ms. Dunlevy was notified of the suit, she failed to respond or to submit herself to the Pennsylvania court's jurisdiction. All other parties appeared.

   2. **Holding in Pennsylvania action:** The Pennsylvania court held that the assignment was not valid. N.Y. Life was ordered to pay the $2,479 to Gould.

   3. **Removal of California claim:** Afterwards, Ms. Dunlevy sued N.Y. Life in California state court for the $2,479. The insurance company removed to federal court, and claimed

that Ms. Dunlevy was estopped by the Pennsylvania interpleader proceeding from claiming that the policy was hers.

4. **Supreme Court affirms:** The U.S. Supreme Court ultimately agreed with Ms. Dunlevy: the Pennsylvania interpleader proceeding ***did not bind*** Ms. Dunlevy.

    a. **Rationale:** The Supreme Court reasoned that the interpleader proceeding was an *in personam*, not a *quasi in rem*, proceeding. Therefore, the proceeding was invalid without personal jurisdiction over Ms. Dunlevy.

    b. **Double obligation:** Ms. Dunlevy was therefore not bound by the interpleader finding that her father, not she, owned the policy. She could thus sue the insurance company for the amount of the policy. As a result, the insurer ended up ***paying the policy amount twice.***

C. **Federal statutory interpleader:** In part because of the result in *Dunlevy, supra* — where the insurer ended up having to pay twice on the policy because of jurisdictional issues — Congress has enacted a ***federal interpleader statute*** that allows for nationwide service of process on multiple claimants to a stake. That statute, today codified as 28 U.S.C. §1335, allows a person holding property which is claimed or may be claimed by two or more adverse claimants to ***interplead those claimants in federal court.***

1. **Jurisdictional problems:** If not for problems of personal and subject matter jurisdiction, there would be no need for the federal interpleader statute: a stakeholder could in most cases avoid double liability without interpleader, simply by ***joining*** (under Rule 20) all potential claimants as defendants to a federal-court declaratory judgment suit concerning title to the property. Three major jurisdictional difficulties may prevent such joinder:

    a. **Personal jurisdiction:** The claimants may be so dispersed geographically that no federal district court (all of which follow local long-arms in diversity actions) could obtain ***personal jurisdiction*** over them.

    b. **Diversity:** *Diversity* might be impossible, as would be the case if one claimant was a citizen of the same state as the stakeholder.

    c. **Amount in controversy:** The ***amount in controversy*** requirement may not be satisfied. The claim in an ordinary diversity case must be in excess of $75,000.

2. **Solution:** 28 U.S.C. §1335's main utility is that it simplifies these jurisdictional problems in the following ways:

    a. **Nationwide service:** *Nationwide service of process* in a §1335 interpleader action is permitted by 28 U.S.C. §2361. That is, a court in which the stakeholder has filed a §1335 suit may serve its process on any claimant, no matter where in the U.S. that claimant resides or is found.

    Note: The nationwide service of process provision would have meant that if the original suit in *Dunlevy* had been brought in (or removed to) federal court, Ms. Dunlevy would have been served, and therefore bound by judgment, no matter where in the U.S. she resided.

b. **Diversity:** Diversity is satisfied as long as *some two claimants are citizens of different states*. See 28 U.S.C. §1335(a)(1). This is sometimes called a requirement of *"minimal diversity."*

> **Example:** Two New York residents and a Californian all claim the proceeds of a particular insurance policy. Since either New Yorker and the Californian form a diverse pair, the diversity requirement for statutory interpleader ("minimal diversity") is satisfied. The citizenship of the insurance company is irrelevant.

c. **Amount in controversy:** The property which is the subject of the suit must merely exceed *$500* in value, not $75,000 as is required for ordinary diversity actions. See 28 U.S.C. §1335(a).

d. **Venue:** The requirements of *venue* are also simplified in §1335 interpleader actions. 28 U.S.C. §1397 allows suit to be brought "in the judicial district in which *one or more of the claimants reside."*

3. **How commenced:** A §1335 suit is commenced by the *stakeholder*, who is referred to as the "plaintiff" in 28 U.S.C. §1335. The stakeholder must, to begin the suit, *deposit into court* the amount of the property in question, or post a bond for that amount.

4. **Right to deny debt:** Even though the stakeholder must deposit the amount of the property with the court, he is not estopped from claiming at trial that he does *not owe the money to any claimant at all*. Wr., 536-37.

5. **Other suits restrained:** To further the goal of protecting the stakeholder from double liability, 28 U.S.C. §2361 allows a court hearing a §1335 action to *enjoin (prohibit) all claimants* from *starting or continuing any other action*, in any state or federal court, which would affect the property.

> **Example:** Insurance Co. is sued in state court by the son of a recently deceased policy-holder; the son asserts that he is entitled to the policy's proceeds. The widow of the policy-holder also files a claim, in federal court. Insurance Co. may bring an interpleader action in the federal court of the district in which either the son or the widow resides, as long as the two are citizens of different states. The federal judge will then enjoin both the son's suit and the widow's suit, and will decide the matter himself.

a. **Must concern property:** The trial court's power to enjoin other lawsuits applies *only* to suits concerning the *property held by the stakeholder* and deposited with the court. This is illustrated by *State Farm Fire and Casualty Co. v. Tashire*, 386 U.S. 523 (1967). In that case, a collision between a truck and a Greyhound bus in California resulted in two deaths and thirty-six injuries, of persons from five states and one foreign country. Suits were filed in California against Greyhound, the truck owner, and the two drivers.

i. **Interpleader sought:** State Farm, the truck-driver's insurer, filed for interpleader in federal court in Oregon (residence of both drivers), claiming it had a limited $20,000 fund available under the driver's policy and wanted all claims against the driver or the fund to be worked out in one proceeding. Alternatively, it claimed that the policy did not cover this particular accident at all.

ii. **Injunction:**   An order was issued, restraining all other suits against the truck-driver or against State Farm. Proper service on all claimants was made as specified in 28 U.S.C. §2361.

iii. **Broadening of injunction:**   Greyhound then successfully sought a broadening of the order to prevent the prosecution in any other court of *any suits against it arising from the accident.*

iv. **Supreme Court limits injunction:**   The U.S. Supreme Court found that the interpleader was proper, but that the restraining order could *only* bar suits against the *$20,000 fund*, and could not bar suits against the insured, or against Greyhound and its driver.

(1) **Effect on insurer:**   The insurer could therefore make sure that its $20,000 fund could not be reached in any other action outside the interpleader, but it could not stop all suits against the insured himself.

(2) **Rationale:**   The Court emphasized that interpleader was not a "bill of peace," and could *not be used to bring together all potential litigation arising from an occurrence*. "The circumstance that one of the prospective defendants happens to have an insurance policy is a fortuitous event which should not of itself shape the nature of the ensuing litigation. For example, a resident of California, injured in California aboard a bus owned by a California corporation, should not be forced to sue that corporation anywhere but in California simply because another prospective defendant carried an insurance policy."

D. **Federal Rule interpleader:**   *Federal Rule 22* provides an interpleader remedy much the same as that of 28 U.S.C. §1335. By the Rule, whenever a person may be exposed to "double or multiple liability," he may demand interpleader. A person may do this by coming into court on his own initiative, as plaintiff, or by counterclaiming or cross-claiming as defendant in an action already commenced against him.

1. **Distinguished from statutory interpleader:**   The chief difference between interpleader under the statute and interpleader under Rule 22 is that *Rule 22 interpleader has no effect on ordinary jurisdictional and venue requirements.*

a. **Complete diversity:**   Diversity must be complete between the stakeholder on one hand and all the claimants on the other (or else there must be a federal question, but this is rare). Wr., 534-35.

b. **Service of process:**   Service of process must be carried out as in any other civil diversity action — that is, within the state where the district court sits, or pursuant to the long-arm of the state. *Supra*, p. 72.

c. **Amount in controversy:**   The $75,000 amount in controversy requirement must be met.

2. **No deposit:**   The stakeholder is *not required*, as he is in statutory interpleader, to *deposit* the property or money into the court.

3. **Denial of liability:**   Rule 22 specifically allows the stakeholder to "aver that he is not liable in whole or in part to any or all of the claimants."

Table 8-3
Comparison: Statutory and Rule Interpleader

	Statutory	**Rule 22**
When there is no federal question, what kind of diversity must exist?	Some pair of claimants must be diverse with each other.	The stakeholder must not have the same citizenship as any claimant.
Where may service of process be made?	Anywhere in the U.S.	Ordinary rules for federal civil suits must be followed.
How much money must be in controversy?	More than $500	More than $75,000 (unless a federal question is present).
Must the stakeholder deposit the amount in dispute in court?	Yes	No
May the stakeholder claim that he is not liable to any of the claimants?	Yes	Yes

Quiz Yourself on
INTERPLEADER

113. A car driven by Xavier hit and injured two pedestrians, Al and Betty. The only insurance policy on Xavier's car was issued by Insurer, and has a $30,000 policy limit. Al is a citizen of the Southern District of New York; Betty is a citizen of the Western District of Oklahoma; Insurer is a citizen of the Western District of New York. Insurer is worried that it will have to defend Xavier in two distinct actions (one brought by Al and the other brought by Betty), and that defense costs plus judgments may total more than $30,000. Also, Insurer is worried that Al, Betty or both may sue in states allowing a direct action against the defendant's insurer. Insurer wants to be sure that it doesn't have to pay out more than $30,000 as the result of this accident. No suit has been commenced yet by either Al or Betty. Tactically, what should Insurer do? _____

114. Same fact pattern as prior question. Can Insurer bring an action pursuant to federal Rule 22 on these facts? _____

115. H and W, a married couple, jointly applied for a homeowner's insurance policy from Insurer. They then got entangled in a nasty divorce proceeding. While this proceeding was pending (and when the status of the marital home was still in doubt), a tornado destroyed the home. H now asserts that he is entitled to the entire proceeds by virtue of a prenuptial agreement signed between H and W; W asserts that she is entitled to the sole proceeds because she is the sole occupant of the house at the moment. W is a citizen of Indiana, where the home is located; H has now moved to Ohio, of which he is currently a citizen. Insurer is a citizen of Kentucky. Insurer's assets are heavily invested in junk bonds, which are relatively illiquid at the moment. Therefore, Insurer would like to delay as long as possible having to pay out the claim or even depositing the $500,000 policy proceeds in court during an interpleader proceeding. Assuming that none of the three states involved (Ohio, Kentucky and Indiana) has helpful interpleader laws, what tactical step should Insurer take? _____

Answers

113. Bring a federal statutory interpleader proceeding, under 28 U.S.C. §1335. That section allows a person holding property claimed by two or more adverse claimants to interplead those claimants. Thus Insurer can commence a federal proceeding "against" both Al and Betty, and say in effect to the court, "Here's the $30,000; you decide how this should be split among Al and Betty. Return any excess to us." Even though this is a suit brought, in essence, in diversity, the amount in controversy requirement is only $500 (not $75,000). Also, the requirement of complete diversity is cancelled, and all that is required is that some two claimants be citizens of different states (satisfied here since Al is a citizen of New York and Betty is a citizen of Oklahoma).

114. No. Federal Rule 22 does allow an interpleader action to be brought by a stakeholder (whether the stakeholder acts as plaintiff, or is already a defendant in an existing proceeding brought by one or more claimants). But Rule 22 interpleader, unlike statutory interpleader, does not give any relief from the normal requirements of personal jurisdiction, subject matter jurisdiction, and venue. In a Rule 22 interpleader action, there must be complete diversity between the stakeholder on the one hand and all of the claimants on the other hand. Since Insurer and Al are both citizens of New York, the required complete diversity is not present. Also, a Rule 22 interpleader action must satisfy the ordinary $75,000 amount in controversy requirement for diversity actions, which the controversy here does not. (What counts for a Rule 22 action is the size of the stake, not the aggregated sizes of the various claims against the fund.)

115. Use Federal Rule 22 interpleader. The most promising place for Insurer to start such a proceeding is in federal court for the district of Indiana where the home is located; H, as a former resident of Indiana and one who still asserts a property interest in Indiana real estate, certainly has minimum contacts with Indiana and is therefore subject to personal jurisdiction (assuming that the Indiana long arm allows him to be served, which is quite likely). Although Rule 22 suits require complete diversity (in the sense that the stakeholder not be a citizen of the same state as any of the claimants), this requirement is satisfied here, since neither H nor W is a citizen of Insurer's home state of Kentucky. The amount-in-controversy requirement is satisfied, since more than $75,000 is at stake. The district where the home is located suffices for venue also, since that is the district where a "substantial part of property that is the subject of the action is situated." 28 U.S.C. §1391(a)(2).

The big advantage for Insurer of Rule 22 interpleader versus statutory interpleader is that under Rule 22 interpleader, Insurer does not have to deposit the "stake" (the $500,000 policy proceeds) with the court at the outset of the proceeding, or post a bond in that amount, as it would for statutory interpleader. Therefore, Insurer gets the use of the money while the suit is pending.

VIII. REAL PARTY IN INTEREST

    A. Assignment: A plaintiff or potential plaintiff may *assign* his claim or "chose in action" to some other party. This assignee may then maintain the suit. At common law, the assignee had to sue in the name of the original claimant; in equity, he could sue in his own name.

    B. Suit in assignee's name: Modern codes, and Federal Rule 17, require that a complaint be in the name of the *"real party in interest."* This means that the *assignee must sue in his own name*, since it is he who will benefit from the judgment.

1. **Subrogation:** The same rule covers *subrogation*. Suppose an insurer has already compensated its insured, who is a tort victim. The insurer is said to be *subrogated* to the rights of the insured, and may sue the tortfeasor just as the insured himself could. Subrogee insurers have been held to be "real parties in interest" under Rule 17, and must therefore *sue in their own name*, not in the name of the insured. Wr., 491-92. (One reason why a subrogee might prefer, if allowed, to sue in the name of the subrogor, is that juries are likely to be more sympathetic to a plaintiff who has actually been injured than to the large insurance company which stands behind him and which is in the very business of sustaining such losses.)

2. **Diversity:** The citizenship of the real party in interest (the assignee or subrogee) controls for diversity purposes.

3. **Rationale:** The reason for requiring the real party in interest to be named relates to the *res judicata* effects of the judgment.

> **Example:** Insurance Company pays off claimant, the victim of a tort allegedly committed by Tortfeasor. Insurance Company is, by the usual common-law rules of subrogation, entitled to sue Tortfeasor just as Claimant could have. If Insurance Company is permitted to sue in the name of Claimant, and loses, it might try to sue again in its own name. Since *res judicata* is often determined, at least preliminarily, from the pleadings, Tortfeasor might have difficulty showing that Insurance Company had already had its day in court, and lost. Therefore, Rule 17(a) requires Insurance Company to sue in its own name. See Advisory Committee's Notes to Rule 17(a).

C. **Representative:** Executors, administrators, bailees, and other types of persons listed in Rule 17(a), are considered as being themselves "real parties in interest," and do not need to bring suit in the name of the person they represent. Wr., 490.

1. **Citizenship of representative controls:** But the citizenship of the represented party (e.g., the estate) generally controls for diversity purposes. *Supra*, p. 124.

IX. THIRD-PARTY PRACTICE (IMPLEADER)

A. **Third-party defendant:** A defendant alleging that a third person is *liable to him* "for all or part of [the plaintiff's] claim against [the defendant]" may "*implead*" such a person as a *"third-party defendant."* Rule 14(a).

> **Example:** An employer who is sued on the theory of vicarious liability wishes to recover from his allegedly negligent employee on an indemnity theory. Rather than wait for a judgment against himself, and then bring a separate action against the employee (and risk losing the second suit as well as the first, since the employee is not bound by collateral estoppel), the employer may choose to bring the employee into the original action. The employer is called a "third-party plaintiff," and the employee is a "third-party defendant."

B. **Claim must be derivative:** For a third-party claim to be valid, the third-party plaintiff may not claim that the third-party defendant is the *only* one liable to the plaintiff, and that he himself is not liable at all. The third-party plaintiff's theory must be one that has the third-party plaintiff's own liability as a ***prerequisite*** for throwing liability on the third-party defendant. Thus, the chief purpose of impleader is to assert claims for ***indemnity, subrogation, contribution***, and ***breach of warranty***. Wr., 548-49.

1. **Alternative pleading:**   However, the third-party plaintiff is not precluded from claiming in an ***alternative*** pleading that neither he nor the third-party defendant is liable.

2. **Partial claim:**   Also, the third-party plaintiff does not have to claim that the third-party defendant is liable for all of the recovery against the third-party plaintiff. He may instead allege that only a ***portion*** of the recovery is due from the third-party defendant.

    > **Example:** Contractors Co. is a partnership composed of two handymen, A and B. The two get drunk one day, and while they are working on repairs at the house of a customer, they cause damage to the property. The customer sues A alone, alleging that he is jointly and severally liable for torts committed by the partnership. A can implead B as a Rule 14(a) third-party defendant, in order to obtain ***contribution*** from him. A will not recover from B the full amount of the tort liability under a contribution theory, as would be the case if B had agreed to indemnify A. Instead, B will pay over to A one-half of the customer's recovery, so that A and B will end up splitting the cost.

C. **When leave of court not needed:**   If an original defendant serves a third-party summons and complaint upon the third-party defendant within ***14 days*** of the time the original defendant served his answer to the plaintiff's claim, no leave of court is necessary for the impleader. Rule 14(a), second sentence.

    1. **Leave necessary:**   After this 14-day period, however, the court's ***permission*** to implead is necessary.

        a. **Grounds for granting leave:** Where the court's permission is needed, courts usually conduct a rough ***balancing test*** in deciding whether to grant it. On the one hand, courts consider the benefits from impleader, mostly the ***judicial efficiency*** that comes from resolving related matters in a single suit. On the other hand, they consider the detriments, most importantly the ***prejudice to the original plaintiff*** in having the waters muddied by the introduction of new parties and issues into the suit. One court listed these factors as among the ones that should be considered:

            ❏ whether ***judicial economy*** would be served by impleader;

            ❏ whether the party seeking leave to implead "deliberately ***delayed*** or was ***derelict in filing*** the [impleader] motion";

            ❏ whether impleading "would ***unduly delay or complicate the trial***";

            ❏ whether impleading "would ***prejudice the third-party defendant.***"

        Too, Inc. v. Kohl's Department Stores, Inc., 213 F.R.D. 138 (S.D.N.Y. 2003).

D. **Impleader by plaintiff:**   Just as a defendant may implead a third-party defendant, so a ***plaintiff*** against whom a ***counterclaim*** is filed may implead a third person who is liable to him for the counterclaim. See Rule 14(b).

E. **Jurisdictional requirements relaxed:**   Both personal and subject matter jurisdictional requirements are relaxed with respect to the third-party claim.

1. **100-mile bulge:** Rule 4(k)(1)(B) allows service of third-party complaints anywhere within the ***100-mile bulge*** surrounding the courthouse, even if the place of service is outside the state, and is beyond the scope of the local long-arm. See *supra*, p. 70.

> **Example:** P sues D in the Southern District of New York, the courthouse for which is located in Manhattan. D wishes to implead X, who lives in Newark, N.J. Since Newark is within 100 miles of the courthouse, X may be served there, even if the New York state long-arm would not reach him.

2. **Supplemental jurisdiction:** A third-party claim generally falls within the court's ***supplemental jurisdiction***. That is, there don't have to be independent jurisdictional grounds for Rule 14 ***impleader*** of ***third-party defendants,*** at least where the claim is by or against a third-party plaintiff, or by a third-party defendant. (But supplemental jurisdiction does ***not*** cover claims by the original plaintiff against a third-party defendant.) See *supra*, p. 149.

> **Example:** P sues D in diversity. D impleads X, a resident of the same state as D, as a third-party defendant. D's third-party claim against X is for less than $75,000. As long as jurisdictional requirements between P and D are met (diversity and amount in controversy) it does not matter that D and X are from the same state, and that the jurisdictional amount is not met by D's third-party claim.

3. **Venue:** Similarly, if ***venue*** is proper between the original parties, it remains valid no matter what the residence of the third-party defendant. However, if this would result in very great inconvenience to a third-party defendant, the court may refuse to allow the impleader at all. Wr., 554.

F. Claims involving third-party defendant: The presence of a third-party defendant may give rise to a welter of different types of claims.

1. **Claim by third-party defendant:** Once a third-party defendant has been impleaded, he may make certain claims of his own. Rule 14(a)(2) allows him to make the following kinds of claims:

   a. *counterclaims* against the third-party plaintiff, which are either permissive or compulsory depending on whether they arise out of the same transaction or occurrence as the third-party plaintiff's claim against the third-party defendant;

   b. *cross claims* (discussed below) against any other third-party defendants;

   c. any claim against the ***original plaintiff*** "arising out of the transaction or occurrence that is the subject matter of the plaintiff's claim against the third-party plaintiff;"

   d. any *counterclaim* against the ***original*** plaintiff, if the original plaintiff has made a claim against the third-party defendant (which can occur in circumstances discussed below);

   e. *impleader claims* against persons not previously part of the suit, if these persons may be liable to the third-party defendant for all or part of the third-party plaintiff's claim against him.

2. **Supplemental jurisdiction:** *All of the above kinds of claims*, except *permissive counterclaims, fall within the court's supplemental jurisdiction*, and thus need no independent federal subject matter jurisdictional grounds.

3. **Defenses:** A third-party defendant may also raise against the original plaintiff the same *defenses* that the original defendant could have raised. See Rule 14(a). "This protects the third-party defendant if the original defendant fails or neglects to assert a proper defense to the plaintiff's claim on which the third party may be liable over." Wr., 552.

   a. **Defenses against third-party plaintiff:** Also, the third-party defendant may of course raise defenses against the third-party plaintiff. He may, for instance, show that no duty of indemnification exists.

4. **Claims by original plaintiff:** The *original plaintiff* may "assert against the third-party defendant any claim arising out of the transaction or occurrence that is the subject matter of the plaintiff's claim against the third-party plaintiff." Rule 14(a)(3).

   a. **Jurisdiction:** A claim by a plaintiff against a third-party defendant does not fall within the court's supplemental jurisdiction, and thus must *independently satisfy jurisdictional requirements*. The court will not allow the possibility of *collusion* between plaintiff and defendant, whereby a plaintiff who could not sue the third-party defendant directly could sue him indirectly by having the defendant implead him. This means that there must be diversity between the plaintiff and the third-party defendant, or a federal question between them, and also that the jurisdictional amount must be met by plaintiff's claim against the third-party defendant. See 28 U.S.C. §1367(b), discussed *supra*, p. 146; see also *Owen Equipment Co. v. Kroger, supra*, p. 145.

      i. **Venue:** Such a claim by plaintiff against third-party defendant is not required to meet the *venue* provisions that would be applicable if the claim were an original, separate, action. Wr., 554-55.

   Note: Observe that "supplementality" is not symmetrical. Although a claim by the original plaintiff against the third-party defendant is not supplemental, a claim by the third-party defendant against the original plaintiff is, since there is no reason to fear collusion between the third-party defendant and the original defendant.

5. **Joinder of claims:** The original defendant may *join* to his third-party claim *any other claims* he has against the third-party defendant. Such joinder falls within Rule 18(a) which, as discussed above, allows a party to join "as many claims as it has against an opposing party."

6. **Illustration:** The many different claims which may arise when a third-party defendant is brought into a suit are illustrated by the following example.

   Example: Servant, on business for Master and driving Master's car, has an accident with a car owned and driven by P. Both drivers are injured, both cars are damaged, and one or both of the drivers was negligent. Master is sued by P. Some of the possible claims are as follows:

(1) P may allege against Master that Master is vicariously liable for Servant's negligence, that P himself was not negligent, and that P therefore has a right to recover for both personal injury and property damage.

(2) Master must allege against P, as a compulsory counterclaim, that P was negligent, that Servant was not (Servant's non-negligence is an integral part of Master's counterclaim, assuming a jurisdiction where contributory negligence is a complete bar, and where it is imputed to the master), and that he, Master, may therefore recover for the damage to his own car.

(3) Master may then implead Servant as a third-party defendant, alleging that if Servant's negligence (and P's non-negligence) results in a judgment against Master, Servant is liable for an indemnity.

(4) Master may join with this an allegation that Servant has been negligent and is therefore liable for the damage to Master's car; he may maintain this claim regardless of the outcome of P's original action, as it has nothing to do with possible negligence by P. On the other hand, under the prevailing tort rule, if Servant is found negligent, Master cannot recover against P on his counterclaim.

(5) Once Servant is in the picture as a third-party defendant, P may choose to file his own complaint for negligence against him.

(6) In that case, Servant must file as a compulsory counterclaim his own claim for injuries against P.

(7) P may then allege contributory negligence as a defense to Servant's counterclaim.

7. **Dismissal of main claim:** If the main claim is ***dismissed*** before or during trial, the court still has the authority to hear the third-party claims based on it, if these are applicable, and if they are within the court's supplemental jurisdiction. Whether to exercise this authority is generally left to the trial court's discretion. See 28 U.S.C. §1367(c)(3).

> **Example:** A third-party claim for indemnity would be meaningless if the original claim for which indemnity is sought is dismissed. If the third-party plaintiff added to his indemnity claim a damage claim against the original plaintiff, however, this claim could be tried after dismissal of the main claim, since it is within the court's supplemental jurisdiction. The court might, however, decide as a matter of discretion (as 28 U.S.C. §1367(c)(3) allows it to do) that a new action meeting all the requirements of jurisdiction would be preferable.

Quiz Yourself on

THIRD-PARTY PRACTICE (IMPLEADER)

116. A commercial aircraft owned and operated by Airline, Inc. crashed into the tip of a peak in the Himalayas while en route from San Francisco to Nepal. Investigation of the "black box" and other instruments found in the wreckage indicated that the pilot believed that he was flying at 20,000 feet above sea level when he was in fact flying at only 9,000 above (less than the height of the mountain). The estate of P, one of the passengers killed in the accident, has sued Airline and Doeing (the plane's manufacturer) in a single federal court diversity action. The suit alleges that Airline was negligent in not discovering the altimeter problem, and that Doeing breached the implied warranty of merchantability by delivering a plane containing an altimeter that would fail.

Doeing's lawyer realizes that if the altimeter was defective, Doeing will be liable even if it behaved without negligence. The lawyer also realizes that if Doeing has breached the implied warranty of merchantability with respect to the altimeter, that warranty has also been breached by Altimeters R Us, the manufacturer of the altimeter (which is not a defendant thus far). What tactical step should Doeing take to ensure that Doeing does not get unfairly saddled with liability for an act (manufacture and delivery of a defective altimeter) that is really the fault of Altimeters R Us? _____

117. Paula, a citizen of Ohio, wished to have a house constructed for her on land she owned in Ohio. She contracted with Dave, a builder who is a citizen of Kentucky; the contract stated that Dave would build a house according to Paula's specifications on Paula's land, for a total construction price of $200,000. Because the capital and risk associated with this project were too much for Dave to deal with alone, he entered into a side-contract with Ted, a financier, whereby Ted agreed to put up half the capital needed for the project, in return for half the profits from the job. This side-contract also provided that the two would share equally in any losses or liabilities that might result from the project. Ted did not contract directly with Paula in any way. Dave is a citizen of Kentucky, and lives in the town of Covington. Ted is a citizen of Ohio, and lives in Cincinnati (about 50 miles from Covington).

Dave constructed the house; Paula paid for it, and moved in. Paula then discovered certain latent defects, which rendered the house substantially less valuable. Paula has brought a suit against Dave in federal court for the Eastern District of Kentucky (where Covington is located); the suit is based in diversity, and seeks $80,000 damages for breach of contract. Paula has not joined Ted in the suit. Dave would now like to bring Ted into the suit somehow, so that if Dave is required to pay up to $80,000 damages, Ted, in the same action, will be required to pay half of this amount over to Dave (so that they will end up having to pay equal shares of any damage award). Although Ted has minimum contacts with Kentucky, the Kentucky long-arm statute is a very limited one which would not allow service on Ted in an action by Paula or Dave concerning either the Paula-Dave or the Dave-Ted contract.

(a) What can Dave do to bring Ted into this action? _____

(b) Describe any procedural intricacies associated with your answer to (a). _____

(c) What special FRCP provision will help you solve a problem relating to jurisdiction? _____

118. Same basic fact pattern as the prior question. Assume that Ted now wishes to file a claim against Paula, alleging that Paula libeled him by writing a letter to the local newspaper, which stated, "Ted secretly and crookedly induced Dave to save them both a few bucks by building my house in a sloppy and dangerous way." Ted's claim is for $100,000. Will the court hear Ted's claim against Paula? _____

119. Same basic fact pattern as the prior two questions. Now, assume that after Paula has sued Dave, Dave has impleaded Ted, and Ted has made a claim against Paula for libel, Paula wishes to make a claim against Ted for deceit — she alleges that Ted conspired with Dave to induce her to pay for an improperly-constructed house. The claim does not involve a federal question, and is for $100,000. Will the court hear Paula's claim against Ted? _____

Answers

116. **Doeing should implead Altimeters pursuant to Federal Rule 14(a).** A defendant may, as a third-party plaintiff, cause a summons and complaint to be served "on a nonparty who is or may be liable to it for all

or part of the claim against it." Rule 14(a)(1). By impleading Altimeters, Doeing is stating that if it is liable for breach of warranty, Altimeters must be derivatively liable to it. (This is a correct statement of warranty law.)

117. (a) Dave can implead Ted pursuant to Federal Rule 14(a). Since Ted will be liable over to Dave for half of anything that Dave is required to pay Paula, Ted's liability is derivative. Therefore, it is appropriate for Dave to bring a third-party action against Ted, even though Paula has not made any claims against Ted directly.

(b) Dave has to solve three problems: (1) diversity; (2) amount in controversy; and (3) personal jurisdiction. As to (1), a claim by a third-party plaintiff against a third-party defendant will come within the court's *supplemental* (formerly ancillary) jurisdiction, provided that it and the main claim concern a "common nucleus of operative fact." The supplemental jurisdiction statute, 28 U.S.C. §1367, does not specifically exclude claims by third-party plaintiffs under Rule 14, as it excludes some claims made by plaintiffs. Thus the fact that Paula and Ted are both citizens of Ohio, and are in a very general sense opposing parties (theoretically nullifying the complete diversity usually required) doesn't matter — so long as Paula and Dave, the original parties, are diverse, the citizenship of the third-party defendant is ignored. As to (2), similarly, the fact that Dave's third-party claim against Ted gets supplemental treatment means that amount in controversy is ignored as to the third-party claim. Therefore, the fact that Dave's claim against Ted is for only $40,000 (half of the up-to-$80,000 claim by Paula) is irrelevant — since Paula's claim against Dave, the original claim, is for more than $75,000, that's all that matters. As to (3), see the answer to (c).

(c) FRCP 4(k)(1)(B)'s "100-mile-bulge" provision. Under ordinary principles, Dave would not be able to get personal jurisdiction over Ted, because he would not be able to make service on him — the federal court sitting in diversity only allows service on out-of-staters to the extent that the long arm of the state in which the federal court sits would so allow. Here, since Kentucky would not allow service over Ted, the federal court would not normally be permitted to allow such service either (even though Ted has minimum contacts with Kentucky). But the special "100-mile-bulge" provision of Federal Rule 4(k)(1)(B) comes to Dave's rescue: according to that Rule, anyone who is brought in as a third-party defendant pursuant to Rule 14 may be served in a place that is "not more than 100 miles from where the summons was issued[.]" Since Cincinnati is within 100 miles of Covington (where the action is pending), Ted may be served at his residence.

118. Yes. Rule 14(a)(2)(D) provides that the third-party defendant "may also assert against the plaintiff any claim arising out of the transaction or occurrence that is the subject matter of the plaintiff's claim against the third-party plaintiff." Since Paula's claim against Dave and Ted's claim against Paula both relate to construction of Paula's house, Ted's claim against Paula will presumably be found to meet this "same transaction or occurrence" test. The bigger potential problem is that Ted and Paula are both citizens of Ohio, and all claims are based solely on diversity. There would thus not seem to be the complete diversity required. However, a claim by a third-party defendant against the original plaintiff falls within the court's supplemental jurisdiction, under 28 U.S.C. §1367, since the claim is closely related to the original claim. Since §1367(b) does not exclude claims by third-party defendants against original plaintiffs, the lack of diversity doesn't matter.

119. No. A claim by the original plaintiff against the third-party defendant does *not* fall within the court's supplemental jurisdiction. The supplemental jurisdiction statute, in 28 U.S.C. §1367(b), specifically bars claims made by the original plaintiff against "persons made parties under Rule 14, 19, 20, or 24." This provision codifies the result of *Owen Equipment Co. v. Kroger*, 437 U.S. 365 (1978). Paula's claim against Ted would have to be brought under Rule 14(b). Therefore, that claim must independently meet the requirements of federal subject matter jurisdiction. Since Paula and Ted are both citizens of Ohio, the requisite diversity is not present, so the claim cannot be heard. (Similarly, Paula's claim against Ted must independently meet the amount in controversy requirement of $75,000, which it does.)

X. CROSS-CLAIMS

A. Definition of cross-claim: Rule 13(g) allows a party to make, in certain situations, a claim against a *co-party*, such as a co-defendant or co-plaintiff. Such a claim against a co-party is called, in federal practice, a *cross-claim*. It is to be distinguished from a counterclaim, which is a claim made against an opposing party. A cross-claim is made only against a party who is on the same side of an already-existing claim as is the cross-claimant.

B. Requirements: There are two principal requirements which a claim must meet before it may be asserted as a cross-claim.

1. **Transaction or occurrence:** First, it must have arisen out of *"the transaction or occurrence* that is the subject matter of the original action or of a counterclaim therein," or else relate to property that is the subject matter of the original action. See Rule 13(g).

   Example: Cabdriver is in an accident with a car driven by Driver and owned by Owner. Cabdriver sues both Driver and Owner, alleging that each is liable for the accident. Owner may bring a cross-claim against Driver for the damage to his car, since Owner and Driver are co-defendants to Cabdriver's initial claim, and since Owner's claim arises from the same occurrence, the accident, as Cabdriver's.

   a. **Compared to compulsory counterclaim:** Observe that the test for allowing a cross-claim is basically the same as that for determining whether a counterclaim is compulsory. But a cross-claim, no matter how closely related to the subject of the existing action, is *never compulsory*. Wr., 575.

2. **Actual relief:** Second, the cross-claim must ask for *actual relief* from the co-party against whom it is directed. Thus, where one defendant claims that he is *blameless* and that the other defendant is liable, no cross-claim can be made. (This is simply a complete defense.)

C. Jurisdiction: Cross-claims are within the *supplemental jurisdiction* of the court, and therefore need no independent jurisdictional grounds. Nor can a cross-claim affect venue. Wr., 577.

Quiz Yourself on
CROSS-CLAIMS

120. Deborah and Dell, each driving a separate car, decided to drag-race one day. While doing so, one or both of them (this is not clear) collided with a car driven by Pete, injuring him. Pete has brought a federal diversity action against both Deborah and Dell, alleging that each, because of negligence, is jointly and severally responsible for his injuries. Pete is a citizen of Michigan; Deborah and Dell are both citizens of Wisconsin. Deborah would like to be able to make a claim against Dell for damage to her car, suffered in

the same accident. However, Deborah does not want to make the claim in the current action, because she thinks that the federal judge assigned to this case is hostile to women drag-racers. If Deborah does not assert her claim against Dell in the present action, will she be able to bring a separate suit against Dell in Wisconsin state court after Pete's case is completed? _____

121. Same facts as prior question. Suppose that Deborah does bring a claim against Dell as part of Pete's original action. Assume that Deborah's claim is for $30,000. Will the federal court take jurisdiction over Deborah's claim against Dell? _____

122. Same basic fact pattern as the prior two questions. Now, assume that Deborah does not want to make any claim against Dell for injuries arising from the accident. Instead, Deborah wishes to assert against Dell a claim for breach of contract. This claim asserts that Dell agreed to sell Deborah his house, and refused to do so when Deborah tendered the purchase price. The claim is for $85,000. Putting aside any problems relating to lack of diversity, may Deborah assert this claim against Dell as part of the action brought by Pete? _____

Answers

120. Yes. If Deborah were to make a claim against Dell as part of Pete's existing action, Deborah's claim would be a *cross-claim* under Rule 13(g). However, Deborah is *not required* to make this cross-claim against Dell — cross-claims under the Federal Rules are always optional, never compulsory (in contrast to counterclaims, which are compulsory if they arise out of the same transaction or occurrence as the original claim). Thus Deborah will not be barred from bringing a separate state-court action against Dell later on (though the doctrine of collateral estoppel will probably prevent her from relitigating issues that were actually litigated by her in the original action).

121. Yes. As discussed in the prior answer, Deborah's claim against Dell would be a cross-claim, asserted pursuant to Rule 13(g). Cross-claims fall within the court's supplemental jurisdiction, under 28 U.S.C. §1367, since they are by definition closely related to the original action and since they are not excluded by subsection (b). Therefore, the ordinary requirements of federal subject matter jurisdiction are ignored. It does not matter that Deborah and Dell are both citizens of the same state, or that Deborah's claim is for less than the $75,000 amount in controversy ordinarily required for diversity suits.

122. No. Since Deborah and Dell are co-defendants, Deborah's claim against Dell must be a cross-claim, asserted pursuant to Rule 13(g). However, Rule 13(g) allows a cross-claim only if it "arises out of the transaction or occurrence that is the subject matter of the original action or of a counterclaim, or if the claim relates to any property that is the subject matter of the original action." Since the Deborah-Dell contract has nothing whatsoever to do with the drag-racing, it does not satisfy this requirement of relatedness, so it cannot be asserted by Deborah even if Dell is willing to have it heard in the basic action.

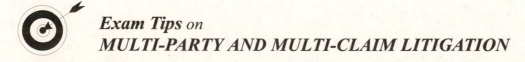

Exam Tips *on*
MULTI-PARTY AND MULTI-CLAIM LITIGATION

This area is a welter of individual procedural devices, and is usually tested from a federal perspective. The one overarching principle is that you must always worry about subject matter jurisdiction and personal jurisdiction; remember that the need for the former will often be eliminated by supplemental jurisdiction. Here are some particular things to watch for:

☛ If the facts involve a *counterclaim* ("cc"), be sure to distinguish between permissive cc's and compulsory ones. Remember that a compulsory cc is one that arises out of the *same "transaction or occurrence"* that is the subject matter of the opposing party's claim. Rule 13(a). [337-341]

     ☞   The need to distinguish between the two types of cc arises most often because you have to decide whether a claim that could have been asserted as a cc in an earlier action is now barred. Remember that a litigant *loses* an unasserted compulsory cc but not an unasserted permissive cc.

     ☞   A sometimes-tested issue is whether, in the second suit, a federal court sitting in diversity must *follow the counterclaim rules of the state* where the district court sits, especially whether the federal court must decline to hear a claim that state law would regard as compulsory (and thus refuse to hear because not asserted in an earlier action), even though the cc would be permissive under the FRCP. Because of the heavy outcome-determinativeness of the issue, the answer is probably that the federal court must follow the state rule.

     ☞   Remember that a *compulsory* cc falls within *supplemental jurisdiction* ("SJ"). Therefore, it does not need to independently involve $75,000. Furthermore, SJ means that D can bring in additional parties to the compulsory cc with whom D is not diverse. (But there probably is *not* SJ for *permissive* cc's, so these must meet the amount-in-controversy and complete-diversity requirements.)

☛ *Joinder of claims* raises few testable issues. Just remember that once P has a valid claim against a particular D, he can add as many additional claims as he wishes against that D. These do not have to independently meet the amount in controversy requirement (since "aggregation" of all claims by one P against one D is allowed). [343-344]

☛ For *joinder of parties,* here are the most testable issues [345-351]:

     ☞   For both plaintiff-joinder and defendant-joinder, you'll need to know the two requirements imposed by FRCP 20: (1) the claims must arise from a *single "transaction, occurrence,* or series of transactions or occurrences"; and (2) there must be a question of law or fact *common* to all Ps or all Ds. You'll usually want to discuss exactly how these two tests are or are not satisfied by your fact pattern. The tests are both pretty easy to satisfy, so normally you should find that joinder is proper (assuming there are no jurisdiction problems).

     ☞   Remember that the requirements of *subject matter* and *personal jurisdiction* must be met as to *each D.* So check that:

        ☞ each D was properly served;

        ☞ each D has minimum contacts with the forum state; and

        ☞ no D is a citizen of the same state as any P (if it's a diversity case)

           ☞ However, supplemental jurisdiction is available in a multi-plaintiff diversity scenario for purposes of the ***amount in controversy*** requirement. So if one P has more than $75,000 at stake, other Ps whose claims are each for less than $75,000 may "piggyback." (Cite to *Exxon Mobil v. Allapattah* on this point.)

☞ Compulsory joinder is often tested. Distinguish between "necessary" parties and "indispensable" ones. [348]

  ☞ A party who is ***"necessary"*** (the "weaker" case for joinder) must be joined if jurisdictionally possible, but the action may go on without him if there are jurisdiction problems.

  ☞ A party who is ***"indispensable"*** (the stronger case for joinder) not only must be joined if jurisdictionally possible, but the action must be dismissed if she cannot be joined.

  ☞ Consult the text of FRCP 19 (and the capsule summary) for analysis of the standards for these two classifications. For a finding of indispensability, the key factors are the degree of ***prejudice to the absentee*** from proceeding without him, and the ***adequacy of P's remedies*** (e.g., state court ones) if the federal action is dismissed.

  ☞ Where there's a "necessary" or "indispensable" party (as with any other type of multi-defendant joinder), supplemental jurisdiction does ***not*** apply, so ordinary requirements of subject matter jurisdiction apply.

☛ Here's what to look for if your fact pattern involves a ***class action.*** [355-395]:

☞ Sometimes the whole idea of a class action will be hidden. Anytime you see multiple (at least 15) people with similar "injuries," you should consider whether they might bring a plaintiff class action.

☞ The ***amount in controversy*** for a diversity class action is one of the most frequently-tested issues in all of Civil Procedure. [138-140]

  ☞ If at least one named class member has a claim exceeding $75,000, but other class members (named or unnamed) don't, ***supplemental jurisdiction*** will apply to take care of amount in controversy for these less-than-$75,000 claimants. (Cite to *Exxon Mobil v. Allapattah*.)

  ☞ A sub-issue is often what kind of a showing each P must make to satisfy the $75,000 requirement. Remember that as long as it's not a "legal certainty" that some P can't meet the requirement, the requirement will be deemed met. This essentially means that if each P has suffered some sort of ***physical injuries***, the amount requirement will usually be deemed satisfied. Another sub-issue is whether the possibility of ***punitive*** damages may be considered — the answer is unclear, but probably little weight should be given to this possibility.

☞ ***"Numerosity"*** and ***"fair representation"*** are frequently-tested elements. If there are more than 25 claimants, "numerosity" is probably satisfied, and if less than 15, it's probably not. To decide "fair representation," look to how much the named Ps have in common with the unnamed Ps. [356-362]

☞ The majority of the time, if there is to be a class action, it will be a *b(3)* action, not a b(1) or b(2) action. In the garden-variety situation of multiple claimants seeking money damages from a solvent defendant, the action will proceed under b(3) or not at all.

    ☞ For a b(3) action, make sure that (1) *common issues* of law or fact *predominate*; and (2) the class action is *superior* to other methods (e.g., individual actions). Thus if there are important issues on which each P varies (e.g., each claimant has a unique set of physical injuries), the class action is probably not superior. [366-371]

    ☞ You'll often have a *mass tort* fact pattern (e.g., an airplane crash or a toxic gas leak/explosion). Here, know that courts often *refuse* to allow b(3) class actions (and to require individual actions instead) because of causation issues and the variety of damages suffered. Cite to *Amchem* on this point. (If D might go broke from thousands of claims, consider the possibility of a b(1) action to preserve a limited fund.)

☞ Remember that absent class members must always be given *notice* (individual, where possible), and that this notice must be paid for by the named plaintiffs. Cite to *Eisen v. Carlisle* on this point. [367]

☞ Class actions questions often require you to say who is *bound* by the judgment. In the usual b(3) action, each class member must be given a chance to *opt out*; if she does so, she's not bound by an adverse judgment or settlement (and can bring her own suit), but conversely, she doesn't get any benefit (including collateral estoppel) from any favorable judgment. *One who doesn't opt out (even if she never got notice) is bound by the judgment.* [368]

    ☞ There's no right to opt out in b(1) or b(2) actions.

☞ Before a c.a. can go to trial, it must be "certified" as a c.a. by the court — i.e., the court declares that the requirements for a c.a. have been satisfied.

    ☞ If on particular facts you conclude that the entire proposed class does not satisfy the requirements (e.g., the named Ps' claims aren't typical, or the named Ps can't fairly represent everyone), consider the possibility that the court could certify a *sub-class* (just one group of Ps), which could go forward.

☞ Remember that any proposed *settlement* must be approved by the court, and, if the action has been certified, *notice* of the proposed settlement must be given to absent class members, at least for b(3) actions. (In b(1) and b(2) actions, the court has discretion about whether to require notice.) [375]

☛ For *intervention*, here are the key points [389-390]:

☞ Sometimes the intervention issue is hidden. Look for a fact pattern in which persons who are not parties might be affected by the outcome, and you're asked how they can protect their interests. For instance, questions sometimes involve a non-party who might someday face a similar lawsuit, and would like to help prevent an adverse precedent that wouldn't be binding on him by collateral estoppel but that would pose *stare decisis* problems. (In this situation, say that permissive intervention is justified but intervention of right is not.)

☞ Always distinguish between *permissive* intervention (FRCP 24(b)) and intervention of *right* (24(a)). Of-right requires much tighter ties to the subject matter of the litigation, among other things. [389]

> ☞ The main consequence of the distinction is that a trial court's denial of permissive intervention is almost never reversed on appeal, but a denial of intervention of right will often be reversed.

☞ Remember that the usual requirements of *subject matter jurisdiction* apply to both types of intervention, i.e., there's no supplemental jurisdiction. Be alert to diversity situations where the would-be intervenor is a citizen of the same state as an opposing party — intervention can't occur no matter how heavily implicated the intervenor's interests are. (Also, in this situation, consider whether the would-be intervenor is an "indispensable" party in whose absence the action must be dismissed.)

☛ Here's what to watch for concerning *interpleader*. [392-396]:

> ☞ Interpleader issues are often hidden. Look for someone in possession of a *"stake,"* where the stakeholder doesn't know *which of two people is entitled* to that stake. Examples: banks that hold bank accounts, insurance companies that hold policy proceeds, contest sponsors that hold prizes, estates that hold assets. Typically, it will be up to you to notice that the stakeholder faces the possibility of double/inconsistent adjudications, and up to you to say that the stakeholder should interplead the competing claimants.

> ☞ If you decide that the stakeholder should use interpleader, always specify whether he should use statutory interpleader or FRCP Rule 22 interpleader. Here are the main differences:

>> ☞ Statutory interpleader (s.i.) affects personal jurisdiction and subject matter jurisdiction; Rule interpleader (r.i.) does not. So nationwide service of process in allowed for s.i. (but not for r.i.). Similarly, diversity is satisfied for s.i. as long as some two claimants are citizens of different states (whereas for r.i. the stakeholder may not be a citizen of the same state as any claimant). And the amount in controversy has to be merely $500 for s.i. (compared with the usual $75,000 for r.i.)

>> ☞ On the other hand, the stakeholder has to deposit the property in court (or post a bond) to use s.i., but does not for r.i.

☛ *Impleader* (third-party practice) issues are very common. [399-403] Here's what to look for:

> ☞ Impleader issues are sometimes hidden. Look for any situation in which an existing party may want to say, in effect, "If I'm liable to so-and-so, then you're liable to me in whole or in part for anything I have to pay to so-and-so." In general, you're looking for claims of *"indemnity"* (whole reimbursement) and *"contribution"* (partial reimbursement). This means that you should think "impleader" in these types of situations (D is the original defendant, and X is a person not yet a party, who D should consider impleading):

>> ☞ D is accused of a tort, and X is D's *insurer*. (X has agreed by contract to indemnify

D.)

☞ P is a tort victim, D made the *product* that injured P, and X made a *component* of that product (e.g., D made the aircraft that crashed and X made the possibly-defective engine).

☞ P is a tort victim injured by a product, D sold it to P, and X is *"upstream" in the chain of sale.* P sues only D, on an implied warranty theory. (*Example:* P sues D, the retailer, and D impleads X, the manufacturer or wholesaler.)

☞ P is a tort victim, D and X were *separately-acting tortfeasors* who have potentially joint-and-several liability and P has chosen to sue only D, not X. (D has a common-law right of contribution from X in this situation.) Example: P is a patient injured while in D, a hospital, and while under the care of X, a doctor not employed by the hospital. P sues only D.

☞ The third-party plaintiff, or TPP (P in the above examples) may *not* claim that the third-party defendant, or TPD (X above) is the *only one* liable to P. The TPD's liability must be "derivative" of the TPP's liability. (On the other hand, TPP doesn't have to prove at the outset that TPD definitely or even probably has derivative liability; it's enough that TPD "may be" liable to TPP is TPP is liable to P.) [399]

☞ When impleader claims are part of the fact pattern, be hyper-alert to *personal and subject matter jurisdiction* issues, which are very frequently present. You'll typically see a TPP and TPD who are both citizens of the same state, for instance. Remember that both types of jurisdictional requirements are relaxed in impleader cases:

   ☞ Most important, impleader claims come within the court's *supplemental jurisdiction*. This means that TPP and TPD *don't have to be diverse* to each other (and TPD doesn't have to be diverse to P), and TPP's claim against TPD doesn't have to be worth $75,000. (The third-party claim can be a *partial* claim, such as a claim for contribution, so this amount-in-controversy relaxation can be important.)[401]

   ☞ Also, *personal jurisdiction* can be relaxed because service of the third-party complaint can occur anywhere within a *100-mile bulge* of the federal courthouse, even if TPD has no contacts with the state where the federal court sits. (Therefore, be on the lookout for service on TPD that takes place in a city close to the courthouse but in another state; the facts will often state the distance between courthouse and point of service, which should tip you to the presence of a "bulge" issue.) [401]

   ☞ You don't have to worry about *venue* for the third-party complaint.

☞ Remember that once a party has been impleaded, there can be additional claims involving the TPD (e.g., TPD against P, P against TPD, TPD against TPP, etc.). Generally, *supplemental jurisdiction will apply* to these, *except* for: (1) P's claim vs. TPD; and (2) TPD's permissive counterclaims against TPP or against P.

☞ Where two people are *already* parties, and are on the *same side* (both Ps or both Ds), one may make a *cross-claim* against the other. [406] Things to remember:

☞ The cross-claim must arise out of the *same "transaction or occurrence"* as the original action;

☞   A cross-claim is ***never compulsory*** (i.e., it's not lost if not asserted in the present action);

☞   Cross-claims come within ***supplemental*** jurisdiction (so D1 doesn't need to be diverse with D2 to cross-claim against him).

CHAPTER 9

FORMER ADJUDICATION

ChapterScope

This Chapter examines the rules that prevent re-litigation of claims and issues that have already been contested (or, in some situations, could have been contested) in an earlier lawsuit. The most important concepts in this Chapter are:

▪ **"Res judicata":** There is a set of rules that prevents re-litigation of claims and issues; the set is sometimes collectively called the doctrine of *"res judicata."* There are two main categories of rules governing re-litigation: the rules of "claim preclusion" and the rules of "collateral estoppel."

▪ **Claim preclusion:** The rules of *"claim preclusion"* prevent a *claim* (or "cause of action") from being re-litigated. They break down into two sub-rules:

❏ **Merger:** Under the rule of *"merger,"* if P *wins* the first action, his claim is "merged" into his judgment. He cannot later sue the same D on the same cause of action for higher damages.

❏ **Bar:** Under the doctrine of *"bar,"* if P *loses* his first action, his claim is extinguished, and he is barred from suing again on that cause of action.

▪ **Collateral estoppel:** The rules of *"collateral estoppel"* prevent re-litigation of a particular *issue of fact or law*. When a particular issue of fact or law has been determined in one proceeding, then in a subsequent proceeding between the same parties, *even on a different cause of action*, each party is *"collaterally estopped"* from claiming that that issue should have been decided differently than it was in the first action. A synonym for "collateral estoppel" is *"issue preclusion."*

❏ **Issues covered:** For an issue to be subject to collateral estoppel, three requirements concerning that issue must be satisfied: (1) the issue must be the *same* as one that was *fully and fairly litigated* in the first action; (2) it must have been actually *decided* by the first court; and (3) the first court's decision on this issue must have been *necessary* to the outcome in the first suit.

❏ **Persons who can be estopped:** Generally, only the *actual parties* to the first action can be *bound* by the finding on an issue.

❏ **Persons who can benefit from estoppel:** But even one who was *not a party* to the first action (a *"stranger* to the first action") may in some circumstances *benefit* from estoppel. That is, the stranger to the first action may assert in the second suit that her adversary, who *was* a party to the first action, is collaterally estopped from re-litigating an issue of fact or law decided in that first action. (Courts are *more willing* to allow the *"defensive"* use of collateral estoppel by a stranger than they are to allow the *"offensive"* use. "Offensive" use refers to use by a stranger who is a *plaintiff* in the second action; "defensive" use refers to use by a stranger who is a *defendant* in the second action.)

■ **Full Faith and Credit:** Where the first and second suits are in different jurisdictions, the second jurisdiction must generally **enforce** the first jurisdiction's judgment (including that judgment's *res judicata* effect), under the doctrine of *"Full Faith and Credit."*

I.　GENERAL PRINCIPLES

A. Scope: All courts agree on the principle that where two parties have fully litigated a particular *claim*, and a final judgment has resulted, that claim may not later be *relitigated* by the loser. All courts are similarly in agreement that if a particular finding of *fact* has been made in the course of a lawsuit between two parties, that issue of fact may not later be retried by the loser, even though the cause of action is different in the second suit. The entire set of rules that prevent re-litigation of claims and issues is often collectively referred to as the doctrine of *"res judicata"* (Latin for "things which have been decided").

1. **Merger and bar:** The rules that prevent a *claim* (or as it is sometimes called, a *cause of action*) from being relitigated are called the rules of *claim preclusion*. Two separate but closely related rules, the rule of *"merger"* and the rule of *"bar,"* make up the doctrine of claim preclusion.

   a. **Merger:** If plaintiff wins the first action, his claim is *"merged"* into his judgment. He cannot later sue the same defendant on the same cause of action for higher damages.

   b. **Bar:** If the plaintiff in the first action loses, his claim is extinguished, and he is *"barred"* from suing again on that cause of action.

   Note: The term *"res judicata"* is sometimes used to refer solely to the rules of claim preclusion. But we use that term in this chapter in its more general sense, to encompass both the rules of claim preclusion and the rules (summarized immediately below) of collateral estoppel.

2. **Collateral estoppel:** If a particular *issue of fact or law* has been determined in one proceeding, then in a subsequent proceeding between the same parties (even on a different cause of action), each party is *"collaterally estopped"* from claiming that that issue should be decided differently than it was in the first action. Thus the doctrine is usually called *collateral estoppel.*

   a. **"Issue preclusion":** The doctrine generally referred to as collateral estoppel is sometimes also called *"issue preclusion,"* to reflect the fact that what is being prevented from relitigation is an issue. The phrase "issue preclusion" has the advantage of contrasting sharply with its opposite, "claim preclusion." Partly for this reason, the Second Restatement of Judgments favors the terms "claim preclusion" and "issue preclusion." See Rest. 2d, Introduction to Chapter 1. Notwithstanding the growing use of the term "issue preclusion," we use the more traditional "collateral estoppel" here.

   b. **Mutuality:** Most courts, until the 1960s, applied the doctrine of collateral estoppel only where the parties in the second action had *both* been present in the first action. A stranger to the first action could not in the second action assert that his adversary (who had been a party in the first action) was collaterally estopped from relitigating an issue decided in the first action — the reason for this was that the stranger could not have been *bound* by a finding of fact in the first action unfavorable to him (the requirements of due process prevent binding a party without giving him a day in court). Therefore, courts reasoned, it was unfair to give the stranger the *benefit* of the first action, where he could not have been saddled with the *burden* of that action. The rule that a stranger to the first action could not assert collateral estoppel against one who had been a party to that first action is known as the doctrine of *mutuality.*

    i.   **Demise of mutuality:** Most courts have discarded the general doctrine of mutuality. Many courts, however, still prevent a stranger to the first action from asserting, in certain situations, collateral estoppel against a party to the first action.

B. **Strangers to the first action:** The rules of claim preclusion and collateral estoppel generally apply to bind only persons who were *parties* to the original action, *not* to *"strangers"* to that action.

    1. **Exceptions:** But there are a few situations in which someone who was not a party to the first action is so closely linked to someone who was, that the stranger will be bound by the first result, for claim preclusion and collateral estoppel purposes, as if she had been a party. For instance, a *successor in interest* to property (e.g., the purchaser of real estate which has been the subject of an earlier quiet-title action), would be bound by the result in the earlier action.

C. **Full Faith and Credit:** The Constitutional requirement of Full Faith and Credit compels the courts of each state to give to a judgment of a sister state the same effect that that judgment would have in the state which rendered it. This requires each state to apply the same rules of merger, bar, and collateral estoppel as the state which rendered the earlier judgment would apply. A statute, 28 U.S.C. §1738, compels the federal courts to give Full Faith and Credit to the judgments of state courts.

D. **Applicable only to new actions:** The rules discussed in this chapter apply only to *new actions* subsequent to the action in which the original judgment was rendered — they do not apply to *further proceedings* in the same action in which the original judgment was rendered. Thus, these rules do not apply to a party who is seeking a *new trial* (in which he hopes the first judgment will be replaced by one of different effect), or to a party who is seeking to have the judgment reversed on *appeal.*

E. **Rationale:** The rules discussed in this chapter are based on the principle that *a party who has been given one fair opportunity to litigate a claim or an issue should not be given a second chance*. This principle is in turn based on two policy considerations: (1) *fairness to the victor* requires that he not be required to relitigate the claim or issue on which he has been victorious; and (2) *judicial economy* requires that litigation arising from a particular controversy not be continued indefinitely.

II. CLAIM PRECLUSION (MERGER AND BAR)

A. **Definition:** If a judgment is rendered for the plaintiff, his claim is *"merged"* into the judgment; that is, it is extinguished and a new claim to enforce the judgment is created. If judgment is for the defendant on the merits, the claim is extinguished and nothing new is created; plaintiff is ***"barred"*** from raising the claim again. Rest. 2d Judgments, §§18, 19; James & Hazard, p. 589. Some illustrations of the operation of merger and bar:

1. P sues D for $1,000 damages resulting from an automobile accident. The verdict and judgment grant P only $500. His claim, or cause of action, is "merged," meaning that P cannot initiate a new suit for the other $500.

2. Same suit as (1), but D is found not to be liable at all. P is "barred" from making the same claim in a second suit against D.

3. P sues D and wins the full $1,000, but finds that D has no property within the state upon which execution can be levied. His remedy is to bring an action "on the judgment" in the courts of whatever state he can find where D does have property. This action will be governed by the rules of Full Faith and Credit; unless D defaulted in the first action and the first court had no jurisdiction over him, the court of the second state must duplicate the judgment of the first court. The two judgments do not merge, and P can levy (or sue in yet a third state) on ***either*** of them.

B. Scope of claim: Since through claim preclusion a judgment is conclusive with respect to the entire "claim" which it adjudicates, it is essential to determine exactly what the dimensions of a claim are.

1. **Rule against splitting of claim:** A claim can include much ***more*** than plaintiff actually chose to state in his complaint. Plaintiff cannot ***"split"*** his claim — if he sues upon ***any portion*** of a claim, the other aspects of that claim are merged in his judgment if he wins, and barred if he loses.

    Example: Plaintiff claims $1,000 due under a single indivisible contract. He thinks there is a three in ten chance that a judge will find in his favor, and so he files ten separate suits, for $100 each, in the hope of winning at least a few of them. He has violated the rule against splitting a claim — the first judgment of the ten will merge with the others if he wins, in which case he has lost the other $900; if the first judgment comes out against him, it bars the others, and he has lost the entire $1,000.

    a. **Strict application:** The rule against splitting a claim applies even where the plaintiff did not split her claim intentionally.

        Example: Assume P has an insurance policy with two distinct parts: Part A entitles P to $100,000, and Part B entitles P to $50,000. Neither P nor her lawyer realizes there is a Part B at the time P's lawyer files suit to collect the $100,000 under Part A. If P wins, she will be barred from later filing to collect on the $50,000 from Part B, since that claim will be considered *"merged"* with the first judgment.

        Note: Where the splitting of a claim occurs through the gross incompetence of counsel, courts will sometimes refuse to strictly apply the rule against splitting, and will permit plaintiff to bring a new suit for the remainder of the claim.

    b. **Installment contracts:** Suppose that the claim relates to payments due under a ***lease*** or ***installment contract***. The general rule is that a plaintiff must sue at the same time for ***all payments*** due at the time the suit is filed, in this lease or installment-contract situation. See James & Hazard, p. 597.

Example: Defendant has made monthly lease payments in January and February, has skipped March, paid for April, and then skipped every month through September. If plaintiff sues in September, he ***must*** sue for March and May-September at once, or else forfeit whatever months he omits, since all the monthly payments are part of the same claim. October's payment, not being due yet, is not part of the same cause of action — if defendant also defaults on it, plaintiff can sue for it at a later date.

    i.   **Acceleration clauses:** Many installment contracts contain ***acceleration clauses***, providing that whenever defendant defaults on one payment, the whole balance becomes due. The courts have disagreed as to whether plaintiff ***must*** sue for the whole balance at once, or whether he may sue for just those months which have actually elapsed. A strict application of the splitting rule would require that plaintiff sue for the entire amount. But such a result is likely to drive the defendant into bankruptcy.

    ii. **Running account:** The same rule requiring suit for all payments due at the time of suit applies where there is a ***"running account"*** between creditor and debtor. For instance, if Merchant sells goods on credit to Consumer, any suit against Consumer must be for the entire amount which Consumer owes Merchant at the time the suit is brought, even though that debt arises out of separate transactions involving separate items. See Rest. 2d, Judgments §24, Comment d.

    iii. **Promissory notes:** But where a debt is represented by ***promissory notes***, a separate suit may be brought upon each note. James and Hazard, p. 607.

2. **Multi-theory actions:** In each of the above instances, plaintiff's claims involved a single contract and a single legal theory. The splitting rule is, however, also applicable to a lawsuit which contains several claims, all arising from the same set of facts and all alleging a violation of the same legal right, but involving a ***variety of theories or remedies.***

    a. **Common law:** At common law, "causes of action" were narrowly construed, and a single act could lead to actions of, say, trespass and trespass on the case, which could not be joined in a single pleading. Claim preclusion was invoked only in such relatively simple cases as those described above. Since plaintiff could not join trespass and case, then the outcome of one action did not "merge" or "bar" the other. (The doctrine of "inconsistent remedies" might have prevented plaintiff's second suit, but that doctrine had nothing to do with claim preclusion, and will not be discussed here.)

    b. **Extension of claim concept:** Procedural reforms within the last century, such as the Federal Rules, have greatly increased a plaintiff's freedom to join several legal theories and remedies in a single pleading. These reforms have correspondingly ***increased the scope of claim preclusion.***

       i. **Transactional test:** The modern approach is to define "cause of action" by a ***"transactional"*** definition. Thus the Restatement Second of Judgments, §24, provides that there will be merger or bar of all of the plaintiff's rights against the defendant "with respect to all or any part of the ***transaction***, or ***series of connected*** *transactions*, out of which the [initial] action arose." What constitutes a "transaction" or "series of transactions" is to be "determined pragmatically, giving weight to such considerations as whether the facts are ***related in time, space, origin, or motivation***, whether they form a ***convenient trial unit***, and whether their treatment as a unit conforms to the ***parties' expectations*** or ***business understanding or usage***."

Example: P files two suits against D, each for violation of the antitrust laws. Suit 1, which is against D as a sole tortfeasor, alleges violations of the Clayton Act. P loses, then brings Suit 2. Suit 2 charges D with conspiring with unnamed persons, and is brought under the Sherman Act.

Held, Suit 2 is barred by the judgment against plaintiff in Suit 1. The "operative facts" alleged by P in Suit 1 were virtually the same as those alleged in Suit 2. Plaintiff "does not get another day after the first lawsuit is concluded by giving a different reason than he gave in the first for recovery of damages for the same invasion of his rights." *Williamson v. Columbia Gas & Electric Corp.*, 186 F.2d 464 (3rd Cir. 1950).

3. **Personal and property damage from accident:**   Where a person suffers both *personal injuries* and *property damage* from the same accident (typically, an auto accident), most states today follow the rule that plaintiff has a *single claim*, not distinct claims for personal injuries on the one hand and property damage on the other. J&H, p. 601. The rationale for this majority view is that a single tortious act has caused all of the injuries, so they should all be litigated together. (The promotion of *judicial efficiency* also argues in favor of this rule.) See *Rush v. City of Maple Heights*, 147 N.E.2d 599 (Ohio 1958) (Ohio follows majority rule). But a handful of states allow the plaintiff to litigate separately her claims for personal injuries and for property damage arising out of a single accident.

4. **Application to equitable remedies:**   The merger of law and equity has resulted in the application of the rules of merger and bar to *equitable* remedies as well as to legal ones. In fact, it will not infrequently be the case that a demand for legal relief (generally, money damages) and a demand for equitable relief (e.g., an injunction or reformation of a contract) will both be deemed to be part of the same "claim," so that both demands must be made in the same action. See Rest. 2d, Judgments, §25, Comment i.

5. **Exception to claim preclusion rules:**   There nevertheless remain instances where two possible legal theories relating to the same incident cannot be joined in any forum, and where as a result claim preclusion is not applicable. Such cases often arise due to statutory *jurisdictional* requirements — if the court trying the first action would not have had subject matter jurisdiction of the theory used in the second action, there will be no bar or merger. Rest. 2d, Judgments, §26(1)(c).

Example: P sues D in state court under a state antitrust law, and loses on the merits. P then sues D in federal court alleging the same facts, and charging a violation of the federal antitrust laws. Because the federal courts have exclusive jurisdiction of antitrust claims, the state court could not have heard the federal claim. Therefore, the second (federal court) action is not barred. Rest. 2d, Judgments, §26, Illustr. 2.

6. **Suits in two different jurisdictions:** Where Suit 1 and Suit 2 are in *two different jurisdictions*, the court hearing Suit 2 must normally apply not its own rules of claim preclusion, but *those of the court that heard Suit 1*.

    a. **State suit followed by federal suit:** This is true not only where Suit 1 and Suit 2 are in two different states, but also where Suit 1 is in *state* court and Suit 2 is in *federal* court, and vice versa. The rule that it is the first court's claim preclusion rules which apply is a corollary to the more general requirement that each court must render "Full Faith and Credit" to the judgments of other jurisdictions. See *infra*, p. 443, for a fuller discussion of this principle.

C. **Adjudication on the merits:** For the rule of "bar" to take effect, the original adjudication for the defendant must have been *"on the merits."* This means that some of the many ways in which plaintiff can lose a case will *not bar future efforts* on his part to relitigate the same claim. See Rest. 2d, Judgments, §20.

1. **Rule 41(b):** Federal Rule 41(b) specifies the following as grounds for dismissal which *never* lead to bar:

    a. *lack of jurisdiction;*

    b. *improper venue;*

    c. *failure to join an indispensable party.*

    d. **Other:** Any other dismissal "operates as an adjudication on the merits" *unless the court specifies otherwise* in its order for dismissal.

    Note: Most states similarly regard the items listed in (a), (b) and (c) above as not leading to bar or merger. See Rest. 2d, Judgments, §20(1). Consequently, it should make no difference whether both actions are federal, both state, or one each — there will never be claim preclusion when the first action is disposed of in one of these three ways.

2. **Failure to prosecute or obey court:** A Federal Rule 41(b) dismissal for failure to *prosecute*, or for failure to *comply* with an order of the court, is apparently *with prejudice* unless the court specifies otherwise. Wright notes that "this is a drastic sanction, and though the courts have the power and must have the power if they are to discharge their responsibility to prevent undue delay in litigation, it is a power that should be exercised only in extreme situations." Wr., 696-97.

    a. **Abuse of discretion:** The failure of the trial judge to specify that such a dismissal is without prejudice is reviewable on appeal and may be reversed as an abuse of discretion.

3. **Failure to state a claim:** Suppose the first action is dismissed for *failure to state a cause of action*, and plaintiff corrected the defects in his pleadings in a second action (rather than through amending the pleadings in the first action). In modern courts, a dismissal for failure to state a claim usually counts as an *adjudication on the merits*, barring the second action.

    a. **Federal system:** Thus in the federal system, a dismissal for failure to state a claim counts as an adjudication on the merits unless the court specifies otherwise. FRCP

41(b). So if the court does not specify otherwise, plaintiff must either amend his pleading (if given leave) or appeal; he may not commence a new action.

    b. State courts and Restatement are in accord: The same is usually true in state courts. Thus the Second Restatement of Judgments, §19, Comment d, provides that a state court adjudication that a complaint is legally insufficient precludes a second suit on the claims asserted in it.

D. Counterclaims: A defendant who pleads a counterclaim is, in effect, a plaintiff with respect to that claim. He is bound by the outcome, just as the plaintiff is bound by the outcome of his original claim.

    1. No splitting: Every jurisdiction now permits a defendant to make a counterclaim on which he may obtain *affirmative recovery*. That is, if plaintiff sues defendant for $10,000, defendant can interpose a counterclaim for $100,000 and hope to win the difference of $90,000, or even the whole $100,000. In such a case, defendant *may not split his counterclaim* into two parts, using $10,000 to offset plaintiff's claim, and later suing for the remainder.

    2. Collateral estoppel danger: A defendant with a claim against one who is suing him has the *option of not using his claim at all* in that action, preserving it for a separate action. He must be careful, however, for if in his *defense* at the first trial he attempts to prove facts which are essential to his own claim, and fails, he will be *collaterally estopped* from pursuing his own claim later on. (See *infra*, p. 427). If his own claim is much greater than the one against him, he may think it worthwhile to *default* at the first trial, since no collateral estoppel effect will attach to a default judgment.

        a. Defendant wins: If the defendant declines to assert his counterclaim, and *wins* as to the plaintiff's claim, he will be able to start a new suit based on the claim he could have asserted as a counterclaim (assuming it was not a compulsory counterclaim, discussed below). For example, assume in Action 1 that D asserts fraud as an affirmative defense, but not as a counterclaim, and wins. D can then bring a fraud claim (Action 2) based on the same actions by his adversary that were at issue in Action 1.

    3. Compulsory counterclaims: Under the Federal Rules, and many state counterparts, a counterclaim which arises from the same transaction as the plaintiff's claim is *compulsory*. Rule 13(a). If the defendant fails to raise it, he is *barred* from using it in a later action. Note that this "transaction" test is similar to the transactional test which is gaining favor for the purpose of defining "cause of action."

        a. State respects federal counterclaim rule: Most states respect the policy behind the federal compulsory counterclaim rule, and thus *bar an action* on a claim that should have been raised as a compulsory counterclaim in a prior federal action. See F,K&M, p. 354.

        b. Settlement: Suppose D does not assert what should be a compulsory counterclaim, and the main action is then *settled*. Is D barred from bringing the claim in a later suit? Courts are split on the question.

E. Change of law: Once a final judgment has been rendered (and either appealed, or the time for appeal passed), *not even a change in the applicable law* will prevent *res judicata* from operating. The fact that the losing party would, because of such an overruling of legal precedent, win the lawsuit if he were allowed to start it again, is irrelevant. Cf. *Federated Department Stores, Inc. v. Moitie*, 452 U.S. 394 (1981).

1. **Major constitutional change:** But where there has been a ***major change*** in ***constitutional law*** between the first suit and the second suit, so that the litigant who lost the first time would win now, claim preclusion may ***not*** be strictly applied, especially if the issue has great public importance. For instance, suppose particular conduct by a school system were found not to constitute intentional (and thus illegal) racial segregation, but then the constitutional definition of forbidden segregation changed; the same plaintiff might be permitted to relitigate the issue of whether the system was illegally segregating. See F,K&M, p. 658.

F. **Persons not party to first action:** Thus far we have limited our discussion of *res judicata* to situations where one of the original parties to the first action is sought to be precluded from relitigation. Normally, ***only parties to the initial judgment*** will be subject to merger or bar.

1. **Exceptions:** But in a few situations, a non-party may be ***so closely tied*** to a party to the first judgment, that he will be both burdened and benefited by that judgment as if he had been a party to it. The six main situations where this can occur are summarized shortly below (p. 424), during the course of our discussion of *Taylor v. Sturgell* and the "virtual representation" doctrine.

2. **"Virtual representation" doctrine rejected:** Prior to 2008, a number of lower federal courts occasionally applied the doctrine of ***"virtual representation,"*** so as to preclude a later claim by a stranger to the first action. The doctrine was used where the court believed that even though the stranger and a party to the first suit did not have such a close relationship that they were in legal privity with each other, the ***practical links*** between the two — such as links of ***friendship*** or a ***shared lawyer*** — were so tight that it was fair to bind the stranger based on the outcome of the first suit; the party was said to have "virtually represented" the stranger. But the Supreme Court ***rejected*** this virtual representation doctrine, at least for federal courts, in ***Taylor v. Sturgell***, 128 S.Ct. 2161 (2008).

   a. **Facts:** The facts of *Taylor* give a good example of the sort of links between a losing party to a first action (call him P1) and a stranger to that first action who now wants to bring his own suit (call him P2) that had sometimes induced lower federal courts to apply the virtual representation doctrine.

      i. **Fellow enthusiasts:** Herrick (P1) and Taylor (P2) were friends and fellow antique-aircraft enthusiasts. Herrick wanted to restore a vintage F-45 airplane he owned, made by Fairchild in the 1930s. He therefore filed a Freedom of Information Act (FOIA) request with the Federal Aviation Administration (FAA) for any technical information in the agency's files about the F-45 model. When the FAA turned down the request on the grounds that the trade secrets exception to FOIA applied, Herrick sued the FAA in federal court and lost, both at trial and on appeal.

      ii. **Links between Herrick and Taylor:** Less than a month later, Taylor brought his own federal FOIA suit for the same documents. It became clear that there were a number of links between Herrick and Taylor beyond friendship and a shared interest in antique aircraft: they were both members of the Antique Aircraft Association (Taylor was the President); Herrick had asked Taylor to help restore Herrick's F-45 (though they had no contract for Taylor to do so); Taylor was represented in a suit by the ***same lawyer*** who had represented Herrick in the first suit; and Herrick gave Taylor documents that Herrick had previously gotten from the FAA during the course of discovery in Herrick's suit.

    iii. **Lower court applies virtual doctrine:** The D.C. Court of Appeals in Taylor's suit ***agreed with Fairchild and the FAA*** that under the doctrine of "virtual representation," Taylor ***had been virtually represented*** by Herrick during the course of the first suit, and was thus ***barred from bringing his own suit***, just as Herrick would be barred from suing again. The Court of Appeals applied a five-factor balancing test, in which such factors as "identity of interest," a "close relationship" between the first party and the present party, and "substantial participation" by the present party in the prior suit were all analyzed. This test led the appeals court to the conclusion that it was fair to bar Taylor.

b. **Doctrine rejected by Supreme Court:** But the Supreme Court, in a (surprisingly) ***unanimous*** opinion, ***completely rejected the virtual representation doctrine***. The opinion was by Justice Ginsburg.

    i. **General rule of against nonparty preclusion:** Ginsburg began by reciting the general rule against applying either claim preclusion or issue preclusion (i.e., collateral estoppel; see *infra*, p. 427) against someone who was not a party to the first action. This rule was justified by the "deeply-rooted ***historic tradition*** that ***everyone should have his own day in court.***"

    ii. **Exceptions:** She then noted that there were six fairly narrow well-established ***exceptions*** to this general rule of no-non-party-preclusion. (In summarizing these, we'll refer to the party to the first suit as "P1" and the non-party who is suing now, and who is proposed to be bound by that judgment, as "P2," even though the party may have been a defendant in the first suit rather than a plaintiff.) Here are the established exceptions to the no-binding-of-strangers-to-the-first-action rule, as listed by Ginsburg:

        [1] P2 ***agrees to be bound*** by the results in the first action;

        [2] P1 and P2 have any of several pre-existing ***"substantive legal relationships"*** with each other (e.g., ***successive owners*** of the same property, or ***indemnitor-and-indemnitee***); these are what are often called ***"privity,"*** though Ginsburg said that she was avoiding using that term because of its potential for confusion.

        [3] P2 is deemed to have been ***adequately represented*** by P1 in the first suit, such as in a properly conducted ***class action***, or in a suit in which the beneficiary of a ***trust*** is represented by the trustee. This category, Ginsburg said, consisted of "certain ***limited*** circumstances."

        [4] P2 ***"assumed control"*** of the first litigation, even though P1 was the named party.

        [5] P1 was the real party in the first suit, and has now ***designated P2 as her rep-***

resentative in the present suit, making P2 P1's ***"proxy."*** So if P2 is now suing as an *agent* on behalf of P1, the suit will not be permitted to go forward because P1, the real party in interest, has already had her day in court.

[6] Under some special *statutory* scheme (e.g., **bankruptcy** or **probate** proceedings), P2 is expressly precluded from relitigating the claim or issue in question, even though P2 was not a party to that first suit.

iii. **No virtual representation:** Fairchild and the FAA (the defendants in Taylor's suit) argued that apart from these six well-established exceptions, a broader, more flexible doctrine of "virtual representation" should be used to cover situations where it would not be ***"equitable"*** to allow the second suit. But Ginsburg ***disagreed***, for several reasons:

[1] the idea of virtual representation goes against "the ***fundamental nature of the general rule*** that a litigant is ***not bound by a judgment to which she was not a party***."

[2] an expansive doctrine of virtual representation would "recognize, in effect, a ***common-law kind of class action.***" In actual class actions (see *supra*, p. 355) there are stringent ***procedural protections*** for non-parties, protections that grow out of ***due process*** considerations (e.g., notice, adequacy of representation, etc.). These protections could be ***circumvented*** if the virtual representation doctrine were allowed to ***"create de facto class actions at will."***

[3] A virtual representation doctrine that balances multiple factors would be ***complicated and time-consuming*** to ***administer***. Claim preclusion and issue preclusion are supposed to reduce the burden on litigants, not increase it; ***"crisp rules with sharp corners"*** are preferable in this area.

iv. **No public-law exception:** The FAA argued that even if the virtual representation doctrine should not be applied to ordinary lawsuits involving private parties, it should be applied to ***"public law claims,"*** that is, suits involving ***government bodies and policies***. The idea was that in public-law domains, there would be a potentially ***limitless number of plaintiffs with standing***, and thus much worse risks of repetitive litigation that would be burdensome to the government. But the Court retorted that massive relitigation was unlikely to be a problem for two reasons: (1) *stare decisis* would let courts swiftly dispose of repetitive suits; and (2) the "human tendency ***not to waste money***" would deter plaintiffs from bringing suits based on claims or issues that had already been adversely determined against others.

v. **Application of test to facts:** The Court then took a quick look at whether, given that a broad virtual representation doctrine would not be recognized, any of the six standard exceptions to non-party preclusion applied on these facts. The only one that was even a possibility was [5] in the above list, that Herrick, having lost the first suit, was using Taylor as his undisclosed ***agent*** to bring the second suit and thus relitigate. On this point, the Court remanded to the lower courts. But Ginsburg stressed that "a ***mere whiff of 'tactical maneuvering'***" would ***not be enough*** for the second suit to be barred; preclusion would be appropriate "only if the putative agent's conduct of the suit is ***subject to the control*** of the party who is bound by the prior adjudication."

    (1) Stringent test: So unless the court on remand found that Herrick was really ***controlling*** Taylor's management of the second suit, Taylor could proceed. The fact that the two were ***friends*** and had the ***same lawyer***, and probably even the fact that Herrick was giving assistance or advice to Taylor, would ***not*** be enough.

  c. Significance: It seems unlikely that *Taylor*'s rejection of virtual representation will turn out to have very far-reaching consequences.

    i. Effect on state court systems: It's not even clear that the holding is binding on ***state court systems***. It's true that the Court refers indirectly to federal constitutional due process concerns: the right of each party to have his own day in court. But the Court in *Taylor* seemed to be speaking in its role as ***supervisor of the federal courts***; in other words, the Court seems to have been making ***federal common law***. If so, a state court system could still apply the virtual representation doctrine as long as the effect on the rights of the stranger to the first action were not so great as to constitute an outright due process violation.

    ii. Not equivalent to *stare decisis*: Notice, by the way, that although a stranger to the first action will have to contend with ***stare decisis*** if she tries to produce a different outcome in the second suit, that's still a somewhat easier task than if virtual representation applied. If the Supreme Court had applied virtual representation to bar Taylor's suit, Taylor would ***never have gotten to the merits at all***, even if he brought suit in a different federal circuit than the one in which Herrick had litigated his suit. But now that Taylor is not precluded, he has two ways to try to ***work around*** the *stare decisis* fact that Herrick lost on the same issue: (1) he can argue that Herrick's suit was a ***wrongly-decided*** holding on an ***important issue of public policy***, so that the usual principle of *stare decisis* should not apply; and (2) he can, perhaps, litigate in a ***different circuit*** than Herrick, in which case the result of Herrick's suit would be possibly persuasive precedent, but not ***binding*** on the court.

Quiz Yourself on
CLAIM PRECLUSION (MERGER AND BAR)

123. P and D, each driving a car, collided. P suffered serious personal injuries, and her car was totally demolished. P brought an action in Ames state court for damages for her personal injuries, but not for any loss of property. P won the suit. P then commenced a second action against D, for the damage to her car, in Ames state court. Will the court hear this second action? _____

124. Pauline and Doug, while each was driving, collided. Pauline suffered personal injuries and damage to her car. Pauline brought a federal court diversity action against Doug, for her personal injuries but not for her property damage. Suit was brought in Iowa federal district court. Doug made a motion under Rule 12(b)(6) for failure to state a cause of action; he asserted that Pauline's claim was barred by the statute of limitations. The federal judge agreed with this assertion, and dismissed the case. The order of dismissal did not say whether the dismissal was with prejudice. Pauline has then brought another action, again in federal court for Iowa, seeking to recover for the property damage she sustained in the accident (in contrast to the personal injury damages she sought in the first action). Should the federal judge hear Pauline's second claim on the merits? _____

125. Same basic fact pattern as the prior question. Now, assume that Pauline's claim in Iowa federal court proceeded to a decision on the merits. The judge applied Iowa state law, which is that contributory negligence by the plaintiff, no matter how small in degree, completely blocks plaintiff from recovering. The judge found in favor of Doug on the grounds that Pauline was slightly negligent. The judge entered a final judgment in favor of Doug. One month later, the Iowa Supreme Court reversed its prior decisions, and held that comparative negligence, rather than contributory negligence, will henceforth be the official doctrine of Iowa. Pauline has now brought a second suit against Doug in federal court for Iowa, for property damage from the original accident. Should the federal judge allow Pauline's action to go forward? _____

Answers

123. **No, probably.** The twin doctrines of *merger* and *bar* (collectively known as *"claim preclusion"*) prevent a plaintiff from "splitting her cause of action" between two suits. If a plaintiff splits a cause of action and wins the first suit, her second claim is said to be "merged" into the favorable first judgment; if she loses the first suit, her second claim is held to be "barred" by the unfavorable first result.

Most courts today follow the "transaction" test for determining what constitutes a cause of action. By this test, both P's personal injury claim and her property damage claim formed a single cause of action, since they stemmed from a single transaction (the auto accident). Therefore, most courts would treat P as losing her property damage claim because it was merged into her previously-asserted personal injury claim. See F,K&M, pp. 634-35.

124. **No.** Claim preclusion only applies where the first suit was resolved *"on the merits,"* so the question becomes whether the dismissal here was on the merits. Under Federal Rule 41(b), an order of dismissal is treated as being on the merits unless either the dismissal order specifies that it is without prejudice, or the dismissal is for lack of jurisdiction, improper venue, or failure to join an indispensable party. Since none of these exceptions applies here, the dismissal is treated as being on the merits. As such, the result is the same as if Pauline had tried her case through to, say, a jury verdict. Her property-damage claim is part of the same cause of action as her personal injury claim, so she is barred by the earlier dismissal from asserting the property damage claim here.

125. **No.** Once a final judgment has been rendered, not even a change in the applicable law will prevent res judicata from operating. The fact that Pauline would have won her original lawsuit if it were brought today, is irrelevant. Since the property damage claim being asserted now and the personal-injury claim asserted then are part of the same cause of action (see the answer to Question 116 above), Pauline's property damage claim will be barred just as if there had been no intervening change of law.

III. COLLATERAL ESTOPPEL

A. Effect: Regardless of which of the parties to an action is victorious, the judgment is "conclusive in a subsequent action between them *upon the issues actually litigated in the action.*"

Rest. 2d, Judgments, §27; James & Hazard, p. 607. A party who seeks to relitigate one of the issues disposed of in the first trial is said to be ***collaterally estopped*** from doing so.

1. **Application:** The principles of collateral estoppel always apply where ***both*** of the parties in the second action were present in the first action. These rules sometimes, but not always, apply where only the person against whom estoppel is sought to be used was present in the first action.

2. **Distinguished from merger and bar:** Whereas claim preclusion applies only where the "claim" in the second action is the same as the one adjudicated in the first action, collateral estoppel applies as long as any ***issue*** is the same, even though the causes of action are different. Also, whereas claim preclusion prevents the second suit altogether, collateral estoppel does not prevent suit, but merely compels the court to make the same finding of fact on the identical issue that the first court made. (Sometimes, of course, this will as a practical matter bar suit, as in a negligence case like *Little, infra*, where the initial finding of plaintiff's non-negligence effectively disposes of a later suit by the defendant.)

   Example: Blue Goose sues Little for damage to its bus resulting from a collision with Little's automobile. Blue Goose is awarded damages of $139. In a subsequent action, Little sues for his own personal injuries.

   Held (in the second suit), "the issue of negligence was necessarily determined" in the first action, and may not be relitigated. The fact that the negligence alleged by Little is 'wanton and willful' negligence (whereas only ordinary negligence was debated in the first action) is irrelevant. The judgment for Blue Goose was definitely a finding that it had not been either ordinarily or willfully negligent (the doctrine of contributory negligence would have barred recovery if it had been.) This finding of non-negligence is binding on Little in the second action. *Little v. Blue Goose Motor Coach Co.*, 178 N.E. 496 (Ill. 1931).

B. **Issues to which collateral estoppel applies:** For an issue to be subject to collateral estoppel, three requirements must be satisfied: (1) the issue must be the ***same*** as one that was ***fully and fairly litigated*** in the first action; (2) the issue must have actually been ***decided*** by the first court; and (3) the first court's decision on this issue must have been ***necessary to the outcome*** in the first suit. Rest. 2d, Judgments, §27.

1. **Same issue:** For the relitigation of an issue to be collaterally estopped, that issue must be ***identical*** to an issue litigated in the earlier trial. However, this requirement of identity is not interpreted with the greatest possible strictness.

   Example: Suppose the first action involves X's negligence to Y's automobile. In a second action, Y will be collaterally estopped from relitigating X's negligence to Y's *person* for injuries arising from the same car accident — the two kinds of negligence will be held to be a single "issue" for collateral estoppel purposes.

2. **Actually litigated and decided:** For collateral estoppel to apply to an issue, the issue must have been ***actually litigated*** and ***decided*** at the first trial. A defendant is thus ***not obligated to raise all of his defenses at one trial*** if he knows that some of them may be relevant to future trials. He does not forfeit these defenses by not raising them as he would forfeit a compulsory counterclaim.

a. Distinguished from merger and bar: This requirement of actual litigation is different from the rules of merger and bar, which can apply not only as to matters which were decided, but also as to all matters which might have been decided.

Example: P sues D for an installment of rent under a lease, and wins. In a later suit for subsequent installments due on the same lease, D denies that the lease was ever executed. Since D did not deny execution in the first action, he will not be collaterally estopped from litigating the execution issue in the second action. Collateral estoppel applies only to issues which were actually litigated previously.

b. "Full and fair" litigation: The party against whom collateral estoppel is sought to be used must have had a ***"full and fair opportunity"*** to litigate the claim. For instance, if he litigated the claim, but important evidence bearing on that issue was rejected by the court without good reason, he would not be bound, on the grounds that he lacked a "full and fair opportunity" to litigate the issue. See Rest. 2d, Judgments, §28(5)(c).

3. Issue essential to verdict: For relitigation of an issue to be precluded, that issue must not only have been litigated and decided in the first action, but the finding on that issue must have been ***necessary to the judgment***. Rest. 2d, Judgments, §27.

Example: Jeffery sues Cambria, and loses. The court's findings of fact state that both parties were negligent, and recovery is denied on the grounds that Jeffery was contributorily negligent. Cambria then sues Jeffery, who claims that Cambria's (contributory) negligence was decided in the first action.

Collateral estoppel is ***not*** applied. Since the court in the first action based its verdict on the fact that Jeffery was contributorily negligent, its finding that Cambria was negligent has no effect in the second action. Collateral estoppel applies only to issues whose adjudication was ***necessary*** to the verdict in the first action. *Cambria v. Jeffery*, 29 N.E.2d 555 (Mass. 1940).

a. Alternate findings: Where a judgment rests upon ***alternate*** findings, either of which would be sufficient to sustain it, there has been much dispute about whether either finding should be given collateral estoppel effect.

i. Restatement denies collateral estoppel effect: The Second Restatement of Judgments reasons that in this situation, it cannot be said that either of the findings was necessary to the judgment, and that therefore ***neither should be given estoppel effect***. Rest. 2d, Judgments, §27, Comments h, i, j.

ii. Additional rationale: Another rationale in support of not giving either finding collateral estoppel effect is that where there are alternative findings, the court ***may not be as careful*** in considering each, thus increasing the possibility of unfairness to the litigant who is bound by one of the findings. (But if both of the determinations are ***upheld on appeal, each*** will have estoppel effect. *Id.* at §27, Comment o.)

4. Foreseeability of future litigation: There is an increasing tendency to apply collateral estoppel in a subsequent action only where that action was ***reasonably foreseeable*** at the time of the initial adjudication of the issue in question. This limitation was suggested by Learned Hand in dictum; he advocated that the estoppel effect of findings be restricted to "future controversies which could be thought reasonably in prospect when the first suit was tried." If this were not done, "Defeat in one suit might entail results beyond all calculation by either party; *a trivial controversy might bring utter disaster in its train.*" *The Evergreens v. Nunan*, 141 F.2d 927 (2d Cir. 1944).

   a.   Followed in Restatement: Hand's suggestion has been followed in the Second Restatement of Judgments, §28(5)(b) and Comment i — relitigation of an issue which was litigated and determined is permitted if it was "*not sufficiently foreseeable* at the time of the initial action that the issue would arise in the context of a subsequent action."

5.   Courts of limited jurisdiction: There is dispute as to whether a court of *limited jurisdiction* can, in deciding a case within its jurisdiction, make findings of fact which are binding in subsequent actions that would be beyond that jurisdiction. The Second Restatement of Judgments recognizes that it will not be appropriate to attach collateral estoppel effect if a redetermination of the issue is "warranted by differences in the *quality or extensiveness* of the *procedures* followed in the two courts or by factors relating to the *allocation of jurisdiction* between them." Rest. 2d, Judgments, §28(3).

   a.   Jurisdictional amount: If the only difference between the two courts is that the first court had a *maximum dollar limit* on claims which it could adjudicate, so that the claim in the second action could not have been disposed of by the first court, this will usually *not* be enough of a reason to deny collateral estoppel effect to the first court's finding.

   Example: A brings a negligence action against B for property damage, in a court whose jurisdiction is limited to $2,000. The rules governing the court's trial procedures are essentially the same as in a court of general jurisdiction. A wins, because the court finds that B was negligent. B now brings a negligence action against A in a court of general jurisdiction, seeking $10,000 for personal injuries arising out of the same transaction. The first suit's finding that B was negligent will have collateral estoppel effect, thus barring B from recovery if the jurisdiction applies the doctrine of contributory negligence. Rest. 2d, Judgments, §28, Illustr. 6.

   b.   Informal procedures: But if the first court not only has jurisdiction limited to a certain dollar amount, but also has *informal procedures*, it will generally not be appropriate to give its finding collateral estoppel effect when the second suit is in a court of general jurisdiction. For instance, in most *small claims courts*, there are no pleadings, no rules of evidence, and usually no counsel present; therefore, findings by such courts will generally not have collateral estoppel effect in a later action in a court of general jurisdiction. Thus on the facts of the above example, if the first suit was in such a court, B would still be able to claim in a second suit that he himself was not negligent. See Rest. 2d, Judgments, §28, Illustr. 7.

      i.   Rationale: The principle denying collateral estoppel effect to small claims court judgments seems reasonable. The purposes of a small claims court may be defeated if people are obliged to either default or to litigate their small claims or defenses to the hilt because of the possibility that large potential lawsuits might later be determined by the outcome.

c. **Surrogate's or probate court:** Sometimes the jurisdiction of the first court is limited not by dollar amount, but by the *subject matter* of the dispute. This is true, for instance, of *surrogate's* or *probate* courts. Generally, the procedures followed in these courts are of comparable rigor to those in courts of general jurisdiction. Therefore, findings made by these courts will generally be *binding* in a later general-court action. See Rest. 2d, Judgments, §28, Illustr. 8.

d. **Second action within exclusive federal jurisdiction:** So far in this chapter, we have generally assumed that both actions take place in the *same jurisdiction*. The rules are generally applicable, however, even if the actions are in the courts of two different states, or one action is brought in state court and the other in federal court. Suppose, however, that the first action is brought in state court, and the second is not only brought in federal court, but involves a *claim as to which the federal courts have exclusive subject matter jurisdiction*. In this situation, the federal court will nonetheless grant collateral estoppel effect to the state court's determination unless, as a matter of statutory interpretation, the court concludes that Congress, in establishing the federal right being sued upon, intended not to defer to the factual determinations of state courts. This issue is discussed more extensively *infra*, p. 444.

6. **Differences in burden of proof:** Differences in the *allocation of the burden of proof* between the first proceeding and the second may dictate that collateral estoppel not apply. If in the first action, the allocation of the burden of proof was more favorable to the party seeking to apply collateral estoppel than it was in the second action, collateral estoppel will not be allowed. Rest. 2d, Judgments, §28(4).

7. **Settlement:** In most jurisdictions, the *settlement* of an action by consent of the parties has *no collateral estoppel effect*. See Rest. 2d, Judgments, §27 (issue must have been "actually litigated" for collateral estoppel to apply).

a. **Minority view:** In a minority of states, however, the settlement may be held to be binding on some or all of the issues which would have been litigated had the suit been tried. Such estoppel effect is of course in conflict with the general rule that only issues which have been fully and fairly litigated are subject to collateral estoppel — nonetheless, some jurisdictions attach collateral estoppel effect to settlements. The parties can avoid this possibility by specifying in the settlement that the agreement is to have no effect on any other cause of action. F,K&C, p. 1160.

8. **Findings of law:** Normally, the question of collateral estoppel arises with respect to findings of *fact*. However, a court's conclusion of *law* is also generally given collateral estoppel effect (assuming, of course, that the other requirements for that doctrine are met). In most situations, "it is unfair to the winning party and an unnecessary burden on the courts to allow repeated litigation of the same issue in what is essentially the same controversy, even if the issue is regarded as one of 'law.' " Rest. 2d, Judgments, §28, Comment b.

Example: Assume that a statute of State X says that a municipality may seize and sell a person's property for unpaid local property taxes only if the municipality "serves a notice of lien" on the person at least 60 days before any sale. Muni, a town, serves D1 by certified-mail only, then seizes and resells his property 70 days later. D1 sues Muni in a State X court of general jurisdiction to have the sale set aside, arguing that the statute required personal, not certified-mail, service, if personal service was feasible. Muni litigates this issue and loses on the merits, so that the sale is unwound. Later, in a matter involving a different property, owned by D2, Muni serves D2 by certified-mail, even though he could easily have been subject to personal service. D2 sues Muni to have the sale set aside.

D2 will be permitted to use collateral estoppel against Muni to bind it to the finding in the D1 action that Muni was required to use personal service where feasible. That is, the fact that the finding in the earlier suit was a ***conclusion of law*** (what the statute requires), not a finding of fact, doesn't prevent collateral estoppel from applying.

a. **Exceptions:** But the Restatement of Judgments recognizes two situations in which a conclusion of law should ***not*** be given collateral estoppel effect: (1) the two actions "involve claims that are ***substantially unrelated***"; or (2) "a new determination is warranted in order to take account of an ***intervening change in the applicable legal context*** or otherwise to ***avoid inequitable administration*** of the laws." Rest. 2d, Judgments, §28(2)(a) and (b).

   i. **Constitutional adjudication:** The "substantially unrelated claims" exception is especially important where the legal issue is a ***constitutional*** one, and the party against whom collateral estoppel is sought to be used is the ***government*** or another party with an ***ongoing interest*** in the constitutional issue. If collateral estoppel were applied to pure conclusions of law in unrelated factual settings in this situation, the result might be to "***freeze doctrine*** in areas of the law where responsiveness to changing patterns of conduct or social mores is critical." *Montana v. U.S.*, 440 U.S. 147 (1979).

b. **Change of legal climate:** If, between the first and second suits, there has been a ***significant change in legal principles***, the court may as a discretionary matter decline to apply collateral estoppel. This is especially appropriate where use of collateral estoppel "would impose on one of the parties a ***significant disadvantage***, or confer on him a ***significant benefit***, with respect to his ***competitors***." Rest. 2d, Judgments, §28, Comment c. See also *Commissioner of Internal Revenue v. Sunnen*, 333 U.S. 591 (1948).

   Example: P, a state liquor licensing agency, sues to have D's wholesale liquor license revoked, on the grounds that D has violated the law governing such licenses by selling only to himself as a retailer. The court finds that D has not violated the law. P then sues X, whose conduct has been the same as D's; a higher court than decided the first case concludes that this conduct violates the statute, and orders X's license revoked. P then brings a second lower-court action against D for revocation. Collateral estoppel effect should not be given to the first P-vs.-D suit, since there has been an intervening change in legal principles, and since use of collateral estoppel would have given D a perpetual, and unfair, advantage over X and other similarly-situated competitors. See Rest. 2d, Judgments, §28, Illustr. 3.

9. **Where second decision fails to apply estoppel:** If for some reason collateral estoppel is not applied in an action where it should have been, and a new judgment results which decides an issue differently from the prior one, the ***second judgment receives binding***

effect by estoppel. The original finding is thus in a sense "overruled", and will not be followed in a third action.

C. Persons bound by collateral estoppel: Where an issue which was litigated in one action reappears in a subsequent action, as a general rule only persons who were parties to the first action will be estopped from relitigating the issue.

1. **Strangers to first action:** Thus a person who is a complete *stranger* to the first action generally *cannot be bound* by collateral estoppel. That is, a person who was not a party to the first action may, in a new action — whether he is the plaintiff or the defendant — litigate any issue, even if that issue was litigated in the first suit. (There are six narrow exceptions, discussed on p. 424 above in the context of claim preclusion.)

   Example: A bus owned by Bus Co. collides with a car driven by Driver. In a suit between these two, Bus Co. is held to have full responsibility. Passenger, who was riding in Driver's car, now sues Driver. Even though the court in the first action decided that Driver was not at all at fault, Passenger is not bound by this finding. This is because Passenger was a complete stranger to the first action, and none of the six exceptions to the "no binding of strangers" rule applies to the ordinary passenger-driver situation. Therefore, the usual rule applies that a stranger cannot be bound by any finding of fact in the first action.

   a. **Due process:** The main reason for not collaterally estopping a stranger to the first action. Such use of estoppel would *violate the stranger's due process rights*; he would be deprived of his *day in court*, by being bound by the results of a lawsuit in which he did not participate.

      i. *Taylor v. Sturgell* **and the rejection of "virtual representation":** For more on a person's right to be free of the binding effect of an earlier suit to which he was not a party, see the discussion of *Taylor v. Sturgell, supra*, p. 423. In *Taylor*, the Supreme Court rejected the "virtual representation" doctrine, a doctrine that would have made it easier to bind someone who was not a party to the first suit. (*Taylor* itself involved claim preclusion, not collateral estoppel, but the Court's analysis applies equally to collateral estoppel.)

   b. **Exceptions:** There are a few narrowly-defined *exceptions* to the general rule that a person who was not a party to the first action cannot be collaterally estopped as to facts found in that action. For instance, if the litigant in the second suit (call him P2) is now acting as an *agent* of a party to the first suit (call her P1), P2 will be collaterally estopped. See *supra*, p. 424, for the Supreme Court's list, in a case involving claim preclusion, of the six situations where this can occur. (The six apply the same way to allow collateral estoppel of the stranger to the first action as they apply to claim preclusion of that stranger.)

      i. **Federal court:** Keep in mind that these six exceptions apply in *federal* litigation; the *states* are free to set up additional exceptions to the no-binding-of-strangers rule, as long as these rules don't violate the non-party's due process rights.

D. Persons who can benefit from estoppel: Who may *benefit* from collateral estoppel? It is not the case that any litigant in the second action may automatically benefit from estoppel.

Any person who was *present* as a litigant in the first action may benefit (assuming the general requirements for estoppel are satisfied). But a person who was a *stranger* to the first litigation may under certain circumstances be deprived of the benefit of estoppel in the second action. However, the limits on a stranger's use of estoppel are far narrower than they used to be.

1. **Mutuality:** It was once held that a party not *bound* by an earlier judgment (because not a party to it) could not use that judgment to bind his adversary who *had* been a party to the former action. The rule prohibiting a stranger's use of collateral estoppel was known as the doctrine of *mutuality.*

    a. **Rationale:** The doctrine of mutuality was rationalized on the grounds that to do otherwise was a violation of the basic principles of fair play. If a litigant could not be burdened with the effect of a prior judgment, it seemed inequitable to allow him to benefit from it.

    b. **Historical exceptions:** Exceptions to the mutuality doctrine were always recognized. For instance, in a master-servant situation where M was entitled to an indemnity from S, and T sued S, lost, and then tried to sue M, M (though not a party to the prior action, nor in privity — an indemnitor may be a privy but not an indemnitee) could use estoppel against T. Restatement of Judgments, §96 (1942).

2. **Demise of mutuality:** Most courts *no longer recognize the general principle of mutuality.* While many courts refuse in particular circumstances to allow the use of estoppel by one not a party to the first action, it is no longer a general rule that a stranger to the first action cannot benefit from findings of fact made against his adversary. See Rest. 2d, Judgments, §29.

    a. ***Bernhard v. Bank of America:*** The first major assault on the mutuality doctrine came in *Bernhard v. Bank of America*, 122 P.2d 892 (Cal. 1942), a decision by Judge Traynor.

        i. **Facts:** Ms. Bernhard sued the executor of an estate to which she was a beneficiary, claiming that he had wrongfully taken money from the deceased's bank account and placed it in his own. It was held that the executor had been the legitimate recipient of a gift from the deceased. Ms. Bernhard then tried to sue the bank for allowing this withdrawal. The bank succeeded in collaterally estopping her from relitigating the issue of whether the withdrawal was legitimate.

        ii. **Holding:** Judge Traynor's opinion stated that "no satisfactory rationalization has been advanced for the requirement of mutuality." The decision went on to state that only three questions are pertinent in deciding whether to allow collateral estoppel: "Was the issue decided in the prior adjudication identical with the one presented in the action in question? Was there a final judgment on the merits? Was the party against whom the plea is asserted a party or in privity with a party to the prior adjudication?" If the answer to each of these questions is "yes", then estoppel is to be allowed in spite of the absence of mutuality.

3. **Offensive/defensive distinction:** *Nearly all jurisdictions* (and the Second Restatement of Judgments — §29) have by now followed *Bernhard's* rejection of the general principle of mutuality. However, many courts have limited *Bernhard's* application so as to prevent

results that appear unjust. Most importantly, some courts have distinguished between the *"offensive"* and the *"defensive"* use of estoppel, allowing the latter but not the former.

a. **Nature of distinction:** This distinction, which was first set forth by Prof. Currie in "Mutuality of Collateral Estoppel: Limits of the *Bernhard* Doctrine," 9 Stan. L.R. 281 (1957), may be summarized as follows: (1) Where a *defendant* in the second action seeks to assert estoppel against the plaintiff, this use of estoppel is said to be *"defensive"* — estoppel is being used as a *"shield"* rather than as a *"sword."* (2) Where a *plaintiff* in the second action seeks to assert estoppel against the defendant, this use is *"offensive."*

b. **Rationale for distinction:** The arguments for allowing defensive use of estoppel are stronger than those for allowing offensive use. In the defensive use case, plaintiff has chosen the second forum and the adversary — he is likely to have had the prospect of the second lawsuit in mind at the time of the first lawsuit, and it is not terribly unjust to hold him to the findings of fact made in that suit. Where the plaintiff in the second action was also a plaintiff in the first action, the arguments for collaterally estopping him are quite strong indeed. If the plaintiff in the second action was a defendant in the first action, and is seeking to assert estoppel, this is still "offensive" estoppel, but the arguments for estoppel are less compelling. Nonetheless, many courts would allow estoppel here.

c. **Offensive use:** The arguments in favor of "offensive" estoppel, by contrast, are weaker. The defendant against whom estoppel is sought to be applied has not had the choice of either forum or adversary; furthermore, it may be assumed that at the time of the first action, he was less aware of the prospect of the second suit than he would have been of a suit which he contemplated bringing as plaintiff. The application of estoppel to bind him might therefore unfairly prejudice him. If the defendant in the second action, against whom estoppel is sought to be applied, was also a defendant in the first action, the case for estoppel is at its weakest.

Example: The best-known example of the injustice of allowing estoppel to be used against a party who was a defendant in both the first and second actions is called the "*multiple plaintiff anomaly*." Suppose D, a railroad company, is involved in a collision in which 50 passengers are injured. The injured persons, instead of consolidating their actions, sue one at a time. If P1 loses, then the other plaintiffs are of course not bound, since they were not parties to P1's action. But if P1 wins, then the application of offensive collateral estoppel will mean that *each of the subsequent plaintiffs automatically wins against the railroad*. If plaintiffs 1-29 lose, but then P30 wins, offensive collateral estoppel will mean that plaintiffs 31-50 all win, even though the railroad won 29 of the first 30 suits. The railroad is thus compelled to defend fully against every suit, or face the loss of all remaining suits. Furthermore, the 50 plaintiffs are likely to get together and agree that the most appealing plaintiff (perhaps the most severely injured, or the one with the most children) should sue first.

It does not take a very refined sense of justice to feel that the railroad is unfairly treated by a scheme which compels it to win each action or face total disaster in the remaining ones. This injustice is coupled with the *judicial inefficiency* inherent in a scheme which gives the plaintiffs a powerful incentive to avoid consolidating their cases, and to sue one at a time, hoping for a positive result in one case. Most courts would therefore probably deny the offensive use of estoppel in such circumstances. But see *Hart v. American Airlines*, 304 N.Y.S.2d 810 (N.Y. Sup. Ct. 1969), an airplane crash case in which the finding of liability of the airline in the first suit to be completed was given collateral estoppel effect in a subsequent case.

4. **Offensive estoppel approved by Supreme Court:** The Supreme Court has held that, in at least some federal cases, *offensive non-mutual estoppel is permissible. Parklane Hosiery Co. v. Shore*, 439 U.S. 322 (1979).

   a. **Facts of *Parklane:*** In *Parklane*, P brought a stockholders' class action against D, based on an alleged false proxy statement issued by the latter. After the suit was started but before it was tried, the SEC brought a suit containing the same allegations, and the trial court found in the Commission's favor. P then sought to use the verdict in the SEC case to collaterally estop D from relitigating the issue of the falsity of the proxy statement.

   b. **Offensive use allowed:** The Supreme Court *permitted* this use of collateral estoppel, even though it was not only non-mutual but also *offensive* (in the sense that the use was sought by a plaintiff, rather than defendant, in the second action). The Court conceded that offensive collateral estoppel may create an incentive on the part of each plaintiff to adopt a "wait and see" attitude, in the hope that the first action by another plaintiff will result in a favorable judgment. Also, the Court acknowledged, offensive use of collateral estoppel may sometimes be unfair to the defendant; this might be the case, for instance, if the first suit was for such a small amount that the defendant had no reason to contest it vigorously, or if the second action "affords the defendant procedural opportunities unavailable in the first action that could readily cause a different result" (e.g., the first action was in a forum inconvenient for the defendant, preventing him from making full-scale discovery or calling witnesses.)

      i. **Case-by-case approach:** Nonetheless, the Court concluded, these difficulties should not be resolved by a ban on all non-mutual offensive use of collateral estoppel, but rather, by a *case-by-case* analysis of the wisdom of allowing such use. In this case, offensive use was reasonable; there was no evidence that P had an incentive to sit out the first litigation (he probably couldn't have joined the SEC suit even if he had wanted to.) Also, D had every incentive to litigate the SEC case vigorously (particularly since it knew about P's case, which had already been filed).

   c. **Right to jury trial:** D also raised the serious objection that offensive use of collateral estoppel here *deprived it of its right to a jury trial in the second action*. (No jury trial was permissible in the SEC action, but would have been in the second suit.) Since mutuality was a requirement for collateral estoppel at common law (as it existed in 1791, the date of the enactment of the Seventh Amendment), allowing offensive collateral estoppel here restricted D's jury rights from what they would have been in 1791.

      i. **Not fatal objection:** The Court conceded that this represented an abridgment, but noted that many other procedural devices developed since 1791 have similarly diminished the civil jury's domain, without being found inconsistent with the Seventh Amendment. The abridgment here was no more severe than in the case of these other procedural modifications (e.g., the modern form of directed verdict, which may be used to take the case away from the jury in a situation where this could not have been done in 1791).

    d. **Dissent:** Justice Rehnquist dissented, first on the grounds that D's Seventh Amendment rights were violated by offensive use of collateral estoppel here. Secondly, he argued, apart from the constitutional issue offensive use here was unfair to D, since the availability of a jury trial could easily lead to a different result from that obtained in the first action. Finally, he noted, a jury would have to be impaneled anyway to resolve other issues in the case (e.g., damages), so that the savings of court time and of litigants' resources would be minimal.

5. **Factors in case-by-case analysis:** As the result of *Parklane*, federal courts (and probably state courts as well, although these are not explicitly bound by *Parklane*) apply a case-by-case analysis in determining whether to allow offensive non-mutual estoppel. Courts should consider the following factors:

    a. **Alignment in first suit:** Whether the party sought to be bound (the defendant in the second suit) was a ***plaintiff*** or a ***defendant*** in the first suit. If he was a defendant, this will militate against use of estoppel, since he was less likely to have had the choice of the forum in which the issue was to be litigated. See Rest. 2d, Judgments, §29, Comment d.

    b. **Incentive to litigate:** Whether the person to be estopped had a reasonable ***incentive*** to litigate the issue fully in the first suit. For instance, as the *Parklane* court noted, the fact that the first suit was for a small amount might mean that the defendant had no reason to contest the issue vigorously. The degree to which the second suit was ***foreseeable*** at the time of the first suit might also be considered in gauging whether there was an incentive to litigate fully in the first suit.

    c. **Discouraging "breakaway" suits:** Whether the plaintiff in the second action could have joined in the first action, and ***"sat out"*** that first action in order to derive a tactical advantage (by which he would be able to use estoppel if his prospective adversary lost, and would not be bound by estoppel if that adversary won). See Rest. 2d, Judgments, §29(3).

    d. **Multiple plaintiff anomaly:** Whether permitting offensive estoppel would present a danger of the ***"multiple plaintiff anomaly"*** (*supra*, p. 435.) That is, if there were numerous potential plaintiffs waiting in the wings, the court would be less likely to permit offensive estoppel, than where the second suit would probably be the last. The court also might look to whether the potential multiple plaintiffs had seemingly gotten together and selected the most appealing plaintiff to sue first.

    e. **Procedural opportunities:** Whether there are ***procedural opportunities*** available to a party in the second action that were not present in the first, which might make a difference in the outcome. For instance, if the court in the second suit allows ***more extensive discovery*** than the first court, this might make a difference. Similarly, if the first case was tried to a judge, and the defendant in the second trial has a Seventh Amendment *right to a jury trial* which would be impeded by collateral estoppel, this may be a factor. (Although the Supreme Court in *Parklane* allowed use of offensive estoppel even though the defendant was deprived of his right to a jury trial on the issue, the Court did not say that the jury trial right could not be considered as a *non-dispositive factor* in deciding whether to allow such estoppel.)

f. Issue of law: Whether the issue is one of *law* or merely of "fact." Where the issue is one of "law" the more flexible doctrine of *stare decisis*, rather than collateral estoppel, should normally be applied. Otherwise, "the court is foreclosed from an opportunity to reconsider the applicable rule, and thus to perform its function of developing the law." Rest. 2d, Judgments, §29, Comment i.

g. Government is party: Whether the defendant in the second action is the *government*. Non-mutual offensive use of collateral estoppel will *virtually never be allowed against the government*. The Supreme Court so announced, as to the federal government, in *U.S. v. Mendoza*, 464 U.S. 154 (1984).

   i. Rationale: In announcing this rule, the Court reasoned that allowing non-mutual estoppel against the government "would substantially thwart the development of important questions of law by freezing the first final decision rendered on a particular legal issue." This would in turn mean that the Supreme Court would not get the chance to follow its current practice of frequently waiting for a conflict to develop between circuits before granting *certiorari*. Also, the federal government would come under pressure to appeal virtually every adverse trial court decision in order to avoid losing the opportunity for reconsideration in a different case presenting the same issue.

   ii. State and local governments: The Court's rule in *Mendoza* only deals with the situation in which the party against whom estoppel is sought to be applied is the *federal* government, and the second suit is in federal court. However, the rationale of that decision also appears applicable to federal court cases in which a state or local government is the defendant, and may in addition be adopted by state courts deciding whether to grant non-mutual offensive estoppel against governmental bodies.

6. Use of criminal conviction: The courts are split on whether to allow estoppel effect to a previous *criminal conviction* of a party. At least one state, California, has given full collateral estoppel effect to a previous criminal conviction. *Teitelbaum Furs, Inc. v. Dominion Insur. Co.*, 375 P.2d 439 (Cal. 1962). Other jurisdictions allow the conviction to be used only as *evidence*; it thus forms a rebuttable presumption. In some jurisdictions (e.g., New York), a conviction for a minor traffic violation may not even be used as evidence, let alone for estoppel.

a. State conviction and federal §1983 suit: The Supreme Court has allowed a state criminal conviction to have collateral effect in a subsequent *federal* case. For instance, the 1871 Civil Rights Act, in 42 U.S.C. §1983, gives a person the right to bring a federal suit against anyone who violates his constitutional rights "under color of" state law. The statute thus allows a federal civil damages suit against state officials who have violated the plaintiff's constitutional rights by false arrest, by search without probable cause or warrant, or by other official misconduct. The Supreme Court has held that a state court's finding in a criminal case that **no constitutional violation** of the criminal defendant's rights occurred may have collateral estoppel effect in a federal §1983 suit brought by that same defendant. *Allen v. McCurry*, 449 U.S. 90 (1983) (also discussed *infra*, p. 445).

Note: *Acquittal* in a criminal case **never becomes binding** in a subsequent civil action. First of all, to grant such estoppel effect would be to allow the criminal defendant to bind a non-party; non-parties may **never** be bound by earlier decisions, even though they may sometimes benefit from such decisions. Secondly, there is a discrepancy between the "beyond a reasonable doubt" standard of proof necessary for a criminal conviction, and the "preponderance of the evidence" standard in civil suits.

Quiz Yourself on
COLLATERAL ESTOPPEL

126. Phillip was injured when a car he was driving collided with a car driven by Doreen. Phillip sued Doreen for negligence in Ames state court. The case was tried before a jury, and the jury found for Phillip, awarding him substantial damages. Judgment was entered. Then, Doreen brought a negligence suit against Phillip for property damage arising from the same transaction. This suit, too, was brought in Ames state court. Ames follows traditional negligence law, by which even a small amount of contributory negligence on the part of the plaintiff prevents the plaintiff from recovering. Ames has no statute or judicial policy making any cause of action a compulsory counterclaim. In Doreen's suit, may she assert, and prove, that Phillip's negligence caused the accident? _____

127. Same basic fact pattern as the prior question. Now, assume that after Phillip sued Doreen in Ames state court for negligence, Doreen declined to answer. A default judgment was entered against her for $100,000 in damages. Doreen then instituted an action, in Ames, against Phillip for negligence. Will the court allow Doreen to assert and prove that Phillip was negligent? _____

128. Same basic fact pattern as the prior two questions. Now, assume that Phillip's suit against Doreen was actively litigated, with Phillip claiming that Doreen was negligent, and Doreen claiming that Phillip was contributorily negligent. The jury found in favor of Doreen. In response to two special interrogatories, the jury stated that Phillip was contributorily negligent and that Doreen was also negligent. (Remember that according to Ames law, even a small amount of contributory negligence bars recovery, even if the defendant was also negligent.) In a second Ames action, Doreen then sued Phillip for negligence. Will Doreen be collaterally estopped from denying her own contributory negligence in this second action?

_____

129. Penny and Dan, each driving a car, were involved in what at first appeared to be a minor fender bender. Penny sued Dan for negligence in municipal court for the town of Langdell, a small claims court whose jurisdiction is limited to cases involving less than $5,000. This court has quite informal procedures; for instance, there is no right to jury trial, and there are no formal rules for the admissibility of evidence. The jurisdiction applies common-law contributory negligence. Penny sought $2,000 for property damage suffered by her. The judge found that Dan drove negligently and that Penny did not; he awarded the full $2,000 to Penny.

Dan shortly thereafter developed back trouble, which in the opinion of his doctor, stemmed from the collision with Penny. Dan sued in a court of general jurisdiction (in the state where Langdell is located) for

$100,000 of compensatory damages for medical expense, and pain and suffering. Penny now asserts that Dan is collaterally estopped from either: (1) showing that Penny was negligent; or (2) denying that Dan himself was negligent. Which, if either, of these assertions is correct? _____

130. Perry sued Denise for negligence, arising out of an auto accident. Since Perry was seeking only a modest sum for actual medical expenses, Denise agreed to settle the case for a $2,000 payment to Perry. The settlement document recited these facts, and made no statement about what effect the settlement would have on any other litigation. A judgment was entered in accordance with this settlement. Shortly thereafter, Xavier, who was injured in the same accident, sued Denise. Putting aside the issue of whether the mutuality doctrine or Xavier's status as a stranger to the first action prevents him from using collateral estoppel, is Denise entitled to deny her negligence as part of her defense of the action brought by Xavier? _____

131. The Agriculture Department of the state of Ames bars any milk wholesaler from selling milk within Ames at a wholesale price of less than $1 per quart. Potter, an out-of-state wholesaler who wanted to sell milk at less than the $1 price, sued the Department of Agriculture in Ames state court. Potter's claim was that the price law discriminated against out-of-state commerce, in violation of the dormant Commerce Clause of the U.S. Constitution. The trial judge who heard the suit agreed with Potter's assertion. Potter, immediately after his victory, began selling milk at 90 cents per gallon. The Agriculture Department did not appeal. Instead, it actively defended a similar suit brought by Xavier, and lost that one at the trial level also. Subsequently, the Department appealed the loss to Xavier to the Ames Supreme Court (the highest court in the state), which found that the price floor was valid as a constitutional matter. Potter continued to sell 90 cent/gallon milk after the decision in Xavier's suit. The Agriculture Department then brought a suit to obtain an injunction against Potter's continuing to sell milk at less than $1 per gallon. Potter asserts that his victory in the earlier suit against him collaterally estops Ames from relitigating that issue with him now. Will Potter get the benefit of collateral estoppel on these facts? _____

132. Peter and Paul were neighbors who agreed to share a cab ride to the airport one night. The cab was driven by David. On a poorly lit city street, the cab smashed into an abandoned car (whose owner was never traced) and Peter and Paul were both seriously injured. Peter brought a suit against David in Ames state court. Peter's lawyer aggressively and expertly litigated the case, but the jury found in favor of David. Special interrogatories given to the jury made it clear that the jury simply believed that David used all due care, and could not have prevented the accident by ordinary precautions. After this verdict, Paul brought a suit against David in Ames state court, also alleging negligence relating to the same accident. Assuming that Paul has no evidence of David's negligence to put forth except evidence used by Peter in the first suit, may Paul nonetheless assert and prove that David drove negligently and caused the accident?

_____

133. Parker was a lifelong smoker. The only two brands he ever smoked were Acme and Baker. On average, he smoked two packs of Acme per day, and one pack of Baker. He contracted lung cancer, and then brought a products liability suit against Acme in Ames state court, asserting that Acme was responsible for his lung cancer. Acme presented evidence that Parker's lung cancer was of a type not usually associated with cigarette smoking, that it was of a type usually associated with asbestos exposure, and that Parker had worked around asbestos for many years. The case was tried to a judge, who concluded that Parker had failed to prove by a preponderance of the evidence that cigarette smoking (regardless of brand) contributed substantially to his getting lung cancer. Parker then brought a suit against Baker, again in Ames state court, making the same type of allegations he had made against Acme. Baker now argues that Parker should be collaterally estopped from asserting that his lung cancer was caused by any brand of cigarette.

Granting Baker's request will result in Parker's claim being dismissed before trial. Should Baker be permitted to use collateral estoppel to bar Parker from claiming that his lung cancer was caused by cigarettes? _____

134. Fred and Greg went one day to a diner operated by Dave. Fred ordered a bowl of clam chowder. The meal went uneventfully, and Fred and Greg left. One week later, Fred sued Dave for strict product liability, alleging that the chowder was dangerously defective, and caused Fred to undergo food poisoning. The suit was tried in a court of general jurisdiction of the state of Ames, and Fred sought $500 in damages. Dave defended by trying to show that Fred's illness was in fact the flu, but the judge found in Fred's favor, and awarded $500 in damages. Nowhere during the trial was Greg mentioned.

Shortly after Fred's verdict against Dave, Greg instituted a suit against Dave in Ames state court. His suit alleges that he drank some of Fred's order of clam chowder, and that he too was food poisoned. Greg's suit seeks $100,000 in damages, stating that while the hospital was treating him for food poisoning, it gave him a drug which caused him to go into convulsions, and that Dave must be liable for all of the resulting injury to Greg. At the trial, Greg seeks to collaterally estop Dave from denying that the clam chowder was dangerously defective (though he is willing to let Dave attempt to prove that the defectiveness was not the proximate cause of Greg's own injuries). Should Greg be allowed to use collateral estoppel in this manner? _____

135. A group of plaintiff lawyers decided that the time was ripe for bringing a serious strict product liability action against one or more of the leading cigarette companies. They singled out the Deadly Tobacco Co. as their primary defendant. They then advertised in consumer magazines for possible plaintiffs who had suffered cigarette-related illnesses. After interviewing dozens of potential plaintiffs, they finally settled upon Angie as their first plaintiff. They picked Angie because her case was especially appealing for several reasons: (1) she began smoking while she was still a minor, and did so in response to repeated television advertising by Deadly and other cigarette companies (this was before the ban on televised cigarette advertising); (2) she tried repeatedly to stop smoking through methods such as hypnosis, but appears to be simply addicted; and (3) she would make a very appealing witness, in part because she has the most serious of all cigarette-related illnesses, lung cancer. Angie's case was tried to a jury in Ames state court. After a long trial, the jury found that cigarettes produced by Deadly were dangerously defective, that Deadly did not issue adequate warnings, and that Deadly should be liable to Angie for $200,000 (a higher figure was rejected since the jury believed that some of the fault was Angie's).

After this victory, the same group of lawyers selected Betty as the next plaintiff. Her case also seems to be strong, though not as strong as Angie's for several reasons (e.g., she did not start smoking until she was an adult, and never saw televised cigarette advertising). Betty's lawyers now propose that Deadly be collaterally estopped from denying that its cigarettes are a dangerously defective product, and from denying that its warning labels (at least during the years that were at issue in Angie's suit) were inadequate. Should this use of collateral estoppel be allowed? _____

―――――――――

Answers

126. **No.** Doreen is *collaterally estopped* from relitigating the issue of Phillip's negligence in the accident. This is because: (1) the issue of Phillip's negligence was *fully and fairly litigated* in the first action; (2) that issue was *actually decided* (since the finding in favor of Phillip, under the substantive law of Ames, was inconsistent with any negligence on Phillip's part); and (3) the finding was *necessary* to the verdict (since if Phillip had been negligent, he could not have recovered under Ames' law on contributory negligence).

127. Yes. Collateral estoppel does not apply here. For collateral estoppel to apply to an issue, that issue must have been actually litigated at the first trial. When a default judgment is entered, no issue is deemed to have been litigated.

128. No. For collateral estoppel to apply to an issue, the disposition of that issue must have been ***necessary*** to the first verdict. Here, once the first jury found that Phillip was contributorily negligent, it didn't matter whether Doreen was negligent (since Phillip couldn't recover even if Doreen were negligent). Since Doreen's negligence was not a necessary component of the first verdict, she will be permitted to relitigate the issue of whether she was (contributorily) negligent during the second suit. See *Cambria v. Jeffery*, 29 N.E.2d 555 (Mass. 1940).

129. Neither. Where the first trial takes place in a court that not only has very limited jurisdiction but also very informal procedures, the findings of that court will generally ***not*** be given collateral estoppel effect. The reason is that the findings of such a court are viewed as insufficiently trustworthy to determine the outcome of a much larger later controversy. (The mere fact that a jury trial was not available would not by itself be enough to deprive the first court's findings of collateral estoppel effect, but the absence of rules of evidence probably would be.) See F,K&M, pp. 681-82.

130. Yes. A ***settlement*** normally has ***no collateral estoppel effect*** on other suits. Therefore, Xavier will not be able to treat the settlement as establishing Denise's negligence, even though a judgment against Denise was entered pursuant to that settlement. (Also, the rule against giving collateral estoppel effect to settlements can be viewed as a specific application of the general rule that collateral estoppel effect will only be given to issues that were litigated in the first action.)

131. No, probably. Collateral estoppel does not usually apply to "pure" issues of law, but does usually apply to "mixed" issues of law and fact, i.e., the application of a given legal principle to a particular fact situation. However, even if the first decision involves (as it does here) a mixed question of law and fact rather than a pure question of law, most courts believe that they have ***discretion*** to decline to apply collateral estoppel where there has been a ***significant change in legal principles*** between the first and second suits. Courts are especially likely to exercise that discretion where use of collateral estoppel would "impose on one of the parties a significant disadvantage, or confer on him a significant benefit, with respect to his competitors." Rest. 2d Judgments, §28, Comment c. Here, use of collateral estoppel would give Potter a perpetual advantage over his competitors (he can undercut their price slightly, and they cannot ever match him). The court is very unlikely to grant Potter, just because of the fortuity of his earlier victory, such a permanent advantage. This is especially true where, as here, the intervening decision was by a higher court than decided the original case in favor of the party now seeking collateral estoppel.

132. Yes. ***A stranger to the first action will never be bound***, either for claim preclusion or collateral estoppel purposes, by the results of that first suit. Peter and Paul were not privies, since their cab-sharing relationship does not fall within any of the traditional relationships recognized as constituting privity by the common law (e.g., master/servant, insurer/insured, etc.). Thus Paul is entitled to get his "day in court," even if that amounts to merely trotting out the same evidence as already used by Peter against David.

133. Yes. Until the 1960s, many courts might have automatically denied Baker's attempt to use collateral estoppel, on the now-discredited doctrine of mutuality (by which since Baker was a stranger to the first action, it could not claim the benefits of collateral estoppel in the second action). Today, virtually all jurisdictions reject the automatic principle of mutuality. Instead, most courts decide on a case-by-case basis whether to allow collateral estoppel use by a stranger. When it is the defendant in the second action who seeks to use collateral estoppel, and seeks to use it against a party who was a plaintiff in the first action, the case for allowing collateral estoppel is at its strongest. Thus here, Parker had the opportunity to fully and fairly litigate the causation issue during his first trial, and Baker is merely trying to use collateral estoppel as a shield rather than a sword in the second action. Nearly all courts would allow Baker to use collateral estoppel here. (This "use by the plaintiff in first action who is also plaintiff in second action" scenario matches the situation in *Bernhard v. Bank of America*, 122 P.2d 892 (Cal. 1942), the major case rejecting mutuality and allowing a stranger to use collateral estoppel.)

134. **No.** Greg is not only a stranger to the first action but is attempting an *offensive* use of collateral estoppel. (That is, he is a plaintiff in the second action.) Therefore, the court will do a case-by-case balancing (similar to that performed by the Supreme Court in *Parklane Hosiery v. Shore*) to decide whether to allow estoppel here. Two factors strongly militate against allowing estoppel here: (1) the first suit was for relatively little money ($500), so Dave did not have an incentive to litigate it to the hilt; and (2) the possibility of a later action by Greg (or anyone else relating to that particular serving of chowder) was quite unlikely from Dave's perspective, so Dave was not at all on notice that issues might be decided as to which collateral estoppel would later be possibly applicable. Together, these factors make it most unlikely that the court would estop Dave from attempting to disprove Greg's allegation of dangerously defective chowder.

135. **No.** Again, we have a situation where a stranger to the first action is proposing to make offensive use of collateral estoppel. Here, we have a stark case of the *"multiple plaintiff anomaly"* — if Deadly wins any given suit, it still has to completely relitigate the merits with the next plaintiff in line, yet under collateral estoppel one defeat by Deadly would cause it to lose against everyone later in line. The unfairness to Deadly from allowing collateral estoppel here is further exaggerated by: (1) the fact that the plaintiffs' lawyers have intentionally chosen the most appealing plaintiff to go first; and (2) the fact that the lawyers intentionally declined to join the additional victims as plaintiffs in the first suit, preferring to have them "wait in the wings." Therefore, it is unlikely that Deadly will be deprived of its chance to relitigate the issue of whether its cigarettes are dangerously defective or its warnings inadequate.

IV. FULL FAITH AND CREDIT

A. Scope: So far, we have generally assumed that both suits take place in the same jurisdiction. We turn now to the special problems that arise when the two suits occur in different jurisdictions. There may be two different states involved, or a state court and a federal court. In either situation, the principle generally referred to as *"full faith and credit"* comes into play.

B. Effect: The Full Faith and Credit clause of the U.S. Constitution (Art. IV, §1) requires each state to give to the judgment of any other state *the same effect that that judgment would have in the state which rendered it*. (A statute, 28 U.S.C. §1738, requires the federal courts to give Full Faith and Credit to state court decisions. See *infra*, p. 445.)

1. **Utility:** This provision is often applicable where a plaintiff has won a judgment in State X, but can find no property in X on which to levy. If he can locate property belonging to the defendant in State Y, he may levy on it by bringing a suit in Y "on the judgment". The courts of Y must accept this judgment at face value, and may not reconsider any issues which it concluded.

2. **Collateral attack on jurisdiction:** The court in which enforcement of the judgment is sought may examine one aspect of the original judgment: *jurisdiction* (either personal or

subject matter), ***provided that the jurisdictional question was not litigated or waived*** in the first action. See the fuller discussion of collateral attack on jurisdiction, *supra*, pp. 95, 121.

    a. Waiver: The jurisdictional question will be held to be ***waived*** if the defendant contests on the merits (as opposed to taking a default judgment), and does not raise the issue of jurisdiction. Thus in *Chicot County Drainage District v. Baxter State Bank*, 308 U.S. 371 (1940), parties to an action were held to have waived their objection to the fact that the court's eventual judgment was made under a federal statute subsequently determined unconstitutional; they were not permitted to collaterally attack the judgment.

C. Misinterpretation of another state's law: State A must give Full Faith and Credit to an adjudication of State B, even if that judgment was based on a ***misinterpretation of the laws of State A.***

D. No duty to decisions of other countries: There is no constitutional requirement that the judgments of ***other nations*** be accorded Full Faith and Credit. The federal courts, and most state courts, will give Full Faith and Credit to the adjudications of ***common-law countries***. As to ***civil law nations***, practice varies.

    1. *Hilton v. Guyot:* In *Hilton v. Guyot*, 159 U.S. 113 (1895), the Supreme Court declined to give credit to a French judgment, on the grounds that the French courts did not give credit to our judgments.

E. Full Faith and Credit to *res judicata effect:* A state must give to the judgment of any other state at least the ***res judicata effect*** that that judgment would have in the state of its rendition.

    Example: A court of State A renders Judgment I, which by the laws of State A would act as a bar to certain subsequent actions. Action II, which is then brought in State B, would, if brought in State A, be barred by Judgment I.

    Even if Action II would not have been barred by Judgment I had both been brought in State B, Action II must nonetheless be barred. In other words, Full Faith and Credit must be given to the *res judicata* effects of a judgment rendered by a sister state — a judgment must be given the same effect, with respect to *res judicata*, that it would have in the state of its rendition.

    1. Greater effect: Some courts have given a ***greater*** effect to another state's judgment than it would have in that other state. Thus in *Hart v. American Airlines*, 304 N.Y.S.2d 810 (N.Y. Sup. Ct. 1969), the court gave collateral estoppel effect to a Texas court's finding of the defendant airline's liability, even though Texas itself, since it required mutuality of estoppel, would not have given the earlier judgment such effect. The giving of greater effect to the first state's judgment does not violate the Full Faith and Credit clause, since that clause merely requires that a court give to a sister court's judgement ***at least*** the same effect it would have in the sister state, not that it be given no greater effect.

F. Federal suit follows state suit: Suppose that the first judgment is in a ***state*** court and the second one is in a ***federal*** court. Several Supreme Court decisions have established that, unless Congress has explicitly or implicitly provided otherwise in a particular context, ***the federal***

court must grant the state court judgment the same res judicata effect it would have in that state.

1. **§1738:** The general rule requiring federal courts to give state court judgments Full Faith and Credit is set forth in 28 U.S.C. §1738, which provides that "The records and judicial proceedings of any court [of] any State ... shall have the same full faith and credit in every court within the United States ... as they have by law or usage in the courts of [the] State ... from which they are taken." Since every federal court is a "court within the United States," the federal courts are bound by this statute to give state court judgments the same effect (including *res judicata*) as the state itself would give them. (But the statute does not say anything about the effect in state court of an earlier federal court judgment — as to this problem, see *infra*, p. 446.)

2. **Partial repeal by Congress:** Since §1738 is a statute rather than a constitutional principle, it is, of course, subject to repeal by Congress. Any statute may be partially repealed, and this partial repeal may be implied as well as express. Therefore, whenever Congress creates a new federal statutory right, it could be argued that this new federal statute implicitly repeals §1738 with respect to any state court determination relevant to the federal right; if this argument were accepted, the result would be that a federal court need not grant to a prior state court judgment the *res judicata* effect of that judgment if doing so would affect a federal right.

3. **View rejected:** But the Supreme Court has held that this argument will normally fail — unless Congress has made it *quite clear* that it wishes to deny the state court judgment *res judicata* effect in the federal court proceeding, the federal court must give the state court judgment the ***same preclusive effect it would have in the state which rendered it.***

    a. ***Allen v. McCurry:*** Thus in *Allen v. McCurry*, 449 U.S. 90 (1980), the Court held that Congress did not intend a partial repeal of §1738 when it enacted 42 U.S.C. §1983, a post-Civil War statute giving a person the right to bring a federal suit for damages against anyone who violates his constitutional rights "under color of" state law. Therefore, a federal court hearing a §1983 action must give to any prior state court judgment the same claim preclusive and collateral estoppel effect as that judgment would have had in the state where it was issued.

4. **Administrative agency findings:** What about state ***administrative agency*** determinations? Must the federal court give these administrative findings the same preclusive effect they would have in the state courts? Section 1738 does not directly require this result, since that section requires the federal courts to give full faith and credit to "judicial proceedings" of any state "court," with no mention of administrative decisions. But the Supreme Court has held that as a matter of federal common law, the ***same result*** should normally occur where a state administrative agency has made a judicial-type decision. See *University of Tennessee v. Elliott*, 478 U.S. 788 (1986), holding that "when a state agency acting in a judicial capacity ... resolves disputed issues of fact properly before it which the parties have had an adequate opportunity to litigate, federal courts must give the agency's fact finding the same preclusive effect to which it would be entitled in the State's courts."

5. **Claim preclusion:** *Allen* and *Elliott* involved collateral estoppel. But the Supreme Court has held that state ***bar and merger*** (i.e., claim preclusion) rules must similarly be applied

in subsequent federal actions unless Congress has affirmatively indicated in creating the federal right that state bar and merger rules are to be ignored. See *Migra v. Warren City Bd. of Ed.*, 465 U.S. 75 (1984).

6. **May not give greater effect to judgment:** Suppose, as we have been doing, that a state suit is followed by a federal suit; suppose further that the facts of the second suit are such that the state court would *not* give preclusive effect to its own earlier judgment, but that general federal principles *would* dictate a preclusive effect. It is now clear that the federal court *may not give preclusive effect* to the prior state court judgment. That is, 28 U.S.C §1738 requires that the federal court treat the state court judgment in the same way as would the state court that rendered it.

   a. **Illustration:** For instance, if the initial state judgment comes from a state that does not allow non-mutual offensive use of collateral estoppel, the federal court hearing the second suit *may not apply such collateral estoppel*, even if the situation is one which under the Supreme Court's *Parklane Hosiery* ruling (*supra*, p. 436) collateral estoppel would be appropriate.

G. **State suit follows federal suit:** Suppose now that the *federal* suit comes *first*, and the *state* suit *second*. As the result of an important 2001 decision, the rule is that where the first decision is by a federal court sitting in *diversity*, the state court in the second suit must give to the earlier federal judgment *the same preclusive effect as such a judgment would have been given by the courts of the state where the first (federal) court sat.* For instance, if the first judgment is by a California federal district court and the second suit is in Maryland state court, the Maryland Court must give to the first judgment the same effect as that judgment would have in the California state-court system. See *Semtek Int'l Inc. v. Lockheed Martin Corp.*, 531 U.S. 497 (2001).

1. **Facts:** The facts of *Semtek* are like an elaborate law school hypothetical.

   a. **Suit 1:** P sued D in California state court on breach-of-contract and other state-law grounds. Because there was diversity, D removed to California federal district court. The federal court properly dismissed the suit on statute-of-limitations grounds, because the suit was barred by California's two-year statute. (See *supra*, p. 261, for an explanation of why a federal court sitting diversity must follow the statute of limitations law of the forum state.) The federal court described its dismissal as being "on the merits."[1]

   b. **Suit 2:** P then filed the same claims in Maryland state court. (The Maryland statute of limitations on the claims hadn't yet expired.) The Maryland trial court dismissed the suit on *res judicata* grounds. The Maryland appeals court affirmed, on the theory that even though California might not have given claim-preclusive effect to a decision by one of its own courts on statute-of-limitations grounds, the *res judicata* effects of a

---

1. Had the suit not been removed, and had the dismissal on statute-of-limitations grounds been made by the California courts, P would not have been prevented from re-filing the suit in some other state that had an unexpired statute. That's because California follows the traditional state-law rule that a dismissal on statute-of-limitations grounds merely bars the *remedy*, and does not extinguish the *substantive right*, so the case can then be brought in a state with an unexpired statute. In other words, in California as in most states, a dismissal on statute-of-limitations grounds has no claim-preclusive effect.

federal diversity judgment is a matter of federal law, and under federal law (as represented by the FRCP 41(b)), dismissals that are on the merits are claim-preclusive.

2. **Supreme Court disagrees:** The Supreme Court, in a unanimous decision, disagreed with both the analysis of and the results reached by the Maryland courts. The Court held that: (1) the claim-preclusive effects of a federal diversity judgment are a matter of ***federal common law***; and (2) the Court was hereby deciding that that federal common law should ***apply the preclusion law of the forum state***, i.e., the state where the federal court that issued the judgment sat (California). The Court took a number of steps to get to this outcome, which are worth reviewing in detail:

   a. **FRCP 41(b) doesn't control:** The Supreme Court first concluded that, contrary to D's assertion, the case was ***not*** governed by FRCP 41(b).

      i. **D's contention:** D contended that the outcome of the case should be determined by FRCP 41(b). 41(b) (see *supra*, p. 287) says that unless the dismissing court "states otherwise," any dismissal (other than for lack of jurisdiction, for improper venue, or for failure to join a party under Rule 19) "operates as an ***adjudication on the merits***." It was clear that the federal court sitting in diversity here had not otherwise specified, so FRCP 41(b) made the dismissal based on statute-of-limitations grounds a dismissal that was "on the merits." According to D, since the dismissal was on the merits, the dismissal was entitled to preclusive effect not only in federal court but in any state court.

      ii. **Contention rejected:** But the Supreme Court disagreed with this last argument. It was simply not true, the Court said, that merely because 41(b) said that the judgment was "on the merits," the judgment was necessarily entitled to claim-preclusive effect in other jurisdictions. Rule 41(b) was merely a "default rule" governing the federal system, i.e., a way of determining whether the plaintiff could refile in the *same federal court* if the prior dismissal was silent about whether it was on the merits or not. 41(b) was *not* a rule that was ever intended to govern what claim-preclusive effect the dismissal would have in some other court, such as a state court.

         (1) **Forum-shopping problem:** Furthermore, the Court said, D's interpretation would ***encourage forum shopping:*** any defendant sued in a state like California (i.e., a state that follows the standard approach of not giving claim-preclusive effects to dismissals on statute-of-limitations grounds)[2] would have an incentive to remove to federal court, obtain a Rule 41(b) dismissal, and be immunized from a refiling of the suit in any state with an unexpired statute. Thus the defendant would have obtained through removal followed by dismissal something (immunity in all other jurisdictions) that it could not have obtained by letting the case remain in the state court where filed. This would be a clear instance of successful forum-shopping.

   b. **Federal common-law applies:** Instead, the Court held, the claim-preclusive effect of a dismissal by a federal court sitting in diversity should be determined as a matter of

---

2. See the prior footnote.

"federal common law," i.e., law as decided by the judges of the federal judiciary (in this case, the Supreme Court). (See *supra*, p. 274, for more about "federal common law.")

c. **Applies law of forum state:**   That still left the Court with the issue of what the *content* of federal common law on this issue should be. Here, the Court decided that the federal common-law rule should be that the *claim-preclusive effect of the forum state* (i.e., the state where the federal diversity court sat) *applies*. The Court acknowledged that there were pros and cons to this approach:

   i. **Not a uniform rule:**   It was something of a negative that this approach would *fail* to yield a *single nationwide rule* about whether Rule 41(b) dismissals on the merits do or do not have claim-preclusive effect. But this was not a serious problem: since state rather than federal substantive law was at issue, "there is no need for uniform federal rule."

   ii. **Discourage forum-shopping:**   On the other hand, the Court noted, applying the claim-preclusion rule of the forum state would have the major positive effect of *discouraging forum shopping*: the Court's solution guaranteed that a suit dismissed after it been removed to federal court would have the *same claim-preclusive effect as if it had been left in the state court* where it was originally filed.

   iii. **Can decline to apply state rule where federal interests are strong:**   But the Court left itself an escape hatch: "This federal reference to state law will *not obtain*, of course, in situations in which the *state law is incompatible with the federal interests.*" But in the statute of limitations context, there was no incompatibility of interests: "There is no conceivable federal interest in giving [the California court's] time bar more effect in other courts than the California courts themselves would impose."

d. **P wins:**   Thus P won the war: since the California courts, following the traditional state-court approach, wouldn't expect to have their dismissal on statute-of-limitations grounds prevent P from bringing suit in some other state with a not-yet-expired statute, Maryland must follow the same approach, and allow the refiled suit to go forward there.

3. **Summary:**   So here's what we know about claim preclusion when Suit 1 is in federal court and Suit 2 is in a state court:

a. **Diversity:**   Where the claim is based on *diversity*, we know from *Semtek* that, as a matter of federal common law, the federal courts choose to have their judgment have the same claim-preclusive effect as it would have had if it had been rendered by the state court of the state where the federal court sits: if and only if the state court would give its judgment claim-preclusive effect are other federal courts, and other state courts, required (or permitted) to do the same.

   Example: Suit 1 is a diversity action brought in federal district court for the Northern District of Illinois. The court dismisses the action for reason X. Suit 2, based on the same claim, is filed in Texas state court. When the Texas court decides whether res judicata applies, it must analyze the matter as follows: (1) If the Illinois state courts would give claim-preclusive effect to a prior Illinois-court dismissal for reason X, then the Texas court must do the same, and refuse to hear the suit; (2) If the Illinois state courts would *not* give (or expect other courts to give) claim-preclusive effect to a prior Illinois dismissal for reason X, then the Texas court not only need not, but may not, give claim-preclusive effect to that dismissal. (The same analysis would be used if Suit 2 was filed in federal district court for some other district other than the Northern District of Illinois.)

b. **Federal question:** Where the claim is based on a ***federal question***, pre-*Semtek* law makes it clear that here, too, the federal courts apply federal common law to determine the preclusive effect that their judgment should have. But in this situation, there is no "forum state" court whose law should be applied. Instead, the federal courts will develop their own case-by-case policies about when their judgment should have preclusive effects (and later state courts will be required to give the same preclusive effect if a case relating to that federal-question claim is brought in state court).

Quiz Yourself on
FULL FAITH AND CREDIT

136. In the courts of the state of Ames, Abel sued Baker for negligence arising out of an automobile accident. The judge concluded that Baker was negligent, and entered judgment in favor of Abel. Shortly thereafter, Conroy sued Baker for negligence arising out of the same auto accident; this suit is taking place in the courts of the state of Bates. The Ames Supreme Court allows broad offensive use of collateral estoppel, and would allow Conroy to make use of collateral estoppel against Baker on the issue of Baker's negligence in the accident, if Conroy's suit had been filed in Ames. The Supreme Court of Bates, by contrast, is a more old-fashioned jurisdiction which almost never allows offensive use of collateral estoppel by a stranger to the first action. Conroy seeks to collaterally estop Baker from denying Baker's negligence in the accident.

    (a) Should Conroy be given the benefits of collateral estoppel here? _____

    (b) Is the answer left to the court's discretion, or is it imposed by some non-discretionary requirement? _____

137. Same basic fact pattern as prior question. Now, however, assume that the second action (by Conroy) was filed not in the state courts of Bates, but rather, in federal district court for the District of Bates. Should/must the federal judge give Conroy the benefit of collateral estoppel against Baker? _____

138. Same basic fact pattern as prior two questions. Now, however, assume that the first suit is in federal court for the District of Ames (sitting in diversity), and the second suit is in the state court of Bates. Again, assume that the Ames courts allow broad use of collateral estoppel, and would therefore allow Conroy to use collateral estoppel against Baker on the issue of Baker's negligence if Conroy's suit was filed in Ames. Must the state court of Bates allow Conroy to use collateral estoppel? _____

Answers

136. (a) Yes.

(b) The answer is required by the Full Faith and Credit Clause of the U.S. Constitution. The Full Faith and Credit Clause of the U.S. Constitution (Article IV, Section 1) requires each state to give to the judgment of any other state the same effect that that judgment would have in the state which rendered it. This requirement extends to the ***res judicata effect*** of the first state court's judgment. Here, therefore, Bates must give to the judgment of the Ames court the same effect that the Ames court system would give to that prior judgment. Since Ames would grant preclusive effect to the judgment against Baker (i.e., Ames would let Conroy collaterally estop Baker), Bates must do the same. This is true even though the Bates courts, if left to their own devices, would prefer not to give collateral estoppel effect to the judgment against Baker.

137. Yes, the federal judge must do so. A federal statute, 28 U.S.C. §1738, requires federal courts to give state court judgments the same effect (including res judicata effect) as the state itself would give them. Except in a very few instances where later, more specific, congressional statutes indicate that Congress does not want the federal courts to have to honor the preclusive effect of a state court judgment, the federal court is bound by §1738 to give the state court judgment the same effect the state itself would give it. Therefore, since no special congressional statute is at issue here, the federal judge must grant collateral estoppel against Baker solely on the grounds that the Ames court would do so.

138. Yes. No congressional statute, and no specific constitutional provision, requires the state court to follow the prior federal judgment's preclusive effect. However, *Semtek v. Lockheed Martin* (*supra*, p. 446) requires the Bates state court to apply the same rule of preclusion as would be applied by the Ames courts (which are the courts of the state where the federal diversity court that rendered the first judgment sits). Since the Ames courts would allow Conroy to make offensive use of collateral estoppel against Baker on this issue if the first judgment had been rendered by an Ames state court, the courts of Bates must allow that same use.

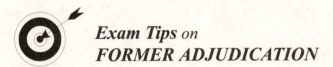

Exam Tips *on* FORMER ADJUDICATION

You will almost always know when you have a Former Adjudication problem, because the fact pattern will have to clue you in to the existence of two suits, one of which has already resulted in a judgment. The trick, of course, is to determine what effect the first judgment should have on the second suit.

☛ Make sure to distinguish between ***claim preclusion*** (sometimes called by the ambiguous phrase "res judicata," which you should avoid unless your professor uses it, or by the preferable terms ***"merger"*** and ***"bar"***) and ***issue preclusion*** (usually called ***"collateral estoppel,"*** which is the preferable phrase to use on exams). [416]

☞ Where the first suit was between the ***same parties*** (or their privies) as the second suit, and involved the same ***"claim,"*** you're interested in ***claim preclusion***. If you find that the requirements for claim preclusion have been met, the case is over — the claim in the second suit is ***"merged"*** into the earlier judgment (if P in the second suit won the first suit), and it's ***"barred"*** by the earlier judgment (if P in the second suit lost the first suit).

☞ Where the second suit involves at least one ***different party*** than the first suit, *or* where you conclude that the second suit involves a ***different "claim"*** than the first suit, then you're interested in issue preclusion / ***collateral estoppel*** (c.e.) If c.e. applies, it resolves a ***particular issue***, but not necessarily the whole claim.

☞ Often, you'll want to examine the possibility of claim preclusion first, then go on to issue preclusion / c.e. if the requirements for claim preclusion aren't satisfied.

☛ For ***claim preclusion***, here are the major sub-issues [417]:

☞ One tip-off for a claim-preclusion problem is ***"claim splitting."*** [418] Typically, P has an accident, and sues in Suit 1 for ***property damage***, and then in Suit 2 sues the same defendant for ***personal injuries*** (or vice versa). In most states, this doesn't work — since both types of damages were suffered in the same incident, they're deemed to be a single "claim." If P won in the first suit, say his second claim is "merged" into the first; if P lost the first suit, say he's now "barred."

☞ Another situation involving claim splitting is the compulsory counterclaim context. When D in Suit 1 fails to assert what is (under the applicable federal or state procedural rules) a compulsory counterclaim, then the mechanism by which D loses the right to bring the claim later is the doctrine of merger and bar.

☞ Many questions involve a person who was ***not a party*** to the first action, but is very cloesly related, somehow, to a person who was a party. Remember that as a general rule, someone who ***wasn't a party*** to the first suit ***can't be bound*** by the result. [423]

☞ And remember that at least in federal courts, there's ***no*** general doctrine of ***"virtual representation"*** by which P1 (plaintiff in the first suit) will be found to be so close to P2 (plaintiff in the second suit) that P2 will be bound because P1 "virtually represented" P2 in the first suit. So, for instance, the fact that P1 and P2 are friends, have a shared interest in the subject matter, and are represented by the same lawyer against the same defendant, won't be enough to make P2 be bound by the result in P1's suit if P2 wasn't a named party to it. [423]

☞ But there are a few ***exceptions*** to the "no binding of strangers" rule. That is, occasionally two people will be so legally-intertwined (i.e., in ***"privity"*** with each other) that one person's presence in the first suit *will* bind the other, even though the latter wasn't a party. That's true where the two are indemnitor-and-indemnitee, or principal-and-agent. [424]

Example: D1 is an ***employee*** charged with a tort, and D2 is D1's ***employer*** (liable for D1's torts under *respondeat superior*). Here, D1 and D2 are "in privity" (D2's liability derives from D1's), so D2 is bound if D1 loses the first suit. (But the converse probably does *not* involve privity — if the employer is sued first, the employee is probably *not* bound as a privy.)

☛ For ***collateral estoppel*** (c.e.), here are the main things to look for [427-439]:

☞ Remember that c.e. applies only to issues that were ***actually litigated and decided*** in the first suit. Anytime you see a fact pattern that involves two suits, look for an issue decided in the first suit that may be relevant to the second suit, and determine whether c.e. may apply to compel the second court to use the first court's finding on that issue.

☞ Because the issue must have been actually litigated and decided, if the first suit ended in a **default judgment**, it has **no** c.e. effect on the absent defendant.

☞ The issue must also have been **necessary to the outcome** of the first suit. So if the first suit would have come out the same way even if the issue had not been decided at all, or decided differently, then c.e. won't apply to that issue. [429]

☞ C.e. questions often involve "who can be **bound**." [433-439] There are two main points to remember:

☞ A true **stranger** to the first action can **never be bound** by c.e., no matter how similar the fact issue, and even if the party who won in the first suit on the issue is now present in the second suit.

☞ However, as with claim preclusion, if a party in the second suit is found to be in **privity** with a party in the first suit, then the former can be bound by the earlier finding. *Example:* If Employee loses in the first suit on an issue of whether he behaved negligently while on the job, Employer will be bound in a second suit because he is in privity with Employee.

☞ C.e. questions also often involve "who can **benefit**" from c.e. Of course, one who was a party to the first action can benefit from c.e. But the key issue — which seems to surface in most c.e. fact patterns —is whether a true **stranger** to the first action can benefit from factual findings made there. Here are the key sub-issues/rules:

☞ Nearly all courts today have **abandoned** the rule of **mutuality**, i.e., the old blanket rule that a stranger to the first action could never benefit from c.e. So when your fact pattern involves a stranger trying to use c.e., you should preface your discussion with something like "Assuming that the jurisdiction follows the majority approach of abandoning mutuality, X may be able to benefit from c.e. …"

☞ Always distinguish between **"offensive"** and **"defensive"** use of c.e., and state which kind of use is proposed in your fact pattern. "Offensive" means use by a first-action-stranger who is the *plaintiff* in the second action; "defensive" means use by one who is a *defendant* in the second action. Remember that courts are **more willing to allow "defensive" use** (but they do sometimes allow offensive use as well).

☞ If the facts involve offensive c.e., check whether P in the second suit **"hung back,"** i.e., declined to join the first suit even though he had a good opportunity to do so. If so, P is less likely to be allowed to use c.e., on fairness and judicial-efficiency grounds.

☞ Determine whether the person to be bound had an **incentive to litigate** the issue the first time. A key aspect is whether that person could reasonably have **foreseen that the second suit would come along** — the less foreseeable, the less incentive to litigate, and the less likely the second court is to allow c.e. Also, check whether the first suit was in a court of **limited jurisdiction**, which would make it less likely that the party to be bound had the requisite incentive to litigate fully. [437]

☞ Check whether the facts involve a danger of the *"multiple plaintiff anomaly"* (a mass tort in which each P sues in turn; once D is found liable in one, c.e. would mean D would lose all subsequent suits.) In this m.p.a. situation, courts usually hold that c.e. is unfair. [437]

☛ Finally, look for *Full Faith & Credit* (FF&C) issues [443-449]:

☞ Any time you have a *judgment* in Suit 1, and Suit 2 takes place in a *different jurisdiction* than Suit 1, you have a potential FF&C issue. You need to ask, "Is the court in Suit 2 bound to follow the judgment issued in Suit 1?"

☞ If Suit 1 and Suit 2 were both in *state* courts, the FF&C clause of the *U.S. Constitution* requires that the Suit 2 court give to the Suit 1 judgment the same effect that that judgment would have in the state that decided it. So State 2 can't allow re-litigation of any factual or legal issues, even if the substantive law of State 2 would have produced a completely different result. Also, State 2 must *"enforce"* the State 1 judgment — it must let the winner of the State 1 judgment seize the loser's State 2 assets without any re-litigation of the merits.

☞ If Suit 1 is in state court and Suit 2 in federal court (or vice versa), FF&C principles similarly require the second court to honor the first court's judgment.

☞ The key exception — frequently tested — is that the second court can reconsider whether the first court had *jurisdiction* (either personal or subject matter), if the jurisdiction issue was *not litigated or waived* in the first suit. This is *"collateral attack."*

☞ FF&C means that the *res judicata* effect of the earlier judgment must also be enforced by the second jurisdiction. So if State 1 would allow, say, offensive use of c.e. by a stranger, State 2 must do the same. (If Suit 1 is in federal court sitting in diversity and Suit 2 is in state court, the state court must give the first judgment the same effect it would have in the court of the state where the federal court that decided Suit 1 sat. [*Semtek v. Lockheed Martin*])

ESSAY EXAM
QUESTIONS AND ANSWERS

The following questions were asked on Civil Procedure Examinations given at Harvard Law School; we have slightly edited some of them. The sample answers are intended to show one possible approach to each question. Page references are to the main text of the outline.

QUESTION 1: Muenster Airways, Inc., is a small airline flying regularly scheduled flights between points in New Jersey, New York, and New England. It is incorporated in New Jersey and has its principal place of business there. Amos Stilton, a passenger on the ill-fated flight described below, is a citizen of Ames, a small midwestern state located between Indiana and Illinois.

In December 2007, Muenster conducted an advertising campaign in Ames and other midwestern states offering a special flying tour of New England in the spring of 2008, featuring stopovers in Tiverton, R.I., Worcester, Mass., and White River Junction, Vermont. Stilton, attracted by the advertisement, bought a round-trip ticket from an independent travel agent in Ames and was put into a group of Ames travelers who would be leaving on the tour on April 1 from Ames City. The agent, after selling the ticket, immediately listed Stilton (care of his Ames address), on Muenster's reservation system as a passenger for the upcoming trip. Transportation to Newark, N.J., the starting point of the tour, was provided to Stilton and other tour participants by another airline.

Stilton and his fellow travelers arrived in Newark on the appointed day and boarded a Muenster plane for Tiverton, but the plane was forced to make an emergency landing in Bridgeport, Conn., and although no passengers were killed, many (including Stilton) were seriously injured.

One of the passengers, Charlene Cheddar, brought a diversity action for $125,000 damages against Muenster in a New Jersey federal court. The case went to trial and the jury found Muenster liable but awarded only $500 to Cheddar, apparently rejecting her claim of serious injury. No appeal was filed.

Stilton has now brought a diversity action of his own against Muenster in an Ames federal court, seeking $100,000 damages. The only portion of the Ames long-arm statute that might plausibly give *in personam* jurisdiction over Muenster in a state-court action is §103(a)(1). Section 103(a)(1) confers on the Ames state courts personal jurisdiction over "any person who acts directly, or by an agent, with respect to a cause of action arising from the person's transacting of any business in this state." Stilton made service of process on Muenster by registered mail (without any acknowledgement-of-service or request-for-waiver-of-service form enclosed) at Muenster's home office in New Jersey; this form of service on out-of-state defendants is authorized by the Ames long-arm.

Stilton, in addition to relying on §103(a)(1) of the Ames long-arm, has sought to establish jurisdiction in the Ames federal court by attachment of an airplane owned by Muenster and currently under two-year lease to Gorgonzola Airways, a company doing business solely in Ames, at an annual rental of $20,000. The Ames long-arm says nothing about the validity of jurisdiction based on such attachments.

A. What are the arguments for and against Muenster's motion to dismiss the action in its entirety for lack of jurisdiction? How should the motion be decided?

B. Assume that all motions addressed to jurisdiction are denied and that Stilton, relying on the New Jersey decision, moves for summary judgment on the issue of liability. Assume that the issue of what effect the New Jersey decision should have on future suits is one of first impression in both the New Jersey state courts and in the federal system. What decision should be made on the motion and why?

QUESTION 2: Staley's Tire Store, Inc., a retail outfit located just across the Rancid River in Langdell City, Langdell, until recently was a franchise dealer for the Plastic Tire Company, Inc., a manufacturer whose principal place of business is here in Ames. Staley's just recently decided to carry a line of tires manufactured by our client, Vinyl Tire Company, Inc., whose plant is also located here in Ames. Staley's has just brought suit under the federal antitrust laws against Plastic in the Langdell federal court, alleging that its franchise agreement with Plastic violated those laws and seeking rescission and damages. Plastic has filed an answer denying any violation of the antitrust laws, and has counterclaimed for damages for breach of the franchise agreement. Plastic has sought to add our client, Vinyl, as a party to the counter-claim, alleging that Vinyl induced the breach. Service of process was made by a federal marshal at Vinyl's home office here in Ames City. Can Vinyl be forced to litigate this case in Langdell, or is there some way we can have the action against it dismissed?

QUESTION 3: Our client, William Byer, entered an agreement with Stanley Cellar to purchase a parcel of Ames land from Cellar for $500,000. A down payment of $100,000 has been made by Byer and the trans-fer was to occur on May 1. Byer claims that he was induced to enter the contract by Cellar's fraud, and when Cellar refused to call the deal off, Byer brought suit in Ames federal court, on April 1, for cancella-tion of the contract and refund of the down payment. (Byer and Cellar are of diverse citizenship). Last week, after getting an extension of time to file his answer, Cellar interposed an answer denying the alleged fraud and counterclaiming for the remainder owing on the contract. He has demanded a jury on all issues triable as of right by a jury. So far as I can tell, the only contested issue in the case is the alleged fraud of Cellar. Does Cellar have a jury trial right on that issue?

QUESTION 4: Our client, Albert Hill, is suing Peter Dale in the Ames federal court for fraud under the federal securities acts. At the trial, there was evidence both ways on the fraud issue, although unfortunately one of our key witnesses was unable to testify because of illness. The judge's charge to the jury, in my view, imposed too heavy a burden of proof on the plaintiff but the jury still came in with a verdict for Hill, awarding substantial damages. After entry of judgment, Dale moved for judgment as a matter of law and, in the alternative, for a new trial, and both motions were denied. I understand that Dale plans to appeal in order to renew two arguments that were raised and rejected in the trial court — (1) that the federal securi-ties acts do not apply to the transaction in controversy and (2) that the evidence was insufficient to take the case to the jury. What procedural steps, if any, should we take at this point? Dale apparently had moved for judgment as a matter of law before the case went to the jury.

QUESTION 5: We are defending a personal injury case and our client has been asked the following Rule 33 interrogatory. "Please give the name and address of all doctors whom you or your attorney have retained, specially employed, or informally consulted concerning the damage aspects of this action." The case is one in which the plaintiff is admittedly totally and permanently disabled by something called Pert's Disease. The issue is whether this condition is causally connected with the blow on the head the plaintiff received as a result of the defendant's alleged negligence. Our medical witness, whose report was made available to plaintiff's counsel two months ago, insists that Pert's Disease cannot be caused or aggravated by trauma and that plaintiff cannot possibly find an expert to support such an absurd claim. Last week I met Dr. Francis Pert, whose research led to the discovery of the disease that bears his name, at a cocktail party. I mentioned the pending lawsuit and asked whether our doctor's opinion was sound. Dr. Pert said that it reflected the general view and was confirmed by Dr. Pert's own published writings. He then added: "But I can tell you, in confidence of course, that my recent research, not yet published, convinces me that the disease can be precipitated by a blow such as you describe in this case." Dr. Pert's distaste for court proceedings is so great that he invariably refuses to appear as an expert witness. How should we answer the interrogatory consistently with the Federal Rules and our sense of professionalism?

QUESTION 6: The State of Ames has enacted the following statute: "No person engaged in the business of a contractor shall be permitted to present any judicial demand before any court of this state for the col-lection of compensation for performance of any act for which a license is required by the law of this state without alleging and proving that he was a duly licensed contractor at all times during the performance of such act." Dauntless Construction Co. is a Thayer corporation engaged in the business of installation and construction of telephone facilities. Dauntless contracted with Pacific Telephone Co., an Ames corporation, to construct certain facilities and install them in Ames. This was a contract for performance of which a license was required by Ames law. Dauntless was a duly licensed contractor in Thayer but neglected to obtain a license in Ames, apparently through ignorance of the Ames requirement. A dispute arose between the parties during the performance of the contract, and Pacific brought an action against Dauntless in the Ames Superior Court for breach of contract. Proper service of process was made. Dauntless removed the action to the U.S. District Court for Ames and filed an answer denying plaintiff's allegations, setting up certain affirmative defenses, and also asserted a counterclaim claiming damages for misrepresentation in the negotiation of the contract and breach of various conditions therein. Pacific has moved to dismiss the counterclaim because of noncompliance with the Ames licensing statute. There is an Ames decision, *McCord v. Dean Waterworks Co.*, 321 Ames 400 (1972), holding that an unlicensed contractor cannot maintain a counterclaim arising out of a contract performed in Ames. You are the law clerk to the federal judge who is about to hear the motion. He has asked you for a memorandum to aid him in dealing with the problem. Prepare the memorandum.

QUESTION 7: Your client, Peripheral Products, Inc., brought a treble damage action against Devious Corp., in the U.S. District Court for Ames under the Clayton Act for alleged antitrust violations. The defendant's answer included a defense based on the four-year statute of limitations provided by Congress for actions arising under the antitrust laws. After a hearing on a motion for summary judgment based on that defense, the court entered this order: "It is ordered, adjudged and decreed that the defendant's motion for summary judgment be, and the same hereby is, granted with costs to be taxed." Peripheral has now brought another action in the Ames Superior Court, alleging virtually the same facts and claiming damages for unfair competition. The Ames statute of limitations allowing six years for such actions has not yet expired. Devious has pleaded *res judicata*. Prepare a memorandum on the problem.

ANSWERS

SAMPLE ANSWER TO QUESTION 1:

Part A: The most difficult jurisdictional questions in this case relate to jurisdiction over the parties. However, there are two preliminary subject matter jurisdictional issues which will be dealt with first: (1) Is there diversity? and (2) Is the amount in controversy requirement met?

(1) *Diversity:* Under 28 USC §1332(c), Muenster is a citizen of New Jersey, since that state is both the state of incorporation and the principal place of business. Stilton is a citizen of Ames, so diversity is established.

(2) *Amount in controversy:* The satisfaction of the $75,000 amount in controversy requirement is clear, at least if the action proceeds *in personam* (rather than *quasi in rem*). Stilton has claimed damages of $100,000; under the *St. Paul Mercury* case (p. 138) this amount will control unless it appears to a legal certainty that Stilton cannot recover more than $75,000. Since Stilton's claim appears to be in good faith, and he is seriously injured, the amount in controversy requirement is satisfied.

However, if the attached airplane is to serve as a source of *quasi in rem* jurisdiction, the amount in controversy requirement may pose a problem. It is only if personal jurisdiction over Muenster turns out to be lacking that the issue of *quasi in rem* becomes important, or available; in that event, the *quasi in rem* action must itself meet the jurisdictional amount. However, it is unclear exactly what it is that must exceed $75,000. Some courts have held that the value of the attached property controls; others have held that it is the value of the claim that matters (p. 83). If the latter measure alone is adopted, the requirement is clearly met. But if it is the value of the attached property that is relevant, a further complication arises. Is it the airplane itself that is being attached, or Gorgonzola's debt for it under the lease? Since the airplane is presumably worth more than the two years of lease payments, Stilton will probably seek *quasi in rem* jurisdiction over the plane itself — if he succeeds, amount in controversy is met as long as the value of the plane exceeds $75,000. But the Ames federal court may conclude that Gorgonzola's interest is unfairly violated by allowing Stilton to attach the plane and levy on it for a claim that has nothing to do with Gorgonzola. In that case, only Gorgonzola's debt to Muenster, $40,000, could serve as the *res* of a *quasi in rem* action (on the theory that a debt owed to the defendant is a sort of property) and this debt does not meet the $75,000 requirement.

Thus, the jurisdictional amount question is doubly complicated if the action turns out to be based upon *quasi in rem* jurisdiction (which would be the case if personal jurisdiction over Muenster is lacking). It would depend first on whether the court views the amount of the attached property, or the amount of the claim, as controlling, and then on whether it is the airplane, or just Gorgonzola's debt, that is the *res*.

(3) *In Personam Jurisdiction:* Turning to the question of *in personam* jurisdiction, the first point to keep in mind is that since this is a diversity action, the federal court for Ames will exercise personal jurisdiction over the out-of-state Muenster only if the Ames *state courts* would exercise such jurisdiction. So even if the Ames courts could constitutionally exercise jurisdiction over Muenster (i.e., even if Muenster had minimum contacts with Ames), if the Ames long-arm wouldn't reach Muenster, the federal court sitting in diversity can't exercise jurisdiction either. (See p. 69, Example 3.)

§103(a)(1) of the Ames long-arm may grant personal jurisdiction over Muenster. Muenster will undoubtedly argue that the travel agent who sold Stilton his ticket was not its agent, and that §103(a)(1) therefore does not apply. Muenster might on this ground escape those decisions holding that where a foreign corporation uses an in-state agent to perform in-state functions (e.g., to advertise in the forum state on behalf of the foreign corporation), the foreign corporation has the minimum contacts necessary for jurisdiction.

In determining whether the travel agent was Muenster's agent within the meaning of §103(a)(1), the volume of Muenster tickets the agent sold, and the existence of communication between Muenster and the agent, should be considered. If the agent sold so many tickets that had he not been in business, Muenster would have set up its own Ames office, the travel agent would likely be found to have been Muenster's "agent." Conversely, if the agent only very rarely sold a Muenster ticket, and few Ames residents took the Muenster tours, the agency relationship would likely be found lacking. Note that §103(a)(1) only applies to those in-state contacts which are related to the *particular cause of action* in question. It is also possible that Muenster's other contacts with Ames, unrelated to the Conn. crash, may be sufficient to confer jurisdiction over Muenster.

Even if the Ames long-arm reaches Muenster on account of the agent's activities, Muenster could still plausibly argue that the Ames federal court's exercise of personal jurisdiction over Muenster, an out-of-Ames corporation, would violate Muenster's right to due process under the 14th Amendment of the U.S. Constitution. As noted, a federal court sitting in diversity won't hear a case that wouldn't fall within the personal jurisdiction of the state where the federal court sits. In this case, it seems likely that the Ames federal court will need to exercise only *"specific"* jurisdiction over Muenster, not "general" jurisdiction. (Specific jurisdiction is jurisdiction for a claim arising at least in part out of the defendant's *in-state activities*.) Ames' claim arises from a flight taken on a ticket that Stilton bought while an Ames resident (and that Muenster *knew* from the beginning was bought by an Ames resident); also, Stilton bought the ticket in response to an in-Ames ad campaign conducted by Muenster. Thus Stilton's claim would likely be found to arise in significant part from Muenster's in-Ames activities, so that specific jurisdiction would suffice. For suits based on specific jurisdiction, an out-of-state corporate defendant's due process rights are not violated so long as the defendant had "minimum contacts" with the forum state. Thus here, there will be no violation of Muenster's due process rights as long as Muenster had minimum contacts with Ames. Here, the combination of Muenster's use of an in-Ames agent to sell tickets in Ames, combined with Muenster's decision to advertise its tour in the state, would almost certainly be sufficient to establish minimum contacts between Muenster and Ames. Thus the federal court should be found to have specific personal jurisdiction to hear the case (assuming that the Ames long-arm was found to apply).

Notice that if the claim *didn't* arise out of any voluntary contacts between Muenster and the state of Ames — as would be the case if Muenster operated and advertised only in New England, and Stilton bought the ticket in New England — then the Ames federal court would need *"general,"* not "specific," jurisdiction over Muenster. General jurisdiction over a defendant corporation may constitutionally be exercised *only* in the corporation's state of incorporation or its state of principal place of business. *Daimler AG v. Bauman.* And Muenster is not incorporated in Ames, nor does it have its principal place of business there. So if general jurisdiction were required (i.e., if the suit didn't arise out of any in-Ames activities by Muenster), the required general jurisdiction *would not* exist.

(4) *Quasi in Rem Jurisdiction:* If it is held that personal jurisdiction over Muenster does not exist, *quasi in rem* jurisdiction may be present. *Quasi in rem* jurisdiction is allowed in federal actions only if: (a) the plaintiff cannot obtain personal jurisdiction over the defendant through reasonable efforts, and (b) the law of the state in which the federal court sits permits such jurisdiction. (FRCP 4(n)). Requirement (a) would be satisfied if §103(a)(1) of the Ames long-arm is interpreted not to reach Muenster by virtue of the travel agent's acts (as discussed above). Requirement (b) raises questions: we're told that the Ames long-arm is silent on the subject of *quasi in rem* jurisdiction. However, if Ames is like most states, it permits such jurisdiction to be exercised over either tangible property present in the state, or over a debt owed by a debtor who is present in the state. Thus the airplane might be treated as the *res*; alternatively, Gorgonzola's debt to Muenster may be the *res*, under an "attachment-of-the-debt" theory. However, Muenster will have a good chance of arguing that under *Shaffer v. Heitner* (pp. 79-82), *quasi in rem* jurisdiction over it is unconstitutional, because Muenster lacks minimum contacts with Ames. This will certainly be the case if *in personam* jurisdiction over it is lacking, since under *Shaffer* the two tests are the same.

An additional issue arises with respect to *notice*. Was registered mail service a sufficient form of notice to Muenster? Federal Rule 4(e)(1) allows service by any method (e.g., registered mail) allowable under the law of the state in which the federal court sits. Since we're told that registered mail service on an out-of-state defendant is acceptable for Ames state-court suits, registered mail service here is sufficient.

Part B: Summary judgment ought to be denied Stilton. He is seeking an offensive use of collateral estoppel. That is, he is, as a plaintiff, trying to apply the finding of liability in the Cheddar case against Muenster in this case. Such offensive use of collateral estoppel was allowed by the Supreme Court in *Parklane Hosiery* (pp. 436-438). But in *Parklane*, only two lawsuits were involved; here, there is the likelihood of not only the Cheddar and Stilton actions, but of actions by each of the other injured passengers as well. It seems unfair to require Muenster to play this "heads you win; tails I lose" game in each of the many possible suits. This is the "multiple plaintiff anomaly" situation (p. 437).

The issue becomes even more stark when one considers the possibility that the jury's finding in *Cheddar* was not really one of liability-but-no-serious-injury, but rather a finding of serious-injury-but-doubtful-liability. In other words, the jury may have mixed elements of liability and damages, and decided to give Cheddar something for her trouble (and save her from paying court costs) even though it didn't really think Muenster was liable. If this is what in fact happened, then there is all the more reason not to hold that the *Cheddar* litigation was conclusive on the negligence issue.

It is true, of course, that to deny the use of collateral estoppel in this instance may promote additional litigation — the negligence issue will be retried, perhaps many times over. But this prospect is somewhat offset by the likelihood that Muenster will not wage as long and desperate a defense. If estoppel were applied, then in the first of a string of suits, the defendant would drag out the litigation as long as possible, and defend as ardently as it could, even if only a few dollars were involved. If estoppel is not applied, then the defendant in Muenster's position can afford to defend a small claim half-heartedly — the amount of increased litigation may thus not be as great as might at first glance be feared.

A further injustice is implicit in allowing the use of collateral estoppel in this situation — Cheddar is effectively penalized for having gone first. Assuming that the jury did in fact render a compromise verdict because of its uncertainty on liability, Cheddar would have been better off waiting until someone else won against Muenster, and then using collateral estoppel. Thus each plaintiff has a powerful incentive to wait for someone else to go first, and to refuse to consolidate with other plaintiffs. When this judicial inefficiency is coupled with the likelihood that the plaintiffs will all agree to let the most appealing plaintiff sue first, it can be seen that Stilton's case for estoppel is about as poor as it could possibly be.

Notice that the question stipulates that neither the New Jersey courts nor the federal district courts have taken any previous position about whether offensive use of collateral estoppel on facts like these should be allowed. If the New Jersey court *had* taken a position on whether offensive use of collateral estoppel should be allowed to be made by a stranger to the first action on facts like these, the Supreme Court's decision in *Semtek v. Lockheed Martin* (p. 446) would require the Ames federal court to apply the preclusion rule that the New Jersey courts would apply, whatever that rule was.

SAMPLE ANSWER TO QUESTION 2:

The question is a very close one, and involves many complexities. Vinyl may or may not be amenable to suit in Langdell federal court; if it is, service may or may not have been valid. If the requirements of personal jurisdiction are met, federal subject-matter jurisdiction is probably present, even though Plastic and Vinyl are citizens of the same state.

Personal jurisdiction: Two issues arise with respect to personal jurisdiction over Vinyl: (1) Is Vinyl *amenable* to suit in Langdell?; and (2) If it is, was service on Vinyl made within the geographical boundaries for service specified by the Federal Rules?

(1) *Vinyl's amenability to suit:* In federal question cases, the federal courts have generally held that a corporation is amenable to suit (i.e., suable) as long as it has minimum contacts with the state in which the district court sits sufficient to meet the *International Shoe* test (p. 23); in other words, the fact that the state courts might not exercise jurisdiction over this particular out-of-state defendant on a state-law claim would be ignored in determining the defendant's amenability to a federal suit. In cases not raising a federal question, however, the prevailing rule is that the federal courts exercise *only* the jurisdiction that would be exercised by the courts of the state in which the federal court sits, even if the state courts do not extend their jurisdiction as far as is constitutionally permissible.

Although the underlying suit here is based on a federal question, the supplemental claim by Plastic against Vinyl is a state-law breach-of-contract claim, so Vinyl's amenability to that claim should probably be analyzed as if the case did not involve a federal question. Under that analysis, if (and only if) the Langdell state courts would have exercised personal jurisdiction over Vinyl had the Plastic claim against it been brought there, the *federal* court in Langdell should also exercise jurisdiction. Plastic's claim against Vinyl seems to involve "specific" jurisdiction. (That is, Plastic's claim that Vinyl induced a breach is probably correctly viewed as growing out of conduct allegedly committed by Vinyl *in Langdell,* namely inducing a Langdell-based company, Staley, to breach a contract connected with Langdell). A state court's exercise of specific jurisdiction over an out-of-state company requires merely that the company have minimum contacts with the forum state. So the Langdell state courts would have constitutionally-sufficient specific jurisdiction over Plastic so long as Vinyl has minimum contacts with Langdell. *Burger King* (pp. 46-49) establishes that an out-of-stater's signing of a franchise contract that's closely related to the forum state is normally enough to constitute minimum contacts between the out-of-stater and the forum state. By extension from *Burger King*, probably an out-of-stater's inducement of a *breach* of a contract that's closely tied to the forum state *also* constitutes minimum contacts with the forum state. By this analysis, the Langdell state courts could constitutionally exercise specific jurisdiction over Plastic for the inducement claim. Consequently, the Langdell *federal* court should and will also exercise such specific jurisdiction, as long as the federal court also believes that the Langdell state courts would elect to *exercise* that specific jurisdiction over Vinyl.

If, on the other hand, the federal court believes that the Langdell state courts would *not* choose to exercise jurisdiction over Vinyl, the issue becomes more difficult. As noted earlier, since the claim against Vinyl is based solely on state law, the federal court should probably treat the problem of amenability as if the claim were based purely on diversity. And in diversity cases, the federal courts will generally not exercise jurisdiction if the courts of the state where the federal court sits would not exercise jurisdiction. So if the Langdell state courts would not exercise jurisdiction over Plastic (even though those courts *could*, consistently with due process, do so), then the federal court for Langdell would not do so either.

(2) *Geographical boundaries for service:* If we conclude through the above reasoning that Vinyl is amenable to service, there is an additional requirement that service be carried out within the geographical limits specified in the Federal Rules. According to Rule 4(k)(1)(A), service on Vinyl may be made anywhere that the laws of Langdell permit. If the Langdell long-arm would permit service on Vinyl's Ames offices, then the federal service which occurred is valid. If Langdell law would not permit such service, the service may nonetheless be valid under the "100-mile-bulge" provision of 4(k)(1)(B). That provision allows service on persons who are brought in as additional parties to a counterclaim pursuant to Rule 19 at a place not more than 100 miles from the court where the action is pending. Thus, if Rule 19 allows Vinyl to be brought in as an additional party to Plastic's counterclaim, and if Vinyl's Ames offices are within 100 miles of the Langdell federal courthouse, service was valid.

It is unclear whether Vinyl may be brought in pursuant to Rule 19. That Rule allows joinder of certain persons who are subject to service of process (is this circular?) and whose joinder will not destroy subject matter jurisdiction. Assuming for the moment that Vinyl meets these two tests (the subject matter question is discussed below), it is joinable under Rule 19 if it "claims an interest relating to the subject of the action and is so situated that disposing of the action in [its] absence may (i) as a practical matter impair or impede [its] ability to protect the interest[.]" Since Vinyl has an interest in having Staley stay in business so that it will continue to distribute Vinyl products, it is arguable that Vinyl satisfies the provision of Rule 19 just cited. If so, service within the 100-mile bulge is permitted.

Subject-matter jurisdiction (supplemental jurisdiction): Plastic and Vinyl are both citizens of Ames. Plastic's claim against Vinyl therefore fails to satisfy independently the requirements of diversity. Unless the claim can be "tacked on" through supplemental jurisdiction, the claim must be dismissed.

The doctrine of supplemental jurisdiction, codified in 28 U.S.C. §1367, allows a federal court which has jurisdiction over an initial claim to also hear a related claim, even though that related claim would not independently satisfy the requirements of federal subject-matter jurisdiction (diversity and amount in controversy). One of the ways supplemental jurisdiction can apply is to allow a court to hear a state-created claim closely related to a federal-question claim that is the "core" claim supplying original jurisdiction. (In other words, supplemental jurisdiction can be used to supply what was known before the 1990 enactment of §1367 as "pendent" jurisdiction.)

For a court to exercise its supplemental jurisdiction, the two claims must form part of the "same case or controversy under Article III" of the Constitution. This test is usually deemed satisfied if the state-created claim and the federal claim derive from a "common nucleus of operative fact"; see *UMW v. Gibbs* (p. 143). Since both the federal claim (that the franchise agreement violated the antitrust laws) and the counterclaim against Staley and Vinyl (alleging that Vinyl induced Plastic to breach the franchise agreement) relate to the franchise agreement, probably the "common nucleus of operative fact" test would be satisfied. Therefore, supplemental jurisdiction would govern the counterclaim against both Staley and Vinyl.

Under pre-1990 law, the addition of Vinyl to the Staley-v.-Plastic counterclaim would probably ***not*** have been allowed under the doctrine of pendent jurisdiction. The Supreme Court's 1989 decision in *Finley v. U.S.* (p. 143), made it very difficult for ***additional parties*** to be brought in to defend a pendent state claim. But §1367(a) expressly overrules *Finley* — that section allows "claims that involve the joinder or intervention of additional parties." So Vinyl does not get any comfort from the subject matter jurisdiction aspect of the case — supplemental jurisdiction as implemented by §1367(a) allows Vinyl to be brought into the counterclaim, even though a claim by Plastic against Vinyl would not independently meet federal subject matter jurisdictional requirements.

All of this assumes, of course, that there is something in the Federal Rules which allows the joinder of Vinyl to Plastic's counterclaim against Staley, apart from questions of jurisdiction. The operative Rule is 13(h), which allows additional parties to a counterclaim to be brought in in accordance with the provisions of Rules 19 and 20. While there is some doubt as to whether Rule 19 would allow such joinder, Rule 20 almost certainly does. That rule allows joinder of persons as defendants "if: (A) any right to relief is asserted against them jointly, severally, or in the alternative with respect to or arising out of the same transaction, occurrence, or series of transactions or occurrences; and (B) any question of law or fact common to all defendants will arise in the action." (A defendant to a counterclaim is presumably a defendant for the purposes of Rule 20.) If the Staley claim and the claim against Vinyl are closely enough related so that the supplemental jurisdiction doctrine applies, then they are certainly close enough so that Rule 20 applies. In that case, Rule 13(h) joinder is allowable. Since such joinder is at the discretion of the counterclaimant, there is nothing Vinyl can do.

SAMPLE ANSWER TO QUESTION 3:

Cellar is raising a legal counterclaim (damages for breach of contract) to an equitable suit (rescission). The question of fraud is a factor affecting both claims, since it would be a defense to the counterclaim and is the basis for the original suit. In *Beacon Theatres*, (p. 310), the U.S. Supreme Court held that a trial judge did not have discretion to order the trial of legal and equitable issues in such a way that the right to jury trial of the former would be lost. Since the issue of fraud will only be tried once (the rules of *res judicata* and "law of the case" require this), it must therefore be tried to a jury, in order to protect Cellar's right to jury trial of his legal counterclaim.

SAMPLE ANSWER TO QUESTION 4:

We should (1) file an answer to Dale's motions in the Appeals Court; and (2) request a new trial on burden of proof in the alternative. The conditional new trial request is necessary to protect ourselves; if the only thing we do is to attempt to refute Dale's arguments, and we fail, the Appeals Court will have no choice but to grant judgment as a matter of law for Dale. It will not be able to grant a new trial, since no party will have made this request on appeal. We should, therefore, specifically state that if the denial of *JML* is found to have been incorrect, we wish a new trial on the burden of proof issue. Such a contention on our part is specifically provided for by Rule 50(e), which allows the Appeals Court either to decide our new trial motion itself, or to remand for a determination of this issue by the trial court. (Of course, if the Appeals Court decides that the federal securities laws do not apply at all, they will dismiss for lack of subject-matter jurisdiction, and will not order a new trial. Our motion under 50(e) would thus make a difference only if the Court finds jurisdiction present, but rules for Dale on the sufficiency of the evidence.)

SAMPLE ANSWER TO QUESTION 5:

The issue is whether the name and address of an expert whom we informally consulted, but whom we did not retain and will not call at trial, is within the scope of discovery. There is virtually no way under Federal Rule 26 that such discovery may be obtained.

Rule 26(b)(4)(B) deals directly with this expert-who-has-been-retained-but-won't-testify scenario:

> "Ordinarily, a party may **not**, by interrogatories or deposition, **discover facts known or opinions held** by an expert who has been retained or specially employed by another party in anticipation of litigation or to prepare for trial and who is **not expected to be called as a witness at trial**. But a party may do so only: (i) as provided in Rule 35(b); or (ii) on showing **exceptional circumstances** under which it is impracticable for the party to obtain facts or opinions on the same subject by other means."

Neither of the exceptions mentioned in 26(b)(4)(B) will likely apply here. The Rule 35(b) exception applies only to a medical examination, and Dr. Pert did not perform one. The "exceptional circumstances" exception might conceivably apply. But nothing prevents the other side from doing the same thing we did — finding Dr. Pert and asking him his off-the-record opinion about whether the blow could have caused the disease. After all, they have the same ability and incentive to discover that the discoverer of Pert's Disease is Dr. Pert, and that he's still alive and might be willing to talk. Therefore, I don't think either the 26(b)(4)(B) exception for "exceptional circumstances," or any professional responsibility on our part, requires us to, in effect, "do the other side's work for them" by disclosing what we know about Pert's off-the-record opinion.

SAMPLE ANSWER TO QUESTION 6:

This is a classic *Erie* problem, in which the federal interest in consolidation of litigation conflicts with a state interest in enforcing licensing requirements. An additional wrinkle is presented by the fact that it is a counterclaim, rather than an original claim, which is in question.

The *Erie* doctrine applies to those situations in which there is no Federal Rule on point, and the underlying claim is a state-created one. That's the case here. If the court decides to follow Ames law, the Dauntless counterclaim will be barred.

The "twin evils" to which the *Erie* decision was addressed are: (1) discrimination against the citizen of the forum state; and (2) forum-shopping (p. 254). Both of these evils would result to a certain extent if the court here refuses to follow Ames common law (the *McCord* decision), and allows Dauntless to pursue its counterclaim. Dauntless, as non-citizen of Ames, has had the opportunity to select a federal forum by means of the right of removal. (Your honor is aware, of course, that a defendant may remove only if he is not a citizen of the state in which the action is originally brought). Dauntless has thus been able to "shop" for a forum which it hopes is the more likely to be hospitable to its claim — it knew that it would fail in Ames state court, so it chose to remove to federal court. If your honor permits Dauntless to prosecute its counterclaim in the face of Ames law, this "forum-shopping" will have paid off.

Prior to the Supreme Court's decision in *Byrd v. Blue Ridge* (p. 262), the problem could have been easily disposed of by resort to the "outcome-determinative" test first espoused in *Guaranty Trust v. York* (p. 261). *Guaranty* held that state law must be followed if it would "significantly affect the result of a litigation for a federal court to disregard a law of a State that would be controlling" had the action been brought in state court. The effect of ignoring Ames law here is nearly the same as the effect would have been in *Guaranty* of ignoring the state statute of limitations. *Guaranty* held that it was "outcome-determinative" to ignore a statute of limitations, since this would allow prosecution in federal court of a claim which would be completely barred in state court. Here, similarly, the effect of ignoring the *McCord* decision would be to allow a claim in federal court which would be barred in Ames state court.

As *Byrd* indicates, however, (1) there are varying degrees of outcome-determinativeness, and (2) the fact that the decision of which law to apply will be somewhat outcome-determinative does not settle the matter — there may be stronger countervailing considerations. Thus, the decision whether to try an issue to a judge or to a jury is less likely to determine the outcome of a lawsuit than is the decision whether to bar an action as untimely. *Byrd* held that the former issue is so little outcome-determinative that strong countervailing federal policies may compel a refusal to follow state decisions on the allocation of judge/jury roles.

It might seem, at first glance, that there is not any strong federal interest in favor of allowing the Dauntless claim. However, there is a strong federal interest in *consolidating* all the related litigation between two parties into one single action. This interest in consolidation is not evident at first — one might argue that if the Dauntless claim is barred, then it can't be brought in either Ames state *or* federal court, and will not reappear to be litigated in a separate, judicially wasteful, action. However, this argument that no consolidation interest is present overlooks a crucial consideration: *the Dauntless claim may be triable as an original action in the state or federal court of some other jurisdiction, perhaps Thayer.* If it is in fact the case that the Dauntless claim can and will be tried elsewhere, then there is a strong federal interest in disposing of all claims between Pacific and Dauntless in one action. Thus, the situation is quite different from that in *Guaranty*, where the federal courts had no strong reason to try a claim time-barred in state court (assuming that no other state court would have allowed the *Guaranty* claim).

It is difficult to tell from the record as it has so far been developed whether the Thayer state courts would entertain the Dauntless claim. Personal jurisdiction over Pacific can be constitutionally exercised by Thayer courts — the making of a contract with a citizen of the forum state is generally a sufficient contact to permit jurisdiction in a suit arising out of that contract. (See *Burger King*, pp. 46-49.) Thus, if the state of Thayer has a long-arm which would reach Pacific, the Dauntless action might be maintainable in Thayer. It is possible, of course, that the Thayer court will defer to the Ames statute (and the *McCord* interpretation of it), and bar the Dauntless claim. This is a question of conflict of laws. If Dauntless would be allowed to sue in Thayer state court, then a federal court sitting in Thayer would have to allow the suit, under the rule of *Klaxon v. Stentor* (p. 259), which compels a federal court sitting in diversity to apply the conflicts rule of the state in which it sits.

It is therefore quite possible that if this court bars the Dauntless claim, it will later be brought in either the state or the federal court of Thayer. In that event, this court will have promoted a kind of "lateral forum-shopping"; defendants in the position of Dauntless will select a forum like Thayer instead of bringing their claims as counterclaims in Ames. Such an inducement to hold back from asserting a counterclaim promotes judicial inefficiency, as well as forum-shopping. This possibility indicates that Ames law should be disregarded, and the Dauntless claim allowed.

However, one additional possibility may negate the above reasoning — if the Dauntless counterclaim is *compulsory*, then it may be waived if it is not brought in this action. Since the counterclaim arises out of the same contract that is the subject of Pacific's claim for breach, it probably meets the "transaction or occurrence" test of Rule 13(a), and is thus compulsory. However, it is not clear whether Dauntless is barred from bringing the claim as an independent action in Thayer if it has done everything it could to assert the counterclaim in this case, and has failed. It would probably *not* be held to be barred from suing on the claim as plaintiff in Thayer state or federal court. Therefore, the fact that the counterclaim arises out of the same transaction or occurrence as the Pacific claim is irrelevant. The above argument for ignoring Ames law and letting Dauntless assert the counterclaim would thus still hold.

One difficulty with this argument, however, is that it compels a district court faced with the kind of problem presented in this case to examine the jurisdictional and conflicts policies of every other potential jurisdiction, in order to determine whether the action will be brought somewhere else if the present court dismisses it. Such an examination may be time-consuming and ineffective. Nonetheless, I think it would not be burdensome for this court to set forth a principle that where the federal court *knows* that there is some other jurisdiction, either state or federal, that will hear the claim, it should not give excessive weight to the door-closing rule of the state in which it sits.

Thus if your honor later determines that Thayer, or some other jurisdiction, would in fact permit the

Dauntless claim as an original action, this court should allow the claim.

SAMPLE ANSWER TO QUESTION 7:

The basic prerequisites for the application of *bar* are the following: (1) The present and former suits must represent very similar "causes of action;" (2) The parties to both suits must have been the same; and (3) The former adjudication must have been "on the merits."

(1) Similarity of causes of action: I think our best hope of defeating the claim of *res judicata* lies in showing that the two claims are not sufficiently identical for bar to apply. While it was formerly the case that absolute identity of the two claims had to be shown, the courts have now adopted a looser test which serves to bar a greater number of claims. Devious will be able to cite the principle that a judgment is conclusive, not only as to matters which were decided, but also as to all matters which *might have been decided*. Of course, this principle does not mean that any claim which could have been asserted in the first action is barred — if that were the case, there would be no hope for us at all, since we could have asserted the unfair competition claim by the doctrine of supplemental jurisdiction (see discussion below). The test for determining whether the second cause of action is so closely related to the previously litigated claim as to be barred by it is a pragmatic one: if two actions allege very similar facts, and claim violation of the same legal right, bar will apply, even though two different legal theories for recovery are involved. The facts of our case are somewhat similar to those of *Williamson v. Columbia Gas*, (p. 420), in which it was held that a claim under the Sherman Act was so similar to a previously litigated Clayton Act claim that the latter bound the former. We should argue that the elements of unfair competition are different from those of antitrust violation, and that the protected legal right is not the same in both cases. However, I am not optimistic.

It should be noted that if the kind of relief we now seek was not available from the court in which we tried the previous action, we will not now be barred. If we can, for instance, show that the unfair competition claim could not have met the requirements of federal subject matter jurisdiction, and could not therefore have been joined with the antitrust claim, we will be in the clear. Unfortunately, the doctrine of supplemental jurisdiction (p. 142 and pp. 145-155) would almost certainly have permitted the unfair competition claim to be joined to the antitrust claim, since the two claims involve a common nucleus of operative fact.

(2) Identity of parties: The parties to both actions are identical.

(3) Adjudication on the merits: Our only remaining hope for avoiding bar is to demonstrate that the original adjudication for untimeliness was not "on the merits." However, this approach is not promising. While a 12(b)(6) dismissal for failure to state a valid claim might arguably be considered not on the merits, a summary judgment is as final and dispositive of the issues as a jury trial. Therefore, I don't think we will get anywhere with this line of attack.

In my opinion, unless we can persuade the court that the two claims are not sufficiently identical for bar to be applied, we will be prevented from litigating the unfair competition claim.

TABLE OF CASES

Principal discussion of a case
is indicated by page numbers in italics.

Adam v. Saenger.. 15
Aetna Casualty & Surety v. Yeatts............................ *304*
Aguilar v. Immigration & Customs Enforcement Div. 233
Allen v. McCurry.. 439, 445
Alyeska Pipeline Service Co. v. Wilderness Soc. *378*
Amchem Products, Inc., v. Windsor............ 358, 361, 376, 378, *380–381*, 382, 410
American Fire & Casualty Co. v. Finn, ... 121
Ankenbrandt v. Richards 124
Asahi Metal Indus. v. Superior Court.................... 9, 29, 43
Asahi Metal Industry Co. v. Superior Court....... 30, *32–34*
Ashcroft v. Iqbal 179, *181–187*
AT&T Mobility LLC v. Concepcion............ 373, *374–375*
Atlantic Marine Constr. Co., Inc. v. United States District Court for the Western District of Texas.............................. *112–114*, 115, 116

Baldwin v. Iowa State Traveling Men's Ass'n............... 96
Beacon Theatres v. Westover........................ *310–311*, 314, 316, 333, 462
Beeck v. Aquaslide 'N' Dive Corp.............................. 194
Bell Atlantic Corp. v. Twombly ... *179–181*, 182, 183, 186
Bernhard v. Bank of America................................ 434, 443
Bernhardt v. Polygraphic Co. of America 258
BMW of North America v. Gore................................. 317
Burger King Corp. v. Rudzewicz *46–49*, 460, 464
Burlington Northern Railroad Co. v. Woods................. 265
Burnham v. Superior Court.......................... *12, 23*, 51, 82
Business Guides, Inc. v. Chromatic Communications Enterprises, Inc................. 173, 174
Byrd v. Blue Ridge Rural Electric Coop., Inc. ... 207, *262–263*, 265, 276, 463

Cambria v. Jeffery 429, 442
Caperton v. A.T. Massey Coal Co., Inc......................... 299
Carden v. Arkoma Associates..................................... 127
Carnegie-Mellon Univ. v. Cohill................................ 163
Carnival Cruise Lines, Inc. v. Shute............................. 16
Cascade Natural Gas Corp. v. El Paso Natural Gas Co. 390
Celotex Corp. v. Catrett..................................... 288–289
Chambers v. NASCO.. 175
Chauffeurs, Teamsters and Helpers Local 391 v. Terry *311–312*
Chicot County Drainage District v. Baxter State Bank 121, 444
Cine Forty-Second Street Theatre Corp. v. Allied Artists.. 242

Clearfield Trust Co. v. United States............................ 275
Coca-Cola Bottling Co. v. Coca-Cola Co.................... 241
Cohen v. Beneficial Indus. Loan Corp. 327
Colgrove v. Battin.. 297
Commissioner of Internal Revenue v. Sunnen 432
Conley v. Gibson 179
Connecticut v. Doehr 90, *90–91*, 93
Cooter & Gell v. Hartmarx Corp. 174

Daimler AG v. Bauman 24, *26*, 46, 51, *56–61*, 62, 63, 64, 68, 459
Dairy Queen v. Wood... *313–314*
Dice v. Akron, Canton & Youngstown R.R. 276
Dimick v. Schiedt *305*
Donovan v. Penn Shipping Co................................... 305
Dyer v. MacDougall 285

Eisen v. Carlisle & Jacquelin................. *88*, 367, 388, 410
Erie Railroad v. Tompkins....... 4, 207, 253, 254, *256–257*, 275, 278, 284, 463
Evergreens, The v. Nunan.. 430
Executive Software North America, Inc. v. United States District Court..................... 154
Exxon Mobil Corp. v. Allapattah Services, Inc. 139, 140, 141, 149, 150, *150–153*, 347, 348, 370, 384, 388, 409

Federated Department Stores, Inc. v. Moitie 423
Finley v. U.S. 144, 146, 152, 153, 157, 462
Franchise Tax Bd. v. Construction Laborers Vacation Trust 131
Fuentes v. Shevin.. 92

Gasperini v. Center for Humanities, Inc. 259, 273, 322
Gomez v. Toledo.. 192
Goodyear Dunlop Tires Operations, S.A. v. Brown 51, *53–56*, 59, 61
Grable & Sons Metal Products, Inc. v. Darue Engineering & Manufacturing........... 134, 135
Gray v. American Radiator Corp........................ 17, 20, 29
Greene v. Lindsey 85
Grupo Dataflux v. Atlas Global Group, L.P. *124–125*, 125
Guaranty Trust Co. v. York .. 175, 257, *261*, 261, 274, 463
Gulf Oil v. Gilbert... 102, 109
Gunn v. Minton.................................... 133, 134, *135–137*

Haas v. Jefferson Bank 349, 350, 355
Hanna v. Plumer 258, 260, 262, *263–265*, 273, 278

Hanson v. Denckla.......................... 26–28, 47, 81
Harnden v. Jayco, Inc. 323
Har-Pen Truck Lines, Inc. v. Mills 274
Hart v. American Airlines...................... 436, 444
Helicopteros Nacionales de Colombia, S.A.
    v. Hall 52–53, 55
Hertz Corp. v. Friend................................. 128
Hess v. Pawloski....................................... 16, 86
Hickman v. Taylor................................. 208, 210
Hilton v. Guyot... 444
Hoffman v. Blaski...................................... 110

In re — see name of party
In the Matter of — see name of party
Insolia v. Philip Morris, Inc. 346
Insurance Corp. of Ireland v.
    Compagnie des Bauxites de Guinee 241
International Shoe Co. v. Washington 21, 23–24,
    27, 67, 81, 82, 460

J. McIntyre Machinery, Ltd. v. Nicastro 29, 30, 31,
    34–39, 40, 41, 42, 45, 67
Japanese Electronic Products Antitrust
    Litigation, In re 314

Keeton v. Hustler Magazine, Inc. 13, 51
Klaxon Co. v. Stentor Electric Mfg. Co. 259, 273, 464
Kramer v. Caribbean Mills 128
Krupski v. Costa Crociere S.p.A 197–198, 201
Kulko v. Superior Court 28

Lauro Lines s.r.l. v. Chasser 327, 329
Leatherman v. Tarrant County Narcotics Intelligence &
    Coordination Unit 177
Liberty Mutual Insur. Co. v. Wetzel.... 290, 324–325, 327,
    331
Little v. Blue Goose Motor Coach Co. 428
Livingston v. Jefferson 101
Louisville & Nashville R. v. Mottley ... 121, 132, 137, 159

Markman v. Westview Instruments, Inc. 313
Mas v. Perry... 14
Masino v. Outboard Marine Corp. 274
Matter of — see name of party
McDonough Power Equipment, Inc. v. Greenwood..... 296
McGee v. Int'l Life Ins. Co. 25–26, 27, 28
Mendoza, U.S. v. 438
Mennonite Board of Missions v. Adams 88
Merrell Dow Pharmaceuticals, Inc. v. Thompson 132
Migra v. Warren City Bd. of Ed. 446
Milliken v. Meyer 13
Mitchell v. W.T. Grant Co. 92
Mohawk Industries, Inc. v. Carpenter 327, 328
Montana v. U.S. 432
Moore v. Baker 196

Mullane v. Central Hanover Bank 50, 86, 87–88

National Equipment Rental v. Szukhent..................... 15
New York Life Insurance Co. v. Dunlevy............ 393–394
Nixon v. Fitzgerald 329
North Georgia Finishing, Inc. v. Di-Chem 92

Oppenheimer Fund v. Sanders........................... 368
Ortiz v. Fibreboard Corp............................... 383–384
Owen Equipment & Erection Co. v. Kroger 145, 147, 158,
    355, 402, 405

Palmer v. Hoffman...................................... 259
Parklane Hosiery Co. v. Shore...... 436–438, 443, 446, 459
Pennoyer v. Neff................................. 11, 24, 51, 77, 84
Perkins v. Benguet Consolidated Mining Co........... 52, 55
Phillips Petroleum Co. v. Shutts............. 49–50, 369, 387
Piper Aircraft Co. v. Reyno 102
Provident Tradesmen's Bank and Trust Co.
    v. Patterson 350

Ragan v. Merchants Transfer 175, 195, 260, 261–262, 264
Rose v. Giamatti 130
Ross v. Bernhard 314, 316
Rush v. City of Maple Heights 420

St. Paul Mercury Indemnity Co. v. Red Cab 138, 138, 457
Saadeh v. Farouki 126–127
Salve Regina College v. Russell 259
Sargent v. Massachusetts Accident Co. 285
Schlagenhauf v. Holder................................. 235
Seattle Times Co. v. Rhinehart 239, 249
Semtek Int'l Inc. v. Lockheed Martin
    Corp. 276, 446–448, 450, 453, 460
Shady Grove Orthopedic Assoc. v. Allstate Ins. Co.... 262,
    265–271, 273
Shaffer v. Heitner................................. 78, 79–82, 84, 459
Shamrock Oil & Gas Corp. v. Sheets 140, 160
Sibbach v. Wilson 235, 263
Singh v. Daimler-Benz 126
Smuck v. Hobson 392
Sniadach v. Family Finance Corp...................... 92
Snyder v. Harris 140, 142
State Farm Fire and Casualty Co. v. Tashire................ 395
State Farm Mut. Automobile Insur. Co. v.
    Campbell.. 317, 318
Stewart Organization, Inc. v. Ricoh Corp................... 271
Strawbridge v. Curtiss................................. 122, 131
Swift v. Tyson......................... 255, 256, 257, 259

Taylor v. Sturgell..................................... 423–426, 433
Teitelbaum Furs, Inc. v. Dominion Insur. Co. 438
Too, Inc. v. Kohl's Department Stores, Inc. 400
Tull v. U.S... 311
Tyler v. Judges of the Court of Registration................ 78

U.S. v. — see opposing party
U.S. Financial Securities Litigation, In re 315
United Mine Workers v. Gibbs............. 143, 146, 162, 461
University of Tennessee v. Elliott 445
Upjohn Co. v. U.S.. 211

Walker v. Armco Steel Corp. 261
Walker v. City of Hutchinson.. 87
Wal-Mart Stores, Inc. v. Duke...................... 357, *358–360*

Williamson v. Columbia Gas & Electric Corp. 420, 465
World-Wide Volkswagen Corp. v. Woodson.... 18, *18*, 29, *30–31*, 45, 66, 67
Wuchter v. Pizzutti 89
Wyman v. Newhouse... 97

Zahn v. Int'l Paper Co.. 388
Zielinski v. Philadelphia Piers, Inc. 191
Zubulake v. UBS Warburg LLC.................................. 234

TABLE OF REFERENCES TO THE
FEDERAL RULES OF CIVIL PROCEDURE

Rule	Page No.	Rule	Page No.
3	175, 195	11(d)	174
4	71	12	94, 178, 193
4(d)	73	12(a)	73, 193
4(d)(1)(G)	73	12(a)(1)(A)(ii)	193
4(d)(2)	73	12(b)	94, 178, 287
4(d)(5)	74	12(b)(2)	74, 94
4(e)	72	12(b)(3)	74
4(e)(1)	72	12(b)(6)	42, 94, 132, 153, 171, 179, 180, 182, 185, 186, 187, 286, 292
4(e)(2)	263		
4(e)(2)(A)	72	12(c)	178, 187
4(e)(2)(B)	72, 85	12(d)	178
4(e)(2)(C)	72	12(e)	187
4(f)	72	12(f)	188
4(h)(1)	72	12(h)(1)	94, 108, 121, 178
4(h)(1)(B)	87	12(h)(2)	178
4(h)(2)	73	12(h)(3)	94, 121, 178
4(k)(1)(A)	68, 69, 70, 154, 193	13	5, 192, 338
4(k)(1)(B)	70, 154, 347, 401	13(a)	149, 338, 339, 422
4(k)(1)(C)	70	13(a)(2)(A)	338
4(k)(2)	68, 69, 71, 72	13(a)(2)(B)	338
4(m)	47, 74, 196, 197	13(b)	337, 339
4(n)	83, 94	13(d)	338
4(n)(2)	83	13(g)	5, 144, 149, 406
7(a)	171	13(h)	149, 150, 339, 344
8(a)	175, 176, 177, 186, 339, 341	14	70, 149, 150, 401
8(a)(2)	182	14(a)	5, 147, 399
8(b)	173, 190	14(a)(2)	401
8(b)(6)	191	14(a)(3)	402
8(c)	192	14(b)	400
8(d)	175, 188	15	193
8(e)	171	15(a)	192
9	177	15(a)(1)(A)	193
9(a)	177	15(a)(1)(B)	193
9(b)	177	15(a)(2)	187, 194
9(c)	177	15(b)	194, 198
9(d)	177	15(c)(1)	200
9(e)	177	15(c)(1)(A)	195
9(f)	177	15(c)(1)(B)	194
9(g)	177	15(c)(1)(C)	196
9(h)	177	15(c)(1)(C)(ii)	197, 200
10(b)	176	15(c)(3)	47
10(b)(5)	275	16	170, 211, 250
11	171, 174, 191	16(a)	250
11(b)	173	16(b)	250
11(b)(3)	173	16(c)	250
11(c)(1)	174	16(e)	250
11(c)(2)	174	16(f)	250
11(c)(4)	172	17	398

Rule	Page No.
17(a)	399
18(a)	5, 337, 343, 344, 402
19	5, 148, 287, 339, 345, 348, 362
19(a)	70, 148, 339, 346, 348, 349
19(a)(1)(A)	349
19(a)(1)(B)	349
19(a)(1)(B)(i)	390
19(b)	148, 348, 349
20	5, 148, 149, 150, 152, 153, 339, 345, 347, 394
20(a)	345
20(b)	346
22	5, 393, 396
23	5, 150, 152, 266, 267, 269, 356, 384
23.1	171
23(a)	265, 268, 356, 362
23(a)(1)	357
23(a)(2)	357, 358
23(a)(3)	357
23(a)(4)	358, 361, 381
23(b)	265, 268, 362
23(b)(1)	357, 362, 366, 368, 382
23(b)(1)(A)	362
23(b)(1)(B)	362, 383
23(b)(2)	357, 363, 364, 365, 366, 369
23(b)(3)	357, 363, 364, 365, 366, 367, 368, 381
23(b)(3)(D)	378
23(c)(1)	371
23(c)(2)(A)	368
23(c)(2)(B)	367
23(c)(3)	366, 368
23(c)(4)	382
23(c)(4)(A)	384
23(e)	375
23(e)(1)	376
23(f)	371
24	5, 149, 389
24(a)	389, 390
24(a)(2)	351
24(b)	389, 390
26	226
26(1)(2)(C)	214
26(a)	205, 219, 220, 242
26(a)(1)	205, 217, 219, 221
26(a)(1)(A)	215
26(a)(1)(A)(i)	212, 217, 218, 220
26(a)(1)(A)(ii)	218, 219, 220
26(a)(1)(A)(iii)	218
26(a)(1)(A)(iv)	216, 217, 219
26(a)(1)(B)(ii)	215
26(a)(1)(E)	217
26(a)(2)	219
26(a)(2)(A)	213, 219
26(a)(2)(B)	214, 219
26(a)(2)(D)	213
26(a)(3)	205, 216, 219
26(a)(3)(B)	227
26(b)	205, 230
26(b)(1)	206, 212, 216, 217, 229, 231, 237
26(b)(2)	219
26(b)(2)(C)	238
26(b)(3)	207, 209
26(b)(3)(A)	209
26(b)(3)(B)	210
26(b)(3)(C)	212
26(b)(4)	207, 213, 215
26(b)(4)(A)	214
26(b)(4)(C)	214
26(b)(4)(D)	214, 215
26(b)(4)(D)(ii)	214
26(b)(5)	221
26(c)	225, 237, 238, 239, 243
26(c)(1)(G)	249
26(c)(3)	241
26(e)	220, 242
26(e)(1)	220, 242
26(e)(1)(A)	220
26(f)	219
26(g)	225
26(g)(1)(B)(iii)	225
26(g)(3)	225
27(a)	171
29	227
30	221, 224, 226, 240
30(a)(2)	226
30(a)(2)(A)	225, 228
30(b)(1)	226
30(b)(2)	226
30(b)(3)(A)	227
30(b)(6)	226, 240
30(c)(1)	226
30(c)(2)	228
30(d)(1)	225, 228
30(d)(3)	229, 239
30(g)	226
31	224, 228, 240
31(a)(4)	226, 240
31(a)(5)	229
32(a)(1)(B)	244
32(a)(2)	244
32(a)(3)	244
32(a)(4)	245
32(a)(6)	246
32(a)(8)	247
32(c)	227
33	224, 228, 234, 240
33(a)	225, 229
33(a)(2)	206, 211
33(b)(4)	237

Rule	Page No.
33(b)(5)	237
33(c)	246
33(d)	229
34	218, 219, 224, 226, 234, 240, 243
34(a)	231
34(c)	234
35	214, 224, 234, 235, 246, 248, 260
35(a)	235, 242
35(b)	214, 235
35(b)(4)	236, 246, 248
36	224, 230, 231, 246, 248
36(a)(1)(A)	211
36(a)(4)	230
36(a)(5)	238
36(a)(6)	230
36(b)	231, 246
37	226, 241, 242
37(a)	239, 241
37(a)(4)	240
37(a)(5)	241
37(a)(5)(A)	241
37(a)(5)(B)	241
37(b)	240, 242
37(b)(1)	242
37(b)(2)	231, 242
37(b)(2)(A)	250
37(b)(2)(A)(vii)	242
37(c)	241
37(c)(1)	220, 242
37(c)(2)	230
37(d)	229, 243
38(a)	308
38(b)	308
41(a)(1)	287
41(a)(1)(i)	174
41(a)(2)	287
41(b)	287, 421, 447
41(d)	287
42(b)	292
45	234

Rule	Page No.
45(c)(3)(A)(ii)	226
45(e)	234
46	320
47	295
47(a)	294
47(c)	295
48	294, 295
49(a)	302
49(b)	302
50	300, 301, 307
50(a)	307
50(a)(1)	300
50(a)(2)	307
50(b)	307, 308
50(c)(1)	308
51(a)(1)	295
51(d)(2)	296
52	291
52(a)	292
52(a)(6)	322
52(c)	287, 292
53(b)	314
54(b)	290, 326
54(c)	177
55(d)	338
56	170, 178, 185, 288, 292
56(b)	292
56(c)(1)(A)	288, 289
56(c)(1)(B)	289
56(c)(4)	288
56(g)	290
58	325
59(a)(1)	302
59(a)(2)	302
60(b)	121
60(b)(4)	121
60(b)(6)	121
61	303
65(b)	172

TABLE OF REFERENCES TO
TITLE 28, UNITED STATES CODE

Section	Page
144 (Judicial Bias)	298
455 (Judicial Bias)	298
455(a)	298
455(b)	298
724 (Conformity Act)	257
1291 (Final Judgment Rule)	324–325
1292(a)(1)	329
1292(b)	326
1331 (Federal Question)	3, 138
1332 (Diversity of Citizenship)	3, 122, 147, 347
1332(a)	126, 138, 141
1332(a)(2)	126
1332(a)(3)	123, 127
1332(b)	138
1332(c)	127
1332(c)(2)	124
1332(d)	125
1332(d)(2)	140, 370
1332(d)(2)(A)	123
1332(d)(4)	371
1335 (Interpleader)	5, 392–396
1335(a)	395
1335(a)(1)	123, 395
1338(a)	160
1359 (Collusive or Improper Joinder)	128–129
1367 (Supplemental Jurisdiction)	350, 390, 142, 144, 145–155, 162, 370, 388
1367(a)	146, 151, 154
1367(b)	146–150, 348, 390, 402
1367(c)	153, 154
1367(c)(3)	163, 403
1391 (Venue)	3, 100, 103–108, 109, 113
1391(a)	348
1391(a)(1)	154, 393
1391(a)(2)	155
1391(b)	348
1391(b)(1)	105, 106, 110
1391(b)(2)	105, 106, 110, 113, 115
1391(b)(3)	106, 107, 108, 111
1391(d)	107, 108, 111
1391(e)	70
1397 (Interpleader Venue)	395
1404 (Change of Venue)	112, 113, 114
1404(a)	108, 109, 110, 111, 115
1406	109, 113, 115
1406(a)	111, 112, 113
1407	384
1441 (Removal)	140, 158
1441(a)	108, 158, 162
1441(b)	158
1441(c)	159, 161–162
1441(e)	160
1445 (Non-removable Actions)	160
1446-50 (Procedure for Removal)	163
1447(c)	162
1447(d)	163
1453(b)	159
1652 (Rules of Decision Act)	254
1655 (Lien Enforcement)	78, 94
1738 (Full Faith and Credit)	445–??, 95, 417, 443
1870 (Jury Challenges)	295
1963 (Registration of Judgments)	95
2072 (Enabling Act)	257
2111 (Harmless Error)	323
2361 (Interpleader — Service of Process)	70, 395–396
2403 (Intervention by U.S.)	389

SUBJECT MATTER INDEX

ABSENCE
Depositions, use at trial, 245

ABSOLUTE IMMUNITY
Discovery
    Distinguished from qualified immunity, 207
    Present rules on, 210

ABSTENTION DOCTRINE
Defined, 124

ACCELERATION CLAUSES
Installment contracts, claim preclusion, 419

ADDITUR
    Generally, 305
Use in state courts, 305

ADJUDICATION WITHOUT TRIAL
    Generally, 286-290
Involuntary dismissal, 287
Judgment on partial findings, 287
Summary judgment, 288-290
Voluntary dismissal, 287

ADMINISTRATORS OR EXECUTORS
Diversity jurisdiction involving, 124
Real party in interest, 399

ADMISSIBILITY
Discovery results, 243-248

ADMISSION
Requests for, 230
Use at trial, 231

AFFIRMATIVE DEFENSES
Pleading, 192

AGENT
Defendant's use of as bearing on personal jurisdiction, 61-65

AIRPLANE
Service of process in, 13

ALIENS
Diversity of citizenship involving, 125-127

AMENDMENT
Pleadings, 193-198
Relation back of, 195
    Change of party, 196-198
    Single "conduct, transaction, or occurrence", 195

AMOUNT IN CONTROVERSY REQUIREMENT
    Generally, 138-140
Aggregation by multiple plaintiffs, 139, 150-153, 347
Class actions, 139, 370-371
Counterclaims, effect of, 140
Diversity jurisdiction, 138
Federal question jurisdiction, 138
Point of view from which measured, 138

Removal jurisdiction, 139, 140
Sum claimed in good faith, 138
Supplemental jurisdiction to satisfy, 150-153

ANCILLARY JURISDICTION
    See SUPPLEMENTAL JURISDICTION

ANSWER
    Generally, 190-192
Time for, 193

APPEALABILITY
Class action, denial of, 371

APPELLATE REVIEW
    Generally, 319-329
Clearly erroneous standard, 322
Collateral order doctrine, 327-329
Deference to trial court, 321
"Final judgment" rule, 323-329
Findings of fact, 293
"Harmless error" doctrine, 322-323
Judgment as a matter of law/JNOV order, 306
New trial order, 302-306
Objection, need for, 320-321
Questions of law, 321
Scope of, 320-323
Trial without jury, 291-292

ASCERTAINING APPLICABLE LAW
    See also ERIE DOCTRINE
    Generally, 253-276
Erie case, 253, 254-257
Federal common law, generally, 274-276
    in diversity cases, 275
    in federal question cases, 274
    in state courts, 276
Where Federal Rule is on point, 263-271

ATTACHMENT
Constitutionality of procedures for, 89-92
In rem jurisdiction, 77
Quasi in rem jurisdiction, 77, 78-82

ATTORNEY CLIENT PRIVILEGE
Work-product immunity, distinguished from, 207

AUTOMOBILE
Driving, as basis for jurisdiction, 16

BANK ACCOUNT GARNISHMENT
Due process, 91

BAR AND MERGER
    See CLAIM PRECLUSION

BIAS OF JUDGE, 298-299

BURDEN OF PROOF
Allocation of burdens, 282
Burden of production, 282
Erie rules on, 259
Preponderance of the evidence, 283, 284-285

CHOICE OF LAW
    See ASCERTAINING APPLICABLE LAW

CITIZENSHIP
    See also SUBJECT-MATTER JURISDICTION,
        DIVERSITY JURISDICTION
Residence compared, 125
Synonymous with domicile, 13

CLAIM PRECLUSION
    Generally, 417-426
Adjudication on merits, requirements of, 421-422
Change of law, 422-423
Federal suit followed by state suit, 446-449
Jurisdictional obstacles, 420-421
Personal and property damage from accident, 420
Splitting a claim, 422
State suit followed by federal suit, 421, 444
Stranger to first action, 423-426
Transactional test for, 419

CLASS ACTION FAIRNESS ACT OF 2005, 123, 140,
370, 384

CLASS ACTIONS
    Generally, 355-385
(b)(1) class actions, 362-363
(b)(2) class actions, 363-366
    Money damages sought in, 364-366
(b)(3) class actions, 366-367
"Absent plaintiff", 49, 384
Amount in controversy rules, 139, 370, 384
Attorney's fees, 378
Binding effect of decisions in, 368-369
Certification as class, 356
Common question test, 366
Common-questions requirement, 358-360
Definition, 355
Determination that no valid class action exists, 371-372
    Appeal from, 371-372
Diversity cases
    Amount in controversy requirement, 370-371
    Citizenship of class members, 369
Due process, 356
Fair-and-adequate-representation requirement, 361-362
Limited-fund rationale, 383-384
Mass tort claims, generally, 378-385
    Aggregation and sampling, 384
    Amount in controversy, 384
    Asbestos case, 379-380
    Definition, 378-379
    Due process problems, 384
    Limited-fund rationale, 383-384
    Opting out, 384
    Partial certification, 384
    Pretrial consolidation, 384
    Problems of, 379-380
    Product liability cases, 380, 381
    Punitive damages, 383
    Requirement of notice, 367-368
    Single-accident cases, 380
    Suitability of class actions, 380-383
    Type of class action used for, 363, 367, 384
Notice, requirement of, 50, 367-368
Opting out, right of, 49, 50, 363, 366, 384
Prerequisites for, 357-362, 362-367
Removal of to federal court, 159
Settlement of, 375-378
Settlement-only class actions, 376

Subject-matter jurisdiction issues, 369-371
Supplemental jurisdiction involving, 149
Table 8-2: Class Actions, 377
Typical-claim requirement, 357
Waiver of right to bring, 372-375

"CLEARLY ERRONEOUS" STANDARD, 322

COGNOVIT NOTE, 16

COLLATERAL ATTACK ON JUDGMENTS
Based on lack of jurisdiction over person, 95, 443
Based on lack of subject-matter jurisdiction, 96, 121, 443

COLLATERAL ESTOPPEL
    Generally, 427-439
Acquittal in criminal case, 439
Administrative agency findings, use of, 445
Burden of proof, allocation of, 431
Criminal conviction, use of, 438-439
Definition, 427-428
Foreseeability of future litigation, 429
"Full and fair" litigation of issue, 429
Government is party, 438
Issue actually litigated, 428-429
Issue essential to verdict, 429
Issue of law, 431-432, 438
Jurisdiction, courts of limited, 430-431
Multiple plaintiff anomaly, 435, 437
Mutuality, 434
Offensive vs. defensive use, 434-436
Persons affected by, 433-439
Settlement, 431
Stranger to first action, 433

"COLLATERAL ORDER" DOCTRINE, 327-329

COLLUSIVE ASSIGNMENT OF CLAIM
Fraudulent joinder to create diversity, 128

COMPLAINT
    Generally, 175-178
Defined, 175
Motion to dismiss (12(b)(6)), 179
Motion to strike (12(f)), 188
Short and plain statement, 176
Special matters, 177
Time for service after filing, 193

COMPULSORY COUNTERCLAIMS
    See COUNTERCLAIMS

COMPULSORY JOINDER OF PARTIES
    See JOINDER OF PARTIES

CONCURRENT JURISDICTION
Between state and federal courts, 254

CONSENT
Basis for jurisdiction, 15
    Over corporations, 81
    Over individuals, 15
"Forum selection" clauses, 15
Inadequate to confer subject-matter jurisdiction, 120

CONSTRUCTIVE SERVICE
Defined, 86
Jurisdiction over the person, 86

CONTRACTS
As basis for *in personam* jurisdiction, 46-49
Choice of law provision, 48

CONTROVERSY, AMOUNT IN
See AMOUNT IN CONTROVERSY REQUIREMENT

CORPORATIONS
Diversity jurisdiction involving, 127
Principal place of business of, 127

COUNTERCLAIMS
Generally, 337-341
Compulsory
Collateral estoppel involving, 422
Definition, 338
Failure to state, effect of, 338, 340, 422
Supplemental jurisdiction over, 154, 340-341, 400-401
Test for, 339
Default by opposing party, 338
Jurisdictional requirements for, 154, 340
New parties to, 339
Permissive
Collateral estoppel involving, 422
Jurisdictional requirements, 341, 402
Quasi in rem suits, 338
Statute of limitations for, 341
Supplemental jurisdiction, 153, 340, 401, 402
Supplemental jurisdiction involving, 149
Third-party defendant to, 339
Who may make, 340

CROSS-CLAIMS
"Ancillary" jurisdiction, 144-145
Between co-plaintiffs, 406
Definition, 406
Distinguished from counterclaim, 406
Supplemental jurisdiction, 153, 406
Supplemental jurisdiction involving, 149
Test for allowing, 406
Transaction or occurrence that is subject matter of original action, 406

DAMAGES
See REMEDIES

"DEATH KNELL" DOCTRINE, 371

DEFAULT JUDGMENT
Collateral attack on, 95, 121, 443

DEFENSES
Pleadings, 192

DENIALS
Based on information and belief, 191
General, 191
Lack of knowledge or information, 191

DEPOSITIONS
Generally, 224-229
Admissibility of, 244-246
Failure to appear, sanctions for, 243
Limits on number and time of, 228
Mechanics of, 226
Non-stenographic version, 227
Objection to, 237
Oral depositions, 226-228
Order compelling, 239-240

Protective order against, 238-239
Recording, means of, 227
Use of at trial, 244-246
Who may be deposed, 225, 226
Written questions, 228

DIRECTED VERDICT
Diversity cases, standard in, 300
Effect of, 299
Federal trials, 300
Judgment as a matter of law, 300
No possible difference among reasonable people, 300
Standard for determining, 300

DISCOVERY
See also individual forms of (e.g., DEPOSITIONS)
Absolute work product immunity, 207, 210-212
Abuse of, 225, 237
Admissibility of fruits of, 243-248
Automatic disclosure, 204
Award of expenses, 240
Compelling, 239-240
Cost shifting by court, 233
Depositions, 224-229
Limit on number of, 225
Non-stenographic version, 227
On oral questions, 226
On written questions, 228
Disclosure, prohibition of, 238
Good faith requirement, 239
Documents, request to inspect, 231
Electronically stored information, 231-234
Expert witness' report, 213, 219
Experts, 213-215
Forms of, 224-236
Impeachment material, 215
"Initial Disclosure", 205
Insurance agreements, 216
Interrogatories, 229
Land, request to inspect, 231
Legal contentions, 210-212
Metadata, 232
Participant experts, 215
Physical examination, 234-236
Constitutionality, 235
Sanctions for not submitting to, 243
"Pretrial Disclosure", 205
Privileged material, 206
Protective order, 237, 238-239
Qualified work product immunity, 207
Request for admission, 230
Request to inspect documents or property, 231
Sanctions, 240-243
Against parties refusing to furnish discovery, 241-242
Gross negligence sufficient for, 242
Scope of, 205-221
Signature requirement, 225
Subpoena, use of against third party, 234
Use of, at trial, 243-248
Use of, in subsequent proceedings, 246
Witnesses
Names of, 212
Statements of, 212
Work product immunity, 207-213

DISMISSAL
Involuntary, 287-288
Voluntary, 287

DIVERSITY
See DIVERSITY JURISDICTION and
SUBJECT-MATTER JURISDICTION

DIVERSITY JURISDICTION
Amount in controversy
Aggregation of claims, 139-140
Class actions, 139
Complete diversity, requirement of, 122-123, 153, 347
Corporations, 127
Nerve center test, 128
Date for determining existence of, 124-125
Partnerships, 127

DIVORCE
Jurisdiction to grant, 28, 77

DOCUMENTS
Request to produce, 231

DOMICILE
Basis for jurisdiction, 13-14
Defined, 13
Prior residence as basis for, 14

DUE PROCESS
Adequacy of notice and hearing, 84-92
Minimum contacts test, 23-49, 79-82
Opportunity to be heard, 89
Punitive damages, 317
Repossession of goods, 89
Statutes going to limit of, 20
Wage garnishment, 91

DURESS
Defense of, to jurisdiction, 96

ENFORCEMENT OF JUDGMENTS
Generally, 94
Full Faith and Credit clause, 95, 443-449
Jurisdiction over the person, 95
Registration, 95
Relitigating issue of jurisdiction, 95, 443-449

EQUITABLE REMEDIES
See REMEDIES

***ERIE* DOCTRINE**
Ascertaining law of particular state, 258-259
Burden of proof, 259
Conflict of law rules followed, 259
Conflict with statute, 271
Constitutional basis for, 257
Federal common law
in diversity cases, 275
in federal question cases, 274-275
in state courts, 276
Federal Rules of Civil Procedure, doctrine not applicable to, 260, 263-265
Forum non conveniens, state law concerning, 263
Forum-shopping, evils of, 254, 255, 256
Obsolete state decision, 258
Outcome-determinative test, 261-263
Right to jury trial, in diversity cases, 262
Rules Enabling Act, 257, 260, 264, 268, 269
State decision obsolete, 258
Statute of limitations, 261
Substantive/procedural distinction, 260-263
Validity of Federal Rules, 260, 263-265

EXCESSIVE VERDICT
New trial because of, 304

EXPERTS
Discovery concerning, 213-215

FAILURE TO STATE CLAIM UPON WHICH RELIEF CAN BE GRANTED
Dismissal for, 179-187

FEDERAL COMMON LAW, 274-278

FEDERAL JURISDICTION
See JURISDICTION OVER THE PARTIES;
SUBJECT-MATTER JURISDICTION

FEDERAL QUESTION JURISDICTION
Generally, 131-133
Amount in controversy not required, 138
Embedded federal issue not appearing in complaint, 133-137
Removal jurisdiction, 158-163
Statutory basis, 131-133

FIGURES
Figure 6-1: Analyzing Erie problems, 277

FINAL JUDGMENT
Necessary for appeal, 306, 323-329

FINDINGS OF FACT
Judgment on partial findings, 287, 292
Separately stated by judge, 291

FORMER ADJUDICATION
See also COLLATERAL ESTOPPEL; CLAIM
PRECLUSION
Collateral estoppel, 427-439
Full Faith and Credit, 443-449
Issue preclusion, 416
Merger and bar, 417-426
Mutuality of estoppel, 434
Splitting of claim, 418-420
Stranger to first action, 423-426
"Virtual representation" doctrine, 423-426

FORUM NON CONVENIENS
Choice of law, 111
Defined, 101
Factors for allowing, 102, 108
In federal courts, 108
Original venue improper, 111
Where action might have been brought, 109

FORUM-SHOPPING
See also *ERIE* DOCTRINE
Evils of, 254, 255, 256, 447

FRAUD
Defense to jurisdiction, 96
Requirement of specific pleading, 177

FULL FAITH AND CREDIT CLAUSE
Administrative agency findings, 445
Enforcement of judgments, 95, 443-449
Obligation to give, 443-449
by federal court to state court's judgment, 444-446
by one state to another's judgment, 443
by state to federal judgment, 449

GARNISHMENT OF DEBT
Due process required prior to, 89

GENERAL APPEARANCE
Conferring jurisdiction, 16

GENERAL DENIAL, 191

"HARMLESS ERROR" DOCTRINE
Defined, 303
New trial not allowed for, 303
Appellate review and, 322

IMMUNITY
From service of process, 97
Work-product, 207-212

IMPEACHMENT MATERIAL
Discovery of, 215

IMPLEADER
Generally, 399-403
By plaintiff, 400
Defined, 399
Derivative claim, requirement of, 399-400
Dismissal of main claim, effect of, 403
Jurisdictional requirements relaxed for, 400-401
Other claims added to, 402
Supplemental jurisdiction, 401, 402
Supplemental jurisdiction involving, 149

IMPLIED CONSENT
Jurisdiction based on, 16, 81

IN PERSONAM JURISDICTION
See JURISDICTION OVER THE PARTIES

IN REM JURISDICTION
See JURISDICTION OVER THE PARTIES

INADEQUATE VERDICT
New trial, 305

INDISPENSABLE PARTIES
Compulsory joinder of parties, 348-351
Defined, 348
Supplemental jurisdiction over, 350

INDIVIDUALS, JURISDICTION OVER
See JURISDICTION OVER THE PARTIES

INJUNCTION
Appeal from order granting or denying, 329

INJUNCTIONS
See REMEDIES

INSTRUCTIONS BY JUDGE
To jury, 295

INSURANCE AGREEMENTS
Discovery, 216

INTERNET
Acts committed on, as covered by state long-arm, 18
Claims not involving in-state activities, jurisdiction for, 45
Website as constituting minimum contacts, 28-44

INTERPLEADER
Generally, 392-397
Comparison chart, 397
Definition, 392-393
Denial by stakeholder of debt, 395
Deposit by stakeholder, 395
Other suits restrained, 395-396
Rule 22 interpleader, 396
Statutory interpleader, 394-396
Table 8-3: Comparison — Statutory and Rule
  Interpleader, 397

INTERROGATORIES
Admissibility at trial, 246
Defined, 229
General verdict with, 302
Objection to, 230

INTERVENTION
Generally, 389-390
Of right, 389-390
Permissive, 390
Supplemental jurisdiction, 390
Supplemental jurisdiction involving, 149

INVOLUNTARY DISMISSAL, 287-288

ISSUE PRECLUSION
See COLLATERAL ESTOPPEL

JNOV
See JUDGMENT NOTWITHSTANDING THE VERDICT

JOINDER OF CLAIMS
Generally, 343-344
Defined, 343
Effect of rule against splitting cause of action, 344, 418-419
Jurisdiction requirements for, 344

JOINDER OF PARTIES
Generally, 345-351
Compulsory joinder, 348-351
  Jurisdiction requirements, 349-350
  "Necessary" and "indispensable" parties
        distinguished, 348-349
Indispensable party, 348, 349
Multi-party product liability cases, use of in, 346
Permissive joinder, 345-348
  Jurisdiction requirements, 346-348
  Test for allowing, 345
Supplemental jurisdiction, 145, 347-348, 350
Supplemental jurisdiction involving, 149

JUDGMENT AS A MATTER OF LAW
Appellate review of grant or denial of, 308
Application, 307
Defenses, applicable to, 307
Definition, 307
Motion for directed verdict, as condition precedent, 306
Motion for new trial combined with, 308
Order reversed on appeal, 308

JUDGMENT NOTWITHSTANDING THE VERDICT
Application, 307
Definition, 307
Federal practice; see JUDGMENT AS A MATTER OF LAW
Standard for granting, 307

JUDGMENTS
Enforcement of, 94

JURISDICTION OVER THE PARTIES
   Generally, 7-117
Agent, use of as giving rise to, 61-65
At-home test, 53-61
Child support claim, 28
Choice of law, constitutional limits on, 51
Collateral attack on, 95
Conducting business, 19
Consent as basis for, 15, 81
   "Forum selection" clauses, 15
Contract as basis for, 46-49
Corporations, generally, 21-51
   Agent present, 22
   Contracts as basis for, 46-49
   Domestic corporations, 22
   "Minimum contacts" test, 23-49, 79
   Out-of-state corporations, 51
Domicile as basis for, 13
Due process, long arm going to the limit of, 20
Federal actions, 68-75
   Amenability to suit, 74-75
   Local long-arm followed in diversity, 70
   100-mile bulge, 70
   Service of process, 72-74
   Service on individuals, 72
   Territory for service, 68-72
   Waiver of formal service, request for, 73
Foreign defendant, 71
Foreigners, 20
Fraud, defense based on, 48, 96
General jurisdiction, 45-46
   Corporation as defendant, 51
   Modern trend as to, 51
   Tougher rules governing, 51
Immunity from service, 97
"Implied consent" doctrine, 16, 81
Individuals, 11-21
   Conducting business by, 19
In personam jurisdiction, defined, 8
In rem jurisdiction, generally, 77
   Actions for specific performance of land-sale contracts, 78
   Constitutionality, 77
   Effect of *Shaffer*, 78
   Federal *in rem* jurisdiction, 78
Internet Website, effects of, 43-44
Internet, acts committed on, 18
Limited appearance, 82
   Federal use of, 83
Long-arm statutes, defined, 17
"Minimum contacts" test, 23-49, 79-82
Motorists, non-resident, 16
Notice and opportunity for hearing, 84-92
Notice requirement, 84-88
   Actual notice not received, 88
   Actual notice received, but statute invalid, 88
   Cognovit, 16
   Garnishment suits, 85
   Hearing, opportunity for, 89-92
   Out-of-state defendant, 86
   Publication, 86
   Service on corporations, 86
   Service on state official, 86
   Substitute service, 85
Opportunity to be heard, 89-92
   Due process, test for, 90
   Prejudgment remedies, 89-92
   State action, 92

Out-of-state acts with in-state consequences, 17-18
Ownership of property, based on, 18
Presence as basis for, 12, 82
Products liability cases, 17-18, 28-43
Purchases made in state, 45
Quasi in rem, generally, 78-82
   Based on debts, 82
   Definition, 78
   Federal suits based on, 83
   Limited appearance, 82
   Minimum contacts required, 79-82
   Res judicata effect of, 79
Residence as basis for, 14
Special appearance, 93
Specific jurisdiction, 45
Stream-of-commerce theory, 54
Torts, based on
   In-state, 17
   Libel, 18
   Out-of-state with in-state consequences, 17, 28-43
   Products liability, 17, 28-43, 380, 381
   Single-accident cases, 380

JURISDICTIONAL AMOUNT
   See AMOUNT IN CONTROVERSY REQUIREMENT

JURY
   Generally, 294-296
Alternates, 295
Challenges to, 294-295
Instructions to, 295
Misconduct of, 296
Number required, 294
Selection of, 294-295
Seventh Amendment, 294
Unanimity requirement, 294

JURY TRIAL, RIGHT TO
   Generally, 308-315
Complex cases, 314-315
Damages, suits for, 311
Deciding whether claim is legal or equitable, 311-313
Declaratory judgment, 314
Legal and equitable claims mixed, 309-311
Patent claims, 313
Seventh Amendment, 308

LAND
Request to inspect, 231
Venue in actions involving, 99

LEGAL THEORIES
Discoverability, 211

LIMITED APPEARANCES
Defined, 82
Federal *quasi in rem* suits, use in, 83
Special appearances compared, 82

LONG ARM STATUTE
   See also JURISDICTION OVER THE PERSON
Basis of jurisdiction, 9
Defined, 17
Illinois Act, 17, 19
Non-resident motorist statutes, 16
Notice by mail, 86
Service on designated state official, 86
Statutes going to limits of due process, 20

MASS TORTS
See CLASS ACTIONS

MERGER AND BAR
See CLAIM PRECLUSION

METADATA
Discovery of, 232

MINIMUM CONTACT
Suit based on products shipped into the forum state, 28-43

MINIMUM CONTACTS
See also JURISDICTION OVER THE PERSON
"Absent plaintiff," not required for, 49, 369
Balancing test, 9
Basis of jurisdiction, 79-82
Defined, 9, 23
Internet Website as constituting, 43-44
Out-of-state tortious act, in-state consequences, 17, 28-43
Products liability cases, 28-43
Quasi in rem jurisdiction, 79-82
Single life insurance policy, 25
Voluntary contacts by defendant required, 26-28

MOTIONS
Defined, 178
For judgment on pleadings, 187
For more definite statement, 187
To dismiss for failure to state claim, 179-187
  Plausibility standard for deciding, 179-187
To strike, 188

MOTOR VEHICLE
Operation of, as implied consent, 16

MULTI-PARTY AND MULTI-CLAIM LITIGATION
See CLASS ACTIONS, IMPLEADER, INTERPLEADER, INTERVENTION, JOINDER OF CLAIMS, JOINDER OF PARTIES, and REAL PARTY IN INTEREST

MULTIPLE-PLAINTIFF ANOMALY
Offensive vs. defensive use of collateral estoppel, 435, 437

MUTUALITY
Collateral estoppel, 434-435

NATIONWIDE SERVICE OF PROCESS
In interpleader cases, 69, 394

NECESSARY PARTIES
Compulsory joinder of, 348-351

NERVE CENTER TEST
For corporation's citizenship, 127-128

NEW TRIAL
Appealability of order granting, 306
Bias discovered after trial, 296
Excessive verdict, 304-305
Grounds for granting generally, 302-303
Inadequate verdict, 305
Jury's error of law, 304-305
Misconduct by jury, 296
Newly discovered evidence, 305-306
Partial new trial, 305
Remittitur and Additur, 305
Verdict against weight of evidence, 304

NEWLY DISCOVERED EVIDENCE
New trial, 305-306

NEWSPAPER PUBLICATION
Service of process by, 86

NOMINAL PARTIES
Diversity jurisdiction involving, 124

NON-JURY TRIAL
Generally, 291-292
Judgment on partial findings, 292

NON-RESIDENT MOTORIST STATUTES
Basis of jurisdiction over individuals, 16

NOTICE AND OPPORTUNITY TO BE HEARD
See also JURISDICTION OVER THE PARTIES

100-MILE BULGE PROVISION
Federal jurisdiction over the parties based on, 70

OPPORTUNITY TO BE HEARD
Test for due process, 90

PARTIAL NEW TRIAL
Issues of liability and damages, 305

PARTICIPANT EXPERTS
Discovery involving, 213

PARTIES, JURISDICTION OVER
See JURISDICTION OVER THE PARTIES

PENDENT JURISDICTION
See SUPPLEMENTAL JURISDICTION

PERMISSIVE COUNTERCLAIMS
See COUNTERCLAIMS

PERMISSIVE INTERVENTION
See INTERVENTION

PERMISSIVE JOINDER OF PARTIES
See JOINDER OF PARTIES

PERSONAL JURISDICTION
See JURISDICTION OVER THE PARTIES

PHYSICAL EXAMINATIONS
Discovery, 235
Report of examining physician, 235

PLEADINGS
See also COMPLAINT, ANSWER, DENIAL, REPLY
Affirmative defenses, 192
Amendment, 192, 193-198
Answer, 190-192
Complaint, 175-177
Conclusory statement insufficient, 176
Counterclaims, 192
Denials, 191
Failure to state claim upon which relief can be granted, 179
Relation back to, 194-198
  Change of party, 47, 196
  Single "conduct, transaction, or occurrence", 195
Reply, 171
Rule 11, 172-175

Sanctions
    For frivolous or harassing pleading, 172-175
    See also SANCTIONS
Short and plain statement, 175
Signing of, 172
Special damages, 177
Special matters, generally, 177
    Failure to plead, effect of, 177
    If not listed in Rule 9, 177
    List of, 177
Timetable for, 193
Types of, 169
Variance of proof from pleadings, 198-199
Verification, 171

PREJUDGMENT RELIEF
Due process, 89-92

PREPONDERANCE OF THE EVIDENCE
    Generally, 284-285
Burden of proof, 283
Definition, 284

PRESUMPTIONS
Definition, 283
Effect of, 283-284

PRETRIAL CONFERENCE
    Generally, 250
Pretrial order, 250
Promoting settlements, policy of, 250
Sanctions, 250
Scheduling order, 250

PRINCIPAL PLACE OF BUSINESS
Of corporation, 127-128

PRIVILEGED MATERIAL
Discovery, 206

PRODUCTS LIABILITY
Class actions, 380, 381
Jurisdiction in cases of, 17, 28-43

PROTECTIVE ORDER
    See DISCOVERY

PUBLICATION
Means of notice, 86

PUNITIVE DAMAGES
Due process issues with, 317-318

QUALIFIED WORK-PRODUCT IMMUNITY
Discovery
    Distinguished from absolute immunity, 208
    Overcome by showing of need, 210

QUASI IN REM
    See JURISDICTION OVER THE PARTIES

REAL PARTY IN INTEREST
    Generally, 398-399

REGISTERED MAIL SERVICE
Constructive service, 86
Non-resident motorist statutes, 17

REGISTRATION OF JUDGMENTS
Generally, 95

RELIEF
    See REMEDIES

REMEDIES
Generally, 316-319
Compensatory damges, 316
Equitable remedies, 318-319
    Injunctions, 318
    Specific performance, 318
Punitive damages, 317
    Due process limits, 317

REMITTITUR
Amount of, 305
Definition, 305

REMOVAL TO FEDERAL COURT
    See also SUBJECT MATTER-JURISDICTION
    Generally, 158-163
By plaintiff, not allowed, 159
Class actions filed in state court, 159
Diversity jurisdiction, 159, 160
Illustrations, 159
Mechanics of, 163
Multiple claims, 159, 161-162
Remand, 162
Waiver, 163

REPLY
Time for, 193

REPOSSESSION OF GOODS
Due process, 92

REQUEST FOR ADMISSIONS
Discovery, 230

REQUEST TO PRODUCE DOCUMENTS
Discovery, 231

RES JUDICATA
    See COLLATERAL ESTOPPEL, CLAIM PRECLUSION

RIGHT TO JURY TRIAL
    See JURY TRIAL, RIGHT TO

RULES ENABLING ACT
Definition, 257
Narrow construction of federal rules, to avoid violating, 265

RULES OF DECISION ACT
    Generally, 254-257

SANCTIONS
Against parties refusing to furnish discovery, 250
Inherent power of court to sanction, 174
Rule 11 sanctions for frivolous or harassing filings, 172-175
"Safe harbor" provision, 174

SERVICE OF PROCESS
    See also JURISDICTION OVER THE PARTIES
Dwelling unattended, 85
First-class mail, 86
Immunity from, 97
Nationwide service, 69

Newspaper publication, 86
Notice to corporate official or manager, 87
Registered mail, 86
State law, federal service according to, 70
State official, service on, 86
Substituted service, 85
Subterfuge, use of, 96
Time for service, 74
Waiver of formal service, request for, 73

SEVENTH AMENDMENT
  See JURY; JURY TRIAL, RIGHT TO

SPECIAL APPEARANCE
Defined, 93
Substitutes for, 94
Waiver of right to, 94

SPECIAL DAMAGES
Pleading, 177

SPECIAL MATTERS
Pleading, 177

SPLITTING A CLAIM
Claim preclusion, 418-420

STATE OFFICIAL
Service on, 86

STATUTE OF LIMITATIONS
Counterclaims, 341
Outcome determinative test, 261-262

STOCKHOLDERS' DERIVATIVE SUIT
Verification requirement, 171

SUBJECT-MATTER JURISDICTION
  Generally, 119-163
Aliens, jurisdiction involving, 123, 125
Amount in controversy; see AMOUNT IN CONTROVERSY
    REQUIREMENT
Ancillary jurisdiction; see SUPPLEMENTAL
    JURISDICTION
Collateral attack on lack of, 121
Diversity jurisdiction, generally, 122-130
    Abolition possible, 122
    Abstention doctrine, 124
    Aliens, 125-127
    Assignment of claim, 128
    Devices to create or destroy, 128
    District of Columbia, citizens of, 125
    Nominal parties, 124
Federal questions, generally, 131-133
    Anticipation of federal defense insufficient, 132
    Claim based on merits, 137
    Must appear in well-pleaded complaint, 132
    New parties brought in, 143
    Removal of multiple claims, 159
    State-created claim, 132
    Supplemental jurisdiction, 132, 142-155
Pendent jurisdiction; see SUPPLEMENTAL JURISDICTION
Removal, generally, 158-163
    By plaintiff, not allowed, 161
    Certain cases not removable, 160
    Devices to defeat, 128
    Diversity cases, 159
    Face of pleadings, determined from, 160
    Mechanics of, 163

Multiple claims, 159, 161-162
    Original state court jurisdiction required, 160
    Remand, 162
    Waiver, 163
Supplemental jurisdiction; see SUPPLEMENTAL
    JURISDICTION
Waiver of, lack of, 121
When objection to lack of may be made, 121

SUBPOENA
Duces tecum, 226, 234
To non-party deponent, 226, 234

SUBSTITUTED SERVICE
Defined, 85
Jurisdiction over the person, 72, 85

SUMMARY JUDGMENT
Meaning and application, 288-290
Movant has burden of proof, 288-289
Partial, 290
Showing by movant, 288-289

SUPPLEMENTAL JURISDICTION
  Generally, 142-154
"Ancillary" jurisdiction, 142
Class action plaintiffs and, 149
"Common nucleus of facts" test, 146
Compulsory counterclaims, 148, 340, 402
Compulsory counterclaims and, 149
Cross-claims, 402
Cross-claims and, 149
Discretionary rejection, 153
Diversity cases, 146-150
Exclusions, 147
Federal question cases, 146
Impleader, 402
Impleader and, 149
Intervention, 390
Intervention and, 149
Joinder of claims, 344
Joinder of parties, 148, 347-348, 350
"Pendent" jurisdiction, 142-143, 146
Permissive counterclaims, 341
Permissive joinder of parties and, 149
Personal jurisdiction, 154
Statute, 145
Venue, 154

TABLES
Table 8-2: Class Actions, 377
Table 8-3: Comparison — Statutory and Rule
    Interpleader, 397

THIRD PARTY PRACTICE
  See IMPLEADER

TORTIOUS ACT
Basis of jurisdiction over individual, 17, 28-43

VARIANCE
Of proof from pleadings, 198-199

VENUE
  Generally, 99-114
Corporations, 107
Federal actions, 103-114
    Defendant's residence, 105
    Diversity cases, 106

Place of events, 105
Forum non conveniens, 101
 Federal suits, 108
 State suits, 101
Local actions, 100
Removal cases, 108
Supplemental jurisdiction, 154
Transfer to different federal court, 108
Transitory actions, 100
Unincorporated associations, 108
Waiver, 108

VERDICT
Against weight of evidence, 304
Directed; see DIRECTED VERDICT
General, 302
Special, 302

VERIFICATION
Pleadings, 171

**"VIRTUAL REPRESENTATION"
DOCTRINE**, 423-426

VOLUNTARY DISMISSAL, 287

WAGE GARNISHMENT
Due process, 91

WAIVER OF SERVICE
Request for, 73

WEIGHT OF EVIDENCE
Verdict against, 304

WITNESSES
Expert, discovery of, 213-215
Names of, discovery of, 212
Statements by, discovery of, 212

WORK-PRODUCT IMMUNITY
Absolute, 208, 210-212
Attorney-client privilege, distinguished from, 207
Legal claims, defenses and conclusions, 211
Qualified, 209
Selection of documents by attorney, 211

WRITTEN QUESTIONS
Depositions upon, 228